Video training courses are available on the subjects of these books in the James Martin ADVANCED TECHNOLOGY LIBRARY from Deltak Inc., 1220 Kensington Road, Oak Brook, Ill. 60521 (Tel: 312–920–0700).

MANAGING
THE DATA-BASE
ENVIRONMENT

TELEPROCESSING
NETWORK
ORGANIZATION

DISTRIBUTED FILE
AND DATA-
BASE DESIGN

STRATEGIC
DATA-PLANNING
METHODOLOGIES

SYSTEMS ANALYSIS
FOR DATA
TRANSMISSION

DESIGN AND STRATEGY
FOR DISTRIBUTED
DATA PROCESSING

COMPUTER
DATA-BASE
ORGANIZATION

(second edition)

INTRODUCTION
TO COMPUTER
NETWORKS

COMPUTER NETWORKS
AND DISTRIBUTED
PROCESSING

PRINCIPLES
OF DATA-BASE
MANAGEMENT

INTRODUCTION
TO
TELEPROCESSING

PRINCIPLES OF
DISTRIBUTED
PROCESSING

AN END-USER'S
GUIDE TO
DATA BASE

COMPUTER

COMPUTER NETWORKS
AND
DISTRIBUTED PROCESSING:
SOFTWARE,
TECHNIQUES,
AND ARCHITECTURE

A *James Martin* BOOK

NETWORKS AND DISTRIBUTED PROCESSING

SOFTWARE, TECHNIQUES, AND ARCHITECTURE

JAMES MARTIN

PRENTICE-HALL, INC., Englewood Cliffs, N.J. 07632

Library of Congress Cataloging in Publication Data

MARTIN, JAMES, (date)
　　Computer networks and distributed processing:
software, techniques, architecture.

　　Bibliography: p.
　　Includes index.
　　1. Electronic data processing—Distributed
　　processing. 2. Computer networks. I. Title.
　　QA76.9.D5M37　　　001.64　　　80-20652
　　ISBN 0-13-165258-3

Computer Networks and Distributed Processing:
Software, Techniques, and Architecture
James Martin

Editorial/production supervision by *Karen J. Clemments*
Jacket design by *Alon Jaediker*
Manufacturing buyers: *Joyce Levatino and Gordon Osbourne*

Printed in the United States of America

10　9　8　7　6　5　4　3　2

PRENTICE-HALL INTERNATIONAL, INC., *London*
PRENTICE-HALL OF AUSTRALIA PTY. LIMITED, *Sydney*
PRENTICE-HALL OF CANADA, LTD., *Toronto*
PRENTICE-HALL OF INDIA PRIVATE LIMITED, *New Delhi*
PRENTICE-HALL OF JAPAN, INC., *Tokyo*
PRENTICE-HALL OF SOUTHEAST ASIA PTE.. LTD., *Singapore*
WHITEHALL BOOKS LIMITED, *Wellington, New Zealand*

TO CORINTHIA

CONTENTS

PART II COMPUTER NETWORKS

PART III NETWORK MECHANISMS

PART **IV** **ERRORS, FAILURES AND SECURITY**

PART **V** **FUTURE**

PREFACE

At certain times a new technology emerges which is destined to change the nature of data processing: stored program control in the early 1950's, magnetic tape in the mid-1950's, large on-line storage in the 1960's, and the use of terminals. Today a technology of immense importance is spreading: *distributed processing in which intelligent machines in different locations cooperate by means of networks.*

This new and vital direction is throwing DP management into one of the worst dilemmas they have faced in the history of computing.

The choices that analysts and managers must make in this new area are complex and have long-lasting implications. Furthermore the financial implications of making the right choice are great. Some corporations appear to the author to be taking the wrong course. He has attempted to estimate the eventual cost of this. There can be little doubt that it will cost millions of dollars in some corporations, in abandoned approaches, redesign, and program rewriting. And this does not count the lost opportunities and inability to obtain information needed by management because of the incompatibility and nonconnectability of separate systems, minicomputers and intelligent terminals.

Large computers, minicomputers, and microcomputers in intelligent terminals are becoming interconnected into all manner of configurations. The corporation of the near future will be laced with networks which handle not only its data processing but also its word processing, mail and message sending. End users on the shop floor, in the sales offices, in the planning departments—in fact everywhere—are beginning to perceive what is happening and are demanding a piece of the action. They want a minicomputer, or an intelligent terminal, or access to distant data bases.

Unfortunately the technology of distributed networks is very complicated. It is easy to perceive the idea of networks, but very difficult to understand the technical subtleties. The subtleties can and must be hidden from the end user. The user perceives merely the dialogue or simple procedure that is provided for him. But that requires network architectures.

Network architectures specify the protocols or sets of rules which are needed to interconnect computers. These protocols are highly complex because there must be precise cooperation between distant intelligent machines.

Herein lies the dilemma. *The various architectures are incompatible.* The network architectures of IBM, Univac, DEC, NCR, Hewlett Packard, etc., are entirely different. Machines from different manufacturers cannot in general be hooked together (in spite of claims to the contrary) without bypassing the architecture and losing its advantages.

To make matters worse, major common carriers are developed or have developed *their* architecture for networks. By far the most spectacular of these is AT&T's A.C.S. (Advanced Communications Service), formally called BDN (Bell Data Network). However, different common carriers have different architectures; for example, Telenet, SBS (the communications satellite subsidiary of IBM, Comsat and Aetna), and PTT's in Europe, Japan and elsewhere (P.T.T. refers to a national telephone administration usually government controlled.)

The networking architectures of the common carriers are fundamentally incompatible with those of some of the computer manufacturers. AT&T's impressive ACS is in head-on collision with IBM's mainstream direction in networking: SNA (Systems Network Architecture). One reason for this is that both perceive networking as *their* territory. AT&T thinks that data networks, like telephone networks, ought to be provided by the carrier. Data concentrators, switches, front-ends, intelligent terminals and terminal cluster controllers are considered the data equivalent of telephone concentrators, PBX's, local switching offices, trunk switching offices and telephone instruments. IBM, on the other hand, derives great revenue from its terminals, cluster controllers, 3705's, network equipment and the many instructions executed in the mainframe to support it. It does not want anyone else dictating how its distributed machines should be interconnected. A great territorial fight is in the making.

Meanwhile DP analysts and executives must make decisions about their corporate networks and how to implement distributed processing.

The end users are clamoring for distributed processing. They have the minicomputer salesman beating at the door. DP management knows that the scattered minicomputers must be hooked together—that 60% of the data stored in one location will be needed in other locations. Sometimes they ignore the problem and hope that new software will emerge that will tie the fragments together. They hear the ARPANET connected incompatible machines. They hear that new standards are emerging like HDLC and X.25, X.3, X.28 and X.29.

The new standards will help, but not completely and not quickly. There is no resemblance between the major architectures from manufacturers and X.25, X.3, etc. Even if there were, neither ARPANET nor the current standards would solve the most important of the incompatibility problems—the Layer 4 control mechanisms described in this book. The best that can be hoped for is a clumsy bridge at the transport subsystem level, but many of the worst problems are external to the transport subsystem.

What should a DP manager do?

He might close his eyes and do nothing. In this case he may deny his organization the very considerable advantages of the new machines. The end users may rebel, as they are doing in many places, and get their own machines.

He may allow a proliferation of incompatibility without counting the future cost.

He could select one manufacturer's distributed architecture and stick with it. There is much to be said for this if the product line in question is sufficiently diverse. The manufacturers with major distributed processing architectures have planned a "migration path" into the future in which many new products will conform to the architecture and can be installed with the minimum disruption to existing application programs. But he may fear being locked into one manufacturer.

He could insist that the computer network conform to the new standards, especially X.25, but this would lock out most of the products of major manufacturers, which are not compatible with X.25.

He may plan a judicious mixture of these approaches, deciding where compatibility is vital, where it can be dispensed with, and where it is possible to build a bridge between different incompatible systems. He may select a manufacturer's architecture such as SNA for a certain set of applications, and a common carrier architecture like X.25 or ACS for all other interconnections.

Whatever he does, he should plan and understand the future implications of his choices. He or his staff need to understand the technical tradeoffs in distributed processing networks. The cost of *not* understanding could be extremely high.

This book explains the technology of computer networks and distributed processing architectures. It will enable readers to understand the issues and perceive what is important in an architecture design. It indicates how the architectures are likely to evolve in the future. This information is vital in making decisions about how to implement distributed data processing.

Part 1 of this book discusses the different types of networks and distributed configurations.

Part 2 explains the concepts of architectures for distributed systems, and what are desirable features of the different layers of the architectures.

Part 3 describes the mechanisms that are used in networking, and particularly those in specifications for the new common carrier (PTT) networks such as the X.25 networks, their X.3/X.28/X.29 interface, and the Bell System ACS network.

Part 4 explains the requirements and mechanisms for dealing with errors, failures of different types, recovery, deadlocks, privacy and security.

Part 5 discusses the future directions of network architectures.

The subject is complex. Many readers will benefit from a fast scan through the book before detailed reading of the chapters which particularly concern them.

After scanning the book, a fast path could be taken as follows:

CHAPTER 2   The Trend to Distributed Processing
CHAPTER 3   Types of Distributed Systems
CHAPTER 4   Private Networks

To understand fully the mechanisms and tradeoffs, the whole book should be studied.

James Martin

PART **I** **THE PROMISE**

1 THE PROMISE
OF COMPUTER NETWORKS

In America's pioneering days, each log cabin in the wilderness was an isolated outpost in a disconnected world. The pioneering days of the computer are still with us. But a new technology is evolving that will change the computer world as much as America changed. It is the technology of distributed processing and computer networks. Instead of being isolated outposts, computers will use programs and data stored by computers in other locations.

The growth of the communications systems that will make this technology economical is taking place at the same time as the spread of vast numbers of minicomputers and microcomputers. The combination of these developments is fundamentally changing the patterns of data processing. Many jobs which used to be done on large, heavily shared computers can now be done on stand alone minicomputers or microcomputers. Data in central storage units can be shared by large numbers of dispersed users, many having a small computer which can process the data or provide an end-user dialogue which simplifies the access to information. Data of interest to one terminal user may reside in multiple distant computers, accessible via networks. When a computer program says GET, it may be accessing a file unit attached to a computer a thousand miles away.

PROTOCOLS To enable the increasing variety of computers to communicate with one another, there must be rigorously defined protocols—i.e., sets of rules about how control messages and data messages are exchanged between machines, and how they control the communication process. Along with the protocol definition, the formats of the control messages and the headers and trailers of the data messages are likewise rigorously defined.

These formats and protocols become quite complex. It is desirable that there should be a widely accepted standard so that all manner of machines can communicate. Unfortunately, several different sets of formats and protocols are emerging from different organizations, as we discuss later in the book.

Some formats and protocols relate just to the transmission process for transporting data from one machine to another via a complex network. Communications, however, consists of more than merely a data transport mechanism. It may be necessary for one machine to load a program into another, to specify how a remote file will be used, to convert from the procedures or characters of one machine to those of another, to specify security procedures, to specify how compressed data should be expanded or edited before printing, to determine how machine usage will be charged, and so on. In some cases an elaborate contract is drawn up between machines before they begin a session of interaction. These processes, which are separate from the transport process, are specified to a greater or lesser extent in the architectures for computer networks and distributed processing.

RESOURCE SHARING   The purpose of many computer networks is to permit a far-flung community of users to share computer resources. Many such users now have their own minicomputers and calculators, so the shared resources have to be interesting enough to warrant access via a network. The facilities accessible by networks are in fact becoming more interesting at a rapid rate.

The remote computer may contain *software* which a user needs to employ. It may be proprietary software kept at one location. It may require a larger machine than any at the user's location. The distant computer may provide access to *data* which is stored and maintained at its location. Sometimes the remote machine controls a large or special printing facility. Sometimes the remote machine compiles programs which are used on smaller peripheral machines.

One of the best known resource-sharing networks is ARPANET, a United States network interconnecting more than fifty university and research computer centers (including a few in Europe). Many universities have interesting, and sometimes unique, computer facilities. These will become more valuable if they can be employed by a larger community of users. The idea behind ARPANET is that a professor or student at one university should be able to employ the facilities at any other university on the network. Usually he does this by means of a terminal, receiving responses from a distant computer almost as fast as if he were at the location of that machine.

A good example of a resource worth sharing is a program at M.I.T. for assisting with mathematics—MACSYMA. It is one of the largest programs written. It can solve simultaneous equations, factor polynomials, differentiate, and evaluate the world's worst integrals. A person needing this help can access it via ARPANET.

Public or semipublic networks can also provide access to highly specialized facilities. The *New York Times,* for example, has automated its archival stores of news stories. Hundreds of millions of abstracts of news items dating back to the early 1960's can be searched with a query language which permits unanticipated queries by linking multiple descriptive words. There are stock market systems which permit users to search for stocks which meet specified criteria of company or financial characteristics—price, earnings, performance, and so on. Encyclopedia companies are working at computerizing encyclopedic bodies of information. A network enthusiast's vision is that vast numbers of information systems like these will become accessible, inexpensively, to network users.

Networks can provide access not only to information systems but also to large numbers of problem-solving facilities. Some corporations have a large number of intricate computerized tools for various types of engineering design or evaluation. These are made available to engineers throughout the corporation via a corporate network. There are cash flow models, market forecasting models, budgetary control models, and so on. One hospital has successfully operated a prediagnosis system for several years. A computer program interviews a patient to make a preliminary diagnosis of his ailment to decide whether he† should see a nurse, doctor, or specialist. Computerized medical diagnosis will not replace that of a doctor but it could provide worried persons with a quick indication of whether they need to see a doctor or to take some simpler remedial action. Similarly there are systems for job counseling, finding employment, booking theater seats, doing tax calculations, and so on.

In general there is such a rich diversity of computer applications and information banks that it is impossible to predict the way networks would be used if easy network access and a high level of sharing made them economically available.

Box 1.1 lists a few of the resources worth sharing via networks.

BOX 1.1   A few of the resources that are accessible via computer networks

- A computer for mathematical operations which solves simultaneous equations, factors polynomials, differentiates, and solves the most complex integrals (e.g., M.I.T.'s MACSYMA).
- Advanced word processing facilities which can handle multiple type fonts, professional print editing, and are on-line to printing equipment.
- Legal search systems which can search and display cases, patents, etc.
- Business directories; corporate annual reports; business analyses.
- Design tools for complex design processes, simulation, etc.

†The author has given much thought to the problem of avoiding words with a sexist connotation. It is possible to avoid words like "man," "manpower," "mankind," but to avoid the use of "he," "his" and "him" makes sentences clumsy. In this book, whenever these words appear, please assume that the meaning is "he or she," "his or her" and "him or her."

BOX 1.1 *Continued*

- Forecasting models, cash flow models, financial models which permit the asking of multiple "what if?" questions.

- Market research information; foreign marketing aids.

- News access machines which can search past news stories or abstracts with given search criteria (e.g., the *New York Times* system)

- Investment information. Large numbers of parameters can be used relating to the past performance of the stock, the financial condition of the firm, its position in the industry, industry performance, etc.

- Information retrieval systems which search for books, technical reports, papers and articles on particular topics.

- A writer's aid; a dictionary, thesaurus, phrase generator, indexed dictionary of quotations, and encyclopedia.

- Games of the type that grow or change with various enthusiasts adding to the complexity or diversity.

- Resources of interest to a home user; domestic applications of the British *Prestel* system (a *Viewdata* system):

  - News reports; weather forecasts.
  - Sports results.
  - Stock market data; ticker tape.
  - Theater, movies, and community events information.
  - Directories; yellow pages.
  - Shopping information, prices, advertisements.
  - Classified advertisements from many sources.
  - Restaurants; good food guide.
  - Consumer reports.
  - Cars for sale.
  - Household magazine, recipes, book reviews, film reviews.
  - Train, bus, plane timetables; journey planning assistance.
  - Holidays, hotels, travel booking.
  - Radio and TV programs.
  - Games, pastimes, jokes, hobbies.
  - Employment directory; job opportunities.
  - Medical assistance service; medical prediagnosis.
  - Tax information; tax assistance.
  - Insurance information.
  - Encyclopedia reference.
  - Computer-assisted instruction.
  - School homework, quizzes, tests.
  - Catalog of *Open University* courses available on television.
  - Message sending service.

CORPORATE NETWORKS   Most computer networks are fundamentally different from ARPANET and the early resource-sharing networks. They are designed for specific applications in business and government data processing. Some of these are for transferring data between separate systems. Some are data entry networks in which computers used for data entry ship their files to distant machines. Some are designed to permit a terminal at one location to have access to data processing systems in different locations.

At a rapidly increasing rate, networks are being built for distributed processing. Intelligent terminals, minicomputers, desktop computers, and programmed devices which control groups of terminals are proliferating. The spread will continue to gain momentum as the power of low-cost microelectronics increases. The small machines in many cases have to be connected to larger machines to exchange data, use centralized data bases, and employ programs stored elsewhere. Computer networks for distributed processing often use quite different protocols from networks like ARPANET.

In some cases a common corporate network has been designed to be shared by a variety of unrelated systems. There are many advantages to this approach, which will become more common as different networking needs develop.

THE NETWORK RESOURCE   A data network can become a resource in its own right. Once in existence it can completely change the planning for computer installations. Given the existence of a network like ARPANET, a university confronted with the new demands for computers should ask, "Ought we to provide the resource or could a resource elsewhere on the network be used?"

In some corporations the existence of a corporate network has had a major effect on the planning of data processing facilities. It gives more freedom to plan the balance between centralized and decentralized computers, files, and data bases. Different locations can specialize in different data processing functions. Such is the case with British Steel, for example, which has a network linking many locations in which computers are used. Similarly a trans-European network called EIN (European Information Network) linking research centers raises questions about where particular computing resources should be located and whether certain ones should be combined. It is often cheaper to have one expensive facility which is shared among locations than to have separate versions of the facility at each location. Sometimes expensive networks have been justified by a calculation of how much it would cost to provide the same facilities without a network.

COST REDUCTION   In its early days teleprocessing was very expensive; it was used only on systems with a special need for it, like airline reservation systems and military systems. As private networks emerged from their pioneering days, the cost dropped. Public data networks are still in their infancy, and as they grow there is scope for major cost reductions.

There are various aspects of technology which are likely to force the price of terminal usage drastically lower. This is important because almost all aspects of telecommunications are characterized by high price elasticity. In other words, when the price comes down, the usage goes up. This has been true with telephony and telegraphy; it is undoubtedly true with data transmission and computer networks. If the price comes down far enough, the usage will grow by leaps and bounds.

Let us summarize some of the reasons for future cost reduction:

1. Computer networks like those we describe in this book are being built. A typical terminal user transmits far fewer bits than the total which a telephone channel can carry. In a dialogue with a distant computer, a typical user causes less than 2500 bits of user data to be transmitted in both directions in five minutes of terminal use. A telephone line can transmit 2,880,000 bits in five minutes. To lower the cost of tranmission, then, networks are needed which permit a very high level of sharing lines between diverse users.

2. Telephone trunk technology is undergoing a change from analog to digital operation [1]. Both transmission and switching are better handled digitally for much of the telephone network. The change is taking place in the interests of telephony, not data transmission, yet it will have a major effect on lowering the cost of data transmission. Common carrier digital telephone channels transmit 64,000 bits per second in both directions simultaneously (with 56,000 bits per second being available to carry user's data in the U.S.). This represents a major increase in the data-carrying capacity of telephone trunks, and modems are not needed on digital circuits. The relative cost of data and voice is swinging dramatically in favor of data.

    More than half of AT&T's wire-pair trunks are now digital lines carrying 1.5, 3.2, or 6.3 million bits per second on each pair of copper wires. Higher-speed digital trunks are also operating, using coaxial cables, digital radio, and optical fibers. AT&T is adopting a bit rate of 274 million bits per second [2] for the high-speed digital channels of the Bell System.

3. Of particular promise are communications satellites. A satellite can provide high-speed digital channels which interlink stations anywhere on one side of the earth at a cost potentially much lower than that of terrestrial trunks and switches.

    SBS, Satellite Business Systems, a subsidiary of IBM, Comsat and Aetna, uses satellites which relay channels of 48 million bits per second, accessible from small earth stations on users' premises. These are small satellites; but the era of the space shuttle is dawning. There are great economies of scale in satellite systems. Satellites launched with the space shuttle could carry higher bit rates and be accessible to earth stations of *much* lower cost. In some exploratory NASA designs for such satellites, terminals communicating directly via the satellites are small enough to be portable [3].

4. Perhaps the most dramatic change taking place in the computer industry is the falling cost of microcomputers and mass-produced microminiature logic and memory (Fig. 1.1). A microcomputer can be installed under the covers of an electric typewriter for much less than the cost of the typewriter. Computer terminals before the mid-1970's were fairly expensive. Some relatively simple and very cheap terminals are now becoming available. Terminals designed for low cost and ease of use can plug directly into the telephone lines

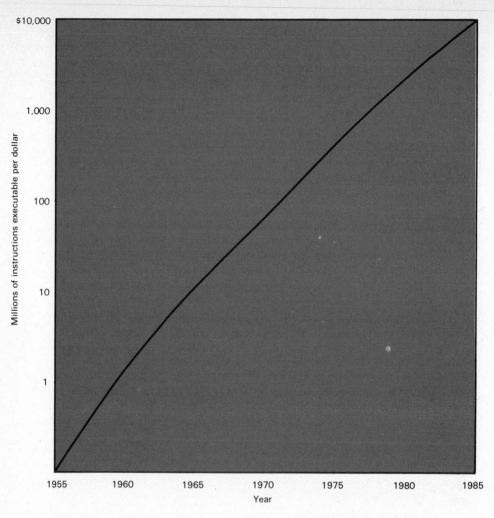

Figure 1.1 The decrease in cost of logic circuitry in terms of millions of instructions per dollar.

without an external modem. They can be cheap, portable, plug-in machines. The telephone lines may be used to dial a local connection to a computer network. Before long *pocket* terminals not much bigger than pocket calculators will be used. Most business people who carry a pocket calculator today will carry a pocket terminal in the future.

5. The standards organizations have created standards for interfacing to digital networks (such as HDLC, X.25, X.3, X.28, and X.29 discussed in Chapters 18, 22, and 23). These will permit the interface between the user machine and the network to be mass-produced inexpensively—eventually on a single VLSI chip. (VLSI stands for "Very Large Scale Integration"—the ability to put hundreds of thousands of electronic components on a silicon chip.)

6. In addition to cheap simple terminals, the latest semiconductor technology is bringing highly sophisticated terminals, many of which are programmable or connected, to a programmable controller. Because they are programmable, many of the functions that were performed by a

distant computer are now performed at the terminal location. The dialogue which must take place between the machine and its user occurs mostly at the terminal location. Not only can the dialogue be better designed for an ordinary user but also the number of bits which are transmitted over communication lines drops—often to a tenth of what it was or even much less than that.

Thus while speech trunks are carrying an order of magnitude more bits, many terminals transmit an order of magnitude less. This, combined with the building of switched data networks which permit many thousands of terminals to share transmission resources, should result in a major drop in the costs of data transmission; and as the price drops, the numbers of users will grow.

Box 1.2 summarizes the reasons why data transmission costs will drop.

**IMPROVED
ACCESSIBILITY**   To facilitate widespread use of networks, accessibility to them needs to be improved. It is desirable to have inexpensive machines in offices, shops, restaurants, and the home—wherever there is a telephone—which can access the data networks as easily and cheaply as making a telephone call.

A major step towards this objective is the creation of a standard interface to shared networks which machines everywhere can use. Such an interface has been defined by the international organization for telecommunications standards, the CCITT (Comité Consultatif International Télégraphique et Téléphonique). This standard is the CCITT Recommendation X.25, and the associated recommendations for the attachment of dumb terminals: X.3, X.28, and X.29. These standards are likely to have wide but not exclusive acceptance. It seems likely that there will be not one, but several families of protocols in general use. Not *all* machines will be directly interconnectable, but large families of machines which employ common protocols (such as manufacturer's protocols discussed in Part V of this book) will be.

Mass-produced, easy-to-use terminals which plug simply into the telephone jack are needed, and these will eventually have very large sales. One such family of terminals is the AT&T Transaction Telephones and the VuSet terminals (Figs. 1.2). Another will be the pocket terminals with built-in modems and dialing capability.

The telephone is ubiquitous, and so is TV. A television set with an attached microprocessor and keyboard like a pocket calculator can form a color display terminal. The combination of telephone and television technology has the potential of providing society with vast numbers of attractive terminals. This is the idea behind a British Post Office development called Prestel (originally Viewdata) (Fig. 1.3). From the home or office, television sets users will be able to dial the Prestel computer network and obtain services such as those listed at the bottom of Box 1.1. The cost of the addition to the television set should be minimal—no more than the cost of today's TV games. There will be many business applications for Prestel and because of the large market for sets, businesses will acquire cheap network terminals.

Cable television can also provide television terminal users with a means of accessing computer networks.

BOX 1.2   Factors which will lead to a substantial reduction in the cost of data transmission

- Mass-produced cheap terminals will become available. Some are derivatives of a telephone handset (like the Bell Transaction Telephones); others are derivatives of pocket calculators; still others are built by adding circuits to a conventional television set (like the British Post Office's Prestel/Viewdata scheme).

- Use of intelligent terminals and controllers lessens the number of messages and bits transmitted, especially in dialogue operations, by a factor of ten or sometimes much more.

- The telephone industry continues its swing from analog to digital (PCM) transmission.

- Satellites and other transmission media provide low-cost bit transmission.

- Techniques such as *data under voice* permit wideband digital channels to be derived from existing microwave and other facilities.

- Computer networks permit massive sharing of transmission facilities, interleaving transmission bursts from many machines. Small users can afford data transmission because they are charged only for what they transmit.

- Large-scale public networks are being built, on which economies of scale will give a low cost per packet: for example, Telenet, TYMNET, and, most important, Bell's ACS.

- Network standards permit mass-produced network interface machines using VLSI circuitry.

- Transmission control operations are removed from the software of mainframe computers into external cheaper units.

- Massive new applications lead to economies of scale in data networks.

Figure 1.2(a) AT&T's VuSet©, an inexpensive desktop terminal linked to the Touchtone® telephone. It displays four lines of 16 characters each, using a 64-character set, and is designed to be highly reliable.

Figure 1.2(b) Data terminals which are an inexpensive extension of the telephone handset could come into very widespread use. It is possible that a high portion of telephones could eventually have data capability. Such devices could be used for innumerable applications, possibly with templates for labeling the keyboard. This figure shows AT&T's Transaction II telephone. It has an 8-character visual display and reads magnetic-stripe cards conforming to ABA standards.

Figure 1.3 The British Prestel (Viewdata) scheme. Television sets in homes and offices become a cheap data network terminal.

Some countries have a public service for data broadcasting to home television sets. The owner of a set with a suitable attachment can receive frames which he selects from a "magazine" of available frames. The frames contain news reports, weather forecasts, stock prices, sports results, shopping information, information about broadcasts, and so on. The contents of each frame change as they are updated and could be changing constantly like the stock market ticker tape. Given the spectrum space of several television channels, an extremely large number of frames could be broadcast. Interactive dialogues could be created by combining data broadcasting with the use of appropriately programmed microprocessors in the television sets. Programs for such processors could be transmitted through the air like the data they would use.

A standard for broadcasting data to television set exists in Europe. It is called Teletext. The Teletext and Viewdata standards are compatible as far as possible and provide a two-shift character set that includes 64 graphics characters from which diagrams, large lettering and attractive screen formats can be created. Characters inserted into the data stream can also create seven different colors and enable selected portions of the display to flash on and off. This character set makes possible attractive displays on a conventional TV set (Fig. 1.4).

Broadcast data can also be picked up by a hand-held device the size of a pocket calculator or transistor radio. In the future, a pocket calculator could be designed to pick up current stock market figures, for example.

More interesting, small radio terminals which transmit have been used. Networks using radio terminals have also been used, experimentally. Such networks connect terminals by radio a distance of a few miles to a station from which they may be linked into a computer network. Protocols which work well with radio networks have been

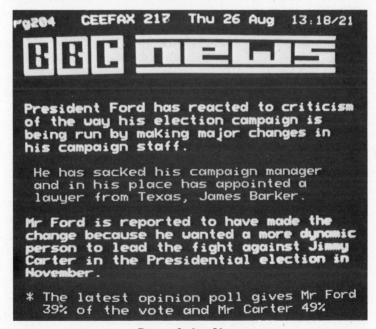

Table of Contents

Part of the News

Figure 1.4 CEEFAX screens. A BBC system for enabling television viewers to display frames of broadcast data on their screens.

demonstrated. Data devices can use radio links much more efficiently than speech devices such as CB radio. In the U.S.A. the FCC (Federal Communications Commission) has made a large block of the UHF spectrum available for new mobile radio applications. It is possible that portable data terminals will come into common use. Some prototypes have been designed for pocket devices a little larger than a calculator, with an extendible antenna. The applications of such devices would be innumerable if their cost dropped like that of pocket calculators. However, unlike pocket calculators, their use is dependent upon whether the common carriers build appropriate facilites.

Box 1.3 lists improved forms of access to networks. As computer networks grow and spread, the means for accessing them will drop in cost and become widespread.

NETWORK APPLICATIONS   As network costs drop, new applications become economical.

The combination of price elasticity and economies of scale leads to exponential growth in technology usage. As new applications bring more traffic, economies of scale will lower the transmission cost; as the transmission cost is lowered, new applications will provide more traffic—a positive feedback condition. Some new applications have potential traffic volumes hundreds of times greater than today's applications

The groups of applications which were a major driving force in the development of the Canadian public data network, DATAPAC, were those relating to the means of making payments—checking a customer's credit, authorizing the acceptance of a customer's check or the use of a magnetic-stripe bank card for making a payment. Some systems transfer funds electronically via networks instead of sending paperwork through the mail.

In the U.S.A. about 30 billion checks are written per year, representing about $20 trillion per year. An electronic fund transfer network could speed up the clearing time for checks by at least one day on average; probably more. One day represents a float of $\dfrac{\$20 \text{ trillion}}{365} = \$54.8$ billion, savable by electronic check transfer.

The number of credit card transactions is almost double the number of checks, and the payment delay with these is much longer. If all credit and transactions required a message sending over a data network, this information would be about a thousand times as much information transmission as that on the ARPA network.

Much larger in its potential is the prospect of electronic mail. A high proportion of the world's mail could be sent electronically. Only 20.2% of all mail in the U.S.A. originates from individuals; the rest is from business and government. Most business and government mail is originated by computer, and much of the rest comes from machines such as typewriters and word processing equipment. Such machines could be connected to networks, on-line or off-line, to avoid the tedious work of manual mail sorting and delivery. Given sufficient volumes, the cost would be much less than conventional mail.

BOX 1.3 Technologies which can improve the accessibility of remote computer resources

- *Viewdata (Prestel).*
  A cheap addition to the home television set which converts it to a color computer terminal linked to the home telephone line. It can access the Prestel network with a *local* telephone call. (Fig. 1.2).

- *Teletext.*
  A low-cost accessory to the home television set which enables it to pick up broadcast data. Teletext is a European standard compatible with Prestel. (Fig. 1.3).

- *CATV.*
  A reverse channel on cable television systems which permits the home television set to be used as a computer terminal.

- *Computer hobbyists.*
  A mass market for cheap equipment to access data networks.

- *X.25 and datagram.*
  Standards for network interfaces which permit large sales of mass-produced interface equipment.

- *Cheap additions to a telephone handset.*
  These convert a telephone into a computer terminal; e.g., AT&T's Transaction telephones (Fig. 1.2).

- *Pocket Terminals.*
  Future, cheap, mass-produced, portable terminals which plug into the telephone's microjack and contain built-in modems and dialing facilities.

- *Packet radio terminals.*
  Cheap equipment for accessing data networks with radio terminals (which may be hand-held portable devices).

- *Ethernet.*
  One of several schemes for the wiring of buildings or providing short-distance networks. A plug in the wall could connect minicomputers, typewriters, word-processing machines, copying machines, fascimile machines, process control equipment, graphics screen, etc., to a computer satellite antenna, or data network interface, with a high bandwidth.

- *Small satellite antennas on private premises.*
  These will give low-cost private networks and high-bandwidth transmission when necessary.

BOX 1.4 Technologies which improve the resources accessible by networks

- Very large on-line storage systems: 10^{12} bits. Later 10^{13}, 10^{14}.
- On-line libraries, avoiding the need for off-line tape and disk libraries.
- Inverted file systems. Software which facilitates information retrieval.
- Data base management systems. Especially those which permit spontaneous access to the data stored.
- Languages for on-line data-base interrogation, searching, and maintenance.
- Text retrieval software and software for managing files in word-processing applications.
- Technologies for automatic reorganization of very large storage systems; e.g., data migration.
- Data storage software appropriate for graphics.
- Hardware for data base management, inverted files, etc. For example, back-end data base management processors, hardware for secondary key operations, hardware file directory modules, associative memory.
- Fast, special-purpose computers; e.g., array processors, Illiac IV, the Grey computer, special-function processors, storage management computers.
- Psychologically effective terminal dialogues.
- Terminal dialogue program generators.
- Intelligent network directory modules.
- Software for distributed files or distributed data bases. Data access protocols.
- Software which enables peripheral machines to automatically obtain the services of remote machines.

Many communications in business need to be faster than mail. There are far more telephone calls placed than letters sent. Networks offer the prospect of very fast delivery of mail or messages. When mail or messages are sent in seconds, the way they are used becomes quite different from that of conventional mail. Bell's ACS network design is especially appropriate for office memos and messages.

When a person is not in his office a computer network can put messages in a queue for him.

In cases where letters or messages need to have signatures or drawings, or to be hand-written, transmission by facsimile can be used, rather than by machines which send characters. There are already more facsimile machines in the United States receiving and transmitting documents than telegraph machines.

**HOME USE
OF NETWORKS**
A further network application is the reference to information of various types. If terminals were widely available and it were cheap to use them, business and private individuals would be likely to make many references to information such as stock market figures, news, weather forecasts, business data, timetables, educational material, and so on. The British Post Office Prestel service has been heralded as ''probably the most significant development in public communications since television'' [4].

Who will provide the data and programs that people will want to use with the Prestel set? The answer to this is perhaps the most important aspect of the Prestel scheme. *Anyone* can provide it. Computer hobbyists or individual entrepreneurs can put data or programs into the Prestel files, and when any of the viewers use it, the originators will be paid a small royalty. Similarly advertising organizations, department stores, government agencies, or big corporations can make their data or programs available. It is, in effect, a new form of publishing. Publishing organizations, large and small, will distribute information via Prestel. But unlike most forms of publishing, the private individual can participate.

One market research study forecast that there could eventually be 10 million Prestel sets in Britain. If this were so the resulting data flow would be hundreds of times that on ARPANET today.

Box 1.4 lists technologies which will improve the resources accessible by networks, and Box 1.5 lists some potentially high-volume network uses.

**MERGING
TECHNOLOGIES**
Much of the potential of networks, then, will arise from having cheap access to distant machines. Low-cost data transmission can be made possible by massive sharing of digital circuits, and the swing from analog to digital telephone trunking. Distributed intelligence can reduce the numbers of bits transmitted in a dialogue. Inexpensive terminals can be created by additions to telephone and television sets.

We have the ingredients of a chain reaction as illustrated in Fig. 1.5.

BOX 1.5 Potentially high-volume applications of computer networks

- Systems for corporate operations of many different types, e.g., order entry systems, centralized purchasing, distributed inventory control, insurance underwriting.
- Corporate information networks, marketing information, customer information, product information.
- Airline reservation, car rental, hotel booking, networks.
- Electronic mail and message sending. Two-way interchange of messages.
- Electronic transfer of financial transactions between banks and via check clearing houses.
- Consumer check and credit verification in stores and restaurants, and, in some cases, consumer electronic fund transfer; bank cash dispensers and customer terminals.
- Intercorporate networks. For example, a computer in one firm transmits orders or invoices to another. Insurance agents have insurance company terminals, possibly via a shared network. Travel agents have terminals from airlines, shipping lines, hotel chains, etc.
- Stock market information systems which permit searches for stocks that meet certain criteria, performance comparisons, moving averages, and various forecasting techniques, all using dialogues which employ graphics.
- Terminal systems for investment advice and management, tax preparation, tax minimization.
- Home information services (such as Prestel or any which use the home TV set).

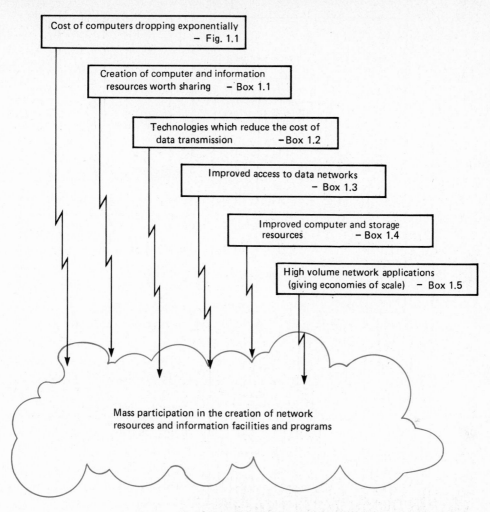

Figure 1.5 Ingredients of a chain reaction.

Most networks to date have been private and much of what we say will relate to private networks. The first public switched-data networks for computers are now operating. When these have matured and user demand is more certain, there will be massive expansion of the public networks probably using the X.25 and related protocols. Perhaps by the end of the century cheap terminals will be as ubiquitous as the telephone is today.

The computer was initially regarded as a machine for scientific and technical calculations. Later it became a machine for business data processing and this form of computing rapidly overtook scientific computing as shown in Fig. 1.6. Business data processing was originally batch processing with no telecommunications. Terminal access to data processing machines came slowly at first and eventually grew to dominate

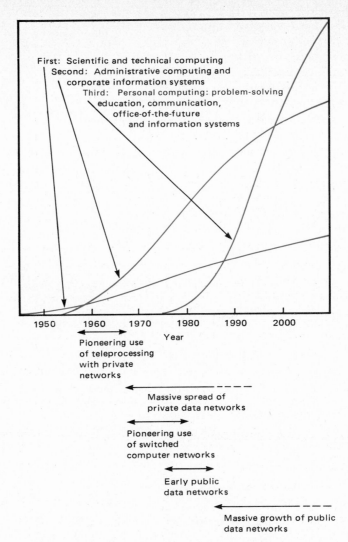

First: Scientific and technical computing
Second: Administrative computing and
corporate information systems
Third: Personal computing: problem-solving
education, communication,
office-of-the-future
and information systems

1950   1960   1970   1980   1990   2000

Year

Pioneering use
of teleprocessing
with private
networks

Massive spread of
private data networks

Pioneering use
of switched
computer networks

Early public
data networks

Massive growth of public
data networks

Figure 1.6 The growth of three types of computer usage.

business data processing. In the future *personal* uses of computing will grow—to solve problems, to collect data, to obtain information. The terminals will be perceived as a communications medium, like television or newspapers or books, and come to be accepted as part of the information fabric of society. Personal computing will become indispensable for work, for education, for medical care, and for dealing with problems, large and small.

Personal computing whether on pocket machines or network terminals may eventually grow in volume to overtake conventional data processing, as shown in Fig.

1.6. The potentials for networks in banking, finance, education, communication between people, problem solving, and the running of corporations are endless.

End users of a wide variety of different types will acquire their own machines or gain access to other machines. These machines will vary greatly in their capabilities, ranging from programmable desktop or pocket machines to fast sophisticated minicomputers. Some end users will program, but not most. Most will use prepackaged applications, prepackaged dialogue, report generators, dialogue generators, inquiry facilities, information retrieval systems, data entry systems, word processing packages, and data base interrogation, manipulation and search languages. Often the local intelligent machines will need programs in distant machines. Much of the data entered or used in local environments, and often *stored* in local environments, will also be used elsewhere. It will have to be transmitted.

This endlessly variable collection of machines made possible by today's microelectronics is growing at a furious rate. Terminals and processors will be scattered everywhere throughout corporations. Most of them will need to communicate. So corporations need networks and network standards that will make this possible.

Distributed processing will eventually spread to every nook and cranny of corporations. It is as inevitable as leaves coming out on a tree in spring. On the other hand, the expansion will be difficult to manage and control. It is difficult now to make the right networking decisions, but the payoff will be huge.

REFERENCES

1. The change from analog to digital operation is discussed in the author's books *Telecommunications and the Computer,* 2nd ed. 1976, and *Future Developments in Telecommunications,* 2nd ed., 1977, both from Prentice-Hall, Englewood Cliffs, NJ.

2. 274 million bits per second is the speed of the Bell T4 carrier, of which there are several implementations using different transmission systems. These are described in the author's *Future Developments in Telecommunications,* 2nd ed.

3. Bekay, I., and H. Mayer, "The Aerospace Corporation 1980–2000: Raising Our Sights for Advanced Space Systems," *Astronautics & Aeronautics,* July/Aug. 1976.

4. Advertising brochure for seminars on Prestel given by Butler Cox and Partners Ltd. in collaboration with the British Post Office, London, 1977.

2 THE TREND
TO DISTRIBUTED PROCESSING

MEANING OF DISTRIBUTED PROCESSING

The term *distributed processing* is used to describe systems with multiple processors. However, the term has different meaning to different persons because processors can be interconnected in many ways for various reasons.

For some authorities, the term refers to a multiprocessor complex in one location. In its most common usage, however, the word *distributed* implies that the processors are in geographically separate locations. Occasionally, the term is applied to an operation using multiple minicomputers which are not connected at all.

LOCAL VS. REMOTE DISTRIBUTION

We can distinguish varying degrees of dispersion of the distributed components:

1. Interconnected by a bus to form a single computer complex.

2. Interconnected by cables in a machine room.

3. Interconnected by in-plant wiring.

4. Interconnected by *permanent* common carrier telecommunications, e.g., a leased telephone line or permanent virtual circuit.

5. Interconnected by intermittent common carrier telecommunications, e.g., a dialed telephone connection or virtual call.

6. Not physically connected.

In cases 3, 4, and 5 we may have a computer network. As we will see there are some fundamentally different types of computer networks. If telecommunication lines were fast enough there would be no difference in function between a distributed computer system in one room and a geographically scattered system. Today, however, telecommunication links in normal use for data transmission are much slower—often 1000 times slower—than the channels which interconnect the boxes in a computer room. Consequently the functions which we distribute geographically are usually different from those which we distribute in one machine room.

The next generation of communications satellite systems may change the distribution of function on some systems because they will transmit brief bursts of data as fast as the buses or channels in a machine room. However, there will be a propagation delay of about 270 milliseconds—the time it takes light to travel to the satellite and back—and this will inhibit some types of function distribution. It could make sense to put devices such as mass storage (library) subsystems or printer subsystems at the other end of satellite links designed to transmit large bursts of data at high speed.

MACHINE COSTS   A major driving force towards distributed processing is the cost of small processors. Until the spread of minicomputers in the early 1970's a commonly accepted rule was Grosch's law which said that the cost per machine instruction executed was inversely proportional to the square of the size of the machine. Economies of scale in computing led to centralization. All work became funneled into centralized factory-like data processing shops.

Grosch's law became questioned in the 1970's. Some people even suggested that it had been reversed because the cost per instruction on some minicomputers was lower than on large computers, and on microprocessors was lower than minicomputers. The reason is related to the use of VLSI (very large scale integration) circuits, which can be mass-produced. Their development cycle is much shorter than that of large machines. Therefore they tend to have later technology which is less expensive because the cost of technology is dropping so rapidly. Tiny mass-produced processors in the future will give a cost per instruction *much* lower than that on large machines; they will, however, use a much simpler instruction set. Many applications require a complex instruction set. The sets do not need floating point arithmetic or elaborate MOVE instructions. The price/performance ratio on all computers will drop greatly throughout the next ten years, but it is likely to drop much more rapidly on small mass-produced machines than on machines costing hundreds of thousands of dollars.

The application load in large corporations is likely to continue to grow rapidly. The millions of instructions per second (MIPS) required for large on-line data base systems is likely to exceed the capacity of the largest commercial computers. The required capacity can be obtained, however, by distributing system functions and applications to peripheral machines. Functions will be distributed both to machines in the computer center and to many machines in user locations. This trend to distribution of processing will continue because the application program and software usage of machine instructions per second is growing much faster than the development of higher-speed machines.

When small computers are available for $10,000 or less, end users have a high incentive to possess their own machine, regardless of possible economies of scale. There are powerful reasons for tying these computers into corporate systems rather than allowing isolated incompatible development [1].

SOFTWARE PATH   In comparing the costs of minicomputers and large com-
LENGTH   puters, the software is often a more important factor than
                      hardware. When a transaction enters a system, is pro-
cessed, and leaves, a large number of software instructions is executed in addition to
the instructions in the application programs. The number of software instructions executed for a transaction is referred to as the *path length*. A typical inexpensive minicomputer handles one transaction at a time, i.e., single-thread operation—no multiprocessing. It reads and writes file records in a simple direct fashion. The path length is often
less than a thousand instructions. On a large computer with a virtual operating system
and data base, data communications facilities, the path length is often greater than one
or two hundred thousand instructions.

The application programs for most commercial jobs execute a fairly small number
of instructions per transaction, often one or two hundred. The total number of instructions executed per transaction in a large computer can therefore be a hundred times
greater than in a cheap minicomputer.

The user gains many benefits from the complex software of large computers, but
the cost in terms of instructions executed is high.

THE NATURE   The term *teleprocessing* was used to imply the use of tele-
OF TELEPROCESSING communications facilities for accessing processing
                       power. When calculators and minicomputers become
cheap, however, what was originally done by terminals and teleprocessing began to be
done on the local machine. The local machine may itself be connected by telecommunications to other machines, and a transaction may then be processed either on the local
machine or on a distant machine.

There are two main reasons why a transaction is sent to a distant machine. First
the local machine has *insufficient power;* the transaction may need the number-crunch-
ing power of a large machine. Second, the transaction needs *data* which are stored
elsewhere. Most commercial transactions—the bread and butter of data processing—
do not need large computer power. Small computers or terminal cluster controllers at
user locations are sufficient to process them. *Therefore the main reason for teleprocessing in commercial data processing is to obtain data, not to obtain processing
power.* The advent of microprocessors has changed the nature of teleprocessing.

PROCESSING, DATA, In general, there are three aspects of systems that may or
AND CONTROL   may not be distributed: *processing, data,* and *control*
                       mechanisms. The arguments relating to the three are dif-

ferent. There may be arguments for centralizing some of the *data* and distributing others. These are different to the arguments relating to the distribution of *processing*. A system may have much of its processing geographically scattered, and yet the overall *management* and *control* mechanisms reside separately.

In some computer networks the control mechanisms are mostly centralized. In others, they are mostly distributed. Where purely centralized control exists, loss of the center puts the entire network out of action. With distributed control any portion of a network can be destroyed and the rest will continue to function. A centralized system may have its reliability enhanced by having more than one center, or more than one computer capable of control at the center.

Both centralized and distributed control are found in nature, often in combination. A city has largely distributed control. Some functions are centralized in the city hall, but the city would go on working if the city hall were destroyed. Some packet-switching computer networks would go on functioning if any single portion were destroyed even though a few management functions are centralized. A human body has vital centralized functions. It can tolerate much damage, but not the destruction of the brain or heart. Some computer networks are equally dependent upon certain critical components. As networks assume increasingly vital purposes, fault-tolerant control mechanisms will become more important.

DISTRIBUTED DATA   Where interlinked processors are geographically scattered, the data they use may be scattered also. However, the constraints which apply to locating of data are different from those which apply to locating processors. In many systems it is the structure and usage of the *data* that determines what is practical in the distribution of processors.

Data can be stored in two types of ways—as straightforward data files or as data bases. A file is data designed to serve a particular application or related group of applications. A programmer's view of file is similar to the file which is physically stored. A data base is an application-independent collection of data from which multiple different programmers' records can be derived by software. There are major advantages in employing data base software but the software is complex and usually operates, today, on data stored at one location. Distributed data is often organized, therefore, in the form of *files* (usually on-line files) rather than as a *data base,* although multiple data base systems may also be interconnected.

Economies of scale in storage systems are different from those in processors. The cost per bit stored on very large storage units is substantially lower than that on small storage units.

Often, however, it is not the cost per bit that determines whether data should be centralized or decentralized. There may be properties inherent in the data itself which lead naturally to centralization or decentralization. For example, if a file is being constantly updated and geographically scattered, users want the current version (as with the airline reservation file), and therefore the file is usually centralized. If the data as a whole are searched, or secondary key operations are performed on them, they are usually centralized. If they are stored in data base form, they are usually centralized. On the other hand, if the data are used only by the peripheral location where they originate, then they can be decentralized. If the update rate is low, or updates can be performed offline, then multiple copies of the same data are usually stored at different locations.

The question of which configurations make sense in specific distributed processing situations is determined to a major extent by what data are used and whether the data should be distributed.

CATEGORIES OF DATA DISTRIBUTION   There are a number of types of ways in which data can be distributed and used. Figure 2.1 shows types of data system configurations. The diagrams apply to either file systems or data base systems, or in some cases to combinations of the two.

The top two diagrams show systems in which the data is centralized. Where multiple hosts are used, these might be either local to the data or remote from it.

The next two diagrams show hierarchical data systems. In the first, labeled *dependent* hierarchical data, the data in the lower-level machines are closely related to those in the higher-level machine. They are often a subset of the higher-level data, used for local application. The master copy of the data may be kept by the higher-level machine. When a change is made to the data in the lower machine, this change must be passed up to the higher machine—sometimes immediately, sometimes later in an updating cycle.

In other systems the lower machine may store some of the data that is in the higher machine and also have some which is its own and which is never passed upwards. The lower machine, for example, might keep addresses of and general information about customers. These bulky data are never needed by the higher-level system. The higher-level system might, however, store customer numbers, names, credit information, and details of orders—redundantly. These are stored by both machines and any modifications to them by the lower machine must be passed upwards.

In the diagram labeled *independent* hierarchical data, all of the processors are independent self-sufficient data processing systems. The structure of data in the lower-level machines is probably quite different from that in the higher-level machine. A common example of such a relationship is one in which the lower-level systems are designed for routine repetitive operations: order entry, production control, inventory, and so on. The high-level machine is an *information system,* possibly at a head office location, designed to answer spontaneous queries from management, planning staff, forecasters, product or strategy designers, etc. All of the data in the higher-level machine may be culled from the lower-level machines, but the data are summarized, edited, and reorganized with secondary indices or other means of searching them to answer spontaneous queries [2].

The next diagram shows a *split-data* system. Here there are multiple data systems containing identical data structures. The system in District A keeps District A data.

That in B keeps B data, and so on. Most of the transactions processed require the data in the system which handles them, but occasionally a transaction originating in one district needs the data in another district. Either the transaction or the data must be transmitted over the network. Some organizations have installed many minicomputers, each with similar split-data files, and a network interconnecting them.

We distinguish between a *split-data* and a *separate-data* system. In the former the application programs and data structures are similar. The multiple machines are planned and programmed by a common group. In the *separate-data* configuration the interconnected systems contain different data and different programs, and are probably installed by different teams. Nevertheless they serve the same corporation or government body. One of the computers might be able to request data from another. An end-user terminal might be connectable to all systems.

In the configuration shown, one of the systems handles *production,* another *purchasing,* and the third *general accounting.* These systems are in different locations. The production system, which might be in a factory, creates purchasing requisitions, and these are transmitted to the purchasing system. Both the purchasing and the production system generate data which must be passed to the general accounting system.

Figure 2.2 shows a working example of a separate-data system installed with large computers, and Fig. 2.3 shows one installed with minicomputers. In the former, the computer systems are 300 miles apart, each system has its own development staff, and both systems are connected to terminals throughout North America. The terminals exist in all locations of a large marketing organization. The transaction is relayed to the system it needs by means of the communications concentrators. The minicomputer system is more truly ''distributed.'' Here each store has its own minicomputer and data files. These minicomputers communicate with the central *purchasing, marketing,* and *general accounting* systems.

The next diagram of Fig. 2.1 shows *replicated data.* Identical copies of the data are stored in geographically separate locations, because this duplicate storage avoids the need for high-volume transmission between the systems and thus is cheaper. Such an organization only makes sense if the volume of updates of the data are low.

The last diagram of Fig. 2.1 shows heterogeneous data systems—independent computer systems set up by different authorities for different purposes, and interconnected by a general-purpose computer network like ARPANET. Each computer keeps its own data and there is no commonality or relationship be among the different forms of data organization. A user can access any computer on the network, but he must know the details of how that particular computer's data is organized.

COMBINATIONS   Figure 2.1 illustrates different forms of data distribution which give different problems. Many configurations contain mixtures of these forms. Figure 2.4 on page 34 shows a typical corporate configuration containing most of them.

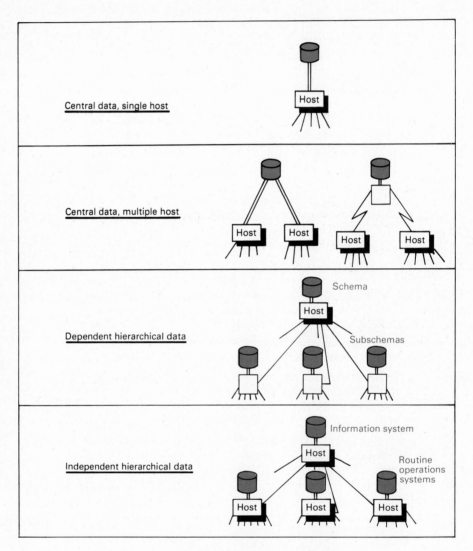

Central data, single host

Central data, multiple host

Dependent hierarchical data

Schema

Subschemas

Independent hierarchical data

Information system

Routine
operations
systems

Figure 2.1   Categories of distributed data systems.

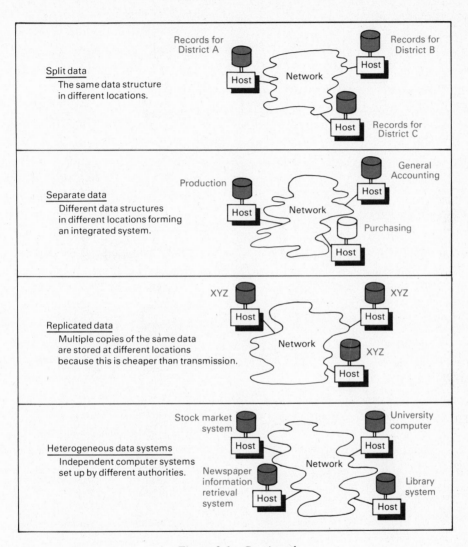

Split data
  The same data structure in different locations.

Records for District A — Host — Network — Host — Records for District B — Host — Records for District C

Separate data
  Different data structures in different locations forming an integrated system.

Production — Host — Network — Host — General Accounting — Host — Purchasing

Replicated data
  Multiple copies of the same data are stored at different locations because this is cheaper than transmission.

XYZ — Host — Network — Host — XYZ — Host — XYZ

Heterogeneous data systems
  Independent computer systems set up by different authorities.

Stock market system — Host — Network — Host — University computer — Newspaper information retrieval system — Host — Host — Library system

Figure 2.1   Continued

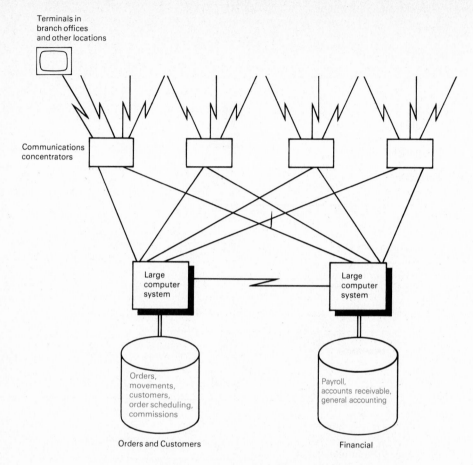

Terminals in
branch offices
and other locations

Communications
concentrators

Large
computer
system

Large
computer
system

Orders,
movements,
customers,
order scheduling,
commissions

Payroll,
accounts receivable,
general accounting

Orders and Customers

Financial

Figure 2.2   An installed example of a large separate-data system.

Data can be divided within a distributed system according to the following criteria:

1. Geography.
2. Type of data.
3. Type of usage.

CENTRALIZATION VS.
DECENTRALIZATION

The new environment of distributed processing confronts data processing managers with a complex set of choices. What operations should be centralized and what decentralized? Where should the data be kept? What configuation of large computers, minicomputers, and intelligent terminals will best serve the end users?

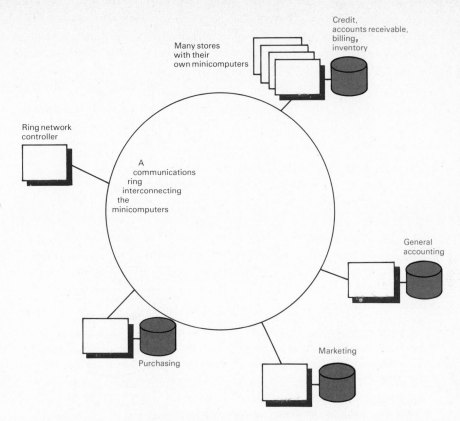

Figure 2.3   A ring network of minicomputers forming both a *separate-data* and a *split-data* system (split data because there are so many stores with similar files).

In addition to the technical aspects of system design—processing, data, and control mechanisms—there are the human aspects. Should the application programming be done centrally or by peripheral groups? Should the overall implementation management be centralized or distributed? What standards should be set centrally?

The costs of hardware militate against a high degree of centralization. Moreover, there are other costs which are often higher than the hardware costs. There are also major human and political arguments for and against centralization. It is often these human and political factors which determine the issue.

The important point is that the technology now gives the system designer a choice. The mix of microcomputers, minicomputers and large computers, and the software architectures for tying them together permit whatever mix of centralization and decentralization is appropriate for an organization.

It is no longer adequate for a system vendor to sell only large mainframe computers. A vendor needs to be able to tailor a distributed system to the customer's organization, and the configuration of such systems will differ widely from one situation to another. A computer manufacturer needs a software architecture which ties the distributed components together into an appropriate computer network. Such architectures are emerging and are discussed later in the book.

Box 2.1 summarizes the forces which are causing the trend to distributed processing.

BOX 2.1 The factors which are causing the trend to distributed processing

- *Low cost processors*.
  Minicomputers and microcomputers have dropped in cost to a level where most end-user groups can afford one. They will increase in power and drop in cost much further.

- *Grosch's law overruled*.
  Grosch's law said that the cost of processing is inversely proportional to the square of the size of the computer. This leads to centralization of all software and processing functions. Today executing an instruction on a micro or minicomputer costs less than on a very large computer. This leads to decentralization of some functions.

- *Increasing sophistication of end users*.
  Some end users are becoming familiar with computers and programming and would like a piece of the action.

- *End-user dissatisfaction*.
  Many end-user managers are dissatisfied with the responsiveness of the central DP group. Their requests for programs or information are ignored or dragged out for too long. They would like to have their own processing facilities.

- *Need for higher availability*.
  Many end users have become dissatisfied because data or processing power is not available from the central system when they need it, either because of failures, software crashes, or scheduling constraints.

- *End-user imagination*.
  Once end users understand computing, they use their imagination about how computers can help them. Many uses of computers that would not come from a central group are being originated by end users. Only the end users are close to the real problems of their location.

- *High cost of phone lines*.
  Telecommunication costs place constraints on usage of a centralized system.

Box 2.1 *Continued*

- *Low bandwidth of phone lines.*
  For some uses of distant systems, high-speed bursts of data transmission are needed at speeds higher than that of a voice line. Distributed systems can avoid this need.

- *Better dialogue.*
  Interactive systems need intelligent terminals or controllers to achieve psychologically effective dialogues with fast enough response times.

- *Central control of remote development.*
  Random, scattered, and decentralized development without overall management can lead to chaos. The separate pieces rapidly become incompatible and are difficult to link together to provide central management information. DP management loses control. Instead, distributed processing networks with appropriate standards are needed.

- *System interlinking.*
  As data processing builds up in an organization, there is an increasing need to interlink separate systems.

- *Remote data base access.*
  Data bases maintained at one location are valuable to users at other locations. It is desirable that programs used at other locations should employ them.

- *Networking software.*
  Software for networking and distributed processing is now available and is improving.

- *Security.*
  Distributed systems may give better security and reliability because they avoid putting all the eggs in one basket.

- *Excessive CPU load.*
  Large installations are running out of computing power on large systems as the applications increase in number and use software which is increasingly expensive in machine instructions. Functions need to be off-loaded from the central CPU and distributed. Large computers are not becoming faster quickly enough to meet the large application backlogs and desire for instruction-gobbling software.

- *Programmer shortage.*
  As end users demand more interactive programs, the manpower of central DP groups often becomes inadequate. It is desirable where possible to give end users facilities to develop their own computing, possibly with high-level software using a remote data base.

- *Centralization and decentralization.*
  There are powerful arguments both for and against centralization [3]. Distributed processing makes it possible to build systems which to a large extent can achieve the advantages of both.

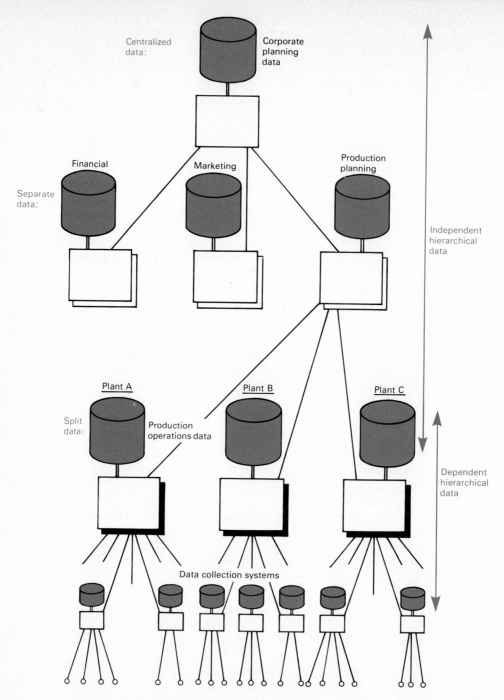

Figure 2.4 The categories of data distribution in Fig. 2.1 are often combined in one system.

This book confines itself to the technology of distributed processing. Human and political aspects of distributed system design are discussed in the author's companion books.

REFERENCES

1. Discussed in the author's forthcoming book *Design of Distributed Data Processing,* Prentice-Hall, Englewood Cliffs, NJ.

2. Discussed in the author's book *Principles of Data Base Management,* Prentice-Hall, Englewood Cliffs, NJ, 1976.

3. Same as reference 1 above.

3 TYPES OF DISTRIBUTED SYSTEMS

There are several types of distributed processing systems in which the components are hooked together by telecommunications. This chapter categorizes them and gives examples.

HORIZONTAL VS. VERTICAL DISTRIBUTION

First we shall distinguish between horizontal and vertical distribution.

By *vertical distribution* we mean that there is a *hierarchy* of processors, as in Fig. 3.1. The transaction may enter and leave the computer system at the lowest level. The lowest level may be able to process the transaction or may execute certain functions and pass it up to the next level. Some, or all, transactions eventually reach the highest level, which will probably have access to on-line files or data bases.

The machine at the top of a hierarchy might be a computer system in its own right, performing its own type of processing on its own transactions. The data it uses is, however, passed to it from lower-level systems. The machine at the top might be a head-office system which receives data from factory, branch, warehouse, and other systems.

By *horizontal distribution* we imply that the distributed processors do not differ in rank. They are of equal status—peers—and we refer to them as *peer-coupled* systems. A transaction may use only one processor, although there are multiple processors available. On some peer-coupled systems a transaction may pass from one system to another, causing different sets of files to be updated.

Figure 3.2 illustrates horizontal distribution. The top diagram shows multiple processors connected to a bus or wideband short-distance channel. The second diagram shows multiple processors connected to a loop, perhaps spanning several buildings in a factory complex, university campus, or shopping center, but in some systems being

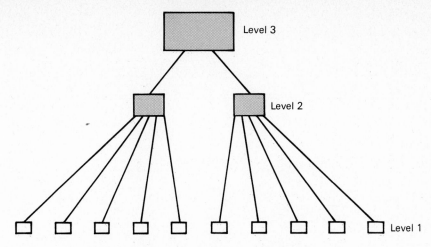

Figure 3.1   Vertical distribution.

comprised of long-carrier connections. The third and fourth diagrams show horizontal computer networks in which a user may access one of many machines.

COOPERATIVE
OPERATION?

In some networks the user has a choice of computer systems available to him, but he normally employs only one computer at a time. The computers are programmed independently, and each computer performs its own functions.

In other networks the computers are programmed to cooperate with one another to solve a common set of problems. This is often the case in a vertical system (Fig. 3.1). The lower-level machines are programmed to pass work to the higher-level machines. This is sometimes true also in a horizontal system. The processing of one transaction may begin on one machine and pass to another. The different computers perform different functions or maintain and update different files. The machines may be minicomputers in the same location or computers scattered across the world on a network.

FUNCTION
DISTRIBUTION VS.
SYSTEM DISTRIBUTION

In some distributed systems, usually vertical systems, *functions* are distributed, but not the capability to fully process entire transactions. The lower-level machines in Fig. 3.1 may be intelligent terminals or intelligent controllers in which processors are used for functions such as message editing, screen formatting, data collection dialogue with terminal operators, security, or message compaction or concentration. They do not complete the processing of entire transactions.

We refer to this distribution as *function distribution* and contrast it with *system*

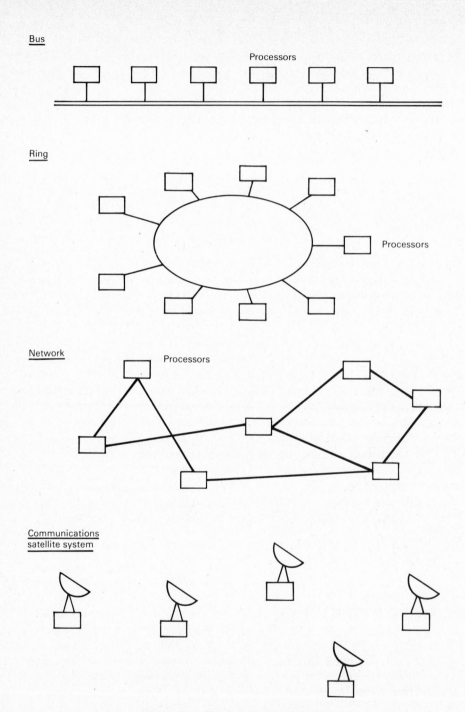

Figure 3.2 Horizontal distribution.

distribution in which the lower-level machines are systems in their own right, processing their own transactions, and occasionally passing transactions or data up the hierarchy to higher level machines.

In a *systems distribution* environment the lower machines may be entirely different from, and incompatible with, the higher machines. In a *function distribution* environment, close cooperation between the lower-level and higher-level machines is vital. Overall system standards are necessary to govern what functions are distributed and exactly how the lower and higher machines form part of a common system architecture with appropriately integrated control mechanisms and software.

COMBINATIONS   *Many configurations of the future will be neither purely vertical nor purely horizontal; neither purely homogeneous nor entirely heterogeneous. They will be combinations of these, and function distribution and systems distribution will be combined in one configuration.*

Figure 3.3 shows a network with both a horizontal and vertical association of machines. It contains both function distribution and vertical systems distribution.

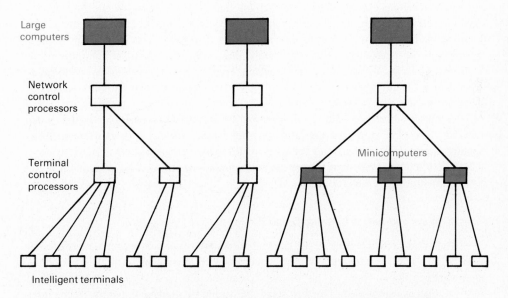

Figure 3.3   Some networks contain both vertical and horizontal combinations of processors, and both function-distribution and distributed system aspects. The shaded machines are processors capable of processing entire transactions.

**FUNCTION
DISTRIBUTION**
When the peripheral nodes are not self-sufficient systems but perform a function subservient to a higher-level distant computer, we speak of *intelligent terminals, intelligent terminal cluster controllers,* or *intelligent concentrators.* These terms imply a vertical distribution of function in which all or most transactions have to be transmitted, possibly in a modified form, to a higher-level computer system, or possibly to a network of higher-level computer systems.

The centralized teleprocessing system of 1970 employed simple terminals and carried out almost all of its functions in the central computer. At first system control and housekeeping functions were moved out, then functions such as data collection, editing, and dialogue with terminal operators, and finally many of the application programs themselves.

Figure 3.4 shows places where intelligence could reside in a vertical function distribution system:

1. In the host computer, B

2. In a line control unit or "front-end" network control computer, C

Many functions are necessary to control a terminal network. If the host computer performs all the operations itself, it will be constantly interrupting its main processing, and many machine cycles will be needed for line control. Some of the line control functions may be performed by a separate line control unit. In some systems, all of them are performed by a separate and specialized computer. The proportion of functions which are performed by a line control unit, which by the host computer hardware and which by its software, varies widely from system to system. Some application functions could be performed by the subsystem computer—for example, accuracy checking and message logging.

A major advantage of using a front-end network-control computer is that when the host computer has a software crash or brief failure, the network can remain functionally operational. Restart and recovery of the network without errors or lost transactions is a tedious and often time-consuming operation, and if it happens often it can be very frustrating to the end users.

3. In the mid-network nodes, D and E

The mid-network nodes or concentrators may take a variety of different forms. They may be relatively simple machines with unchangeable logic. They may have wired-in logic, part or all of which can be changed by an engineer. They may be microprogrammed. Or they may be stored-program computers, sometimes designed solely for concentration or switching, but sometimes also capable of other operations and equipped with files, high-speed printers, and other input-output equipment.

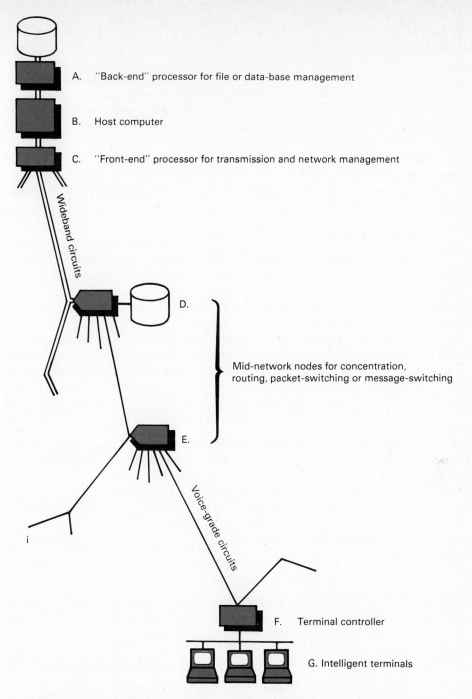

A. "Back-end" processor for file or data-base management

B. Host computer

C. "Front-end" processor for transmission and network management

Wideband circuits

D.

Mid-network nodes for concentration,
routing, packet-switching or message-switching

E.

i

Voice-grade circuits

F. Terminal controller

G. Intelligent terminals

Figure 3.4 Places where intelligence can reside in a distributed-intelligence network.

4. In the terminal control unit, F

Terminal control units also differ widely in their complexity, ranging from simple hardwired devices to stored-program computers with much software. Increasingly they are computers with storage units and there is a trend towards greater power and larger storage. They may control one terminal or many. They may be programmed to interact with the terminal operator to provide a psychologically effective dialogue in which only an essential kernel is transmitted to or from the host computer. They may generate diagrams on a graphics terminal or interact with the operator's use of a light pen. They are often the main component in carrying out the assortment of distributed functions which this chapter will list.

5. In the terminal, G

"Intelligent terminals" are becoming more intelligent. Their processing functions range from single operations such as accumulating totals in a system which handles financial transactions, to dialogues with operators involving much programming. Some intelligent terminals do substantial editing of input and output data. Some terminals perform important *security* functions.

Where several terminals share a control unit, F, such functions are probably better performed in the control unit, leaving the terminal a simple inexpensive mechanism in which the main design concern may be tailoring the keyboard and other operator mechanisms to the applications in question.

6. In a "back-end" file or data base management processor, A

File or data base operations may be handled by a "back-end" processor. This can carry out the specialized functions of data base management or file searching operations. It can prevent interference between separate transactions updating the same data. It can be designed to give a high level of data security protection.

"Back-end" processors, where they exist today, are normally cable-connected to their local host computer. They could, especially when high-bandwidth networks or communications satellite facilities are available, be remote from the host computers which use them.

CHOICE OF FUNCTION LOCATION   The designer, faced with different locations in which he could place functions, may choose his configuration with objectives such as the following:

1. *Minimum total system cost.* There is often a trade-off between distributed function cost and telecommunications cost.

2. *High reliability.* The value attached to system availability will vary from one system to another. The systems analyst must evaluate how much extra money is worth spending on du-

plexing, alternate routing and distributed processing to achieve high availability. On some systems reliability is vital. A supermarket must be able to keep its cash registers going when a communication line or distant host computer fails.

3. *Security*. In some systems function distribution is vital for system security (as we discuss later).

4. *Psychologically effective dialogue with terminal users*. Function distribution is used to make the dialogue fast, effective and error-free.

5. *Complexity*. Excessive complexity should be avoided. The problems multiply roughly as the square of the complexity.

6. *Software cost*. Some types of function distribution occurring throughout a network incur a high programming expenditure. The use of stored-program peripheral machines may inflate cost.

7. *Flexibility and expandability*. It is necessary to choose hardware and software techniques that can easily be changed and expanded later, especially because telecommunications and networking technology are changing so fast. Some approaches make this step difficult.

REASONS
FOR FUNCTION
Box 3.1 lists the main reasons for function distribution. They fall into three categories:

1. Reasons associated with the host

Many machine instructions are needed to handle all of the telecommunications functions. The load on a central machine could be too great if it had to handle all of these functions. A single computer operates in a largely *serial* fashion executing one instruction at a time. It seems generally desirable to introduce parallelism into computing so that the circuits execute many operations simultaneously. This is the case when machine functions are distributed to many small machines.

2. Reasons associated with the network

There are many possible mechanisms which can be used to make the network function efficiently. We will discuss them later in the book. These mechanisms are used to lower the overall cost of transmission and increase its reliability. The network configuration is likely to change substantially on most systems, both because of application development and increasing traffic, and because of changes in networking technology which are now coming at a fast and furious rate. Function-distribution may be used to isolate the changing network from other parts of the system so that the other parts do not have to be modified as the network changes. The term *network transparency* is used to imply that changes which occur in the network be not evident to and not affect the users.

BOX 3.1   Reasons for function distribution

1. Psychologically Effective Dialogues

- *Local interaction.*
  Much of the dialogue interaction takes place locally rather than being transmitted, and hence can be designed without concern for transmission constraints.

- *Local panel storage.*
  Panels or graphics displayed as part of the dialogue can be stored locally.

- *Speed*
  Local responses are fast. Time delays which are so frustrating in many terminal dialogues can be largely avoided. The delays that do occur when host response is needed can be absorbed into the dialogue structures.

2. Reduction of Telecommunications Costs

- *Reduction of number of messages.*
  In many dialogues the number of messages transmitted to and fro can be reduced by an order of magnitude because dialogue is carried on within the terminal or local controller.

- *Reduction of message size.*
  Messages for some applications can be much shortened because repetitive information is transmitted.

- *Reduction of number of line turnarounds.*
  Because the number of messages is reduced; and because a terminal cluster controller or concentrator can combine many small messages into one block for transmission.

- *Bulk transmission.*
  Nontime-critical items can be collected and stored for later batch transmission over a switched connection.

- *Data compaction.*
  There are various ways of compressing data so that fewer bits have to be transmitted. This effectively increases the transmission speed.

- *Minimum cost routing.*
  The machine establishing a link could attempt first to set up a minimum-cost connection, e.g., a corporate tie-line network. If these are busy it could try progressively more expensive connections (e.g., WATS, direct distance dialing).

- *Controlled network access.*
  Terminal users may be prevented from making expensive unauthorized calls.

Box 3.1 *Continued*

3. Reliability

- *Local autonomy*.
  A local operation can continue, possibly in a fallback mode (using a minimal set of functions), when the location is cut off from the host computer by a circuit, network, or host failure. On certain systems this is vital.

- *Automatic dial backup*.
  A machine may be able to dial a connection if a leased circuit fails.

- *Automatic alternate routing*.
  A machine may be able to use an alternate leased circuit or network path when a network failure occurs.

- *Control procedures*.
  Control procedures can be used to recover from errors, or failures and to ensure that no messages are lost or double-processed.

- *Automatic load balancing*.
  A machine may be able to dial an extra circuit or use a different computer to handle high traffic peaks.

4. Less Load on Host

- *Parallel operations*.
  The parallel operation of many small processors relieves the host computer of much of its work load, and lessens the degree of multiprogramming. In some systems this is vital because the host is overburdened with data base operations.

- *Permits large numbers of terminals*.
  Some systems require too many terminals for it to be possible to connect them directly to a host computer. Distributed control and operations make the system possible.

5. Fast Response Times

- *Process mechanisms*.
  Local controllers can read instruments rapidly and give a rapid response to process control mechanisms when necessary.

- *Human mechanisms*.
  Fast reaction is possible to human actions such as the use of a plastic card or the drawing of a curve with a light pen.

Box 3.1 *Continued*

- *Dialogue response times.*
  Dialogues requiring fast response times (such as multiple menu selection) can be handled by local controllers.

6. Data Collection

- *Data entry terminals.*
  Many inexpensive data entry terminals (for example, on a factory shop floor) can be connected to a local controller which gathers data for later transmission.

- *Local error checking.*
  Local checks can be made on the accuracy or syntax of terminal entries. An attempt is made to correct the entries before transmitting them to the host.

- *Instrumentation.*
  Local controllers scan or control instruments, gathering the result for transmission to a host computer.

7. More Attractive Output

- *Local editing.*
  Editing of output received at terminals can lay out the data attractively for printers or screen displays. Repetitive headings, lines, or text, and page numbers can be added locally. Multiple editing formats can be stored locally.

8. Peaks

- Interactive and real-time systems often have peaks of traffic which are difficult or expensive to accommodate without function distribution. Storage at the periphery allows the peak transactions to be buffered or filed until they can be transmitted and processed economically.

9. Security

- *Cryptography.*
  Cryptography on some systems gives a high measure of protection from wiretapping, tampering with magnetic-stripe plastic cards, etc. Cryptography is vital on certain electronic fund transfer systems.

- *Access control.*
  Security controls can prevent calls from unauthorized sources from being accepted, and prevent terminals from contacting unauthorized machines.

Box 3.1 *Continued*

10. Network Independence

- *Network transparency.*
  Programmers of machines using networks should not be concerned with details of how the network functions. They should simply pass messages to the network interface and receive messages from it.

- *Network evolution.*
  As networks grow and evolve, and as different networks are merged, programs in machines using the networks should not have to be rewritten.

- *New networks.*
  Network technology is changing fast. As applications are switched to new types of networks (e.g., DDS, value-added networks, Datadial, satellite networks), the programs in the using machines should not have to be rewritten.

11. Terminal Independence

- *New terminals.*
  Terminal design is changing fast. If a new terminal is substituted, the old programs should not have to be rewritten. Software in terminal controllers may make the new terminals appear like the old.

- *Virtual terminal features.*
  Application programs may be written without a detailed knowledge of the terminal that they will use. For example, the screen size or print-line size may not be known. The programmers use specified constraints on output, and the distributed-intelligence mechanisms map their output to the device in question.

Mechanisms relating to the network may reside in any of the locations indicated in Fig. 3.4. A terminal or a controller for a cluster of terminals may have mechanisms intended to minimize the transmission cost. A front-end communications processor may relieve the host of all network functions, and maintain network operations without loss of data if the host or its software fails. Intelligence may also reside in mid-network nodes such as packet-switching devices, concentrators, intelligent exchanges, or telephone company equipment in systems such as AT&T's ACS. The phrase "intelligent network" is increasingly used to imply that the network itself uses computers to share transmission links or other resources in an efficient, dependable manner.

3. Reasons associated with the end user

Probably the most important of the three categories is that associated with the end user. On many systems built prior to the era of function distribution, the dialogue that takes place between the terminal and its operator is technically crude. It is often difficult for the user to learn, and clumsy and frustrating in operation. The user is forced to learn mnemonics and to remember specific sequences in which items must be entered. The response times are often inappropriate. The majority of the users who should be employing terminals are unable to make the machines work, and generally discount the possibility of ever using them because they perceive them as being difficult—designed for technicians, programmers, or a specially trained and dedicated staff. One psychologist describes many of these user-terminal interfaces as ''unfit for human consumption.''

In the past there has been good reason for the crudity of terminal dialogues. The terminals had no intelligence. Every character typed and displayed had to be transmitted over the network. The network often used leased voice lines serving many terminals, and to minimize the network cost, the number of characters transmitted was kept low. The response times were often higher than psychologically appropriate because of the queries on the lines.

With intelligent terminals or controllers the dialogue processing can take place in the local machine. Most of the characters are not transmitted over the telephone lines. The only characters transmitted are those which take essential information to the central computer and carry back essential information to the terminal. These characters will often be only a small fraction of the total characters typed and displayed in a psychologically effective dialogue.

Much of the future growth of the computer industry is dependent on making the machines easy to use and understand for the masses of people in all walks of life who will employ them, and distributed intelligence can play a vital part in this.

HIERARCHICAL DISTRIBUTED PROCESSING   So far this chapter has discussed *function distribution* in which the peripheral machines are not self-sufficient when isolated from their host by a telecommunications or other failure. Now let us expand the discussion to *processing distribution* in which the peripheral processors keep their own data and can be self-sufficient, but which are connected to higher-level systems.

There is not necessarily a sharp boundary line between function distribution and system distribution. In some cases there has tended to be growth from function distribution to system distribution, with more and more power being demanded in peripheral machines. In other cases the peripheral machines started as standalone minicomputers and became linked into a higher-level system.

The application programming steps for most (but not all) commercial transactions do not require a large computer. Small, inexpensive, mass-produced processors such as those discussed in the previous chapter could usually handle the whole transaction. They would handle it with a *much* smaller software path length than a large computer. The difference in software path length greatly reinforces the arguments about there no longer being economies of scale. Some large mainframes with complex data base management systems use more than 100,000 *software* instructions per transaction and only a few thousand *application* instructions per transaction.

In some cases there are good reasons for storing the *data* which a transaction requires *centrally*. In other cases the data also can be kept in storage attached to the local machine.

As we commented earlier, criteria for determining whether a transaction is transmitted could be:

1. *It needs the power of a large computer*
2. *It needs data which are stored centrally*

If one of these criteria does not apply, then the transaction is processed locally. Most commercial transactions and many scientific calculations do not need the power of a large computer. There are exceptions such as simulations and complex models. Many of these exceptions would not use the teleprocessing anyway. But the second criterion—centralized data—is important to some, but not all, data. Consequently data base and data communications techniques are closely related, and computer manufacturers produce *data base, data communications (DBDC)* software.

EXAMPLES OF HIERARCHICAL CONFIGURATIONS

Some examples of hierarchical configurations are as follows:

1. Insurance

The branches of an insurance company each have their own processor with a printer and terminals. This processor handles most of the computing requirements of the branch. Details of the insurance contracts made are sent to a head office computer for risk analysis and actuarial calculations. The head-office management has up-to-the-minute information on the company's financial position and exposure, and can adjust the quotations given by the salesmen accordingly.

2. A chain store

Each store in a chain has a minicomputer which records sales and handles inventory control and accounts receivable. It prints sales slips (receipts) for customers at the time of sale. Salesmen and office personnel can use the terminals to display pricing, inventory and accounts receivable information, and customer statements. The store management can display salesman performance information and goods aging and other analysis reports (Fig. 3.5).

The store systems transmit inventory and sales information to the head office system. At night they receive inventory change information. The fast receipt of inventory and sales information enables the head office system to keep the inventory of the entire organization to a minimum.

The store systems run unattended. Any program changes are transmitted to the systems from the head office computer.

3. Production control

Various different production departments in a factory complex each have a minicomputer. Work station terminals on the shop floor are connected to the minicomputer and the workers enter details of the operations they perform. The task of scheduling

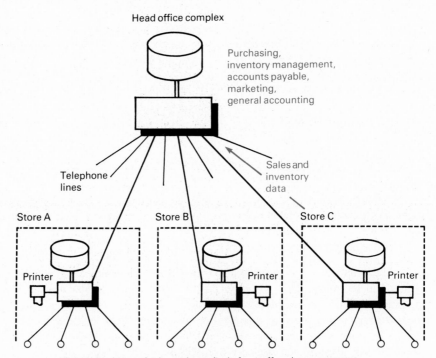

Figure 3.5 A hierarchical configuration in a chain store. Each store has a standalone minicomputer system, with files and terminals which handle the store operations. It transmits sales and inventory summaries to the head office where nationwide planning is done. Any program changes in the store computers are made and tested at the head office and are transmitted to the store computers.

the operations so as to make the best utilization of men and machines is done by the minicomputer. The shop foreman displays these operations schedules and often makes changes to them because of local problems and priorities. He frequently makes a change and instructs the machine to reperform its scheduling program.

Details of the work to be done are made up by a higher-level computer which receives information about sales and delivery dates, and performs a gross and net breakdown of the parts that must be manufactured to fill the orders. The central computer passes its job requirements to the shop floor minicomputers, and receives status reports from them.

PROCESS CONTROL   Hierarchies of processors were common in process control applications before they were used in commercial data processing. Many instruments taking readings in an industrial or chemical process are connected to a small reliable computer which scans the readings looking for exceptions or analyzing trends. The same computer may automatically control part of the operation, setting switches, operating relays, regulating temperatures, adjusting values, and so on.

Response time must be fast on some process control applications. A local minicomputer is used to ensure fast response. Increasingly today, tiny cheap microprocessors are being employed in instruments and control mechanisms. Many such devices may be attached to a minicomputer which stores data relating to the process being controlled.

A higher-level computer may be concerned with planning the operations, optimization, providing information for management control, or general data processing. Figure 3.6 shows a configuration in a steel mill, with different processors each having its own two-level process-control system, with these systems being linked to a higher production planning system.

In hospitals, the elaborate patient instrumentation used in intensive-care wards is monitored and controlled by small, local and highly reliable computers. These in turn are linked to higher-level machines which can perform complex analyses, provide information to stations, record patient histories, and so on.

CAUSALLY COUPLED?   In some configurations the design of the peripheral systems is largely independent of the design of the higher-level systems. In others the periphery and the center are so closely related that they are really separate components of the same system.

An example of a *causally coupled* configuration is a corporate head-office *information system* which derives its data from separate systems, separately installed in different corporate departments. These systems transmit data at the end of the day to the control system where it is edited, reformatted, and filed in a different manner to

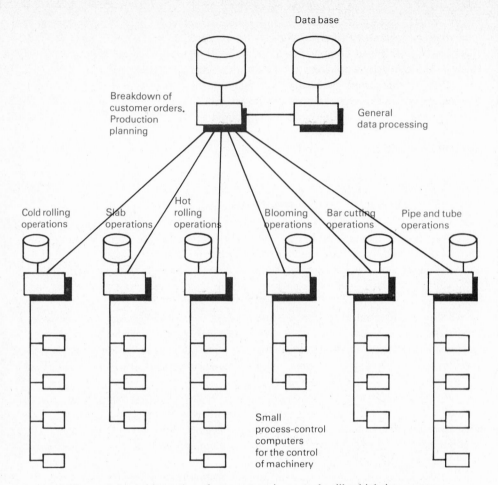

Data base

Breakdown of
customer orders.
Production
planning

General
data processing

Cold rolling
operations

Slab
operations

Hot
rolling
operations

Blooming
operations

Bar cutting
operations

Pipe and tube
operations

Small
process-control
computers
for the control
of machinery

Figure 3.6 A hierarchy of computers in a steel mill which integrates
the process control in several plant areas, and production planning.
The system gives higher productivity of plant operations and permits
immediate response to customer orders.

that in the peripheral systems, to serve a different purpose. The installers of the peripheral systems designed them for their own needs and were largely unaware of the
needs of the central system.

An example of a closely coupled design is a banking system in which all customer
data is stored by a central computer. (This does not apply to all banks. Some have
loosely distributed systems.) A small computer in each branch, or group of branches,
serves the processing needs of that branch, providing the tellers and the officer with the
information they need at the terminals. Customer data is also stored in the branch com-

puters, largely in case of a failure of the central system or the telecommunications link to it. The peripheral files are strictly subsets of the central file. The programs developed for the peripheral computers are compiled on the central computer, and loaded from it into the peripheral computers. Changes in the peripheral programs are made centrally and transmitted. Account balancing requires tight cooperation of the peripheral and central machines.

MULTIPLE LEVELS   Vertically distributed configurations may contain more
                             than two levels of processor. In some there may be as
many as four levels (Fig. 3.7).

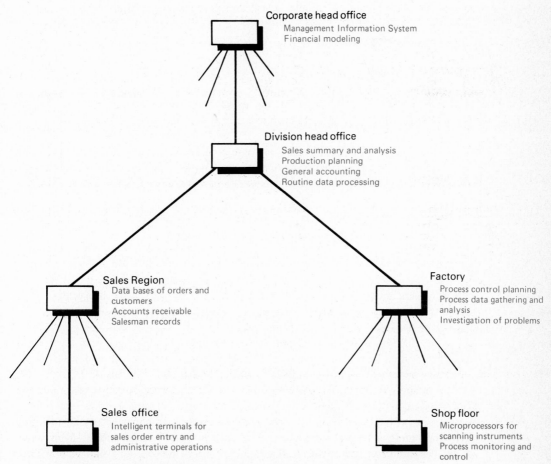

Figure 3.7 There may be as many as four levels in a vertical distribution of applications.

The lowest level may consist of intelligent terminals for data entry, or microprocessors in a factory, scanning instruments.

The next level may be a computer in a sales region assembling and storing data that relates to that region, or a computer in a factory assembling the data from the microprocessors and being used for production planning.

The third level is a conventional large computer system in the divisional head office, performing many types of data processing and maintaining large data bases for routine operations. This computer center receives data from the lower systems and sends instructions to them.

The highest level is a corporate management information system, with data structured differently from that in the systems used for routine operations. This system may be designed to assist various types of high-management decision making. It may run complex corporate financial models or elaborate programs to assist in optimizing certain corporate operations, for example, scheduling a tanker fleet. It receives summary data from other, lower systems.

REASONS FOR HIERARCHIES

Reasons for using hierarchical systems distribution are summarized in Box 3.2. The set of reasons should include those in Box 3.1 on function distribution.

An important group of reasons on some configurations is related to data—where it is kept and how it is maintained. Also of great importance are arguments relating to human, political, and organizational reasons, in addition to technical reasons [1].

HORIZONTAL DISTRIBUTION

So far we have discussed vertically distributed systems. Now we will consider horizontal distribution.

Some software, control mechanisms and system architectures are primarily oriented to vertical distribution, and some are primarily for peer-coupled systems. A transport subsystem which merely transmits data between computers *could* be designed to serve a horizontal or vertical configuration equally well. The differences are more important in the higher-level activities such as file management, or data base management, intelligent terminal control, data compression, editing, man–machine dialogues, recovery, restart, and so on.

In reality, major differences are found in the transport subsystems also. A transport subsystem designed for vertical distribution can have simpler flow control and routing control mechanisms, and hence simpler recovery procedures. It may use elaborate concentrators or other devices for maximizing network utilization, and may employ some of the function distribution features listed in Box 3.1. We discuss these mechanisms later in the book.

BOX 3.2 Technical reasons for using hierarchical distributed processing

(Note there are also human, political, and organizational reasons which are often more important than these technical reasons.)

- *Cost.*
  Total system cost may be lower. There is less data transmission and many functions are moved from the host machine.

- *Capacity.*
  The host may not be able to handle the workload without distribution. Distribution permits many functions to be performed in parallel.

- *Availability.*
  Fault tolerant design can be used. Critical applications continue when there has been a host or telecommunications failure. The small peripheral processors may be substitutable. In some systems high reliability is vital; e.g., a supermarket system, or hospital patient monitoring.

- *Response time.*
  Local responses to critical functions can be fast; no telecommunications delay; no scheduling problems; instruments are scanned and controlled by a local device.

- *User interface.*
  A better user interface can be employed, e.g., better terminal dialogue, when the user interacts with a local machine; also better graphics or screen design; more responses, faster response time.

- *Simplicity.*
  Separation of the peripheral functions can give a simpler, more modular system design.

- *More function.*
  More system functions are often found because of ease of implementing them on the peripheral machines. Salary savings often result from increased peripheral functions.

- *Separate data organizations.*
  The data on the higher-level system may be differently organized from those on the peripheral systems (e.g., corporate management information organized for spontaneous searching versus local detailed operational data tightly organized for one application).

See also Box 3.1 on distributed intelligence and function distribution.

Box 3.3 lists major reasons for horizontal distributed processing.

BOX 3.3   Reasons for horizontal computer networks

- *Resource sharing.*
  Expensive or unique resources can be shared by a large community of users, as on ARPANET.

- *Diversity.*
  Users have access to many different computers, programs, and data banks.

- *Transaction interchange*
  Transactions are passed from one system to another or from one corporation to another: e.g., financial transactions passed between banks on SWIFT; airline reservations or messages passed between computers in separate airlines, as on SITA.

- *Separate systems linked.*
  Separate previously existing systems are linked so that one can use another's data or programs, or to permit users to access all of them.

- *Local autonomy.*
  Local autonomous minicomputer systems are favored, with their own files, and some transactions need data which reside on the file of a separate system.

- *Functional separation.*
  Instead of one computer center performing all types of work, separate centers specialize in different types. For example, one does large-scale scientific computation. One does information retrieval. One has a data base for certain classes of application. One does mass printing and mailing.

- *Transmission cost.*
  Separate systems share a common network designed to minimize the combined data (and possibly voice) transmission cost.

- *Reliability and security.*
  When one system fails, others can process transactions. If one system is destroyed, its files can be reconstructed on another.

- *Load sharing.*
  Unpredictable peaks of work on one machine can be off-loaded to other machines.

- *Encouragement of development.*
  A corporate network can permit small data processing groups to develop applications.

PATTERNS OF WORK   Because of the mechanisms built into software or systems architecture, designers sometimes try to make all configurations vertical, or all configurations horizontal. This can result in excessive overhead, system inflexibility, or clumsy control. Whether or not a configuration *should* be vertical, or horizontal, or both, depends upon the *patterns of work* the configuration must accomplish and the *patterns of data usage*.

In designing a distributed system we are concerned with such questions as:

- Where are the units of processing work required?
- How large are these units? What size of processing machine do they need?
- Are the units independent, or does one depend on the results of another?
- What stored data do the work units employ?
- Do they share common or independent data?
- What transactions must pass between one unit and another? What are the patterns of transaction flow?
- Must transactions pass between the units of work immediately, or is a delay acceptable? What is the cost of delay?

The answers to these questions differ from one organization to another. The patterns of work are different. The patterns of information flow between work units are different. Different types of corporations tend, therefore, to have their own natural shapes for distributed processing. What is best for an airline is not necessarily best for an insurance company.

The nature of the work units may be such that they can be independent of one another and have no need to know what each of the others is doing. They may be standalone units having no communication with any other unit—possibly standalone minicomputers. On the other hand, they may need to share common data which resides centrally. In this case there are vertical links to a common data store. There may be multiple such data stores which themselves pass information to a higher system. Alternatively the work units at one level may be such that they need to pass information to other units at the same level. This situation may lead naturally to horizontal communication; but it could also, if necessary, be handled vertically with a centralized processor relaying transactions between the units.

EXAMPLES   1. An airline reservation system requires a common pool of data on seat availability. Geographically scattered work units use, and may update, the data in this pool. Each of them needs data which is up-to-date second by second. This data needs to be kept centrally. The bulkiest data are those relating to passengers. A passenger may telephone the airline in cities far apart; when he does so the agent to whom he talks must be able to access needed data. In order to find the data it is easier to keep it centrally also.

2. A car rental firm may permit its customers to pick up a car at one location and leave it at another. When the car is picked up a computer terminal prepares the contract. When the car is left a terminal is used to check the contract and calculate the bill. If a minicomputer at each location performed these functions, horizontal communication would be needed between the destination location and the location where the car was picked up. However, some centralized work is also needed because it is necessary to keep track of the company's cars and ensure that they are distributed appropriately for each day's crop of customers. Credit and other details about regular customers may also be kept centrally.

   The shape of the work therefore indicates both vertical and horizontal distribution. However, because the centralized (vertical) links are needed, the customer contracts may also be kept centrally and the same links used to access them. The rental offices may then use intelligent terminals rather than complete minicomputers.

3. Insurance companies have offices in different locations. They keep details about customers and their policies. An office does not normally need to share these data with another office or pass transactions to it. The offices could therefore use standalone machines. Customers in different locations may have different requirements. In the U.S. different states have different insurance regulations and tax laws. The different machines may therefore be programmed somewhat differently. The insurance company's head office, however, needs to know enough details of all customers policies to enable it to evaluate the company's cash flow, and risks, and to perform actuarial calculations which enable it to control the company's financial exposure. Enough data for this purpose is therefore passed upwards to the head office. This vertical communication does not need to be real-time, as in the case of an airline reservation system. It can be transmitted in periodic batches.

   Although the pattern of the work in an insurance company is appropriate for a decentralized system, that does not necessarily mean that a decentralized system will be the cheapest or best. There are various arguments for centralization, among them economies of scale, centralized control of programming, and use of data base software. A function-distribution rather than a processing-distribution configuration is used in some insurance companies.

4. In a group of banks, each handles its own customers with its own data processing system. A customer in one bank, however, can make monetary transfers to customers in other banks. A network is set up by the banks to perform such transfers electronically. The money is moved very rapidly and hence is available for use or interest-gathering by banks for a longer period. The use of this "float" more than pays for the network. In this example we have a peer-coupled configuration with need for a horizontal transfer between the work units.

DEGREE OF HOMOGENEITY

We may classify horizontal configurations according to the degree of homogeneity of the systems which communicate. This affects the design, the choice of software and network techniques and, often, the overall management.

At one extreme we have identical machines running the same application programs in the same corporation. In other words the processing load has been split between several identical computers. At the other extreme we have incompatible machines running entirely different programs in different organizations, but nevertheless interconnected by a network. One of the best known examples of this is ARPANET, interconnecting university and research centers, as shown in Fig. 3.8.

A logical map of ARPANET in 1972 showing the various incompatible computers that it interconnected:

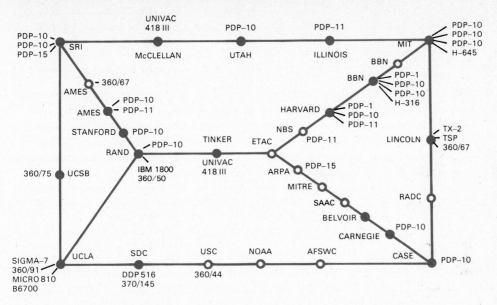

A physical map of ARPANET two years later. ARPANET continued to grow and change and was the pioneering system that paved the way for horizontal heterogenous networks.

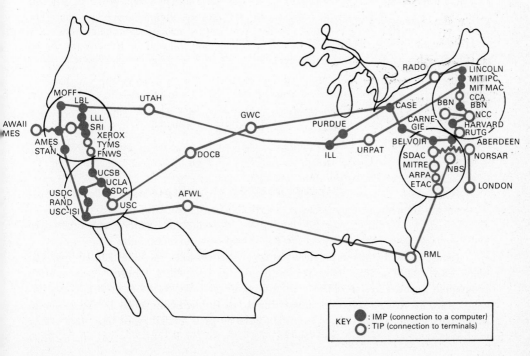

Figure 3.8

NONCOOPERATIVE SYSTEMS

We may subdivide configurations into those composed of *cooperative* and *noncooperative* systems. A noncooperative configuration consists of computer systems installed independently by different authorities with no common agency controlling their design, but linked by a common shared network.

When the networking capability becomes accepted and understood by the various system development groups, there may be slightly less noncooperation. Developers know that a certain data base exists on another system. They may learn to think in terms of interchanging data, sharing resources, and establishing compatible transaction formats.

Because the cost and ease of networking will improve greatly in the future, some corporations have attempted to impose certain standards on their diverse systems groups, which will eventually make interconnection of the systems more practical or more valuable. Among the types of standards imposed or attempted have been the following:

1. Standardization of transaction formats.

2. Standardization of line control discipline.

3. Use of compatible computers (one large corporation decreed that all minicomputers should be DEC machines, possibly anticipating future use of DEC's network architecture).

4. Standardization of data field formats and use of an organization-wide data dictionary.

5. Standardization of record or segment formats.

6. Use of a common data description language (e.g., CODASYL DDL, or IBM's DL/I).

7. Use of a common data base management software.

8. Use of a common networking architecture.

COOPERATING SYSTEMS

Cooperating systems are designed to achieve a common purpose, serve a single organization, or interchange data in an agreed-upon manner. We can subdivide cooperating systems into those in which the separate systems are used by the same *organization* and those in which *separate corporations* are interlinked.

Networks which interlink separate corporations are found today in certain industries. In the future they may become common in most industries to bypass the labor-intensive steps of mailing, sorting, and key-entering orders, invoices, and other documents which pass from a computer in one organization to a computer in another.

Industries with intercorporate computer networks today include banking and airlines. Most major airlines have reservation systems in which terminals over a wide geographic area are connected to a central computer. Worldwide airlines have worldwide networks. Many booking requests cannot be fulfilled completely by the airline to which they were made. The airline might have no seats available, or the journey may necessitate flights on more than one carrier. Booking messages therefore have to be passed from the computer in one airline to the computer in another, and often the response is passed back swiftly enough to inform the booking agent who initiated the request at his terminal. In order to achieve this linking of separate systems all partici- pating airlines must agree to a rigorously defined format for the messages passing be- tween the airlines. This format is standardized by an industry association, ATA in the United States and IATA internationally. To operate the interlinking network, the air- lines set up independent nonprofit organizations, ARINC (Aeronautical Radio Incor- porated) in the U.S., and SITA internationally (Societé International de Telecommuni- cations Aéronautique). The separate airlines must send ATA- or IATA-format mes- sages using the ARINC or SITA protocols. These networks began as networks for sending low-speed off-line telprinter messages. As the need arose they were upgraded to handle fast-response messages between computers as well as conventional teleprinter traffic. Figure 3.9 shows the computer-to-computer network of SITA (including future proposed links).

Networks have also been designed to connect bank computers for moving money

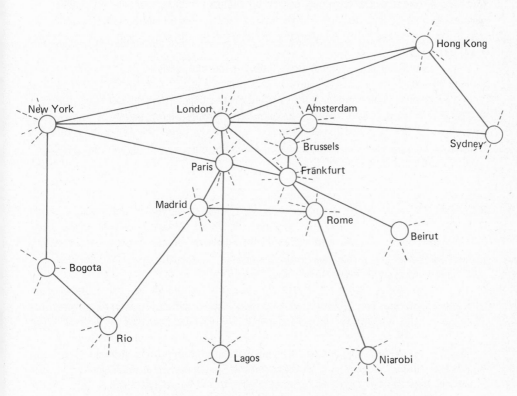

Figure 3.9 The SITA network's present and proposed trunks. Many smaller, lower-level centers are connected to those shown.

and messages almost instantaneously between banks. As with the case of airlines, the bank computers are differently programmed, incompatible machines, set up by widely different corporations in different countries. Like the airlines the banks must send rigorously formatted messages and observe precise network protocols. In this case a very high level of security must be built into the cooperative procedures because sums exceeding a million dollars are transmitted between computers.

SYSTEMS UNDER ONE MANAGEMENT   Much of the use of distributed computing is within one corporation under one management. This could result in a compatible configuration using a common networking architecture. Often, however, the systems to be linked were installed separately in separate locations without any thought about eventual interconnection. The files or data bases are incompatible; the same data field is formatted differently in different systems; programs cannot be moved from one computer to another without rewriting; where teleprocessing is used the terminals are incompatible; and even the line control procedures are different so the terminals cannot be changed without a major upheaval in the systems they are connected to. In this environment a major reprogramming and redesign effort is needed before networking becomes of much value, and often this effort is too expensive.

It is necessary that systems in different functional areas of a corporation be developed by different groups. Corporate data processing is much too complex for one group to develop more than a portion of it. The current trend to decentralization is resulting in more and more autonomous groups carrying out application development. This a valuable trend because it results in more people being involved in application development, and the development being done locally where the application problems are understood.

INTERFACES   In order to make computer networking of value, it is desirable that the *interfaces* between the separately developed systems be rigorously defined and adhered to. *If the interfaces are preserved, each development group can work autonomously.*

There are several levels of interface:

1. Interface to the transport subsystem which permits blocks of data to be moved between distant machines. This interface can be defined independently of the application or the firms which use the network.

2. Interfaces for the software services which are external to the transport subsystem but not part of the application programs; for example software for remote file access, compaction, conversion, cryptography, setting up sessions, editing messages, and so on.

3. Applications interfaces defining what transaction types are interchanged between different application systems. These can be defined independently of the choice of networking software or hardware.

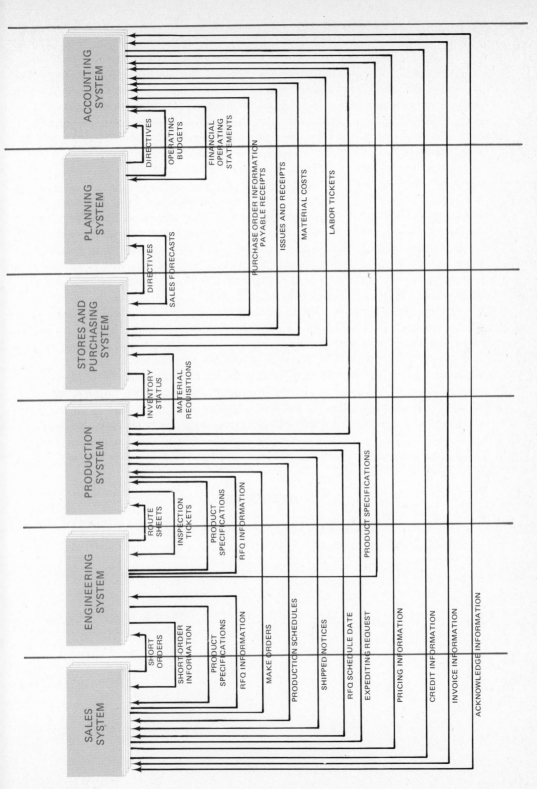

Figure 3.10 Messages passing between separate application systems in a network need to have their content specified by the systems analysts. These messages travel in envelopes having formats rigorously defined by the network software architecture.

Interface 1, above, is provided by some common carrier systems for computer networking (the CCITT X.25 standard, for example). Interfaces 1 and 2 are provided by some of the manufacturers' protocols for computer networks and distributed processing (for example IBM's and DEC's architectures for networks). Interface 3, above, is usually up to the systems analysts. Figure 3.10 gives an illustration of computers serving six functional areas in a corporation, and shows the transaction types flowing between them. A typical transaction would be given a rigorously defined format. When they are transmitted between machines, data would be in the format with additional headers and a trailer prescribed by interfaces 1 and 2.

As changing costs take the computer industry increasingly toward distributed processing, one highly desirable characteristic is portability of programs. Programs should be capable of being moved from one processor to another and gaining access to distributed data instead of centralized data. There are arguments for, and against, distributed processing, and there are many possible distributed configurations. It is advantageous for a manufacturer's product lines to possess the flexibility to change system configurations without the need to rewrite programs.

The interfaces and protocols that are desirable for distributed processing make the software complex, as we shall see. Furthermore there are so many different configurations, functions, machines, operating systems, access methods and data base management systems that need to be supported that it will be years before the software for distributed systems can do everything that is theoretically desirable. New machines, operating systems, and other software will increasingly be designed to plug into the rigorously defined architectures for distributed systems.

Computer networks and distributed processing are a vitally important and fundamental step in the growth of the computing and telecommunications industries. There is a long road ahead, and the journey will take years to come.

REFERENCES

1. See the author's companion books to this one on distributed processing from Prentice-Hall, Englewood Cliffs, NJ.

4 PRIVATE NETWORKS

Data networks fall into two broad classes: public networks and private networks.

Public networks are built by common carriers—in many countries the government telecommunications administration. Their transmission and switching facilities are shared by the computers and terminals of many corporations and other organizations. Any one machine using the network may send data to any other (if permitted by security and software constraints). Many nations are building data networks for this purpose and these will become a vital part of a nation's service infrastructure.

Private networks are built within one corporation or government organization. The implementors lease circuits for private use, usually telephone circuits, and construct a network which may or may not have its own switching facilities. The majority of corporate networks today use *private* leased lines rather than *public* switched data networks. One reason for this is that public data networks are still in their infancy. As they grow the incentive to use them will increase.

The argument has been frequently expressed that public data networks rather than multiple private networks would be better for a nation. Public networks would carry greater traffic volumes and would benefit from economies of scale. Greater traffic volumes would lead to a higher line utilization, and to the use of wideband trunks which would give a faster response time. Public networks can afford diversity of routing which enables faulty trunks or equipment to be circumvented. On the other hand, the line utilization of many private networks is higher than the early multiple-user switched networks because they are tightly designed for a given relatively stable traffic pattern.

Corporations and government departments are generally free to choose whether to build their own private network or use public networks. Their choice will depend upon the relative cost. The designer uses techniques to adjust the network configuration and choice of circuits so as to achieve a given result at a minimum cost. Today costs still often favor the use of leased circuits, and hence the widespread use of private networks. In the future, lower tariffs and greater availability of public switched data networks will increase their use—at least in some countries. To achieve economies of scale in public networks it might pay a telephone administration to adjust its prices so that users are encouraged to desert the private lines and use the public network. This is being done in some countries. Another factor affecting the choice will be whether the software of a chosen manufacturer is compatible with the public network protocols.

For the next few years private networks will probably remain in more common use than public networks.

This chapter describes private networks; the next deals with public networks.

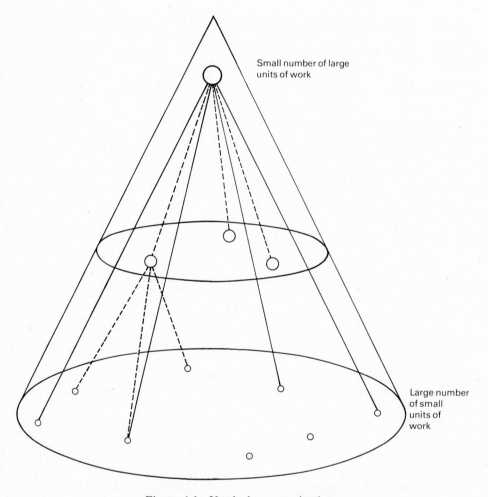

Figure 4.1   Vertical communication.

PRIVATE NETWORK STRUCTURES   Most private networks are vertical rather than horizontal. This was natural when data processing systems were highly centralized. Even with distributed processing there is usually a hierarchy of work activities. An organization tends to have many relatively simple repetitive jobs at its lower levels. Higher in the organization there tends to be a few complex jobs. The lower levels interchange data with the higher levels as shown in Fig. 4.1, but there is often little interchange among the lower-level units themselves. Sometimes the lower work units share common data which is maintained at a higher level.

Because of the vertical patterns of data flow most private networks are star-structured or tree-structured. A growing proportion of private networks interconnect separate self-sufficient computer centers, and these may be horizontally structured networks. Sometimes there are separate vertical networks with horizontal links between their tops as shown in Fig. 4.2.

The network mechanisms for hierarchical or star-structured networks are fundamentally simpler in certain respects than those for horizontal or mesh-structured networks. Some types of software have been designed for star-structured networks only,

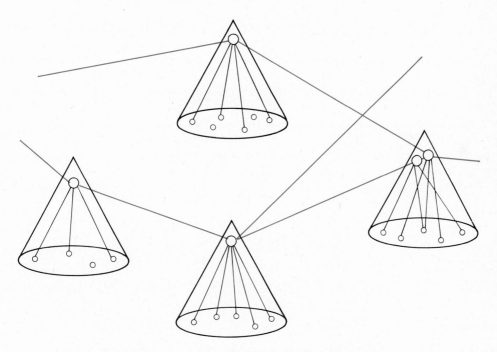

Figure 4.2 Separate vertical networks linked horizontally at their tops.

avoiding the complexities which mesh-structured networks have, such as alternate routing, deadlocks, flow control, and distributed network management.

There are various mechanisms used to implement hierarchical networks:

- Multidrop lines with polling.

- Frequency division multiplexers.

- Time division multiplexers.

- Looped lines.

- Concentrators.

- Multidropped concentrators.

These were all in use prior to the era of computer networks and distributed processing and are described in the author's books *Teleprocessing Network Organization* and *Systems Analysis for Data Transmission*.

Many large corporations have a proliferation of leased-line networks. Separate networks have been implemented by different teams for different purposes, some for different divisions or subsidiaries of a corporation. Most governments have a much greater proliferation of separate networks.

Figures. 4.3 to 4.12 show typical private networks. In this illustration they have all grown up in the same corporation. (The systems described are fictional but are based on the systems of an existing corporation, simplified somewhat for reasons of clarity.)

The systems shown cover the information needs of the corporation from selling the products and maintaining them, to deciding what to manufacture, giving instructions to the plants, and controlling the manufacturing process. They handle accounting operations, provide networks for relaying administrative messages between most corporate locations and data between computer locations and gather together, for management, many types of information, which they endeavor to make conveniently accessible. In addition, they provide terminal services for staff ranging from scientists to secretaries and give remote batch access to large computers.

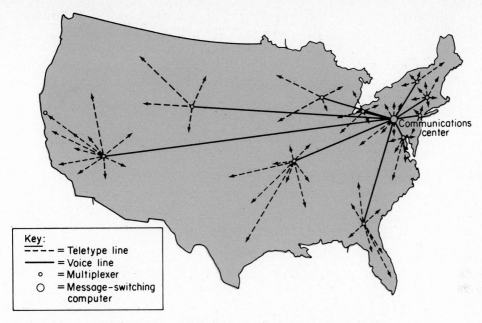

Figure 4.3 Administrative message-switching network.

A system linking leased teletype lines from major corporate locations to a communications center, in which messages are forwarded by a message-switching computer. Several teletype channels are multiplexed onto the leased voice lines, and many terminals may be "multidropped" on each teletype channel.

This network was the first to be installed and remains separate from those installed later. Its purpose is to relay administrative messages from any major location in the corporation to any other, at high speed. Such locations have machines like teleprinters for receiving or transmitting the messages. A message will normally reach its destination in a few minutes. The sending of a message is equivalent to the sending of a commercial cable except that it is quicker and more accurate, and the messages are stored for future reference and can be broadcast to many locations. More important, the overall cost per message is substanially lower than that of commercial cables.

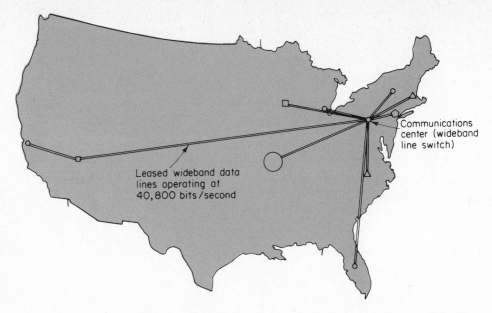

Leased wideband data
lines operating at
40,800 bits/second

Communications
center (wideband
line switch)

Figure 4.4   Switched wideband network.

A second network established in the same corporation as that in Fig. 4.3, designed to transmit batches of data at high speed between the corporation's major computer centers. Wideband lines from the computer centers are connected to a slow,
electromechanical, crossbar switch. Operators can manually dial a wideband circuit
from any one computer center served by this network to any other. When the connection is established transmission can begin.

Whereas the network in Fig. 4.3 is for people sending messages to people, this
network is for machines sending data to machines. Sometimes tape-to-tape transmission is used; sometimes disk-to-disk. The lines are not *physically* switched in the Fig.
4.3 network; here they are. There is a great difference in line speed: 150 bits per
second in Fig. 4.3; 50,000 bits per second here.

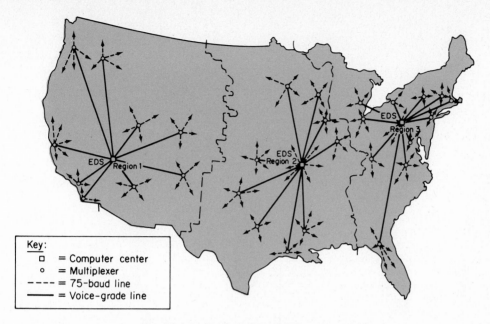

Key:
□ = Computer center
○ = Multiplexer
---- = 75-baud line
—— = Voice-grade line

Figure 4.5 Engineering division system.

The engineering division of the same corporation is divided into three regions, each of which has a computer center. Interactive typewriter-like terminals were installed to give support to the field engineers. Initially a system was installed in one region on a pilot basis and, when successful, was duplicated in the other two regions. The field engineers can obtain a variety of services from their terminals. For instance, they can make inquiries about technical information and, in some cases, receive lengthy instructions.

They can order components that are needed and obtain delivery-time estimates. They report full details of all failures. The computers analyze the failure reports and the repair activity. They maintain inventory control of the spare parts kept at all locations in each region, with terminals being used for this purpose in all the stores, where spare parts are kept.

The system was designed and the networks optimized without consideration of the existing networks in Fig. 4.3 and 4.4.

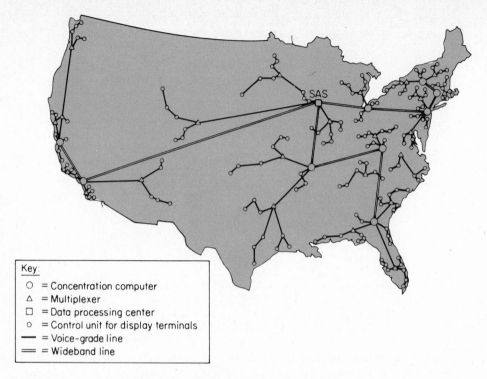

Figure 4.6   Sales administration system.

A separate real-time system providing display screen terminals in the branch offices was installed by the sales division.

These terminals are used to enter details of all orders taken, of all customer payments, and of all customer requirements, such as training course bookings.

The sales staff can inquire about the status of all orders. The branch offices now have little of the paperwork that they required before this system was installed, and much clerical and administrative manpower has been saved. Customer inquiries can be answered immediately. Details of sales proposals can be planned, priced and varied—with the aid of the computer—before the proposal is made. This process is valuable, for the proposals are highly complex. The computer will check that the items proposed conform to regulations and constraints applicable at that time. The availability of the computer screens in the branch offices means that more complex selling can be contemplated in future plans. The communications network again consists of permanently leased lines; however, the configuration is very different from the one in Fig. 4.5. Voice lines link the screen units to concentration computers and the latter are linked to the Sales Administration System computers with wideband lines. The network is designed so that the terminal users receive a response time of about 2 seconds to most of their terminal actions.

The sales division is organizationally separate from the other divisions and designed its own network without reference to them.

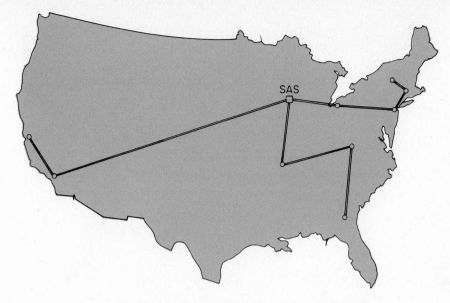

Figure 4.7 Evening transmission on sales division lines.

After the branch offices shut down, the concentration computers of this diagram, at district centers, become batch-processing machines with direct-access files and high-speed printers. The wideband links to the Sales Administration System data processing center are used for transmitting data to them for customer mailings. Invoices and other documents are composed, mailed, and controlled at the district centers where the concentration computers are located. Backup information in case of failure is stored at the district centers, and this information is transmitted to them at night from the data processing center.

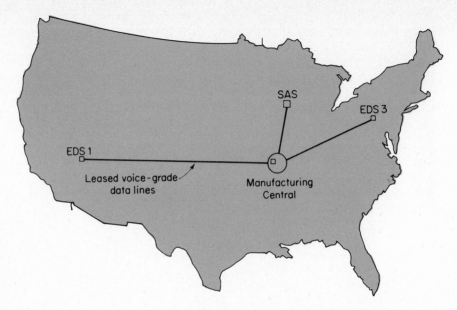

Figure 4.8 The manufacturing central system.

The corporation has several manufacturing plants. The planning of what should be manufactured takes place centrally at the location of one of the largest plants and is handled with the aid of a data processing system called the Manufacturing Central System.

The input for the decision of what to manufacture comes from market forecasts, and from day-to-day knowledge of what orders have been taken and what spare parts are needed. The latter two are kept by the Sales Administration System (SAS) and the Engineering Division Systems (EDS). These are transmitted, once daily, to the Manufacturing Central System.

The Manufacturing Central System, in return, transmits details of the manufacturing status of orders and when they will be completed to the SAS and EDS systems.

Voice lines are used for these transmissions. The transmissions are sufficiently long that leased lines have a lower telecommunication cost than the use of public telephone lines. The leased voice lines shown in Fig. 4.8 are therefore permanently connected.

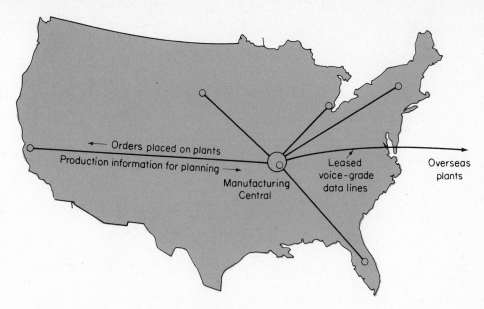

Figure 4.9 Transmission to the plant information systems.

A two-way interchange takes place between the Manufacturing Central System and the data processing systems at the plants. The former sends the plants orders of what to manufacture. The plants return progress details, estimates of completion dates, and information about plant schedules which will aid the central planning process.

The orders are now processed by the plant computer. Here breakdowns into individual components are fed into the production shop schedules. The plant computers maintain files giving order and stock status, plus other files that can be interrogated by the staff at the manufacturing central location.

The information interchange between the plant computers and the Manufacturing Central System was again designed to take place over leased voice lines, because this was the cheapest form of connection if done without consideration of other systems.

Some of the plants themselves have an internal network linking shop-floor minicomputers to the main plant computer. This uses links within the plant which are privately installed and maintained.

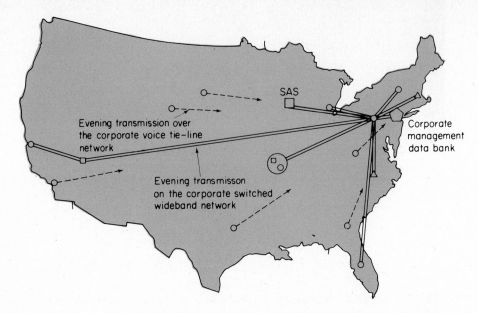

Figure 4.10   The corporate management data bank.

A large data bank of corporate information is kept at the corporate headquarters in New York. This bank contains details of personnel salaries, sales, forecasts, customers, suppliers, and other relevant information. It is organized in such a way that a variety of management questions can be answered as quickly as possible, and this necessitates a file organization quite different from that of the separate systems, where the information is compiled (e.g., the Sales Administration System). Much of the data are processed to provide summaries and statistical digests in anticipation of management needs.

The corporate management data bank is built up from information transmitted daily from plant locations, the Manufacturing Central System, the Sales Administration System, the laboratory locations, and several other sources. Transmission to this system takes place over the switched wideband network, where possible. Some locations, however, are not connected to this network. In general, such sites have smaller quantities of information to send, so they transmit over the corporate voice tie lines.

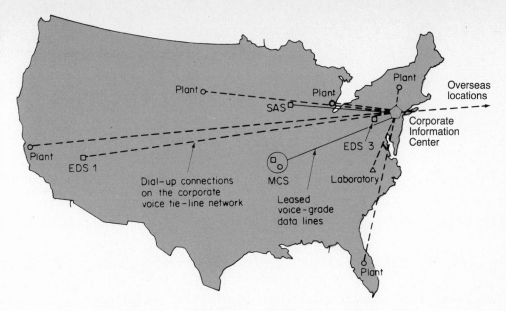

Figure 4.11 The Corporate Information Center.

The mission of the Corporate Information Center is to provide the information needed by functional and strategic management. Much of this information is needed "immediately" or at least very quickly by the management in question. A group of specialists in the center is familiar with all the sources designed to satisfy this need. Much of the information comes from the files maintained at the information center, such as the management data bank mentioned above. However, for many queries, it is necessary to go farther afield and inspect other files or question the staff of other information centers.

Each plant has an information center for its own management. The Manufacturing Central System has a group of specialists who are able to interrogate its files, and so has the Sales Administration System. The staff of the Corporate Information Center call on these specialists when necessary, converse with them, and link their terminals into those systems.

In some cases, the staff of the specialized systems do the file interrogation with their own terminals and then switch the results to the terminals of the Corporate Information Center. The staff here, in turn, display the information they have located on the screens or terminals used by management. Several mechanisms for doing so exist. The manager in question may have a compatible terminal, and so the data are switched for display on it. There may be a low-speed printer in his locality, thus providing him with a printout. Some of the managers in the corporate headquarters building, which houses the Corporate Information Center, have closed-circuit television links to the information room. On these screens they can see the face of the staff member who assists them, plus whatever printouts or displays he may generate. The boardroom and other meeting rooms are equipped with display terminals, printing terminals, and closed-circuit television.

The Corporate Information Center needs links to other systems for this purpose. Only the links to the SAS and MCS are used frequently enough to make a permanent leased line economical. The other locations are accessed by a dial-up telephone line.

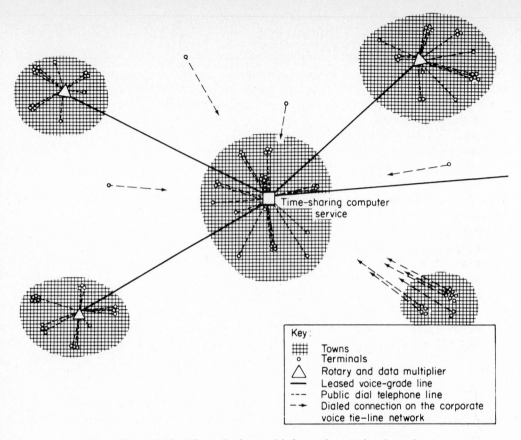

Key:
- ⊞ Towns
- ○ Terminals
- △ Rotary and data multiplier
- — Leased voice-grade line
- --- Public dial telephone line
- --→ Dialed connection on the corporate voice tie-line network

Figure 4.12   Time-sharing and information retrieval services.

The corporation has a growing set of services to which employees can gain access with typewriter-like terminals. These include programmed tools of various types, the capability to search for and retrieve technical information, financial and accounting packages, text editing capability, library services, statistical analysis packages, and so on. Some users have their own programs available on time-sharing computers. Some maintain their own files at the computer center. Some scientists and secretaries have such terminals at their desks, and in many locations there is a room with communally used terminals.

Different computers can be dialed from the terminals. At present such computer systems cover a community of users in a limited geographical area. Several such systems exist in different parts of the country. Users in the same city as the computer location dial it on the public telephone network or, sometimes, on tie-lines. Users in certain distant cities dial a number that connects them to a leased voice line shared among many users by means of time-division multiplexing. The dialed call reaches a scanning device that searches for a free data channel on the multiplexed link shown as a △ symbol on Fig. 4.12. This leased-line facility serves only those locations with a suitably high density of users. Locations without such a line may dial the computer directly, either on the public network or on the corporate tie-line network.

It is clear that for many of these services a higher speed terminal and often a visual display unit would give a far more satisfactory man–machine dialogue. This is resisted, however, because of low speed of the multiplexing subchannels.

AN INTEGRATED NETWORK

The proliferation shown in Figs. 4.3 to 4.12 involves wasteful duplication of routes. There is a desire in many such corporations today to replace the separate networks with a common network. Figure 4.13 illustrates what this might be like. The common network may have a lower overall cost. It also has better reliability because it can use alternate routes when failures occur. Further, it gives greater flexibility of interconnection. One terminal can reach many computers, and information can be interchanged between the separate computer systems.

As the diversity of information resources grows in a corporation, it becomes less predictable what remote computers are likely to be used at any given location. It therefore becomes more desirable to have a horizontal network spanning the major locations, rather than a collection of disjoint vertical networks as in Figs. 4.3 to 4.12. Also, with the growth of word processing, there is a need to transmit mail and documents between locations. The network in effect, acts as a switch interconnecting the locations. In Figs. 4.3 and 4.4 the switch is in one place. In Fig. 4.13 it is distributed.

Conversion from separate networks to an integrated network has in practice proved to be a difficult task. The message formats and protocols of the integrated network are different from those used in the earlier networks. New software is needed and

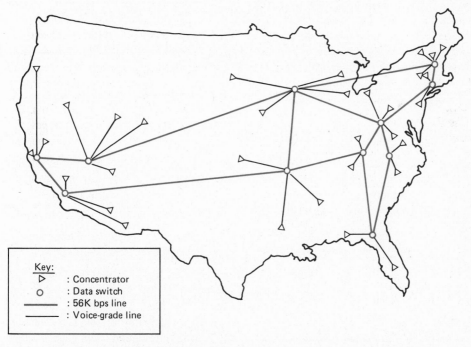

Key:
▷ : Concentrator
○ : Data switch
——— : 56K bps line
——— : Voice-grade line

Figure 4.13 An integrated corporate network replacing the separate networks of Figs. 4.3 and 4.12.

usually terminals have to be changed. This usually requires modification to application programs. Sometimes the use of a new terminal necessitates a new man–terminal dialogue structure which causes major application program rewriting. Because of these difficulties, there are often arguments from groups who want to retain their old network. To make matters worse, sometimes the performance aspects of the new network are worse—longer software path lengths, more main memory needed, and longer response times.

Figure 4.13 may be described as an integrated network for *data* transmission. *Telephone* transmission, however, costs much more than data transmission in most organizations. Many organizations have a telephone "tie-line" network of leased private lines for telephone calls. An integrated network designed to minimize communication costs should take into consideration telephone traffic and mail as well as computer traffic. In many countries the cost of a *channel group* with the capacity of 12 telephone circuits or of a *supergroup* with the capacity of 60 telephone circuits is substantially less than the cost of the individual circuits. Groups of circuits may therefore be leased and organized so that they can handle telephone, mail, and data traffic. The trunk groups may follow all or some of the red line routes in Fig. 4.13. Data circuits will be derived from the trunk groups. The economics of trunk routing for telephone traffic may affect the topology of the data network.

Communication satellite technology is rapidly evolving and is dropping in cost much faster than land-based circuits. The red line network in Fig. 4.13 could be replaced by satellite usage as shown in Fig. 4.14. Here, a small satellite earth station, with an antenna of 7 meters or less in diameter, is used at each location which has a high traffic load. The control equipment at each earth station permits that station to transmit to or receive from any other station on Fig. 4.14. The station equipment may permit voice and data traffic to share the same facilities. This sharing helps to cost-justify the use of satellite earth stations. Some corporations are now installing satellite networks using the facilities of SBS (Satellite Business Systems). The network planning often takes two years.

Some countries have satellites for domestic use and others do not. Some satellite users have their own earth stations; others lease circuits from a satellite common carrier which routes them via its own earth stations. The use of satellites can result in substantially different network mechanisms.

THE NETWORK RESOURCE   Once an integrated network exists it often becomes a valuable corporate resource. Figure 4.15 shows such a network in use by the British Steel Corporation. The trunks shown linking major locations are supergroups with a bandwidth of 240 kHz—enough to carry 60 simultaneous telephone calls, but costing substantially less than 60 telephone circuits. Of this, 48 kHz is used to form a data network between the locations using packet-switching (discussed later). The economics of combining telephone, fac-

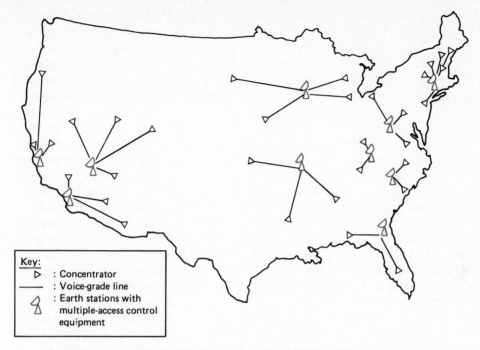

Figure 4.14   A corporate network integrating the data transmission capabilities of Fig. 4.13 with telephone trunking and image transmission via a satellite, using small corporate earth stations with demand-assigned multiple-access capability.

Figure 4.15   The corporate network for British Steel. The links are 240 KHz supergroups (having the capacity of 60 voice channels). Most of this bandwidth is used for telephone traffic, with a little document transmission. 48 KHz is used to provide a corporate data network interconnecting host computers. Distant terminals are attached via concentrators. The host computers use front-end protocol converters which emulate local terminals. The network has permitted specialization in the use of computer centers.

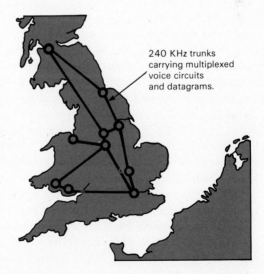

240 KHz trunks carrying multiplexed voice circuits and datagrams.

simile (mail) and data traffic make it possible to obtain the wideband data circuits at what is effectively a low cost.

Once such a network exists in an organization it can have a major effect on the planning of computer resources. Different locations may specialize in different functions, giving economies of specialization. In a corporation, one computer center may specialize in scientific computing or operations research needing a powerful processor. Another may do corporate-wide payroll; another may handle mass mailing operations. Different systems carrying out specific operations—such as inventory control, production scheduling, order processing, etc.—may pass data via the network to a separate system which stores summary data with indices appropriate for providing management information. Separate systems may transmit financial figures to a head-office computer for cost accounting control. One location may have a system for providing patent and legal information to lawyers throughout the corporation.

Figure 4.16 illustrates a corporate network with specialized facilities at different locations. Networks in university and research environments, such as ARPANET in the USA (Fig. 3.8) and CYCLADES in France (Fig. 24.3) give access to a variety of general-purpose or specialized computers, to research data banks, to systems which permit the searching of technical abstracts, libraries, patents, legal documents and so on.

MULTICORPORATE NETWORKS

A few private networks link computer centers in multiple corporations. Two leading examples are the SITA network illustrated in Fig. 3.9 which passes messages between airline computers around the world, and the SWIFT electronic fund transfer network which passes financial transactions between banks (Fig. 4.17).

To operate multicorporate networks, a separate service corporation is sometimes set up which creates and operates the network. SWIFT, Society for Worldwide Interbank Financial Transactions, is a nonprofit-making organization set up and wholly owned by banks which are connected to it. SWIFT implemented and currently operates the network shown in Fig. 4.17, the purpose of which is to send money, messages, and bank statements, at high speed between banks. The participating banks finance the system, and a tariff structure charges for its use on a per-message basis plus a fixed connection charge and an annual charge based upon traffic volumes. The banks range from very small to banks with 2000 branches.

The SWIFT system is a message-switching network which originally had two switching centers as shown in Fig. 4.17. Several hundred banks are connected to the system. It can expand without functional redesign to have multiple centers. It uses voice-grade circuits and most traffic is delivered in less than one minute. All traffic is stored at the switching centers for ten days after transmission and during that period can be retrieved if necessary. Transactions can be entered into the system regardless of whether the recipient bank's terminals are busy or not. The originator of an urgent message will automatically be informed by the system if there is a delay in delivering the message.

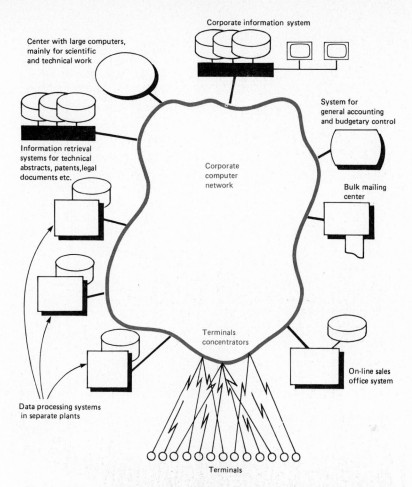

Center with large computers,
mainly for scientific
and technical work

Corporate information system

Information retrieval
systems for technical
abstracts, patents, legal
documents etc.

System for
general accounting
and budgetary control

Corporate
computer
network

Bulk mailing
center

Terminals
concentrators

On-line sales
office system

Data processing systems
in separate plants

Terminals

Figure 4.16   A corporate network may permit economies of specialization.

Early in its history the SWIFT traffic was about one third of a million messages per day. The initial switches were each designed to handle 23 transactions per second. The system can accept either single messages or bulk traffic from computers or magnetic tape. Transactions can have priorities allocated to them.

For multicorporate networks to be useful it is necessary that the corporations using them agree on message formats and application procedures. There must be a set of corporate standards for network use over and above the standards for the transmission. SWIFT imposes such standards on its users. They enable the banks to send and receive messages between countries in computer-readable form. Fig. 4.18 shows typical SWIFT messages.

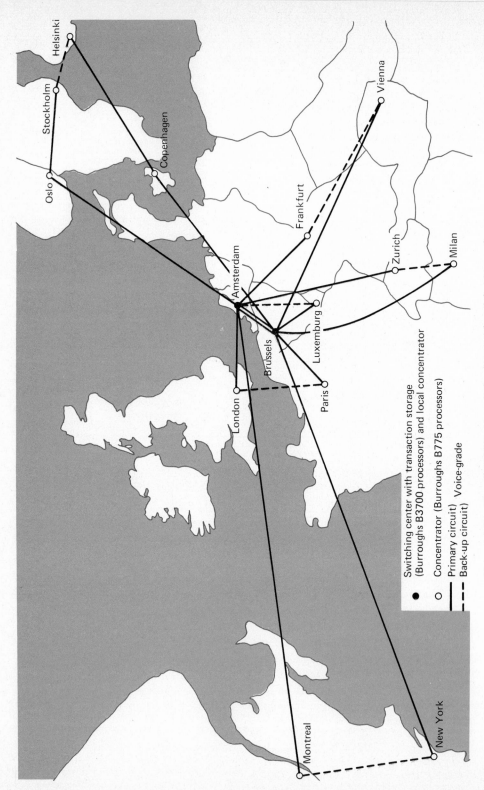

Switching center with transaction storage
(Burroughs B3700 processors) and local concentrator

Concentrator (Burroughs B775 processors)

Primary circuit) Voice-grade

Back-up circuit)

Figure 4.17 The **SWIFT** network for international fund transfer.

Figure 4.18 An example of a transaction being handled by the
SWIFT network. A customer, John Loeb & Co., asks their bank
in Paris, the Banque de France, to transfer $750,000 in U.S. cur-
rency to the account of the customer J. Blanagan in Swiss Credit
Bank in Zurich. Because the currency is that of neither the sender
nor receiver country, a third bank, the Chemical Bank in New
York, is involved. Both the sender and receiver banks have accounts with this third bank which handles the reimbursement.
The Banque de France first sends a message to the Swiss Credit
Bank with details of the transaction. It then sends a related message to the Chemical Bank in New York asking it to debit the
Banque de France's account with $750,000 and credit the Swiss
bank's account.

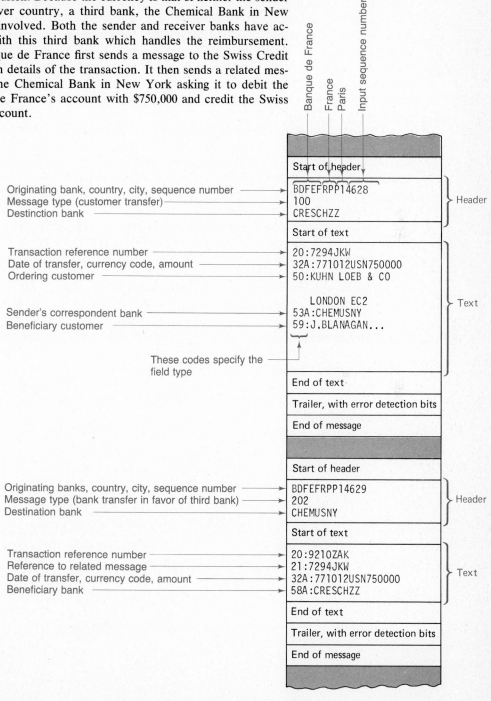

There is much scope for other multicorporate networks.

Approximately 70% of all *first class* mail in the U.S. is originated by computer. Most of this, invoices, orders, receipts, payments, etc., is destined to be fed into another computer, often in another firm. It should be transmitted directly in alphanumeric form. Instead it is usually printed, burst, fed in envelopes, sent to a mail room, stamped, sorted, delivered to a post office, sorted again, delivered to the destination post office, sorted again, delivered to a corporation, handled in the mail room, opened, and laboriously keyed into a medium which the receiving computer can read. All this—when a packet sent on a value-added network costs a small fraction of one cent.

The corporation, like SWIFT or SITA, which provides the service of multicorporate networking is, in essence, a private common carrier. In countries where all mail and electronic transmission is handled by government post and telecommunications administrations such a corporation may not be allowed to operate. SWIFT has had severe political problems with the European PTT's.† Its political problems have been far more difficult to solve than its technical ones.

Multicorporate transmission of the future may employ public data networks, where these exist, rather than private networks. In those few countries where the laws allow freedom of choice on this issue, private multicorporate networks may still be built if this gives lower transmission costs than the public tariffs.

There is massive scope for the interconnection of computers in different organizations. In the United States there is a potential of several hundred million messages per day (contrast with SWIFT's one third of a million per day). The difficulty is achieving agreement among organizations on message formats. Most computer salesman sell to *single* organizations, and systems designers work for single organizations, where one man is responsible—not multiple organizations.

Sooner or later, however, the machines in separate organizations will become linked and the world will be laced with networks over which corporate and government computers exchange information.

†PTT is the abbreviation commonly used for a government telecommunications administration (Post, Telephone and Telegraph).

5 PUBLIC NETWORKS

During the mid-1970's furious debates ensued among the major common carriers of the world about whether they should build a public data network, what form it should take, and how much they should spend on it.

The common carriers (this term includes the telecommunications administrations of countries with government-controlled telecommunications—the PTT's) desired to provide better service to the computer community. They also perceived that there was a revenue which would grow to tens of billions of dollars worldwide, which could go either to themselves or to the computer industry. This is the revenue from the switches, concentrators, multiplexers, polling equipment, line control equipment, etc.—the various devices used in the interconnection of machines. Common carriers operate the equipment for switching and routing telephone calls; it seemed natural that they should operate the new equipment for switching routing data.

Once computers were used for switching the desire grew to use them for other functions also. AT&T developed its plans for ACS (Advanced Communications Service, Chapters 6 and 7) in which the nodes would not only switch data but provide a variety of functions which need processing and storage. The British Post Office created its Viewdata schema (subsequently called Prestel) for operating public data bank accessible with television sets in homes or offices, initially via the telephone network.

CIRCUIT-SWITCHING AND PACKET-SWITCHING

There are two main categories of public computer networks: *packet-switching* networks and *circuit-switching* networks.

A *packet-switching* network divides the data traffic into blocks, called "packets," which have a given maximum length (for example, 128 bytes). Each packet of user data travels in a data envelope which gives the destination address of the packet and a variety of control information. Each switching node in a minicomputer reads the packet into its memory, examines the address, selects the next node to which it shall transmit the packet, and sends it on its way. The packets eventually reach their destination, where their envelopes are stripped off. Then, they may have to be reassembled to form the original user messages. It is rather like a postal service in which letters in envelopes are passed from one post office to another until they reach their destination. The typical delivery time on today's packet networks is about a tenth of a second.

We describe these two forms of network construction in detail later in the book.

A *circuit-switching network* establishes what is in effect, a physical circuit between the communicating machines. The circuit is set up rapidly under computer control; it remains set up while the data passes, which might take a second or less, and may then be disconnected so that other users can employ the same facilities. The reader might think of a copper path, carrying electricity, which is set up for a second or so between the communicating machines and is then disconnected. In fact the path is not a simple copper circuit because time-division switching is used in which many streams of bits flow through an electronic switch, all interleaved with one another. Circuit switching has been used for decades in telephone exchanges and in the worldwide telex network. The difference with computer networks is that the user circuit is set up and disconnected very quickly. The switched connection is often used only for the time it takes one message to pass, or for one message and an interactive response; sometimes it remains connected for the transmission of a batch of data. This rapid computer-controlled switching is sometimes called *fast-connect switching*.

PACKET-SWITCHING NETWORKS

Many advanced nations now have a public packet-switching network, either working or talked about. These are becoming interconnected into multinational networks so that packets can travel around the world or at least part of it.

The first major public packet-switching network was Telenet, shown in Fig. 5.1. This derived its techniques (and its management) from ARPANET, the first private packet-switching network (Fig. 3.8). Telenet was bought by GT&E, the second largest U.S. telephone company in 1979.

Figure 5.2 shows examples of national packet-switching networks. Figure 5.3 shows a transnational network, Euronet, which can carry packets between the national networks in Europe.

In Figs. 5.2 and 5.3 the packet switches and lines interconnecting them are shown in red. Many subscribers are a long distance from a switch, so concentrators are used to bring the user traffic to and from the network. The concentrators may form a small start network linked to a packet switch, like the private networks of the previous chapter, linking many users to the nearest packet switch. Most users are linked to the

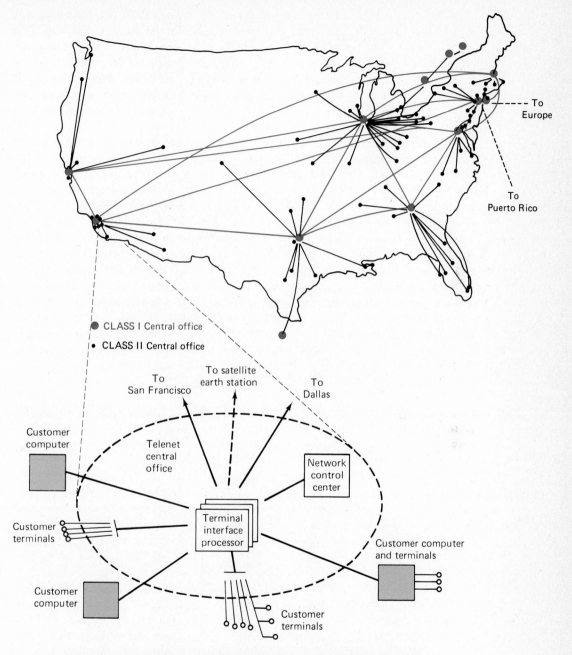

Figure 5.1 (a) Telenet's rapidly changing packet-switching network—one of the first "value-added common carriers." (b) A physical map of Telenet.

1. Bell Canada's DATAPAC, the X.25 packet switching system of the Trans Canada Telephone System.

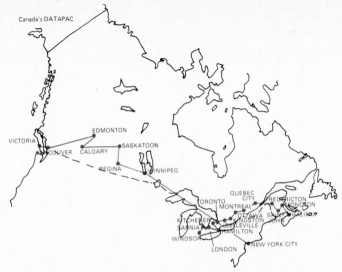

2. TYMNET became a value-added common carrier in 1976 and has been growing rapidly ever since. TYMET competes with Telenet shown in Fig. 5.1.

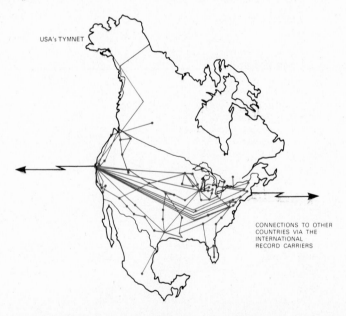

Figure 5.2 Most industrial countries are now building public data networks using the CCITT X.25 and related standards. These are interconnected via the international record carriers and via EURONET (Fig. 5.3). These networks can add new links and switches quickly. Before long the industrial world will be laced with X.25 networks.

3. TRANSPAC, the public packet-switching network of France. Whereas TYMNET and Telenet are private corporations offering value-added service, the networks of European countries are operated by the government telecommunications organization like their telephone networks.

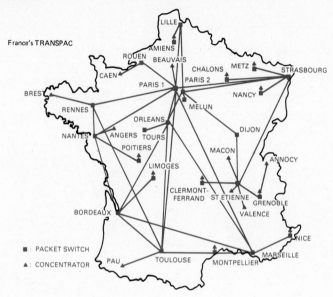

France's TRANSPAC

■ : PACKET SWITCH
▲ : CONCENTRATOR

4. United Kingdom PSS network.

U.K. PSS NETWORK

——— OPENING DATE
----- 1981 EXTENSION

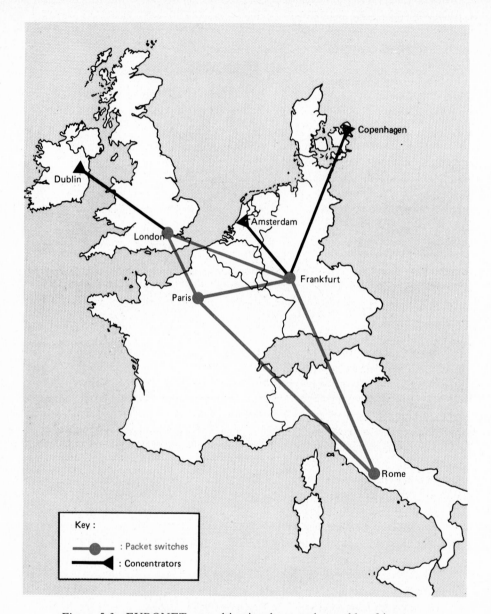

Figure 5.3 EURONET, a multinational network capable of interconnection with national networks. EURONET uses packet-switching protocols compatible with TRANSPAC (Fig. 5.2), and other national networks.

networks by telephone lines going directly to a switching node or else to a concentrator. This restricts their maximum data rate to that of a telephone line: 9600 bits per second. In North America some users can have higher-speed digital links into their premises.

User machines connected to a packet-switching network need to observe a rigorous set of rules for communicating via the network. It is desirable that networks in different countries should follow the same set of rules so that user machines around the world can employ the same software and control mechanisms, and so that packets can pass easily from one network to another. There has been a high degree of international agreement on the rules—the protocols and message formats—for public packet-switching networks, centering around Recommendation X.25 of the CCITT, (Comité Consultatif International Télégraphique et Téléphonique) the international standards organization for telecommunications. X.25 networks are described later in the book.

FAST-CONNECT CIRCUIT-SWITCHED NETWORKS

The first public circuit-switched network was built by the Datran Corporation in the United States, and was subsequently taken over by Southern Pacific Communications. Southern Pacific no longer offers the Datran type of switching publicly.

Whereas Datran built a digital microwave trunk specially for the purpose, other circuit-switched data networks use conventional wideband circuits between the switching nodes. Figure 5.4 shows a good example, the Nordic data network of Scandinavia. The data switches are interconnected by trunks operating at 64,000 bits per second. Multiplexers and concentrators carry users, traffic to the nearest switching node. These also are connected to the network by 64 Kbps trunks. There may be two or more trunks connecting two switches, or connecting a concentrator and a switch. More trunks are allocated to a data network as its traffic builds up.

The network provides switched synchronous data circuits at speeds of 600, 2400, 4800 and 9600 bits per second. Asynchronous (start–stop) terminals at speeds of 110, 150, 200, 300 and 1200 bits per second may be connected to the network.

The call set-up time is normally 100 to 200 milliseconds—very fast compared with the telephone network, and fast enough to make it economical to disconnect after each message and response in a man–machine dialogue.

Any circuit-switched network can encounter a "busy" condition, just as there are busy signals from the telephone when all circuits are in use. The designer of a circuit-switched network adds trunks and switching facilities until a sufficiently low proportion of the calls encounters a *network busy* condition. The probability that an attempted call will be unsuccessful is a basic design parameter of a circuit-switched network. The Nordic network is designed so that less than 0.5% of calls will fail to be connected due to network faults or congestion. This figure is determined by the numbers of

The structure and components of the Nordic data network

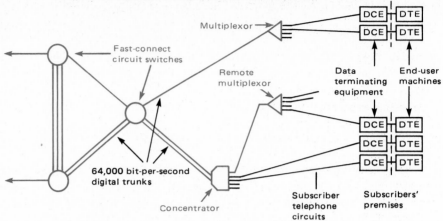

The geography of the Nordic data network. The first phase uses 88 concentrators and 84 multiplexors not shown here

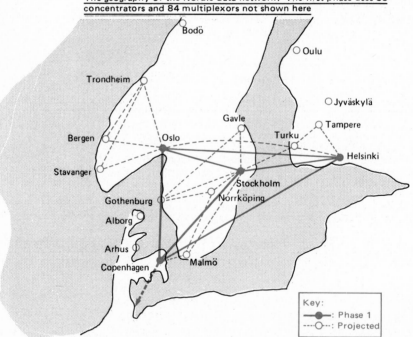

Figure 5.4 The Nordic public data network using fast-connect circuit switching.

trunks. Because the call set up time is fast and most calls are brief, the unit which controls the user connection to the network can retry an unsuccessful call quickly and have a high probability of succeeding on that attempt.

DTE's AND DCE's   The end-user machine—terminal, computer, controller, etc.—is referred to by the telecommunications administrations as a DTE, Data Terminal Equipment. This machine must plug into a unit which is the termination point of the communications circuit. This is called a DCE, Data Circuit-terminating Equipment. This plug-in connection forms the interface between the user's equipment and the common carrier equipment. DTS's and DCE's are drawn on Fig. 5.4.

For a leased telephone line the DCE is normally a modem. For a public (dial-up) telephone line a modem and telephone handset are often used, with the handset being employed by a human operator to establish the connection. With a fast-connect circuit-switched network a different unit is needed for establishing and disconnecting the calls. A switched connection can be established either automatically or by hand. The interface to packet-switching networks is more complex Packets with precise formats must be interchanged to set up a call and to control the flow of data. The formats and protocols of CCITT Recommendation X.25 are commonly used as described later in the book.

CONNECTIONS   Sometimes it is desirable to employ more than one type of
BETWEEN NETWORKS   network to achieve a given connection. A dialed telephone call may be made to access the concentrator of a packet-switched network. A multinational call may be set up involving a packet-switched network in one country and a circuit-switched network in another. Not all packet networks have identical formats, and messages may need to pass from one network to another.

To deal with network connections, interface machines are needed. The connection between different data networks is called a *gateway*. It consists of a minicomputer which appears to each network as though it were a normal node of the network. It takes data in the format of one network and puts it in the format expected by the other.

In Fig. 5.5, where a machine connected to Network A communicates with a machine connected to Network C, an addressing scheme will be needed which permits the connection to be set up to the right network and also to the requisite node on that network. Problems involved in the interconnection of networks are discussed later in the book.

Euronet (Fig. 5.3) could evolve into a "hypernetwork" designed to interconnect other networks. Worldwide hypernetworks will also be needed if efficient public networking is to take place worldwide.

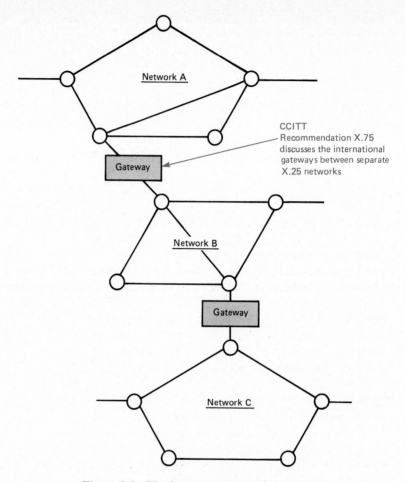

Figure 5.5   The interconnection of networks.

EIGHT TYPES
OF TARIFFS

The switched networks provide two types of connections between machines: first a connection switched through the network so that a machine can request a switched path to any other machine connected to the network; and second, a connection which is permanently established between two machines. A "permanent" connection does not imply a permanent physical path between the machines. On a circuit-switched network it implies a continuous stream of bits or bytes derived by submultiplexing. On a packet-switched network it means that when one of the connected machines sends a packet it is routed automatically to the other machine with no preliminary call set-up.

In the future, then, there could be eight main types of basic tariff associated with telephone and telegraph circuits and the two types of data networks:

	Switched	Nonswitched
Telegraph	Telex, TWX	Leased subvoice-grade circuit
Telephone	Dialed telephone connection	Leased telephone circuit
Packet-switched data network	"Virtual call	"Permanent Virtual Circuit"
Circuit-switched data network	Fast-connect circuit-switched path	Permanent submultiplexed bit stream

In some cases the virtual path through a circuit-switched and packet-switched network can be made to appear identical.

A few countries already have all eight of these types of tariffs. Some countries have a packet network but not yet a circuit-switched data network. Some countries have a fast-connect circuit-switched network but not yet a packet network. Most countries with a circuit-switched data network are saying that they may also acquire public packet-switching facilities.

We could be working toward a time when advanced countries will have them all. The designer of corporate systems will then attempt to select that mix of communication facilities which meets his objectives at minimum cost.

In addition to the above forms of tariff there will be tariffs for other services which are not pure communications, such as those associated with processing and storage in the nodes as in AT&T's ACS (next chapter).

VALUE-ADDED NETWORKS

The concept of *value-added common carriers* was important in the development of computer networking. A value-added carrier leases communications facilities from conventional common carriers and uses these in conjunction with computers to build a network which offers new types of communications services and tariffs. These are called *value-added networks* (VANS). Graphnet offered services for delivery of documents, often in facsimile form. Telenet built a network for the interconnection of data processing machines, like the ARPA network although the software and hardware mechanisms eventually became substantially different from ARPANET. Telenet delivers packets of data between computers or terminals in a fraction of a second, and charges by the packet. TYMNET offering similar services evolved from a private time-sharing network to a value-added common carrier.

In 1971 the United States Office of Telecommunications Policy recommended a policy of *first-tier* and *second-tier* common carriers. The first-tier carriers construct and own telecommunications links, and lease channels to their customers. They typically own 50% to 100% of the channel miles in service and lease the remainder from another carrier. The second-tier carriers are the value-added carriers. They add equipment, including multiplexers and computers, to channels leased from first-tier carriers and sell services that they create in this way, including message-delivery services, computer networks, and possibly information retrieval services and computer timesharing devices. It seems likely that second markets will develop in many telecommunications areas. The second-tier carrier may minimize investment in terminals by letting the customer provide these.

Legislation in favor of second-tier carriers has increased the diversity and competitiveness of the telecommunications industry in those countries where it has been passed. In most countries, such legislation does not yet exist.

Telecommunications systems use computers in different ways. Some use them for switching; some for sorting messages which are transmitted; some for processing the data transmitted. At one extreme the computer merely switches the circuits; at the other the circuits are merely links into a data-processing system. The term "computer utility" became used for describing public access to computer networks, and in 1966 the United States Federal Communications Commission (FCC) initiated a lengthy inquiry to determine whether public computing services should be regulated. The inquiry terminated in 1973 and defined the six categories of operation shown in Fig. 5.6 (FCC Docket #16979). Local and remote data processing services are not to be regulated, whereas communications systems are. There is a *hybrid service* between these two in which a subscriber sends data, which is processed and transmitted to another subscriber. If the data processing is the primary part of this operation, it is not regulated. On the other hand, if the operation is primarily one of communication between the parties, it *is* regulated. The former is referred to as *hybrid data processing* and the latter as *hybrid communications*. There is a gray area between these two about which lawyers will argue. The FCC is now conducting a new inquiry into the subject partly because of the uses of distributed intelligence. It is difficult to say whether certain intelligent functions are "computing" or "communications" functions.

Hybrid communication services must be completely tariffed and regulated by the FCC. Common carriers may not offer data processing services (hybrid or otherwise) except through a separate corporation with separate facilities, officers and accounting. AT&T has been excluded from offering any such unregulated services under an earlier consent decree.

Most countries do not have these legislative problems because the state telecommunications authority rigorously enforces its absolute monopoly over all telecommunications, no matter how bad its service may be.

**STANDARDS
AND CAPABILITY**
For computer networks to be useful as possible it is desirable that they should employ standard interfaces so that many different machines can connect to many different networks. Just as telephone devices can connect to telephone networks everywhere, so data devices should be able to connect to data networks everywhere, and the data networks themselves should be linked up worldwide.

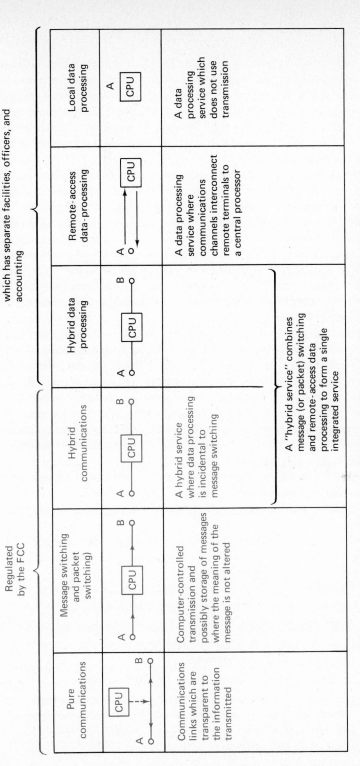

Figure 5.6 Range of services defined by the first FCC computer inquiry final decision.

The interface to a data network is likely to be more complicated than that to a telephone network because it cannot rely on any human intelligence as does the making of telephone calls. It must be completely automatic. However, if the interface is rigorously defined it can be built into mass-producible VLSI machines and quantity production will make the cost low. It can reside in inexpensive terminals and in computers. One of the distributed logic elements employed by a computer can be the standard network interface unit.

Perceiving this, as we mentioned earlier, telephone administrations (common carriers) of the world used their international standards organization, CCITT, to agree upon an internationally recognized set of protocols for making calls on data networks. This is referred to as CCITT Recommendation X.25. X.25 defined the formats of packets of data which will be used both for carrying information and for setting up and disconnecting calls on data networks, and for dealing with the errors and failures. It is likely that many countries of the world will build X.25 data networks in addition to those already in use. A wide variety of machines using the X.25 protocols will be manufactured. We will refer to X.25 frequently throughout the book. Chapter 22 discusses it in detail.

Producing a standard interface to data networks is complex, and requires different layers of control which we will discuss in the following chapters. X.25 does not attempt to define all of the protocols that are desirable for computer communication or distributed processing. It is concerned with the sending of packets across the network interface. Further, it would not be suitable for all types of transmission networks. Other protocols are likely to continue to exist for inexpensive machines like AT&T's transaction terminals, or the British Post Office's Prestel television sets. Other protocols will exist for circuit-switched networks and wideband networks.

Other protocols will continue to exist in computer manufacturers' architectures for distributed processing, and for new or specialized forms of data networks including networks using communications satellites, simple inexpensive networks, networks for facsimile transmission, networks with radio terminals, networks using cable television, and so on.

Network protocols have been created by the following types of organizations:

- CCITT and standards authorities.

- Common carriers with networks simpler and cheaper than X.25, like AT&T's TNS network (discussed later), and leased line networks.

- AT&T, with the introduction of its Advanced Communications Service (ACS).

- Common carriers with technology different from that for which X.25 was created, e.g. communications satellite networks.

- Value-added carriers such as Telenet, TYMNET, Graphnet.

- Computer or minicomputer manufacturers with architectures for interconnecting their software and hardware products, e.g., IBM's SNA (Systems Network Architecture), DEC's DECNET, Sperry Univac's DCA (Distributed Communications Architecture).

- Industry groups creating protocols for specific applications such as electronic fund transfer or airline reservations.

- Large corporations which develop their own computer network and networking software (sometimes purchased from a software vendor).

COMMON PRINCIPLES   In spite of the diversity of network types, there are many common principles which can be applied to these networks. The different networks have problems in common such as flow control, transmission errors, user interfaces, congestion, recovery from failures, network management, security, etc. Often they use similar mechanisms for solving these problems. The similarities among ARPANET, new common-carrier networks, DEC-NET, and IBM's SNA are as striking as the differences. We spend much of this book considering the principles and mechanisms.

6 AT&T's ADVANCED COMMUNICATIONS SERVICE

The most interesting of the public network architectures at the time of writing is AT&T's Advanced Communications Service (ACS). An earlier version of this was referred to as the Bell Data Network (BDN).

ACS is intended to provide the virtual circuits and virtual calls of the CCITT X.25 Recommendation, possibly with modifications; and also a form of datagram service and services for message switching, electronic mail, remote batch operations, and data entry.

It differs from most other public network architectures in that it provides processing power and storage at its nodes, which customers can employ for their own purposes. The programs in these nodes can be provided both by the telephone company and by customers. Telephone company programs will be shared by many customers. Customer-provided programs will be locked and usable only by the customer but may be shared by multiple user terminals and computers. This amounts to a form of time-sharing of those operations which we described as *function distribution* or *distributed intelligence*. We will refer to it as *distributed intelligence time-sharing,* and discuss its applications in the following chapter.

The user can perceive the structure of ACS as being, in effect, like that in Fig. 6.1. User machines—terminals, computers, or controllers—are connected to an ACS node which can carry out processing and storage functions. A major regulatory argument may revolve around what functions are permitted in the node computers.

VIRTUAL PRIVATE NETWORKS   ACS is to be a large-scale nationwide network from which multiple virtual subnetworks can be derived. Each subnetwork will have the appearance of being private and separately managed. A corporation can have one or more virtual private subnetworks.

Many corporations today have separate networks which were separately designed for different applications or different divisions. The collections of separate networks

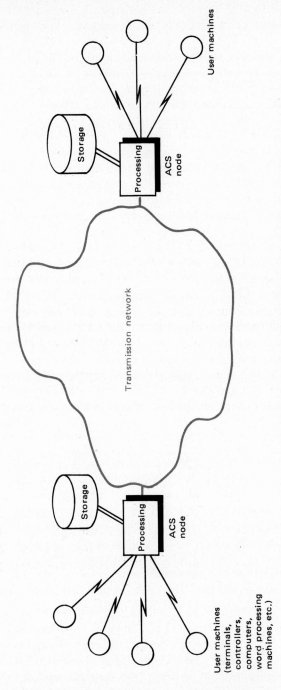

Figure 6.1 A logical view of ACS as seen by the users. What can the processing and storage be used for?

illustrated in Figs. 4.3 to 4.12 are typical. One large car manufacturer at the time of writing has 20 such networks. Another car manufacturer has six coming into one building.

These separate networks are generally incompatible, using different line control procedures and different network mechanisms. A terminal on one of them often cannot be connected to another. In offices where the networks intersect there are often multiple terminals, side by side, each connectable only to its own network. This incompatibility seriously limits the flexibility of use, and it is expensive to have multiple networks in parallel.

Many corporations have attempted to integrate their separate networks, or at least some of them, into a common corporate network, like those in Figs. 4.13 to 4.16. The modification of existing networks, however, has proved remarkably difficult, and the compromises involved have sometimes led to clumsy, expensive structures.

The 1980's will be characterized by corporate networks serving multiple computers and applications, just as the 1970's were characterized by separate single-computer networks. The problem corporations face is what architecture to select. The selection of IBM's architecture would tend to lock one into IBM. This is also true for some other manufacturers' architectures. Some corporations have written or acquired their own networking software which is manufacturer-independent, but this can be troublesome. The result is often expensive, inelegant, and generates major difficulties or software expense in attaching new computers to the network. As small, cheap computers proliferate this becomes an increasingly serious problem. Many attempts at creating corporate-wide networks have been scrapped or drastically modified.

AT&T's view is that elegant, highly flexible, virtual private networks can be provided by ACS (Fig. 6.2) and that the ACS protocols will become a standard, or at least an AT&T standard, which all manufacturers who have any sense will interface with.

OFFICE
OF THE FUTURE

Office administration has resisted automation so far. In the last ten years the productivity of office personnel has risen by only five percent. Their turn is now coming. Word processing, automated filing, soft-copy memos, electronic mail, etc., will possibly be the largest growth area for the application of electronics for the next ten years. The common corporate network should be as effective as possible at providing electronic mail, access to remote files, text processing services, and so on. Most existing computer networks do not handle this well.

ACS provides elegant solutions for mail, memos, and office-of-the-future networking.

STARTUP COSTS

The startup costs and difficulty of implementing networks have been high. Often the cost of adding new applications to an existing network are high. This tends to result in networks being used only for high-payback applications. ACS is designed to make the startup easy and

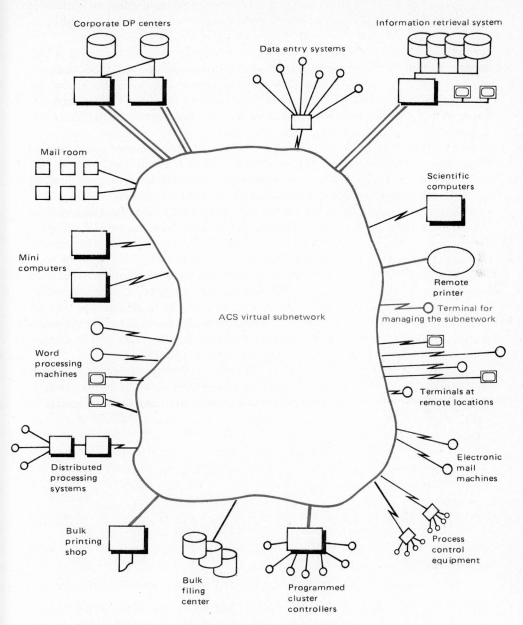

Corporate DP centers

Data entry systems

Information retrieval system

Mail room

Scientific computers

Mini computers

Remote printer

ACS virtual subnetwork

Terminal for managing the subnetwork

Word processing machines

Terminals at remote locations

Distributed processing systems

Electronic mail machines

Bulk printing shop

Process control equipment

Bulk filing center

Programmed cluster controllers

Figure 6.2 ACS is designed to provide virtual private networks serving a variety of different types of transmission needs.

inexpensive. ACS can be added simply to an existing computer without much software writing, because it can emulate existing teminals.

SMALL USERS   ACS is particularly appropriate for small users, many of whom have avoided teleprocessing so far because of the perceived difficulties and cost. It is easy for a small user to subscribe. As with any large, public, packet-switching network, the cost per packet is likely to make low-volume usage much cheaper than the alternative of employing telephone connections. Furthermore, ACS has features which can make a cheap, dumb terminal appear like a sophisticated expensive one.

ACS is appropriate for hundreds of thousands of small businessmen. Similarly, if it were widespread, it would be appropriate for low-volume terminals or small offices of a large organization. These small offices are often not linked to the corporate network today because of cost. ACS virtual links could give a low-cost connection.

INCOMPATIBILITY   There are many different types of terminal line control and consequently many different types of terminals which cannot communicate with one another. It would be useful to be able to send data between incompatible terminals. ACS will interface with many (but not all) types of terminals, and hence can act as a link between incompatible machines.

NETWORK   The management of corporate networks has become in-
MANAGEMENT   creasingly complex, expensive, and time-consuming. A substantial number of personnel are involved in network management especially in corporations with multiple networks. It is difficult to obtain the right skills to manage this function well. Expensive network monitoring equipment is needed to measure traffic, provide information for designing the growth of networks, for detecting and isolating trouble conditions, and for assisting in restoring operations.

ACS has extensive network management, monitoring, and diagnostic features. It removes the burden of network management from the customer. It provides detailed reports on the performance of each virtual subnetwork and provides cost reports with cost breakdown by terminal or type of usage, making possible the allocation of costs to individual users.

TWO-LEVEL NETWORK   ACS users are connected to the nodes shown in Fig. 6.1 These nodes, in turn, are connected with a higher-level trunking network.

ACS thus has two levels of switches: the node illustrated in Fig. 6.1 and a higher-level switch which is referred to as a *tandem*. These are shown in Fig. 6.3.

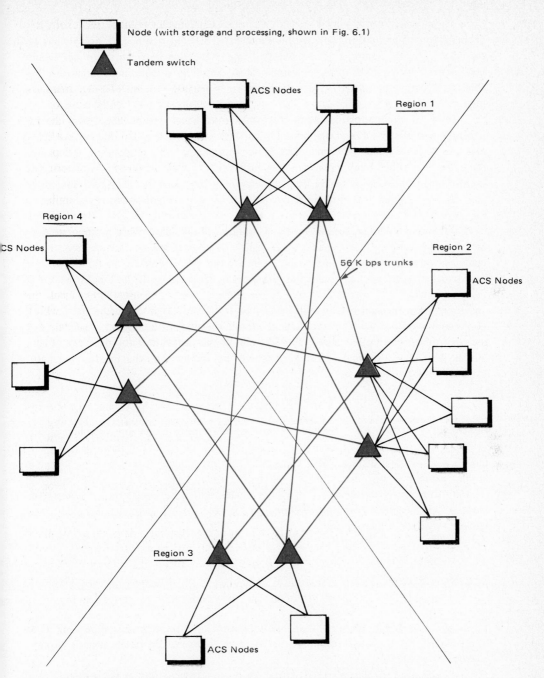

Figure 6.3 The ACS network. Two disjoint paths between each node, containing not more than two tandems.

107

The nodes are interconnected with a packet-switching network in the current implementation. The *tandems* are packet switches. This will not necessarily always be the case. If in the future a circuit-switched interconnection between the nodes would give better service, this may be implemented. Similarly a communications satellite connection might be used for part of the traffic when the volume of usage becomes high.

In the current implementation the trunks over which the packets travel are intended to be mostly DDS (Dataphone Digital Service) circuits of 56,000 bps. ACS is thus an overbuild of the DDS network. No new trunks need be constructed; the service is created by adding computers to the existing DDS network shown in Fig. 6.4, possibly supplemented by existing analog trunks operating at the same speed. AT&T intends to place nodes in about 100 cities initially, these being approximately the cities shown in Fig. 6.4.

ACS must deliver certain types of traffic *rapidly*. The trunk configuration is therefore designed so that any two nodes can be interconnected via not more than two tandem switches. A packet taking the longest route would travel over three 56-Kbps trunks and two end circuits connecting the users to their nodes. If the longest packet is that recommended by the CCITT X.25 Recommendation—255 user bytes—then the end-to-end transmission time would usually be less than 200 msecs when the network is not congested and 56 Kbps (DDS) end circuits are used. If analog telephone circuits are used for end-user connections, then the end-to-end packet delivery time would usually be less than a second. Most packets will be shorter than the maximum length, giving shorter delivery times.

RELIABILITY   Reliability is of prime importance in any switched public network. ACS trunks therefore follow the rule that there must always be two disjoint paths connecting any two nodes. It will be seen that that is the case in Fig. 6.3. Every node must be connected to at least two tandems, using separate trunks. As the network grows the nodes will be grouped into *regions* with tandem switches in each region as shown in Fig. 6.3. All nodes are connected to all tandem switches in their region.

ACCESS TO ACS   Users of ACS may access their nearest node by a variety of different types of connections as shown in Fig. 6.5:

1. *An ACS access line.* When the customer is located within an ACS serving area, an ACS access line may be used. When this is not the case, access may be via one of the following types of circuits.

2. *Public telephone circuits.* Terminal users at locations everywhere may dial their nearest ACS node. They may dial either a shared ACS port or a port dedicated to that customer.

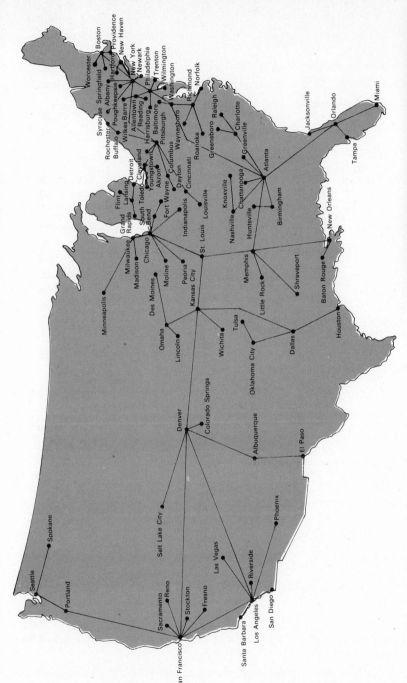

Figure 6.4 DDS network.

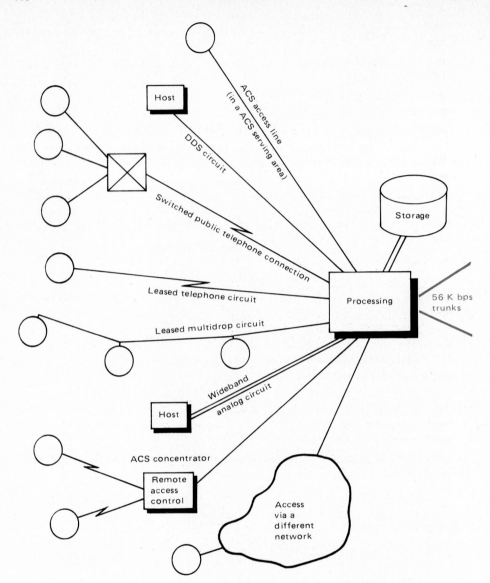

Figure 6.5 Types of circuit by which users may access their nearest ACS node.

3. *WATS.* Terminal users may dial an ACS node on a WATS line, sometimes at lower cost than via a public telephone network.

4. *Leased telephone circuits.* For locations constantly transmitting via ACS, a leased telephone may be used at speeds up to 9600 bps.

5. *Multidrop circuits*. Polled terminals may be connected to an ACS node on a leased multidrop circuit.

6. *DDS circuits*. The leased digital circuits of DDS may be used at speeds of 2400, 4800, 9600, and 56,000 bps.

7. *Wideband analog circuit*. A computer or device needing high-speed communications may be connected to its ACS node on a wideband circuit at a speed of 56,000 bps.

8. *Concentrator*. In most cases access will be to the ACS nodes shown in Fig. 6.1. Sometimes for customers far from such a node, an ACS concentrator-like device will be provided. This is labeled a *remote access control* unit in Fig. 6.5, and may itself be accessed by a dial or leased telephone line.

9. *Network interconnection*. ACS may be accessed via other data networks, for example, Telenet, TYMNET, X.25 networks of other countries, the Japanese Venus network, etc. AT&T's stated objective is to make every practical effort to permit a broad range of interconnection between ACS and other networks and carrier services.

TERMINAL COMPATIBILITY   It is intended that ACS should support most of the common types of general-purpose terminal, but not special-purpose terminals such as graphics and facsimile terminals. The latter may be connected via computers or controllers which *can* connect to ACS. Less common forms of terminal will not be supported initially. Box 6.1 lists the intended types of terminal support.

One of the attractive features of ACS is that it will permit incompatible types of terminals to be interconnected via the network. A binary synchronous polled visual display unit can send messages to a start–stop unbuffered contention teleprinter. Each of these perceives only the interface to its ACS node.

It is intended that ACS should be expanded in the future to meet any emerging standard protocol.

COMPUTER INTERFACE   Computers are connected to the network with three types of protocol support:

1. Emulation

The computer may interface with the network as though it were communicating directly with conventional terminals. The ACS node *emulates* these terminals. This is called *emulation support* and has the advantage that it requires no (or few) changes to the computer's teleprocessing software. It thus makes the startup cost of using the network very low.

The network will emulate start–stop ASCII terminals, binary synchronous interactive terminals, cluster controllers, or batch terminals.

BOX 6.1 Types of terminals supported by ACS

Terminal class 1: Asynchronous contention—character mode

Protocol:	Start–stop contention, using ASCII code.
Speed:	110 to 1800 bps.
Examples:	Teleprinters, portable unbuffered terminals.

Terminal class 2: Asychronous contention—block mode

Protocol:	Start–stop transmitting blocks, ASCII code.
Speed:	110 to 1800 bps.
Examples:	Start–stop buffered display terminals.

Terminal class 3: Asynchronous polled

Protocol:	Polled start-stop; PTTC/EBCD (Paper Tape Transmission Code/Extended Binary Coded Decimal).
Speed:	110 to 1800 bps.
Examples:	Typical terminal is 134.5 bps polled paper tape and typewriter-like devices.

Terminal class 4: Synchronous polled

Protocol:	Binary synchronous polled, as defined in ANSI X3.28— 1976 subcategories 2.4 & B2, plus RVI & WACK.
Speed:	2400 to 9600 bps.
Examples:	Cluster controllers and stand-alone terminals.

Terminal class 5: Synchronous contention

Protocol:	Binary synchronous contention, as defined in ANSI X 3.28—1976 subcategories 2.3 & B2, plus RVI & WACK.
Speed:	2400 to 9600.
Examples:	Batch terminals, remote job entry terminals, cluster controllers.

2. Character-oriented Messages

This is a binary synchronous message protocol designed to allow the host to carry out the message sending and receiving functions of ACS (described below).

3. Bit-oriented Interface

This is designed to be consistent with the CCITT Recommendation X.25; however it has many additions to X.25 to permit the full range of ACS functions.

CALL AND MESSAGE SERVICE
ACS provides two types of service, referred to as *call* and *message* service (Box 6.2).

Call service provides the virtual calls and permanent virtual circuits of X.25, with some improvement over X.25. It also provides a form of datagram service referred to as the *fast select* feature.

Message service makes use of the nodes' processing and storage facility to provide message switching, electronic mail, data entry, data retrieval, remote batch, data editing, and dialogue functions.

CALL FEATURES
The *call* features provide a customer with a bidirectional logical path between stations. Call service is most appropriately used for real-time and interactive communications. It permits communication between terminals, between computers, or between a terminal and a computer.

Box 6.2   Summary of ACS capabilities

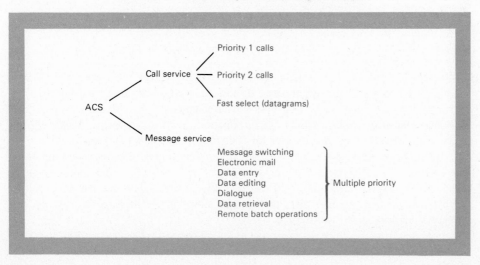

There are three levels of call:

PRIORITY 1:   Transmits the data with minimum delay.

PRIORITY 2:   Provides for transmission where efficiency of data throughout is preferred over minimum delay.

FAST SELECT: A datagram option. For fast transmission of single short messages with no call setup or disconnect operations. (The other call options require either a *virtual call* establishing or else a *permanent virtual circuit*.)

There are several call features which can be specified (most of which are not in the CCITT X.25 Recommendation):

- CALL ORIGINATE—PRIORITY 1.
- CALL ORIGINATE—PRIORITY 2.
- CALL ORIGINATE—FAST SELECT.
- RECEIVE CALL.
  In one mode calls can be connected only if the receiving station is not busy. In another mode the busy station can be *alerted* to the fact that a call is waiting. It then has a given interval in which it may prepare to receive the call, disengaging from its current transaction.
- CALL HOLD.
  A call can be temporarily placed on "hold" while another call is accepted or originated. A station may have multiple calls on "hold."
- CALL FORWARD.
  A station with this feature may forward incoming calls to another station.
- ACCEPT COLLECT CALLS.
  This feature allows a station to authorize the receipt of collect (reverse charge) calls.

MESSAGE FEATURES   *Message* features use the message processing and storage capabilities of the ACS nodes to prepare messages for transmission and to store or access messages after transmission. Message features are used for one-way transmission of information, with appropriate acknowledgments. They also have interesting uses for dialogues in interactive systems.

The area in which messages are assembled before transmission is called the *Message Storage Area* (MSA), and the area in which they are stored after transmission is called the *Message Arrival Area*, (MAA) (See Fig. 6.6). If data are sent to a station which is not ready to receive them they can be stored in the message arrival area for delivery at an appropriate future time.

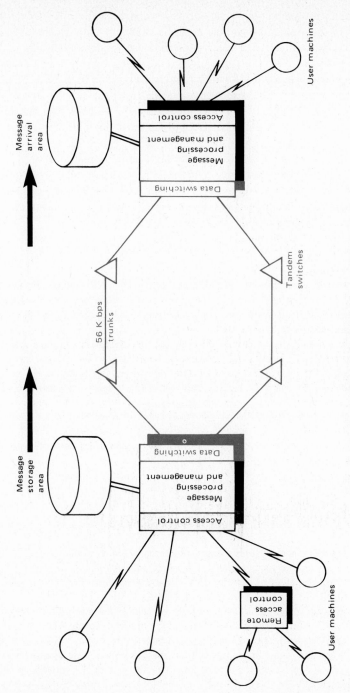

Figure 6.6 Functional layout for message services.

115

The sending station can store data at its local node while it works on the data, editing it, correcting it, inserting new records, building up a batch, and applying integrity or auditing controls. The receiving station can inspect data stored for it when the user wishes.

In a data entry system, the data to be sent can be built up in the sending node, and transmitted when complete. In an interactive system a dialogue may be carried out in the sending node, resulting in a possibly complex transaction which is then transmitted. In an electronic mail system, mail can be stored at the receiving node; the user may come into his office, see a blinking light indicating that there is mail for him, and display it on his screen. He may inspect his mail from a terminal at a different location if he is travelling, or at home. (Of course, security controls are needed.)

A reporter of the future may possibly enter his copy into ACS, using text-editing facilities for perfecting it, and instruct the system to deliver it at a given time. Up to that time he can modify it.

As with calls, there are some basic functions for transmitting messages:

- SEND MESSAGE.

     Messages can be sent with different grades of service offering different *priorities*. The highest priority results in messages of 1000 characters or so being delivered to the destination node in seconds. Lower priorities are appropriate for the delivery of batches of data or electronic mail.

     A message can be stored, either at the sending end or the receiving end. The originator specifies whether the message will be released to the network immediately or stored. Until the message is released, the originator retains access to the message. He may continue to adjust it, build it, add records to a batch, or otherwise manipulate it. He may then specify immediate delivery or delivery at some future time. If the latter, he may continue to change the message until it is sent.

     The sender may also specify the earliest time the message is to be made available to the destination address. After it is sent it may reside in the destination storage node until this specified time.

- RECEIVE MESSAGE.

     The receipt of a message may be in one of three modes: *automatic, scheduled,* and *demand.*

     Automatic mode causes conventional immediate delivery with the specified priority.

     Scheduled mode causes messages to be delivered to an idle station at a prespecified *time.* (This time refers to delivery from the *destination* node storage; the time in the SEND function refers to delivery to the trunking network from the *origination* node storage.)

     Demand mode causes a message to be held in the destination storage until the destination station requests it—for example, a user employing his office terminal to request the display of any mail that is waiting for him.

     When messages are delivered from the destination node storage, they are not destroyed. A *copy* is delivered. The users determine when the network should discard the message.

- COPY TO.

    A copy of messages can be sent to specified addresses as well as to the primary destination. This is like addressing a letter to a given individual with *copies* to other persons. The practices of office administration as well as telephony have been studied in designing to functions of ACS.

- MESSAGE FORWARD.

    A receiving station may instruct its local node to forward incoming messages to a different address. Messages for a person, for example, may be forwarded to a different location if he is visiting there.

- ACCEPT COLLECT MESSAGES.

    A destination station may authorize its ACS node to accept and store *collect* (reverse charges) messages.

- NOTIFICATION OF DELIVERY.

    This feature provides for users to be notified of successful delivery of messages both to the destination *node's* storage, and to the destination *station*. Reports may be requested showing transmission times and arrival times. Reports are generated listing any messages whose delivery has not been confirmed.

- MESSAGE RECORD KEEPING.

    ACS offers the capability to keep a journal of messages sent for sending stations, and of messages received for receiving stations. The journals can be selective, for example by listing all messages received from a given station.

ACS STORAGE

ACS nodes have two types of storage *general storage* and *protected storage*. General storage preserves messages being sent or received. Protected storage stores programs used for manipulating messages, assisting the end users, or providing ACS functions.

Message storage may be dedicated to a single station or shared between stations. If shared, multiple stations may participate in the building up of a message at an originating node, or may have access to message queue at a destination node.

Storage may be *reserved* for a given station, or provided on a *demand* basis, as required and when available.

ACS users *subscribe* for the use of storage in the same way that they subscribe for telephones, lines, and virtual circuits.

The storage is used for storing messages, as described, and also for message record keeping (journals), logs of abnormal conditions, and notification of message delivery.

PERFORMANCE

The FCC filing for ACS made little comment about the performance of the network or delivery times. As noted above, the use of 56-Kbps lines with not more than two tandem nodes should give fast delivery for top-priority messages—generally faster or at least as fast as the ARPA delivery times illustrated in Fig. 29.5

Information on the forerunner "Bell Data Network" indicated the following priorities:

Top priority.
A 0.99 probability of delivery in 200 millisecs or less. This is to be expected with network structure described for top-priority *calls.*

Priority 2.
A 0.99 probability of delivery in 15 seconds or less. This is appropriate for fast data entry and document delivery applications. Documents might be exchanged by two persons who are conversing by telephone at this speed, for example. It seems appropriate for top-priority *messages* but not for second-priority *calls.*

Priority 3.
A 0.99 probability of delivery in 30 minutes. This is suitable for sending batches of data, and human messages which replace telex or cable services.

Lowest priority.
A 0.99 probability of delivery in 4 hours. This is appropriate for most mail and some batch processing.

A different price is charged for different traffic priorities. Associated with the priorities are time ranges for messages which have to be delivered at specified times.

REPEATED ATTEMPTS AT DELIVERY   When a destination station is busy or off-line, the destination node may attempt repeatedly to deliver messages to it. The service details may specify how frequently the node keeps trying and for how long. When it finally stops trying, it may ask the sending station what to do. The sending station may give it instructions such as the following:

1. Delete the message.

2. Keep trying to deliver it.

3. Reclassify the delivery mode to *on-demand* delivery.

ADDRESSES   Four types of addresses can be used by ACS:

1. *Standard addresses.* These are numbers allocated to each station, like telephone numbers.

2. *Mnemonic addresses.* These are symbolic addresses—a word or phrase chosen by a customer to refer to a given station. For example, one station may address another with the word "WAREHOUSE" or "PALO ALTO."

3. *Multiple-address mnemonics.* A customer-chosen word or phrase may refer to an address list, for example "PROJECT 74" or "BOARD OF DIRECTORS" or "PROSPECT MAILING LIST." ACS will send the data in question to every station on the list.

4. *Implied address.* This is used when a station communicates with only one other station, for example a hot-line, or a terminal which uses only one computer center. ACS automatically inserts the requisite address into the messages or packets from that station.

NETWORK MANAGEMENT

As we have noted, corporations with multiple networks and an incompatible mix of equipment spend a horrifying amount of DP effort on network management. ACS will provide a complete network management service for each virtual subnetwork. This service includes the capability to monitor the network and adjust it as necessary, to detect and deal with problems, to allocate charges, and to activate and deactivate network components.

Each customer is assigned a single Bell System work center where one individual has the responsibility for the entire subnetwork. Troubles are reported to that center, regardless of where they occur.

Certain terminals can be designated *control terminals.* From these a variety of commands can be issued to control and manage the network. These include the ability to:

- Activate or deactivate stations anywhere on the virtual subnetwork.

- Activate or deactivate function sets—that set of capabilities including storage and processing.

- Activate or deactivate the entire subnetwork.

- Modify the rights which a station has to use programs and message storage areas.

- Assign and change passwords which are issued to network users to prevent unauthorized access.

- Assign and change charge codes. Charge codes are allocated to different functions so that bills can be prepared summarizing the charges for different uses of the network.

- Modify forwarding addresses for CALL FORWARD and MESSAGE FORWARD functions.

In addition to these *control terminals,* one or more terminals (possibly the same terminals) may be designated *customer network information centers.* These stations will receive management reports about the network, relating to configuration, usage, performance, maintenance, and service information. The reports can be delivered on demand, or at scheduled times, or, for some reports, when an incident occurs.

These facilities, in combination, allow the customer to manage and control his virtual subnetwork in a simple fashion.

TROUBLES

The network has been designed to detect automatically most of the troubles that occur through the use of automated testing and diagnostics. Normally the trouble is detected quickly and isolated. Often it can be bypassed by alternate routing. The diagnostics determine the cause of the trouble so that it can be corrected quickly. If the problem is in customer equipment the customer will be notified promptly.

The management and diagnostic facilities (along with the duplicate path structure) should give a high network availability and reduce the need for customers to report troubles and dedicate resources to network monitoring, management, and testing.

When troubles do affect the customer there is one center to which they will be reported, which is well equipped to isolate and correct them. This center will provide detailed reports of the action taken.

EFFECT
ON THE DP INDUSTRY   If ACS passes its legal hurdles and is deployed with nodes in a hundred U.S. cities, what effects will it have on the DP industry?

1. For large corporations it will provide a means to build a single corporate network which can replace the chaos of multiple, disjoint, and incompatible networks.

2. As the number of minicomputer and microcomputer installations increases and distributed processing strategy requires a means to interconnect them, ACS could provide a common networking solution. This could greatly enhance the usefulness of distributed data processing.

3. Its low entry cost will make it practical to use a network for applications for which this is not economical today.

4. It is especially appropriate for electronic mail and message sending systems. This is a vast market which would grow rapidly if ACS were widespread.

5. It is particularly appropriate (like Telenet) for the small business or individual user who wants to contact distant computers from a cheap terminal. The cost of sending packets with an ACS-like network will be much lower than the alternative of connecting via long-distance telephone lines.

6. The user interface to ACS would probably emerge as a North American standard for networking, incorporating the CCITT standards, but providing many extra facilities. Such a standard would greatly enhance the uses of data communications as cheap microelectronic machines become commonplace.

7. It would be used for data transfers between different corporations. These are often avoided today because of networking difficulties. There is a great need for intercorporate networking for uses such as the following:

   • A corporation sends its orders for supplies directly to the computers of the supplier corporation, thus avoiding the need for keying them into the supplier system.

   • Invoices are transmitted directly to customers' computers.

   • Payroll checks and other money are transmitted directly to the requisite bank computers.

   • Freight shipment documents are transmitted directly between shippers, freight carriers, and consignees.

   • Claims are transmitted from the offices of doctors, dentists, and hospitals, directly to insurance company computers.

- Insurance brokers have a terminal which is linked to the computers of multiple insurance companies.

- Reservations can pass automatically between travel agents, airlines, hotels, motels, car rental firms, etc.

Intercorporate networking can represent a major increase in automation by avoiding today's mail and data entry functions.

In summary, the widespread deployment of a network like ACS is badly needed and will greatly stimulate new uses for data processing technology.

7 DISTRIBUTED INTELLIGENCE TIME-SHARING

The biggest question mark about ACS is what programs should be placed in the nodes to assist users?

The most innovative and interesting aspect of the Bell design is the capability to have both Bell-provided programs and customer-provided programs in the nodes. These programs could be used for a wide variety of functions. Network users employ a high-level language called FDL for creating features for the nodes. This was originally called "Feature Definition Language" and was called "Form Definition Language" in the FCC filing.

A sentence from an earlier description of the Bell Data Network was, "The functions available to the user are only limited by his ability to program his requirements in FDL."

REGULATORY UNCERTAINTIES
The risks involved in introducing new telecommunications services in the U.S. are not only the risks of the marketplace, but also the risks of unpredictable decisions from the regulatory authorities. This most innovative aspect of ACS is unfortunately that most likely to cause regulatory or legal problems. If the various government bodies permit, there should be free competition between the uses of intelligence in the network, and the uses of similar functions in end-user machines of all sizes.

Freedom for everyone to invent functions that the network will perform appears to be desirable, because a preliminary examination of what these functions might be indicates that a very rich and useful set is possible. AT&T's ACS filing with FCC omits many of the interesting uses of processing and storage. It is clear that these uses, and many that were mentioned in the filing, are in competition with the data processing industry's marketing of intelligent terminals, network control functions, and distributed processing architectures.

AT&T was constrained in a 1955 consent decree to not market any *computing,* such as time-sharing services. Since then the technology has changed so that computing and transmission are inextricably mixed in efficient data communications facilities. It is very difficult to define where data processing ends and communications services begin. The reader might ask himself which of the following functions, for example, are data processing, and which are communications?

- Concentrator functions.

- Storage of messages for later delivery.

- Compacting data for more efficient transmission.

- Programs enabling a user to fill in a format so that only variable data is transmitted.

- Assistance with data entry for transmission.

- Transmission security functions.

- Deriving virtual private networks from a shared networking facility.

- Providing virtual terminal functions.

- Conversion operations which permit incompatible machines to communicate.

- Network auditing controls.

- Network monitoring, billing, and management functions.

- Controls permitting a batch to be entered, validated, and modified before transmission.

- Dividing long messages into packets for transmission, and reassembly of the messages before delivery to a user machine.

- Dialogue functions to facilitate network sign-on.

- Functions for standard user dialogues such as menu-selection dialogues (e.g., those dialogues which permit a domestic television set to be used for transmission in the British Post Office Prestel [Viewdata] network).

- Directory functions which permit one subscriber to locate another subscriber.

- Conversion of symbolic, list, abbreviated, or hot-line addresses into real addresses.

- Functions equivalent to those in a computerized PABX.

- Functions permitting a user to request display or delivery of a message sent some time previously.

It makes *technical* sense to allow telephone companies to put *any* functions they think useful into network nodes, but to insist that they also provide simple virtual circuit and call facilities. The user then has a choice between buying distributed intelligence functions from the telephone company and using similar functions in intelligent terminals, controllers, or computers. We need regulatory structures which permit the best technologies to win, and that is usually achieved with maximum competition.

Because of the regulatory uncertainties it is not clear at the time of writing how quickly ACS will evolve and exactly what services it will provide. Equally uncertain is how quickly such networks will be adopted by other carriers in North America and PTT's abroad. ACS makes it clear that a new round of international standards are needed to facilitate worldwide networks with similar functions.

CUSTOMER PROGRAMS

Customer programs will reside in a protected storage area in the nodes where they are used. These programs will be of two types: *interactive* and *noninteractive*.

Interactive programs will be used by terminal operators. They can provide message editing functions, data entry assistance, data validation sequences, dialogues to assist in creating transactions or formulating a request to a remote machine, assistance in signing on to a remote machine, and so on. They can also be used to establish and receive calls, and to send and retrieve messages.

Noninteractive programs are used to assist in the preparation of messages. They can also take totals of certain fields in batches of data entered (to serve as a check on batch integrity). They can add serial numbers to messages, build batches ready for transmission, permit the retrieval and modification of records in a batch before transmission, create auditors' journals, automatically distribute messages to multiple stations, and assist in message management and network management.

TERMINAL USER DIALOGUES

A common use of customer programs will be the provision of dialogues to assist in data entry or to guide an operator through the steps that are necessary in using the network, using a terminal, or using a remote machine. There are several types of standard dialogues that can be provided to serve multiple different applications. For example:

Form Filling

The network displays a form on the terminal screen, and the user fills in the form. Only the data which is entered is transmitted.

Menu Selection

The node displays a menu and the user selects one item from the menu. On the basis of this choice the node then displays another menu. This continues until a message is built up, which is transmitted.

Command Sequence

The node displays a sequence of commands or questions to the terminal user. The user responds to each and the set of responses is transmitted. Before transmission the node program may apply validity checks or completeness checks to the set of responses and display further instructions to the operator if necessary.

Text Editing

The user is given the capability to enter text, to inspect it on a screen, and to modify what he has entered. The facilities of advanced word processing machines can be provided, including spelling checks, thesaurus use, right justification, automatic insertion of repetitive phrases or blocks of text, etc.

Batch Build-up

The user is given assistance in building a batch of records. He may insert, delete or modify records as he wishes. The program automatically totals certain fields, applies completeness checks, creates an auditor's journal, etc.

Entry Validation

The programs carry out specified tests on field values. Fields can be tested for range (the value falls within specified limits), length, character set, field set membership (the field is one of a set of fields), and structure (e.g., letter ''B'' is followed by a numeric subfield). A set of field values may be added, for example, a column totaled on an accountants' listing, and tests may be applied to the total. Separate fields may be compared, added or otherwise combined, and tests may be added that are based on multiple fields. Tests may be made contingent on passing other tests.

Data Base Dialogue

A program assists the user in formulating a query for a data base or information retrieval system. The program uses a data base interrogation dialogue which assists the user in knowing how the query should be formulated, what the names of record types and field types are, what types of data the user is allowed to inspect, etc. The node may contain some data dictionary or data occurrence information to assist in this. When the query is correctly formulated it is transmitted to a distant data base system.

The formulation of the query may be a complex operation which is carried out without inspecting the data base itself. Languages for this are now in use, such as IBM's Query-by-Example for simple data base usage, and STAIRS for information retrieval. Standard manufacturer-independent, data base query languages are beginning to evolve.

Sign-on Dialogues

Signing on to use a remote application is remarkably difficult on some networks. Often the sign-on requires three states: sign-on to the network, sign-on to the remote computer, and sign-on to the application or program in that computer. The user has to know a precise procedure which is difficult to memorize in order to sign on. Dialogue techniques can make signing on simple, the operator being instructed how to proceed at each step. Easy-to-use sign-on dialogues should be part of the assistance the nodes give to users.

In addition to interactive programs, many types of noninteractive programs may be customer-written: for example, report generators. A report format or a screen display may be specified. A group of fields is transmitted and a program in the destination node creates the report that contains these fields. Different reports may be created from the same message at different locations.

FUTURE GROWTH OF NODE SOFTWARE

Some distributed-intelligence facilities are user-independent; the same program can be employed with many different customers. Others are user-dependent, designed by a customer for a specific application. Both types of programs can reside in the ACS nodes.

What is likely to happen, if ACS comes into general use, is that all manner of customers will create programs for the nodes. So will software houses. Some of these programs will have wide general applicability. They will be made available either by software vendors or customer associations, or by the telephone company as official ACS features.

ACS, or systems like it, could thus cause a chain reaction in which distributed-intelligence features become widely available in public networks. It is highly desirable that such networks should harness the immense creativity of the computer community in producing user features.

NETWORK LANGUAGE SUPPORT CENTER

The ACS filing specifies a *network language support center* which assists customers in their creation of features to reside in the nodes. This enables customers to enter their source programs into the network. It compiles the source program which the customer writes in the high-level FDL language, and provides facilities enabling the customer to test the program. It transmits reports on the compilation to the customer. It loads the program into the protected storage of those nodes which the customer specifies, and manages all customer programs used in the network.

If the user requires the customer-written programs to operate in different ACS nodes to serve different terminals, he gives appropriate instructions. The programs are then transmitted to the requisite nodes and loaded. Similarly customer-written programs can be deleted from the network.

The programs provided by AT&T will be written in the same language, FDL, as that which customers use. Customers may therefore modify the standard ACS programs. The modified version will be handled by the network language support center like any other customer-written program.

PARAMETERS In some cases the program may be used with parameters which modify its operation. These parameters may be stored in the general storage area rather than locked in protected storage. The parameters can then be changed from a terminal.

Many AT&T-provided programs will be parameterized in this way so that they have the widest general applicability.

The parameters to be used by a terminal can be prespecified and fixed on a per-application basis. Alternatively they can be specified for each call when it is set up or for each message before it is sent.

The combined abilities to place customer programs in the nodes, and to use parameters to select program actions, give great flexibility in using ACS.

COMPETITION The distributed-intelligence features we have described place networks like ACS in competition with the computer industry. Similar functions can be provided in computer manufacturers' architectures for distributed processing and in the software for intelligent terminals and controllers.

Where will be the best place for such functions? In the network, in host computers, or in intelligent terminals and controllers built with microprocessors? Nobody can be sure. It depends on future costs, network deployment, and service. There will be cheap dumb terminals in use for a long time, and these need the services of intelligent networks.

It is *very* desirable that many such features be standardized. Standards, *de facto* or official, may be more likely to emerge from the telecommunications industry than from manufacturers of intelligent terminals, minicomputers, mainframes, and software vendors, who are too busy creating new innovations to have much time to create standards.

The best course in the long run will probably be that some distributed intelligence should come from the computer industry and some from common carriers. Different functions are appropriate for each. The reader might glance again at Box 3.1, which lists reasons for wanting to use distributed intelligence (function distribution). Some of these reasons can be satisfied with an intelligent common-carrier network like ACS, but some of them can only be satisfied with intelligent terminals or controllers. The data processing community needs both. *A legal framework is necessary therefore which encourages both.*

COMPARISON WITH COMPUTER INDUSTRY ARCHITECTURES How does ACS compare with the architectures of the computer manufacturers like IBM's SNA or DEC's DECNET? First, it is incompatible with them. It is *competitive* with them. It does not (at the time of writing) support IBM's SDLC terminals. The incompatibility will present difficult management decisions in the future because many of the features of the manufacturers' architectures are highly desirable and are not in ACS. The question for big corporations is not whether to use *either* SNA *or* ACS, but how to use both. What type of bridge will be built between them?

ACS could provide a *ubiquitous* transport network with some Layer 4 functions that make it *easy to use*. It should give great *flexibility of interconnections*. It appears *easy to begin to use* and has *low start up costs*. It assumes the burdens of *network management, monitoring,* and *trouble diagnosis*. It provides *fast* interconnections that should be of *high reliability*. In addition, it offers an excellent set of mechanisms for electronic mail and message switching, with on-demand retrieval of messages.

Any public packet-switching network built on a large enough scale should give a low cost per packet, and this will greatly lower the cost of using terminals for those users who are not connected to a leased-line concentrator network or other private network designed to handle a high traffic volume. Today if you are fairly near a Telenet node and want to use interactively a computer a thousand miles away, the cost is a fraction of what it was a few years ago when you would have had to use the toll telephone network. Public packet-switching networks on a large scale will greatly stimulate the use of terminals by individuals, small businessmen, and small offices of large corporations.

A good computer manufacturer's architecture, on the other hand, should have many functions which could not easily be put into a common carrier network. They include the following:

- A program in one machine should be able to call functions in a remote machine.
- A program in one machine should be able to use files in a remote machine.
- A machine should be able to control the *pacing* of remote operations such as printing and file accessing.
- The operating system of one machine should be linkable to the operating system in a remote machine.
- A data base language operated in one machine should be able to use a remote data base.
- Distributed data base functions will eventually be part of computer networking.
- Tight security needs end-to-end cryptography and management of keys.
- Remote machines can set up sessions which enable them to cooperate in complex ways.

We might use the terms *tight cooperation* and *loose cooperation*. *Tight cooperation* requires precise cooperation between complex machines or complex software. The mechanisms in the cooperating machines are sufficiently complex that they need to be part of the same manufacturer's architecture or an intricate and precise copy of it. *Loose cooperation* requires machines to interpret each other's messages or packets, provided they follow a protocol for doing so that can be quite differently architected and from different manufacturers. There is no sharp distinction between "tight" and "loose" cooperation, but rather a scale of varying complexity.

In general, common-carrier architectures of the future can facilitate loose cooperation. Computer manufacturer architectures like SNA, DCA, and DECNET can facilitate tight cooperation.

It is likely that future transport networks (Layer 3) will be more flexible and more reliable if they are major implementations of common carriers. Functions requiring *tight* cooperation will be the province of computer manufacturers. Functions requiring *loose* cooperation may be up for grabs.

The telecommunications industry should be encouraged to go ahead as fast as possible with networks like ACS. They will make a *major* difference to the use of computing. At the same time the computer industry should be free to compete, putting distributed intelligence into *its* machines, and using simple virtual circuits or leased lines where this appears best.

8 TYPES OF COMPUTER NETWORKS

There are many different types of computer networks. The diversity is caused by the different types of distributed processing, the different needs of users, the different types of organizations owning or operating the networks, and the emerging new requirements of the office-of-the future.

There are major differences in the mechanisms of a horizontal network and a vertical network, or between an amorphous network serving incompatible computers like ARPANET and a tightly designed network serving the machines and software of one computer manufacturer or one user corporation.

ORGANIZATIONS   Different organizations create networks for different purposes, and we may categorize these as follows:

1. Single Application

Many networks have been built in a single corporation for a single application, for example, airline reservations. Such networks are designed and tuned to the application in question.

2. Multiple Application

Many corporate networks are designed for multiple applications which can share a common data base or data processing center. These are often vertical networks, like those in the figures in Chapter 4, constrained in design for reasons of efficiency, cost, or ease of implementation.

3. Corporatewide Networks

Large corporations have many computer centers and sometimes design networks to interconnect them. A corporate network may be designed as a general-purpose network to serve the corporation and give data-processing designers more freedom to employ remote facilities. Different groups in large corporations have often implemented separate networks, and a corporate network is an attempt to integrate these, provide economies of scale and better services.

4. Multiorganization Networks

Some networks have been constructed to serve groups of similar organizations such as banks, airlines, universities, etc. These are often horizontal networks such as those in Figs. 3.8, 3.9 and 4.17. Sometimes they are general-purpose like ARPANET (Fig. 3.8); sometimes they are special-purpose like the SWIFT electronic fund transfer network (Fig. 4.17), in which case they can usually be designed more economically.

5. Value-added Carriers

A value-added carrier provides a network constructed with leased lines to serve many customers in selected geographical areas. It may be a general-purpose computer network like Telenet or TYMNET. Special-purpose value-added networks are also feasible.

6. Common Carriers

Common carriers such as telephone companies provide nationwide data networks of several different types. Some of them are essentially the same as networks provided by value-added carriers, usually designed to move packets of data between subscribers in a fraction of a second. A telephone company has advantages that a value-added company does not if it chooses to use them. It can employ its high-speed digital pathways and switches directly rather than having to lease the tariffed subchannels. Digital PCM trunks operate at speeds of millions of bits per second (in North America 1.5, 6.3, 43, and 274 million bits per second) [1].

Telephone companies also operate leased digital facilities or circuit-switched networks.

7. Multiple Common Carriers

Multiple common carriers agree on network protocols with which to interconnect their data networks, just as telephone networks are interconnected. The common protocols permit the buildings of multinational, and eventually worldwide, computer networks.

8. Wideband Networks

Networks capable of carrying high bandwidth traffic are coming into existence for use such as copying machines transmitting to copying machines, remote slide presentations, and teleconferencing.

SPECIALIZED NETWORKS

It would be appealing to have a vast general-purpose network that could serve all types of distributed processing needs. These needs, however, are diverse and conflicting. One system demands very fast response times; another can tolerate message delivery taking hours, but needs it cheap. One system needs brief interactive transmission; another requires batch transmission of lengthy records and files. The needs of typewriter-like terminals are different from those of visual-display terminals with large screens. The requirements for facsimile documents are different from those of telegrams. Some machines can afford massive software overhead; others are very limited. On some networks the main thrust of the design must be to miminize cost.

Particularly diverse are those software requirements external to the message transport mechanism. There are many important functions of this software, as we discuss later, and they differ widely from one type of system to another.

There is a great number of computers, minicomputers, microcomputers, terminals and peripherals which need to be connected into distributed systems. The variety is too great for any general-purpose network to serve the needs of all these devices. Therefore, we find many forms of specialized computer networks, often operating more economically than a general-purpose network. Networks may be specialized in the following ways.

Specialized by Computer Manufacturer

Many computer (and minicomputer) manufacturers have a wide array of machines and software which they wish to interconnect. Most computer manufacturers have network architectures for this purpose. The first were the architectures of the Digital Equipment Corporation (DECNET), IBM (SNA), and Sperry Univac (DCA). All of these are quite different, designed to serve the networking needs of the particular manufacturer's equipment. Much future hardware and software from such manufacturers will be designed to conform to the manufacturer's network architecture, employing its unique formats and protocols.

Specialized by Application

Some networks are designed for one application, for example electronic funds transfer (Fig. 4.17) or airline reservations (Fig. 3.9). This gives a specific type of requirement which often results in simpler and cheaper control mechanisms than with a general-purpose network.

Specialized by Message Parameters

Some networks handle only messages shorter than a certain length. This substantially simplifies their mechanisms. We will discuss the concept of *datagram* networks in Chapter 24; this is an important and simple class of packet transmission network. Some networks are designed for slow traffic—no fast response times—but give secure or inexpensive transmission of messages or batches. Some networks are code-sensitive, transmitting only data in a given code.

Specialized by Machine

Networks from a computer manufacturer are sometimes designed to interconnect that manufacturer's machines. Some other networks are designed to interconnect computers but not terminals. They may connect any computer which has the correct protocols programmed into its software. Some networks handle specific types of terminals such as telex machines, or machines which conform to a precisely specified protocol.

Particularly important in the future may be networks which permit the interconnection of large numbers of inexpensive machines. AT&T's Transaction Network System is an example, permitting the inexpensive deployment of devices not much larger than telephones, which have a small display, keyboard, and possibly magnetic-stripe card reader. The British *Prestel* network using television sets is another. There will soon be vast numbers of microcomputers and cheap VLSI devices in need of simple data networks, rather than telephone communications.

Specialized by Transmission or Switching Technology

Many networks are built to use a particular type of transmission link or switching mechanism. Many are designed to use voice lines, and their throughput or response time, and hence application, is thus limited. Some have been designed to use public switched circuits. Some have been designed to use packet switching mechanisms, described later, which are ideal for messages of certain lengths but may be expensive for very short messages, large batches of long records, or facsimile transmission. Some networks have been designed to exploit special transmission technologies such as packet radio and communications satellites (Chapter 27).

Many networks employ complex message headers and protocols so that only machines capable of handling that complexity can be connected to them. Simple terminals have to be connected to them via an interface computer.

WIDEBAND NETWORKS   Most office machines have required transmission facilities of voice-grade speed or lower. That is not surprising because nothing else was generally available. Now wider bandwidth facilities are emerging, at least in North America. These include AT&T's DDS network offering data rates up to 56 kbps, Xerox's XTEN network taking channels of 256 kbps into users' premises, SBS (Satellite Business Systems) offering user channels up to 6.3 mbps, and American Satellite.

Along with the higher bandwidth capability, office machines using high data rates are reaching the market place and are in the development laboratories. These include intelligent copying machines which transmit to one another, displays for giving remote still-video presentations, teleconferencing facilities using freeze-frame or full-frame video, and high-speed computer printers and graphics displays. It also makes sense to have computer-to-computer transmission or computer-to-storage transmission at high speeds for some applications.

Box 8.1   Types of Network

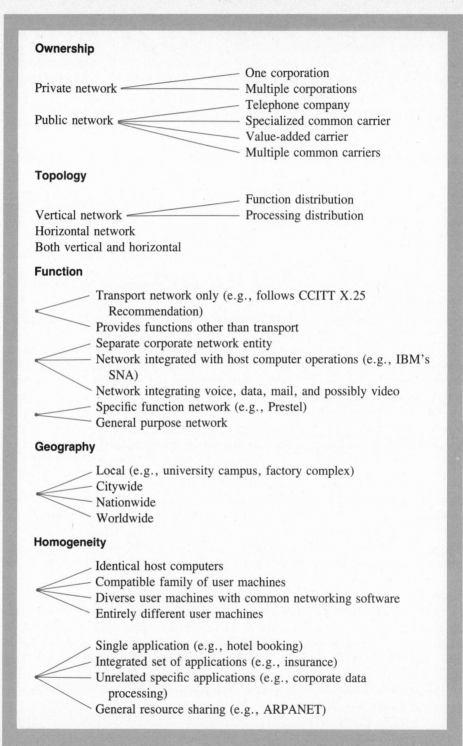

Ownership

Private network
- One corporation
- Multiple corporations

Public network
- Telephone company
- Specialized common carrier
- Value-added carrier
- Multiple common carriers

Topology

Vertical network
- Function distribution
- Processing distribution

Horizontal network

Both vertical and horizontal

Function

- Transport network only (e.g., follows CCITT X.25 Recommendation)
- Provides functions other than transport

- Separate corporate network entity
- Network integrated with host computer operations (e.g., IBM's SNA)
- Network integrating voice, data, mail, and possibly video

- Specific function network (e.g., Prestel)
- General purpose network

Geography

- Local (e.g., university campus, factory complex)
- Citywide
- Nationwide
- Worldwide

Homogeneity

- Identical host computers
- Compatible family of user machines
- Diverse user machines with common networking software
- Entirely different user machines

- Single application (e.g., hotel booking)
- Integrated set of applications (e.g., insurance)
- Unrelated specific applications (e.g., corporate data processing)
- General resource sharing (e.g., ARPANET)

Box 8.1 *Continued*

Switching Technique

No switching; multiplexor network
Concentrator network
Telephone switching
Fast-connect circuit switching
Message switching
Packet switching
Datagram switching

Multiple access
Voice line (polling)
CATV
In-plant wideband
Radio
Satellite

Coupling of User Nodes

Causal coupling. User nodes interchange any user messages.
Coupling with predefined application transactions
Coupling with macroinstruction (e.g., GET for remote storage use)
Specific addressing (like a telephone number)
Generic addressing (the originating node refers to the required node symbolically or generically and the network directory mechanism finds it)
Implied addressing (the station always transmits to the same address, e.g., a hot-line, or a terminal always connected to the same computer.)

Bandwidth

Sub-voice grade (e.g., telex or TWX)
Voice grade
56 kbps or 64 kbps (e.g., AT&T's DDS. The speed of digitized PCM voice)
$1/4$ to $1/2$ mbps (for applications such as copying-machine to copying-machine transmission or still frame video)
1.5 mbps and higher (for moving image video)
Virtual bandwidth derived from 56 kbps or similar speed circuits (today's generation of packet-switching networks).
Virtual bandwidth derived from 1.5 mbps or similar speed circuits (e.g., built on T1 circuits. Such networks might handle packetized *voice* and data).

As well as employing nationwide links some of these machines employ local links using in-plant or cable television circuits.

Wideband networks will eventually form an important resource of the office-of-the-future.

Box 8.1 summarizes differences between different network types. Some of the terms in Box 8.1 are explained later in the book.

Networking systems vary in the types of functions they provide. Some merely provide a transport mechanism for moving data from one node to another. Some provide many services in addition to a transport subsystem. If only a transport mechanism is provided, it is up to the system designers to determine what protocols the user machines employ once data is passing among them.

Sometimes the network software provides macroinstructions such as GET or CALL so that a program in one machine can employ programs or files elsewhere in the network. Sometimes each user machine must give a specific network address of a distant machine before it can be contacted. On other networks a generic or symbolic statement is made of the requirement, and a network mechanism contacts the requisite machine.

More detailed differences between networks will emerge when we discuss their mechanisms later in the book.

REFERENCE

1. Martin, J., *Future Developments in Telecommunications,* 2nd ed., Chapter 27, Prentice-Hall, Englewood Cliffs, NJ, 1977.

PART **II**   COMPUTER NETWORKS

9 BASIC NETWORK FUNCTIONS

We are concerned with networks for communication between intelligent machines—some more intelligent than others. The public telephone system is a network for communication between intelligent *people* (some more intelligent than others). The similarities and differences are instructive.

A person placing a telephone call has to know a telephone number. He has a formal procedure for requesting that a call be established to that number. After a short delay the network informs the caller of whether the call was completed and, if not, indicates one of several reasons why—called party's telephone is in use, busy network, called party did not answer the telephone, invalid number dialed, equipment failure, etc. After the electrical connection is made there is a brief period of human protocol in which the required person is found, identifies himself, and listens while the caller identifies himself. The communicating parties then have a *session* of conversation.

We will use the word *session* for machines in communication. The machines may be executing a one-way transfer of data or a dialogue. Like a telephone call, the session may go on for an extended period. One computer may be using another computer's data base. An operator may be entering data into a remote machine. A terminal user may be carrying out a dialogue with a distant computer. There are three main phases to communication: establishing the session, conducting the session, and terminating the session.

As with a telephone call, establishing the session involves two separate operations. The first is the process of establishing the telecommunications path so that information can be interchanged. The second is the process of identifying the parties and having them agree to communicate, using specified procedures and facilities. On the telephone system the latter may require a secretary or an operator, who drops out of the link as soon as the parties are in session.

There are thus five processes:

1. Connecting the transmission path.}   (physical process)

2. Establishing the session.

3. Conducting the session.   (logical process)

4. Terminating the session.

5. Disconnecting the transmission path.}   (physical process)

TRANSPORT SUBSYSTEM

Connecting and using the transmission path is an operation entirely separate from that of setting up the session once the path is connected. On the telephone system the former involves the transmission and switching equipment. In computer networks the transmission links and their operation can be regarded separately from the session services and applications which employ them. We will refer to a *transport subsystem* in computer networks which passes messages between the communicating machines. External to this are the *session services*.

We discuss the transport subsystem in more detail in Chapter 12. It is sometimes referred to as a *transport network, transport subnetwork, transmission subnetwork,* or *transmission subsystem*.

TERMINATION SUBSYSTEM

When simple terminals transmit simple data messages the facilities which they need, such as buffering, can be simply defined and allocated. In the world of distributed processing many different types of facilities to aid communication are provided by the distributed software and hardware. Most of the valuable ways of using distributed intelligence require the machines at each end of the link to be working in precise cooperation. One may be editing or formatting data on the basis of characters placed in it by the other. One may be compressing data so that it can be sent more economically, and the other expanding it to its original form. One may encypher data for security reasons and the other must decypher it. One may ask for a file of data and the other transmits a succession of records from the file without further instructions. Control of the *rate* of transmission is needed to ensure that one machine does not outpace the capability of the other.

The software that is used for functions such as data-base operation and time-sharing services is highly complex. Before the advent of distributed intelligence this software resided entirely in a central computer. Now, increasingly, there are good reasons to distribute certain functions. In order to use distributed software it is necessary when establishing a session to ensure that the machines at each end of a connection employ matching or complementary functions.

A terminal is likely to be used to access different software at different times. At one time it might be connected to a data base system, at another to interactive computing facilities, and so on. The same applies to intercomputer communication. There are *many* different types of software, with differing requirements, and the proliferation is rapidly increasing.

In dialogues between machines different protocols are observed about who speaks when. In some cases the machines alternate their transmissions; one speaks and then the other, like a polite human conversation. In other cases both machines can speak at once. One may transmit data while the other transmits control signals, or they may both transmit data at once. Sometimes one machine is allowed to interrupt the other; sometimes not. Before message interchange begins, the protocol of the conversation must be specified.

Because the facilities and protocols employed by intelligent machines can vary, the establishment of these facilities and agreement on protocol must take place when the *session* is established. We will refer to the collection of services or functions which exist *external to the transport subsystem* as the *termination subsystem* (see Fig. 9.1). The termination subsystem provides a set of session services, which differs from one architecture to another.

The termination subsystem consists of software (and possibly some hardware or microcode) in any of the following five places:

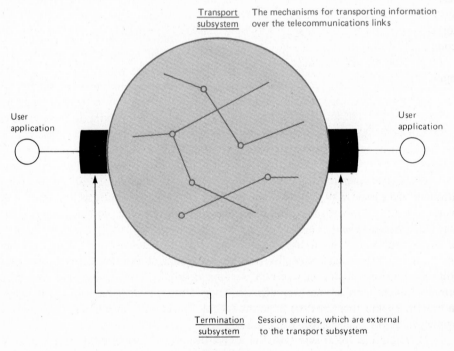

Figure 9.1

1. A host computer.

2. A front-end communications controller.

3. A terminal concentrator.

4. A terminal controller.

5. An intelligent terminal.

In some architectures the transport subsystem and the termination subsystem are in different machines. There is a machine-to-machine interface between these subsystems. In other architectures, portions of the transport and termination subsystems are in the same machine with a software interface between them.

SESSION SERVICES   Session services fall into two types: those used when setting up the session and those used when the session is in progress. Most human telephone calls do not use any services external to the transmission system when the call is in progress, although they could. Scramblers could be used to ensure privacy, for example. Networks for distributed processing and computer resource sharing can employ many types of services external to the transmission subsystem. They include the editing of data, code conversion, data base services, cryptography, or other techniques for achieving security. We discuss this and give a more complete list in Chapter 13.

Session services are used prior to the interchange of data to ensure that the communicating parties

- are authorized to communicate,
- have the facilities they need to communicate, and
- agree upon the manner in which they shall communicate.

Authorization is necessary when a terminal or application program attempts to use a remote data base, file system, or computer. It is an important process because networks could allow terminals or computers anywhere to gain access to these facilities. Unauthorized access could be expensive, could violate privacy or secrecy, or could result in damage to data or programs.

The facilities which user processes require when they communicate vary greatly from one user process to another. They may require different hardware, such as buffering, different software such as editing or file access modules, and different options in employing the software. That they are ready to use the requisite facilities must be agreed on before data transfer begins.

Different user processes communicate with different protocols. The protocols to be used must be agreed upon before the session begins.

On some networks *all* nodes have the capability to set up a session. On other networks only certain nodes, or possibly only one node has the capability. In a horizontal network, all nodes may have the *same* network capabilities (with the exception of the node which carries out administrative functions like collecting traffic statistics and maintaining information about the status of the network). In a vertical network, the nodes sometimes have widely differing capabilities. The machines lower in the hierarchy have relatively little memory or computing power. The job of setting up the session is done by the machine or machines at or near the top of the vertical configuration. When a machine low in the hierarchy wants to participate in a session it contacts the higher machine which has the responsibility of establishing the session.

Like a telephone operator, the node which establishes the session may drop out

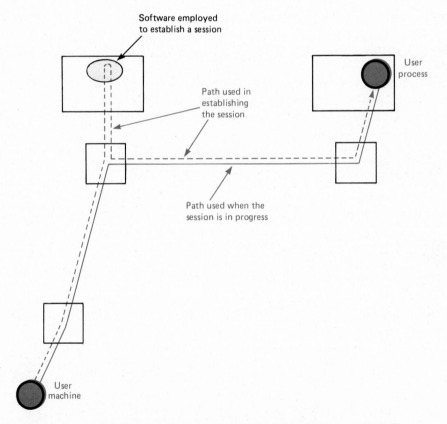

Figure 9.2 A third party sets up a session and establishes a route for it. After the session is established the third party drops out, but may be responsible for recovery actions. Contrast with Figure 9.3.

of the communication as soon as the session is set up. This is illustrated in Fig. 9.2. A terminal requiring a session communicates with its local host computer, asking for a session with a distant computer. The session-establishment software in the first computer communicates with that in the second. The session is agreed upon and the first computer drops out, leaving transmission to proceed as shown by the parallel line.

Sometimes the machine which establishes the session is the same as the machine which sets up the transmission path. That might be the case in Fig. 9.2, even if the transmission path is more complex than that shown. In Fig. 9.3 the nodes drawn in red circles set up the transmission path. The using computers set up the session.

It is possible to give the *front-end proscessors* the capability to establish sessions. This has the advantage that the host computers are independent of network software. If a host fails or has a software crash, the network keeps operating.

VARIETIES OF USERS   We will frequently refer to "users" of networks. *By "user" we mean the source or destination perceived by the network of the information transmitted. "Users" employ the transmission facilities and session services.*

The term "end user" is employed in some literature and manufacturers' manuals to refer to a user process or user machine. This is an unfortunate choice of

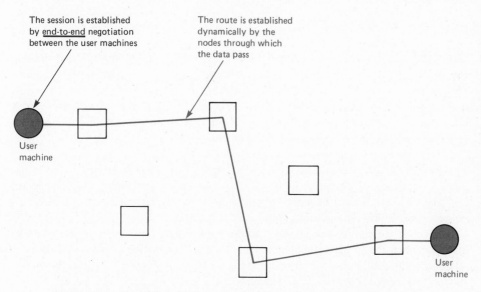

Figure 9.3   A session set up without the assistance of a third party or manager. The route is selected dynamically by the nodes which relay the data to its destination.

wording. "End user" should refer to the persons or departments who utilize the system as a whole. We will employ the term only with this meaning. The programs or mechanisms which constitute the sources and sinks of information handled by the network software will be called *users, user processes,* or *user mechanism.*

Before the advent of distributed intelligence, the term "user" had a clear meaning in data communications. It referred to the user of a simple terminal, often a typewriter-like device or a visual display unit. Now, however, terminals or their controllers can contain application programs, and these programs become "users" of the transmission facilities and session services. An application program could be either in a host computer or in a peripheral device. Both are "users" of the network.

On the other hand, a user could be a very simple mechanism. It could be an indicator light or a sensor or actuator in a process control application. It could be a disk or cartridge, or other removable media which stores data on a terminal.

A user, then, can be:

1. A person at a simple terminal.

2. A sensor or actuator.

3. Removable media.

4. An application program in a terminal or controller.

5. An application program in a host computer.

6. A function built into a chip or microcode.

DIFFERENCES FROM THE TELEPHONE SYSTEM   The differences between computer networks and the telephone networks are great. First, apart from telephone sets, almost all of the electrical equipment of the telephone network is the *transmission (transport) subsystem.* For computer networks and distributed processing the *termination subsystem,* external to the transport subsystem, is very important.

There are few differences among telephone sets, and they are used in much the same way. There are enormous differences between the user processes and user machines interlinked by computer networks. The user processes employ different end-to-end protocols which must be agreed upon, and they need different facilities which must be available, before data is exchanged.

Even if we confine our attention to the transmission links there are major differences between the needs of telephone and the needs of computer networks. Box 9.1 summarizes the differences in needs between telephone subscribers and machines, and the top half relates to the transmission links.

Telephone callers all need the same capacity channel—a channel with enough bandwidth to facilitate human conversation. For machine transmission we would like (but often cannot obtain) transmission capacities ranging from a few bits per second up to the capacities of the machines' own channels—millions of bits per second. Machines sometimes transmit data in one direction, sometimes in each direction alternately, and sometimes in both directions at once. Machines sometimes need fast response times and sometimes their data can be delivered later, when convenient. The time taken to dial and connect a telephone call is typically 20 seconds or more. For some machine applications the connection time should be fast—say a second or less.

Telephone callers are tolerant of noise on a channel. Human speech is highly redundant and its meaning can usually be understood when small portions of it are damaged. Background noise has to be very bad to prevent comprehension. With some machine applications accuracy is vital. *Every bit* sent must be received without error.

BURST TRANSMISSION   Probably the most important difference is that people need transmission that is *continuous* so that a person talking can be heard without interruptions. A dialogue between machines often takes place in *bursts*, and the periods of silence between the bursts are much longer than the bursts.

While many applications of data transmission are for one-way delivery of batches of data, the most common and fastest growing use of networks is for *interactive* systems. It is because interactive systems make different types of demands on transmission and switching facilities that new types of public networks are coming into existence around the world.

When a continuous telephone circuit is used for typical interactive transmission between two machines, that circuit is very inefficiently used. This is illustrated in Fig. 9.4. The transmission takes place in a sporadic fashion. The user will often pause to read a response or to think. When he types he may do so slowly. The terminal has a buffer so the transmission line is not occupied during the keying.

The number of characters transmitted in both directions in a half-hour dialogue between a person at a typewriter-like terminal and a computer is typically less than 21,000 bits with ASCII coding. The figure varies substantially from one dialogue to another. A dial-up voice line can transmit at 4800 bits per second; in half an hour it can transmit 8,640,000 bits. Many speech trunks now use PCM techniques in which one telephone channel becomes 56,000 bits per second in each direction (64,000 if the overhead is included) [1]. This is 201,600,000 bits in total in half an hour. It might be said that with a typical dialogue at a typewriter-like terminal, this represents a transmission efficiency of

$$\frac{21,000}{201,600,000} = 0.0001.$$

To achieve a high efficiency over today's trunks, many transmitting machines have to *share* the circuit. This is what happens on computer networks. Computer networks are designed to permit a high degree of *resource sharing*. Many users share the computing, data base, and transmission resources. In the 1960's it was important to

BOX 9.1 Telephone users and users of computer networks have very different characteristics, so that different architectures are needed

THE TRANSPORT SYSTEM

TELEPHONE USERS	USERS OF COMPUTER NETWORKS
• Require a fixed-capacity channel.	• Require a very wide spread of channel capacities ranging from a few bits per second to (ideally) millions of bits per second.
• Always carry out a two-way conversation.	• One-way or two-way transmission.
• Tolerant of noise on the channel.	• Data must be delivered without errors.
• Transmit or listen *continuously* until the call is disconnected.	• In a man–computer dialogue transmission is in bursts.
• Require immediate delivery of the signal.	• In nonreal-time data transmission the data can be delivered later, when convenient.
• Have a constant transmission rate.	• In a man–computer dialogue, mean number of bits per second is usually low, but the peak requirement is often high. The peak to average ratio is often as high as 1000.
• The time to set up the connection can range from a few seconds to one minute.	• Sometimes it is desirable that the connection should be set up in a second or less.
• Switching is carried out only at the start of a conversation.	• Efficiency can be improved if the messages which constitute a dialogue are individually switched with a very low switching time.
• Telephone dialing is manual.	• Setting up a connection between machines is often automatic.
• Telephone callers employ simple compatible instruments.	• Incompatible machines may intercommunicate giving a need for code or signal conversion.

BOX 9.1 *Continued*

• Different priorities are not used on the public telephone network.	• It is valuable to have several levels of priority.

EXTERNAL TO THE TRANSPORT SUBSYSTEM

TELEPHONE USERS	USERS OF COMPUTER NETWORKS
• Users employ human to telephone protocol.	• Users employ a variety of protocols for information interchange.
• Most calls require no services external to the transmission subsystem.	• A wide variety of session services is employed.
• No special facilities or agreement on protocol are needed.	• Establishment of session facilities and agreement on end-to-end protocol must occur before the user session begins.
• Telephone calls have little or no security protection.	• Security protection is important for some calls.
• Equipment failure or malfunction is annoying but generally not harmful.	• Procedures must be designed so that equipment failures cannot cause loss or double-processing of transactions.
• Reverse-charge calls are handled by operator intervention.	• Reverse charges are handled automatically.

share the computers and there was major development of multiprogramming operating systems and *time sharing*. Now minicomputers and microcomputers have become low in cost and the big need is to share the transmission facilities; hence the development of computer networks.

Many different transmissions such as those in Fig. 9.4 can be interleaved on the same communication line. The interleaving is made more practical by the fact that the bursts shown in Fig. 9.4 can be delayed slightly if necessary. Bursts from many machines can queue for the transmission links.

There are several different types of mechanisms for building computer networks, which we discuss later, but all their transport subsystems operate by handling *bursts* of transmission, and interleaving the bursts from many users. This is fundamentally different from the telephone network which operates with channels which transmit *continuously* so that the human ear can listen continuously. Many telephone users share one physical trunk but they do so by having subchannels which transmit *continuously*, not in bursts.

It is not only interactive traffic that requires burst multiplexing and burst switching. Much traffic which is essentially one way, such as the sending of telegrams or mail, or electronic fund transfer, also requires brief bursts of transmission, with acknowledgements of correct delivery.

PEAK-TO-AVERAGE RATIO   Some interactive data transmission is more bursty by nature than others. A measurement of its burstiness can be made by dividing the *peak transmission rate* that is desirable by the *average transmission* rate during a session. This is measurement of the need for *burst* multiplexing and *burst* switching (as opposed to multiplexing and switching which is continuous for the duration of a session, as on the public telephone system). It is noteworthy that the terminal–computer dialogues in use by the computer industry are increasing in their peak-to-average ratio. *Distributed intelligence often gives a need for a higher peak-to-average ratio than with earlier, simpler applications of data transmission.*

Table 9.1 lists six applications of terminals and gives estimates of their peak-to-average ratio. The dialogues in question have been selected to be typical of the patterns of responses found in terminal–computer dialogues. They are given in detail in the author's *Telecommunications and the Computer*, 2nd edition.

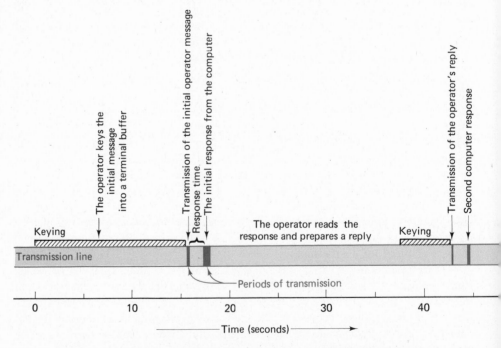

Figure 9.4 Most man–computer interactions make highly sporadic use of the transmission facilities.

The peak transmission rate is determined by the response time needs of the dialogue user. In some cases he needs to receive a screen of information in about two seconds, requiring a transmission rate of several thousand bits per second. How many characters are on that screen depends on the structure of the dialogue. This peak is divided by the average bit rate during the session. The average bit rate is often low because of the lengthy periods of silence, as illustrated in Fig. 9.4.

With teletype machines or typewriter-like terminals, the peak-to-average ratio is often between 10 and 25.

With nonprogrammable visual display units the peak-to-average ratio is often between 100 and 250. It is higher because the dialogue is designed to display screens of information which contain many bits and should be displayed with a fast response time.

With programmable visual display units much of the dialogue may take place within the terminal so the average number of bits transmitted is lower. Periodic references to data stored in a distant machine require fast responses, and this makes the desirable peak rate high. Hence the peak/average ratio is higher. The peak/average ratio with programmable terminals often exceeds 1000.

Graphics terminals used on computer networks normally have local programming capability. The network may be required to deliver a substantial piece of program or graphic display rapidly, again giving a high peak/average ratio.

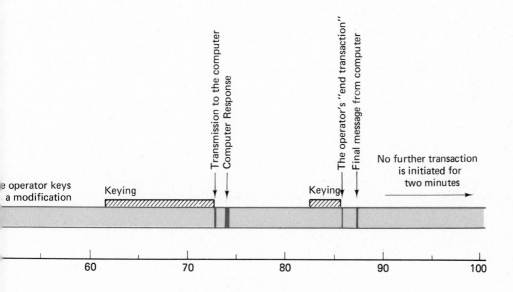

Table 9.1 Six dialogue applications with terminals, giving estimates of their peak-to-average ratios. These dialogues were selected as typical of response patterns found in terminal–computer dialogues.

	Average Rate (bits/sec)	Desirable Peak Rate (bits/sec)	Peak/Average Ratio
1. Average calculation evaluating an equation using the language BASIC on a typewriter like terminal.	8	100	12.5
2. A stockbroker analyst using a typewriter-like terminal to do a calculation involving a data-base.	10	150	15
3. A data entry operation in which an operator calls up different ''forms'' and fills them in, working rapidly on a visual display unit.	15	1500	100
4. An airline reservation using nonintelligent terminals and a tightly designed dialogue on a visual display unit.	10	2000	200
5. A sales order system permitting enquiries and updates			
a. using nonintelligent visual display terminals	40	4000	100
b. using programmable terminals	2	4000	2000
6. A complex graphics system in which a person is using a light-pen to design circuits.	200	200,000	1000

A high peak/average ratio can be handled efficiently when a large number of users share a transmission subsystem. Usually the subsystem is shared by many different types of application operating simultaneously.

HIDING THE COMPLEXITY The mechanisms of the *telephone* system are highly complex. The user neither needs nor wants to understand them. He perceives only the interface to the network which is built into the telephone set, and this interface is designed to be as simple as possible. The mechanisms of computer networks are complex and likely to change, and so the user should say, like the telephone subscriber, ''Don't tell me how it works; tell me how to use it—and make that as simple as possible.''

Making complex operations appear simple to the user can itself be a complex process.

REFERENCE

1. PCM trunks are explained in the author's *Telecommunications and the Computer*, 2nd ed., Prentice-Hall, Englewood Cliffs, NJ, 1976.

10 LOGICAL, VIRTUAL, AND TRANSPARENT FACILITIES

There are three important terms which relate to the hiding of complexity in software and hardware facilities:

- Virtual
- Transparent
- Logical

(Readers familiar with these words may skip this chapter.)

- *Something virtual appears to exist but does not.*
- *Something transparent appears not to exist, but in fact does.*
- *A logical facility is in some way different from reality, either virtual or transparent. The logical facility is what is perceived by a program or user.*

The words *real* and *physical* are used to contrast with these words. A *real* facility or a *physical* facility exists in actuality. It is part of the physical world.

The terms *virtual* and *logical* can sometimes be used interchangeably. For example, "logical terminal" and "virtual terminal" could mean the same.

Terms used in this book, incorporating these words, include the following:

- Logical message; physical message.
- Logical link; physical link.
- Logical unit; physical unit.
- Logical display space.
- Virtual circuit; physical circuit.

- Virtual call.
- Virtual network terminal.
- Network transparency.

VIRTUAL FACILITIES   The word *virtual* referring to computer facilities or to data indicates that the item in question *appears to exist to the application programmer* when in fact it does not exist in that form. The programmer may, for example, write his program as though he has infinite main memory when in fact memory is limited, but the computer overcomes the shortage by means of a paging mechanism which transfers blocks of data or program backward and forward between main memory and the peripheral storage devices. A programmer may similarly refer to virtual data which appear to exist but in fact do not, at least in that form; the computer generates them in some way, possibly using a more compact form of storage, every time the programmer refers to them.

An application or systems program may refer to data as though they were on a disk when in fact they are on a cartridge of a mass storage device; a control program quickly moves them to a disk, thus simulating a *virtual* disk unit.

In this way we can speak of virtual memory, virtual disks, a virtual communication link, or a virtual computer.

A virtual computer is a machine which *appears* to have certain properties so that it can run certain programs; it is made to exist by software inside what is really a quite different computer. Different users could employ different virtual machines simultaneously, each apparently existing inside one powerful computer.

Similarly a *virtual circuit* is a communications circuit which *appears* to exist. There is no such physical circuit. There is a mechanism which may use multiple physical circuits for transporting messages between user machines. The user machines plug into precisely defined virtual circuit interfaces and transmit messages almost as though they had a physical circuit all to themselves. In fact the physical circuits will be shared by transmissions from many different user machines.

A *virtual call* is a call which is set up between two user machines, rather like a telephone call, but which uses a virtual circuit.

NETWORK TRANSPARENCY   Whereas something virtual appears to exist but does not, something *transparent* appears *not* to exist but in fact does. Many of the complex mechanisms used in data storage and data transmission can be hidden from the programmer so that he does not have to understand or even know about them. In this way his work can be made simpler and his programs easier to understand.

The complex ways in which bits are manipulated in a communications network can be made transparent to the programmer or user.

It is only by using transparency that we can afford to build some of the complex structures that we will discuss. Without it, application programming and maintenance would be too difficult.

We speak of *network transparency*, meaning that the transport network and its complex mechanisms are invisible to the end users. The end users might as well be connected by a simple point-to-point channel (except perhaps for the slight delay when the network is used).

Network transparency often implies that the network is interchangeable. Because the network is made invisible to the users, a different type of network using different mechanisms can be substituted. Network transparency is sometimes described as being a characteristic of the software packages. It can be valuable because both network configurations and the mechanisms used are likely to change. It is desirable that such changes should not affect the end users' programs or mechanisms.

LOGICAL FACILITIES   The word "logical" is often used in computing software and architecture. We speak of a logical communication link, a logical message, a logical data base structure, and so on.

When the reader sees the word "logical" he might substitute in his mind the word "make-believe"—a make-believe communication link, a make-believe data base, a make-believe terminal. The software (that "master of illusion") will cause the make-believe to come true (Fig. 10.1).

There are three reasons for wanting to indulge in make-believe. First, the reality has become much too complicated for ordinary programmers, systems analysts, or users. The data network mechanisms and data bases which are used today are very complex. The record and message structures are often in a different form from that which the application programmer wants. Therefore instead of showing the programmer or user the horrifying reality we show him a make-believe world which is simple to comprehend. We do not say, "Your terminal is connected to the computer in Los Angeles via a cluster controller which compresses the data and sends it to a concentrator on a multidrop type 3002 line with Paradyne modems which is hub-polled by a front-end processor which passes the messages to. . . ." Instead we say, "Your terminal has a logical connection to the application program you asked for."

The more complicated the real world becomes the greater the need for this type of make-believe. We find several layers of make-believe in a modern data base–data communications system. The *logical* statements made by a programmer or user are converted into the physical reality by software, by microcode or, on some devices, by hardware. Much of the complexity in software is designed to make the complex mechanisms *transparent* to the persons who use them.

The second reason for make-believe is that the technology or use of it is changing fast. The optimum network design in 1981 will be entirely different from that in 1978. A leased-line concentrator network is replaced by use of a value-added network. A data base structure evolves into new shapes to accommodate new uses of

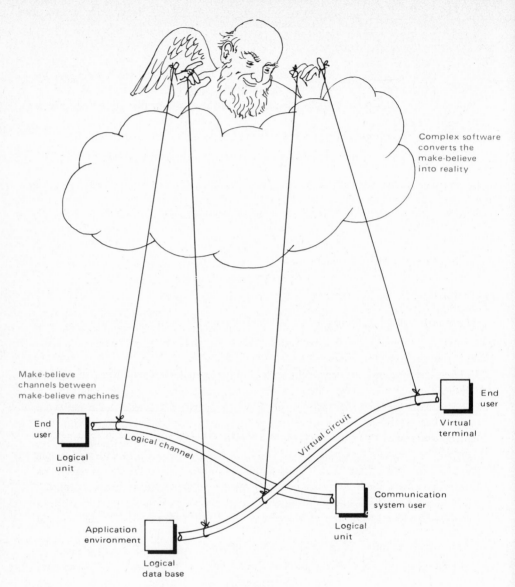

Complex software
converts the
make-believe
into reality

Make-believe
channels between
make-believe machines

End
user

Logical
unit

Logical channel

Virtual circuit

End
user

Virtual
terminal

Application
environment

Logical
data base

Communication
system user

Logical
unit

Figure 10.1

data. Since it is desirable not to keep rewriting the application programs, we pretend
to those programs that nothing has changed. They continue to use the same *logical*
facilities. We continue to maintain the same *logical* interfaces in the software.

Logical operation protects the programs and users from the future. In many organizations this protection is important because a major portion of the development

effort and budget is spent on rewriting the past in some way instead of forging ahead with new applications. The more man-years an organization has invested in its programs the greater the need to protect them from rapidly changing technology and system usage. As time goes by the number of invested man-years grows until it becomes unthinkable to have to rewrite the programs.

The third reason for employing make-believe facilities is to pretend to the users or programmers that the equipment is better than it really is. We let a programmer think the computer has a main memory of many million bytes when its *real* memory is much smaller. The programmer perceives a *virtual* memory, or *virtual* machine.

LOGICAL AND   The message which the application programmer thinks he
PHYSICAL MESSAGES   sends is not necessarily the same as that which is physi-
                         cally transmitted.

Many readers will be familiar with the concept of *logical* vs. *physical* records on tape and disk. The *logical record* is the input or output of an application program. The *physical record* is what is actually written on tape or disk, and sometimes it contains many logical records blocked together.

We will use similar wording to describe messages which are transmitted. A *logical message* is an end-user message, or is the input or output of an application program. It is what that program receives from or sends to a terminal with one input or output instruction. If the transmission equipment does not convert the data, but merely transmits it, as is often the case on a switched telephone circuit, then the logical message will be transmitted from one end of the circuit to another.

Often however, the blocks of data which are transmitted are different from the logical messages in some way. These are *physical messages*. The physical messages are the self-contained collections of bits which travel on the communication lines. Their structure and format differ from one type of network to another.

The following are some of the ways in which the physical messages may differ from the logical messages:

1. The physical message has an envelope when synchronous transmission is used, which contains information used to control the transmission (for example, the HDLC envelope illustrated in Fig. 18.2). In the simplest case a physical message may consist of one logical message with an envelope to control the transmission.

2. The physical message may contain more than one logical message. There is an optimum size for physical messages which can maximize the throughput of a transmission system. Nontime-critical logical messages are sometimes stored and batched together for transmission in one or a small number of physical messages. When interactive terminals are used, often a cluster of terminals may be connected to one controller. If more than one terminal has data to send, these data may be combined into one physical message. Similarly a block of logical messages may be transmitted *to* the cluster.

3. The opposite is more common: A long logical message is cut up into smaller slices for phys-

ical transmission, because some transmission mechanism is designed to handle messages no greater than a given size. This is done to save buffer storage and to speed up the delivery. When a logical message is cut up into slices there must be some indication of how to connect the slices back together again. The physical messages will contain an identification and sequence number for this purpose.

4. There are many ways to compress messages so that they can be transmitted in a smaller number of bits. Some data compaction techniques are quite complex but can double the throughput of a communication link. The logical message is converted to a compact physical form before transmission and converted back again after transport.

5. Some transmissions, especially those handling financial data or classified data, require a high level of protection from possible wiretapping. Cryptography is used on some systems. The logical message is enciphered so that it cannot be derived from the physical message without the correct deciphering circuit and the (temporary) key that was used for enciphering. Cryptography is vital for the rapidly spreading electronic fund transfer systems.

6. Some logical messages are composed of some variable and some unchanging data. The unchanging data could be stored at the ends of the communication links and not transmitted. An editing procedure may be used which permits the physical message to be expanded into the requisite logical message, for example with suitable headings, lines, and tabular spacing for display on a screen.

7. The physical message may contain a header which controls the routing and transport mechanisms.

8. The physical message may contain a header which relates to the control of peripheral hardware and sessions.

    Box 10.1 summarizes the differences between logical and physical records.

    Often the term *message* is used by itself. This normally means a logical message. When the term *message* is used by itself in this book it will always mean a user's message or application program message. The physical message is commonly called a *block, frame,* or *packet.*

BOX 10.1 Reasons why physical messages are different from logical messages

1. Header for synchronous data link control.

2. Header for routing and network control.

3. Header for control of sessions and peripheral hardware.

4. Blocking several logical messages into one physical message.

5. Slicing logical messages into small blocks or packets.

6. Compaction.

7. Editing facilities.

8. Cryptography.

9. Dialogue control.

10. Sequence or integrity control.

The physical message is referred to as a *block, frame,* or *packet.*
The logical message is often referred to as simply a *message.*

11 LAYERS OF CONTROL

Advanced computer systems have software which has grown up in layers rather like the skins on an onion. Different layers relate to different types of functions and services. This applies to operating systems, to data base or storage software, and also to teleprocessing software.

INCREASING USEFULNESS

Each layer that is added is an attempt to increase the usefulness or ease of use of the machines, or to introduce modularity by dividing the complex set of functions into discrete layers. Figure 11.1 shows the growth of software layers around the central processing unit.

For distributed processing, in which distant machines are interconnected, layers of software (or hardware or microcode) are needed around the telecommunications links to make these more useful, to hide the complexity from the network users, and to separate the functions into more manageable slices.

Figure 11.2 illustrates four types of layers which are fundamental to advanced teleprocessing systems.

The innermost layer is the *physical (electrical) connection* between the data machine and the telecommunications circuit.

The next layer is the *link control* which relates to how data are transmitted over a physical line. Throughout the history of teleprocessing there have been many different forms of link control. Some were character-oriented—telex line control, start-stop line control with an ASCII character set. Some were oriented to blocks of characters— binary synchronous line control, line control for specific terminals such as the IBM 2260, line control for specific applications such as airline reservations. More recently the bit-oriented line control procedures which we describe in this book have emerged— HDLC, SDLC, etc.

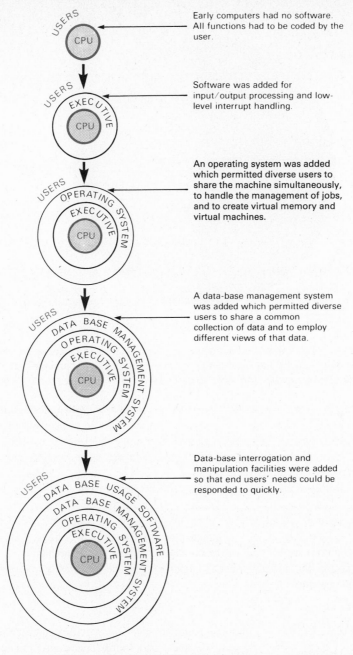

Early computers had no software. All functions had to be coded by the user.

Software was added for input/output processing and low-level interrupt handling.

An operating system was added which permitted diverse users to share the machine simultaneously, to handle the management of jobs, and to create virtual memory and virtual machines.

A data-base management system was added which permitted diverse users to share a common collection of data and to employ different views of that data.

Data-base interrogation and manipulation facilities were added so that end users' needs could be responded to quickly.

Figure 11.1 Layers of software. Each layer that was added made the machine more capable and more useful.

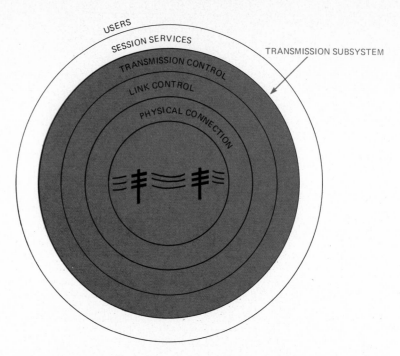

Figure 11.2 In a similar manner to Figure 11.1 the layers of control for communications are intended to make the physical communications links more capable and more useful.

The third layer, *transmission control,* in conjunction with inner layers, provides the transmission network—the transmission subsystem. The transmission network can be regarded as an entity which the higher levels employ for moving data from one user machine to another through multiple intermediate nodes such as concentrators, packet switches, line controllers, etc.

The layer external to the transmission subsystem in Fig. 11.2 provides a variety of services which are used to establish and operate sessions between the using machines. As we will see later, a rich array of such services is possible and desirable.

These four layers are fundamental to data networking and distributed systems. They are found in all of the computer manufacturers' architectures for distributed processing. Their detail differs somewhat from one manufacturer to another especially in the outermost layer.

ISO'S SEVEN LAYERS   In some manufacturers' architectures for distributed processing the third and fourth layers are split into sublayers. However the layers are defined, they form a standard with that manufacturer. Many different machines incorporate the same standard layers. They form the basis for communication between machines which are otherwise diverse.

It is highly desirable that machines of different manufactures should be able to communicate. For this to be possible they have to use the same layers, and the formats of data and control messages which pass between the layers have to be compatible.

Given the immense proliferation of machines that is now occurring, one of the activities most important to the future of data processing is the setting of standards to enable machines of different manufacturers and different countries to communicate. As a start in the setting of such standards ISO, the International Standards Organization, has defined seven layers, further subdividing the four layers of Fig. 11.2. These are shown in Fig. 11.3.

Their functions are as follows:

Layer 1: Physical Control

The innermost layer relates to setting up a physical circuit so that bits can be moved over it. It is concerned with *the physical, electrical, functional, and procedural*

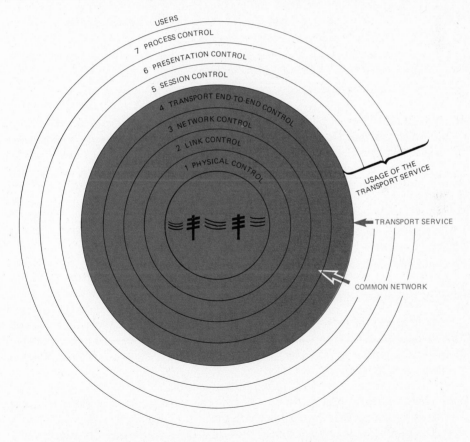

Figure 11.3 The International Standards Organization's seven layers of control for distributed processing.

characteristics to establish, maintain, and disconnect the physical link [1]. If the user machine employs an analog circuit like a conventional telephone line, it will be connected to a modem. Its interface with the modem is a generally accepted standard, e.g., EIA RS 232-C and CCITT Recommendation V.24 [2]. If a digital circuit is used, a newer Recommendation for the physical interface, CCITT Recommendation X.21 can be used, or support for a V.24 interface can be achieved through the use of X.21 *bis* [3].

Layer 2: Link Control

This layer relates to the sending of blocks of data over a physical link. It is concerned with issues such as:

- How does a machine know where a transmitted block starts and ends?
- How can transmission errors be detected?
- How can recovery from transmission errors be accomplished so as to give the appearance of an error-free link?
- When several machines share one physical circuit how can they be controlled so that their transmissions do not overlap and become jumbled?
- How is a message addressed to one of several machines?

The transmission of physical blocks of data requires a *physical link control* procedure which specifies the headers and trailers of blocks which are sent, and defines a protocol for the interchange of these blocks. Such procedures have been used since the earliest days of data communications. For distributed processing a more efficient line control procedure than start–stop or binary synchronous is desirable, which permits continuous transmission in both directions, of data which can contain any bit pattern. The International Standards Organization has specified such a line control procedure, HDLC (Higher-level Data Link Control). The American Standards Organization, the CCITT, and various computer manufacturers, each have their own variants of this which differ slightly in subtle details.

Layer 3: Network Control

Prior to 1975, Layers 1 and 2 were all that were specified. These were adequate for communication between machines connected to the same physical line. The world of distributed processing and computer networks requires more layers, and these are substantially more complex.

Layer 3 relates to *virtual circuits,* sometimes called *logical circuits* or *logical links.* These are make-believe circuits. They do not exist in physical reality but Layer 3 pretends to the higher levels that they do exist.

The path between computers may at one instant be via a number of physical lines as shown in Fig. 11.4. Each physical line spans two network machines which must use

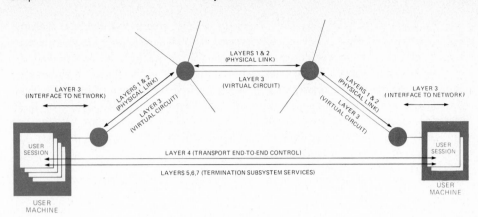

Figure 11.4

the Layer 1 and Layer 2 procedures to exchange data. The users do not wish to know what route the data travels or how many physical lines it travels over. The user machines want a simple interface to a virtual circuit. The Layer 3 layer of control creates the virtual circuit and provides the higher levels with an interface to it.

On some systems, the route on which data travels between two user machines varies from one instant to another. The network machines may require that users' messages be divided into slices, called packets, no greater than a certain length. The packets must be reassembled into messages after transmission. On some networks the packets fall out of sequence during transmission. The rules for Layer 3 state that the network must deliver the packets to the user machine in the same sequence as that in which they were sent by a user machine.

There are many such complications in the operation of a virtual circuit. Layer 3 provides a standard interface to the virtual circuit, and as far as possible hides the complex mechanisms of its operation from the higher layers of software.

Layer 4: Transport End-to-End Control

The inner three layers of Fig. 11.3 represent a common network which many machines may share, independently of one another, just as many independent users may share the postal service. It is possible that a postal service might occasionally lose a letter. To ensure that this has not happened, two users might apply their own end-to-end controls, such as numbering their letters. Layer 4 is concerned with similar end-to-end controls of the transmission between two users having a session.

Figure 11.4 illustrates that whereas Layer 3 is concerned with the interface between the user machine and the network, Layer 4 (and the higher layers) is concerned with the end-to-end interaction between user processes. The functions executed in Layer 4 may include end-to-end integrity controls to prevent loss or double processing of transactions, flow control of transactions, and addressing of end user machines or processes.

The lower four layers provide a *transport* service. They are concerned with the transport of blocks of bits from one user process to another, but not with the manipulation of those bits in any way. Some of the higher layers manipulate the bits.

The transport service in the future will take many different forms. Sometimes it will be a packet-switching network using the international standards from Layer 3 and below (CCITT Recommendation X.25, discussed later). Sometimes it will be quite different—wideband point-to-point circuits, the Xerox XTEN networks, satellite circuits, and so on. The interface from higher layers or from user machines to Layer 4 is intended to provide a *standard interface to users of the transport service independent of what network type is used*.

Layer 5: Session Control

The task of setting up a session between user processes can be complex because there are so many different ways in which machines can cooperate. Like two businessmen agreeing to a joint venture, they must agree beforehand on the rules of the game. In effect they sign a contract stating the manner in which they will cooperate. We will describe this later in the book.

Layer 5 standardizes this process of setting a session and of terminating it. If something goes wrong in mid-session, Layer 5 must restore the session without loss of data, or if this is not possible terminate the session in an orderly fashion. Checking and recovery are thus functions of Layer 5.

In some types of sessions a dialogue takes place between machines and a protocol must regulate who speaks when and for how long. In some cases the two machines speak alternately. In others one machine may send many messages before the other replies. In some sessions one machine may interrupt the other; in other cases not. The rules for how the dialogue is conducted need to be agreed upon when the session is set up.

Layer 6: Presentation Control

Layer 6 contains functions relating to the character set and data code which is used, and to the way data is displayed on a screen or printer. A stream of characters reaching a terminal will result in certain actions to give an attractive display or print out. The character stream will contain characters which cause editing of the data, line skipping, tabbing to position the data in columns, adding fixed columns headings, highlighting certain fields, use of colon, and so on. Formats may be displayed into which an operator enters data, and then only the entered data is transmitted. A coded number sent to an intelligent terminal may cause it to select a panel for display and enter variable data into that display.

There are many possible functions concerned with the presentation of data. These are carried out by Layer 6. Many of them relate to the character stream, its codes, and the ways they are used.

In some cases application programmers perceive a *virtual terminal* or *virtual display space*. Input/output statements relate to this make-believe facility, and the Layer 6 software must do the conversion between the virtual facility and the real terminal.

It is desirable that devices with different character sets should be able to communicate. Conversion of character streams may therefore be a concern of Layer 6.

The character stream may be compacted into a smaller bit stream to save transmission costs. This may be Layer 6 function.

Encryption and decryption for security reasons may also be a Layer 6 function.

Layer 7: Process Control

Layer 7 is concerned with higher level functions which provide support to the application or system activities, for example operator support, the use of remote data, file transfer control, distributed data base activities, higher level dialogue functions, and so on. The extent to which these are supported in the network architecture and in the software external to the network architecture, such as data base software, will differ from one manufacturer to another.

When distributed files and data bases are used various controls are needed to prevent integrity problems or deadlocks. Some types of controls for this are strongly related to networking, for example the timestamping of transactions and delivery of transactions in timestamp sequence (sometimes called pipelining) [3].

Pacing is necessary with some processes so that the transmitting machine can send records continuously without flooding the receiving machine, or so that an application can keep a distant printer going at maximum speed.

SUBSYSTEMS The lower four layers are all concerned with the transport of bits between one user process and another. We will refer to them collectively as *the transport system*.

Layers 5, 6, and 7 provide a variety of services which are employed by the user sessions. We will refer to these layers collectively as the *session services subsystem*.

Chapter 12 discusses the transport subsystem and Chapter 13 discusses the session services subsystem.

MANUFACTURERS' ARCHITECTURES The architectures for distributed processing from the various computer and minicomputer manufacturers contain all or part of the seven layers we have described. Layers 1, 2, and 3 are usually clearly distinguished, but the functions of Layers 4, 5, 6, and 7 may be intermixed and not broken into those layers recommended by the International Standards Organization. Increasingly as distributed processing technology evolves the clean separation of the layers will be necessary.

International standards exist, and are widely accepted, for Layers 1, 2, and 3. They are employed not only by the computer industry but by the telecommunications industry in creating public data networks. We will describe these standards and their use in Part III of this book.

Partly because of the telecommunications industry use of Layers 1, 2, and 3, the computer industry is building hardware and software which employs these layers. Some computer vendors (notably IBM, Univac, and DEC) have created their own incompatible versions of Layer 3. Old versions of Layer 2 are in use and likely to remain so because old protocols take a long time to die.

At the higher layers different manufacturers are going their own way, and creating their own in-house standards. These are perceived by individual manufacturers as being extremely important because they make the many different machines in the product line interconnectable. But although machines of one manufacturer are interconnectable, those of different manufacturers cannot be interconnected at the higher layers. They can be interconnected only at Layers 1 and 2, and sometimes Layer 3.

The layers are being applied not only to computers and conventional terminal controllers but also to electronic "office-of-the-future" equipment such as intelligent copy machines, word processing equipment, electronic mail machines, document storage and retrieval equipment, process monitoring and control facilities, security facilities, and so on. It is clear that these product lines are merging and require to be connected by networks.

DIFFERENT MACHINES   In a distributed processing network the layers may be spread across a variety of different machines. Figure 11.5 shows several types of machines. A central processing unit may be designed to contain all seven layers like the computer on the left in Fig. 11.5, or, probably better, some of the layers may be removed to a separate *front-end* processor. A front-end processor may handle the lower three layers or it may handle Layer 4 functions also.

Terminals containing microprocessors may have enough power to handle all the layers like the intelligent terminal in Fig. 11.5. This is less complex than the networking software at a computer site because the terminal supports only one session at a time, uses only one logical channel, and contains few management functions. In many cases the terminals are simpler machines connected to a terminal cluster controller, and it is this controller which contains the networking software, as shown at the bottom of Fig. 11.5. The terminals may be in the immediate vicinity of the controller, or they may be far away, connected by telecommunications, in which case the controller may be regarded as a concentrator. A concentrator may contain only the lower three layers.

Figure 11.5 does not show mid-network nodes such as packet-switching machines or concentrators. These may be part of the transport subsystem, with no Layer 5, 6, 7, or even Layer 4 functions.

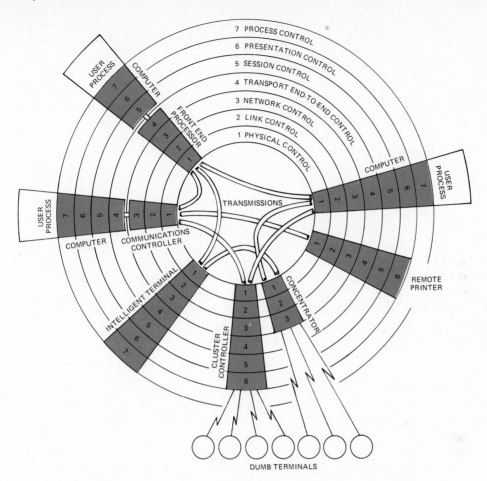

Figure 11.5 The layers of control are allocated between machines in different ways.

FUNDAMENTAL LAYERS

The concept of using separate layers of control is fundamental to all architectures for distributed processing. The layers used however differ from one manufacturer to another.

Some of the layers are fundamental and widely accepted even in architectures which are otherwise entirely different. Layers 1, 2, and 3 are found in almost all architectures. They are fundamental: the existence of an electrical interface to the transmission circuit (Layer 1), the existence of a link control procedure (Layer 2), and the separate existence of a common network to which many different machines can be connected (Layer 3).

The common network may be a public network or may be private. Layers 1, 2, and 3 are vital to public networks. Private networks may use the same standards and then they can be interconnected to public networks also.

End-to-end control of the movement of data in a particular session is often (but not always) important. This is done by Layer 4. Where one module of Layer 3 is needed in a machine which connected to a network, one module of Layer 4 is needed *for each session* in that machine.

Session services are also needed for each session. The concept of a session services subsystem is fundamental. However in software architectures it is not always broken into Layers 5, 6, and 7. The architecture may have one layer for providing session services.

Figure 11.6 illustrates the common network, the transport end-to-end control, and the session services. These are three fundamental concepts, along with link control (Layer 2) and the electrical interface (Layer 1).

Because a session needs transport end-to-end control (Layer 4) as well as session services (Layers 5, 6, and 7), these are sometimes built into one module—the module which supports the session.

This separation of Layers 1, 2, 3 and (4 + 5 + 6 + 7), or Layers 1, 2, 3, 4, and (5 + 6 + 7) is found in architectures for *vertical* networks connecting intelligent devices to computers, and in *horizontal* networks which interconnect peer-related computers.

DIFFERENT NAMES   Different organizations use different names for the layers. Box 11.1 lists some of the alternate names used. Univac uses the term *Transport Network,* and IBM *Transmission Subsystem.* IBM uses the term *Path Control* for Layer 3, DEC *Network Services Protocol* for Layers 3 and 4. The session services subsystem is called *Function Management* in IBM, *Dialogue Layer* in DEC, and *Termination System* in Univac; the session services provided differ in these three cases. Univac splits Layers 3 and 4 combined into three sublayers.

SYMMETRY   In some cases, the networking layers are symmetrical. In other words when a certain level of software exists at opposite ends of a link, both ends carry out the same functions. In Fig. 11.4 the outermost machines execute all seven layers; the inner machines drawn as circles execute only transport subsystem functions; but the layering is symmetrical. In a horizontal computer network all machines may contain the same networking software (with the exception of functions such as network monitoring and statistics gathering).

On the other hand, vertical networks are often nonsymmetrical. For reasons of economy the machines lower in the hierarchy have simpler software or control mechanims than those at the top (at least at the higher level layers). In Fig. 11.5 the computer and terminals at the left are in communication. However, the higher level software

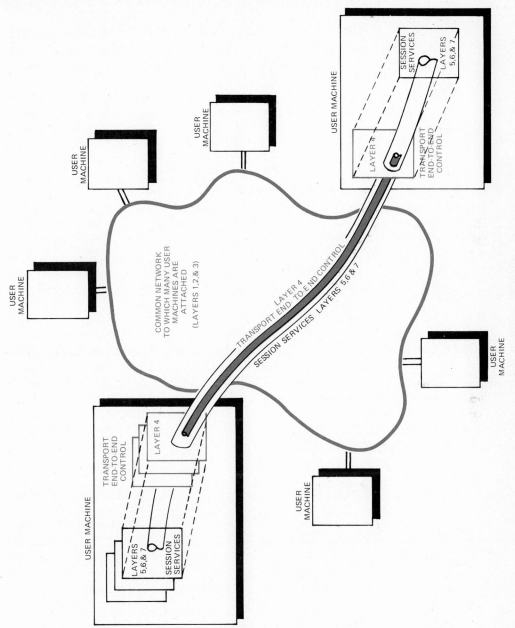

Figure 11.6 Use of the layers.

169

BOX 11.1   Terms used in different architectures. The functions of the layers are not exactly the same in the different architectures.

Names used by the International Standards Organization	Other Terms Used in This Book	Terms Used by Telephone Companies, Following the CCITT Recommendation X.25	Terms Used in IBM's SNA Architecture	Terms Used DEC's DECNET Architecture	Terms Used in UNIVAC's DCA Architecture
Layer 7 Process control		—			
Layer 6 Presentation control	Session services subsystem	—	Function management	Dialogue layer	Termination system
Layer 5 Session control		—			
Layer 4 Transport end-to-end control	Transport subsystem	—	Transmission control	Network services protocol (NSP Layer)	Transport network system
Layer 3 Network control		Level 3	Path control		
Layer 2 Link control	Common network	Level 2	SDLC (Synchronous Data Link Control)	DDCMP (Digital Data Communications Management Protocol)	UDLC (Universal Data Link Control)
Layer 1 Physical control		Level 1			

may be designed to be much simpler in the terminal than in the computer or its front-end network machine.

In some networks the terms *primary* and *secondary* are used to describe unsymmetrical relationships between machines. In some, the terms *master* and *slave* are used. In links between a computer and terminal controller, or large computer and minicomputer, a *primary/secondary* relationship is often employed. The management of the link is the responsibility of the *primary* machine. This machine takes most of the initiative. It sends messages and the secondary machine responds. The primary machine is responsible for recovery when failures or problems occur.

We will see examples of symmetrical and nonsymmetrical relationships later in the book. Symmetry is generally appealing in horizontal networks. In vertical networks it may be unnecessarily expensive.

MESSAGES, PACKETS AND FRAMES   Different *units* of data are exchanged between the different layers. The lowest layer is concerned with the transmission of *bits*. Layer 2, the physical link control (such as HDLC, IBM's SDLC, and similar protocols), transmits *frames*. A frame is a group of bits which constitutes a single recoverable block transmitted over a physical line. It has a header and trailer, which are necessary for controlling the physical transmission. They identify where it begins and ends. The header contains a physical link address and control information. The trailer contains redundant bits for detecting transmission errors.

Layer 3 passes blocks of data to Layer 2 for physical transmission. They are sometimes called *packets*. They do not contain the *frame* header and trailer as this is of no concern to Layer 3. A packet may be defined *as a group of bits addressed to a network destination, which is routed to that destination as a composite whole; the packet may contain data and control signals, while some packets contain only central signals*. A packet is routed to its destination by means of packet-switching, which we discuss later. It could however be routed by concentrators or mechanisms different from those on today's packet-switched networks. The concept of a packet is of general value independently of whether packet-switching is used. It is a grouping of data which travels to a destination over a virtual circuit. It must carry a network destination address like the address on a letter, which is different from the addresses of the physical nodes through which it passes on its way. Like a letter it also contains an origination address so that it may be returned to its sender if something goes wrong and it cannot be delivered. Packets contain control information which regulates the end-to-end delivery.

Layer 4 communicates via the common network with Layer 4 in a *session* at the other end, as shown in Fig 11.6. We will refer to the messages it sends as *session messages*. A session message may be too large to be transmitted as a single packet. Layer 4 may slice one such message up into multiple packets and reassemble the session message after transmission. In some cases the session messages may be very small and for efficiency several of them could be (in theory) combined into one packet for Layer 3 before transmission. On simpler systems there is no slicing or combining of session messages; the session message becomes the data portion of a packet.

The users of the communications system exchange *user messages*. A user message might be the same as a session message. Often it is not, however, because the Layer 6 software changes it by encyphering, code conversion, compaction, or editing.

We thus have five types of data units, transmitted by the different layers as shown in Fig. 11.7:

1. Bits.
2. Frames.
3. Packets.
4. Session messages.
5. User messages.

Typical manipulation of a user message before transmission is shown in Fig. 11.8. Different systems use different names for the data units, as shown in Box 11.2, and may take somewhat different actions from those in Fig. 11.8 when handling them.

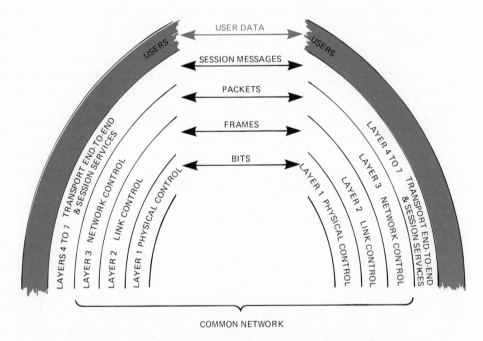

Figure 11.7 The types of data units that are interchanged between the layers. Different names are used for these in different network architectures, as shown in Box 9.2.

BOX 11.2 Names used for different data units

Data Units Interchanged Between:	Terms Used in This Book (See Figs. 11.5 and 11.6)	Terms Used by CCITT Recomendations	Terms Used in IBM's SNA Architecture	Terms Used in DEC's DECNET Architecture	Terms Used in UNIVAC's DCA Architecture
Users	User data; user messages	User messages	User data	User data	User data set
Layers 4 to 7	Session messages	—	Basic information unit	DAP message	Port data unit
Layer 3	Packets	Packet	Path information unit	NSP message	Network data unit
Layer 2	Frames	Frame	Basic link unit	DDCMP message	Frame

173

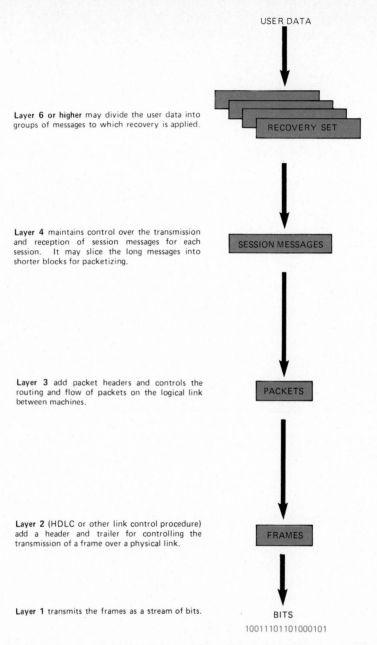

USER DATA

Layer 6 or higher may divide the user data into groups of messages to which recovery is applied.

RECOVERY SET

Layer 4 maintains control over the transmission and reception of session messages for each session. It may slice the long messages into shorter blocks for packetizing.

SESSION MESSAGES

Layer 3 add packet headers and controls the routing and flow of packets on the logical link between machines.

PACKETS

Layer 2 (HDLC or other link control procedure) add a header and trailer for controlling the transmission of a frame over a physical link.

FRAMES

Layer 1 transmits the frames as a stream of bits.

BITS

10011101101000101

Figure 11.8 User data may be manipulated as shown before transmission.

Figure 11.9 summarizes the main communication between the layers.

COMPARISON   When data is transmitted on a communication line, or
WITH DATA BASE   stored on a storage unit, it becomes a serial stream of
                        bits. In both cases layers of software exist between the
user program and the physical storage or transmission. Conversion between the data
the user perceives, and what is physically transmitted or stored, ranges from simple to
complex, depending on the sophistication of the system. Figure 11.10 shows the layers
used for data bases and networks. The layers closest to the user process provide user
services, and represent data in the form most useful to the user. As we move to the
outer parts of Fig. 11.10, the data become more abstract. The bit streams stored or
transmitted serve multiple applications, and are manipulated to suit the diverse mechanisms which are employed. The bit streams may be sliced or converted into different
forms for reasons of economy, efficiency, reliability, or security.

INDEPENDENCE   A principle of a layered architecture is that the layers
                        ought to be kept entirely independent.
Layer 1 (e.g., the standards EIA RS 232-C or CCITT V24) is extensively used
for all types of data transmission, many of which do not employ HDLC, SDLC, or
related procedures, and most of which have no networking software.
Layer 2, the physical link control procedure (e.g., HDLC, SDLC, etc.), is also
independent of the higher layers, and is used for many data communications links
which do not have higher level software.
The common network architecture should likewise be a self-contained set of procedures which can be employed by many different types of systems. It will be used by
different types of Layer 4 and higher software, and by systems with no higher level
software. Application programs, data base software, or other types of software, often
plug directly into Layer 3 or Layer 2. The interfaces to Layers 2 and 3 should therefore
be rigorously defined and preserved, independently of what goes on in the other layers.
Teleprocessing technology is changing rapidly and is likely to continue changing
because new facilities are being installed or planned for data transmission. Satellites,
microcomputers, value-added carriers, PCM transmission, data radio, and fast computerized switching create great opportunities as well as pressure for change [4]. It can
be expected therefore that the mechanisms of the transport subsystem will change, in
some cases beyond recognition. The interface to Layer 4 needs to remain constant to
protect the users. As a system changes from using, say, a leased-line concentrator
network to a common-carrier virtual-circuit network, this change should be hidden
inside the transmission subsystem. It should be transparent to higher level software,
and especially to the application programs, so that these do not have to be rewritten.
The layers should thus be completely *separate and independent,* and *their interfaces rigorously defined.* In addition to facilitating change this is a great aid to debug-
ging and to the diagnosis of network faults.

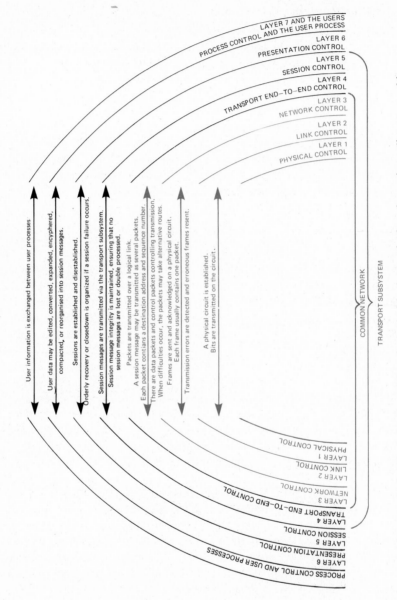

LAYER 7 AND THE USERS
PROCESS CONTROL AND THE USER PROCESS
LAYER 6
PRESENTATION CONTROL
LAYER 5
SESSION CONTROL
LAYER 4
TRANSPORT END—TO—END CONTROL
LAYER 3
NETWORK CONTROL
LAYER 2
LINK CONTROL
LAYER 1
PHYSICAL CONTROL

User information is exchanged between user processes

User data may be edited, converted, expanded, encyphered, compacted, or reorganised into session messages.

Sessions are established and disestablished.

Orderly recovery or closedown is organized if a session failure occurs.

Session messages are transmitted via the transport subsystem.

Session message integrity is maintained, ensuring that no session messages are lost or double processed.

Packets are transmitted over a logical link.
A session message may be transmitted as several packets.
Each packet contians a destination address and sequence number.
There are data packets and control packets controlling transmission.
When difficulties occur, the packets may take alternative routes.

Frames are sent and acknowledged on a physical circuit.
Each frame usually contains one packet.

Transmission errors are detected and erroneous frames resent.

A physical circuit is established.
Bits are transmitted on the circuit.

COMMON NETWORK

TRANSPORT SUBSYSTEM

PHYSICAL CONTROL
LAYER 1
LINK CONTROL
LAYER 2
NETWORK CONTROL
LAYER 3
TRANSPORT END—TO—END CONTROL
LAYER 4
SESSION CONTROL
LAYER 5
PRESENTATION CONTROL
LAYER 6
PROCESS CONTROL AND USER PROCESSES

Figure 11.9 Each layer communicates with the equivalent layer in a distant machine and is unconcerned with the complexity of lower layers which make the communication possible.

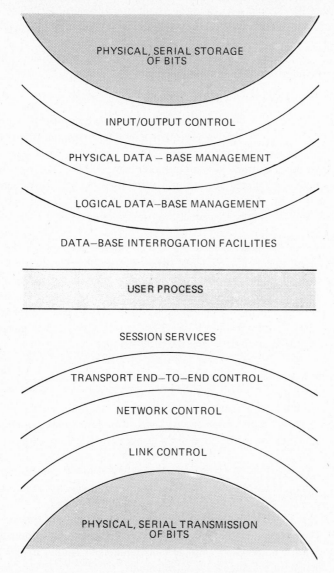

Figure 11.10 Layers of control separating the application programs or user process from (i) the physical, serial storage of bits, and (ii) the physical, serial transmission of bits.

There is often pressure during implementation to violate the separation of the layers or tamper with the interfaces between them to gain a performance advantage. It is important that this should not be done. To do so could make further development in the future extremely expensive, perhaps so expensive that it would prevent desirable improvements.

However, while the interfaces are preserved, some implementations may drop down to a lower interface to lessen the overhead.

DISADVANTAGE   The disadvantage of layered control is that it increases the total overhead required for communication. The Layer 2 frames, Layer 3 packets, and higher layer session messages, each need headers, and the total of these headers often adds up to more than 100 bits. Many of the bits would be required whether a layered architecture were used or not. However, when each layer is designed to be of general use independent of the other layers, the overhead is usually higher, and the number of processing instructions needed to control the transmission is higher.

When general-purpose layers are used, there may be some overlap of function. This may occur, for example, when the interfaces between the layers are standards adopted by a manufacturer, or common carrier, or by the standards organizations. We will see examples of this duplication of function later in the book. It is not a serious problem, hit merely causes an increase in overhead. In terms of processing cost it may be offset by placing Layer 2 and possibly Layer 3 in peripheral microprocessors—distributed systems within the machine room.

In all layered architectures there is a trade-off between the advantages of layering, and the increased overhead it incurs. The duplication of function is likely to be less if all the layers are designed by one design team to form part of a common architecture.

The overhead can be lessened by designing the mechanisms and message headers so that the more complex functions are *optional*. Simple networks should have simple mechanisms. Complex networks have more elaborate mechanisms and longer message headers. Both integration of the layers and variation in the degree of complexity and overhead are accomplished effectively, for example, in the Digital Equipment Corporation's architecture, DECNET. DECNET, being an architecture for minicomputers, needs to be especially careful about incurring avoidable overhead.

Layer 3 and Layer 4 and the session service layers are not needed for all communications. They may therefore be designed so that they can shrink to nothing or almost nothing when not needed. Simple communications should not be penalized by mechanisms designed for complex communications.

ADVANTAGES   The advantages of layering are immense. They are summarized in Box 11.3 There is no doubt layered architectures and standard interfaces between the layers will lead to a much greater interconnectability of machines.

Box 11.3 Advantages and disadvantages of layering

Advantages of Layered Architectures

1. Any given layer can be modified or upgraded without affecting the other layers.

2. Modularization by means of layering simplifies the overall design.

3. Different layers can be assigned to different standards committees, or different design teams.

4. Fundamentally different mechanisms may be substituted without affecting more than one layer (e.g., packet switching vs. leased-line concentrators).

5. Different machines may plug in at different levels.

6. The relationships between the different control functions can be better understood when they are split into layers. This is especially true with the control actions which occur sequentially in time from layer to layer.

7. Common lower level services may be shared by different higher level users.

8. Functions, especially at the lower layers, may be removed from software and built into hardware or microcode.

9. Plug compatible connections between machines of different manufacturers are made easier to accomplish.

Disadvantages of Layered Architectures

1. The total overhead is somewhat higher.

2. Two communicating machines may have to use certain functions which they could do without.

3. To make each layer usable by itself there is some small duplication of function between the layers.

4. As technology changes (e.g., as cryptography and compaction chips become available, or these functions can be built on to VSLI chips) the functions may not be in the most cost-effective layer.

IN GENERAL THE ADVANTAGES ARE GREAT, THE DISADVAN-TAGES SLIGHT.

REFERENCES

1. The words in italics are taken from the description of the Layer 1 interface in the CCITT Recommendation X.25.

2. Described in Chapter 17 of the author's *Telecommunications and the Computer,* 2nd ed., Prentice-Hall, Englewood Cliffs, NJ, 1976.

3. Rothnie, J. B., and Goodman, N., *An Overview of the Preliminary Design of SDD.1: A System for Distributed Data Bases.* Computer Corporation of America, Technical Report CCA-77-04. Cambridge, Mass., 1977.

4. Described in the author's *Future Developments in Telecommunications,* 2nd ed., Prentice-Hall, Englewood Cliffs, NJ, 1977.

12 INTERFACES

Particularly important in a layered architecture are the interfaces between the layers. These must be precisely defined and adhered to rigorously. They are candidates for standardization, either in the international standards arena or in the architectural standards employed by a major common carrier or computer manufacturer. Intensive international standards activity has occurred relating to the Layer 1, 2, and 3 interfaces. Work is in progress on the higher layers. These are more difficult because their functions vary greatly from one system to another. Ideas are evolving rapidly about what session services should be provided.

The *mechanisms* of each layer will change as the technology develops. The interfaces between the layers are often designed to accommodate new mechanisms and, as far as possible, new functions when they may arise. As new mechanisms and network functions come into use, it is highly desirable that previously written programs should continue to work. This is achieved by designing the interfaces appropriately and preserving them.

COMMUNICATION BETWEEN LAYERS

Each layer in an architecture for distributed processing communicates with an equivalent layer at the other end of a link. The reader might think of the communicating machines as layer cakes, as shown in Fig. 12.1. Each layer contains a different set of functions.

Sessions take place between user processes. The higher layers (4, 5, 6, and 7) relate to these sessions. The lower layers are not concerned with the sessions, but with the movement of data through a network shared by many machines. Figure 12.2 illustrates this. Layers 4, 5, 6, and 7 provide end-to-end communication between the sessions in user machines. Layers 1, 2, and 3 provide communication with the nodes of a shared network. These nodes may be packet switches, communications controllers, concentrators, or other machines designed to make a data network operate.

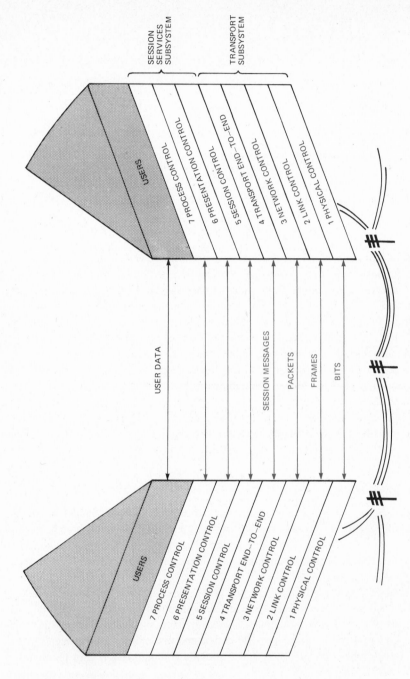

SESSION SERVICES SUBSYSTEM

TRANSPORT SUBSYSTEM

USERS

7 PROCESS CONTROL
6 PRESENTATION CONTROL
5 SESSION CONTROL
4 TRANSPORT END-TO-END
3 NETWORK CONTROL
2 LINK CONTROL
1 PHYSICAL CONTROL

USER DATA

SESSION MESSAGES

PACKETS

FRAMES

BITS

USERS

7 PROCESS CONTROL
6 PRESENTATION CONTROL
5 SESSION CONTROL
4 TRANSPORT END-TO-END
3 NETWORK CONTROL
2 LINK CONTROL
1 PHYSICAL CONTROL

Figure 12.1 Each layer contains different functions. Each layer communicates with its peer in another machine.

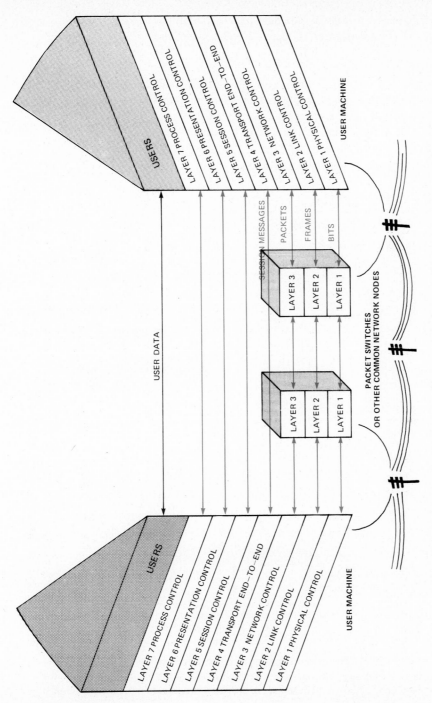

Figure 12.2 Layers 4 to 7 provide end-to-end communication between session software. Layers 1 to 3 provide an interface to a shared network.

There are two forms of communication between the layers in separate machines, *headers* and *control messages*. Figure 12.3 illustrates these.

HEADERS   Each layer of a layered architecture (except Layer 1) may add a header to the messages sent. This header is interpreted by the equivalent layer at the other end of the link.

Layer 2 frames contain a header to be used by the Layer 2 mechanisms at the

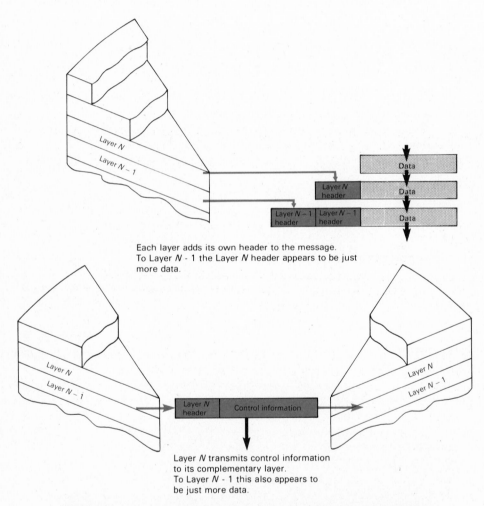

Each layer adds its own header to the message.
To Layer *N* - 1 the Layer *N* header appears to be just
more data.

Layer *N* transmits control information
to its complementary layer.
To Layer *N* - 1 this also appears to
be just more data.

Figure 12.3   There are two firms of communication between equivalent layers: message headers for that layer, and control messages passed between the layers. These are, or will become, the basis of international standards.

other end of a physical link. They also contain a trailer which is used to indicate the end of the frame and to check whether the frame contains any transmission errors.

Layer 3 packets contain a header which directs the packet to its destination and is used by Layer 3 at that destination. Layer 4 messages may contain a header intended for use by the distant and complementary Layer 4. And so on.

In general, the Layer N header is not inspected by Layer $N-1$. It appears like any other data being transmitted. Layer $N-1$ then adds its own header (shown in Fig. 12.3).

Figure 12.2 shows transmission between two user machines via a network node which contains only transport subsystem software.

CONTROL MESSAGES   In addition control messages are used which travel like data messages but whose sole function is to carry control signals between the control layers. Separate types of control messages are exchanged by the different layers. They have functions such as setting up communication, dealing with errors or procedure violations, regulating the rate of flow, and so on. In general, signals which occur frequently are carried in the message headers; signals which occur only infrequently or which require more than a few bytes are sent as separate control messages.

Control messages may be used when it is necessary to send a signal to the destination without delay. They travel with higher priority than data messages in most systems, bypassing the queues of data messages like ambulances screaming through the streets of a city.

The international standards define the control messages and the headers which each layer uses. This defines how the layers intercommunicate. Machines of different manufacturers may communicate if they use the same headers and control messages and interpret them in the same way.

INTRA-NODE   Layers above and below each other in the same node may
COMMUNICATION   communicate by means of parameters. These are passed
                      between the layers when the message is passed from
one layer to the next. They give information such as what address to send the message to, or what type of control is required. Figure 12.4 shows parameters being passed between layers in a node which is transmitting. The reverse direction of flow would be used when it is receiving.

The internal workings of a node, such as that in Fig. 12.4, does not need to be known in order for different nodes to communicate. For this purpose only the formats of the message headers and control messages are required. The international standards therefore avoid specifying the intra-node communication. It is desirable to leave implementors as much freedom as possible in designing their nodes. This is especially true because of the rate of change of technology. Layer N in Fig. 12.4 might be in software today but in microcode or chips tomorrow. The layers might be in the same machine

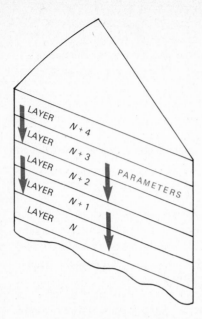

Figure 12.4 A manufacturer's architecture may define parameters which are passed from one layer to another in the same node. The interface between layers in a node is *not* defined in the international standards in order to leave the maximum freedom in architecture implementation.

today but split between machines tomorrow. These changes should effect the resulting messages perceived by a distant machine.

Although definition of the parameters in Fig. 12.4 should not be in the international standards, it may be part of a manufacturer's architecture definitions.

The behavior of each layer should be self-contained and not dependent on the operation of other layers. The other layers may change. It might be tempting for the designers of one layer to use information in the header used for another layer. Layer N 1 could examine the Layer N header and obtain information which affects the actions of Layer N 1. This, however, may prove expensive in the future because it would violate the principle of keeping the layers independent. Layer N and its header could not be changed without concern for Layer N 1. The Layer 3 header, for example, contains information about the destination of the Layer 3 message on the logical link. This might be used by Layer 2 for addressing the message on the physical link. However, the logical link layer might then be drastically changed, perhaps to employ a value-added network or virtual-call tariff rather than a leased-line network, and it becomes desirable to change the Layer 3 header, perhaps to conform to a new international standard. This change would force a rewriting of Layer 2 also if Layer 2 used the Layer 3 header.

The layers should be kept entirely separate and independent.

PROTOCOLS   Data communications systems need a set of rules which the communicating parties will obey when they send signals to one another. These rules are called *protocols*. The word protocol originally referred to the rules and customs of diplomatic, court, or military communications. Protocols between communicating machines enable them to set up calls between one another, interpret each other's data, deal with error conditions and perform various functions which aid the end users of a network. The protocols consist of controlled exchanges of precisely specified commands and responses.

In early data transmission systems the protocols were relatively simple and related to sending data across a single link. Today, with distributed processing, multiple layers of control, and mesh-structured networks, the protocols become highly complex and must be thought out with meticulous care. As we will see later, flaws in protocol design have occasionally led to subtle problems such as networks jamming with deadlocked traffic, or occasional messages being lost.

The protocols define the control information that is used for communicating between the layers as illustrated in Fig. 12.3 and how this control information is acted upon.

FOUR-LAYER   Most manufacturers at the time of writing do not have the
ARCHITECTURES   full seven layers of ISO. Many have four layers in which
                        the session services and end-to-end integrity control are
encompassed in one layer. The bottom three layers may follow the CCITT Recommendation X.25, described in Chapter 22.

Figure 12.5 shows the use of headers in a four-layer architecture. Two user machines are communicating via a network node. The user machines have all four layers. The network node uses only the lower three layers needed for routing the data to its destination and controlling the physical transmission.

What is shown as a single Session Services Layer in Fig. 12.5 may be split into two or more layers. The exact layering at the higher levels differs from one manufacturer to another.

OVERHEAD   If all seven layers are used then all of these except Layer
                        1 will create its own header, as shown in Fig. 12.6.
This usage appears to incur a large overhead both in terms of the extra bits transmitted and the processing required to handle the layers. The former can be minimized by using a bit structure which permits optional fields to be omitted when not in use (including *all* of the fields for session services). More serious has been the machine cycles and memory needed to execute the software. As microminiature circuitry grows in power and the standards for architectures stabilize, so increasingly the functions will be built into cheap mass-produced chips. This will occur both within one manufacturer's product line and in industrywide manufacture of independent chips.

Already chips exist for executing the Layer 2 control (HDLC, SDLC, or nonstandard forms of Layer 2 such as the Digital Equipment Corporation's DDCMP), and for Layer 3 control (CCITT X.25 Layer 3). As chips increase in component density other functions will be moved outside of computers so that they do not have to be executed in software.

An interface between machines needs to be defined in terms of the layers: the layer headers and control messages that are passed between layers as shown in Fig. 12.3. An application programmer may know nothing of these; he uses a higher-level language, and a compiler or interpreter creates the headers and control messages. The language may use commands such as GET, PUT, OPEN, and CLOSE, which refer to data or facilities in a distant machine.

This is shown in the first illustration of Fig. 12.7. The programmers perceive only the interface to the outermost layer and use a high-level language to communicate with this layer.

In some cases the programmers drop down to the Layer 4 interface as shown in the second illustration of Fig. 12.7. This may be done for reasons of efficiency; the programmers can control the transport subsystem more directly. The interface to the transport subsystem is also defined in terms of control messages and message headers. Again, a high-level language may provide the programmer's means of communication with the transport subsystem.

The transport subsystem, looking out, perceives data messages (and in some cases, parameters) sent to it by those who employ it. It does not know whether they come from Layer 5 or 6 software or user processes, and does not know whether a compiler or interpreter has been used. It knows only the precisely defined transmission subsystem interface.

In many cases the programmer uses Layer 3 rather than Layer 4; he uses the interface to a packet-switching network (third diagram of Fig. 12.7). He will usually employ input/output commands which generate the requisite packets and reassemble the input messages.

On older and simpler systems, there is no Layer 3 or 4—no logical links, only physical links. A program may use the Layer 2 software directly as in the fourth diagram of Fig. 12.7. It may use it by passing packets to Layer 2 ready for framing, or it may use a high-level language which employs commands such as SEND and RE-CEIVE, in which case an operating system generates the control and data packets.

INTERFACE
TO OUTER LAYER The user's or application programmer's interface to the outermost layer is designed to make the network and its complexities as transparent as possible.

There are two degrees of transparency. First the network may be completely transparent. There is no difference between a program which uses the network and one which does not; both use the same commands. A remote file or printer is used in the same way as a local file or printer. This is sometimes called *local/remote transparency*.

Second, there may be partial transparency. The programmer uses high-level commands for setting up a connection and for disconnecting it, and for sending and receiving messages.

Ideally, the application programmer should not have to know that a network

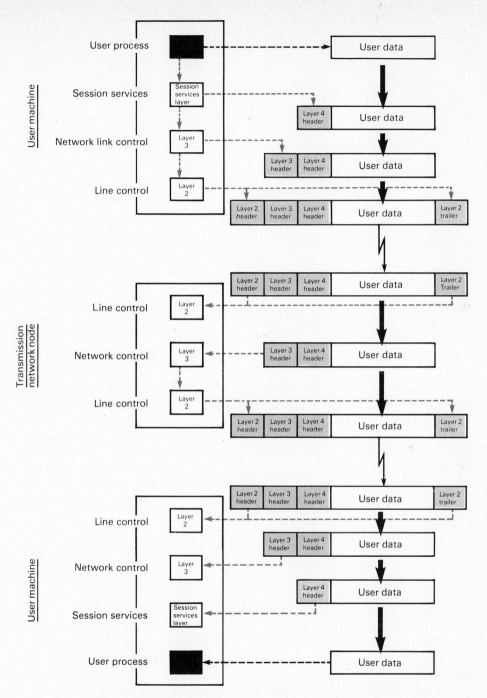

Figure 12.5 Use of headers as data is relayed through a network, for an architecture with four layers.

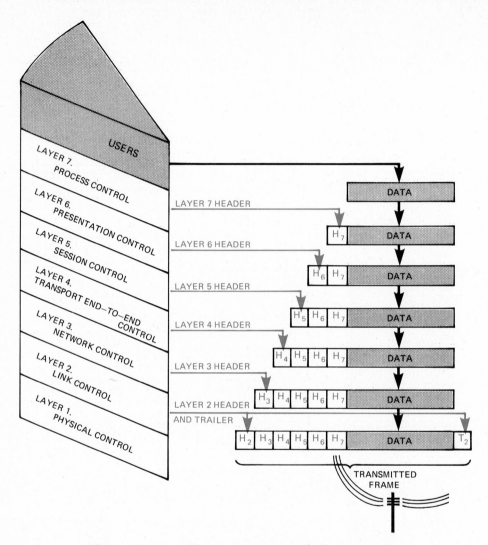

Figure 12.6   Use of headers in the ISO 7-layer architecture.

exists. He writes input/output instructions into his programs, employing symbolic addresses as with any other input/output unit. The software must employ a table of network resources with which it can convert the symbolic references to network units into network addresses which can be used with the transport subsystem.

When a file record is requested which is stored in a different location, it will take some time to retrieve. The computer operating system will make the application pro-

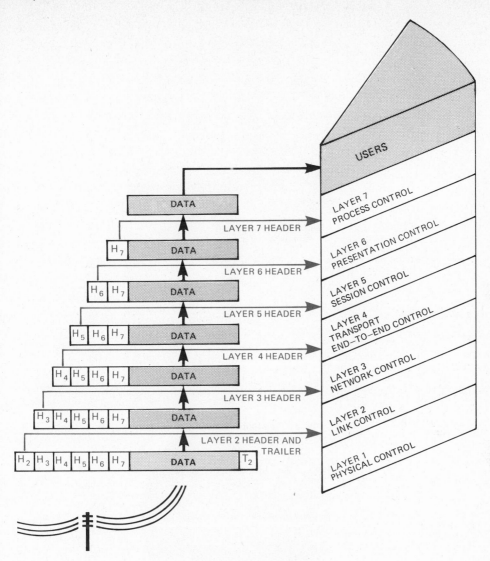

Figure 12.6   Continued.

gram which made the request *wait* while other work continues. This happens with any storage unit operation; the difference is that the wait is longer. How long depends upon the design of the transport subsystem.

In a transparent interface, commands such as OPEN, CLOSE, GET, PUT, and DELETE are used. An application programmer's commands for the DECNET network, for example, employ them as shown in Box 12.1.

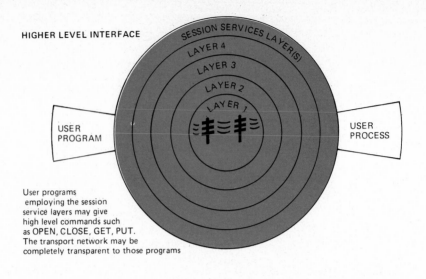

HIGHER LEVEL INTERFACE

SESSION SERVICES LAYER(S)

LAYER 4

LAYER 3

LAYER 2

LAYER 1

USER
PROGRAM

USER
PROCESS

User programs
employing the session
service layers may give
high level commands such
as OPEN, CLOSE, GET, PUT.
The transport network may be
completely transparent to those programs

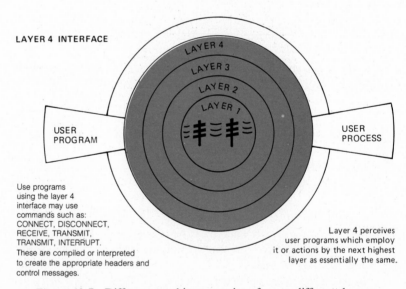

LAYER 4 INTERFACE

LAYER 4

LAYER 3

LAYER 2

LAYER 1

USER
PROGRAM

USER
PROCESS

Use programs
using the layer 4
interface may use
commands such as:
CONNECT, DISCONNECT,
RECEIVE, TRANSMIT,
TRANSMIT, INTERRUPT.
These are compiled or interpreted
to create the appropriate headers and
control messages.

Layer 4 perceives
user programs which employ
it or actions by the next highest
layer as essentially the same.

Figure 12.7 Different machines may interface to different layers.

LAYER 3 INTERFACE

Programs, software or chips using the Layer 3 interface directly create and accept the requisite data and control packets

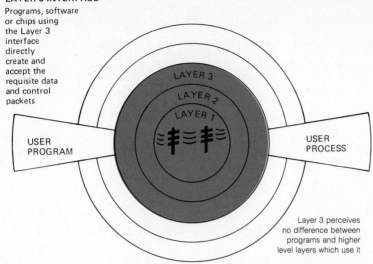

Layer 3 perceives no difference between programs and higher level layers which use it

LAYER 2 INTERFACE

Simple devices may use the layer 2 interface (HDLC, SDLC ,etc.) without using the higher layers. They employ the physical circuit directly, composing a suitable header and trailer for the frames that are sent.

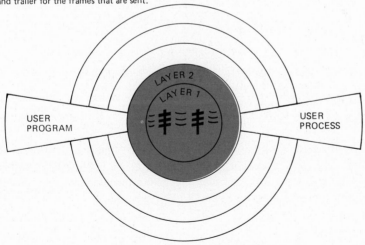

Figure 12.7   Continued.

BOX 12.1 A high-level user program interface: an illustration of an interface to DECNET's Session Service subsystem

OPEN (5, 'FACTORY-A ', 'PAYROLL [50,100]')

This command causes the file called PAYROLL stored under user account 50,100 on the computer system at location 'FACTORY-A' to be opened, and referred to as logical unit 5 by the program that issued the command. A similar command is used for access to printers, card units, and other devices.

GET (5, BUFFER)

This command causes data to be transferred from the remote file or device now known by this program as 5 into the user's buffer.

PUT (5, DATA)

This command causes data to be transferred from the user's buffer to the remote file or device known as 5.

CLOSE (5)

This command causes the remote file or device known as 5 to be closed and the link the remote system terminated.

DELETE ('FACTORY-A ', 'OLD-CUST [90,70]')

This command causes the file called 'OLD-CUST stored under user account 90,70' on the system at location 'FACTORY-A' to be deleted; i.e., removed from the file directory for that account.

A somewhat less transparent interface would be one in which the application program sets up a connection and then uses that connection. Box 12.2 illustrates such use, also with commands from DECNET.

LAYER 3 INTERFACE   Layer 3 provides the interface to the common network. Sometimes this is a public packet switching network; sometimes it is a network structure built into a manufacturer's architecture. The *user* packets transmitted and received are of two types:

1. Data Messages

These contain user information to be relayed through the network. (The users of the transport subsystem could be higher layer software modules, for example, interchanging messages which establish a user session.)

BOX 12.2 A somewhat less transparent interface than that in Box 12.1; also a DECNET program

CONNECT (3, 'FACTORY-A ', 'INVENTORY')

This causes a connection to be established between the issuing program and a program called 'INVENTORY' in a computer at a location called 'FACTORY-A.' In subsequent commands the program will refer to the connection with the number 3. The remote program must agree to complete this connection.

SEND (3, DATA)

The program which set up connection 3 indicates that specified data be sent to the program at the other end of that connection.

RECEIVE (3, BUFFER)

The program which set up connection 3 indicates its willingness to receive data from the program at the other end of that connection. No data will be transmitted until the program at one end of the connection indicates that it has data to send and the other side indicates it has a buffer to receive it.

DISCONNECT (3)

The program which set up connection 3 indicates its desire to terminate it.

2. Control Messages

These are used for actions such as requesting or terminating a virtual call, indicating when a called machine is busy or unavailable, regulating the rate of flow, maximizing the speed of a distant printer, controlling a distant file operation, dealing with failures, traffic jams, and breaches of protocol. The control messages are usually short—often only one byte of user information—and usually they need to reach their destination *fast*.

Some control signals are not sent as separate messages, but are "piggybacked" in data messages which are traveling to the same location.

Figure 12.8 illustrates a Layer 3 interface, showing typical control and data messages. The diagram is based on the CCITT Recommendation for a Layer 3 interface, which is used by many of the public packet-switching networks of the world and many manufacturers' architectures. The headers and control messages shown in black and white give complete instructions to the network software and no other parameters have to be passed. They are discussed in more detail later in the book.

When user programs interface directly with the transport subsystem, they may

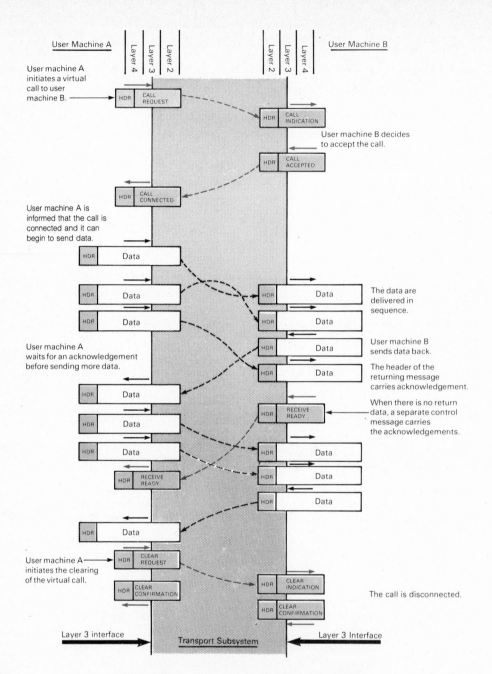

Figure 12.8 An example of a Layer 3 interface.

BOX 12.3 Commands for a Layer 3 Interface employed by DECNET

CONNECT
> Establishes a logical link to a distant user-machine. The distant machine acknowledges its participation in the link.

DISCONNECT
> Disestablishes the logical link, freeing the buffers and other facilities that were employed.

RECEIVE
> This indicates that a machine is in RECEIVE status, i.e., is ready to receive a message, and has a buffer allocated to its reception.

TRANSMIT
> This requests that data be sent over the link. Data can only be sent to a node in RECEIVE status, which has allocated the necessary buffers. The burden of buffering is thus put on the users, which is not usually the case when Layer 4 software is employed.

TRANSMIT INTERRUPT
> This is used to forcefully send a small message to a destination which is not necessarily in RECEIVE status. The message is small enough that no special buffer allocation is needed for it. It bypasses any queues in the network and goes directly to its destination.

employ transmission-subsystem commands which are compiled or interpreted to create messages such as those in Fig. 12.8. DEC software, for example, has five transmission-subsystem commands which users of DECNET can employ:

CONNECT
DISCONNECT
RECEIVE
TRANSMIT
and TRANSMIT INTERRUPT   (see Box 12.3).

The reason why small machines may interface directly to the transport subsystem is that more efficient operation may be achieved and the overhead or complexity associated with higher layers can be avoided.

LAYER 2 INTERFACE   In some cases machines drop down to the Layer 2 interface, *physical* data link control, as shown in Fig. 12.9, i.e., they have no Layer 3 or higher layer. Layer 2 control is often built into a terminal.

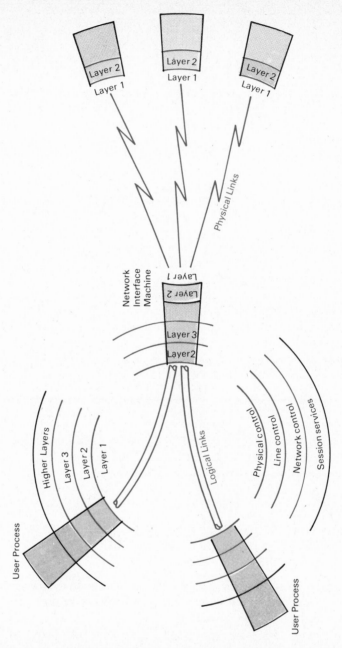

Figure 12.9 Terminals without Layer 3 software (or hardware) are connected to physical circuits going to a network interface machine.

Terminals are often connected to a computer via a network interface machine as shown in Fig. 12.9. They may be remote from this network node; connected to it via a physical link such as a leased or dial telephone line. On this circuit Layer 2 link control is used. However, it might be different from the Layer 2 link control used by the network. Most networks employ an advanced data link control procedure (such as HDLC, SDLC, UDLC, etc.). Terminals may use simpler or older procedures. They may be *binary synchronous* or *start–stop* terminals. In this case the Layer 2 procedure on the network of Fig. 12.9 would be different from that used by the terminals on the right. The network interface machine handles the links to terminals with one link control procedure, and the links which comprise the network with another.

LAYER 1 INTERFACE   The innermost interface, Layer 1, is usually the well-established 25-pin plug connection to a modem or other transmission equipment. Any data machine, with or without software can send bits over it. A simple terminal may use start-stop transmission. If this terminal is connected to a computer network it will be via a concentrator or gateway processor such as that in Fig. 12.10, and this machine will use the higher software layers.

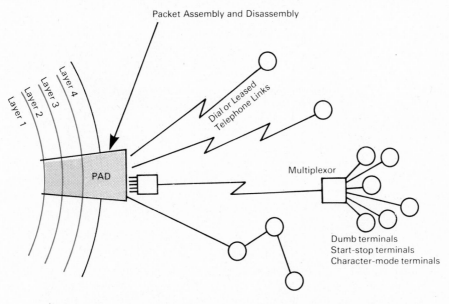

Figure 12.10 Dumb terminals connected to the network via a PAD (Packet Assembly and Disassembly) interface.

BYPASSING
THE INNER LAYERS

Lastly, a channel of a distributed processing system may bypass all or some of the inner layers when components can be connected more directly. Two machines in the same building may be connected by a high capacity channel rather than a virtual circuit. Figure 12.11 shows user processes which employ the Session Services layers but these modules are directly interconnected, bypassing the normal transmission subsystem layers. The session services subsystem uses the standard interface to Layer 4.

The transmission media used in Fig. 12.11 might be a point-to-point connection, or circuit-switched connection which does not need messages to be sliced into packets and which avoids the complications of Layer 3. It might be a communication satellite channel, an office-of-the-future network like Xerox's XTEN, a local wideband network (Chapter 26), cable television, or merely a conventional computer channel connecting machines in building. Some digital circuit-switched facilities use CCITT X.21

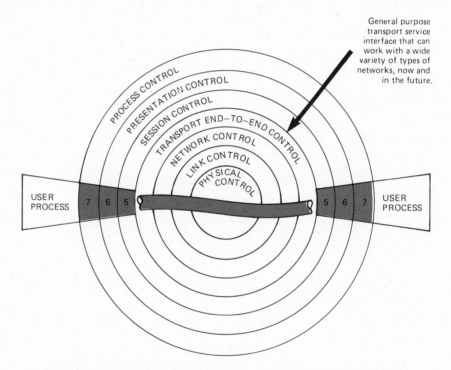

Figure 12.11 A system which uses the session services layers but not the transmission subsystem layers. It employs the *standard interface to Layer 4,* but transmission does not use CCITT X.25 or similar mechanisms. It may be a wideband point-to-point channel, CATV, communication satellite network, office-of-the-future network, Ethernet (Chapter 24), or merely a computer channel connecting machines in a building.

physical control. The interface to Layer 4 is intended to be a general-purpose transport service interface which can work with a wide variety of different types of networks.

To the user processes it may make no difference whether or not Layers 4, 3, 2, or 1 are used. The user processes may be kept waiting less if the inner layers are bypassed, but the code they use is unchanged. A well-designed architecture for distributed processing should make the details of how distribution is accomplished transparent to the users.

13 PHYSICAL LINK CONTROL

This chapter and the next two describe the three main layering subdivisions, first link control (Layer 2), then the transmission subsystem (Layers 1 to 4), and then the termination subsystem (Layers 5, 6, and 7). Boxes 13.1, 14.1, and 15.1 summarize the functions of these subdivisions.

The purpose of a physical link protocol is to transfer blocks of data without error between two devices connected to the same physical circuit. The reader might imagine the physical circuit to be a pair of copper telephone wires, although in reality the circuit could be more complex and include different transmission media.

In many cases the two devices will be at opposite ends of the physical circuit and no other device will transmit on that circuit. Sometimes, however, there will be multiple devices attached to the single physical circuit. The former is called a *point-to-point* circuit and the latter a *multidrop* circuit. With a multidrop circuit a device will receive, electrically, all transmissions including those which are not addressed to it. It must recognize those which *are* addressed to it and reject the others.

The bits transmitted are sometimes changed by transmission errors. A telephone line has far more noise and errors than the circuits within a computer room. The physical link protocol must be able to detect transmission errors, and react to them by having the transmitting device resend the faulty packets.

The receiving machine must be able to detect when a message begins and when it ends. Some form of demarcation is needed because messages are of variable length.

The conventional connection between a data machine and a modem is the CCITT V.24 interface or the EIA RS 232-C interface in the United States. For a data machine with automatic dialing these are extended and become the CCITT V.25 and EIA RS 366 interfaces. New standards, EIA RS 422 and EIA RS 423 are coming into use to replace the EIA RS 232-C interface. They use an electrical connector interface EIA RS 449.

The above standards are for *analog* transmission. Increasingly lines are being

BOX 13.1 Functions of Layer 1 and 2 control mechanisms

Layer 1

- Provide an electrical interface between the data machine (computer, terminal, concentrator, controller, etc.) and the data communication equipment (modem, line driver, etc.).

- Establish and disconnect a physical transmission path.

- Transmit bits over that path.

- Make the data machine aware of path failures.

Layer 2

- Transmit frames over a physical transmission path.

- Indicate which are the first and last bits of the frame.

- Detect transmission errors.

- Retransmit frames which were damaged by transmission errors.

- Permit frames to be of any length, up to a given maximum, and to contain any pattern of bits.

- Ensure that no frames are lost.

- If more than two data machines are connected to the physical path, (i) address the frames to the correct machine; (ii) maintain discipline over the time when each machine transmits; (iii) the controlling machine should detect a failure to respond in any of the other machines.

- Where necessary, permit data to be transmitted in both directions at once.

- Where desirable, maximize the throughput of the line with techniques such as continuous ARQ or selective repeat ARQ (discussed in Chapter 31).

---

used which transmit end-to-end in a *digital*, not analog, fashion. No modems are used; an interface is needed to a digital line driver. The CCITT X.21 and X.21 BIS Standards specify such interfaces.

It is desirable to have a miniature version of such an interface so that every pocket calculator, television set, and cheap terminal can have a cheap chip inside it which enables it to be connected to the conventional four-pin telephone outlet in the wall. Such an interface is sometimes referred to as a *mini-interface*.

When failures occur or problems are detected, such as a receiving machine not being ready, the machines must send control messages to initiate corrective action. Such messages are defined in the physical link protocol.

INTELLIGENT   None of the foregoing is new. These processes have been
MACHINES   carried out in some form or other since the dawn of data
                                    communications. In the mid-1970's, however, one factor
was new. Mass-produced microminiature circuitry made it reasonable to assume that communicating devices would have a buffer and a limited logic capability. In other words, in a world of *distributed intelligence* communicating machines would have a certain amount of intelligence, perhaps on one microelectronics chip.

Given this assumption it was possible to design physical link protocols which were more efficient than the earlier ones. They would make a higher transmission

BOX 13.2 Physical link control protocols similar to the International Standards Organization HDLC

Protocol	Organization Which Specified It
HDLC Higher-level Data Link Control	ISO International Standards Organization
ADCCP Advanced Data Communication Control Procedures	ASA American Standards Associaton
Recommendation X.25 Level 2 of this Recommendation (now identical to HDLC)	CCITT Comité Consultatif International Téléphonique et Télégraphique
SDLC Synchronous Data Link Control	IBM
UDLC Universal Data Link Control	Sperry Univac
CDLC (replaced by HDLC)	CDC
BDLC (replaced by HDLC)	Burroughs

throughput possible on a given physical link, and would permit data to be sent in both directions at once on a full duplex link.

Several organizations specified protocols for this environment which are similar in essentials, but have had minor differences in detail. These are listed in Box 13.2.

The three standards organizations listed in Box 13.2 have stated that they intend to agree on one protocol. We will use the ISO name for it: HDLC, Higher-level Data Link Control.

Meanwhile IBM has made extensive use of its protocol, SDLC, Synchronous Data Link Control. Much of IBM's data communications software and hardware since 1974 has employed SDLC. However, there are many IBM terminals still in existence using the older *binary synchronous* protocol, and so some of the new software must still accommodate this protocol.

The principles of HDLC and SDLC are essentially the same. SDLC is an allowed subset of HDLC. We will describe HDLC and then indicate how SDLC differs from it. Other manufacturers use other subsets.

Several other computer manufacturers have their own protocols similar to HDLC, but sometimes with minor differences in detail.

Another entirely different physical link protocol is used by the Digital Equipment Corporation for minicomputer networks—DDCMP, Digital Data Communications Management Protocol.

DATA TRANSPARENCY   The data which is transmitted can be of any length and any pattern of bits. The data may not have any characteristics which are designed to assist the transmission protocol, and transmission must not interfere with *any* pattern of data. This property is referred to as *data transparency*.

How, in this case, is the end of a variable-length packet to be recognized? There are three possible ways:

1. A Count

The header of the packet could contain a count of bits or bytes, saying how long the packet is. This method is used in the Digital Equipment Corporation's protocol, DDCMP.

2. Character Stuffing

The data, although transparent, could be divided into character lengths of, say, 7-bits each. Certain bit patterns could be designated as *control characters* as they are in the ASCII code. Any of these control characters may occur by chance in the data. The data may, for example, contain the bit combination 1110100, which in the ASCII code is an ETB character meaning END OF TRANSMITTED BLOCK. The receiving machine must not interpret this as the end of transmission.

The bit sequence 1110100 cannot be used by itself to mean end-of-transmission. Consequently each control signal is composed of two characters, the first of which is DLE (DATA LINK ESCAPE, 0000100 in ASCII code). DLE ETB (0000100 1110100) is then interpreted as END OF TRANSMITTED BLOCK, and similarly with other control characters. DLE (0000100) could occur by chance in the *data* stream. In this case it must be sent as DLE DLE (0000100 0000100). This is referred to as *character stuffing*, and permits any combination of data bits to be sent without being confused with control signals.

Character stuffing with DLE characters is used in IBM's *binary synchronous* line control protocol.

3. Bit Stuffing

HDLC and SDLC use a special bit combination called *flag* 01111110, to indicate both the start of a packet and the end of a packet. Again, 01111110 might crop up by chance in the data stream. To prevent this causing problems, the data is scanned by the transmitting and receiving machines. Whenever five consecutive 1 bits are detected in the data stream the transmitting machine inserts an extra 0 bit. Whenever five consecutive 1 bits are detected by the receiving machine, it examines the next bit to see whether it is a 0 or 1 bit. If it is a 0 bit the machine deletes it. If not, the receiving machine looks for the flag, 01111110. This procedure is illustrated in Fig. 18.1. It enables the receiving machine to detect the flag no matter what data bits were sent. This insertion of 0 bits is called *bit stuffing*.

**MANY
CONFIGURATIONS**   When the devices connected to a line have some logic and buffering capability, a wide variety of configurations is possible (Fig 13.1). It is desirable to have a physical link protocol which can handle all, or almost all, of these.

It should handle point-to-point and multipoint lines. On multipoint lines it should handle roll-call and hub polling [1] (with polling, a ''go-ahead'' signal is passed from device to device on the line; with the more usual roll-call polling only the controlling master station sends ''go-ahead'' signals). It should handle loops of devices and other forms of multiple access line.

It should be efficient on both slow and fast lines, and lines with a long turnaround time or propagation delay. It should be efficient on both half duplex and full duplex lines. In a full duplex line, data messages should be able to flow in both directions at once, and if it is a multidrop line, data from different terminals should be able to be interleaved. Half duplex and full duplex devices should be able to operate simultaneously on the same physical link.

On some systems the terminals are constantly in an active condition. On others they can be dormant or off-line some of the time. The protocol needs to be able to handle a terminal which is not constantly being polled, or one which changes from a dormant to an active condition.

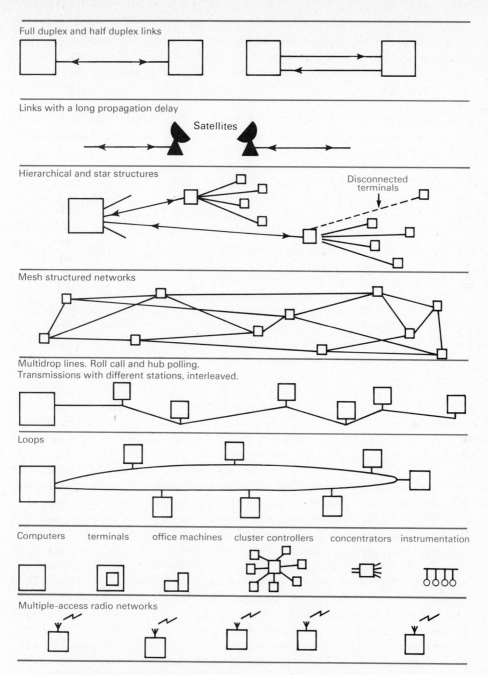

Full duplex and half duplex links

Links with a long propagation delay

Satellites

Hierarchical and star structures

Disconnected terminals

Mesh structured networks

Multidrop lines. Roll call and hub polling.
Transmissions with different stations, interleaved.

Loops

Computers   terminals   office machines   cluster controllers   concentrators   instrumentation

Multiple-access radio networks

Figure 13.1   The physical link protocol ought to handle a wide variety of different configurations.

Some overhead is unavoidable in achieving this degree of generality. The protocol should handle all configurations as efficiently as possible, permitting high line throughputs. There is a case to be made for specialized protocols also handling specialized types of physical links (e.g., very high-speed satellite channels).

HIGH RELIABILITY   The physical link control mechanism should be able to deal with errors or temporary busy conditions without involving higher authority or higher layers of control.

As discussed in Chapter 31 polynomial codes for error detection can be powerful. A 16-bit code is used in most cases, and with this the rate of undetected errors on telephone lines is typically about 1 bit in 10^{12}. A telephone line transmitting 4800 bits per second for 8 hours every day would have one undetected bit error every 20 years on average. A typical interactive dialogue uses a much lower *average* bit rate, and if it had been used from the time of Christ until today there is a good chance that no undetected error would have occurred in it!

Bit errors can occur not only in data fields but also in control bytes, addressed bytes, the flag pattern 01111110, and in any supervisory message. All of these should be protected with the error detecting code. The recovery procedures should be foolproof so that when any of these errors occur they do not cause user messages to be accidentally lost or delivered twice. (Double delivery may be serious in some systems; for example with financial transactions.)

PHYSICAL BLOCK   On a given physical link there is a certain optimum length
LENGTHS   for the blocks of data, which will maximize the throughput possible on that link. If a block is very long the probability of its containing an error and having to be retransmitted will be high. If the blocks are very short the overhead and time taken in line turnarounds will be high. The optimum length can be calculated for a given link and is often a few thousand bits. Other network considerations often lead to a much shorter block length.

Switched data networks usually have their own maximum packet size. This is based on factors such as users' message lengths and buffering costs. Agreements exist between common carriers concerning packet sizes in packet-switching networks. CCITT Recommendation X.25 recommends that the maximum data field length in a packet should be 128 8-bit bytes. It states that 16, 32, 64, 256, 512, or 1024 bytes, or, exceptionally, 255 bytes, may be used by some organizations.

When user messages exceed the maximum packet size, they must be sent a piece at a time and joined together after transmission. This is not the concern of the *physical link* protocol, however. The physical link protocol merely sends the pieces. The physical link protocol may take into consideration that packets are sent in groups, and may require an acknowledgement of correct receipt when the last packet in the group is sent, rather than when every packet is sent.

SEQUENCING It may or may not be a requirement of the physical link protocol that it always delivers messages in the same sequence as that in which they were sent. Most physical links do deliver the messages in sequence. However, where there is a long propagation delay as on a satellite link, the most efficient form of recovery from errors is *selective repeat* error control, discussed in Chapter 31. This retransmits the packet that was in error and does not retransmit the correct packets which followed it. The result is packets being delivered in a different sequence from that in which they were sent.

Selective repeat error control is often avoided because of the delivery sequence problem.

PARALLEL CIRCUITS Normally a physical link consists of one transmission circuit connecting the data machines. Occasionally two or more circuits are used in parallel. This is usually done to achieve a higher throughput. It can also improve reliability—if one circuit fails another is still usable. It may be done to handle peak loads—an extra dial-up circuit is added when the traffic exceeds a certain volume.

In most systems each parallel circuit requires its own physical link control. *How* the traffic is distributed to use the circuits is the concern of a higher-level layer of control. It is also possible to regard the pair or group of circuits as *one* physical link between two machines. In this case the physical link protocol will distribute the traffic among the circuits. It will make the group of parallel circuits *appear* as though they were *one* higher-speed circuit. Most physical line control mechanisms do not do this. One which does is the Digital Equipment Corporation's physical line protocol, DDCMP (Digital Data Communications Management Protocol).

WHAT THE PHYSICAL LINK PROTOCOL DOES NOT DO The physical link protocol is merely a means of delivering packets over a single physical link. It has no concern with what happens beyond that link, for example how packets are routed through a multilink network, concentration techniques, device status and device control, end-to-end control functions, security techniques, how long messages are sliced into packets or how short messages are gathered into blocks for transmission. It is not concerned with the establishment, maintenance, or disconnection of a switched path between stations.

REFERENCE

1. Roll-call and hub polling are explained in the author's *Systems Analaysis for Data Transmission,* Prentice-Hall, Englewood Cliffs, NJ, 1972.

14 THE TRANSPORT SUBSYSTEM

The purpose of the transport subsystem is to permit many users to share the same transmission facilities. The mechanisms which permit this sharing may be complex, so the transport subsystem presents an interface to each user which makes it *appear* that it is using a simple point-to-point link.

In some cases a transport network is an entity in its own right, entirely separate from the machines which employ it. In other cases it is a subsystem of a computer communications architecture which also incorporates higher level facilities and services.

Transport subsystems range from simple to highly complex. At one extreme is a system with leased lines for connecting a few terminals to a computer. At the other extreme is a multinational packet-switching network using different types of lines to interconnect many incompatible computers and terminals. All such transport subsystems should be transparent, giving users the appearance of a point-to-point link. The same higher level software (Layers 4 to 7) may be used on both, so, ideally, both should present the same transport subsystem interface.

Transport subsystems are provided by computer manufacturers, by common carriers offering a switched data network, and, in countries where the law permits it, by independent organizations offering value-added or time-sharing networks. Some of these different organizations use different mechanisms and provide entirely different interfaces from the transmission subsystem. The CCITT X.25 Recommendation for a standard network interface is doing much to encourage compatibility between at least some networks.

HIGHER-SPEED BURSTS

Table 9.1 made apparent the need for line sharing in interactive systems. An interactive terminal has periods of silence which are much longer than its bursts of transmission. The *average* transmission rate during an interactive session is usually less than 20 bits per second for both directions of transmission combined. Even a simple voice line is less than 0.5% utilized when employed for one interactive session. Yet we would like to employ line speeds higher than those of a voice line for delivering to a user a screen full of information quickly, or for delivering a program routine, a piece of a data base, or a facsimile image or copy of a document.

A very attractive feature of a high level of sharing is that it makes economical the use of high-speed lines, and these permit faster response times. Fast delivery makes possible the transmission of program routines when needed for interactive use, fast interchange of portions of a data base, remote display of facsimile documents, and use of more attractive screen displays in man–computer dialogues.

In general, as computer technology evolves into distributed processing, computer networks, and better services for end users, so the need for transmission of high-speed bursts rather than low-speed bursts increases. To make this economical, a high level of line sharing is needed. This may come from common carrier services such as value-added networks or communications satellite systems. It may come from the design of private systems employing leased lines to provide corporations or government departments with networks serving many computers in many locations.

BURST MULTIPLEXING AND SWITCHING   All telecommunications operations are characterized by major economies of scale. The greater the sharing, the lower the potential cost per user channel. This is true both of the telephone network and of data transmission. They are fundamentally different, as we stressed before, in that telephone users want continuous channels whereas most computer users want burst transmission. Figure 14.1 illustrates the difference between continuous-channel sharing and burst sharing.

The outside rectangle of Fig. 14.1 represents a total communicating capability: channel capacity × time. The channel capacity of physical trunk circuits is much greater than that required by a telephone call. The mechanisms of the telephone system therefore allocate a portion of the capacity, which is continuous in time, to a telephone call. This is illustrated by the horizontal band in Fig. 14.1.

For computer networks we would like to be able to use the entire capacity for a brief instant in time to transmit a burst of data. Then, some time later, we would transmit another burst. This is illustrated by the vertical bands in Fig. 14.1. Bursts from many different users would be interleaved, as on a computer's burst multiplexer channel. To interconnect users at scattered locations a communications network needs both transmission and switching capability. The argument about continuous channels and bursts applies both to the transmission and the switching.

Transmission on telephone channels employs continuous-channel multiplexing— traditionally frequency-division multiplexing. For computer operations a different form of multiplexing is needed, which interleaves high-speed bursts.

Similarly the switches on the telephone network connect continuous telephone channels. A data network needs switches which route bursts of data to their destination.

BOX 14.1 Functions of transmission subsystem software

- Establish a logical link to a remote machine. The logical link may employ multiple physical links.
- Disconnect the logical link after use.
- Deliver messages over the logical link.
- Provide a precisely defined interface to higher levels of software (or application programs).
- Select a route through the network which is efficient.
- Ensure that no message is lost. If a message, or part of a message, is undeliverable, notify the sender or return the message to the sender.
- Deliver the messages in the sequence in which they were sent (First-in, first-out).
- Avoid delivering any message twice (e.g., after a failure has occurred).
- If necessary divide long messages into multiple packets to shorten the delivery time or to lessen the buffering needs of intermediate nodes.
- If messages are sent as multiple packets, reassemble the messages correctly.
- Avoid links or nodes which have failed, by means of *alternate routing*.
- *Dynamic alternate routing* may be used (i.e., different packets in the same session could travel by different routes) to minimize congestion and balance the traffic load.
- Permit the receiving machine to regulate the rate at which it receives messages so as to avoid overloading.
- Permit the network to regulate the flow of traffic so as to avoid problems caused by congestion, buffer shortage, or message reassembly.
- Prevent any one user-machine overloading the transmission resources so that other users are excluded.
- If necessary use parallel routes between user-machines or parallel physical links between nodes to increase the throughput.
- Short interrupt-messages may be sent which bypass the queues and do not need buffer reservation.
- Messages may be sent with different priorities, e.g.,

HIGHEST PRIORITY: Control messages.

PRIORITY 2:   Real-time or fast interactive messages.

PRIORITY 3:   Slow interactive messages.

BOX 14.1 *Continued*

PRIORITY 4:   Batch-processing traffic.

PRIORITY 5:   Traffic which can be deferred, e.g., mail.

- Address conversions may be performed when user machines do not employ full or absolute network addresses.

- Access to a user machine may be restricted to a specified group of users for reasons of security or cost control.

- Traffic statistics may be accumulated for network monitoring.

- Information may be collected for billing users for transport subsystem usage.

- The mechanisms should be designed to avoid deadlocks.

STORE-AND-FORWARD ROUTING AND CIRCUIT SWITCHING

Burst switching can be done in two ways.

First the switch can connect together transmission circuits, as do telephone switches, *but for a very brief time*—the time that it takes the burst to flow and no longer. This is called *fast-connect circuit switching*.

Secondly, the switch can have memory. It reads the burst of data into its memory, examines its address, and then transmits it on the appropriate channel. This is called *store-and-forward* operation.

There are several types of store-and-forward devices:

- A concentrator.
  This is usually used in a vertical network or subnetwork to connect multiple lines from lower-level machines to one line going to higher-level machines.

- A message switch.
  This reads in messages, examines their address, and forwards them down an appropriate outgoing line. Traditional message switching is used for relaying administrative traffic, and the switching machine files the messages so that they can be retrieved later if necessary.

- A packet switch.
  Packet-switching networks slice messages into packets of a given maximum length (typically 128 bytes). They relay the packets individually through store-and-forward nodes to a destination node where the original message must be reassembled from the packets.

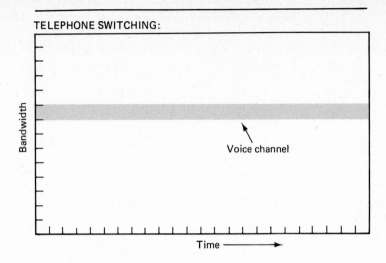

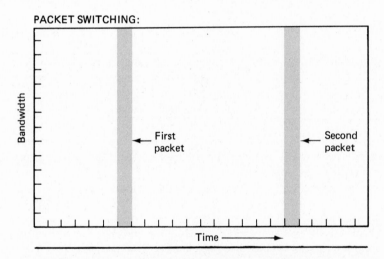

Figure 14.1 The circuit-switched telephone network slices up the available information-carrying capacity in a different way from a packet-switched network. The shaded blocks show the allocation to one user.

Any of these devices could be a small high-speed computer. With circuit switching, an end-to-end path is set up through computerized switches before the data is sent, as on the telephone system, though the time to connect the path is several milliseconds rather than several seconds. The path is disconnected as soon as the burst is transmitted, and the switching capacity can then be allocated to other bursts. With store-and-forward switching each message or packet carries information which enables the switch to detemine how to route the packet. There is no setting up a path before transmission. After transmission the storage in the switch can be allocated to other traffic.

TREE AND MESH   As we have noted, transport networks may vary from very
STRUCTURES   simple to extremely complex. It is desirable that control
                           procedures should be devised which work well
with complex networks, but which can be subsetted for use with simple networks so that simple networks do not have unnecessary overhead.

Computer manufacturers with architectures for computer networks sometimes install systems in which only two computers are connected. Often they will install tree-structured networks in which all transmission paths go up or down the tree. There is no alternative routing.

Figure 14.2 shows a tree. A tree is composed of a hierarchy of nodes. The uppermost level of the hierarchy has only one node, called the *root*. With the exception of the root, every node has one node related to it at a higher level, and this is called the *parent*. No node has more than one parent. Each node can have one or more nodes related to it at a lower level. The top node is often the large computer center. The lowest nodes are often terminals. Nodes in between may be computers, concentrators, or terminal controllers, as in the vertical networks illustrated in Chapter 6.

A large tree-structured network is shown in Fig. 14.3. Such a network often uses store-and-forward concentrators. Sometimes a tree-structured network built with leased lines can use public switched circuits for backup when a lease line or node fails.

Figure 14.4 shows a large mesh-structured network. Here there is no hierarchical

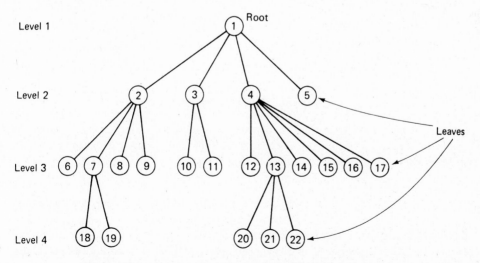

Figure 14.2   A tree. (No element has more than one parent.)

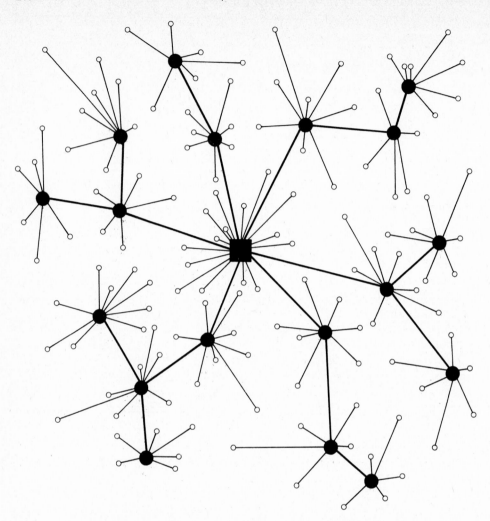

Figure 14.3   A tree-structured network. No alternate routing.

relationship. The term *peer-coupled* network is sometimes used because it connects computers which are peers, i.e., of equal status (although possibly differing greatly in size and importance).

VARIABLE ROUTING   Between any two nodes in Fig. 14.4 there are many possible routes, although one may be more direct than others. The route that a message takes may vary from one time to another depending upon the degree of congestion on different routes, and upon whether any lines or nodes are inoperative.

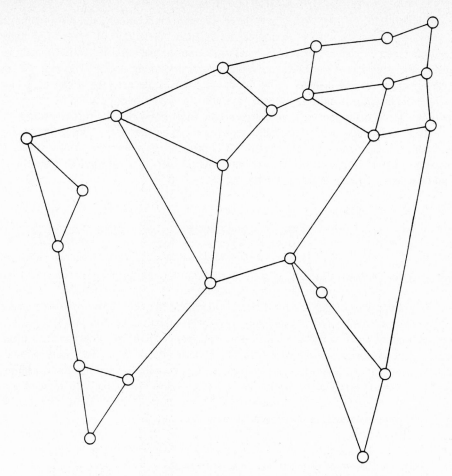

Figure 14.4 A mesh-structured network interconnecting computer centers.

Variable routing introduces a variety of complications which we discuss later in the book. It is necessary to have an algorithm which decides which route a message or packet should take. That algorithm needs information about the conditions in the network which affect what would be the best route. Different slices of a message (packets) may be sent by different routes, and so might arrive at their destination out of order. It is necessary to reassemble them before they are delivered to the message user. The reassembly process needs buffer storage. There is a danger that a receiving node may run out of such storage when the traffic converging on it is exceptionally great. Some networks have encountered deadlocks caused by traffic overloads. When failures occur, message recovery is more difficult if variable routing is used, especially if different slices of the same message can travel by different routes.

FLOW CONTROL   To lessen the problems with deadlocks and traffic jams, it is desirable to regulate the flow of traffic. A high-speed computer is capable of pouring messages into the network at a speed which far exceeds the capacity of the lines, concentrators, or switching nodes. The input needs to be regulated so that sudden traffic floods do not jam the network. Even if no one machine sends an exceptional volume of traffic, a traffic overload could still occur when by chance many messages converge on the same network node or destination.

The mechanisms needed for traffic regulation can be simple or complex depending upon the overall structure of the network. It is desirable to make them straightforward; on some of the early networks they were not entirely successful and serious traffic jams would occasionally lock up the network.

QUEUES   Because of the fluctuating load on networks, queues build
AND PRIORITIES   up. With a circuit-switching network the queues can be held at the outside of the network, possibly in transport/subsystem buffers, possibly external to the transport subsystem. With a store-and-forward network there are queues in the switching nodes and concentrators.

Different types of traffic have different timing requirements. Some messages need to be delivered rapidly to their destination, but with others speed does not matter. If a queuing system handles traffic in a first-in, first-out fashion, and the traffic is originated at random as in most data networks, then the utilization of queue "servers" such as lines and nodes cannot exceed a certain amount without the queues becoming lengthy. To maximize the utilization of the servers the traffic may be divided into different priorities. High-priority traffic passes through the network as quickly as possible. Low-priority traffic is not sent until there is idle capacity.

If a network is to handle a variety of traffic types, as most networks do, then the needs of the users are best met by multipriority mechanisms. Today's mix of traffic can employ five levels of priority, shown in Box 14.2.

NETWORK ADDRESSES   Networks need *addresses* for the various devices or user modules which they interconnect. A network address is analogous to a telephone number. A user wishing to contact another user states that user's address in the session initiation procedure, like dialing a telephone number, and the network makes the connection. The simplest form of address is a single unique number in a large enough range of numbers to encompass all possible users. IBM's SNA (System Network Architecture) uses 16-bit addresses, presumably hoping that no SNA system will have more than 2^{16} (= 65,536) separate addresses. A *datagram* network proposed by a group of common carriers in Canada used 32-bit addresses, not because they expected 2^{32} (>4 billion users—slightly less than the world's population) users, but because 32 bits can represent any 10-digit North American telephone number (the second digit of the area code is 1 or 0) and a datagram machine (discussed in

Chapter 24) could be connected to any telephone outlet. The Digital Equipment Corporation uses network addresses which can be any number of 8-bit bytes. Each byte contains seven bits of the address. The eighth bit is set to 1 if the following bit contains more of the address. Other systems use variable-length addresses and employ a count field to indicate the number of bits in the address. Variable-length addresses allow small networks to be handled with low address overhead, but permit large addresses for large networks.

AREAS
AND SUBAREAS

Large networks are usually divided into *areas* of smaller size and these may be divided into subareas. A user may employ an area or subarea address rather than the complete address when contacting another user in the same area or subarea. For example we dial a 7-digit telephone number when contacting a telephone in the same area. To dial a telephone a thousand miles away we have to preface the 7-digit number with a 3-digit area code. To call a number on the same exchange it may be possible to use 4 digits. Similarly, on some computer networks an abbreviated address is used within a localized area. When a packet with a full network address reaches a localized area it must go to a node in that area which has the task of converting the full network address to the area address, and passing it onwards. This is sometimes called a *boundary* node. The function of converting from full network protocols to localized area protocols is called the *boundary function* (Fig. 14.6).

Some terminals are manufactured with a short fixed address. A cluster controller, line controller, or concentrator converts between this terminal address and the full network address.

In some networks, user machines address each other *symbolically*. Each network *user* has a unique name, and the users refer to each other with these names. The machine which sets up the session converts these names into binary addresses which are employed during the session.

The binary address of the destination is carried by each transmitted packet so that it can be routed correctly to that destination. The packet also carries the address of the sender so that undelivered messages can be returned, and so that recovery from failures can be accomplished without loss of messages.

NONEXPLICIT
ADDRESSING

In some networks the messages do not carry the explicit addresses of the users. Instead they carry some form of *session identification* and the address of a network node near the destination, such as a network interface machine, a concentrator, or a terminal cluster controller. This network node uses the session identification to pass on the message either to the destination user, or to a machine in contact with the destination user.

Nonexplicit addressing has two advantages. First, the address carried by the

BOX 14.2   Desirable priority levels

HIGHEST PRIORITY: *Critical network control messages*

These are not *user data* messages. They are messages which affect the functioning of the network itself or the devices connected to it. They are needed for regulating the flow, pacing, sending urgent control signals, avoiding traffic jams, and breaking up deadlocks if they occur. They must jump the queues of user messages because they are needed to break up these queues when they are excessive. Like ambulances in city streets they should scream through the traffic to where they are needed. They are generally short and do not have the buffering requirements that user messages have. Small buffers can be permanently allocated for them.

PRIORITY 2: *Interactive or real-time traffic*

This is user traffic which must be delivered quickly, often in a fraction of a second so that a total response time of less than 2 seconds, say, can be achieved. This traffic often dominates the design of the queuing mechanisms and buffers. The need for the fast response time has dominated the topology of many packet switching networks and mandated their use of widebank circuits. A typical design criterion is that the majority of this class of packets (say 99%) will be delivered in 200 milliseconds or less. To calculate the total response time it is necessary to add together the times for all the packets constituting a message and the response to it, and various other times such as compute time, file-access time, and terminal-editing time.

The wider the bandwidth of the lines the shorter the delivery time. But networks with high bandwidth lines need a high volume of traffic to be justifiable.

Priority 3: *Slow interactive traffic*

Psychological studies of user behavior when operating with different response times show that some responses ought to be less than two seconds. Others can take substantially longer. Priority 3 is for those messages which are interactive but which do not need a two-second response time. Five seconds, 10 seconds, or even longer, is appropriate. For Priority 3 the design criterion might be that 99% of the packets are delivered

BOX 14.2 *Continued*

within 2 seconds. (Again two or more such one-way delivery times are included in the overall response time).

PRIORITY 4: *Batch and noninteractive traffic*

This waits in the queues until higher priority traffic has been sent. When all the resources are needed for Priority 3 and higher, it can be kept out of the network until capacity is available. In extreme circumstances, to make way for higher priority traffic or to unlock traffic jams, it can be eliminated from the network queues and then resent later. Checkpoint restart mechanisms are designed to permit safe recovery from loss of such traffic.

LOWEST PRIORITY: *Deferrable traffic*

If any network (including a corporate telephone network) is designed solely for traffic which must be sent fairly quickly (at least in an hour or two), then the network is likely to be idle for much of the day. Figure 14.5 illustrates this. The network must be designed to carry the peak traffic of the peak day. The shaded portion of Fig. 14.5 is the time-critical traffic of an average day. The white area surrounding it represents unused network capacity. Traffic which can be deferred until the start of the following day can be sent in the white area. This can include electronic mail, nontime-critical batch traffic, file dumps, logs for auditors, and so on.

This deferrable traffic fills in the idle time. Higher priority traffic can blast its way through the deferred traffic if necessary. In the future, *mail* will be the largest class of non-time-critical traffic on networks.

packets can be shorter. Second, it enhances security. An unauthorized person obtaining a data packet by wire-tapping or other illicit means could not identify the destination or the originating user.

Often a user machine has multiple *ports*. In other terminology, it has multiple *logical channels* allocated to it. When it places a call it selects a logical channel. Each logical channel has a number. The responding machine does not need to know the number of the logical channel. Instead the machine which sets up the session allocates an address to the session. Communicating user machines may then address each other

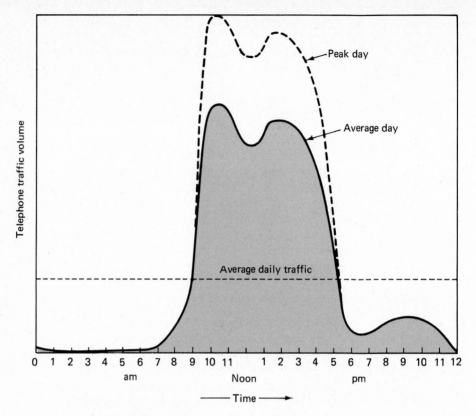

Figure 14.5 Telephone traffic. The unshaded part of the chart represents idle channel capacity.

with the session number, and the nodes of the transport subsystem use this number to select the transmission path and the port of the receiving machine.

TRANSPORT HEADERS   When a packet or message sets off on its journey through a transport network it must carry with it certain information like the paperwork which accompanies a freight shipment. This information is carried in Layer 3 and Layer 4 headers.

It must carry a *destination address* so that the various network machines can route it to that destination. This is different from the address in the Layer 2 header which gives merely the next stop on the journey rather than the ultimate destination. It should also carry an *origination address* so that if it becomes undeliverable for some reason it can be returned to its sender, or at least its sender can be notified. It should carry a

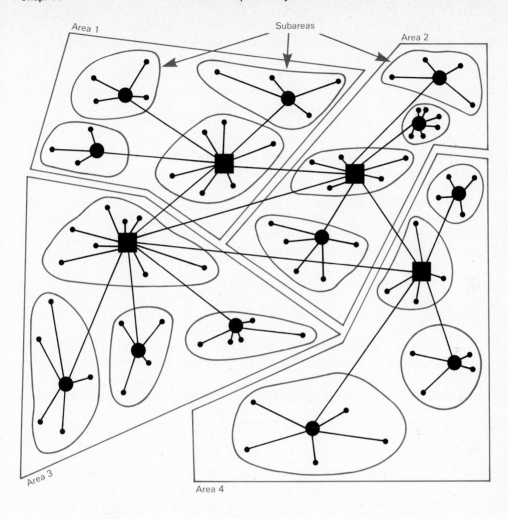

■ : Area controller, or boundary node to an area.

● : Subarea controller, or boundary node to a subarea.

Figure 14.6   Areas and subareas.

serial number so that it can be traced or referred to if lost due to a machine malfunction.

Many virtual circuits share the same physical circuits, and so the packet or message should carry the *virtual circuit number* to which it relates, or a *session number*. On that virtual circuit there may be a means of regulating the rate of flow so that the receiving devices do not become overloaded. The flow control mechanisms commonly use two serial numbers which we will discuss later—a *Send Sequence Number* N_S and a *Receive Sequence Number* N_R.

When long messages are sent on the virtual circuit they are cut into slices and sent in multiple packets. The packets must contain information which enables the receiving node to join the slices together in the right sequence to form the original message. The *Send Sequence Number* may be sufficient for this when used in conjunction with a bit in a packet which indicates that *more data* is to follow.

The transport subsystem should use a priority scheme so that some messages have higher priority than others. A packet or message, then, may contain a *priority indicator,* and higher-priority items jump the queues of lower-priority items.

Different types of messages or packets may have different formats. A data message may be different from a control message. Again, different types of messages or packets may be routed to different software modules for handling. The item may therefore carry an indication of what *type of item* it is or what *format* is used.

TWO TRANSMISSION HEADERS

As we have indicated, two levels of transmission control are desirable:

- Layer 3: This relates to the mechanisms of a common shared network and is unconcerned with the problems of individual sessions in the machines which use the network.
- Layer 4: This relates to specific sessions, is concerned with the end-to-end control of transmission for these sessions, and is unconcerned with the mechanisms of the common network.

Box 14.3 lists the types of information desirable in the Layer 3 header. The bits which carry this information travel with each packet that is transmitted. In addition other control packets are needed to establish the virtual circuit indicating the addresses the sending and receiving machines, disestablish the circuit, and deal with any failures.

The international standard for Layer 3, CCITT Recommendation X.25 is strongly oriented to packet-switching networks. Fig 14.7 shows its header. It can function with other types of networks such as leased-line concentrator networks, but is not appropriate for all networks. Circuit-switched or digital leased-line networks, possibly using the CCITT Recommendation X.21 (Chapter 25), do not require the complexity of X.25. X.25 would be very inefficient with digital facsimile applications which will assume greater importance as office-of-the future technology and electronic mail spread and converge with data processing.

The sessions using Layer 4 require a standard interface to a transport service. The formats and protocols used should work with different forms of transport service and not be oriented to one particular form such as packet-switching. A given session may

BOX 14.3   Types of information desirable in the Layer 3 header

- Identification of virtual circuit (logical channel) to which this packet relates.

    NOTE: To deliver the packet the network must know the *destination address*. In case the packet is undeliverable the network must know the *origination address*. Neither of these relatively lengthy fields need be carried in a data packet. The network can deduce them from the number of the virtual circuit (logical channel or session). They must be sent in the packet which originally sets up the virtual circuit. Not including them in every packet shortens the packet headers and improves security.

- Packet type (so that the network knows whether to merely transmit the packet or to take some special action).

- Header format (so that the network knows which bits are which in the packet header. This might be deduced from the packet type).

- Send Sequence Number $\left.\right\}$ To control the flow on the virtual circuit and
- Receive Sequence Number   ensure that no packets are lost.

- More-data bit. To indicate that this packet is not the last packet of a message which is being sent.

- Priority indicator. To indicate whether the packet should jump the queues (or possibly be stored for off-peak transmission).

- Diagnostic indicator. To indicate that this packet should be returned to its sender, or traced, i.e., its journey logged for diagnostic purposes.

at one time operate via a packet-switching network and at another via a leased line, X.21 circuit, satellite circuit, or non-packet-switching network. Network technology is changing fast. Layer 4 should work with the many different network technologies of the future, including some which do not use Layer 3 (such as digital circuit-switched networks)—Fig. 14.8.

The communication with Layer 4 sends and receives messages, not packets (i.e., the messages are not chopped up into slices). It applies end-to-end controls to the messages to ensure that none are lost or received twice. These controls may require that messages be serial-numbered separately for each session. The serial numbers are used to control restart and recovery after failures. The messages must contain an indication of which session is sending and receiving them. They may be directed to soft-

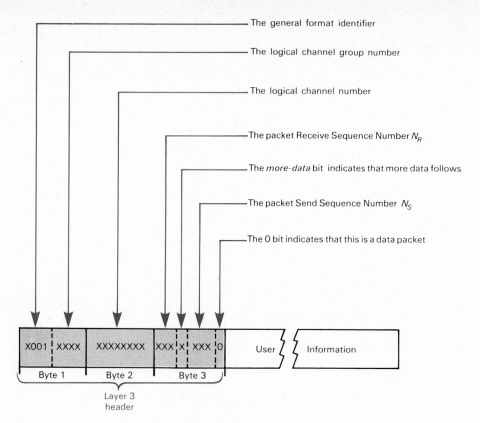

Figure 14.7 The Layer 3 header in the CCITT X.25 protocol containing most of the functions listed in Box 14.3.

ware other than *user* sessions, for example the software which sets up and controls sessions or performs overall network control. Bits in the header would indicate this routing.

Layer 3 (at least in the X.25 Recommendation) does not allow data messages of different priorities. It allows short control messages to be transmitted with higher priority than the data messages. The levels of priority listed in Box 14.2 are desirable and may be a Layer 4 function if Layer 3 does not handle them. Layer 4 may store the low priority items until transmission capacity is available.

ADDITIONAL
OVERHEAD

To some extent the functions placed in Layer 4 in manufacturers' architectures result from the deficiencies in Layer 3. If an X.25 virtual circuit could be trusted to *never* lose a message then end-to-end integrity control could be dispensed with in Layer 4. If Layer 3 handled priorities, Layer 4 need not. (It would be better to handle prior-

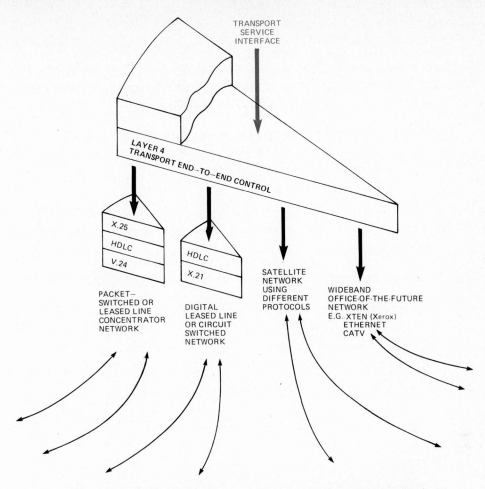

Figure 14.8 The Transport Service Interface (to Layer 4) is independent of the network technology and will work with a diversity of future
networks including some which do not employ a Layer 3.

ities in Layer 3 because the common network should enable high priority items to jump
the queues).

The X.25 Layer 3 has been criticized from both sides. It has been attacked because it duplicates some of the functions in Layer 2 (HDLC) [1]. (More about this in
Chapter 22). It has been attacked because it omits functions which cause additional
controls to be necessary in Layer 4 [2]. The problem arises because the different layers
have been defined by different organizations with slightly different perceptions of the
requirements. The main perception of the designers of X.25 was the building of public
packet-switching networks which would handle the types of computer usage common

in the late 1970's (e.g., *not* digital facsimile, mail, voice, teleconferencing, or high bandwidth office-of-the-future applications).

We have stressed that the building of widespread X.25 networks will be of great value to the future of computing. It is extremely beneficial that a standard exists and is coming into widespread use. That the use of the standard involves somewhat higher overhead will be offset by the mass production of microelectronic circuitry to handle that overhead.

Some manufacturers may choose not to use X.25 and possibly to integrate Layers 3 and 4 into one transmission subsystem layer. As part of their integrated design they may subdivide this layer into their own sublayers.

SUBLAYERS   Univac's DCA (Distributed Communications Architecture)
                            for example divides its integrated equivalent of
Layers 3 and 4 into three sub-layers called *Trunk Control, Route Control,* and *Data Unit Control* (Fig. 14.9). *Data Unit Control,* the highest layer, chops the session messages into packets, performs flow control on the packets (like X.25), and converts machine addresses to logical channel numbers and back again. *Route Control* determines the route through the network, and sometimes joins small messages together to

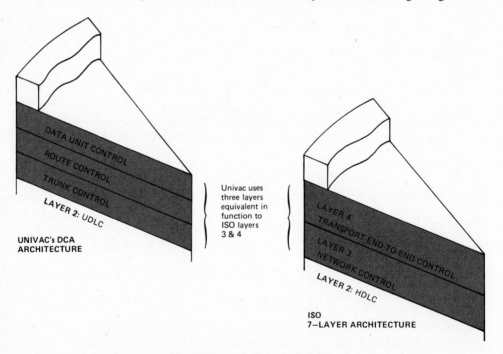

Figure 14.9 Some manufacturers integrate ISO layers 3 and 4 into one layer. This layer may be split into sublayers for implementation. Univac's DCA architecture uses three sublayers as shown here.

travel over the same route as one packet. *Trunk Control* queues packets to and from the communications links, performs initialization and recovery, and manages the communications resources.

**NETWORK
TRANSPARENCY**
One of the reasons for a layered architecture is that the design of the transport subsystem will probably change, and it is desirable that the user programs should not have to change with it.

The most common change is that the network configuration changes, but uses the same techniques. On some systems this happens every few weeks. With more potentially disruptive alterations, the techniques themselves change. Variable routing is introduced into a system which previously had fixed routing. Use of public telephone links is replaced by leased lines and concentrators. A concentrator network is replaced by a packet-switching network. The change, especially if it occurs within the network architecture of one manufacturer, may be done in such a way that the external interface to Layer 4 remains the same.

One change in which the network transparency is less easily preserved is when new common carrier protocols, such as those in the CCITT X.25 Recommendation, are substituted for previously used network protocols of a different form. The change from a private leased line network to a public packet-switching network is likely to bring a different external interface to Layer 3. It is the task of Layer 4 to preserve the network transparency when this happens.

**NETWORK
CONVERSION**
In the future there are likely to be multiple types of transport networks. There will be public packet-switching networks with a CCITT X.25 interface. There will be economic reasons still to use leased circuits, both digital and analog, with concentrators. There will be circuit-switched networks—both the telephone network and some circuit-switched data networks. Value-added networks like TYMNET will continue. A new generation of satellites offers interesting possibilities for new forms of networking. These different networks require different protocols, and also the various manufacturers' network architectures use fundamentally different protocols.

The software will sometimes have to convert from one type of transport network to another. It may have the function of *selecting* which type of network is employed for a session to a given destination. Is it cheaper to go via a public packet-switched network, a leased line facility or a satellite network? These will have fundamentally different pricing structures and *least-cost routing* may be a feature of the software. This might all take place within the Transmission Subsystem.

Unfortunately networks have properties which have an effect external to Layer the Transmission Subsystem. For example satellites have a long propagation delay which affects the *pacing* control. Different networks permit different maximum message sizes. Some networks can provide a high bandwidth; others cannot.

Layer 4 software, then, may be involved in network interconnection and minimum-cost routing, and may have to vary its end-to-end control from one network to another.

PAYMENT FUNCTIONS Network users must be billed for their use of network resources. Transport subsystem software may record details of what each user has employed, and pass this information to a billing program (which is itself a user program).

Some users may request that the party they want to communicate with pays—like a collect (reverse charges) telephone call. The Transport software may issue requests for reverse charging, and respond to such requests from distant nodes.

SUMMARY OF MECHANISMS To summarize, there are some basic types of mechanisms which a transmission subsystem for computer networking needs. They are listed in Box 14.4 along with the chapter which discusses them further. These mechanisms are found in the network architectures of both computer manufacturers and common carriers.

BOX 14.4 Basic mechanisms required in transport subsystems, with an indication of which chapter discusses them later in the book

- Physical link control. *Chapter 18*
- Switching. *Chapters 19 and 25*
- Traffic routing. *Chapter 21*
- Message slicing and reassembly. *Chapter 19*
- Flow control. *Chapter 20*
- Queuing. *Chapter 19*
- Priorities. *Chapter 20*
- Network management. *Chapter 16*
- Error control. *Chapter 31*
- Recovery. *Chapters 31, 32, and 33*
- Security. *Chapter 35*
- Billing. *Chapter 16*

REFERENCES

1. Pouzin, L., "A Restructuring of X.25 into HDLC," *Computer Communication Review,* ACM 7, No. 1, January 1977: 9–28.

2. "Further Study of Packet Mode Operation on Public Data Networks," *CCITT Study Group VII Contribution No. 60-E,* January, 1977.

15 THE SESSION SERVICES

Whereas Layers 1, 2, 3, and 4 have an overall objective which can be concisely stated, the session services subsystem is a collection of diverse activities. Just what services are provided external to the transport subsystem differs greatly from one system to another. While the standards organizations can specify complete standards for Layers 1, 2, 3, and probably 4, they will have a more difficult time with the higher layers. These higher layer standards, however, are extremely desirable and important. When they exist and are widely accepted they will greatly enhance the usefulness and value of networks.

The session services provided differ from one type of network to another. Different types of distributed processing need different types of services. So do different types of user software, like data-base software for example. The Session Services Subsystem differs widely from one computer manufacturer's architecture to another. If different transport subsystems were to become similar in the future, solving a common problem, the personality of different manufacturers' network software would reside largely in the session services subsystem. The main sales arguments of the future will probably relate to Layers 5, 6, and 7.

Box 15.1 lists the possible functions of the higher layers. We can divide them into three groups:

1. Functions required when setting up or disconnecting a session.
2. Functions used during the normal running of a session.
3. Functions employed when something goes wrong such as a node failure or a protocol violation.

Box 15.1 is a lengthy list—not necessarily complete—and no manufacturer's networking software comes close yet to providing the whole list. In the development of networking there is a long road ahead. We can perceive what is needed but the protocols will be complex. As new protocols become accepted, new machines will come into existence which use them and it will become steadily easier and cheaper to implement computer networks and distributed processing. This applies both within one manufacturer with a diverse assortment of machines, and within the computer and telecommunications community in general.

SETTING UP A SESSION

The process of setting up a session differs widely from one type of usage to another. At its simplest it is merely a matter of sending a connection request to a distant node, and accepting its confirmation. The Layer 5 software may generate messages for this purpose such as the CALL REQUEST and CALL ACCEPTED packets shown in Fig. 12.5. After the session it sends messages such as the CLEAR REQUEST and CLEAR CONFIRMATION packets of Fig. 12.5.

In networks other than the simplest, an authorization procedure is needed to determine whether an incoming request for a session is from an authorized user. This may be done simply or it may be an elaborate security procedure.

Particularly important with intelligent machines is the process of *binding* to make sure that machines have the capability and correct protocols for communication.

BINDING

The term *bind* refers to the agreement which two parties make saying that they will work together with certain protocols to achieve a particular result. One party may send a BIND instruction to another; the other either agrees and sends a BIND instruction back or else disagrees and sends a negative response back. It is rather like the signing of a contract between the two parties. Before the contract is signed, some details of what is in it have to be agreed upon.

In order to BIND a coffee machine you press a button or put a coin in it. The machine gives a positive response to the BIND by switching on a light or making a buzzing noise. Before that you may have had to establish certain *parameters* which govern its work, such as CREAM, SUGAR, EXTRA SUGAR, LARGE, etc. The machine may respond negatively, possibly because of lack of authorization (foreign coin), possibly because your parameters were invalid (CHICKEN SOUP with EXTRA CREAM and SUGAR), possibly because of lack of resources (no cream left) and possibly because of breakdown.

A beverage machine has a limited range of resources and parameters. A computer may have a vast range. The computer can enter into communication with many different users which may require different resources, different Layer 6 or 7 protocols, or different parameters within one protocol. A BIND command, or statements which pass between machines prior to that command for the purposes of setting up a session, contain details of the parameters and resources to be used in the session. A response to

BOX 15.1 Possible functions of the session services subsystem

(A few of these functions are also listed as transport subsystem functions, because some transport subsystems perform them and some do not.)

1. *Assistance in Establishing a Session*

- Determine where a requested function is performed, or where requested data reside.
- Establish communications with the node which owns or controls the requested function or data. Obtain its agreement to establish a session.
- Check that the communicating nodes have the resources, such as buffering, necessary for the communication.
- Check that the communicating nodes have the software necessary for the communication.
- Exchange information about protocols to be used in the communication.

2. *Basic Networking Functions*

- Convert the high-level statements or requests of the user programs into the protocols of the transport subsystem.
- Correlate the requests and responses to those requests.
- Queue the messages.
- Prioritize the messages.
- Divide messages into slices when they are too long for the transport subsystem and reassemble them after transmission.
- Use serial numbers to maintain the correct sequence of messages, if this is not guaranteed by the transport subsystem.
- Perform flow control to prevent overloading the user programs.
- Control the timing of when messages are sent in order to make efficient use of distant mechanical devices with their own timing, such as printers and storage units. This is referred to as "pacing."

3. *Application Macroinstructions*

- Process macroinstructions of programs written in conventional languages, e.g., GET, PUT, OPEN, and CLOSE in COBOL programs which now refer to distant facilities.

BOX 15.1 *Continued*

- Provide remote/local independence, i.e., the same program is used whether the facility it refers to is local or remote.

- Process application program instructions referring to virtual terminals, virtual presentation space, etc.

- Process macroinstructions which are more network-oriented, e.g., CONNECT, DISCONNECT, TRANSMIT, and INTERRUPT.

- Process commands from user processes which do not employ conventional programming, e.g., report generators, data base interrogation languages, graphics dialogues, and special-purpose machines such as bank customer terminals.

4. *Program Control Facilities*

- Down-line loading and execution of programs.

- Up-line dumping.

- Portability of programs.

- Job control commands for network machines.

- Interface to job control language of operating systems.

5. *File Access Functions*

- Provide access to single records (read, modify, delete, or insert new records).

- Transfer whole files or portions of files. The node which has the file accepts one command to transmit the file and then sends it in a sequence of messages with appropriate control of pacing.

- Insert and interpret end-of-record and end-of-file indicators in the messages.

- Search a file or multiple dispersed files to find information specified with secondary keys.

- Facilitate distributed data-base operations (e.g., determine what physical records are needed to provide the logical data a user needs; determine where these data are located; access the data via the transport subsystem).

- Find the physical location of data which are referred to symbolically.

6. *Recovery and Error Control*

- Perform end-to-end acknowledgments and sequence-number checking, if it is felt necessary to have an additional check external to the transport subsystem.

BOX 15.1 *Continued*

- Operate batch controls (e.g., both ends of the link take totals of the records transmitted and compare them).

- Recover from a *reset* or *restart* condition in the transport subsystem. Layer 4 attempts to recover, retransmitting what is necessary, *without breaking the session.*

- Provide orderly session closedown if that becomes necessary, and preserve data integrity when the session restarts.

- Checkpoint restart. The messages are divided into recoverable groups. If something goes wrong the transmission is restarted at the beginning of the group—a checkpoint.

- Provide operator controls which bridge periods of failure, e.g., a cash count in a banking terminal.

7. Editing and Translation

- Perform code conversion.

- Format the data for preprinted stationery.

- Format the data to fill a screen, print tables, etc.

- Add user appendages to data, such as page headers, dates, page numbers, and repetitive information.

- Format the data for maximum clarity and attractiveness.

- Use graphics to create graphs or charts.

- Format the data to meet the record specifications of an application program.

8. Dialogue Software

- Store frequently used wording and panels, and display these upon receipt of an identifying code.

- Insert variable data into stored panels, and display them.

- Facilitate and control data collection.

- Facilitate and control data entry by a terminal operator.

- Operate menu selection, command-and-response, or other form of application-independent dialogue in which only the results of the dialogue are transmitted.

- Conduct data base interrogation dialogues which assist a terminal operator in formulating data base queries or operations.

BOX 15.1 *Continued*

9. *Virtual Operations and Transparency*

- Permit users to refer to virtual terminals. The Layer 4 software does the conversion between the virtual and real terminal formats and control signals.

- Permit the use of virtual machines other than terminals.

- Permit programmers to use *logical* input/output or display spaces, and map these to the characteristics of specific machines.

- Possibly provide user access to more than one transport subsystem (e.g., a leased line system with Layer 3 software, and a value-added carrier network).

- Select the network end protocol to use on the basis of least-cost routing.

- Make the operation of the transport subsystem or subsystems invisible to the users.

10. *Compaction*

- Perform code conversion to reduce the number of bits transmitted (e.g., compaction of ASCII code characters, zero and blank suppression, Huffman encoding).

- Use editing to reduce message lengths.

- Substitute coded identification numbers for repetitively used screens, formats, messages, or segments of text.

11. *Payment Functions*

- Record resource usage for billing purposes.

- Record usage of copyright programs, data, or text, for the establishment of royalties.

- Issue or respond to requests for reverse charging.

12. *Security and Audit Functions*

- Screen incoming calls, permitting only those from authorized users.

- Control access, i.e., one machine or user can have a session only with certain specified machines or users.

- Issue or check passwords.

- Use cryptography to encipher and decipher messages transmitted where high transmission security is needed (e.g., with electronic fund transfer).

- Maintain journals or audit trails.

the BIND agrees, disagrees, or possibly modifies the request. The *resources* may include buffer storage, logging file space, a suitable communications path, software modules, cryptography, etc. The *protocols* agreed upon may be protocols for end-to-end error control, end-to-end flow control, editing, specified virtual terminal operations, conversion, etc. The *parameters* may include timing parameters, or specify whether data interchange proceeds in a full-duplex or half-duplex fashion, what formats are to be used for editing, etc.

Once both parties have signed the contract in this way, communication between the applications environments begins.

We have described binding which takes place when a session is initiated. Binding *could* take place at the following times:

1. In the factory. In other words the machines always communicate in the same way.

2. When the system software is generated.

3. When a network is started up or a machine or software ("logical unit," "virtual terminal," application environment") is initiated.

4. When a session is established.

5. In mid-session when a particular interaction is initiated.

BASIC NETWORKING　　　Part of the Session Services Subsystem may execute func-
FUNCTIONS　　　tions which are necessary in order to utilize the transport
　　　subsystem.

If Layer 4 reassembles long messages it must have some form of *message numbering* to control this. The sequential numbering will also be used to ensure that messages are not lost or duplicated. Sequential numbering may also be needed at Layer 6 to correlate session messages with the responses to those messages. In some manufacturers' architectures the Layer 4 functions are integrated with Layer 6 functions.

PACING　　　We mentioned the importance of regulating the rate of
　　　flow in the transport network to prevent congestion and
traffic jams. Control of timing is also needed in the Session Services Subsystem to make efficient use of the machines and processes which are connected to the network. For example a line printer has a cycle time—the time to print one line. If the data are not ready at the start of the print cycle it misses a complete cycle. On the other hand, it has a limited buffer. Suppose that the buffer on a remote printer can hold three lines of print. If data are sent to it too fast the buffer capacity will be exceeded; data will be lost and have to be retransmitted. So sending data too fast or too slowly causes a drop in performance. Furthermore the timing varies because the printer skips blank lines and skips from one page to another. To use the remote printer efficiently there needs to be an end-to-end exhange of timing signals. This is called "pacing."

Pacing control is needed when any continuous electromechanical process is used remotely. A storage unit has variable access times and if a file is being written the sending machine must know when to send records. This control of timing is quite separate from the Layer 3 control of flow. In an integrated architecture common timing mechanisms could be used. More often the transport network has *its* flow control mechanism and the higher layer pacing mechanism is separate. We discuss this in Chapter 20.

HIGH-LEVEL   As we commented in Chapter 12, applications programs
MACROINSTRUCTIONS   should employ high-level macroinstructions for using the network, such as OPEN, CLOSE, GET, and PUT. In general, it is desirable that the macroinstructions for using a local peripheral device should be the same as those for using a remote device. There should be *local/remote transparency*. The programmer need not necessarily know the location of the file or printer that his program employs.

It is necessary for interpreters or compilers to translate the high-level commands into the commands which the network can accept. This may be regarded as a Layer 4 function; it may be a function of layers external to Layer 4, or it may be a function of application software. If the interface to the transport network is that in the CCITT X.25 Recommendation, then Layer 4 must ranslate whatever high-level commands it receives into X.25 packets such as those shown in Fig. 12.8. The outer layers must correlate the responses with the commands and deliver the data in whatever form the user process requires.

There is a rapidly increasing number of user processes which do not use conventional programming languages with instructions like GET, PUT, etc. Instead there are report generators, data base interrogation languages, information retrieval dialogues, graphics dialogues, and machines for special purposes such as bank customer terminals, teaching machines, and home television sets connected to Viewdata-like networks. A layer of software (hardware or firmware) is needed which will connect the mechanisms or programs of these to the transport network interface.

DOWN-LINE LOADING   Intelligent terminals, cluster controllers, and minicomputers connected to networks often have their programs loaded from a larger distant machine. A data processing center in charge of a network may manage, store, test, and maintain the programs throughout the network. Session services software has the capability to transmit a program to a distant machine, and initialize its use: transmit, load, and go.

UP-LINE DUMPING   Conversely a dump may be taken of a distant program for testing or security purposes. The program is transmitted to a parent computer which prints it, stores it, or displays it.

These functions are called *down-line loading* and *up-line dumping*.

PROGRAM PORTABILITY   It is often desirable that a program can be moved easily from one machine to another, or distributed from a parent machine to many others. If the machines are exactly compatible this merely requires facilities for down-line loading and up-line dumping. If the machines have different instruction sets, the programs will have to be recompiled for the different machines and the network software must manage the separate copies, down-line loading them as required.

JOB CONTROL STATEMENTS   A conventional computer with no network is controlled with a set of commands and statements sometimes known collectively as a job control language. A broadly equivalent set of commands and responses is used on some networks to link the job control interfaces of major operating systems. These control both batch jobs and single transaction processing. On Sperry Univac's Distributed Communications Architecture, for example, these job control commands and responses are part of the Port Presentation Services for each logical port on the network (equivalent to ISO Layer 6).

The future of network architectures will be related to the future of operating systems. Rather than having an operating system in one room controlling jobs, we need distributed control with the operating systems of many machines cooperating. Now that major network architectures have been defined, operating systems and other software will evolve to encompass the distributed environment. A logical link on a network is similar to a channel in a machine room, only slower. Distributed network-wide operating systems are theoretically possible. However, it may be better to have disjoint autonomous operating systems in separate machines with protocols linking them. It would be possible to build future operating systems to employ networking primitives.

FILE ACCESS   A particularly important function of networks is to provide access to remote storage units.

This requires a command set for reading or writing complete files, and for reading, writing, deleting and inserting single records. It needs the ability to communicate end-of-file and exception conditions. Where data bases are used, it needs the various data base commands and exception conditions to be handled on a network basis.

When more than one machine or user can update the same file (or data base), controls must be devised to prevent them interfering with one another. While one user is making a change the others must be briefly locked out, but in locking them out the possibility of deadlocks must be avoided (as discussed in Chapter 34).

Data base management systems are complex. It is much more complex to extend them to a distributed environment. Much of the complexity comes from the need to preserve data integrity when multiple users may be updating the same data, and when a variety of types of failures can occur. Because of this there will always be strong arguments for centralizing certain types of data [1].

In some networks a machine may make a reference to data, addressed symbolically, without knowing where that data resides. A function of the network software is then to find the data, using a directory.

RECOVERY
AND ERROR CONTROL

The transport subsystem, as we have commented, has its own error and recovery control. This usually has to be supplemented with *end-to-end* error control external to the transport subsystem.

Error control is built into Layer 2 protocols for physical link control, such as HDLC, SDLC, etc. It is also built into Layer 3 logical link control such as the CCITT X.25 standard. Most major architectures also have end-to-end error control in Layer 4. The Session Services Subsystem may also have forms of error control. Why all of these? It is a principle of layered architectures that errors or failures should be taken care of at the lowest level possible. If a physical link control mechanism can deal with a transmission error, it should not allow the error to cause problems at higher levels. The types of failure that the different layers can cope with are different. Layer 2 deals with bit errors in transmission. Layer 3 deals with failures of circuits or switching nodes, bypassing them if possible. Layer 4 deals with higher-level problems like failures which cause sessions to be terminated. In addition the Session Services Subsystem may deal with errors in protocol usage which disrupt communication between two users: printers running out of paper, invalid requests, and so on.

Chapter 33 discusses outer layer errors and recovery.

EDITING

In the days of punched-card installations, the clanking machines had changeable panels which the operators wired with masses of plug wires rather like colored spaghetti. These were used for editing. The relatively small number of characters compressed into a punched card were distributed on to preprinted stationery, constant fields were added, and totals taken as directed by the panel wiring.

In networks the data are not squeezed into a punched card; they are squeezed into a *packet*. As with punched cards, the data in packets can be edited to produce attractive printouts, invoices, statements, and screen displays. The editing is not done by a plug-wired panel but by an intelligent terminal, controller, or minicomputer. A coded format is used to control the operation. The machine which does the editing can store many such formats. The format to be used may be selected when a session is set up, or it may be selected dynamically in mid-session. A data entry operation or a dialogue with a screen can employ many different formats. The Session Service message headers may contain a code saying which format is to be used with that message.

One sometimes sees printouts from terminals which are unattractive or confusing because of attempts to minimize the number of characters transmitted (including blank characters). I receive terminal-printed statements from a stockbroker which are barely intelligible. There is no longer an excuse for unattractive printouts or displays. Peripheral intelligence should be used to format the data with clarity.

For some uses of data, graphs and charts are a particularly informative type of display. Although they are slow to transmit over telephone-speed lines, they may be created rapidly at a peripheral machine.

COMPACTION

Processing costs are dropping much more rapidly than transmission costs. Increasingly it will be economically advantageous to compress data so as to lower the number of bits transmitted. The editing of messages for printing or display helps to reduce the numbers of bits transmitted. There is also a variety of compaction techniques, discussed in Chapter 28.

In addition to saving transmission cost on some networks, compaction can reduce response times significantly when the data are long enough to take many seconds to transmit.

DIALOGUE

The primary consideration in dialogue design should be to make the system as easy to use and as psychologically effective as possible. To do so requires fast responses at times and sometimes a large number of characters for displaying. Some of these characters are standard verbiage or display panels which can be stored peripherally. Instead of transmitting them, the network transmits a coded reference to them—five characters perhaps instead of five hundred.

The panels which are displayed in a screen dialogue may be standard panels but with some variable information in them. The message transmitted contains the variable information, and identification of the panel. Associated with the panel are some instructions or an editing format saying how the variable information is to be inserted into the panel. The panel filing and editing capability may be part of the Layer 6 software.

The terminal software may control basic definable operations such as data collection, job entry, menu selection dialogues, file searching, or data base inquiry. These can each form the basis of a predefined Layer 6 protocol. The Layer 6 software may be able to employ many such protocols. The ones to be used are selected when the session is established.

In some network architectures, users can either use standard *presentation services* or else define their own, to be invoked when a session is set up.

VIRTUAL TERMINALS

It would be useful if a person at any terminal could connect to the facilities of a network. The problem is that a great diversity of terminals exist. They employ different control procedures, different-size screens and different mechanisms. The computer which the person wishes to use may not know what control procedures to use to communicate with his terminal. It is therefore desirable that there should be some standardization of the terminals in use (or at least the interfaces to them).

As the cost of electronics drops the diversity of terminals will increase. Standardization should not inhibit the introduction of better terminal mechanisms and designs. Therefore network authorities refer to a make-believe terminal—a *virtual network terminal*. This has defined control procedures and display areas. A programmer can be told exactly how to communicate with the virtual terminal. The real terminal at which an end user is sitting may be different, so that Layer 6 software converts the control signals and data for the virtual terminal into those for the real terminal, and vice versa. A wide variety of different terminals can then communicate with the same application program.

Figure 15.1 illustrates this. The application process communicates using the virtual terminal protocols. The Layer 6 software (or firmware) at the terminal converts these to whatever local conventions are used. Host computers from different manufacturers unfortunately use different virtual terminal protocols. The terminal controller may therefore store more than one conversion procedure. At one time it communicates with Manufacturer A using his protocol. At another time it communicates with Manufacturer B using a protocol defined by a standards committee.

In some cases the terminals may be simple unintelligent machines connected by telephone lines to a controller with a buffer and software which makes them appear like a defined virtual terminal.

Terminals differ greatly in their basic characteristics. There is not much resemblance between a credit checking terminal with a bank-card reader, and a visual display unit with a light pen. Furthermore there may be not one but many widely accepted standards for terminals in the future—telex machines, ASCII visual display units, electronic fund transfer terminals, home Viewdata-like television sets, and so on. Because of this, host computers should have multiple standard or virtual terminal interfaces. The agreement about which to use must be made when a session is established.

Part of the conversion process is sometimes the conversion from one character set to another, e.g., telex to ASCII.

SECURITY   Several techniques are used for making a network secure. These are discussed in Chapter 35. They include the encyphering of messages, controlling access to the network, allowing one machine to have sessions only with certain specified machines, and thoroughly checking the authorization of network users. Audit trails or logs may be maintained for security purposes. Tightly controlled communication with security officers' consoles may be provided.

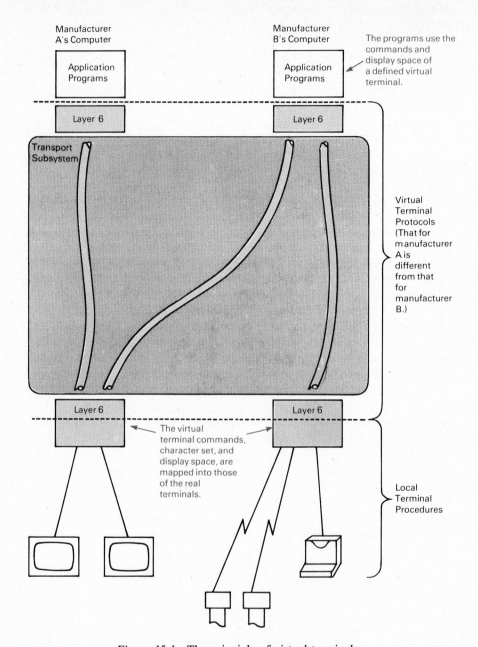

Manufacturer
A's Computer

Application
Programs

Manufacturer
B's Computer

Application
Programs

The programs use the
commands and
display space of
a defined virtual
terminal.

Layer 6

Layer 6

Transport
Subsystem

Virtual
Terminal
Protocols
(That for
manufacturer
A is
different
from that
for
manufacturer
B.)

Layer 6

Layer 6

The virtual
terminal commands,
character set, and
display space, are
mapped into those
of the real
terminals.

Local
Terminal
Procedures

Figure 15.1   The principle of virtual terminals.

TRANSPARENT AND NONTRANSPARENT SERVICES

Many of the functions listed in Box 15.1 can be invisible to the application programmer. He does not need to know whether compaction or cryptography is being used, or how it is used. He does not need to know that long messages are cut into slices before transmission. Some of the functions cannot be invisible. For example, if repetitive phrases, headers, or panels are stored remotely from the program and referred to by brief identifiers, then the programmer must understand this and have a list of the formats and identifiers that are used. If dialogue software is used at a remote terminal location and only the results of the dialogue transmitted to the application program, then the application programmer must have specifications of the resulting messages which his program will receive.

One way of subdividing the Session Services software could be to split it into transparent and nontransparent layers as shown in Fig. 15.2. The nontransparent outmost layer contains services which need a special interface to the application program which must be specified in detail. The transparent layer is invisible to the application program.

Exactly how the diverse functions of Box 15.1 are allocated to the ISO layers or the layers of manufacturers' architectures will be the subject of many years' debate and systems evolution.

PUTTING IT ALL TOGETHER

To summarize, Fig. 15.3 shows the modules of software (or microcode or chips) which would exist in a full-function node following the ISO 7-layer proposed standards.

There is one module of Layer 1 and 2 control for each circuit. Layer 2 is HDLC. In most systems today Layer 1 is CCITT V.24 but as common carriers and PTT's provide digital circuits or digital interfaces to their circuits, it will increasingly be the cleaner, simpler interface of CCITT X.21 (with no modems).

Layer 3 is the interface to a common network shared by all the machines in a system or all the machines in many systems. This may be a packet switching network,

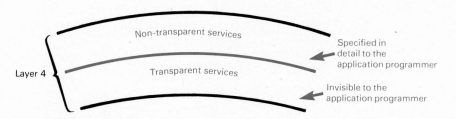

Figure 15.2   Session Services software divided into transparent and nontransparent sublayers.

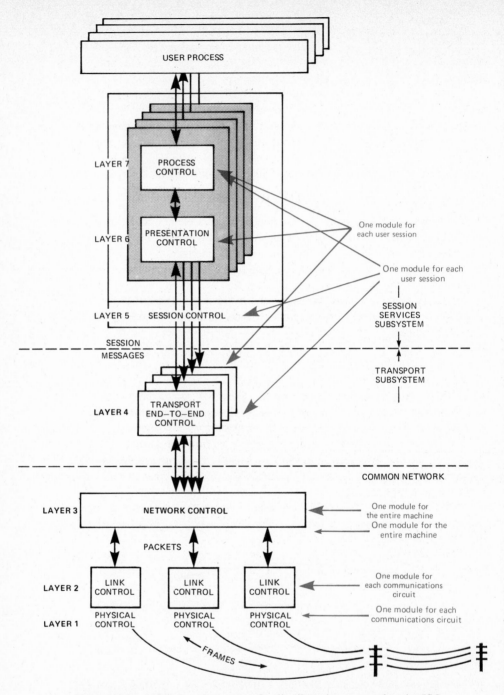

Figure 15.3 A full-function node of a distributed system using the ISO
7-layer architecture.

or a leased-line concentrator or other network with a CCITT X.25 interface to it. One module of Layer 3 exists for the entire machine handling the transmission and reception.

The higher layers are session oriented. Layers 4, 6, and 7 have one module for each session using common code but maintaining separate data, registers, etc. The interface between the higher layers and Layer 4 is the interface to a Transport Service which would be the same with a wide variety of types of transmission resources. In particular it might use an X.21 digital leased line or circuit-switched network with no packet interface, possible no Layer 3.

Layer 5 manages the establishment and disestablishment of users' sessions, and manages the restart and recovery after failures.

Exactly how the diverse functions of Box 15.1 are allocated to the ISO layers or the layers of manufacturers' architectures will be the subject of many years' debate and systems evolution.

At the time of writing the manufacturers' architectures do not map exactly into the breakdown of function in Fig 15.3, although there is some similarity. Fig. 15.4 shows a full-function node of IBM's SNA (Systems Network Architecture).

Layer 1 is identical. Layer 2 uses SDLC, a permissible subset of HDLC. Layer 3, *Path Control,* is broadly equivalent to Layer 3 of X.25 but bears no resemblance in detail.

SNA's *Transmission Control* contains more functions than those in the ISO Layer 4. It contains functions which relate to more than merely the transport service, and which ISO would place in Layer 6. For example the *Transmission Header* (TH) contains bits for session *pacing* control, agreements about who speaks when (Must every message have a user response or can several messages be transmitted before there is a response?), grouping of separate messages into *chains, bracketing* of dialogue messages and responses which represent one transaction, and an indication of whether there is a higher level header. The reason why so much has been included in the *Transmission Header* is that many messages do not have a higher level header.

The major activity of SNA's *Function Management* is called *Presentation Services* which corresponds to ISO's *Presentation Control.* Layer 7 functions may be in software, such as distributed data base software, external to SNA.

ISO Layer 5 has its equivalent in SNA: *Logical Unit Services* and *Physical Unit Services* which set up and serve the SNA sessions.

All manufacturers who want to market an advanced product line for distributed processing must create components (software, microcode, or chips) broadly equivalent to Fig. 15.3.

The problem at the time of writing is they are creating different ones. There is no manufacturer-independent standardization yet at the higher layers. Instead there are IBM standards, DEC standards, Univac standards, and so on. This creates a severe dilemma for DP management. Which standards should they select? How can machines of different manufacturers be linked? What should be their corporate strategy for distributed systems? [2]

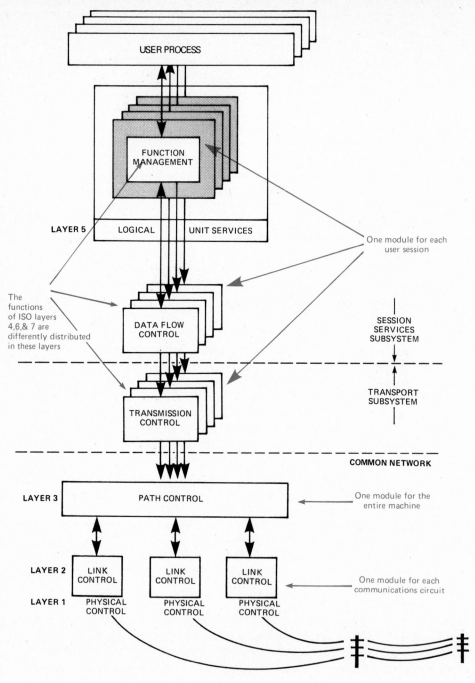

USER PROCESS

FUNCTION MANAGEMENT

LAYER 5 LOGICAL UNIT SERVICES

One module for each
user session

The
functions
of ISO layers
4,6,& 7 are
differently distributed
in these layers

DATA FLOW
CONTROL

SESSION
SERVICES
SUBSYSTEM

TRANSPORT
SUBSYSTEM

TRANSMISSION
CONTROL

COMMON NETWORK

LAYER 3 PATH CONTROL

One module for the
entire machine

LAYER 2 LINK
CONTROL   LINK
CONTROL   LINK
CONTROL

One module for each
communications circuit

LAYER 1 PHYSICAL
CONTROL   PHYSICAL
CONTROL   PHYSICAL
CONTROL

Figure 15.4

REFERENCE

1. See the author's forthcoming book *Design of Distributed Data Processing*.

2. James Martin, *Corporate Strategy for Distributed Processing*. Savant, 2 New Street, Carnforth, Lancs., LA59BX, England, 1980.

16 NETWORK MANAGEMENT

An office needs a variety of control and management functions to make it operate with the correct flow of paperwork. The same is true of a computer network. Some are low-level repetitive functions performed by a clerk each minute he is working at his desk. Others are slightly less repetitive and are needed to initiate the handling of a new customer, terminate the handling of an older customer, and deal with simple problems in a mechanical predefined manner. Others need intelligence and are not predefined. These fall into two categories: those concerned with operation and maintenance, i. e., keeping the existing system working, and those concerned with modifying, auditing, or overseeing the existing system.

In discussing computer networks the following four terms are used: *control, management, maintenance,* and *administration.* These words are sometimes used rather loosely. For clarity we will define them as follows:

- *Control* refers to the second-by-second operation of hardware or software functions that are repeated continuously for an extensive time: for example, the normal flow of data through the transport subsystem; or the normal operation of a session which is already established.

- *Management* refers to software functions which are not part of the second-by-second repetitive control of operations. These functions could cease and the *control* mechanisms would continue to work, at least for a time. Management functions include the setting up of sessions, the termination of sessions, accounting and charging for sessions, programmed recovery, automatic switchover, and checkpoint-restart.

- *Maintenance* refers to the mainly human activity of keeping the network running—diagnosing failures, making and testing repairs, routine maintenance. To assist this human function a variety of machine facilities are needed including diagnostics, error logging, and terminals and programs which enable the service engineers to check the network, run the diagnostics, and correct problems.

- *Administration* refers to the *human* work associated with operating the network. A network administrator starts up the network, shuts it down, monitors its performance, brings up new circuits or reconfigures the network when necessary, brings new user machines on-line, and is concerned with potential security violations. The network administrator requires a terminal and computer programs, and is a special type of network end-user. Software is needed throughout the network to assist in network administration.

NETWORK OWNERS AND USERS

The distinction between owners and users is important. The owners operate the network as a service for the users. They are not interested in how the users employ it providing that they obey the rules. The owners bill the users for their employment of the network resources.

The owners employ different management facilities from the users. The owners are concerned with billing, network performance, reliability, and fast correction of problems. The users are concerned with end-to-end protocols and file usage, end-to-end session control and services, accuracy control, availability, end-to-end pacing, and security.

The management and administrative functions may be divided into modules serving these two groups.

DISTRIBUTION OF MANAGEMENT

Individual networks differ in the extent to which they distribute or centralize the above functions.

Control decisions, such as which way to route the packets, can be entirely centralized, partially centralized, made by multiple centers, or completely distributed.

Management decisions may be centralized to a greater extent. Some, such as changing the routing when failures occur, could be decentralized. Networks other than simple onces often have multiple management modules which intercommunicate for puposes of setting up and disconnecting sessions, dealing with failures, maintaining accounts for billing, and so on.

Maintenance engineers like to access the network from any user node and run tests or diagnostics. The diagnostic programs may reside only in certain computers, but can be invoked from anywhere on the network. Network information which the engineers need, such as failure reports and error statistics may be transmitted to a central location.

Administration of the network as a whole may take place at one location. This center maintains statistics on network use, congestion, and performance. The staff there may start up and close down the network (though some networks never close). They reconfigure the network, possibly run simulations of it, deal with failures, sometimes telephoning a remote location to get a failure fixed, bring new devices, circuits, and

BOX 16.1 Facilities which may exist in network management and administration software

1. Session services

- Request to have sessions are received.
- The session requests are validated.
- Resources are allocated to sessions.
- Subchannels, table entries, session identifiers, etc., are assigned.
- The route for the session is selected. Alternative routes in case of failure may also be selected. (This is for systems without dynamic routing of packets.)
- The communicating parties are *bound* and their session initiated.
- When it is over the communicating parties are *unbound* and their session terminated.
- When failures occur, session recovery is initiated.
- Accounting information is gathered for billing purposes.
- Requests for network sessions with devices of foreign architecture are handled.

2. Handling of physical resources

- A directory of physical resources is maintained (processors, terminals, cluster controllers, peripherals, channels, circuits, line groups, etc.)
- The management software permits these physical resources to be activated and deactivated.
- Dynamic reconfiguration may take place when failures occur.
- Recovery action may be initiated.
- Information is provided to the network operators to enable them to deal with the physical resources.
- Information is provided to the maintenance engineers about the physical resources.
- Resources are monitored for performance measurement.

3. Maintenance

- Terminal facilities are provided for maintenance engineers to access the network.
- Errors and failures are logged.
- Reports and analyses of the errors and failures are done and made available at the engineer terminals.

BOX 16.1 *Continued*

- Problems are automatically reported to a network operator.
- Diagnostics and confidence tests are run, possibly triggered automatically, possibly by an operator or engineer.
- Decisions to take down network components or circuits are made, based on the severity or frequency of errors.

4. Security

- A surveillance log is maintained of all security procedural violations.
- The surveillance log is analyzed for the security officer, highlighting occurrences needing immediate attention.
- Triggering of alarms on detection of certain types of procedural violations.
- Files of passwords, cryptography keys, or other security information are securely managed.
- Terminals are provided for security officer functions.

5. Administration

- Terminals are provided for network operators.
- The operators can display details of the network and its various resources.
- The operator can start and stop the network.
- An operator can activate and deactivate network components.
- An operator can start and stop application programs.
- An operator can reconfigure the network dynamically (i.e., without shutting it down).
- An operator can change specifications of network control mechanisms.
- An operator can down-line load programs.
- An operator can initiate a dump of programs in peripheral machines, possibly transmitting the dump to a larger machine for printing.
- An operator can initiate trace or statistics-gathering programs.
- An operator can initiate performance measurement aids.
- Network performance can be measured, analyzed, and possibly experimented with.
- Information is collected for billing users and bills are prepared.

end users on-line, and are generally aware of the operational status of the network as a whole.

In complex networks there may be multiple administration centers, each dealing with a portion of the network. When a network is a vertical and horizontal combination as in Fig. 4.2, the computer at the top of each vertical portion may perform management and administration functions for that portion. In IBM's Systems Network Architecture (SNA) the vertical groupings are called *domains*. A host computer at the top of each domain carries out management functions for its domain, and communicates horizontally with management modules at the top of other domains. Administration for each domain may be done at the top of that domain; administration for the horizontal links or the entire network could be done at one specific computer center. There may be multiple administrator terminals, each at any point in the network, and each having jurisdiction over a defined set of links and devices in its own domain or in other domains. The administrator terminals report to a parent (VTAM or TCAM) at the top of their domain.

Security is handled in different ways by different organizations. Sometimes the security officer is different from the network administrator. He or she needs a terminal from which to monitor the network and be provided with reports on network problems, misuse, and violations of security procedures whether they are accidental or possibly deliberate. Sometimes different security officers are concerned with different portions of a network.

Box 16.1 summarizes the various features for management and adminstration that a network might employ.

CONTROL MECHANISMS

Control mechanisms are the subject of Part III of this book. It is necessary to have error control, flow control, and routing control as data pass through Transport Subsystem, and pacing control and control of protocol usage in the Session Services Subsystem.

MANAGEMENT MODULES

Network management often resides in several different places in modules which communicate across the network.

There needs to be some form of manager in or close to end-user environment. It may have to make a request to central management for a session to be set up. If we were concerned only with the transmission subsystem the user management would have the task of setting up and disconnecting the calls. It would be a person saying to a secretary, "Get me a call to Fred in Hong Kong." With a CCITT X.25 network this could mean sending the packets which set up and disconnect a virtual call, as shown in Fig. 12.8. Usually, however, we are also concerned with higher layer functions, and these need various allocating resources and protocol agreements establishing when a session is set up.

As we commented earlier, in setting up a session the management must ensure that the communicating parties

- are authorized to communicate,
- have the facilities they need to communicate, and
- agree upon the manner in which they shall communicate.

Buffer space must be allocated, control of timing (pacing or flow control) must be agreed upon, security authorization must be checked, use of virtual network terminal protocols or file transfer protocols must be agreed upon, procedures for editing, compaction, conversion, or encryption may have to be agreed upon, and so on—in fact any of the functions listed in the previous chapter.

CENTRALIZED VS DECENTRALIZED MANAGEMENT
Where should the above management functions take place?

In some architectures the setting up and management of a session is done by the machines which participate in the session. In others it is done by a third party—centralized management.

In general there are four types of approaches to control or management; these are shown in Figs. 16.1 and 16.2

First, there may be no separate manager. The communicating machines take care of their own problems. This situation is shown in the top two diagrams of Fig. 16.2.

In this situation there may be a *primary-secondary (master-slave)* relationship. One of the two machines is designated the primary (master) and the other the secondary (slave). The primary initiates the exchange, and when something goes wrong the primary is responsible for the recovering action.

Alternatively the two communicating machines may be equal, with no primary-secondary relationship between them (second diagram of Fig. 16.2). They are *peer-coupled*, i.e., of equal status. Either machine can initiate the exchange. When a failure occurs the machine which initiated the exchange (or initiated the transaction that is affected) is responsible for recovery.

Until the mid-1970's most teleprocessing used a primary-secondary relationship between the communicating machines. This was because usually one of the two machines was rather dumb. It was a terminal or secondary (slave) device designed to respond in a fairly simple fashion to the commands from the primary (master) which was usually a computer. By the late 1970's intelligent terminals, intelligent controllers, and computer-to-computer communication were common, and so peer-coupled protocols were practical. A peer-coupled protocol is usually a *balanced* or *symmetrical* protocol in which both machines have the same algorithms. The advantage of this is that any such machine can communicate with any other and hence there is greater flexibility. With primary-secondary systems one secondary station usually cannot com-

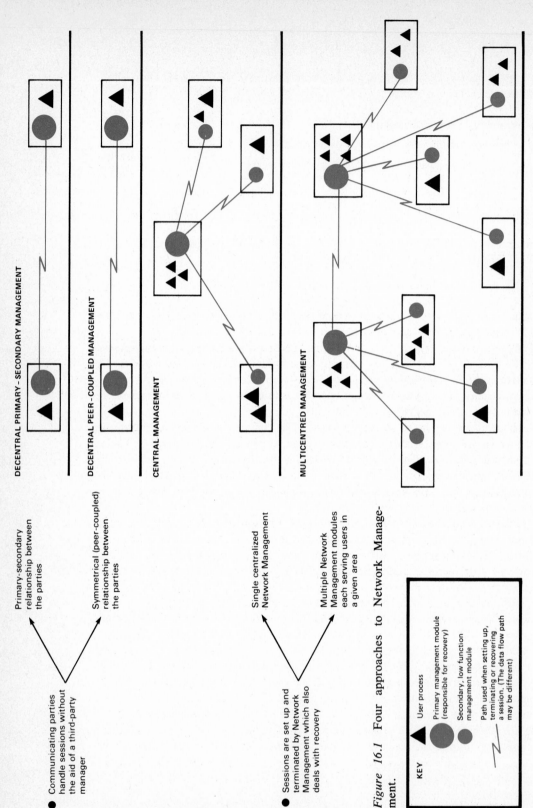

Figure 16.1 Four approaches to Network Management.

Figure 16.2 Four approaches to Network Management.

municate with another secondary, except via a primary. A computer may have to be-have as a primary for some communications and a secondary for others.

It is neater, and not necessarily more complicated, to avoid primary-secondary relationships and give each computer and terminal controller the same set of protocols.

Second, there are architectures in which a separate manager is employed. These are shown in the second two diagrams of Fig. 16.2. These fall into two categories: centralized systems with one network manager, and systems with multiple network managers as in the bottom diagram of Fig. 16.2.

If the using machines are dumb they need the help of network managers to set up their sessions. If they are intelligent they *could* set up their own sessions without the help of a network manager. As microprocessors gain more power and machines gain more intelligence, there becomes less reason for having a separate network manager to set up sessions and handle recovery. Networks interconnecting computers, such as AR-PANET, do not have separate machines for session management. Nor do most network architectures for minicomputers. Some large computer manufacturers such as IBM and Univac *do* have centralized or multicentered session management. Powerful host computers manage the interconnection of peripheral, less powerful machines.

An argument for centralized session management is that the network manager can allocate the network resources in an optimal manner. The manager can make sure that there are enough trunks and buffers for the session. It may select the route that the session traffic shall use. If there are more session requests than can be handled, it may give priority to the important ones. However, routing, trunk and buffer control, and priority can also be handled in a distributed fashion. Centralized session management can greatly assist in achieving an orderly recovery from failure. However, it has the disadvantage that when the central machine fails or has a software crash a large number of sessions may be affected. Centralized session management can control security, al-lowing processes to communicate only if they are authorized, and possibly allocating the cryptography keys.

The use of a session manager separate from the communicating parties can in-crease the *complexity* of setting up and terminating sessions and session recovery. Similarly, primary-secondary relationships can increase the complexity. The achievement of high availability is more complex with primary-secondary centralized management. Some of the architectures for distributed peer-coupled networks are rela-tively simple.

There are furious arguments among network architects about whether centralized or decentralized session management is the best. In practice both are working well. Decentralized session management appears cleaner and more flexible. Any ma-chine can set up a session to any other. But it needs more capability in the communi-cating parties. The need for primary–secondary relationships and centralized or multi-center management stems from the need to handle nodes of limited power. As the power of microprocessors grows, distributed, symmetrical protocols look more attrac-tive.

As the chips improve session management may increasingly be done in a symmetrical fashion with no need for a third-party manager. The type of configuration in Fig. 16.3 is attractive. All machines have a standard interface to a common network. Any machine can initiate a session to any other machine which has the requisite attributes. Each pair of communicating machines is responsible for its own session security and recovery.

Small, simple machines may have a parent which does session management for them, as at the bottom left of Fig. 16.3.

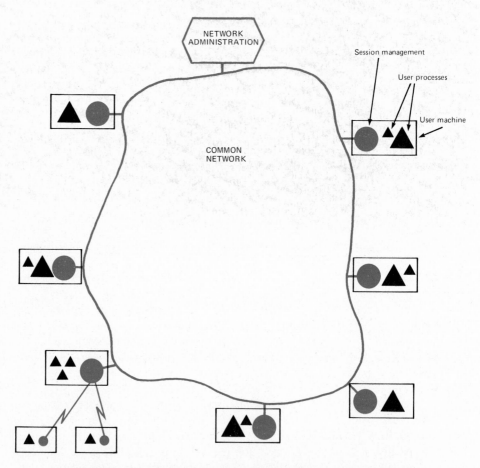

Figure 16.3 As chips and networks improve this form of management appears increasingly attractive. Any machine has the capability to have a session with any other machine without third-party management. All are connected to a common network which has its own network administration. Small, simple machines, as the bottom left-hand corner, may have a parent machine to set up and manage their sessions.

The management functions of the network *owners* are quite separate from those of the network *users*. The owner functions of network maintenance and administration may be centralized or bicentralized.

PERMANENT SESSIONS   If a management module in a user machine has to contact a centralized management module in order to set up sessions, there is usually a permanent session in effect between these two management modules. Every decentral management module is permanently in session with the requisite central management module. This is illustrated in Fig. 16.4. The purpose of this is so that a user can request a session at any time and it will be set up quickly.

The fact that there is a permanent session does not mean that any transmission capacity or buffer space is being used. That will only be the case when communication takes place over the session path. It does mean that requisite registers, linkages, or table entries are set up to enable the two management modules to communicate without delay.

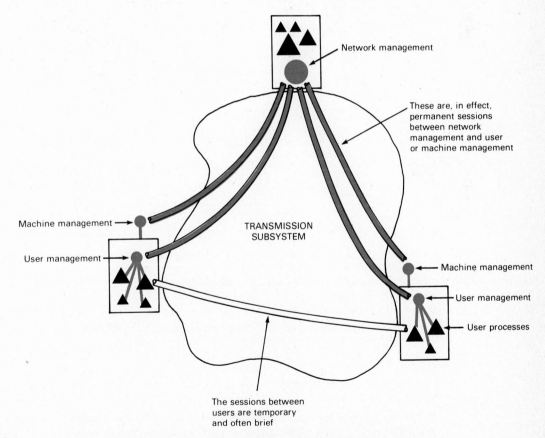

Figure 16.4 Permanent sessions for network management communication.

The central management, in addition to communicating with decentral session management, may also have links to the modules which manage *machines*. The purpose of this is to deal with problems such as printers running out of paper, machines not ready, storage units having long, unpredictable access times, and so on. Some architectures have permanent sessions in effect between machine management and network management modules.

If the network administrator module is separate from the network management, there may also be a permanent session between the network management module and network administrator module. Sperry Univac's architecture has three types of network

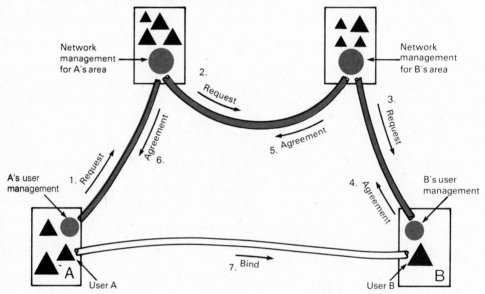

User A wants to have a session with User B in a part of the network controlled by a different manager. The setting up of the session proceeds as follows:

1. (Labeled "1" above) A's User Management uses its permanent session with its Network Management to request the user session.

2. The Network Management sends the request to the Network Management which controls B. (There is a permanent session between the Network Management modules).

3. The request is passed on to B's User Management.

4. B's User Management agrees that B can enter into the session with A. It allocates the appropriate resources and sends a message to its Network Management saying that it agrees.

5.& The Network Management modules pass the agreement message to A's User Management,
6. allocating any network resources that are necessary.

7. A's User Management allocates the session resources and issues a BIND command. The session can begin.

Figure 16.5 Managing the establishment of a session with multicentered Network Management. (Different network architectures use different words for software modules which accomplish this.)

management modules: local, area, and global network management services. The *local* module is used to serve each major group of *machines*. The *area* module serves the *user* Management (AMS, Application Management Services) with which it is permanently in session. The global module serves the network *administrator* for the entire network. The user management and local network management modules are permanently in session with the area network management, and the area network management modules are permanently in session with the one global network management module.

Figure 16.5 shows a session being set up between two users which report to different network managers. The request for the session is passed on between the network managers, and the agreement travels back by the same route. The user management allocates the necessary resources in the user environment. The network management allocates the necessary network resources and may establish the route through the network that the session traffic uses.

Different architectures use different words for this process. In IBM the network management modules are the SSCP (System Services Control Point) of TCAM (Tele-Communications Access Method) or VTAM (Virtual Telecommunication Access Method) residing in the host computers. The modules which act for the users are called Logical Units (LU). In Sperry Univac the network management modules are the area NMS (Network Management Services) and the modules in the user environment are the AMS (Application Management Services).

In a completely distributed system there are no centralized or higher-level facilities for the setting up of sessions. Establishing a session may still be a complex process in which protocols have to be agreed upon and resources allocated. This is the case in the Digital Equipment Corporation's DECNET architecture for interlinking minicomputers.

In a network which provides *only* the transport function, for example, a common carrier X.25 network or a corporate data service network, it is necessary to set up Layer 3 sessions (transport sessions). An exchange of commands such as that shown at the top and bottom of Fig. 12.8 might be sent from the user machines to request a *virtual call* or *logical circuit*. This operation could be managed in a centralized, multiple-center, or distributed fashion.

In an integrated architecture both Layer 3 and higher aspects of the session may be established by the same machines. If the transport network is architecturally separate from the Session Services Subsystem, it may be separately managed. This might be the case where the transport network is a separate X.25 facility which users plug into. The management of the X.25 virtual calls and permanent virtual circuits might be in a separate module from the session management. The former could be decentralized and the latter centralized.

SESSION FAILURE An important function of the management modules is to deal with failures.

Bit errors in transmission are dealt with automatically by the Layer 2 mechanism—physical link control (HDLC, SDLC, BISYNCH, etc.). Higher-level mechanisms must deal with problems such as lost packets, irretrievably damaged messages, node failures, line failures, security breaches, and harmful errors in protocol.

We discuss the ways in which these problems are handled in Part IV of the book. It is desirable that a management module be responsible for initiating the recovery action. This module will attempt to recover without terminating the session if possible. Failing this, it should attempt to close down the session in an orderly fashion without losing or damaging data, if possible.

THE NETWORK OPERATORS

A network operator has many functions to perform. He or she watches over the network with a console rather like the operator of an on-line computer. The console is often a terminal and can be located anywhere. There may be several network operators in different places, each with jurisdiction over a different set of nodes and facilities. This is often the case where a network serves several divisions of a corporation. Each division has its own computers and terminals, and these are administered separately from any other division.

The operator console is connected to network administration software which is in one or multiple centers. This software permits the network to be controlled in two types of ways. First, it may allow an administrator to *define* a network and *generate* the systems programs which control and manage the network. This tailors the network and places an upper bound on its facilities such as numbers of trunks, terminals, and buffers. Second, the software permits a network operator to monitor or control the network or part of the network. The operator can display the status of the various facilities, activate and deactivate nodes, start and stop various facilities, may be able to adjust priorities, and so on.

NETWORK OPERATOR COMMANDS

The operator uses a set of *network operator commands*. These are provided by the network administration software, for example IBM's VTAM. The commands enable the operator to take actions such as the following:

- Display the status of categories of network entities.

In this way all terminals, all lines, all major nodes, all application programs, or all of the above within a given portion of the network, could be checked.

The display for all terminals might be a list of the names, addresses, types of all terminals, and whether they are active; and for logical units or virtual terminals the name of the associated physical unit and whether it is active, the names of the major node to which the terminal is connected, the name of the line or channel to which it is connected, or entities on the path to an associated host computer.

The display for all lines might include a list of the lines in each portion (area, domain) of a network, whether they are active, line type, which nodes they are connected to, which node manages them, and possible summary figures for their load, failures, and transmission errors.

The display for applications programs might include the names of all applications programs, which node(s) they reside in, and whether they are active. Another display might show all nodes which can contain application programs and list the programs in them.

From these summary listings an operator could display more detail of individual entities, as follows:

- Display the status of individual network entities.

The condition of a particular terminal, a terminal cluster controller, a line, a trunk group, a part, switching equipment, a network control program, an application program, a session, and possibly files could be verified.

The display for a terminal might show whether it is active, whether it has power, the name of the application program (if any) to which it is connected, the name of the node to which it is connected, the name of the line or line group to which it is assigned, details of the path which connects it to a host computer, the identification of the session it is participating in, and possibly a count of its activity.

The display for a line might show its type, whether it is active, what nodes it is connected to, whether it is switched or nonswitched, name of a line group to which it is assigned, which machine controls it, statistics of its traffic load, error retransmissions, and failures, whether its traffic is currently being counted or monitored, and parameters relating to its control such as specifications for polling delay, time-outs, and maximum number of error retransmissions.

The display for an application program might include whether it is currently connected to the network software, its job and step names, the terminals connected to it, the terminals with requests for connection queued to it, and statistics of its usage.

- Activate and deactivate network entities.

Before a node can be used in a network it must be declared to the control program as "active." The same may be true with lines, logical or virtual units, and so on. The operator can activate and deactivate these.

- Start and stop application programs.

Sometimes an application program is started by a user at a terminal with a command such as LOG ON. Others users employ the terminal for a given application without logging on. A bank customer uses a cash-dispensing terminal, for example, without logging on. A network operator must start and stop programs which are not activated by their users.

- Load programs into remote nodes.

In a vertical network programs are often maintained and stored in a central node. From there some of them are transmitted and loaded into peripheral machines. In a horizontal network programs may be passed from one node to another. An operator may control the down-line loading of programs.

- Activate a remote network control program.

The network control programs in peripheral nodes may be activated, and possibly loaded, by a network operator. A peripheral node may be switched from one host computer to another when failures occur and it may then need a modified control program.

- Activate and deactivate files.

Where the network management encompasses distributed files the operator may be able to activate and deactivate files, and possibly create files. This is often in the province of *user* rather than *network* management.

- Activate and deactivate links to foreign equipment.

It is a usually desirable to connect foreign devices to a network, i.e., devices which do not conform to the network architecture. Sometimes these are older terminals or machines with protocols which predate those of the network architecture. The network software may permit these to be linked to the network and the operator can activate and deactivate them.

- Reconfigure the network.

Additional circuits may be added to a network, additional machines connected, and the connections between machines modified. A peripheral node may be switched from one host to another. In practice many networks grow and change substantially. Within the limits of a given system generation which determines the scope of the software in use, the software changes for these reconfigurations can be made by the operators.

- Enter messages for users.

The operator may be able to enter messages which will be displayed to users when they log on.

- Change transmission parameters.

Adjustments may be made to parameters on lines, such as polling delay, limit on negative responses to polling, time-outs, maximum number of retries when an error occurs.

* Start and stop traffic monitors or testing aids.

The operator may initiate the recording of traffic statistics or performance measurement data, and may initiate on-line testing or traces.

* Initiate a dump.

A program can be *down-line loaded* from a host computer to a smaller machine. The smaller machine can be *up-line dumped,* i.e., the contents of its memory at a given time transmitted to the larger machine and printed or stored. The operator may initiate a dump—either an up-line or a dump on a printer attached to the machine being dumped.

MAINTENANCE

For maintenance purposes the network software should log all errors and failures. The logs should be analyzed and summarized, and prepared for the maintenance engineers. The management software may make decisions to automatically close down certain components or circuits when the severity or frequency of errors or failure exceeds a certain threshhold. It may automatically run diagnostics and confidence tests.

The maintenance engineer needs to be able to inspect the network, examine the error and failure logs, and run diagnostics. This would be done from terminals and so requires some of the facilities listed above for operators.

SECURITY

For security reasons the network may be monitored for procedural violations made by the users. Violations of more than a certain level may trigger alarms at the location of a security officer. All security procedure violations will be logged, and the logs should be analyzed for patterns or usual frequencies of violations. The security officer should be able to inspect the violation logs and analyses at any time from a terminal.

Users may have to key in passwords or secret numbers to gain access to programs or network facilities. These should be maintained with maximum security by the security officer. Similarly if keys are used for cryptography, these need to be maintained with maximum security. This is discussed in Chapter 35.

There may be one security officer or several. There may be one for the network as a whole and other persons with security responsibility in the various user environments. These persons need terminals with secure access to the facilities the network employs for security.

OTHER ADMINISTRATIVE FUNCTIONS

In addition to the functions mentioned, the network should have facilities for billing its users.

Some networks have a center where network measurements are made and performance is studied. Tools may exist in this center for analyzing the performance, and summarizing and charting the network measurments. In some cases experiments are carried out during the quieter periods and weekends and night to test the capacity of the network configuration. Tools may exist for simulating the network and evaluating how to reconfigure it for optimal performance.

17 STANDARDS, AGREEMENTS, AND CCITT RECOMMENDATIONS

The great potentials of computer networks will unfold only if there are widely accepted standards and agreements which enable machines to communicate. Without these the spread of micro- and mini-computers would be chaotic. What differentiates civilization from a primitive rabble is the ability of its members to communicate, and communication needs agreements and standards.

Bodies for standardization exist both worldwide and within various countries. Figure 17.1 shows the main organizations concerned with standards for data communications, internationally and in the United States. In addition to those shown there are organizations, both national and international, concerned with communications standards within a particular industry such as banking, airlines, shipping, etc.

Computer manufacturers making a range of equipment for networks or distributed processing must have their own internal agreements for the interfaces, protocols, and message formats that are used. These form the basis for their network architectures. They are not described as "standards" because they do not originate in the standards organizations. They often exist many years before equivalent standards come into existence, and form a vital part of the industry development. Often many manufacturers create "plug-compatible" machines which conform to the formats and protocols of another manufacturer's architecture. The formats and protocols of a large manufacturer like IBM can therefore become a *de facto* standard.

Similarly the leading telecommunications organizations create innovative networks which require unofficial standards for interconnection. In the U.S. AT&T sets most of the standards for the telephone industry and has a large staff keeping the independent telephone companies informed. The operations of a telephone company are spelled out in *Bell System Practices* (BSP) and the independents adopt this with a few modifications of their own.

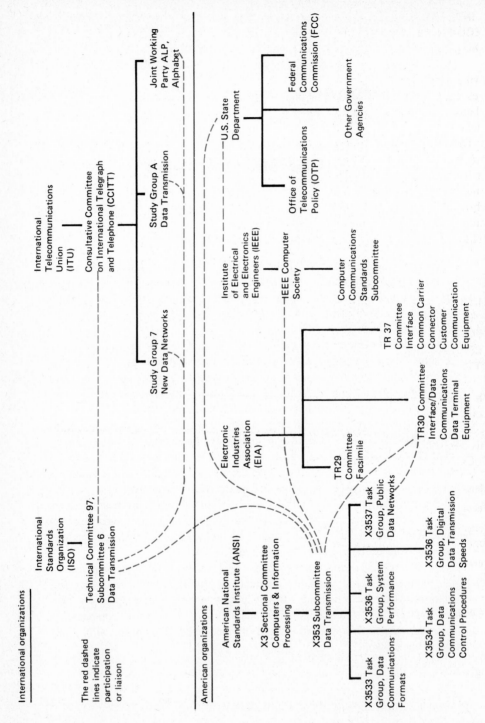

Figure 17.1 Organizations concerned with standardization for data communications. In addition there are organizations related to specific industries.

THE INTERNATIONAL TELECOMMUNICATIONS UNION (ITU)

Although incompatibilities exist, the degree of compatibility is remarkable in international telephone and telegraph networks. This is largely due to the International Telecommunications Union. This organization, centered in Switzerland, has 124 member countries throughout the world. Its consultative committees carry out very detailed studies of world telecommunications and make recommendations for standardization. The recommendations are put into practice widely throughout the world, with some notable dissensions.

There are three main organizations with the ITU: *The International Registration Board,* which attempts to register and standardize radio-frequency assignments and to assist in the elimination of harmful radio-frequency interference on the world's radio communcation circuits; *The Consultative Committee on International Radio* (CCIR), which deals with other standards for radio, especially long-distance radio telecommunications; and *The Consultative Committee on International Telegraphy and Telephony* (CCITT). Figure 17.2 shows the organization and functions of the ITU.

COMITÉ CONSULTATIF INTERNATIONAL TÉLÉGRAPHIQUE ET TÉLÉPHONIQUE (CCITT)

The Consultative Committee on International Telegraphy and Telephony, based in Geneva, is divided into a number of study groups which make recommendations on various different aspects of telephony and telegraphy. There are study groups, for example, on telegraphy transmission, performance, telegraph switching, alphabetic telegraph apparatus, telephone channels, telephone switching and signaling, noise, and several others.

Figure 17.1 shows three of the study groups which are concerned with the subject of this book.

CCITT has five categories of members:

1. Member country telecommunication administrations (A members).

2. Recognized private agencies such as AT&T (B members).

3. Scientific or industrial organizations such as equipment manufacturer associations (C members).

4. International organizations such as the International Civil Aviation Organization and the ISO (D members).

5. Specialized agencies operating in related fields such as the World Meteorological Organization (E members).

Only A-type members have voting powers at the plenary sessions where decisions are made, so the *Recommendations* produced, which have the effect of standards, are strongly related to the needs and economics of the national common carriers.

Of particular relevance to this book are the CCITT X series of Recommendations, listed in Box 17.1. These relate to data transmission over *digital* networks. The V

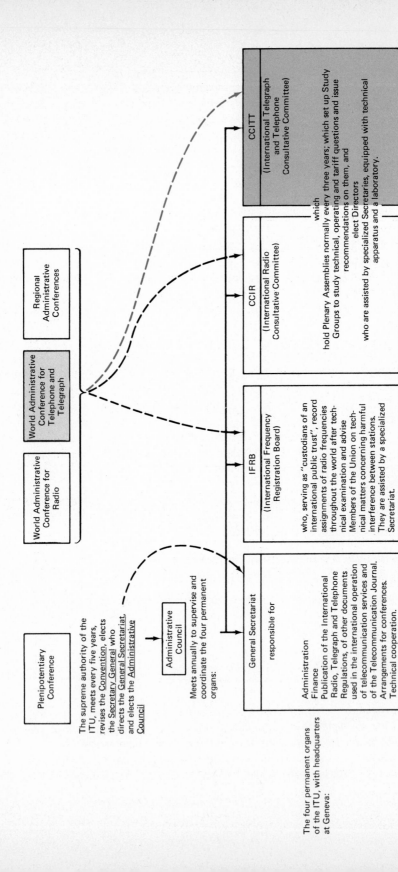

Plenipotentiary Conference

The supreme authority of the ITU, meets every five years, revises the Convention, elects the Secretary General who directs the General Secretariat, and elects the Administrative Council

World Administrative Conference for Radio

World Administrative Conference for Telephone and Telegraph

Regional Administrative Conferences

Administrative Council

Meets annually to supervise and coordinate the four permanent organs:

The four permanent organs of the ITU, with headquarters at Geneva:

General Secretariat

responsible for

Administration
Finance
Publication of the International Radio, Telegraph and Telephone Regulations, of other documents used in the international operation of telecommunication services and of the Telecommunication Journal.
Arrangements for conferences.
Technical cooperation.

IFRB

(International Frequency Registration Board)

who, serving as ''custodians of an international public trust'', record assignments of radio frequencies throughout the world after technical examination and advise Members of the Union on technical matters concerning harmful interference between stations. They are assisted by a specialized Secretariat.

CCIR

(International Radio Consultative Committee)

CCITT

(International Telegraph and Telephone Consultative Committee)

which

hold Plenary Assemblies normally every three years; which set up Study Groups to study technical, operating and tariff questions and issue recommendations on them, and
elect Directors
who are assisted by specialized Secretaries, equipped with technical apparatus and a laboratory.

Figure 17.2 The organization and functions of the International Telecommunications Union, ITU.

BOX 17.1 The X series of CCITT Recommendations, relating to data transmission over public data networks

Number	Title
X.1	International user classes of service in public data networks.
X.2	International user facilities in public data networks.
X.4	General structure of signals of International Alphabet No. 5 code for data transmission over public data networks.
X.20	Interface between data terminal equipment and data circuit-terminating equipment for start-stop transmission services on public networks.
X.20*bis*	V-21—compatible interface between data terminal equipment and data circuit-terminating equipment for start-stop transmission services on public data networks.
X.21	General-purpose interface between data terminal equipment and data circuit-terminating equipment for synchronous operation on public data networks.
X.21*bis*	Use on public data networks of data terminal equipment which are designed for interfacing to synchronous V-series modems.
X.24	List of definitions of interchange circuits between data terminal equipment and data circuit-terminating equipment on public data networks.
X.25	Interface between data terminal equipment and data circuit-terminating equipment for terminals operating in the packet mode on public data networks.
X.26	Electrical characteristics for unbalanced double-current interchange circuits for general use with integrated circuit equipment in the field of data communications.
X.27	Electrical characteristics for balanced double-current interchange circuits for general use with integrated circuit equipment in the field of data communications.
X.30	Standardization of basic model page-printing machine in accordance with International Alphabet No. 5.
X.31	Characteristics, from the transmission point of view, at the interchange point between data-terminal equipment and data circuit-terminating equipment when 200-baud start-stop data-terminal equipment in accordance with International Alphabet No. 5 is used.
X.32	Answer-back units for 200-baud start-stop machines in accordance with International Alphabet No. 5.
X.33	Standardization of an international text for the measurement of the margin of start-stop machines in accordance with International Alphabet No. 5.
X.40	Standardization of frequency-shift-modulated transmission systems for the provision of telegraph and data channels by frequency division of a primary group.
X.50	Fundamental parameters of a multiplexing scheme for the international interface between synchronous data networks.
X.51	Fundamental parameters of a multiplexing scheme for the international interface between synchronous data networks using 10-bit envelope structure.
X.60	Common channel signaling for synchronous data applications–data user part.
X.70	Terminal and transit control signaling system for start-stop services on international circuits between asynchronous data networks.
X.71	Decentralized terminal and transit control signaling system on international circuits between synchronous data networks.
X.92	Hypothetical reference connections for public synchronous data networks.
X.95	Network parameters in public data networks.
X.96	Call progress signals in public data networks.

BOX 17.2 The V series of CCITT Recommendations, relating to data transmission over analog networks

V.1	Equivalence between binary notation symbols and the significant conditions of a two-condition code.
V.2	Power levels for data transmission over telephone lines.
V.3	International Alphabet No. 5 for transmission of data and messages.
V.4	General structure of signals of the 7-unit code for data and message transmission.
V.10	Use of the telex network for data transmission at the modulation rate of 50 bauds.
V.11	Automatic calling and/or answering on the telex network.
V.13	Answer-back unit simulators.
V.15	Use of acoustic couplers for data transmission.
V.21	200-baud modem standardized for use in the general switched telephone network.
V.22	Standardization of modulation rates and data-signaling rates for synchronous data transmission in the general switched telephone network.
V.22B	Standardization of modulation rates and data signaling rates on leased telephone circuits.
V.23	600/1200-baud modem standardized for use in the general switched telephone networks.
V.24	Functions and electrical characteristics of circuits at the interface between data terminal equipment and data communication equipment.
V.25	Automatic calling and/or answering on the general switched telephone network.
V.26	2400 bits/second modem for use on four-wire leased point-to-point circuits.
V.26B	2400 bits/second modem for use on the general switched telephone network.
V.27	Modem for data signalling rates up to 4800 bits/second over leased circuits.
V.28	Electrical characteristics for interface circuits.
V.30	Parallel data transmission system for universal use on the general switched telephone network.
V.31	Electrical characteristics for contact closure-type interface circuits.
V.35	Transmission of 48 kilobits/second data using 60 to 108 kHz group bank circuits.
V.40	Error indication with electromechanical equipment.
V.41	Code-independent error control system.
V.50	Standard limits for transmission quality of data transmission.
V.51	Organization of the maintenance of international telephone-type circuits used for data transmission.
V.52	Characteristics of distortion and error rate measuring apparatus for data transmission.
V.53	Limits for the maintenance of telephone-type circuits used for data transmission.
V.56	Comprehensive tests for modems that use their own interface circuits.
V.57	Comprehensive test set for high transmission rates.

series of Recommendations, mostly older, relates to data transmission over *analog* networks, i.e., conventional telephone systems (Box 17.2).

CCITT
RECOMMENDATIONS
X.21 AND X.25

Of particular importance to our subject are CCITT Recommendations X.21 and X.25.

As we mentioned earlier CCITT Recommendation X.25 defines the user interface to transport networks; it specifies the interface to Layers 1, 2, and 3. New data networks are coming into operation around the world which are designed to provide this interface. Data processing manufacturers are creating software and hardware for computers, terminals, cluster controllers, and concentrators, which link to X.25 networks or transport subsystems.

While the CCITT X.25 Recommendation is designed primarily for packet-switching networks, CCITT Recommendation X.21 is a Layer 1 interface for *digital* networks. This is used with either digital leased lines or circuit-switched lines. It can be thought of as being a digital-line equivalent of the EIA RS 232-C or CCITT V.24 interface to analog circuits. It will be increasingly important as circuit-switched and nonswitched digital transmission circuits spread.

CCITT Recommendation X.25 is explained in Chapter 22, and CCITT Recommendation X.21 in Chapter 25.

It is likely that vast national and international data networks will grow up and interlink, as did the telephone networks of an earlier era, using the X.21 and X.25 protocols in their present or an improved form.

As microprocessors and VLSI drop in cost, small and inexpensive machines will connect to these networks. X.25 networks will form one of the most important transport subsystems for distributed processing.

ISO

ISO, the International Organization for Standardization, has a subcommittee concerned with digital data transmission (Technical Committee 97, Subcommittee 60). Membership for ISO activities is provided by the national standards organizations of participating countries.

ISO is responsible for the physical link protocol (Layer 2), HDLC (High-level Data Link Control). As mentioned in Chapter 12, this is similar to the physical link protocols of the American National Standards Committee, ANSI. As of today minor subtle differences exist between these protocols. HDLC is identical to Layer 2 of X.25.

Most major computer manufacturers now use a line control procedure similar to HDLC (see Box 14.1), but again with some minor subtle difference. Many of these implementations are permissible subsets of HDLC. The subsets are not necessarily compatible with one another.

Of great importance in the future is the ISO model for distributed processing nodes consisting of the seven layers discussed earlier in the book (Figs. 11.3, 11.9, and 12.6).

ANSI	Sectional Committee X3 of the American National Stan-
dards Instiute is responsible for computers and information
processing. Subcommittee S3S5 of this is responsible for data transmission and has a
number of task groups as shown in Fig 17.1.

Often the work done for international standards originates in national standards
committees such as ANSI. ANSI specified a physical link protocol, ADCCP, Advanced Data Communications Control Procedure, which became the basis for the ISO
work resulting in HDLC. ANSI created a 7-layer model of a distributed processing
node which led to the ISO 7-layer model.

EIA	EIA, the Electronic Industries Association, is the U.S.
national organization of electronic manufacturers. It is a
trade association member of ANSI.

Its Committee TR30 is responsible for the development and maintenance of industry standards for the interface between data processing machines and data communications equipment. This includes the Layer 1 interface—the interface between user
machines and modems, signal converters, etc., the quality at the interface, and the
signaling speeds. The Committee was responsible for the EIA RS 232-C interface which
is employed by most data machines and modems (and is similar to the CCITT V-24
interface) and its RS 422 and 423 replacements. This committee liaises with and has
joint meetings with the ANSI Subcommittee X3S3 on data transmission.

INDUSTRY	In addition to the generally applicable standards of bodies
AGREEMENTS	like ANSI, EIA, ISO, and CCITT, agreements between
industry groups about their communications protocols
are extremely important. Several industry organizations are concerned with data communications and computer networks. These include ICAO, the International Civil Aviation Organization which has a committee concerned with industry standards for data
communications used in international air traffic control, IATA, the International Air
Transport Association which is concerned with reservations and administrative messages transmitted between airline computers, and banking associations which are concerned with traffic between bank computers, including electronic fund transfer and cus-
tomer-operated terminals and cash-dispensing machines.

If generally accepted formats and protocols were available for efficient *transport*
networks, industry groups would be primarily concerned with formats and protocols
for Layer 4 or for user applications. For example, procedures today define what fields
and codes are used in an electronic fund transfer message or an airline reservation
message, and what responses must be sent to these messages.

There is much need for further development of industry agreements.

PART III   NETWORK MECHANISMS

18 HDLC, SDLC, ETC.

This chapter describes the International Standards Organization physical link protocol HDCL (Higher-level Data Link Control). The American Standards Association's protocol, ADCCP, is similar. CCITT Recommendation X.25 Layer 2 is one of the permissible options of HDLC. Various manufacturers have their own derivative of HDLC (see Box 13.2), the most common of which is IBM's SDLC (Synchronous Data Link Control).

HDLC is likely to become the most widely accepted physical link protocol for distributed processing and computer networks. It will steadily replace binary synchronous line control and other forms of line control for buffered terminals. (Start–stop line control for unbuffered devices will continue to exist.) The HDLC standard permits several variations in its implementation. Because these are different, one version of it may not be able to communicate with another version. IBM's SDLC, for example, may be slightly different from another vendor's version.

OBJECTIVES

The objectives of HDLC, SDLC, etc., are as follows:

1. The data field carried can be any number of bits and any pattern of bits. This is not a *character-oriented* data field as with earlier protocols. Distributed processing networks need to carry *any* pattern of bits, not merely a specified character set.

2. A powerful means of protecting the tranmissions from errors is needed.

3. The operation should be fail-safe. When failures occur, including failures in control mechanisms, the protocol should not lose a packet, deliver the same packet twice, or deliver garbled packets.

4. The same protocol should be able to handle point-to-point, multidrop, or looped physical links.

5. The same protocol should operate on half-duplex or full-duplex lines. Half-duplex and full-duplex terminals may be connected to the same physical link at the same time.

6. Full-duplex operations should be as efficient as possible, permitting the maximum throughput of data on the link. On a multidrop link, transmission to one station and from another should be able to occur simultaneously.

7. The protocol should be able to operate efficiently on links which have a long propagation delay or turnaround time.

8. The protocol should be able to operate efficiently on wideband links, up to very high transmission rates.

9. Improper link control procedures, or inoperative machines, should be reported. Such faults may be referred to a high-level protocol for recovery.

FLAG BYTE   HDLC, etc., uses bit stuffing, as described in Chapter 11, to achieve data transparency. Each message begins and ends with a *flag byte* 01111110. The 0 bit is inserted after every five 1 bits in the data so that the flag byte† pattern can never occur by chance. This technique, illustrated in Fig. 18.1, permits any pattern of bits to be sent.

Figure 18.1   Bit stuffing in HDLC, SDLC, etc.

FRAME FORMAT   In HDLC terminology, the packet is called a *frame*. Figure 18.2 shows the frame format.

The frame starts and ends with a *flag* byte, 01111110. At the start of the frame is a 3-byte header; at the end is a 3-byte trailer. These form an envelope, and any number of bits can be carried between the header and trailer. There are two types of frames: a *data-carrying* frame and a *control* frame. A control frame may have *no* bits between the header and the trailer.

---

†The HDLC standards use the term "octet" meaning 8 bits of data. We have used the word "byte" because it is more common in the computer industry.

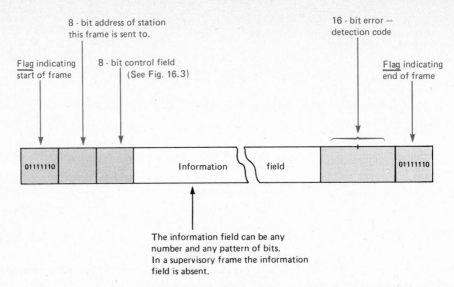

Figure 18.2 The HDLC frame format. A fully variable information field is enclosed in the HDLC envelope.

The three bytes of the header are as follows:

Byte 1:   the *flag,* 01111110, which indicates the start of the frame.

Byte 2:   an 8-bit address, permitting up to 2555 addresses on a physical link. This number can be expanded in HDLC if necessary by using an extra byte or bytes.

The address is usually that of an individual station. However, it could also be a *broadcast* address so that a single frame is received by all stations on the link, or it could be the address of a *group* of stations. One station, then, might have several addresses. It inspects the address byte and if it is any of those addresses it accepts the frame.

Byte 3:   an 8-bit byte containing information for controlling the link, which we discuss later. This can also be extended by one byte.

The trailer bytes are as follows:

Bytes 1 and 2:   a powerful 16-bit error detecting code.

Byte 3:   the *flag,* 01111110, which indicates the end of
the frame. When that is detected the receiving
machine examines the previous two bytes and
executes its error detection algorithm.

The zero bit insertion and deletion which we described applies to all bits between
the flag bytes—including the *address, control,* and *error check* bytes. The error check
also relates to all of these bits.

If there are less than 32 bits between the flag bytes, the frame is not valid and so
the receiving machine would reject it.

BETWEEN FRAMES   Usually the channel remains in *active state* between the
transmission of frames. In this state continous flag bytes
are sent. The receiving machines detect each flag byte, and if it is not followed by
another flag, they assume that a frame transmission has started. Thus:

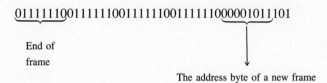

End of
frame

The address byte of a new frame

IDLE STATE   The transmitting machine can abort a frame which it has
AND FRAME ABORTS   started to send by transmitting at least seven contiguous 1
bits (with no inserted 0 bits).

A channel is defined as being in an *idle state* when the transmission of 15 or
more contiguous 1 bits is detected. In this state a primary must repoll a secondary
before transmitting an *I*-frame to it.

A station can abort a frame without throwing the link into an idle state by transmitting eight contiguous 1 bits followed by a flag. This merely causes the frame to be
abandoned, and another frame can then be sent in the normal fashion.

There are thus two types of *abort:*

11111111   1111111:   Puts the link into *idle state* so that the primary
must repoll the secondary.

11111111   10000001:   Abandons the current frame in such a way that
another *I*-frame may be sent immediately.

FRAME EXTENSIONS

Optional extensions to the frame are permitted, as follows:

Address Extension

The address byte may be extended by adding an extra byte. Normally one 8-bit byte is used for the address and all 256 combinations are usable addresses. By prior arrangement, the first transmitted bit (low-order bit) of the address byte can be reserved; if it is "0" this indicates that the next contiguous byte is also an address field. Similarly the first bit of this can be "0" to indicate a further address byte and so on. Thus the address byte may be recursively extended. If the first bit of the first address byte is "1," this indicates that there are no extra address bytes and a range of 128 addresses is usable.

Address extension is rarely used. It is rare that more than 256 stations would be attached to a single physical channel. It is possible in packet radio (Chapter 27) or cable television and short-distance broadband networks (Chapter 26).

Control Field Extension

The 8-bit control byte in most frames contains one or two 3-bit counts for controlling the link, as will be described shortly. The control field can be extended by one extra contiguous byte so that 7-bit counts are used. This gives modulo 128 rather than modulo 8 counts.

For most terrestrial links 3-bit counts are adequate. 7-bit counts are desirable on wideband satellite links because those have a propagation delay of about 270 milliseconds, and the actual throughput falls far below the nominal throughput unless a link control procedure with large counts is used [4].

Frame Checking Sequence Expansion

The 16-bit error detection check is adequate for most transmission. The HDLC standard says that the number of bits used could be increased by one or more bytes if a higher degree of protection is found necessary in the future.

THREE TYPES OF FRAMES

HDLC, etc., uses three types of frames. These are designated:

I-frame: *Information transfer frame*.
This is the frame which carries users' data.

S-frame: *Supervisory frame*.
This is used for supervisory control functions such as acknowledgments, requesting transmission, and requesting a temporary suspension of transmission.
Normal routine operation uses only *I*-frames and *S*-frames.

U-frame: *Unnumbered frame*.

This is used to provide additional link control functions. The frame is called "unnumbered" because it contains no sequence numbers. In SDLC it is called a *nonsequenced* frame, *NS* frame, for the same reason.

The first bits in the control byte indicate what the frame type is, as shown in Fig. 18.3.

> *I*-frame: The first bit is 0.
>
> *S*-frame: The first two bits are 10.
>
> *U*-frame: The first two bits are 11.

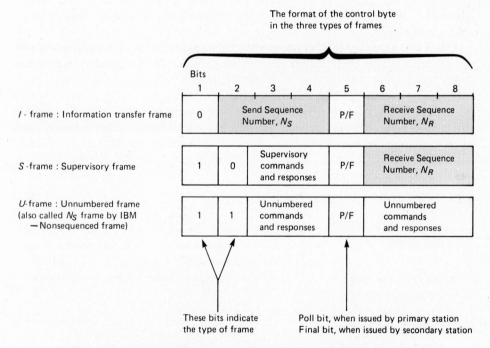

Figure 18.3 The format of the control byte—the third byte in the header (see Fig. 18.2). [*Note:* This is sometimes drawn reversed with bit 8 on the left. The bits are sometimes numbered differently from this CCITT numbering. However it is drawn, the bit on the left (above), is the first bit to be transmitted.]

PRIMARY AND SECONDARY STATIONS   For control purposes one station on a physical link is designated a *primary* station; the other(s) are *secondary* stations. The primary station assumes responsibility for the organization of data flow and for error recovery operations on the link.

A frame sent from a primary station to a secondary is called a *command*. A frame from a secondary to a primary is called a *response*. Normally when a command is sent, a response, or a string of responses is expected in reply.

A multidrop link usually uses polling, and the station which polls the others is the primary. On a point-to-point link either station could be the primary. The primary station needs more logic capability than the secondary, and so when terminals are connected to a computer, the computer is normally the primary station.

A station may have several links connected to it. In certain configurations it must act as a *primary* for some links and a secondary for others. For example, a concentrator is a primary station on its low-speed links connected to terminals and a secondary on its high-speed link connected to a computer. The nodes on a mesh-structured network have to be primaries for some lines and secondaries for others. The choice of whether a station is primary or secondary is normally made when a system is designed.

It is not necessary that all information transfers be initiated by a primary station (as was the case on some earlier line control procedures). A secondary station can initiate transmission when desirable. In some systems it has to wait until polled, and in others it can send an unsolicited response.

Some stations can combine the functions of a primary and a secondary. Such a station is called a *combined* station. The protocols used for transmission between combined stations can be symmetrical, i.e., both stations on a link perform the same set of transmission control functions. This is referred to as *balanced* operation and is important on computer networks.

MODES OF OPERATION   A secondary station normally operates in one of two modes: *normal response mode,* in which it never transmits unless the primary station instructs it to, and *asynchronous response mode* in which it may begin transmission without being instructed to by the primary station.

Normal Response Mode

In normal response mode a secondary station can transmit only in response to a command frame from the primary station. Its response may consist of one or more frames and must indicate which is the last frame of the response. It then cannot transmit again until it receives another command. This is the conventional mode of operation for terminals, terminal controllers, and polled lines. The primary station is responsible for the link and must keep polling or sending commands to the secondary station(s). The primary station is responsible for time-outs, retransmission and all forms of recovery action.

Asynchronous Response Mode

In asynchronous response mode the secondary station can initiate the transmission of a frame or group of frames. These frames may contain information or may be sent solely for control purposes. The secondary station is then responsible for time-out and retransmission if the frame it sends is not acknowledged correctly.

A secondary station in asynchronous response mode could be dormant for periods of time, and not be polled by the primary. When it is used it must then initiate transmission to the primary. Such a station may possibly be on a multidrop line with other stations in either asynchronous or normal response mode.

Asynchronous response mode is necessary for the control of *loops* of stations, or of multidrop lines with *hub polling*. In both of these configurations a secondary can receive a "go-ahead" message from another secondary and transmit in response to it. The "go-ahead" signal progresses around the loop or down the line.

Some special types of physical link controls employ primary and secondary stations but require the secondary stations to initiate transmissions. This is true, for example, of the ALOHA family of protocols which is used on packet radio systems.

BALANCED MODE   For mesh-structured computer networks it is desirable to have high volumes of traffic traveling in both directions between the nodes. It is important that transmission efficiency should be as high as possible, and transmit times as low as possible. Asynchronous response mode has been used for such an environment, permitting any node to initiate transmission. To achieve greater efficiency, however, HDLC defines a *balanced class of procedures* [5].

With balanced operation each station assumes the role of *both* a primary and a secondary, i.e., it is a *combined* station. All stations have the same set of protocols. Any station can send and receive both commands and responses. The stations have equal responsibility for error recovery.

There is one mode of operation for balanced procedures. It is called *asynchronous balanced mode,* ABM, because any station can initiate transmission at any time. Sometimes it is simply referred to as *balanced mode*.

In many packet-switching networks of the future it is likely that the nodes which relay packets will communicate in balanced mode. Unbalanced procedures were originally devised with the assumption that it would be economical to put primary functions (especially the responsibility for recovery) in big nodes only. Secondary stations would exist in large quantities and should be less expensive than primary stations. Most communication would be between computers and terminals, for which the computer is naturally a primary and the terminal a secondary. Now two changes are occurring. First, computer networks and distributed processing require full-duplex, asynchronous, high-volume, fast transmission between computers. Second, microelectronics is dropping in cost so that it has become economical to put primary station functions in small machines such as terminal controllers. It is likewise economical to mass-produce LSI circuitry which puts the *same* set of control functions in every machine. Hence the desirability of a *balanced class of procedures*.

Figure 18.4 illustrates the main modes of operation.

CONTROL BYTE   Figure 18.3 shows the control byte. It serves various functions in controlling the exchange of information.

The fifth bit of the control byte is called a *poll bit* when it is issued by a primary station, and a *final bit* when issued by a secondary station. The poll bit is set to 1 on *commands* when a response is required. More than one frame may be sent in response. The last frame in response to a command has the final bit set to 1, and this requires an acknowledgment.

The interchange between stations is controlled by sequence numbers. They are usually 3-bit numbers (and optionally 7-bit numbers, as discussed above), shown in Fig. 18.3. The 3-bit numbers count from 0 to 7 and then back to 0.

Every information frame is identified by a sequence number N_S, in bits 2 to 4 of its control byte. The receipt of information frames is confirmed by sending an acknowledgment which contains the sequence number of the *next information frame which the receiving station expects to receive, N_R*. This implies that all frames prior to N_R have been received correctly. The supervisory frames which can carry acknowledgments have N_R in their last three bits. Acknowledgments can also be carried by a returning information frame. The information frame therefore carries two sequence numbers: its own number, N_S, and the number which acknowledges frames received, N_R.

Two bits in the *S*-frame identify the type of *S*-frame. There can therefore be four types of *S*-frames.

The *U*-frame has no sequence numbers and so five bits are available for identifying types of *U*-frames. There could be, therefore, up to 32 types of *U*-frames, but not all are in use.

SUPERVISORY FRAMES   The *S*-frames are used for initiating and controlling the information transfer that takes place in the *I*-frames. An *S*-frame has no bits enclosed between its header and trailer. In other words it is normally a 6-byte (48-bit) frame. There are four types of *S*-frame, and they can each be either commands or responses. The type is indicated by bits 3 and 4 (see Fig. 18.3). Each *S*-frame contains a receive sequence number, N_R.

Normal Response Mode (NRM)

1. The primary station initiates the interchange :

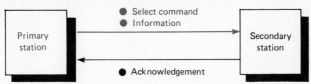

2. The secondary station initiates the interchange :

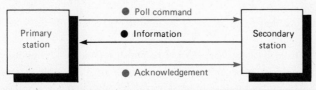

Asynchronous Response Mode (ARM)

The secondary station can initiate an exchange without first being selected or polled by a primary station:

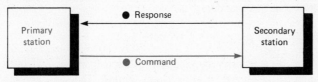

Asynchronous Balanced Mode (ABM)

The stations have identical protocols. Both stations on a link can send both commands and responses. Either can send a command to initiate an exchange:

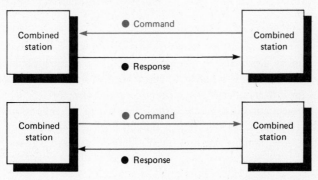

Figure 18.4   The three modes of information interchange in HDLC.

Bits 3 and 4 indicate the type of S-frame, as follows:

00:	RR	Receive Ready
01:	REJ	Reject
10:	RNR	Receive Not Ready
11:	SREJ	Selective Reject

RR (Receive Ready)

This is sent by a primary or secondary station to:

1. *acknowledge* that it has received frames numbered up to $N_R - 1$ correctly,
2. indicate that it is now ready to receive frame number N_R. It is used as the normal mechanism for controlling the flow of error-free information frames.

It may be used by a primary station to *poll* a secondary station, saying, in effect: "I-frame number N_R is expected next; if you have such a frame to send, send it." If the secondary station has no data to send, it replies with another RR frame which says, in effect: "I have no I-frame to send yet; the next I-frame I expect to receive from you is number N_R." On a multidrop line the primary station might poll each of the secondary stations in turn in this manner.

RNR (Receive Not Ready)

This is sent by a primary or secondary station to indicate it is temporarily in a *busy* condition and can accept no information frames. The sequence number N_R is the number of the frame expected next after the busy condition ends, and may be used to acknowledge that frames prior to N_R have been received correctly. The end of a busy condition may be signaled with any other valid S-frame, and with certain types of U-frames.

REJ (Reject)

This is sent by a primary or secondary station to request transmission or retransmission of information frame number N_R and those that follow it. It implies that information frames prior to number N_R have been received correctly.

Only one reject condition may be established at any one time for a given direction of transmission on a physical link. The condition is cleared upon the correct receipt of an I-frame with an N_S number equal to the N_R number of the REJ frame.

SREJ (Selective Reject)

This is used by a primary or secondary to request transmission of a single I-frame, numbered N_R. It acknowledges that the frames up to N_R have been received correctly but that N_R has not. After a station has transmitted a Selective Reject it will accept only the *I*-frame numbered N_R and those that follow it. The SREJ exception condition is cleared (reset) when the requested I-frame is received.

Selective Reject is intended for the type of error control known as *selective-repeat continuous ARQ*. This is discussed in Chapter 31 and illustrated in Fig. 31.2. The transmitting station continuously transmits the acknowledgments of the transmission lagging behind. When a frame is in error, that frame alone is retransmitted.

Selective-repeat ARQ is not used on the majority of terrestrial links. It can improve the efficiency of a satellite link somewhat, but is more costly in its buffering requirements [4].

ACKNOWLEDGMENTS   When a station transmits a frame, it requires an acknowledgment saying that the frame was received correctly. The receiving station need not, however, send a separate acknowledgment for *every* frame. The acknowledgment gives the serial number of the next frame it expects to receive, in the N_R field. Because this implies that every frame prior to the one with that serial number has been received correctly, it can be an acknowledgment for one or several frames.

The serial number usually has 3 bits, and so up to 7 frames can be transmitted before an acknowledgment is received. In earlier forms of physical link control a sending machine had to receive an acknowledgment to *every* frame before it sent the next one. This procedure slowed down the traffic somewhat, especially on half-duplex links (which can only transmit in one direction at a time) and especially when there was a lengthy propagation delay or line turnaround time. This is one of the reasons why a higher throughput can be achieved with HDLC than with earlier procedures such as binary synchronous line control. Most high-speed modems have a substantially longer line turnaround time than their earlier slower counterparts, which makes it particularly desirable to avoid frame-by-frame acknowledgment.

Transmission via satellite, which is rapidly dropping in cost and increasing in use in some countries, results in a long propagation delay—about 270 milliseconds for a one-way hop. At least 540 milliseconds will elapse between the sending of a message and the receiving of an acknowledgment. With a delay of this magnitude it is often desirable that a station should be able to send for more than 7 frames before receiving an acknowledgment [4]. In such circumstances the optional extra control byte is used to give a modulo 128 count permitting up to 127 frames to be sent before acknowledgment.

Any of the four types of *S*-frames could act as an acknowledgment. For efficiency, a frame carrying data can also act as an acknowledgment. Any of these acknowledgments carries the number N_R of the information frame that that acknowledging station expects to receive next.

A point-to-point line between the nodes of a computer network will often carry data in both directions simultaneously. The data frames will each serve as an acknowledgment of frames traveling in the opposite direction. HDLC can thus give a highly efficient use of such a full-duplex line.

Carrying acknowledgments or other control information in the data messages is sometimes referred to as *piggybacking*.

CONTROL
OF INFORMATION
EXCHANGE

When a primary or secondary station sends *I*-frames, it may send one, or a group of up to 7 (or 127 with the extra control byte). The last (and sometimes the only) frame in the group has the bit 5 of the control byte— the bit labeled P/F in Fig. 18.3—set to 1. When the frame is a *command* sent by a primary station, this bit is called the *poll* bit and it requests a response from the addressed secondary station. When the frame is a *response* sent by a secondary station the bit is called the *final* bit and it requests an acknowledgment from the primary (which could be an information frame). The P/F bit, then, serves a similar function in each case. It indicates that a station expects a response before it transmits another frame.

Figures 18.5 and 18.6 show situations in which one station sends data and the receiving station responds with more data. In Fig. 18.5 a primary station sends data first; in Fig. 18.6 a secondary sends it first.

At the top of Fig. 18.5 the primary station, shown in red, sends one *I*-frame. Its *poll* bit is set, so it is requesting the secondary to respond. The secondary responds with one *I*-frame. This has its *final* bit set and so the primary sends an acknowledgment. There is no information frame on which to piggyback this acknowlegment so the primary sends an RR (Receive Ready) *S*-frame.

At the bottom of Fig. 18.5 an exchange takes place which is similar except that the primary sends *several I*-frames. The last frame of each of these groups has the *poll/ final* bit set and so elicits a response.

Figure 18.6 shows the same information exchange as Fig. 18.5 except that the roles of primary and secondary station are reversed. In normal response mode the secondary cannot initiate the exchange so the primary keeps polling the secondary to see whether it has anything to send. If not, the secondary station responds to the poll with an *S*-frame, normally an RR (Receive Ready) *S*-frame. When it does have something to send, it sends it in an *I*-frame.

FULL-DUPLEX
OPERATION

Prior to the use of distributed processing and computer networks, half-duplex operation of physical links was common, and full-duplex operation was exceptional. With computer networks or multiple processing locations, it is often desirable to have data flowing in both directions at once on a physical link.

Figure 18.7 shows variable-length data messages traveling in both directions. The data flowing in one direction is independent of the data flowing in the other. Either station could be the primary. There are few *S*-frames in Fig. 18.7; the signals control-

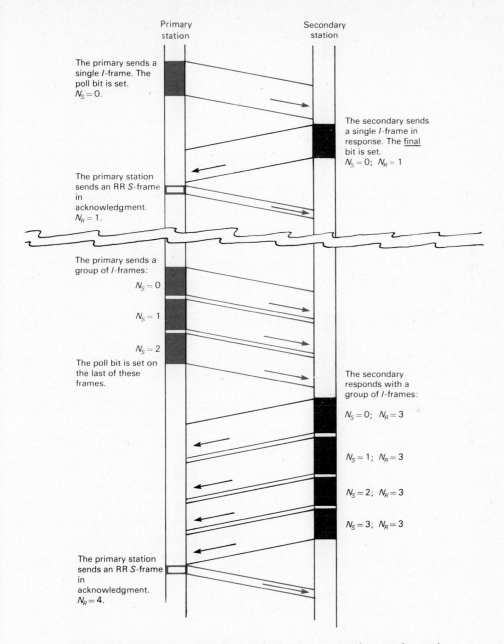

Primary
station

Secondary
station

The primary sends a
single *I*-frame. The
poll bit is set.
$N_S = 0$.

The secondary sends
a single *I*-frame in
response. The <u>final</u>
bit is set.
$N_S = 0$; $N_R = 1$

The primary station
sends an RR *S*-frame
in
acknowledgment.
$N_R = 1$.

The primary sends a
group of *I*-frames:

$N_S = 0$

$N_S = 1$

$N_S = 2$

The poll bit is set on
the last of these
frames.

The secondary
responds with a
group of *I*-frames:

$N_S = 0$; $N_R = 3$

$N_S = 1$; $N_R = 3$

$N_S = 2$; $N_R = 3$

$N_S = 3$; $N_R = 3$

The primary station
sends an RR *S*-frame
in
acknowledgment.
$N_R = 4$.

Figure 18.5 A primary station sends data to a secondary station and
wants a response.

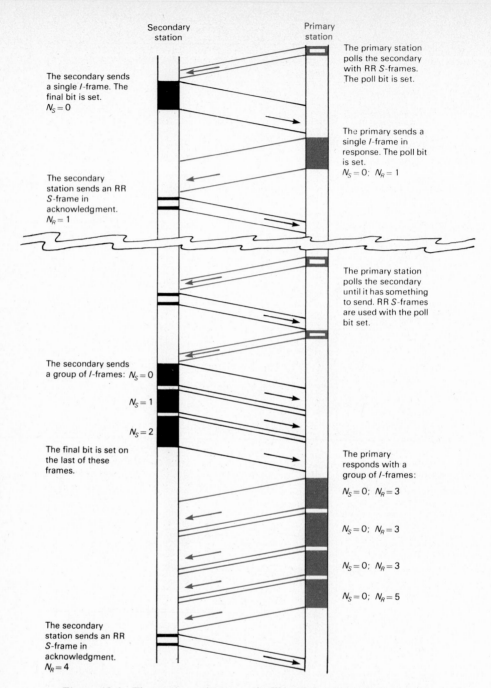

Secondary
station

Primary
station

The primary station
polls the secondary
with RR S-frames.
The poll bit is set.

The secondary sends
a single I-frame. The
final bit is set.
$N_S = 0$

The primary sends a
single I-frame in
response. The poll bit
is set.
$N_S = 0; \ N_R = 1$

The secondary
station sends an RR
S-frame in
acknowledgment.
$N_R = 1$

The primary station
polls the secondary
until it has something
to send. RR S-frames
are used with the poll
bit set.

The secondary sends
a group of I-frames: $N_S = 0$

$N_S = 1$

$N_S = 2$

The final bit is set on
the last of these
frames.

The primary
responds with a
group of I-frames:

$N_S = 0; \ N_R = 3$

$N_S = 0; \ N_R = 3$

$N_S = 0; \ N_R = 3$

$N_S = 0; \ N_R = 5$

The secondary
station sends an RR
S-frame in
acknowledgment.
$N_R = 4$

Figure 18.6 The same exchange as in Fig. 18.5, except that the secondary station speaks first.

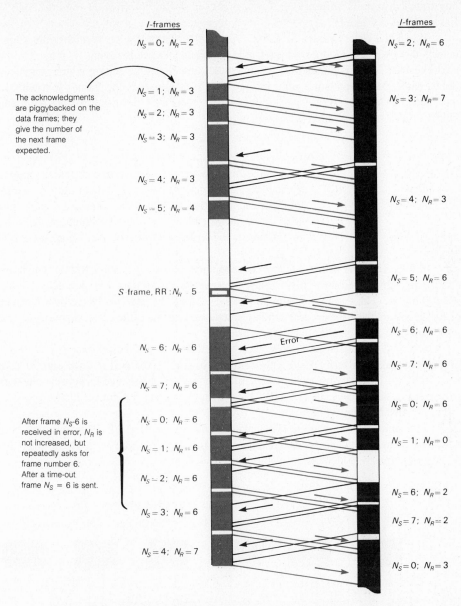

I-frames

$N_S = 0$; $N_R = 2$

$N_S = 2$; $N_R = 6$

The acknowledgments are piggybacked on the data frames; they give the number of the next frame expected.

$N_S = 1$; $N_R = 3$

$N_S = 3$; $N_R = 7$

$N_S = 2$; $N_R = 3$

$N_S = 3$; $N_R = 3$

$N_S = 4$; $N_R = 3$

$N_S = 4$; $N_R = 3$

$N_S = 5$; $N_R = 4$

$N_S = 5$; $N_R = 6$

S frame, RR : $N_R = 5$

$N_S = 6$; $N_R = 6$

$N_S = 6$; $N_R = 6$

Error

$N_S = 7$; $N_R = 6$

$N_S = 7$; $N_R = 6$

$N_S = 0$; $N_R = 6$

After frame N_S-6 is received in error, N_R is not increased, but repeatedly asks for frame number 6. After a time-out frame $N_S = 6$ is sent.

$N_S = 0$; $N_R = 6$

$N_S = 1$; $N_R = 0$

$N_S = 1$; $N_R = 6$

$N_S = 2$; $N_R = 6$

$N_S = 6$; $N_R = 2$

$N_S = 3$; $N_R = 6$

$N_S = 7$; $N_R = 2$

$N_S = 4$; $N_R = 7$

$N_S = 0$; $N_R = 3$

Figure 18.7 HDLC or SDLC in operation on a full-duplex line with *I*-frames traveling in both directions at once, carrying both data and control signals. This could be the link between two nodes of a computer network such as that in Fig. 14.4.

ling the exchange of information are piggybacked on the information frames. Each I-frame carries the number N_R of the I-frame expected next.

When the error occurs in frame $N_R = 6$, the station which receives this frame detects the error and so does not update its N_R count. It keeps saying $N_R = 6$, i.e., the next expected frame is number 6. After a preset time delay the station which originated the damaged frame sends it again. In Fig. 18.7 it also resends the frames following it; they need not have been resent if the receiving station were designed to store them and put them into sequence when errors occur.

FULL-DUPLEX MULTIDROP OPERATION

On a multidrop line transmissions to the different secondary stations may be interleaved. With a full-duplex multidrop line, such as that in Fig. 18.8, interleaved transmissions in both directions can occur simultaneously as shown in Fig. 18.9. This is sometimes called *multi-multidrop* or *multi-multipoint* operation.

In Fig. 18.9 the primary station is sending to secondary station B data which are divided into three frames. Only the last of these frames solicits a response by having the poll bit on. The three frames do not follow each other immediately, perhaps because of the nature of the user process, and so interleaved between them are supervisory and information frames for other stations on the line.

Roll-call polling is commonly used to multidrop lines; the primary says to each of the secondaries in turn "Have you anything to send?" The poll is a Receive Ready, RR, S-frame. The response may be an I-frame or may be a negative response—another RR S-frame, which says, in effect, "I have nothing to send but am ready to receive I-frame number N_R from you."

Hub polling is often more efficient than roll-call polling [6]. With this, the poll is passed from secondary to secondary. A U-frame is therefore used rather than the sequenced primary-secondary exchange.

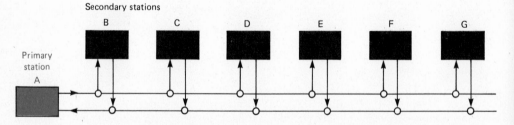

Figure 18.8 On a full-duplex multidrop line, such as this, HDLC or SDLC can handle transmissions in both directions at once, with messages from different stations interleaved as shown in Fig. 18.9.

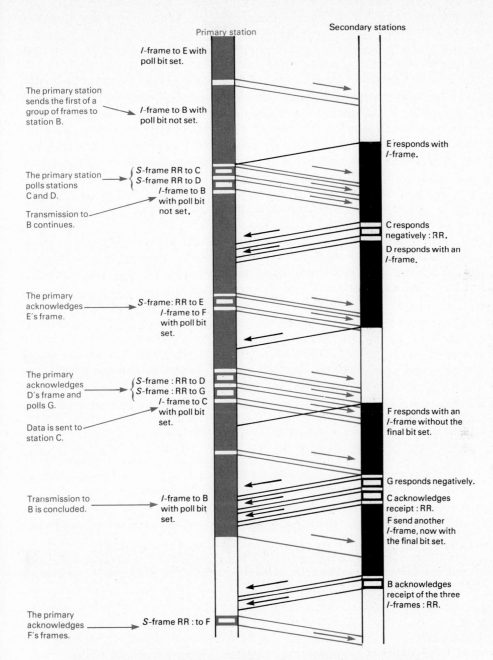

Primary station

Secondary stations

I-frame to E with
poll bit set.

The primary station
sends the first of a
group of frames to
station B.

I-frame to B with
poll bit not set.

E responds with
I-frame.

The primary station
polls stations
C and D.

{ *S*-frame RR to C
  S-frame RR to D
  I-frame to B
  with poll bit
  not set.

Transmission to
B continues.

C responds
negatively : RR.

D responds with an
I-frame.

The primary
acknowledges
E's frame.

S-frame: RR to E
I-frame to F
with poll bit
set.

The primary
acknowledges
D's frame and
polls G.

{ *S*-frame : RR to D
  S-frame : RR to G
  I- frame to C
  with poll bit
  set.

Data is sent to
station C.

F responds with an
I-frame without the
final bit set.

Transmission to
B is concluded.

I-frame to B
with poll bit
set.

G responds negatively.

C acknowledges
receipt : RR.

F send another
I-frame, now with
the final bit set.

B acknowledges
receipt of the three
I-frames : RR.

The primary
acknowledges
F's frames.

S-frame RR : to F

Figure 18.9   On a full-duplex multidrop line, transmissions to and from
different stations can be interleaved.

TIME-OUTS When a primary station transmits a frame with the *poll* bit on in the control field, it expects a reply within a specified time. If it does not receive the reply it expects it will retransmit the frame which solicited it.

This is referred to as a *time-out*. The primary station has a clock which enables it to detect when the line has been idle for a time long enough to indicate that something is wrong. Often the absence of a reply was caused by a transmission error. Retransmission will solve the problem. If the problem persists, the primary station will retransmit it a given number of times. If repeated retransmissions do not succeed, then the situation is not recoverable by the physical link protocol and the problem is referred to a higher authority.

Two time-outs are used. The first relates to a secondary failing to respond; the second to a received signal being present but undetectable. The first is called an *idle detect* time-out; the second a *nonproductive receive* time-out.

Neither the duration of the time-outs, nor the number of retries, is specified by HDLC. They vary from one implementation to another, depending upon the nature of the transmission link and the duration of response processing. Error recovery is discussed further in Chapter 31.

U-FRAMES The illustrations we have given employ *I*-frames and *S*-frames. These frames always relate to transmission controlled by sequence numbers. The third type of frame, the *U*-frame (unnumbered frame), has no sequence numbers. The purposes of this extra type of frame are as follows:

1. They provide a mechanism for sending information which bypasses the sequence-numbered exchanges. There could be up to 32 types of *U*-frames (the *type* being encoded in 5 bits). This makes possible a wide variety of commands and responses for supervisory purposes. It means that the control capability of HDLC can be expanded if necessary. *U*-frames could have an information field if necessary, which *I*-frames do not.

2. The *U*-frames provide commands which can initialize a station, change transmission modes, and disconnect a station. This is particularly useful with dial-up lines or stations which are not permanently connected.

3. The *U*-frames provide a mechanism for rejecting invalid commands or dealing with special error conditions such as information frames which are too long for a station's buffering capability.

COMMANDS AND RESPONSES Several types of *U*-frames are specified. Some are *commands* and some are *responses*.

The basic *U*-frame commands are used to set the transmission modes and to disconnect a secondary station:

SNRM:　　Set Normal Response Mode

SARM:　　Set Asynchronous Response Mode

DISC:　　Disconnect

A *disconnect* (DISC) command terminates the operational mode. In switched networks it causes the addressed secondary to go "on hook," like putting down the telephone handpiece. In nonswitched networks it informs the secondary that the primary is suspending operation with it.

The basic *U*-frame responses are:

UA:　　Unnumbered Acknowledge

CMDR:　　Command Reject

The *unnumbered acknowledge* (UA) is used by the secondary to acknowledge the receipt and acceptance of *U*-format commands from the primary.

A *command reject* (CMDR) is a response which a secondary station sends when it receives a command which is nonvalid for reasons such as the following:

1. There is no such command.

2. The command is not implemented at the receiving station.

3. The *I*-field is too long to fit into the receiving station's buffers.

4. The N_R received is incongruous with the N_S that was last sent.

The command reject frame has an information field that gives details of why the command was rejected.

LOOP OPERATION　　　　IBM employs a variant of SDLC which is used when stations are arranged in a loop, as in Fig. 18.10. A primary station controls the loop. Each secondary station acts as a repeater and relays every frame it receives to the next station on the loop. It examines the address of every frame, and captures those frames which are addressed to it.

When it originates a frame, a secondary station must briefly suspend its repeater function and transmit the frame. It is permitted to do this only when it receives a special *go-ahead* pattern. This pattern consists of a 0 bit followed by seven 1 bits, 01111111. It is a unique bit pattern used only in loop operations. The secondary station receives the pattern and if it wants to transmit, it changes the seventh 1 bit to 0, thereby creating a flag pattern, 01111110. This becomes the starting flag of the frame which the station originates.

When the primary station originates a *go-ahead* pattern, 01111111, it is relayed around the loop until it reaches a station which wants to transmit, and which converts it to a flag pattern, 01111110. The station then transmits one or a group of

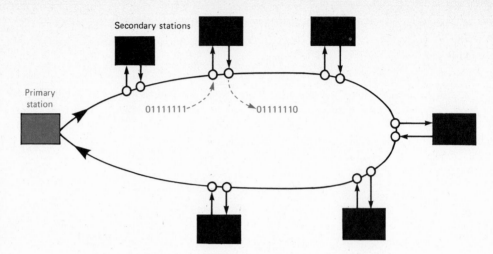

Secondary stations

Primary
station

01111111
01111110

Figure 18.10 Loop operation. The secondary station can originate
transmission only when it receives the unique GO-AHEAD pattern
01111111. If it wants to transmit, it changes the seventh 1 to 0 and thus
produces the flag byte which becomes the start of its message.

frames. When it has finished, it transmits the go-ahead pattern again so that secondary
stations downstream might also transmit. When the go-ahead pattern reaches the primary station, the cycle is complete.

The primary station can invite a secondary station to transmit by polling it in the
normal manner with an *I*-frame or *S*-frame. It can also send a poll in a *U*-frame—an
ORP command (Optional Response Poll). An ORP is unrelated to the use of sequence
numbers. A secondary station does not have to respond to it; it can if it wishes. The
ORP may be addressed to a specific station, or it may be addressed to all of the stations
on a loop and multidrop line.

When the primary sends a poll command of any type, it must follow it with a
go-ahead pattern, 01111111, so that the secondary can respond. To poll the entire
loop it sends an ORP followed by 01111111. The first station receiving this which has
something to send changes the 01111111 to a flag and transmits.

ADDITIONAL MODES   During normal operation the original versions of HDLC,
OF OPERATION   SDLC, etc., have two basic modes of operation (Fig.
                              18.4):

                              NRM: Normal Response Mode.
                              ARM: Asynchonous Response Mode.

Some other modes have been added and proposed, of which the most important is the Asynchronous Balanced Mode (Fig. 18.4) discussed earlier in this chapter. The additional modes include the following:

INITIALIZATION MODE (IM)

A station may be in this mode before it becomes operational. Special U-frame commands can change it to one of the operational modes.

NORMAL RESPONSE MODE EXTENDED (NRME)

Similar to NORMAL RESPONSE MODE but with two control bytes in the frame header, giving 7-bit (modulo 128) counts instead of 3-bit counts.

ASYNCHRONOUS RESPONSE MODE EXTENDED (ARME)

Similar to ASYNCHRONOUS RESPONSE MODE but with two control bytes in the frame header, giving 7-bit instead of 3-bit counts

NORMAL DISCONNECTED MODE (NDM)

Similar to NORMAL RESPONSE MODE except that the secondary station is logically disconnected from the data link. No I-frames or S-frames can be transmitted or accepted. Certain U-frames can be transmitted or accepted, in order to change the mode, cause a secondary station to identify itself, or poll a secondary station.

ASYNCHRONOUS DISCONNECTED MODE (ADM)

This is similar to NORMAL DISCONNECTED MODE except that (as in ARM) the secondary can initiate a response without being polled by the primary. In NORMAL DISCONNECTED MODE (like ARM), it can only respond when it receives a command from the primary.

Disconnected modes are needed when a secondary is to be prevented from appearing on the link unexpectedly while another interchange is taking place. It might cause unintended contention, a sequence number mismatch between primary and secondary, or ambiguity in the primary as to the secondary's status.

A disconnected secondary can be sent a command, or sequence of commands, which brings it to a fully operational mode.

ASYNCHRONOUS BALANCED MODE (ABM)

Combined stations (primary and secondary functions combined) using identical protocols communicate in a symmetrical fashion over a point-to-point link.

Similar to the above but with two control bytes in the frame header, giving 7-bit instead of 3-bit counts.

In the various proposals for additional modes of HDLC operation, the main additions are new types of *U*-frame, i.e., new types of commands and responses. These are described in References 5 and 7. They are relatively minor additions to what we have described in this chapter.

INCOMPATIBILITY   The increasing variety of commands and responses means that several dialects of HDLC are coming into use which are not fully compatible. This is not *necessarily* harmful providing that they are compatible for the basic functions.

If one machine sends a nonbasic command and the receiving machine rejects it because it is not implemented, the sending machine should confine itself to a more basic form of interchange (which is generally adequate). There are, however, machines which do not adjust downwards in this way. These are unable to work with machines containing simpler HDLC implementations.

If a machine, possibly an SDLC machine, does not work with balanced operations, extended addresses or extended control fields, for example, that would not be particularly serious. Machines communicating with it would have to adjust to its forms of operation. However, if a machine violated the basic rules of HDLC, that would render it unable to communicate with other HDLC machines.

REFERENCES

1. ISO documents number 3309 and 4335, available from American National Standards Institute Inc., 1430 Broadway, New York, NY 10018.

2. ANSI document number X3534/589 (see above address).

3. IBM General Information Manual of SDLC, Poughkeepsie, NY.

4. Martin, James, *Communications Satellite Systems,* Prentice-Hall, Englewood Cliffs, NJ, 1978.

5. ISO documents number 1339, 1340, 1341 (address in Reference 1).

6. Martin, J., *Systems Analysis for Data Transmission,* Prentice-Hall, Englewood Cliffs, NJ, 1973.

7. ISO document number 1300 giving definitions of NDM, ADM, and IM modes (see address in Reference 1).

19 PACKET SWITCHING

As we discussed in Chapter 14, packet switching is one way to build a switched data network capable of handling the *burstiness* in interactive computer traffic.

Figure 19.1 shows a typical packet-switching network. Each of the circles in Fig. 19.1 is a packet-switch node to which data machines can be attached. The diagram shows only three of the many data machines which are using the network. When machine A wants to send a message to machine B, it passes it to its local packet-switch node. If the message is longer than 128 bytes the node divides it into packets of maximum length 128 bytes (a typical figure). Each packet is then sent through the network a link at a time. Each node receiving a packet examines its address and determines which node to pass it on to. Eventually the packets reach the node which serves machine B. This node reassembles the packets into the original message and delivers it to machine B.

The CCITT definition of a *packet* is as follows: *A group of binary digits including data and call control signals which is switched as a composite whole. The data, call control signals, and possibly error control information are arranged in a specified format* [1].

The associated CCITT definition of *packet switching* is: *The transmission of data by means of addressed packets whereby a transmission channel is occupied for the duration of transmission of the packet only. The channel is then available for use by packets being transferred between different data terminal equipment. Note: The data may be formatted into a packet or divided and then formatted into a number of packets for transmission and multiplexing purposes* [1].

These definitions apply to the networks for which the terms were originally used, such as the ARPA network, the Telenet network, the Datapac service in Canada, and the British Post Office EPSS (Experimental Packet-Switched Service), but they apply also to network protocols or to conventional message switching networks. A major difference between such networks is the geographical layout. A network such as ARPA

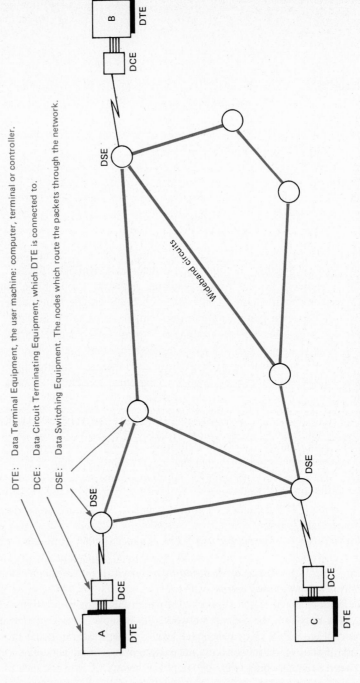

DTE: Data Terminal Equipment, the user machine: computer, terminal or controller.

DCE: Data Circuit Terminating Equipment, which DTE is connected to.

DSE: Data Switching Equipment. The nodes which route the packets through the network.

Figure 19.1 A typical packet-switching network, showing three user machines connected to it.

or Telenet serves many computer centers with a mesh-structured line layout such as that in Fig. 19.1. A typical data concentrator network has a tree structure, taking traffic to or from one computer center, or possibly a few interlinked centers.

MESSAGE SWITCHING   Packet switching is a form of *store-and-forward* switching in which messages are stored at the switch nodes and then transmitted onwards to their destination. Store-and-forward switching has existed for decades in telegraphy where it is called *message switching* [2]. There are, however, major differences between packet switching and conventional message-switching.

Whereas message switching is intended primarily for nonreal-time people-to-people traffic, packet switching is intended primarily for fast machine-to-machine traffic, including terminal-to-computer connections, and is employed to build computer networks. These differences in purpose are such that there are major differences in operation between message-switching and packet-switching networks. One important difference is in the speed of the network. A packet-switching network may be expected to deliver its packet in a fraction of a second, whereas a message-switching system typically delivers its message in a fraction of an hour. Each node passes the packet to the next node quickly, like passing on a hot potato. Another important difference is that message-switching systems usually file messages for possible retrieval at some future time. A packet-switching system deletes the message from memory as soon as its correct receipt at the next node is acknowledged. Because a message-switching system files messages, usually at one location, it tends to use a *centralized* star-structured or tree-structured network. A packet-switching network usually has a mesh-structure with no particular location dominating the structure.

In many message-switching systems, fairly long messages are sent as a single transmission. In packet-switching systems long messages are chopped up into relatively small slices, typically 128 8-bit bytes. Because the packets are of limited size, they can be queued in the main memory of the switching nodes and passed on rapidly from node to node. At its destination the original message has to be reassembled from the slices.

PUBLIC AND PRIVATE   The first large-scale packet-switching network was the
NETWORKS   ARPA network shown in Fig. 3.4. Much of the explor-
                         atory work on packet-switching techniques was done in
universities with grants form ARPA (the U.S. Department of Defense Advanced Research Projects Agency). A great amount of work went into building, modifying, tuning, simulating, analyzing, and monitoring ARPANET. From this a body of theory emerged which led to the building of public packet-switching networks, first by the value-added carrier Telenet, and then by traditional common carriers. Today there are several common-carrier, packet-switching networks around the world, with tariffs

which charge by the packet rather than charging for duration of connection as on telephone networks.

Packet-switching can be used as a technique for the transport subsystem of computer manufacturers' network architectures. It can be used for large private corporate networks, as well as for public networks. However, a network like ARPA needs a large traffic volume to make it *economically* justifiable.

One of the requirements of ARPA was that it should deliver its packets *quickly* to its users, sufficiently quickly that a person using a terminal would perceive little difference whether the terminal were connected to a computer in the same building or a computer thousands of miles away. This requirement applies to public data networks also. ARPANET achieved a fast delivery time by using lines which transmit at 50,000 bits per second. It used about 50 such lines. To achieve a reasonably economical utilization, such a resource needs a very large traffic volume. We have commented that much of the use of such networks will be for *interactive* traffic—to serve terminal users. A typical terminal operator transmits less than 10 bits per second averaged over his terminal usage (see Table 9.1). So ARPANET would need many terminal users to keep its 50 50,000 b/s lines busy.

VALUE-ADDED CARRIERS   A common carrier serving a large number of customers has sufficient traffic to keep a fast packet-switching network busy. Figure 5.1 shows the network of Telenet, the first such carrier. Figures 5.2 and 5.3 show European packet-switching networks.

The nodes of the Telenet network are called *central offices*. Like the ARPA nodes they perform two main functions. First they act as a link between the network and the data processing equipment which uses the network. Second they carry out the switching operation, determining the route by which the data shall be sent, and transmitting them.

A wide variety of user machines must be connected to such a network, as illustrated at the bottom of Fig. 19.2. Some locations connected are large computer centers; some have many terminals linked to a cluster controller; some have a single terminal connected to a telephone line.

The term IMP was used for the nodes in the ARPA network, meaning *Interface Message Processor*. The user's computer, referred to as a *host* computer, is connected directly to an IMP. The IMP receives its messages and formats them into packets. The orginal ARPANET used only IMP's, and then a second type of interface machine was added to connect terminals with no host to the network. This was called a TIP, *Terminal Interface Processor*. In Telenet the central office acts as the IMP. TIP's can be remotely connected to it, as shown in Figure 19.2, along with other forms of terminal interconnections.

Packet-switching networks serving a similar market to Telenet are now operating in several countries.

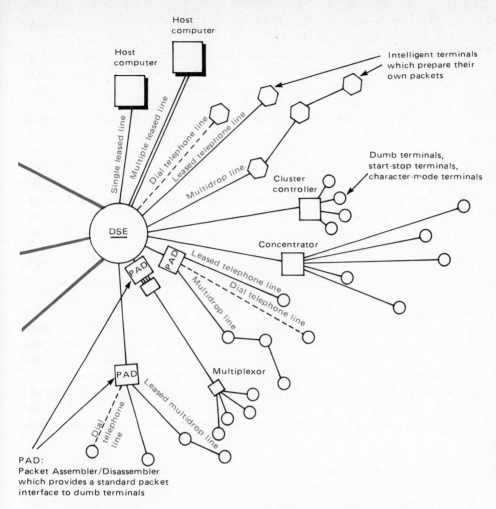

Figure 19.2 A wide variety of lines and data communications devices can provide access to a packet-switching network.

PACKETS   When user data are first received by a network node, that node formats them into packets. Like an envelope in which mail is sent, the packet must have a destination address, origination address, and various control information such as that in Box 14.2. Figure 14.7 shows the packet header used on ARPANET.

The transport network computers shunt the packets to their destination but should not interfere in any way with the data inside the envelopes. In fact, networks should be designed with security safeguards so that network computers cannot pry into the contents of the envelopes.

The final network computer strips the transmission control information from the packets, assembles the data, and passes them to the appropriate user machine.

A network computer receiving a packet places it in a queue to await attention. When the packet reaches the head of the queue, the computer examines its destination address, selects the next network computer on the route, and places the packet in an output queue for that destination. A packet-switched network is usually designed so that each network computer has a choice of routing. If the first-choice routing is poor because of equipment failure or congestion, it selects another routing. The packet thus zips through the network, finding the best way to go at each node of the network and avoiding congested or faulty portions of the network.

PACKET SIZE   The size of the packets affects how rapidly a message is relayed through a store-and-forward network. This is illustrated in Fig. 19.3. The passage of time is shown on the vertical axis going from top to bottom.

A packet is completely received into the storage of a node before it can be checked for transmission accuracy, acknowledged, and then retransmitted. If the packet is large its reception will take longer, so there will be a longer delay before it is transmitted onward. The two parts of Fig. 19.3 show the same message being transmitted. It reaches its destination faster on the right-hand side because it is sliced into smaller packets. The delivery time for a large message is longest when it is not sliced at all but transmitted and stored whole, which occurs in most *message-switching* systems.

There are two penalties to be paid for the slicing. First the slices have to be reassembled. There must be sufficient storage available to Layer 3 for reassembly of all the messages it is receiving. Reassembly is a relatively simple operation if the slices arrive in sequence. On networks with alternate routing or selective-repeat error control (discussed later), the slices can arrive out of sequence, and on rare occasions a slice may be missing. The reassembly software may be handling many messages simultaneously and there is a danger that *deadlocks* could occur (discussed in Chapter 34).

The second penalty is that the packets must carry headers. Typical headers are from 8 to 16 bytes in length. If a message is sliced into many small packets the overhead due to headers will be high. The packet size, then, should be neither too small nor too long. There is an optimum packet size. Some network designers have found a size of about 1000 bits to be appropriate. CCITT Recommendation X.25 recommends that the maximum data field length be 128 bytes. The 128-byte field is large enough that a high proportion of the messages for interactive systems fits into one packet.

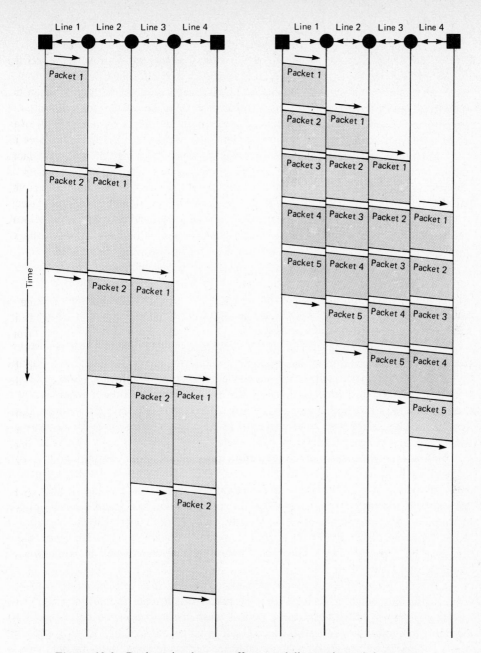

Figure 19.3 Packet size has an effect on delivery time. A long message reaches its destination more quickly when divided into five packets (on the right) than when it is divided into two packets (left). Message switching would give a still longer delivery time because the message is not divided into packets.

TYPES OF CONTROL   Several types of control are needed on a packet-switching network. It is necessary to control the effects of transmission errors, line failures, and equipment failures, while at the same time maintaining security. These forms of control, discussed in Part IV of this book, are indispensable on all data networks. Packet-switching networks need two forms of control which become much more complex than on simpler networks: *routing control* and *flow control*.

Each node relaying a packet must decide on which outgoing line to send it. The means of making this decision can become complex when alternate routes are used, depending upon the conditions in the network. A variety of routing strategies is possible.

A scheme in which the routes selected vary with the conditions of the network is called *adaptive routing*. ARPANET used adaptive routing. Most public packet-switching networks also use adaptive routing, but of a simpler form than ARPANET.

Adapting routing sometimes results in oscillatory behavior, with the routing pattern oscillating rapidly backwards and forwards under peak conditions. Minor changes in the routing algorithm can affect the routing behavior under heavy loading in ways which are difficult to predict without simulation of the network, but which can substantially affect the peak network throughput.

It is possible that packets in such a network could fail to reach their destination because of temporary equipment failure or a data error in the address. Such packets might be passed indefinitely from one node to another if something did not stop them. To prevent this, a count field is used in each packet and the number of nodes that have relayed that packet is recorded in it. When the count exceeds a certain number, the packet is returned to its point of origin. This process protects the network from becoming clogged with roving, undeliverable messages.

Flow control is desirable to prevent too many packets from converging on certain parts of the network so that traffic jams occur. The control messages which are passed between nodes to control the packet routing play a part in avoiding traffic jams. However, if too many packets enter the network heading for a given destination, the routing control alone will not prevent a traffic jam. Traffic congestion can be harmful because packets bounce around from node to node occupying an excessive share of the transmission capacity. The network performance degenerates out of all proportion to the increased load.

Packets in a mesh-structured network are rather like cars traveling across a city. At various points a decision must be made: which route should one take? This decision becomes difficult and more critical when traffic congestion builds up. It is desirable to avoid flows of traffic which result in major traffic jams. When congestion starts to slow down the traffic it is desirable for packets to avoid the congested area if possible. But how do you get information about the congested areas to other areas where routing decisions must be made? To optimize the flow of traffic through a city at rush hour, minimizing the journey times would be a complex job. Network designers attempt this optimization and must specify algorithms which work under all conditions. Flow control and routing control have been the subject of much university research. They are discussed in the next two chapters.

The subject is made particularly critical and intriguing by the fact that on working networks a variety of traffic deadlocks have occurred, occasionally locking an entire network solid. It is like a city traffic jam in which no driver behaves intelligently but follows precise rules which he has been given. Under rarely occurring traffic conditions the rules result in a jam which spreads and does not unlock. Network protocols must avoid this (see Chapter 34).

REASSEMBLY PROBLEMS

Alternate routing strategies can cause major complications in message recovery and message reassembly. It would be easy to reassemble the packets into messages if they always arrived in sequence and there were always enough buffers available. However, with alternate routing the packets may arrive out of sequence because some routes are more congested than others. A message may be ready to be reassembled with the exception of one packet which is stuck in a traffic jam somewhere. This causes the buffers in the reassembly node to be tied up when they are needed for other traffic. It may not matter if only one message is involved but there may be many such messages tying up the buffers and on rare occasions there may be insufficient buffers for a node to continue functioning.

Chapter 20 and 34 discuss reassembly problems futher.

TWO TYPES OF PACKET SWITCHING

Because of the complexities of message reassembly, flow control and the reservation of buffer space, two types of packet switching have been proposed. One, like ARPA and Telenet, allows users to send messages long enough to need slicing into multiple packets. We will refer to this as *conventional* packet switching.

The other type is much simpler. It never divides a message into slices so there is no reassembly problem. Because of this, messages cannot exceed a certain length (255 bytes has been proposed). If they do exceed their limit, the user process or higher level software has to do the slicing and reassembly. Virtual calls are not used. Instead each message is on its own. It sets off into the network carrying its destination address and may occasionally have to wait in a node until buffer space is available at the next node. No call setup or reservation messages have to be sent ahead to prepare for it. This type of network is referred to as a *datagram* network, and the messages are called *datagrams*. A datagram is *a one-packet message which appears to the network to be unrelated to any previous message or any future message*. Given the latter criterion the protocols needed to make the network function become much simpler.

Chapter 24 discusses datagram networks.

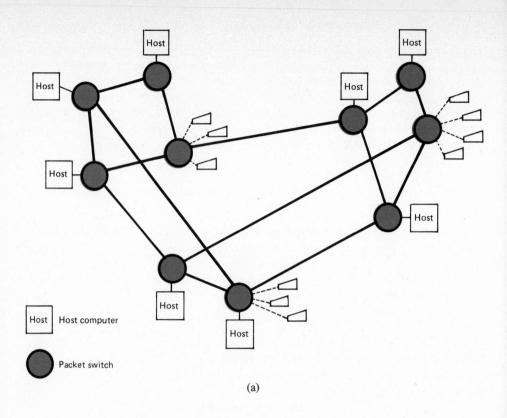

(a)

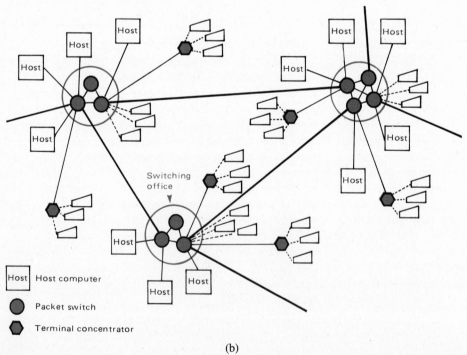

(b)

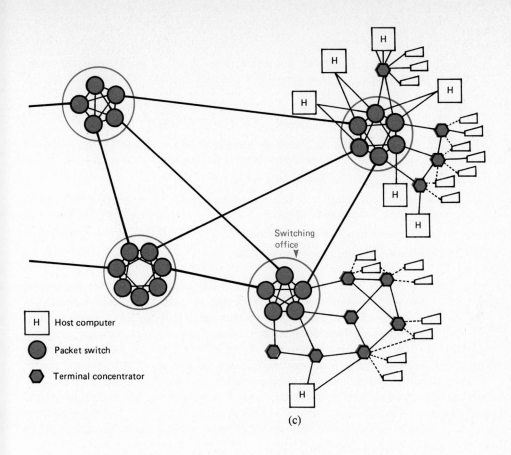

H   Host computer

●   Packet switch

⬡   Terminal concentrator

Switching
office

(c)

Figure 19.4   Three generations of packet switching. (a) First generation packet switching, e.g., ARPANET, CYCLADES. Vulnerable to
failure of the switching computer which typically is down 1% of the
time. (b) Second generation packet switching, e.g., Telenet, DATA-
PAC, TRANSPAC, EPSS. Unaffected by single switch failures in the
switching office but vulnerable to failures of the concentrator link. (c)
Mature packet switching, e.g., Telenet 1980. Switching computers use
multiple microprocessors. There are multiple routes to concentrators.
(Diagram from Telenet.)

HOW TO SIMPLIFY PACKET SWITCHING

There are several ways in which packet-switching transport subsystems can be simplified. They include the following:

- No message slicing and reassembly.
- No mechanisms which can change the sequence of packet delivery, i.e., all portions of a message are sent by the same route with no selective repeat error control.
- Routing is fixed for the duration of a virtual call.
- No setting up of virtual calls, i.e., each packet travels to its destination independently with no prior setup or reservations.
- User messages all have the same priority.
- No guarantee of delivery or return to sender.

One or more of these criteria can simplify the protocols and lower the cost of software, and often, of hardware. Many networks or transmission subsystems apply one of these simplifications. ARPA had no message priorities. Some manufacturers' network implementations have no alternate routing. Some networks have no guarantee of delivery. The latter is not necessarily as bad as it sounds. An interactive terminal user who does not receive a response will resend the message which required the response. A batch system should put checkpoints at frequent intervals in a batch to verify whether the previous portion of the batch has been sent correctly. If not, the system will resend it.

In order to avoid unnecessary overhead some software specifies certain of the above simplifications as options for the network, as a whole, or options for sessions which employ the network.

THE USER INTERFACE

As data networks spread, the usability of these networks will be enormously enhanced if they have a standard user interface. Just as telephones can plug into telphone networks everywhere, so data machines should be able to plug into data networks everywhere. The interface to data networks is much more complex, but lends itself to LSI mass-production.

The most important effort to standardize the user interface is the CCITT X.25 Recommendation, described in Chapter 23. This was rushed through the CCITT committee in record-breaking time in 1976 by common carriers from different countries which were building packet-switching networks.

The X.25 interface is for Layers 1, 2, and 3. It is likely that it will become widely accepted throughout the world with many X.25 networks coming into existence, and a wide variety of machines and software accommodating it. It can be built not only into *host* computers but also into intelligent terminals. Many terminals will remain devices which use much simpler protocols than X.25, and these will be connected to cluster controllers, concentrators, or other interface machines which do employ X.25.

To make data communications flourish as it should, it is desirable that terminals everywhere should be able to dial a data network access point with a local telephone call, or else be inexpensively polled or scanned by machine such as that in Fig. 25.6 which connects them to a data network.

In designing X.25 many lessons were learned from ARPANET and the first TELENET implementation. X.25 adopted the good features of ARPANET protocols while improving upon the mechanisms for flow control, message reassembly, buffer allocation, and establishing calls. No doubt X.25 will itself be refined as its use grows.

The network architectures of some major computer and minicomputer manufacturers have a transport subsystem entirely different from X.25. Software bridges have been developed so that some of these machines can transmit via the world's public packet-switching networks.

THREE GENERATIONS OF PACKET SWITCHING

Packet switching has evolved through three generations, shown in Fig. 19.4. The first, typified by ARPANET, had single minicomputers acting as the switching nodes. The second had multiple smaller minicomputers acting as nodes. Each node was protected from the failure of individual minis, because its separate minis could each switch the traffic and they were mesh-connected within the node. The second generation provided virtual circuits and virtual calls. The third generation increased the reliability of the concentrator links by having alternate routes to its concentrators. The switching nodes were built with multiple microcomputers, giving further protection against failure, and greater reliability.

REFERENCES

1. CCITT Fifth Plenary Assembly, Green Book Volume VII, Telegraph Technique, published by the International Telecommunications Union, Geneva, 1973.

2. Message switching, and its differences from packet switching, are described in the author's *Telecommunications and the Computer*, 2nd ed., Prentice-Hall, Englewood Cliffs, NJ, 1976.

20 FLOW CONTROL AND PACING

The purpose of *flow control* is to permit traffic to move as rapidly as possible through a network and to avoid overloading the network or its users.

On a tree-structured network, overloading can cause excessive queues to build up. On a mesh-structured network traffic jams can occur like those in a city at rush-hour. In a city the drivers use human intelligence to unlock the traffic jam. In a network, however, the procedures for avoiding or unlocking traffic jams must be thought out rigorously in advance. Some of the early networks locked solidly on occasions because the flow control procedures were not quite good enough.

The machines which use networks operate at their own speed. A transmitting machine could possibly send traffic too fast for the receiving machine. The receiving machine may run out of buffers, or be unable to process the traffic that rapidly. The receiving machine must have some means of regulating the rate at which the sending machine transmits. The process of regulation is sometimes referred to as *pacing*.

THREE LAYERS Flow control, like other forms of control, can operate at the different network layers, as illustrated in Fig. 20.1.

At Layer 2 it is usually simple. A small group of frames is transmitted; an acknowledgment is received saying that frames up to a certain number have arrived correctly; then more frames can be transmitted. Frame flow control and error control are combined into one operation, as shown in Figs. 18.4, 18.5, and 18.6. Over a satellite link it can become somewhat more complex because of the large propagation delays.

At Layer 3 the complexity of the flow control mechanism depends upon the structure of the network. A mesh-structured network is more difficult to control than a tree-structured network. On a tree-structured network the flow is orderly, to and from the top of the tree. Flow control consists mainly of regulating the *rate* of flow. On a mesh-

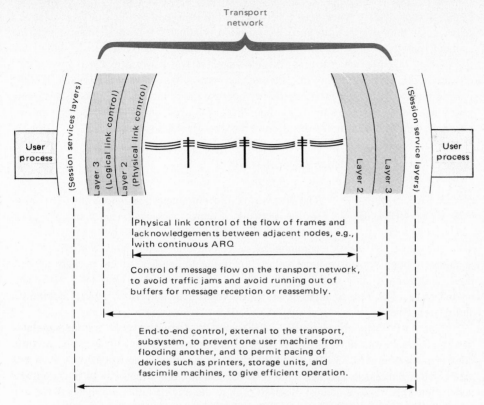

Figure 20.1   Flow control is needed at the three functional layers of a network. The procedures at the three levels may be different.

structured network, converging traffic goes in diverse patterns and causes subtle forms of lockups which we will discuss shortly. The flow control function must include protocols to avoid lockups and to back out of them if they do occur. Packets can arrive out of sequence and have to be put back into sequence again before delivery to a user process. Flow control must relate to the sequencing process. If one packet of a multi-packet message is delayed, the flow of further packets may be stopped until the message in quesiton is delivered.

Even if the transport network has elaborate flow control for its own purposes, *end-to-end* timing control is needed between the machines which employ it. This is necessary to prevent one machine from sending data faster than another can handle it, to achieve efficient utilization of a remote printer or other device, and to synchronize machines which utilize data at a fixed rate.

Pacing in the Session Services Subsystem is particularly important for the control of machines which operate synchronously because of some mechanical component. Suppose that the network is being used to transmit to a remote line printer. The printer

cannot accept data at more than a certain rate. If data comes too slowly it misses a
print cycle. It is desirable to keep the machine printing at full speed without missing
cycles if possible. A buffer is associated with the machine and the pacing signals tell
the sending machine when to transmit, slowing it down if a print cycle is missed and
possibly requesting retransmission if a message arrives too early for the printer. Timing
is even more critical on a facsimile printer because the printer has continuously moving
paper and cannot make up for a lost line. Pacing is used similarly to read or write on
a storage unit with seek times or different duration for each record.

**REQUEST
FOR NEXT MESSAGE**
The best way to prevent congestion is to control the *input*
to the network. Control messages can warn all input
nodes that congestion is beginning to build up. The most
common cause of potential traffic jams is that one host
computer suddenly sends a large volume of traffic to another. If the packets for this
traffic follow each other at the speed of the input machine, there may be a traffic jam
on the route. The rate of input needs to be controlled rather than merely opening a
sluice-gate wide.

The ARPA network controlled such surges by permitting only one message at a
time to be sent from an originating point to any one destination. The message could
consist of up to eight packets. When the destination node has completely received and
assembled the message and delivered it to the machine for which it was intended, the
destination node sends a control message back to the originating node saying that it can
take another message. This is called *"ready-for-next-message"* signal, RFNM (pro-
nounced "Rufnum"). The RFNM is formatted similarly to the other packets, and finds
its way through the network using the same protocols as any other packet.

Figure 20.2 shows the passage of a message through the original ARPA network. The message goes from the host machine on the left of the diagrams to the host
machine on the right. Three switching nodes, or IMP's, are shown. The first IMP is
connected directly (i.e., not over a telephone company line) to the originating host
machine. The host sends a message, which on the ARPA network can be up to 8063
bits, to its local IMP with a header saying where the message is to be sent.

The IMP chops the message into packets. The IMP determines which line to
transmit on, and sends the first packet. When it receives an acknowledgment from the
next IMP saying that the packet was received correctly, it sends the next packet. The
packets eventually arrive at the destination IMP, the third IMP in the figure. They may
have come by different routes and hence could possibly arrive out of sequence. The
destination IMP waits until it has received all the packets for this message; it assembles
the message, removes the packet envelopes, adds a message header, and delivers the
message to the destination host. The receiving IMP then sends a RFNM addressed to
the originating IMP on the left. The RFNM is relayed like any other packet to the IMP
to which it is addressed. When the left-hand IMP receives the RFNM correctly it tells
the host that it is ready to accept another message for transmission.

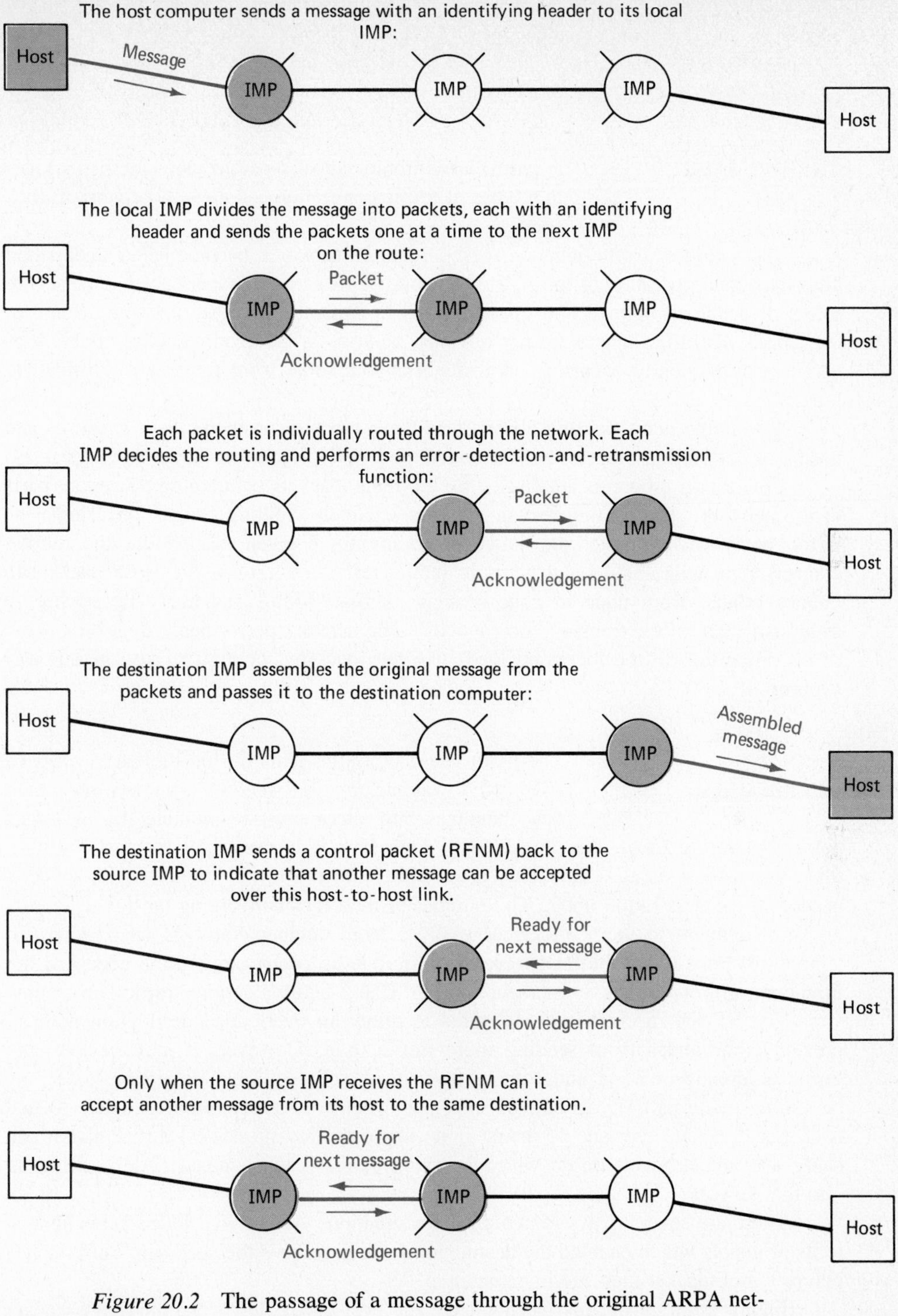

The host computer sends a message with an identifying header to its local IMP:
Host
Message
IMP
IMP
IMP
Host
The local IMP divides the message into packets, each with an identifying header and sends the packets one at a time to the next IMP on the route:
Host
Packet
IMP
IMP
IMP
Acknowledgement
Host
Each packet is individually routed through the network. Each IMP decides the routing and performs an error-detection-and-retransmission function:
Host
Packet
IMP
IMP
IMP
Acknowledgement
Host
The destination IMP assembles the original message from the packets and passes it to the destination computer:
Host
IMP
IMP
IMP
Assembled message
Host
The destination IMP sends a control packet (RFNM) back to the source IMP to indicate that another message can be accepted over this host-to-host link.
Host
Ready for next message
IMP
IMP
IMP
Acknowledgement
Host
Only when the source IMP receives the RFNM can it accept another message from its host to the same destination.
Host
Ready for next message
IMP
IMP
IMP
Acknowledgement
Host

Figure 20.2 The passage of a message through the original ARPA network.

The RFNM mechanism shown in Fig. 20.2 is neat and simple, *but it proved to be inadequate.* Traffic jams occurred.

TRAFFIC JAMS A particularly problematical aspect of networks is that certain types of traffic congestion can cause a network to lock solidly.

The nature of traffic jams on mesh-structured networks became better understood after the actual operation of the ARPA network. This network experienced some severe forms of deadlock both in live operation and in simulations of the network. Some of the causes of traffic jams were not obvious, at first. Some occurred very rarely, triggered by infrequently occurring coincidences. And some were remarkably difficult to prevent.

Nonsimple networks will always face these types of problems, so the causes and means of controlling them should be understood. We discuss deadlocks in Chapter 34.

Congestion problems are caused by too many packets converging on certain parts of the network. The routing techniques play a part in avoiding congestion. However, if too many packets enter the network heading for a given destination, the routing control alone will not prevent a traffic jam. Traffic congestion can cause packets to bounce around from node to node seeking alternate routes and hence occupying an excessive share of the transmission capacity. The network performance degenerates out of all proportion to the increased load, like the roads out of a large city on a Friday evening.

MESSAGE REASSEMBLY The main cause of traffic jams during the early years of ARPANET was *message reassembly.* Any network which cuts messages into slices must reassemble the messages before delivering them. As illustrated in Fig. 19.3 it is desirable, for fast response time, to cut the messages into fairly small slices. To reassemble them, buffer space is needed in the destination node. The number of messages converging on this node varies from moment to moment. Occasionally a large number converge on it so that it temporarily runs out of buffer space. A traffic pile-up occurs around the node and the flow control protocol has its moment of truth: Can it avoid a serious traffic jam or not?

The RFNM mechanism is intended to allow an overloaded destination node to prevent other nodes from sending more traffic to it. However, it may be too late; traffic is already in flight and coming from many sources. The destination node may be storing many partially assembled messages when it runs out of buffer space so that it cannot complete any one of them. If it cannot destroy messages, this situation can cause a deadlock, with traffic which is trying to reach the jammed node backing up into the network.

There are several ways to avoid such a situation. ARPANET added a mechanism to its protocols which enabled the destination node to *reserve* the necessary buffer space before a mulitpacket message is transmitted.

Figure 20.3 shows this mechanism. The host on the left is sending an 8-packet

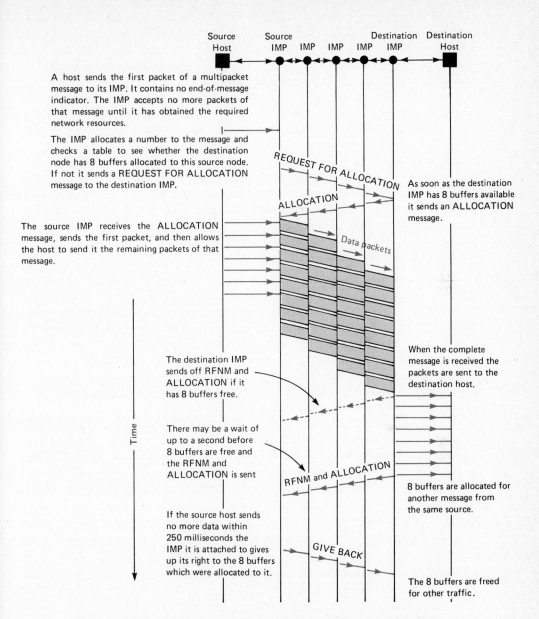

Source Host   Source IMP   IMP   IMP   IMP   IMP   Destination IMP   Destination Host

A host sends the first packet of a multipacket message to its IMP. It contains no end-of-message indicator. The IMP accepts no more packets of that message until it has obtained the required network resources.

The IMP allocates a number to the message and checks a table to see whether the destination node has 8 buffers allocated to this source node. If not it sends a REQUEST FOR ALLOCATION message to the destination IMP.

REQUEST FOR ALLOCATION

ALLOCATION

As soon as the destination IMP has 8 buffers available it sends an ALLOCATION message.

The source IMP receives the ALLOCATION message, sends the first packet, and then allows the host to send it the remaining packets of that message.

Data packets

When the complete message is received the packets are sent to the destination host.

The destination IMP sends off RFNM and ALLOCATION if it has 8 buffers free.

There may be a wait of up to a second before 8 buffers are free and the RFNM and ALLOCATION is sent

RFNM and ALLOCATION

8 buffers are allocated for another message from the same source.

If the source host sends no more data within 250 milliseconds the IMP it is attached to gives up its right to the 8 buffers which were allocated to it.

GIVE BACK

The 8 buffers are freed for other traffic.

Time

Figure 20.3 The sequence of events on ARPANET for multipacket transmission. If many multipacket messages are to be sent as rapidly as possible the control events for one message need to be overlapped with those of the next.

317

message to the host on the right. When its local IMP receives the first packet it sends a REQUEST-FOR-ALLOCATION control message to the destination IMP. The destination IMP reserves 8 packet buffers if it can, and informs the source IMP that it has done so by sending an Allocation control message to it. Only then may the source IMP start transmitting data. Furthermore, in order to preserve its own buffers it now refuses to accept more than one packet of the message from the originating host until it has been given the Allocation that it needed.

When the destination IMP has received all 8 packets it reassembles the message and passes it to the destination host. When it returns the RFNM to the source IMP, this is now combined with a new Allocation signal saying that it has set aside 8 more buffers so that the source IMP can send another 8-packet message if it wants to. The reason for this automatic Allocation without request is that usually a user sending an 8-packet message will follow it with another message; it is part of a longer transmission. If the source IMP does not in fact receive another message to send within 250 milliseconds it will give up the space reserved for it. It does this with the Giveback message shown at the bottom of Fig. 20.3.

VIRTUAL BANDWIDTH   Flow control procedures are needed not only to avoid traffic jams, but also to maximize the throughput of a network. For interactive systems we are concerned with the response time of a network. For file transmission we are concerned with its *virtual bandwidth*. What is the overall speed of file transfer in bits per second across the logical link?

Suppose that the source host in Fig 20.3 is transmitting a file, or possibly a very long message such as a facsimile document. It is desirable to send the next message as quickly as possible after the message in Fig. 20.3.

The destination sends a new Allocation with the RFNM, but even so there will be a gap between the sending of one message and the next. To avoid any such gap in transmission the new buffer allocation needs to be made earlier, in advance of the source node being able to send the message. ARPA introduced a further complication to permit this. A simple and more flexible technique is pacing using two parameters, M and N.

M AND N PACING   When a source node requests to transmit continuously, the receiving node tells it to send N packets, or possibly N messages. N is a parameter of the flow control procedure which is related to the buffer availability in the receiving machine.

The destination node will not necessarily wait until it has received all N packets before it sends the request for another N. This would cause a break in the transmission. Instead it sends its request when there are still M outstanding packets from the previous request. The size of M depends upon the time delays in relaying the data and control messages through the network.

M and N pacing is illustrated in Fig. 20.4. It is shown here as applying to a

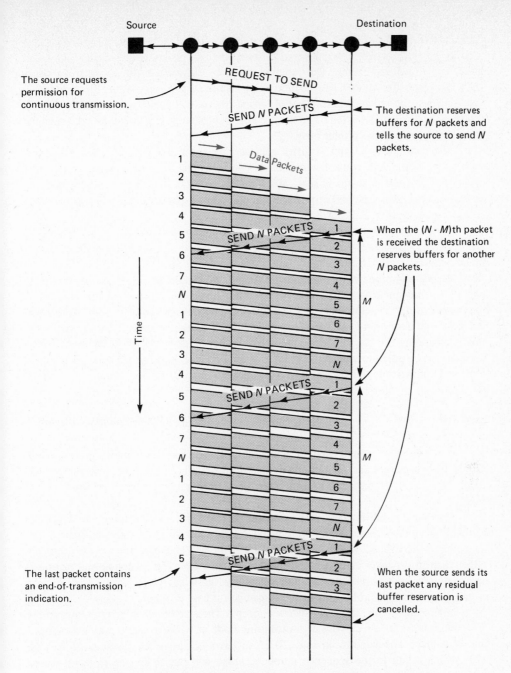

Source   Destination

The source requests permission for continuous transmission.

REQUEST TO SEND

SEND N PACKETS

The destination reserves buffers for N packets and tells the source to send N packets.

Data Packets

1
2
3
4
5
6
7
N
1
2
3
4
5
6
7
N
1
2
3
4
5

Time

SEND N PACKETS

SEND N PACKETS

SEND N PACKETS

1
2
3
4
5
6
7
N
1
2
3
4
5
6
7
N
1
2
3

When the (N - M)th packet is received the destination reserves buffers for another N packets.

M

M

The last packet contains an end-of-transmission indication.

When the source sends its last packet any residual buffer reservation is cancelled.

Figure 20.4 Continuous *M* and *N* flow control. This type of pacing can be used in Layers 2, 3, and 4. It is used on packet-switching networks and networks of other types.

packet-switching network. It is also used on other types of networks. In particular it is used in Layer 4 control. Consider transmission to a line printer with a buffer which can hold four lines of print. The source may be instructed to send three lines ($N = 3$). When the second one arrives, it is instructed to send another three ($M = 1$). As long as the printer goes at full speed there will be buffer space available for each line when it arrives. The source keeps sufficiently far ahead of the transmission delays to keep the printer busy.

The parameters M and N differ substantially from one network situation to another. On simple link control where blocks are sent one at a time and each block is checked before the next one is sent, $N = 1$ *and* $M = 0$. On the ARPA network data are sent a *message* at a time and a message can consist of 8 packets, $N = 8$ and $M = 0$. On some architectures N and M are variables.

N should not be too large, otherwise much buffer space is needed in the nodes, and recovery procedures require more to be retransmitted. Typical values are likely to range between 1 and 16.

Where high apparent bandwidth is needed, M should be large enough to permit continuous transmission. This value varies from one network situation to another. If the control signal is returned on terrestrial telephone lines without passing through intermediate nodes, $M = 2$ or 3 may be adequate. If there are several packet-switching nodes separating the origin and destination, a larger value of M might be used. If the network uses a satellite channel operating at 56,000 b/s, 30 or so packets could be on their way by the time the control signal is returned. M may be 30 or more.

THE WINDOW CONCEPT

When one user process sends traffic to another it is desirable that the traffic should arrive in the same *sequence* as that in which it is dispatched. The transport subsystem should be transparent and should not jumble up the traffic. On ARPA and similar networks sequencing is performed on the span of up to 8 packets which can form a message.

A more flexible concept of sequencing is referred to as the *window* concept, a form of M and N control first introduced by the Canadian Datapac designers. Sequencing is performed within a variable-size window, and can operate continuously rather than in 8-packet chunks as on the ARPA network. The reception and transmission of sequenced packets is controlled by a *window* at each end of the connection. Flow control regulates the transmission between these windows.

Figure 20.5 illustrates the window concept. The size of the window relates to the available buffers of a receiving or transmitting node at which packets may be arranged into sequence. The window in Fig. 20.5 can have 128 possible positions, 0 through 127, which relate to the sequence numbers which are carried by the packets. Those packets at a receiving node which fall within the window can be arranged into sequence by that node. When sequenced, the packets at the left of the window can be delivered

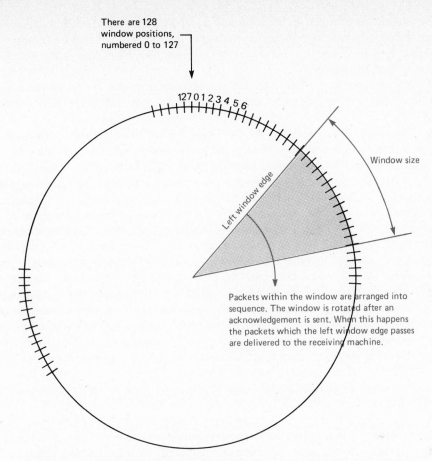

There are 128
window positions,
numbered 0 to 127

127 0 1 2 3 4 5 6

Window size

Left window edge

Packets within the window are arranged into
sequence. The window is rotated after an
acknowledgement is sent. When this happens
the packets which the left window edge passes
are delivered to the receiving machine.

Figure 20.5   The window concept used for flow control. This is a 128-
position counter with a window size of 9. Figure 20.6 shows an 8-po-
sition counter with a window size of 3.

to the user process. As that happens the window rotates and an acknowledgment of the
delivered packets is transmitted to their sender.

If a packet is received which does not fall into the current window position of the
receiving node, it cannot be handled because of buffer size limitations. It is discarded. The packets which fall within the window are sequenced by the receiving
node, and duplicates are discarded. If a packet in the sequence is missing the window
cannot be rotated past that point. To deal with these situations error messages relating
to the window are sent.

To control the transmission the sending machine maintains a window which is the
same size as the receiving machine. An acknowledgment to the sending machine con-

tains a sequence number giving the position of the receiving machine's left window edge which indicates what packet the receiving machine expects to receive next. The sending machine rotates its window to this position, thereby making buffers available for continued transmission.

The transmitter can only transmit sequence numbers that are inside the transmit window. The receiver can only accept sequence numbers that are inside the receive window.

Virtual calls will normally be full-duplex. There must then be both a receive window and a transmit window at each end of the link-four windows in all. One node may have many calls in operation, requiring many windows.

Seven bits are needed to represent the window position in Fig. 20.5. A station using such a scheme would put two 7-bit numbers in the messages it sends, one being a sequence number of the message itself, and the other the sequence number of the *next message the station expects to receive*. The former is called a *send* sequence number N_S, and the other a *receive* sequence number N_R. The former indicates the position of the *send window,* the other the *receive window*. If a receive window fails to move as expected because of an error, the receiving machine will inform the sending machine. If no data packets are being transmitted which can carry this information, a separate control packet will be sent (an acknowledgment). If the sending machine does not receive an acknowledgment allowing it to rotate its window within a specified time, it will retransmit one or more of the packets in its send window.

For many terrestrial networks, 8 window positions are used rather than the 128 of Fig. 20.5. N_S and N_R are then each 3-bit numbers. Figure 20.6 illustrates flow control with 8-position counters and a window size of 3. It shows the synchronization of the send and receive windows.

Glancing ahead, Fig. 22.7 shows Layer 3 flow control on an X.25 network with windows of size 3 in a system which uses 8-position windows.

The window size may be changed, if desired, to help control congestion, or because different *sessions* have different requirements. Protocols should have the capability to send information about the two window parameters, and to change the window sizes when necessary.

If the window size is too large, more buffering is needed and it is possible that a delayed packet might be accepted incorrectly because of the wrap-around count. If the window size is too small the effective throughput of the logical link will be restricted. This is especially so if the time for packets to traverse the link is long. If high virtual bandwidth is needed, or if the packet propagation time is long, a large window size and a large counter are needed. If satellite transmission is likely to be used, a 128-position counter is desirable because of the long delay on satellite channels. On the Japanese public packet-switching network [1], a 128-position counter is being used, partially because future transmission may be via satellite. Most packet-switching networks in Europe, where satellite transmission seems unlikely, are using 8-position counts.

Whatever priority scheme is used, flow control procedures may employ it to lessen traffic jams, increase response times for interactive traffic, increase network throughput for certain types of traffic, or to lower the total network cost of handling a given quantity of traffic.

In general, flow control is a complex subject. Much research on and simulation of flow control mechanisms has been done. This is discussed in the reference listed below.

REFERENCES

1. Kahn, R. E., and W. R. Crowther, "Flow Control in a Resource-Sharing Computer Network," *IEEE Transactions on Communications,* June 1972.

21 ROUTING TECHNIQUES

Imagine that you are driving through a city. There are many ways to reach your destination. On the map it may appear that one particular route is the best. But suppose that certain streets are closed and that traffic jams exist in a few areas. You reach an intersection. Which is the best way?

The situation is similar to that with a packet-reaching node of a mesh-structured network. The packet may carry a destination or logical-channel address. Which way should the node route it?

In order to make this decision you would like to have detailed knowledge of the situation elsewhere. The better your knowledge the better your routing decision can be. However, it would be expensive to give you complete up-to-the-second information of the situation elsewhere, so you have to make the routing decision under conditions of imperfect knowledge.

In a network a switching node can only acquire knowledge of the conditions elsewhere if this information is transmitted to it. This transmission uses up circuit capacity. It is as though you could only acquire knowledge of the city traffic jams by means of information carried to you in other *cars*. These could be cars carrying other passengers or they could be special small cars which exist solely to circulate routing information. Obviously there cannot be too many of the latter or they would worsen the traffic congestion.

You cannot make a *perfect* routing decision. It is rather like the Heisenberg Uncertainty Principle. To acquire nearly complete knowledge for routing would require so much overhead that the traffic throughout would be substantially reduced. What, then, is a good routing strategy?

If there is minimal traffic, the network path with the minimum number of links will normally be the best. If a circuit or node has failed, then the path with the minimum number of links which bypasses the failure will be the best.

As the traffic builds up, however, this simple routing strategy can give poor results at times because the shortest path may happen to be congested. The network as a whole should employ a routing strategy that would bypass areas of congestion. Much research has been devoted to network routing strategies (see end-of-chapter references).

OBJECTIVES There are several possible objectives of a network routing strategy:

1. Minimize the packet transit times.
2. Minimize the packet transit costs.
3. Maximize the network throughput capability.

To some extent there is a conflict between these objectives. To minimize the packet transit times under conditions of changing load, many control messages (overhead) would have to be sent, so that the network throughput would be reduced. On the other hand, maximizing the throughput could be done at the expense of packet transit times.

A specific network design or architecture might have a compromise objective such as "minimize the cost of a given throughput with 95% of the packets having a transit time of less than 200 milliseconds."

DIFFERENT TARIFFS In a packet-switching network the routing decision relates simply to which of several similar routes to take. In a corporate network there may be another complication, especially in countries with multiple carriers like the USA. Which *type* of circuit should be used?

The routing software (Layer 4 in this case) will attempt to select the lowest cost route. This may be a satellite circuit; it may be a corporate tie-line trunk, which is used mainly for voice traffic; it may be a specialized common carrier circuit or a wideband facility such as a cable television circuit or facsimile circuit which is available for computer data some of the time only.

The routing mechanism checks which trunks are available from the building to the destination, or to a node near the destination. It selects whichever can be used at lowest cost. Bulk transmission may be deferred until night when lower cost trunks are available. The utilization patterns of a voice network or satellite network might vary greatly and this may vary what circuits are used for data.

STATIC AND DYNAMIC ROUTING When a network node receives a packet addressed to another node it must determine to which of its adjacent nodes to send it. It may have a routing table for this purpose. It then examines the destination address of the packet and looks up the route to that location in its routing table. If the addressing structure is designed for a large network it may employ the address, *not of the final destination, but the destination subarea.*

The routing table may be *static* or *dynamic.*

By *static* we mean that the table is fixed and does not vary with the traffic patterns. Figure 21.1 shows a possible form of such a table. The table shown gives a first choice and second choice path. If the first choice path is blocked or inoperative, a node will use the second choice path. (There is no need for the table in the illustration to give a third choice because no node has more than three lines going from it.)

Dynamic routing uses a table which changes as the traffic loads change, attempting to give the best routing at different times. This is referred to as *adaptive routing*— the network adapts its behavior to varying traffic patterns.

Figure 21.2 shows a network with figures marked on the links, which are proportional to the network delays. It shows a routing table for node *C* which takes these delays into consideration. Because part of the delay is caused by queuing, the delays and hence the routing table will change as the traffic patterns and volumes change.

At one end of a scale the routing could be completely static, never changing. At the other end it could be dynamic, changing almost instantaneously in response to different traffic patterns.

There are many points on this scale between completely static and highly dynamic routing. Static routing could be used, but changed when there is a failure, or changed when large queues build up, or changed periodically. The routing could be fixed for a *session.* At the beginning of a session a route is selected for that session, and the same route is maintained for the duration of the session provided that no circuit or node fails on that route. The node would build a routing table with the session identifier as the input.

Completely dynamic routing would keep each node's tables constantly updated as to what is the best route. The ARPA network nodes receive information for updating their routing tables about twice a second. Very frequent updating requires substantial network overhead. Somewhat less dynamic routing could use less frequent updating.

**INFORMATION
FOR ROUTING**

To construct the best routing tables in the nodes, information is needed about the instantaneous state of the network and its traffic. Unfortunately, it is not possible for the nodes to have up-to-the-nanosecond information about the entire network. To provide it would require too great an overhead. The nodes must therefore make do with information which is out-of-date, perhaps only by half a second, perhaps by much more. Furthermore, the information will probably be incomplete in that it does not cover the entire network and its traffic, but rather is more localized in extent.

We can use another scale to describe the routing, which indicates the extent of the knowledge on which the routing decisions are based. At one end of the scale the routing entity has global network information. At the other end it can observe only its own traffic.

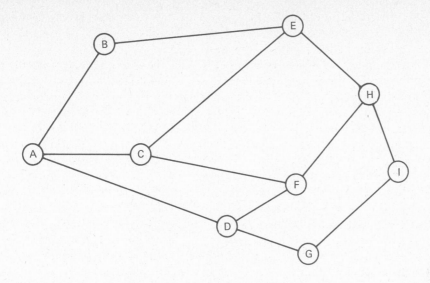

Packet destination	First choice node	Second choice node
A	A	F
B	A	E
D	A	F
E	E	A
F	F	A
G	F	A
H	E	F
I	E	F

Figure 21.1 A static routing table for node C in the above network, giving the node to which C should route a packet for a stated destination.

The numbers are proportional to the delays
occurring on the network:

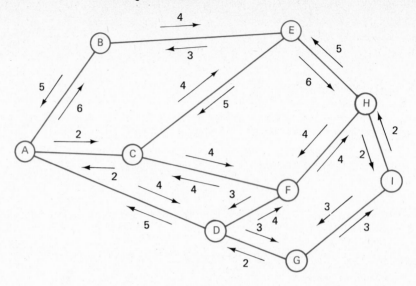

Figure 21.2   A dynamic routing table for node C intended to minimize
transit delays under current network conditions.

Figure 21.3 illustrates this range of routing strategies. The vertical scale indicates how extensive the routing information is. The horizontal scale indicates how dynamic. Routing in the top right-hand corner would be ideal, but would require far too much overhead. Some networks are close to the top of the diagram at the expense of being relatively static. Some are near the right of the diagram at the expense of having to use fairly localized information.

The most *cost-effective* routing technique is not necessarily highly dynamic or fully informed. This depends upon the relative cost of the transmission links and the cost of making the routing decisions. In some networks simple inexpensive routing algorithms are the best.

CENTRALIZED Routing tables can be updated by each switching node or
OR DECENTRALIZED? possibly by each computer which initiates a session.
Alternatively, they can be updated by a central network management facility and the changes transmitted to the switching nodes.

A centralized routing authority usually uses global network information in making the routing decisions. However, it may take some time to collect this information, so the information will not be immediately up to date. A switching node making its own decisions will have up-to-date information about local conditions, but may be ignorant of what is happening two nodes away. Centralized routing is, therefore, often towards

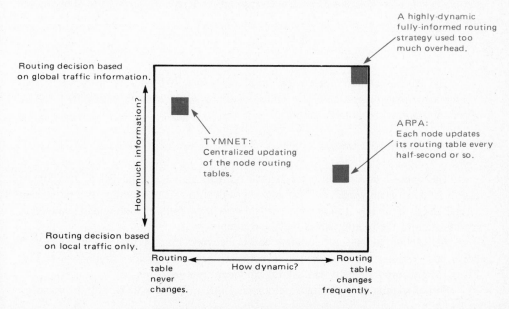

Figure 21.3 Routing strategies.

the top and left of Fig. 21.3. Decentralized routing may be towards the right but not near the top.

Most early systems used either purely centralized or purely decentralized routing. Most networks from major computer manufacturers determine the route before the data is sent. On the other hand, networks such as ARPA and Telenet let each node decide the outgoing circuit it will use for each packet. These nodes are autonomous and the term ''Markovian constraint'' is used to imply that the routing decision for a packet is independent of the previous routes taken by that packet.

PACKET-ROUTING,
MESSAGE-ROUTING,
AND SESSION-ROUTING

The routing decision can be made to apply to each packet, each message, each session; or to each logical circuit:

• *Packet routing.*

The routing decision applies to one packet: the next packet to the same destination might go by a different route.

• *Message routing.*

All packets of one message go via the same route. There is then no shuffling of out-of-sequence packets during message reassembly. Recovery procedures apply to entire message.

• *Session routing.*

The route is chosen when a session is established. All packets in the session go via the same path unless there is a failure of a link or node on that path. If a failure occurs a new session route is chosen.

• *Logical circuit routing.*

The route is chosen when the logical (virtual) circuit is established. If a logical circuit is used for only one session this is equivalent to session routing. If a permanent virtual circuit links two machines this would be a static form of routing and some other modification of the routing tables may be desirable.

ARPANET and several common carrier networks employ packet routing. TYMNET and various other commercial networks employ session routing (see Fig. 21.3). Many corporate networks use logical circuit routing.

Packet routing gives a higher probability that a packet will be able to avoid an area of congestion. The average network transmission time, therefore, tends to be slightly less when packet routing is used than when session routing is used. This difference is observed on simulated studies of network routing. Session routing or message routing may be used, however, because it keeps the packets of a session in sequence and hence avoids the resequencing problems discussed in Chapter 20. Logical circuit routing is used because it is simple and has low overhead.

The main disadvantage of packet routing is that packets can arrive out of sequence, causing message reassembly problems. The main disadvantage of session routing is that sessions can be long and to fix the routing for such a long period lowers the network adaptiveness. Logical circuit routing may be worse. Message routing may be the best compromise in certain networks; session routing in others. The packets comprising the message then arrive in sequence (unless some other desequencing mechanism *like selective repeat* error control is used).

Message routing requires that the switching algorithm knows which packets belong to which messages. The Layer 3 header often carries the number of the logical circuit and an indication of the last packet in a message, from which it can be deduced what packets are parts of the same message.

There are other options concerning when the routing decision is made. Rather than being made at the start of a packet, message, session, or logical circuit, the determination of the route between two given points, or the route for a logical circuit, might be made:

- When the network is started up.
- After links or nodes fail.
- When there are major shifts in workload patterns.
- When changes in network configuration occur.
- At periodic intervals.
- When an operator intervenes.

Reoptimization of routes on a *slowly* changing basis has the advantage that there is time to measure to delays and use them to heuristically evaluate the optimum routing. The disadvantage is inability to adapt quickly enough to changes in traffic and congestion patterns.

HOW AUTOMATIC? The act of changing the routing is automatic, fast, and self-optimizing on some systems. In much distributed system software, however, operator intervention is needed either to change the routing, or to change the routing tables.

With nonautomatic routing the routes may remain fixed until an operator intervenes. Such intervention may not happen until a failure occurs.

Other systems automatically reroute the traffic when they detect that it is failing to reach its destination. The table showing what alternate routes to take, however, has to be entered manually.

Automatic routing schemes are used not only to automatically reroute but to determine what is the route to take. In some they only do this when a failure occurs.

The best is a system which continually examines and optimizes the routing.

EXPLICIT   An important class of routing techniques is called *explicit*
PATH ROUTING   *path* routing. With this form of routing the messages trav-
                                      elling inform the switching nodes what route to use. The
originating machine (or the subarea computer which manages its sessions) selects the route.

Each message could carry details of the route it is to use in its header. However, for a complex network this would require too much overhead in the header. Therefore, the routing instruction may be sent to the switching nodes at the start of a session and remain the same throughout that session unless a failure occurs. The switching nodes insert the routing instruction into a table telling them where to send each packet.

In another version of explicit path routing each message may carry a group of bits indicating whether it takes a primary route or an alternate route. Four bits would permit a choice of 16 possible routes, and the switching node might have 16 entries in its routing table instead of the two in Fig. 21.1. Some of them would be the same if the node has less than 16 paths leaving it. The table look-up can be shortened by having each switch examine only some of the routing bits. Different bits apply to different groups of switches.

The advantage of explicit path routing is that the computer which manages the session can control the type of route that is used. It may select a different type of route for different types of session. Some sessions may send bulk data with no response time constraints. These data can be sent by an inexpensive route and delayed if necessary. Some sessions may use a satellite circuit but on some this may be avoided because the propagation delays affect the pacing or other control mechanisms. Some sessions may transmit facsimile messages of 200,000 bits or so, and routes would be avoided on which this overloads the buffers. An objective of explicit path routing may be to prevent the bulk transmissions from degrading the fast interactive transmissions.

With explicit path routing a computer which manages sessions can measure the *end-to-end* delay associated with different routes, not merely the delay on individual links. This can be used as a criterion for choosing the routes.

Explicit path routing is appropriate for a tightly controlled corporate network handling widely different types of traffic. It is sometimes especially appropriate in a multinational environment. It is not appropriate for a general purpose common carrier or PTT network.

STOCHASTIC ROUTING   Another important class of routing technique is that in which each switching node makes its own routing decision. There are many possible algorithms which that node could use. Some of these algorithms are very simple and require little network overhead. Others are complex and expensive. Much study and simulation of these algorithms has been done. (See references at end of chapter).

If a routing algorithm in each node dynamically modifies its operation to reflect changing traffic patterns, the routing technique is said to be *stochastic*.

Some examples of distributed or stochastic routing are as follows:

1. A technique called *hot-potato* routing passes the packet on immediately, down the shortest route if possible (first choice path in a fixed routing table), and if not down the second choice path, and so on. If no path is free, i.e., there is a queue for every path, the path with the *shortest queue* is selected [2].

2. Various constraints (biases) can be applied to shortest-queue routing. In one, a count is carried by the packet to indicate how many nodes it has passed through. This and the queue size are used to determine the route [3, 4]. Such methods do not employ information about conditions elsewhere in the network. They are at the bottom of the square in Fig. 21.3.

3. In one proposed method each node attempts to obtain information about the delays on routes going *from* it by measuring the delays incurred by packets *arriving* on that route. Each packet is time-stamped when it sets off on its journey and from this time-stamp each node compiles a table of information about delays. Unfortunately, the delays measured are incurred by packets travelling in the opposite direction to that of concern. If the same volume of traffic flowed in each direction this could be a useful method of obtaining delay information. However, many networks have highly unsymmetrical traffic loads. It is like estimating the delays that cars will incur when leaving a city at rush hour by measuring the journey time of *incoming* cars.

4. *Proportional routing*. A choice between two or more routes is made at random except that the proportion of traffic sent down the various alternative links to a destination is varied. The lower the path delay, the higher the proportion of traffic sent down that path. The proportions may be set and periodically adjusted by a central network management facility which, to a greater or lesser extent, is familiar with the network delays. Or, the proportions may be set by the node itself, based on whatever information it can deduce about network delays.

5. The routing may be adaptive only at a gross level in that the nodes react only to circuit failures or major traffic blockages. Each node may employ a routing table like that in Fig.

21.2, which is rarely changed. When an indication is received by the node of a failure or blockages on a route involving the *first-choice* node, it sends the packet to the *second-choice* node instead.

6. In a major class of techniques, the nodes exchange information about delays by sending control messages to one another.

   For all the nodes in a large network to keep each other fully informed would require too many messages. Therefore, various forms of limited exchange are sought. Each node may pass messages to adjacent nodes only. In ARPANET and several networks using ARPANET-like techniques *minimum delay vectors* are exchanged [4], giving estimates of the minimum delay to other nodes in the network. Each node receiving delay vectors adds estimates of its own delay if the route with the minimum delay is taken. In this way delay information propagates throughout the network. The ARPANET nodes exchange this information at half-second intervals.

   Delay vectors may be exchanged at regular intervals (synchronously) as on the ARPA network. Alternatively, they may be exchanged asynchronously, i.e., only when the estimated delays change by more than a certain amount. Simulation studies have indicated that asynchronous exchange gives better network performance.

7. The nodes send information about traffic and delays to a central control location which correlates the information and sends changes to routing tables back to the nodes. More than one central location might be used for reliability reasons.

8. A combination of node-to-node and central routing information may be used. On complex networks it is likely that a combination of distributed and central routing control will be better than either by itself.

OSCILLATIONS AND LOOPS

As with any feedback control system there is a danger that oscillations can occur. With stochastic routing some smoothing of the measurements of delays is desirable to prevent this rather than very fast reactions to delays.

In some cases loops occur in which a packet passes through some node more than once. Looping was a problem on ARPANET. It tends to happen when the network can least afford it—when the traffic is heaviest.

It is generally desirable that the algorithms should be designed to *reduce the long-term average delay* per packet rather than the immediate delay for the packet currently being routed. Solely paying attention to the routing of one packet often has an adverse effect on the routing of other packets [14].

COMBINED STRATEGIES

Combinations of the above strategies are often more effective than any one strategy by itself.

In a combined strategy a centralized mechanism may maintain a global picture of the network traffic and use this to pass routing information to the nodes. This is a relatively slow mechanism which cannot respond quickly enough to local conditions. The nodes, therefore, have their own mechanism for reacting to instantaneous local traffic peaks and failures.

Such a scheme could operate synchronously. Every T seconds the nodes send messages containing traffic information to the routing center. The center compiles this data and sends instructions back to the nodes. T can be varied. If T is small, the scheme is quick to adapt but requires large network overhead. If T is large, fewer messages are needed for network control but the network will react less quickly to congestion. Simulation studies can indicate what value of T gives the best network performance.

Alternatively the scheme could work asynchronously, and only significant *changes* in traffic or routing instructions are sent. One hybrid algorithm of this type is called delta routing [5]. Delta in the name refers to the degree, δ, of independent authority which is given to the nodes. If δ approaches zero the nodes have no authority and we have centralized control. If δ is very large we have decentralized control. An intermediate value of δ would be found which gives the best overall network performance.

It is also possible to combine *explicit path routing* with updating of the routing tables by the network management. The routing tables giving multiple alternate routes are modified by one of the above techniques *when necessary*. The explicit path bits in the messages then select one of the alternate routes. The session managers may continually measure the end-to-end delay associated with their route options.

SIMPLE   Some of the more ingenious routing techniques are
IMPLEMENTATION   complex to implement and some incur excessive over-
head. For these reasons the routing techniques in some manufacturers' network software are relatively simple. They often use a table to establish a route for an entire session, and use an alternate route only if there is a link or node failure.

SUMMARY   Box 21.1 summarizes routing techniques. It could assist
the reader is asking the right questions about the routing techniques used when selecting software for networking.

BOX 21.1 A summary of routing techniques

Objective of Routing Technique

- Minimize the network cost.
- Minimize the message transit time.
- Maximize the network throughput.
- Combinations of the above such as:
  Minimize the network cost with a 0.99 probability the packets will be delivered in 200 millisecs.

Broad Classes of Routing Technique

Technique	Advantages and Disadvantages
• Fixed routes.	Inadequate protection from failures.
• Routing tables in switching nodes changeable manually.	Adaption to failures and congestion is so slow that user sessions are disrupted.
• Routing tables in switching nodes updated by a central computer.	Good on networks with centralized usage. Vulnerable to failure of the central computer.
• Explicit path routing (Route predetermined by session management).	Advantage: Takes into account the fundamentally different requirements of different types of sessions. Disadvantage: Less adaptive than stochastic routing.
• Distributed stochastic routing (There are many variants on this technique).	Advantage: Can adapt quickly to changes in load, and to failures. Disadvantage: Does not take the total network situation into consideration (without excessive overhead).
• Combination of central and distributed stochastic routing.	Advantage: Highly adaptive. Can take total network situation into consideration. Disadvantage: Complex.
• Combination of explicit path and stochastic routing.	Advantage: Highly adaptive. Can take the different requirements of different types of sessions in consideration. Disadvantage: Complex.

Where Are Routing Decisions Made?

- The node which originates the traffic.
- The node which manages the session.
- The switching node.
- A network control center.
- Combinations of the above.

BOX 21.1 *Continued*

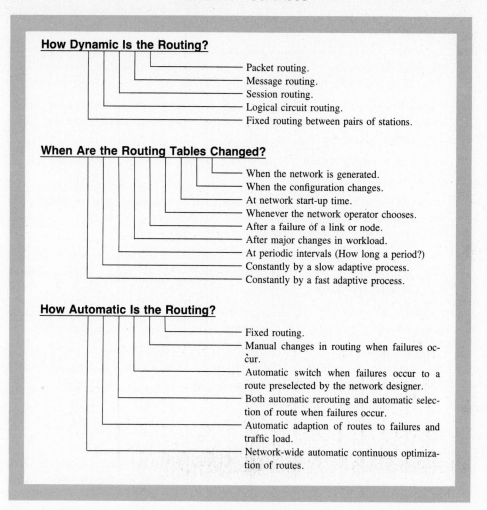

How Dynamic Is the Routing?

- Packet routing.
- Message routing.
- Session routing.
- Logical circuit routing.
- Fixed routing between pairs of stations.

When Are the Routing Tables Changed?

- When the network is generated.
- When the configuration changes.
- At network start-up time.
- Whenever the network operator chooses.
- After a failure of a link or node.
- After major changes in workload.
- At periodic intervals (How long a period?)
- Constantly by a slow adaptive process.
- Constantly by a fast adaptive process.

How Automatic Is the Routing?

- Fixed routing.
- Manual changes in routing when failures occur.
- Automatic switch when failures occur to a route preselected by the network designer.
- Both automatic rerouting and automatic selection of route when failures occur.
- Automatic adaption of routes to failures and traffic load.
- Network-wide automatic continuous optimization of routes.

REFERENCES

1. Boehm, B. W., and R. L. Mobley, "Adaptive routing techniques for distributed communications systems," *IEEE Trans. Commun. Technol.,* Vol. COM-17, No. 3, pp. 340–349, June 1969. See also Rand Corp. Rep. RM 4781-PR, Feb. 1966.

2. Boehm, S. P., and P. Baran, "On distributed communications: II. Digital simulation of hot-potato routing in a broadband distributed communications network," Rand Corp. Rep. RM 3103-PR, Aug. 1964.

3. Fultz, G. L., "Adaptive routing techniques for message switching computer-communication network," School of Engineering and Applied Science, University of California, Los Angeles, UCLA-ENG-7252, July 1972.

4. Fultz, G. L., and L. Kleinrock, "Adaptive routing techniques for store-and forward computer-communication network," in *Proc. 1971 Int. Conf. Communications,* June 1971, Montreal, pp. (39-1)–(39-8).

5. Rudin, H., "On routing and delta routing: A comparison of techniques for packet-switched networks," in *Proc. 1975 Int. Conf. Communications,* paper 41E, June 1975, San Francisco.

6. Frank, H., and W. Chou, "Routing in computer networks," *Networks,* Vol. 1, pp. 99—112, 1971.

7. Chou, W., and H. Frank, "Routing strategies for computer network design," in *Proc. Symp. Computer Communications Networks and Tele-traffic,* April 4–6, 1972, Polytechnic Institute, Brooklyn, pp. 301–309.

8. Gerla, M., "Deterministic and adaptive routing policies in packet-switched computer networks," in *Proc. Third Data Commun. Symp.,* Nov. 1973, St. Petersburg, Florida, pp. 23-28.

9. Schwartz, M., and C. K. Cheung, "Alternative routing in computer-communication networks," in *Proc. 7th Hawaii Int. Conf. System Sciences,* Jan. 1974, pp. 67–69.

10. Jueneman, R. J., and G. S. Kerr, "Explicit Path Routing in Communications Networks," in *Proc. Third International Conference on Computer Communications,* Aug. 1976, Toronto.

11. "Explicit Path Routing for Switching Network," *IBM Technical Disclosure Bulletin* 18, No. 9, Feb. 1976.

12. McQuillan, J. M., "Adaptive Routing Algorithms for Distributed Computer Networks," Report No. 2831. Cambridge, Mass: Bolt, Beranek and Newman. Available from the National Technical Information Service, AD 781467.

13. Rudin, H., "On Alternate Routing in Circuit Switched Data Networks," Research Report RZ801. IBM Zurich Research Laboratory, Switzerland.

14. Gallager, R. G., "Local Routing Algorithms and Protocols," in *Proc. IEEE 1976 Communications Conf.,* Philadelphia, June 1976.

22 CCITT RECOMMENDATION X.25

One of the most important standards for the computer industry is the CCITT Recommendation X.25. This defines the relationship between a transport subsystem, or common carrier packet-switching network, and user machines which employ it. This chapter describes the X.25 techniques, and shows how user machines employ this type of packet-switching network.

Figure 22.1 illustrates the concept of X.25 networks. Many user machines are interconnected by *virtual circuits* on which they communicate by means of packets. The virtual circuits are derived by sharing common communication facilities. The X.25 Recommendation says nothing about how the network shall be constructed, but it is oriented to conventional packet-switching on terrestrial lines of the types available in today's common carrier tariffs. It may need modification for satellites, packet radio, data broadcasting, or networks in advance of today's state of the art.

The virtual circuits illustrated in Fig. 22.1 can be either temporary or permanent. The term *virtual call* is used to refer to a temporary virtual circuit. Like a telephone call there are three phases to a virtual call:

1. The call is set up.
2. The user machines exchange data over the virtual circuit that is established.
3. The call is disconnected.

PERMANENT VIRTUAL CIRCUITS Users of telephone circuits can obtain either a dial-up circuit which they set up when they want and disconnect after use, or they can lease a channel which is permanently connected. Many computer systems have employed leased voice circuits. The X.25 Recommendation gives equivalent options for data. The user can either set up a *virtual call* when he wants and disconnect it after use, or else can have a *permanent virtual*

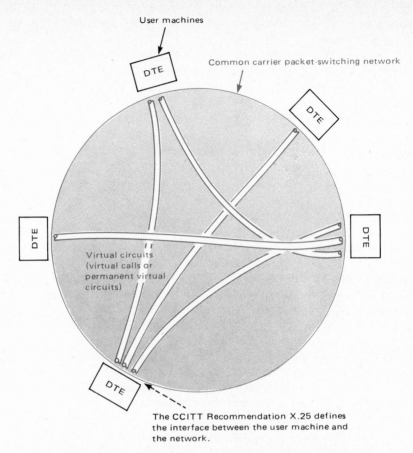

Figure 22.1 User machines (called DTE's, Data Terminal Equipments) send packets with formats and protocols specified by the CCITT Recommendation X.25.

circuit which is permanently connected like a leased telephone line.

In setting up a *virtual call* a logical channel group number must be assigned, and a logical channel number within that group. With a *permanent virtual circuit* the logical channel group number and logical channel number are assigned when the customer leases the facility from the common carrier. The number remains effective for the duration of the lease. A user machine can have available up to 15 logical channel groups (addressed with 4 bits) and up to 255 logical channels within each group (addressed with 8 bits). A given user may employ some logical channels for permanent virtual circuits and some for virtual calls, which are, in effect, *switched virtual circuits*.

When a permanent virtual circuit is used there is no call setup operation before data is sent, or disconnect operation afterwards.

ACCESS TO THE NETWORK   When a subscriber signs up with a common carrier employing the X.25 protocol, he will be provided certain access points to the network. He may have an access point at his location. He may dial the network access point on a conventional telephone line. He may sign up for a certain number of permanent virtual circuits interconnecting the user machines, or a user machine may be authorized to use up to a given number of simultaneous virtual calls (temporary virtual circuits). This is like a computer having a given number of ports. The virtual calls may be placed to another user machine and that machine may accept or refuse the call. Some user machines may be inaccessible by the network for security reasons, and may be called only by members of a specified group of machines.

In CCITT terminology the user machine is referred to as a DTE (data terminal equipment). The user machine is connected to a DCE (data circuit-terminating equipment). The DCE refers to the modem or digital interface which links the user machine to the network. The X.25 Recommendation describes the DTE/DCE interface. Figure 22.2 shows the DTE and DCE. The DTE can be a computer like the *host* machines of the ARPA network. It can be a terminal controller or a concentrator which handles remote terminals. It can be a machine which provides an interface to a different form of teleprocessing or network. With the dropping cost of microminiature circuitry, terminals will be built which execute the X.25 protocols themselves.

To avoid excessive use of acronyms we will refer to the DTE as the *user machine* and DTE/DCE interface as the *user/network interface*. We will use the term DCE for the data circuit-terminating equipment.

THE PAD INTERFACE   Many terminals transmit characters rather than blocks of data or packets. In some cases they use start-stop line control. Sometimes they are inexpensive devices. These terminals need to be connected to an interface machine which buffers the data they send and assembles and disassembles the packets needed for X.25 operation.

The interface machine could be a control unit controlling multiple terminals, which is part of a computer manufacturer's product line. It could be a concentrator to which remote character-oriented terminals are connected by either leased or dialed telephone lines.

Most common carriers operating X.25 networks provide an interface machine for connecting character-oriented terminals to the network. A standard for such an interface has been proposed. It is an extension to (but not part of) the CCITT Recommendation X.25, and is called the PAD (Packet Assembly/Disassembly) interface. It is illustrated at the bottom of Fig. 22.2. The PAD machine receives characters for network transmission and assembles them into a packet. Conversely it disassembles packets and

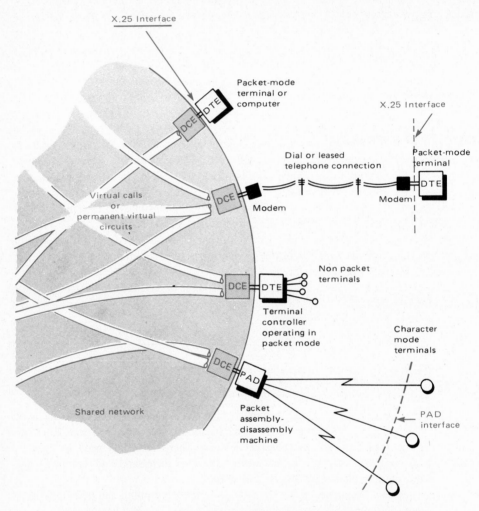

Packet-mode
terminal or
computer

X.25 Interface

Packet-mode
terminal

Dial or leased
telephone connection

Virtual calls
or
permanent virtual
circuits

Modem

Modem

DCE

DTE

DCE

DTE

Non packet
terminals

DCE

DTE

Terminal
controller
operating in
packet mode

Character
mode
terminals

DCE

PAD

Shared network

Packet
assembly-
disassembly
machine

PAD
interface

Figure 22.2 The user machine, DTE, can be a computer, terminal, terminal controller, or interface to another form of teleprocessing. The PAD, packet assembly/disassembly machine, buffers characters to and from character-mode terminal (e.g., start–stop machines) and forms the requisite packets.

344

sends the resulting characters to the terminal which needs them. A protocol is defined for communication between the PAD machine and the character-oriented terminal. This protocol defines how characters are used for indicating the start and end of messages, requesting and confirming connections, and dealing with errors.

There can thus be *packet-mode* user machines which execute the X.25 protocols, and *character-mode* user machines which communicate via a PAD interface. Different types of character-mode machines can be used including HDLC machines and start-stop machines which use delimiter characters from CCITT alphabets to indicate the start and end of messages.

LAYERS OF CONTROL   The user/network interface is concerned with control Layers 1, 2, and 3 (Fig. 22.3).

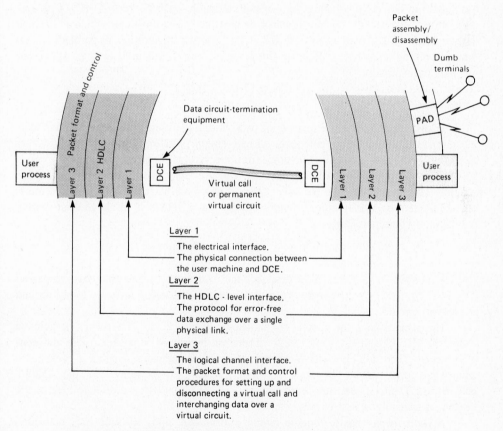

Figure 22.3 The CCITT X.25 user/network interface is subdivided into three levels of interface.

Layer 1: Physical Control

This describes the plug and wires for establishing contact and sending bits between the user machine and the DCE. There is nothing unique to X.25 about this layer. It applies to all *synchronous* data transmission. It defines the interface between the user machine and the line termination of a digital line, similarly to the way the RS #232-C standard defines the interface between a user machine and a modem. Its functions are to pass data, synchronization, and control signals between the user machine and DCE and to handle failure detection and isolation procedures. The recommended form of this interface to digital (as opposed to analog) circuits is described in CCITT Recommendation X.21.

Layer 2: Link Control

This is essentially the HDLC layer of control described in Chapter 18. CCITT has stated an objective of achieving general compatibility with the ISO HDLC procedure. The physical link layer of control defines the frame envelope which is used to carry a frame of data over a physical link and ensure that it is not lost or garbled. Again there is nothing unique to X.25 about this layer of control; it is used in much synchronous data transmission.

Layer 3: Network Control

This layer describes the formats of packets that are used for setting up and clearing a virtual call, sending data over virtual circuits, controlling message flow, sequencing, and interrupts, and recovering from the various problems that might occur.

This layer of control is unique to X.25 and it is described in the remainder of this chapter. In conjunction with the other layers it describes what is equivalent to a transport subsystem in manufacturers' architectures, but is intended for large-scale implementation by common carriers.

PACKET FORMAT X.25 describes the formats of packets that shall be passed between a user machine and DCE in order to set up and use virtual circuits.

The packets have the general format shown in Fig. 22.4. This format is included inside the HDLC envelope (Fig. 18.2). There are two types of packets: *data* and *control* packets. The last bit of the third byte (Fig. 22.4) indicates whether a packet is a control or data packet. (8-bit bytes are referred to as octets in the CCITT documents. Their bits are numbered 0 through 7. Bit 7, which we refer to here as the last bit, is transmitted first in that octet.

A *data packet* has a variable length information field, carrying user data (and possibly user control information for use external to the X.25 layers of control).

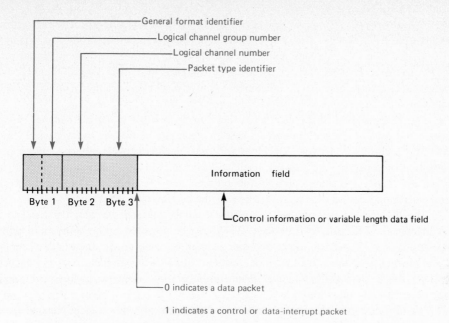

Figure 22.4 The general format of X.25 packets. This is included inside an HDLC envelope.

A *control packet* can be of many different types, and the type is indicated by the third byte. Some types of control packets have their own information field following the third byte. This may be one or more bytes.

A special type of control packet is called the INTERRUPT DATA packet. This contains one byte of user information, which may be used for user machine control purposes not defined by X.25. This packet jumps the queues of normal flow and travels as rapidly as possible to its destination.

The first four bits of a packet are a *general format identifier*. The first bit may be set to 1 or 0 on data packets to give two levels of data transmission. This bit is referred to as the *qualifier bit, Q.* X.25 does not say how the two levels of data packet may be used. One might carry user control information external to X.25. This is the case with the CCITT concentrator (PAD) described in the next chapter.

The third bit is set to 1 if modulo 128 counts are used. The fourth bit is set to 1 if modulo 8 counts are used. (We describe these counts later.)

The general format identifier can thus take the following forms:

	Modulo 8 counts	Modulo 128 counts
Data messages	X001	X010
Control and interrupt messages	0001	0010

LOGICAL CHANNEL NUMBERS

When a user machine sets up a virtual call it selects a free logical channel number from the set of logical channel numbers that are allocated to it. A permanent virtual circuit has a logical channel number permanently assigned to it. The logical channels are arranged into groups of up to 255 channels. A user machine can employ up to 15 such groups.

The identification of the channel is therefore in two parts: *logical channel group number* and *logical channel number*. These numbers are carried by every packet (Fig. 22.4) and enable both network machines and user machines to identify the source and destination of packets. The network itself will have to add additional addressing information to identify the source and destination machines, but this is left to the network implementor and does not concern the user or the user/network interface.

The logical channel numbers constitute a numbering scheme which is local to a user machine and its network interface. They may be regarded as the numbers of ports for that machine. The machines at opposite ends of the same virtual circuit use different logical channel numbers. The network machine to which the user machine is attached translates that user machine's logical channel numbers into whatever addresses are necessary for network operation.

When a user machine initiates a virtual call it selects a free logical channel from those available to it. The number of this and its logical channel group are passed to the local DCE which then attempts to set up the virtual call using that logical channel. If it completes the set up then the channel is available for data transfer until it is disconnected. In the DATA TRANSFER state there is no difference between a logical channel used for a virtual call and that used for a permanent virtual circuit.

INITIATING A VIRTUAL CALL

When a computer or terminal controller attached to an X.25 network wants to initiate a virtual call, it selects a free logical channel and sends a CALL REQUEST packet to its local DCE. Figure 22.5 shows the CALL REQUEST packet.

The packet normally contains the address of the destination device and may contain the address of the originating device. Both addresses are variable in length and thus long addresses could be used if necessary. Each digit of the address is encoded in a half-byte in the address field. The address field is preceded by two half-bytes which state how many digits are in each address.

The addresses may be followed by a *facilities* field which is also of variable length. This field is present when the originating machine wants a call with some optional characteristic which must be communicated to the destination machine. For example, reverse charging may be requested. A maximum data length might be specified because of limited buffer size. A specific window size for flow control might be specified. Other optional facilities may be specified in the future. For each optional facility

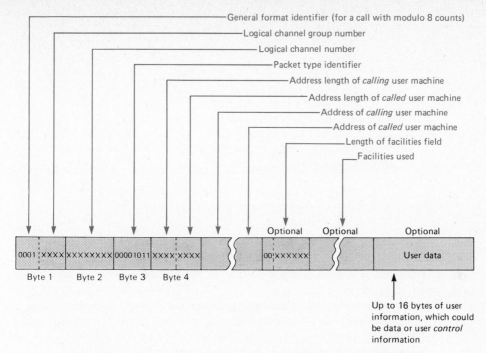

Figure 22.5 The format of the CALL REQUEST and INCOMING CALL packets used when setting up a call.

the facilities field contains a pair of bytes. The first byte of the pair indicates the *type of facility* request, and the second gives a *parameter* applying to it, such as maximum data length.

For efficiency, the CALL REQUEST packet may carry user data. This might be control data relating to a layer of control external to the X.25 subsystem (Layer 4) and concerned with functions such as those in Chapter 15. However it is used, the X.25 protocol is unconcerned with the contents of the data field.

When a CALL REQUEST is sent on a logical channel, that channel changes its *state* at the user/network interface from READY to DTE WAITING. The data machine waits while the network attempts to set up the connection.

The request is transmitted through the network and is passed as an INCOMING CALL packet to the destination machine. The INCOMING CALL packet has the same format as the CALL REQUEST packet. The called machine decides whether it can accept the call. If it can it sends a CALL ACCEPTED packet, which has the format shown in Fig. 22.6.

The CALL ACCEPTED packet travels back to the originating DCE and this transmits a CALL CONNECTED packet (which is the same) to the originating user ma-

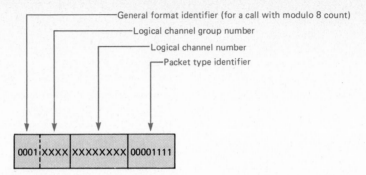

General format identifier (for a call with modulo 8 count)
Logical channel group number
Logical channel number
Packet type identifier

0001 XXXX XXXXXXXX 00001111

Figure 22.6 The format of the CALL ACCEPTED and CALL CONNECT packets which confirm that a virtual call is established.

chine. The requested logical channel is then in the data transfer state, and both user machines can send data over it. The virtual call has been set up.

It is possible that a DCE might receive an INCOMING CALL packet from a distant machine at the same time as a CALL REQUEST packet from a local machine, and both request the same logical channel. It cannot satisfy both requests. It is in a CALL COLLISION state. It cancels the incoming call and responds normally to the CALL REQUEST.

If the attempt to set up a call is unsuccessful, the DCE responds to the calling user-machine by sending a CLEAR INDICATION packet which gives the reason why the CALL REQUEST was not compiled with.

PRIORITY An optional feature of X.25 allows a virtual call to be set up with two priority levels. A user machine can request that a call it places have *high priority*. A call for interactive data interchange might be made at the high priority; a call for batch transmission might be made without the high-priority indication. High priority, if used, is indicated in a *facility* field of the CALL REQUEST and CALL INDICATION packets.

THE FLOW Figure 22.7 shows the flow of packets on a brief virtual
OF PACKETS call. The shaded packets are *control* packets. The white ones are *data* packets. The shaded ones at the top of the figure are those which set up the call. The shaded ones at the bottom are those which disconnect it.

Each user machine perceives merely the packets it sends to the network and the packets which leave it.

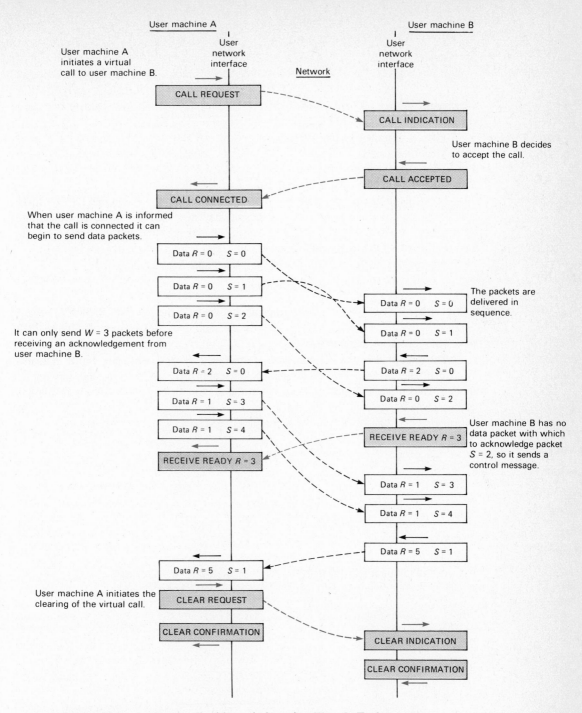

Figure 22.7 A virtual call with a window size $W = 3$. Each user machine perceives merely the packets entering and leaving the network.

**DISCONNECTING
A VIRTUAL CALL**   A user machine may decide to disconnect a virtual call at any time. To do this it sends a CLEAR REQUEST packet to its DCE. The DCE responds when it is ready to clear the channel with a CLEAR CONFIRMATION packet. Both packets contain the number of the logical channel in question.

The DCE transmits the clear request to the DCE at the other end of the logical link. That DCE sends a CLEAR INDICATION packet to the user machine in question. The user machine responds with a CLEAR CONFIRMATION packet. The cleared logical channel is then back in the READY state.

Normally it is the user machine that initiates the clearing of a call. When there are network problems the network equipment may need to initiate the clearing. The DCE sends a CLEAR INDICATION packet to the user machine and the latter responds with a CLEAR CONFIRMATION packet.

Figure 22.8 shows the formats of the packets used for clearing.

DATA TRANSFER   Once a logical channel is in the DATA TRANSFER state, a user machine can send data packets over it. Figure 22.9 shows the format of the data packet.

The data field is of variable length, demarcated by the HDLC *flag* which indicates the end of the packet. The maximum packet length may differ from one network to another. When a user's data is longer than the maximum packet size, the user divides

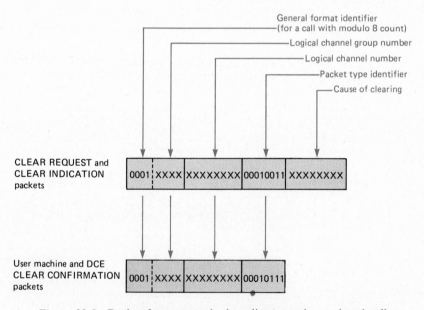

Figure 22.8   Packet formats used when disconnecting a virtual call.

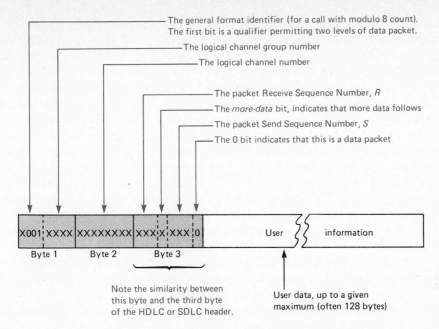

The general format identifier (for a call with modulo 8 count). The first bit is a qualifier permitting two levels of data packet.

The logical channel group number

The logical channel number

The packet Receive Sequence Number, *R*

The *more-data* bit, indicates that more data follows

The packet Send Sequence Number, *S*

The 0 bit indicates that this is a data packet

X001 XXXX	XXXXXXXX	XXX X XXX 0
Byte 1	Byte 2	Byte 3

User ⌇⌇ information

Note the similarity between this byte and the third byte of the HDLC or SDLC header.

User data, up to a given maximum (often 128 bytes)

Figure 22.9   The format of the X.25 DATA packet (with 3-bit counts).

it into several packets, which the network delivers in sequence. The third byte of the header contains a *more data* bit (Fig. 22.9) which, if set, indicates that more of the same data record follows in a subsequent packet. The *more data* bit can only be set in a maximum length packet.

CCITT Recommendation X.25 suggests that the maximum data field length should be 128 bytes. It states that some telecommunications administrations may support other maximum data lengths: 16, 32, 64, 256, 512 or 1024 bytes, or, exceptionally, 255 bytes. Different networks may use different packet sizes. In this case the DATA packets may have to be split or combined as they pass from one network to another. The *more data* bit would be used in conjunction with this.

Data packets can be of two types, as designated by the *Q* bit in general format identifier. The X.25 Recommendation does not specify how the two types should be used. It is likely that one type will carry normal user data and the other will carry control information employed by the end-user machines external to the transport network.

SEQUENCE NUMBERS   As in the other link protocols, the data packet contains sequential message numbers for flow control. The *Send Sequence Number, S*, is a sequential message number composed when the messages are sent. The *Receive Sequence Number, R*, is composed by the receiver when it is ready to receive another message; it gives the Send Sequence Number of the message it expects next. These numbers are usually modulo 8 (3 bits). They reside in the third byte of the header of the DATA packet, which is similar to the third byte of the HDLC header except for the *more-data* bit.

A window mechanism is used to regulate the flow of data, as illustrated in Fig. 22.10. A user machine can transmit packets with sequence numbers within the window. When these packets are received and acknowledged the window rotates.

When a user machine first transmits on a logical channel the lower edge of its window is set to zero, and the Send Sequence Number of its first message is zero. If the window size is W, it can transmit up to W packets before receiving an acknowledgment. The acknowledgment can be either a data message or a control message. It contains a Receive Sequence Number, R, which is the number of the next packet which the receiver expects to receive. When this reaches the sender, the lower edge of the sender's window is set to R. The sender can then send messages numbered up to, but not including $R + W$.

The window size is fixed for a given user machine and is agreed between the subscriber and the common carrier at subscription time.

Sequence numbers can be used for acknowledgement sequencing, and flow control. In the X.25 protocol these functions are combined into a simple integrated procedure.

Figure 22.9 shows 3-bit sequence numbers giving a modulo 8 count. This corresponds to the modulo 8 window shown in Fig. 22.10. If high-speed lines are used (such as T1 carrier or PCM links following CCITT Recommendations A.732 or A.733), or if the propagation delay is long, as on satellite channels, a modulo 8 count is too small. A modulo 128 count can be used by employing a fourth byte in the header in Fig. 22.9 to extend each of the count fields by 4 bits. Figure 20.5 illustrates a modulo 128 window.

The general format indicator which starts each packet (Fig. 20.4) shows whether a modulo 8 or modulo 128 numbering scheme and window is used. Most networks are being implemented with modulo 8 numbering. When traffic volumes build up so that high bit-rate links are needed, and when satellite links come into use, modulo 128 numbering will probably be employed.

If user machines are exchanging data, the flow control signals containing the receive sequence number can be piggy-backed on the returning DATA packets. If not they must be sent by a separate control message. A RECEIVE READY packet is used to indicate willingness to receive W DATA packets starting with the value of the receive sequence number, R. Figure 22.7 shows a RECEIVE READY packet in use.

A RECEIVE NOT READY packet is returned by a user machine when it is temporarily unwilling to receive further DATA packets. It sends a subsequent RECEIVE READY packet when it is once again ready to receive data. Figure 22.11 shows RECEIVE READY and RECEIVE NOT READY packets.

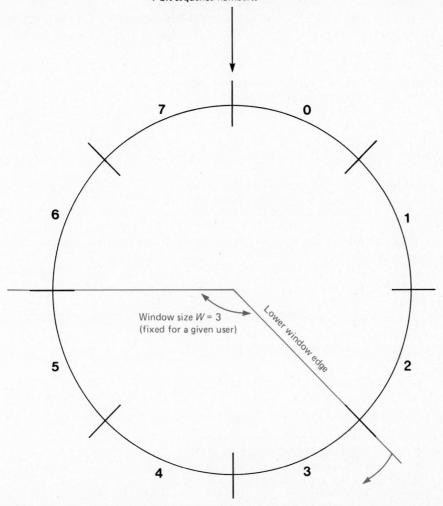

There are 8 window positions and hence
3-bit sequence numbers. Alternatively a
128-position window can be used with
7-bit sequence numbers.

Window size $W = 3$
(fixed for a given user)

Lower window edge

Packets are acknowledged with the Receive Sequence Number, R, which indicates the number of the *next* packet the user machine expects. The lower window edge is then set to R. The sender may send packets up to but not including $R + W$ (in this illustration $R + 3$ because the window size is fixed at $W = 3$). The receiving network machine arranges the packets within the window into sequence, if necessary, before delivering them.

Figure 22.10 The window mechanism used for flow control. Its use was illustrated in Figure 20.6.

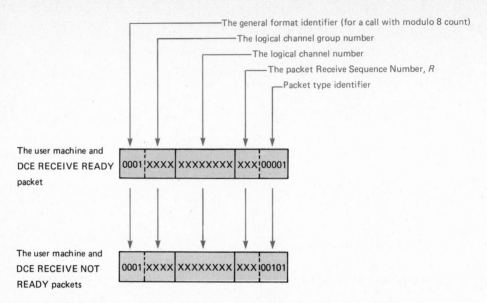

Figure 22.11 Packets used to acknowledge a DATA packet (with 3-bit counts).

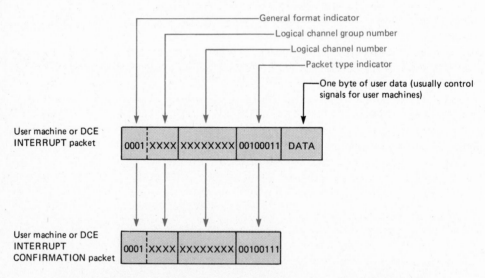

Figure 22.12 The formats of the INTERRUPT and INTERRUPT CONFIRMATION packets.

INTERRUPT PACKETS   A user machine can send an INTERRUPT packet which bypasses the flow control procedures used for normal DATA packets. The INTERRUPT packet contains only one byte of user data. It is transmitted as quickly as possible to its destination, jumping the queues of normal DATA packets. The INTERRUPT packet is delivered to a user machine even when it is not accepting DATA packets.

The INTERRUPT packet *could* carry user data, but normally it is employed for user *control* information rather than data. If, for example, a user of a typewriter-like terminal presses the *break* key to stop a flow of data from a distant computer, this action could be relayed with an INTERRUPT packet to the computer.

The INTERRUPT packet contains no sequence numbers because the sequencing of such packets is of no concern and the packet bypass the normal flow control procedures. Because of this there must be a separate means of acknowledging INTERRUPT packets. An INTERRUPT CONFIRMATION packet is used for this purpose. A user machine is not permitted to send a second INTERRUPT packet on a given logical channel until it has received an INTERRUPT CONFIRMATION packet. Figure 22.12 shows INTERRUPT and INTERRUPT CONFIRMATION packets. These are the same whether they pass from the user machine to the DCE or vice versa.

RESET   Certain types of problems on a virtual circuit can cause that circuit to be *reset*. Resetting does not disconnect the virtual circuit; it reinitializes it. The lower edges of the windows for both directions of transmission are reset to zero so that the next data message will have a Send Sequence Number and Receive Sequence Number of zero. Any DATA or INTERRUPT packets in transit at the time of the reset are discarded.

A reset could occur for a variety of reasons. For example, the remote user machine might be out of order. The subscriber link might not be functioning. The local or remote user machine might have sent a packet with a procedural error. The network might have congestion conditions on that virtual circuit which temporarily prevent data transfer from taking place.

A reset can be initiated either by a user machine or by a network machine. A user machine does so by sending a RESET REQUEST packet to its DCE. The network indicates that a virtual circuit is being reset by sending a RESET INDICATION packet to the machines using that virtual circuit. This packet contains a byte which gives the cause of the resetting. Machines receiving either of the above packets respond by returning a RESET CONFIRMATION packet. The link is then in *data transfer* state waiting for new transmission to begin. Figure 22.13 shows these RESET packets.

RESTART   A *restart* condition is more drastic than a *reset*. It provides a mechanism to recover from major failures. A restart is equivalent to clearing all of the virtual calls that a user machine has connected,

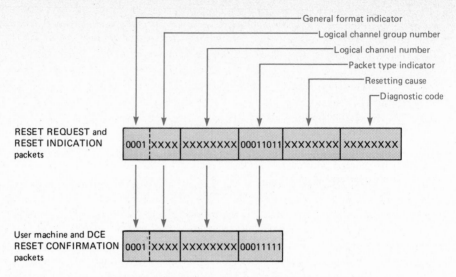

Figure 22.13   The format of packets used for resetting.

and resetting the permanent virtual circuits (because these cannot be cleared). The user machine may then attempt to reconnect its calls. The restart procedure thus brings the user/network interface to the state it was in when the service was initiated.

A user machine may initiate a restart by sending a RESTART REQUEST packet to its DCE. The network may initiate a restart because of a catastrophic network failure, or because a user has failed to follow a correct restart procedure, by sending a

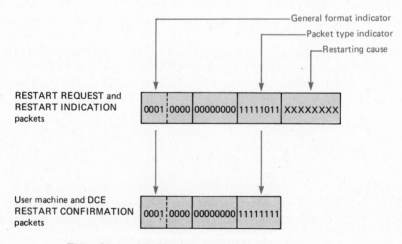

Figure22.14   The format of packets used for restart.

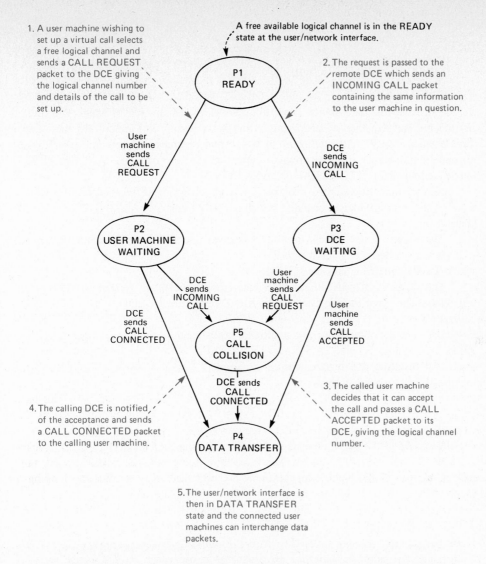

1. A user machine wishing to set up a virtual call selects a free logical channel and sends a CALL REQUEST packet to the DCE giving the logical channel number and details of the call to be set up.

A free available logical channel is in the READY state at the user/network interface.

P1 READY

2. The request is passed to the remote DCE which sends an INCOMING CALL packet containing the same information to the user machine in question.

User machine sends CALL REQUEST

DCE sends INCOMING CALL

P2 USER MACHINE WAITING

P3 DCE WAITING

DCE sends INCOMING CALL

User machine sends CALL REQUEST

User machine sends CALL ACCEPTED

DCE sends CALL CONNECTED

P5 CALL COLLISION

DCE sends CALL CONNECTED

3. The called user machine decides that it can accept the call and passes a CALL ACCEPTED packet to its DCE, giving the logical channel number.

4. The calling DCE is notified of the acceptance and sends a CALL CONNECTED packet to the calling user machine.

P4 DATA TRANSFER

5. The user/network interface is then in DATA TRANSFER state and the connected user machines can interchange data packets.

Figure 22.15   A state diagram for the call set-up phase. A normal call set-up follows the numbered steps shown in red.

RESTART INDICATION packet across the user/network interface. This packet gives a reason for the restart. The response to either a RESTART REQUEST or RESTART INDICATION packet is a RESTART CONFIRMATION packet. These packets are illustrated in Fig. 22.14.

STATE DIAGRAMS   Each of the logical channels which a user machine has available to it can be in one of several *states*. If it is free—i.e., no call is in existence on it—then it is in the READY state. When a call is in existence it is in the DATA TRANSFER state.

Several other states occur in the transition between the READY and DATA TRANSFER states, i.e., in the call setup and disconnect phases. Figures 22.15 and 22.16 are *state* diagrams which show the setting up and clearing of calls. The figures list the normal sequence of operations. Double-state transition arrows are exceptional circumstances—e.g., *call collisions* in which two machines request the same logical channel simultaneously, or a situation in which a user machine does not respond quickly enough to a DCE CLEAR INDICATION.

Neither the setup nor the clearing operation is used with *permanent virtual circuits*. These employ logical channels which normally remain in the DATA TRANSFER state.

There are seven states used for normal operation, designated p1 through p7. They are listed along the top of Table 22.1. This table shows the types of packets which the user machine can send in each state.

The DATA TRANSFER state has three substates related to the *reset* operation. These are FLOW CONTROL READY, the normal condition when a logical channel is in use, DTE (user machine) RESET REQUEST and DCE RESET INDICATION. Similarly there are two additional states used by the *restart* operation: DTE RESTART REQUEST and DCE RESTART INDICATION. Fig. 32.1 shows state diagrams for resetting and restart. Tables 22.2, and 22.3 show the types of packets the user machine can send in these states.

OPTIONAL FACILIITES   We have described the standard features of the X.25 protocol. There are also some optional features, and there may be more optional features in the future. A user machine may request an optional facility when a call is set up, by using *facilities* byte-pairs in the CALL REQUEST packet (the last shaded field in Fig. 22.5). The optional facilities are as follows:

1. *Reverse charging* (already mentioned). A user machine originating a call may request reverse charging. The called machine may be designated as one which accepts reverse charging, otherwise the network will not deliver to it a packet with a reverse charging request.

2. *High priority* (already mentioned). This permits data packets to have a higher priority than normal.

3. *Closed user group.* A closed group of users may share an X.25 network with other users, but members of the closed user group can communicate *only* with one another. This restriction of network use may be done for security reasons, or it may be done to control costs. A computer with sensitive information on its files may be callable only by certain specified machines. A terminal user may be restricted in the computers he can call.

     A user machine can be a member of more than one closed user group. In this case a CALL REQUEST packet must specify which user group that call relates to.

     A user machine may be permitted to make unrestricted outgoing calls, but have incoming calls only from a closed user group.

4. *One-way logical channel.* On a logical channel with this optional facility a user machine will

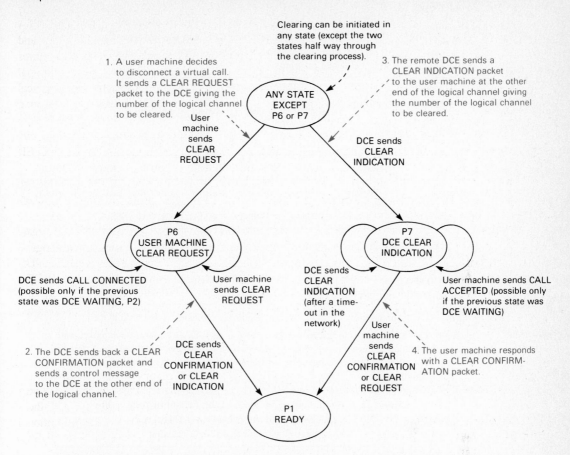

Figure 22.16 A state diagram for the clearing process. A normal disconnect of a virtual call follows the four numbered steps shown in red.

be permitted either to place calls but not accept calls from other users, or to accept calls but not place them.

5. *Packet retransmission.* A user machine can ask its DCE to retransmit one or several data packets. It does this by sending a REJECT packet to the DCE containing the Receive Sequence Number, R, of a packet received. The DCE retransmits packet R and those following it. The number of packets for retransmission cannot exceed the flow-control window size. This is not an end-to-end mechanism. The request for retransmission of a data packet cannot be relayed to the user which originated that packet.

6. *Flow control parameter selection.* A network normally has a given maximum window size and maximum data length. A user machine may optionally operate at less than these because it has limited buffer size or control capability. The window size and maximum data length is referred to as a *throughput class* and may be indicated in the *facilities* field of a CALL REQUEST packet. If there is no such indication, the call is connected with the highest attainable values.

Table 22.1 Action taken by the DCE on receipt of packets from the user machine (DTE) in a given state of the packet level DTE/DCE interface: call setup and clearing

State of the interface / Packet from the DTE	Ready pl	DTE waiting p2	DCE waiting p3	Data transfer p4	Call collision p5	DTE clear request p6	DCE clear indication p7
Call request	NORMAL	ERROR	NORMAL	ERROR	ERROR	ERROR	ERROR
Call accepted	ERROR	ERROR	NORMAL	ERROR	ERROR	ERROR	NORMAL
Clear request	NORMAL	NORMAL	NORMAL	NORMAL	NORMAL	NORMAL	NORMAL
DTE clear confirmation	ERROR	ERROR	ERROR	ERROR	ERROR	ERROR	NORMAL
Data, interrupt, reset or flow control	ERROR	ERROR	ERROR	See Table 22.2	ERROR	ERROR	NORMAL

NORMAL: The action taken by the DCE follows the normal procedures as described in the text.

ERROR: The DCE indicates a clearing by transmitting to the DTE a *clear indication* packet, with an indication of Local Procedure Error. If connected through the virtual call, the distant DTE is also informed of the clearing by a *clear indication* packet, with an indication of Remote Procedure Error.

Table 22.2 Action taken by the DCE on receipt of packets in a given state of the packet level DTE/DCE interface: flow control and data transfer

State of the interface / Packet from the DTE	Data Transfer (p4)		
	Flow control ready (d1)	DTE reset request (d2)	DCE reset indication (d3)
Reset request	NORMAL	NORMAL	NORMAL
DTE reset confirmation	FLOW CONTROL ERROR	FLOW CONTROL ERROR	NORMAL
Data, interrupt or flow control	NORMAL	FLOW CONTROL ERROR	NORMAL

NORMAL: The action taken by the DCE follows the normal procedures as described in the text.

FLOW CONTROL ERROR: The DCE indicates a reset by transmitting to the DTE a *reset indication* packet, with an indication of Local Procedure Error. The distant DTE is also informed of the reset by a *reset indication* packet, with an indication of Remote Procedure Error.

Table 22.3 Action taken by the DCE on receipt of packets in
a given state of the packet level DTE/DCE
interface: restart

State of the interface / Packet from the DTE	Any state p1 to p7 and d1 to d3	DTE restart request state	DCE restart indication state
Restart request	NORMAL	NORMAL	NORMAL
DTE restart confirmation	ERROR	ERROR	NORMAL
Data, interrupt, call set-up and clearing, flow control or reset	See *Note*	ERROR	NORMAL

NORMAL: The action taken by the DCE follows the normal procedures described in the text.

ERROR: The DCE indicates a restarting by transmitting to the DTE, a *restart indication* packet with an indication of Local Procedure Error.

Note—See Table 22.1 for call setup and clearing; see Table 22.2 for data, interrupt, flow control, and reset.

23 THE PACKET ASSEMBLY/DISASSEMBLY INTERFACE: CCITT RECOMMENDATIONS X.3, X.28, AND X.29

The X.25 protocols are fairly complex, though not too complex to put on one VLSI chip. Terminals are beginning to emerge with builtin X.25 interfaces, but there are large numbers of dumb terminals in existence, and still being made, which ought to have access to X.25 networks. Many start–stop terminals, such as teletype machines, are owned by the common carriers. It is desirable that teletype networks and dumb terminals on telephone lines should be connectable to the X.25 networks.

THE CCITT PAD The CCITT has created three standards for connecting start–stop terminals to X.25 networks. Other standards are being proposed for connecting synchronous terminals, and specifying virtual terminals.

The CCITT Recommendations for start–stop terminal connection specify a PAD (Packet Assembly/Disassembly) facility. A start–stop terminal has no message buffer, so it transmits one character at a time. The interval between one character and the next is highly variable because it depends upon when the operator presses the character keys. The characters reach the PAD and the PAD provides a buffer for them. The PAD assembles the characters until a packet is ready to send. It adds the requisite headers and trailer, and sends the packet using the X.25 protocol (with minor additions).

When the PAD receives a packet via the X.25 network, it strips off the headers and trailer, and sends the characters one at a time to the start–stop terminal. A PAD facility may handle many terminals simultaneously, and thus acts as a concentrator.

VIRTUAL CONCENTRATOR A host computer may have many start–stop terminals in session via an X.25 network. They may be connected via one PAD or many. The host is unaware of the location or number of PAD facilities. It perceives the terminals as though they were connected via a conceptual concentrator, comprised of the X.25 network and its PAD facilities (Fig. 23.1).

Start–stop terminal users may dial a PAD on the telephone network. If the terminal usage is heavy the terminal may be permanently connected to the PAD with a leased telephone or subvoice-grade line.

Figure 23.1 shows the terminals all using the same host computer. In reality each terminal using the same PAD facility could be communicating with a different computer.

Three CCITT Recommendations relate to the PAD facility:

* *Recommendation X.3*, which describes the functions of the PAD and the various parameters which can be used to specify its mode of operation.

* *Recommendation X.28*, which describes how start–stop terminals are connected to the PAD via a telephone or other line, and how they can control the functioning of the PAD.

* *Recommendation X.29*, which describes the interaction between the PAD and a host machine using X.25 protocols, and how the host can control the PAD.

These standards are accepted in most of the world. This means that simple terminals can dial the PAD facilities and gain access via worldwide packet networking to hosts in other countries. Large numbers of hosts can share what is becoming a worldwide virtual concentrator.

There are a few functions other than simply relaying characters which any such concentrator should provide.

The PAD may recognize Carriage Return characters from the terminal and relay the packet when these occur. It also relays the packet when the terminal indicates an End-of-Transmission condition, or when the packet is full, or when the delay between characters transmitted from the terminal exceeds a certain value. The PAD addresses the packet to the host and sends it into the network (Fig. 23.2). The terminal may expect the characters it transmits to be echoed back for error checking purposes. The PAD can do this as shown with the terminal on the lower right of Fig. 23.2.

While some buffers in the PAD are assembling packets for transmission to the host, others may be holding packets from the host and transmitting them one character at a time to the requisite terminals. When this is done the character stream may have to be modified slightly. For example, a certain number of fill characters may be inserted after each Carriage Return so that the next printed character is not sent too soon. Carriage Return characters may be inserted to prevent too long a line of characters being sent to the terminal. Different start–stop terminals operate at different speeds, so that the characters must be sent by the PAD at different rates.

There are thus several variations necessary in the behavior of the PAD when handling different terminals. These variations arise both because of the differences in terminals and because of the differences in application.

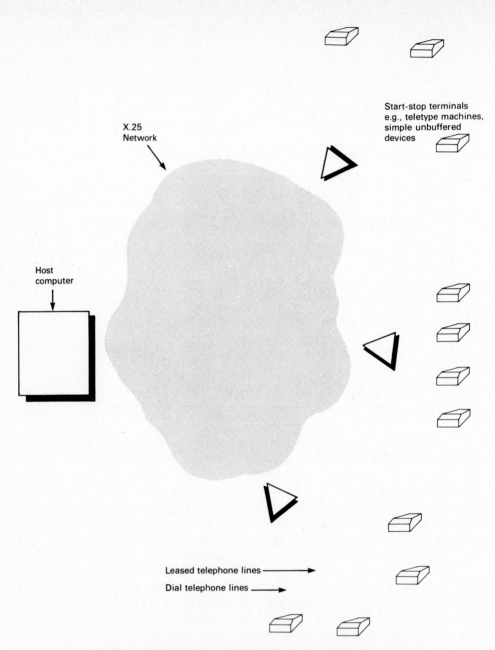

Figure 23.1 PAD facilities are used to connect dumb start–stop terminals to an X.25 network. Several PAD facilities may be perceived by an X.25 host as being like a virtual concentrator.

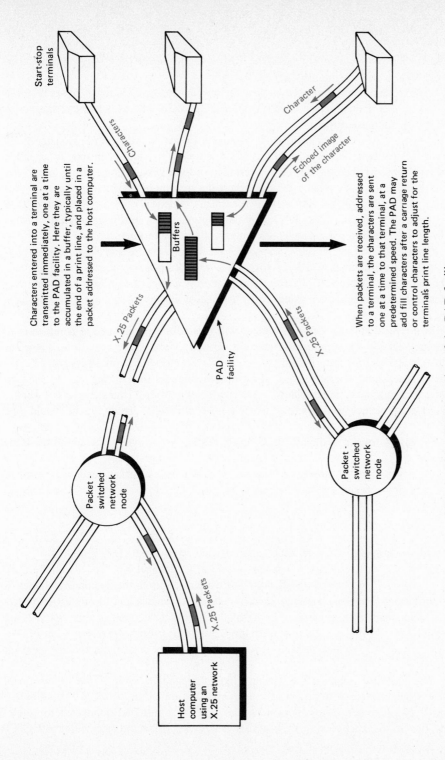

Start-stop terminals

Characters entered into a terminal are transmitted immediately, one at a time to the PAD facility. Here they are accumulated in a buffer, typically until the end of a print line, and placed in a packet addressed to the host computer.

Characters

Buffers

X.25 Packets

PAD facility

Character

Echoed image of the character

X.25 Packets

When packets are received, addressed to a terminal, the characters are sent one at a time to that terminal, at a predetermined speed. The PAD may add fill characters after a carriage return or control characters to adjust for the terminals print line length.

Packet-switched network node

X.25 Packets

Host computer using an X.25 network

Packet-switched network node

Figure 23.2   The operation of the PAD facility.

To accommodate the differences needed there are 12 functions of the PAD which are variable. They are listed in Box 23.1.

Twelve parameters are used to specify the 12 variable functions. A set of these 12 parameters is maintained in the PAD *for each terminal*. Box 23.1 shows the possible values of the parameters.

When a PAD is initialized, each parameter is set according to a predetermined set of values called a "standard profile." This initial set of values can then be changed for any terminal by the operator of that terminal or by a host computer using the PAD.

For example, a terminal user may adjust the maximum line length of a terminal, rather as a typist might do with a typewriter. This is done by setting Parameter 10 to the requisite line length. The PAD will then automatically insert appropriate format control characters into the character stream it sends to the terminal.

CCITT Recommendation X.3 specifies the 12 parameters and their possible values. CCITT Recommendation X.28 specifies how a terminal operator can read or modify the parameter values. CCITT Recommendation X.29 specifies how a host computer can read or set the parameter values for a terminal it wishes to communicate with (see Fig. 23.3).

In a typical session a host computer will routinely set some of the parameters to values suitable for the programs in question. Usually these values remain the same for the whole session. On rare occasions they might be changed in mid-session. For example if a terminal operator goes from manual line-at-a-time data entry to batched cassette data entry, he might change PAD parameter 3 from 2 (transmit packet when a carriage return occurs) to 0 (transmit when the packet is full). To do this he would type SET 3:0.

In most cases the terminal user does not need to set or even know about the PAD parameters.

No doubt more parameters will be added to the list as further needs are specified and agreed upon by the standards committees.

CCITT
RECOMMENDATION
X.28 CCITT Recommendation X.28 specifies how a start–stop terminal communicates with the PAD (Fig. 23.3).

It uses the CCITT Alphabet No. 5 of which the U.S. ASCII code is a variant. This is the standard alphabet of 7-bit characters (8 bits with parity) used by teletype machines and most start–stop terminals other than telex machines. Some of the control characters in this alphabet are recognized by the PAD, including Carriage Return (CR), End-of-Transmission (TC4), and DC 1 and DC 3 which indicate Ready and Not Ready conditions and are used for flow control.

The interface between the terminal and the modem used is the conventional CCITT V.21 interface with electrical characteristics specified in the CCITT Recommendation V.28. In other words, it is a normal start–stop terminal connected to a telephone line in the normal way. The access path is set in accordance with the CCITT

BOX 23.1 PAD functions which are selectable for each terminal by the use of 12 parameters

Parameter Number	Function	Description	Selectable Values of the Parameters
1.	PAD recall by escaping from data transfer phase	This parameter determines whether or not the terminal operator can initiate an escape from the data transfer phase in order to send commands to the PAD.	0: Not possible. 1: Possible.
2.	Echo	Indicates whether an *echo* form of checking is used by the terminal. If it is, each character from the terminal is transmitted back to the terminal for checking (as with the terminal at the bottom right of Fig. 21.2).	0: No echo. 1: Echo.
3.	Selection of data forwarding signal	Indicates whether the PAD should recognize defined character(s), or the "break signal," received from the terminal as an indication to complete the assembly of the packet and forward it.	0: No signal. (The data is transmitted when the packet is full.) 2: Transmit packet on carriage return. 126: Transmit packet on receipt of certain specified control characters.
4.	Selection of idle timer delay	When the delay between characters transmitted from the terminal exceeds the value specified by this parameter, the PAD stops the assembly operation and forwards the packet.	0: No time-out, i.e., the packet will not be forwarded because of a delay between characters. 1 to 255: The value of the delay

BOX 23.1 *Continued*

		which triggers forwarding, in twentieths of a second (255 means that a packet is forwarded when the gap between characters transmitted exceeds 12.75 seconds).
5. Ancillary device control	This parameter indicates whether there is flow control of the terminal by the PAD. If flow control is used the PAD indicates whether or not it will accept characters from the terminal by using the DC1 and DC3 control characters of the CCITT No. 5 (like ASCII) alphabet.	0: No flow control. 1: Flow control used.
6. Suppression of PAD service signals	This parameter indicates whether service signals can be sent from the PAD to the terminal. Service signals, if sent, acknowledge PAD command signals or inform the terminal of the call progress, for example ''Reset,'' ''Status free,'' ''Clear confirmation.''	0: No service signals. 1: Service signals can be sent.
7. Selection of operation of PAD on receipt of ''break signal''	On receipt of a ''break signal'' from the terminal the PAD can take one of various actions, as indicated by this parameter value. Combined values may be permitted, e.g., 21: this causes the PAD to take actions 1,4 and 16.	0: Nothing. 1: Interrupt. 2: Reset. 4: Send the host a control message containing an ''indication of break.'' 8: Escape from the data transfer state.

BOX 23.1 *Continued*

		16: Discard any output to the terminal.
8. Discard output	This parameter indicates whether a PAD may discard user data being sent to a terminal.	0: Normal delivery. 1: Discard.
9. Padding after carriage return	After a carriage return, a number of padding characters are added to the character string sent to a terminal to give the carriage time to return before printing starts again. This parameter specifies the number of characters.	0: A number of padding characters determined by the terminal data rate. 1 to 7: The number of padding characters inserted.
10. Line folding	A packet may be longer than a terminal print line. If so the PAD can automatically insert appropriate format characters to prevent overprinting at the end of the terminal line. This parameter specifies the length of the terminal print line.	0: No automatic insertion. 1 to 255: Number of characters per line.
11. Binary speed	The host can read this parameter giving the speed of the terminal, but cannot change it.	0: 110 bps. 1: 134.5 bps. 2: 300 bps. 8: 200 bps. 9: 100 bps. 10: 50 bps.
12. Flow control of the PAD by the terminal	This parameter indicates whether there is flow control of the PAD by the terminal. If flow control is used the terminal can indicate whether or not it is ready to accept characters from the PAD by using the DC1 and DC3 control characters of the CCITT No. 5 alphabet.	0: No flow control. 1: Flow control used.

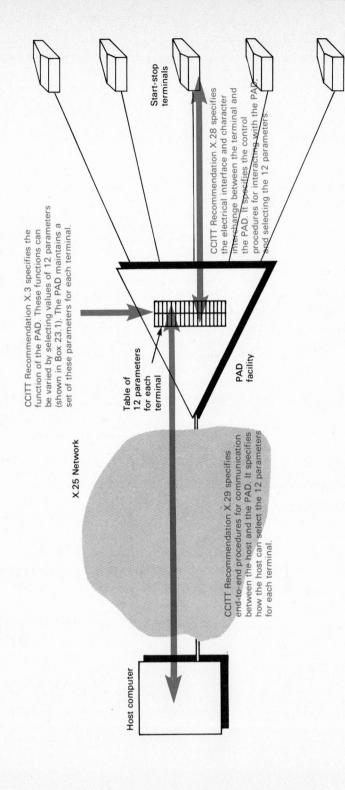

CCITT Recommendation X.3 specifies the function of the PAD. These functions can be varied by selecting values of 12 parameters (shown in Box 23.1). The PAD maintains a set of these parameters for each terminal.

Start-stop terminals

CCITT Recommendation X.28 specifies the electrical interface and character interchange between the terminal and the PAD. It specifies the control procedures for interacting with the PAD and selecting the 12 parameters.

X.25 Network

Table of 12 parameters for each terminal

PAD facility

CCITT Recommendation X.29 specifies end-to-end procedures for communication between the host and the PAD. It specifies how the host can select the 12 parameters for each terminal.

Host computer

Figure 23.3 CCITT Recomendations X.3, X.28, and X.29.

Recommendation V.25—again the conventional use of analog telephone lines (or sub-voice-grade lines).

The terminal can send a "break" signal to the PAD without loss of character transparency. This signal is defined as the transmission of a binary 0 condition continuously for more than 150 millisecs. The PAD can also send a "break" signal to the terminal. The action which the PAD should take when a terminal sends a break signal is given by Parameter 7. It may send a "Reset" packet to the host.

The terminal can send a number of commands to the PAD, and the PAD can send certain service messages to the terminal.

The commands which the terminal can send are used to do the following:

- Set up a virtual call.

- Clear a virtual call.

- Request the status of a virtual call.

- Transmit an interrupt mode packet to the host.

- Read the values of the parameters which the PAD is using for that terminal.

- Set a parameter to a given value (as illustrated above).

- Select a set of parameters known as a standard profile. Two standard profiles are specified.

The service signals which the PAD can send to the terminal are used to do the following:

- Acknowledge the above commands to the PAD sent by the terminal.

- Indicate that a command from the terminal is in error.

- Transmit information about the operation of the PAD to the terminal.

- Transmit information about progress or problems setting up a call as follows:

OCC:	The number called is occupied with other virtual calls and cannot accept another.
NC:	Network congestion temporarily prevents the requested virtual call from being completed.
INV:	Invalid facility requested.
NA:	Not accessible. The terminal is not permitted to obtain a connection to the called number, possibly because it is in a closed user group.
ERR:	Local procedure error.
RPE:	Remote procedure error.
NP:	Not obtainable. The called number is not assigned, or is no longer assigned.

DER: The called number is out of order.

PAD: The PAD has cleared to call following the receipt of an invitation to clear from the host.

CCITT RECOMMENDATION X.29

CCITT Recommendation X.29 specifies how an X.25 machine (i.e., normally a host computer) communicates with the PAD.

Two categories of packets are interchanged between the PAD and the host: the conventional X.25 data for control packet types described in the previous chapter, and packets for controlling the PAD and its relations with the host. The latter are called PAD messages. They are sent as a packet having the Q bit (the first bit in Fig. 22.4) set to 1. The conventional X.25 packets have the Q bit set to 0.

There are several types of PAD messages, as follows:

- SET PARAMETERS. A packet from the host, setting the value of one or more of the PAD parameters, for a given virtual call.

- READ PARAMETERS. A packet from the host requesting the value of one or more of the PAD parameters, for a given virtual call.

- SET AND READ PARAMETERS. Using one packet, the host sets some parameters and reads others, for a given virtual call.

- PARAMETERS INDICATION. A packet from the PAD to host giving parameter values in response to a READ PARAMETERS command.

- INVITATION TO CLEAR. A packet from the host which requests the PAD to clear a virtual call after transmission to the terminal of all data sent so far.

- INDICATION OF BREAK. If the terminal sends a "break" indication and Parameter 7 allows the PAD to deal with it, the PAD sends an interrupt message to the host followed by this PAD message, which indicates that the PAD is discarding the data it has from that terminal.

    Before resuming transmission the host sends a PAD message setting Parameter 8 to "0": "normal data delivery."

- ERROR. A packet indicating an invalid PAD message.

24 DATAGRAMS

Many of the problems and complexities in packet-switching networks arise from the need to send multipacket messages, or to deliver the packets in sequence. If the packets could be sent by themselves so that each packet is unrelated to any other packet, then the network protocols could be relatively simple and less buffering would be needed in the interface nodes.

It has been concluded in several studies of common carrier networks that much of the traffic would indeed be single-packet messages, especially if the packet size was longer than that sent on ARPA network (1008 bits). Some 96% of all messages sent on ARPANET were less than 1008 bits and most of the longer messages were file transfers which could be deferred to a later time [1]. There are some network applications with gigantic potential traffic volumes in which the messages would be less than 1008 bits, for example credit checking, check authorization and fund transfer networks, connecting stores, restaurants, supermarkets, gasoline stations, and banks; inquiry applications; stock quotations; airline, car, hotel and theater reservations; and so on.

Because of this the Canadian authorities who designed Datapac devised the concept of a network which could give two levels of user service [2]. The lowest level transmits single packets and makes no attempt to sequence them. The higher level sets up a virtual call in which the information transmitted must be delivered in sequence, and can consist of messages of any length.

The single packets were named *datagrams* and the network which transmits them a *datagram network*.

A datagram network would be simpler and cheaper to implement than a virtual call network. The datagram user protocol permits simpler terminals or software to be connected to the network.

Datagram enthusiasts have imagined inexpensive terminals which can be plugged into telephone extensions everywhere with a simple telephone plug. The user may dial or may be permanently connected by leased line to a datagram network access node. Some applications could employ vast quantities of such terminals. There are many applications that need nothing more sophisticated. An inexpensive interface unit could convert the home television set into a datagram terminal.

The Canadian originators did not build their datagram network because they wished to conform to the new CCITT X.25 Recommendation. Nevertheless the term *datagram* entered the networking vocabulary and a datagram network remains an important concept. It is unfortunate that common carriers have not provided inexpensive datagram tariffs. There would be many applications of these. The existence of public datagram networks would lead to many new users. It has been proposed that datagram protocols should become an international standard [3, 4].

PROPERTIES OF A DATAGRAM

A CCITT study group [2] defined a datagram as follows: *A message which can be contained in the data field of only one packet is delivered to the destination in its address field. No referral is noted by the network to any other datagram previously sent or likely to follow.*

It is recommended that a datagram should contain up to 128 bytes of data. It is transmitted between user machines without the preamble of setting up a virtual call. It contains a destination address and travels quickly to that destination. It is transmitted between user machines completely independently of any other packet transmitted before or after it. The datagram protocol makes no attempt at sequencing packets or grouping them into messages.

If there is no virtual call setup, and each datagram is independent of every datagram that has gone before or that will go in the future, then the protocols can be very simple. Much of the complexity of ARPANET or X.25 networks is avoided. Consequently datagram machines could be simple, reliable, inexpensive devices, for example, hardwired terminals for financial application, inquiries, reservations, brief message sending, etc. Box 24.1 lists the properties of datagrams.

SECURITY

A datagram network allows any two users to communicate unless they are prevented from doing so for security reasons. For security, users can establish *closed user groups*. Members of a closed user group can communicate with one another, but the network prevents other users from receiving messages from the group or sending messages to its members.

DATAGRAM FORMAT

The datagram format that was proposed originally was very simple. It is shown in Fig. 24.1. More recently a more complex format has been proposed to fit in with X.25 networks. The original datagram had an 8-bit control byte called TYPE, a 32-bit address, and a variable-length data field.

The address placed in the datagram by the sender is the destination

BOX 24.1 Properties of datagrams

- Datagrams are transferred between the network and user machines.

- They have a simple format and use simple protocols, so that datagram machines could be simple.

- They contain up to a given number of user characters (128 bytes maximum was recommended).

- They are sent to the destination in their address field with minimum delay.

- Each datagram is self-contained and is handled independently of any previous or subsequent datagram.

- Datagrams may arrive in a different order from that in which they entered the network.

- There is no virtual call setup needed prior to sending a datagram. A datagram travels to its addressee with no preamble.

- A datagram is delivered to its destination with a high probability of success, but may possibly be lost. Therefore for some applications, user machines will apply their own end-to-end controls.

- If the addressee cannot be reached by a datagram due to situations such as a nonexistent address, failure of addressee's device, or network failure, the datagram will be returned to the sender with the appropriate code in the header.

- A user machine may request the network to prevent another address from sending datagrams to him.

- Protocols for handling sessions, file transfer, longer messages or virtual circuits can be built on top of the datagram facility if needed.

address. When the datagram is delivered *the address has been changed to that of the sender* (Fig. 24.2). This change may take place a stage at a time as the datagram passes through the network.

The address field is large. Thirty-two bits could accommodate four billion users. This was proposed, not because the population of the world is four billion, but so that the address field could contain any 10-digit telephone number (of which the second area code digit is 0 or 1).

There are various meanings for the TYPE code. The meanings for the sender and receiver are different, and are listed in Box 24.2.

Normally datagrams will have the type code DATA. The type codes, of which there could eventually be many, indicate that a normal transfer has failed to take place. The datagram might not be accepted by the network, possibly because it has an invalid address or invalid type code, or because it is too long. It may be returned, possibly

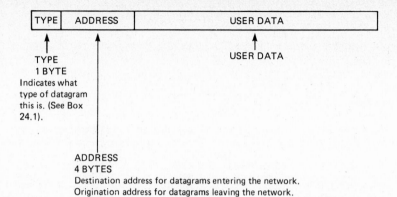

Figure 24.1 The structure of a datagram. In the original proposal only these fields were needed. The current CCITT proposal uses a more complex structure, shown in Figure 24.7 so that X.25 networks can handle datagrams.

because the recipient is busy and not available, or because of network congestion. The TYPE code indicates the reason.

CYCLADES/CIGALE   The first implementation of a datagram-switching computer network was in France—the CYCLADES network (Fig. 24.3). CYCLADES interconnects universities and research centers with a set of objectives similar to ARPANET (Fig. 3.9). The transmission net of CYCLADES is called CIGALE and this is a datagram-switching network. It has proven to be simple

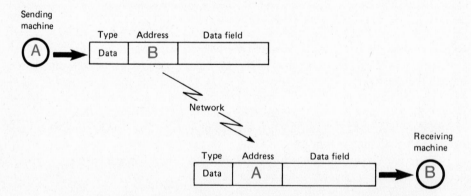

Figure 24.2 The network changes the address as shown. This change may take place a stage at a time as the datagram passes through the network.

BOX 24.2 The TYPE codes of datagrams sent to and received from the network

Type Codes for Datagrams Sent to Network

Number	Name	Meaning
0	DATA	Datagram to be sent to destination in address field.
1	IDENTIFY	Ignore destination address and send this datagram back to originator with his own address.
2	ECHO	This datagram is to be returned from the destination node.
3	BLOCK	Prevent transfer of datagrams to this device from user whose address is in the address field.

Type Codes for Datagrams Received from Network

Number	Name	Meaning
0	DATA	Datagram received from user identified by address field.
1	IDENTIFICATION	This datagram is being returned with originator's address in the header.
2	ECHO	This datagram has been returned from the destination node.
3	BLOCKED	No longer send datagrams to the user identified by the address field!
4	BAD-ADDRESS	This datagram is being returned because the address is invalid.
5	BAD-LENGTH	This datagram is too short to have a valid header, or it has a data field longer than allowed.
6	BAD-TYPE	This datagram is being returned because the type code is invalid.
7	NOT-ACCEPTED	This datagram is being returned because the addressee is not accepting datagrams.
8	NOT-DELIVERABLE	This datagram is being returned because a network failure prevents delivery.
9	PADDED	This datagram is being delivered with padding in the last byte to accommodate the byte nature of the access data link (e.g., BSC).
10	CONGESTING	A large queue of datagrams is awaiting delivery over this link. This datagram is generated inside the network.

and reliable, and provides a simple interface to its host computers. Host protocols are needed as on any computer network, and here they must perform the division of messages into datagrams and reassembly, where this is necessary.

One of the arguments cited against datagrams has been that congestion could occur because a host could send excessive traffic. There are no RFNM's or reservation

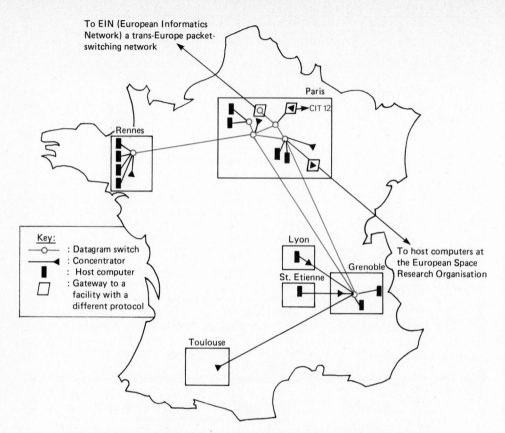

To EIN (European Informatics
Network) a trans-Europe packet-
switching network

Paris

CIT 12

Rennes

Key:
—○— : Datagram switch
�—◀ : Concentrator
▮ : Host computer
▯ : Gateway to a
facility with a
different protocol

Lyon

St. Etienne

Grenoble

To host computers at
the European Space
Research Organisation

Toulouse

Figure 24.3 CYCLADES, a French computer network with objectives similar to ARPANET, serving universities and research organizations. Its transmission subnet is called CIGALE and consists of the
seven switches and eight concentrators shown. CIGALE is a *datagram*
network, and as such gives simple, reliable service. Host interfacing is
simpler than with an ARPANET-like or X.25 network. Higher level
host protocols are needed, like any packet net, but these are independent from the CIGALE interface.

messages as on ARPANET. Each datagram node merely limits the input rate to a certain level. Simulations carried out at the British National Physical Laboratory indicated
that datagram switching is a viable technique and the CYCLADES/CIGALE experience
confirmed this.

VIRTUAL CALLS   When a user has a datagram to send he simply sends it.
There is no need to make reservations for it or to take any
action to establish a connection. When a user wants to send a multipacket message or

group of messages which must be delivered in sequence, he must set up a *virtual call*.

The datagram proposal advocated that where a virtual call facility *is* implemented, this should be as a layer of control on top of the datagram layer, as shown in Fig. 24.4.

A virtual call would employ datagrams to carry its traffic. Both control messages required for the virtual call and data would be carried by the datagrams.

A datagram carrying a virtual call header is used to set up the call, clear the call when it is completed, and send other control messages if necessary. Datagrams also carry the data traffic of the call.

The virtual call protocol is a full-duplex protocol. Like those of ARPA or X.25, it can be used for all forms of data processing. A higher-level protocol (Layer 4) can be used with it.

The virtual call protocol would:

- Establish a call for subsequent exchange of streams of datagrams in both directions.
- Have many calls in progress at the same time.
- Correctly sequence datagrams belonging to a given call.
- Identify and eliminate duplicate datagrams.
- Control the flow of datagrams in both directions.

ADDITION OF A   Many organizations implementing a virtual circuit network
DATAGRAM LAYER   are in fact building a datagram system as the transport
                           mechanism, and then building the virtual circuit protocols
on top of the datagram facility, as in Fig. 24.4. This approach is in keeping with the
principles of good system design. The complexities of the virtual circuit protocol are
decoupled from the means of moving packets around. The virtual circuit protocols

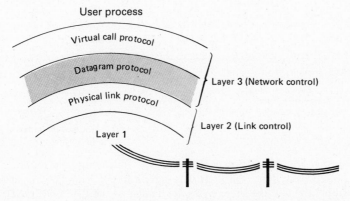

Figure 24.4 A virtual call protocol could be built on top of a datagram facility.

could operate over a packet-switched network, a fast-connect circuit-switched network, a leased-line concentrator network, a radio network, or a simple pair of copper wires, providing they transport packets.

Both common carrier networks (e.g., Telenet in the U.S., EPSS in Britain) and other networks (e.g., EIN in Europe) are using a datagram network as the foundation for a virtual circuit network.

Because datagrams are now perceived as being an adjunct to X.25 networks, a new CCITT proposal gives the datagram a more complex structure than that in Fig. 24.1. [3, 4]. It is shown in Fig. 24.5. This structure fits into the family of X.25 packets illustrated in the previous chapter. Its first four bits indicate that it is a DATAGRAM packet. It has a 12-bit identification number. It contains addresses of both the sending and receiving user machines, and both can be variable length, as with the X.25 packets which set up a virtual call (Fig. 24.5). Also like these packets it can have certain optional facility indications such as throughput class, closed-user group, non-delivery indication, priority indication, reverse charging indication, and so on.

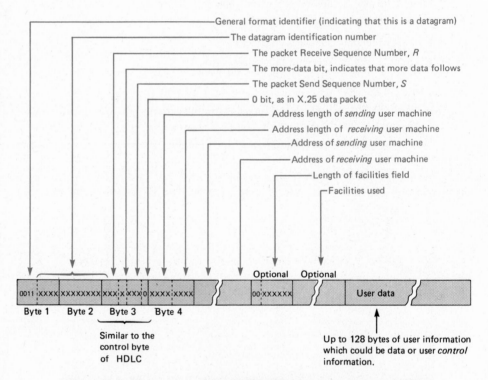

Figure 24.5 The proposed DATAGRAM format for use on CCITT X.25 networks. Note that byte 3 is similar to the X.25 DATA packet (Figure 22.9) and the other bytes are similar to the CALL REQUEST and INCOMING CALL packets (Figure 22.5).

Conforming to the X.25 flow control mechanism using the *window* concept, the third byte of the datagram carries *send* and *receive* sequence numbers, as in an X.25 DATA packet.

This form of datagram contains more overhead than the original concept in Figs. 24.1 and 24.2, especially if equally long addresses are used. Its advantage is that it allows a network operator to provide either X.25 or datagram service (or both) to each customer.

Most X.25 networks carry their own traffic in datagram form, and this is the reason for the packet structure of Fig. 24.5. Given this mechanism it is desirable that users should be able to use the datagram interface directly, as illustrated by the datagram machines in Fig. 24.6.

Figure 24.7 shows a public data network, like Telenet, with two levels of operation. The higher-level trunking network carries datagrams, its nodes being datagram packet-switches. The lower-level network has nodes in more locations and provides the X.25 virtual call and permanent virtual circuit interface.

The user machines in Fig. 24.7 have several options:

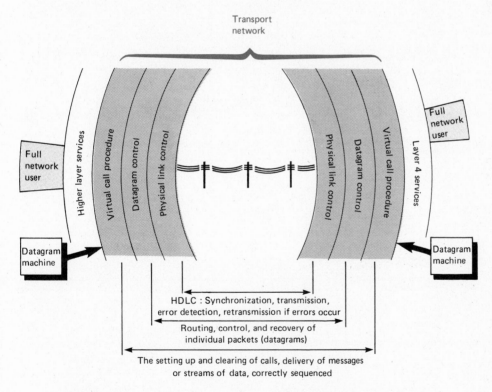

Figure 24.6   Layers of control on a virtual call network with datagrams.

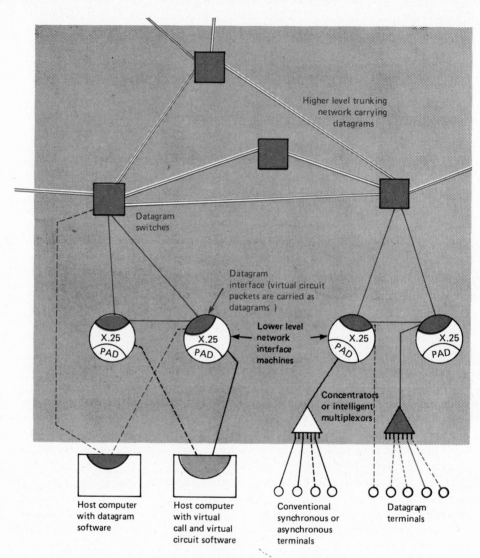

Figure 24.7 An X.25 network which allows datagram access as well as virtual call, permanent virtual circuit, and PAD access. (The dotted lines are dialed telephone connections. Datagram facilities are colored red.)

- A permanent virtual circuit with leased lines to the nearest network node.

- Virtual calls with leased or dial telephone lines to the nearest network node.

- Conventional asychronous terminals connected either directly or via a concentrator or multiplexor to a PAD (packet assembly/disassembly) interface.

- Conventional synchronous terminals connected to an interface which creates the packet headers.

- Datagram machines which bypass the virtual call and permanent virtual circuit software and use the datagram switching facilities directly.

ADVANTAGES   There seems everything to be gained by letting the users employ *either* virtual circuits *or* the underlying datagram protocols, as shown in Fig. 24.6. Access to the datagram protocols would permit the widespread use of inexpensive mass-produced terminals. These could be as simple as the AT&T Transaction® telephone, or a microprocessor interface to the home television set. Datagram networks could form the basis of vast applications such as check authorization and electronic fund transfer.

There is another reason for the common carriers providing a datagram facility. Many users and computer manufacturers need to implement their own end-to-end flow control procedures and checks for lost or duplicated messages, when they are using common carrier virtual circuits. They may have a special flow-control need such as precise timing of a remote printer. They may need the additional message checks because of the critical nature of the application. They may employ software such as IBM's SNA, Univac's DCA, and DEC's DECNET, which performs these functions. In these cases functions are being duplicated. The overhead over the virtual circuit protocol, e.g., X.25, is compounded with a user's end-to-end protocol. There would be less overhead in total if the end-to-end controls were employed on a datagram network rather than on a virtual circuit network. Why duplicate end-to-end controls which are expensive in buffering and software?

In spite of these arguments it seems possible that many common carriers will *not* provide a datagram facility, even if they have one under the covers of their virtual circuit network. Pouzin in a much quoted paper [5] explains that this is because the carriers do not want to be confined to the business of merely moving packets around; they want a more glamorous piece of the action which would otherwise go to the computer manufacturers. In this Frenchman's phrase: "There is something else than technical under the rug."

REFERENCES

1. Kleinrock, L., and W. E. Naylor, *On Measured Behaviour of the ARPA Network,* AFIPS Conference Proceedings, Vol. 43, AFIPS Press, Montvale, NJ, 1974.

2. CCITT Report on Packet-Switching, Report of Meeting in Oslo, CCITT COM VII, Document, Aug. 1974.

3. ISO/TC 97/SC6/WG2 *Datagram Service and Interface,* Contribution to CCITT Com VII Document (Revised Cologne 26) Cologne, Dec. 1977.

4. *USA Proposal for the Datagram Interface,* Contribution to CCITT Com VII Document, Dec. 1977.

5. Pouzin, L., *Virtual Circuits vs. Datagrams: Technical and Political Issues,* INWA General Note #106 & NCC June 1976, AFIPS Press, Montvale, NJ.

25 CIRCUIT-SWITCHING AND HYBRID NETWORKS

The previous chapters have been concerned with store-and-forward operation, mainly packet switching. Computer networks which use circuit switching are also in operation and this can have major advantages.

A traditional circuit switch is one which connects different wire-pair paths by moving electromechanical contacts [1]. This is the way most (old-fashioned) telephone exchanges work. Because the switch is made by moving electromechanical parts, it is slow. Modern circuit-switching equipment uses solid-state electronics with no moving parts. Bits or characters are routed through high-speed computer circuits from the input line to the requisite output line [2]. Whereas a traditional telephone exchange takes seconds to set up the switched path, a solid-state switch takes milliseconds or less. To differentiate, this is sometimes referred to as *fast-connect* switching. The tree-structured or mesh-structured networks of previous illustrations could be built with fast-connect circuit switches. The path between two users would be set up by the switches, the user data sent, and then, milliseconds later, a new path would be connected for different users.

PACKET SWITCHING VS. CIRCUIT SWITCHING

We might compare a telecommunications network with a railroad network. With circuit switching there is an initial switch-setting operation. It is like sending a vehicle down the track to set all of the switches into the desired position: the switches remain set and the entire train travels to its destination.

With packet switching the cars of the train are sent separately. When each car arrives at a switch, the decision is made where next to send it. If the network is lightly loaded the cars will travel to their destination by a route which is close to the optimum. If the network is heavily loaded, they may bounce around or take lengthy or zig-zag paths, possibly arriving in a sequence different from that in which they departed. A train with only a single car can head off into the network with no initial setup operation. However if the train has many cars it should not start its journey until it is sure that there is enough space for the cars to be shunted into sequence at the destination. So an engine has to be sent to the destination and returns with a go-ahead message before the train can set off.

Figure 25.1 shows a comparison of fast-connect circuit switching and packet switching over a route which employs four physical links. The passage of time is shown on the vertical axis going from top to bottom.

With circuit switching a command must be sent through the network to set the switches. A signal returns indicating that they are set correctly and then the entire message is transmitted. When it has been received, an acknowledgment is transmitted to the sender.

With packet switching the preliminary step of setting the switches is not needed. A packet could travel immediately to the first node, which would examine its address and route it onward. Usually however, the sender has to contact the recipient before transmission to reserve the buffering needed for message reassembly or to ensure that the recipient is ready to receive. The right-hand side of Fig. 25.1 therefore shows a REQUEST-TO-SEND message travelling to the destination, which responds with a PERMISSION-TO-SEND message. Then the packets travel to the destination and an acknowledgment is returned to the sender.

ADVANTAGES OF CIRCUIT SWITCHING

Figure 25.1 indicates that fast-connect circuit switching sometimes gives a faster overall delivery time than packet switching. This is true if switching can be done in a few milliseconds, as shown. If the switching took seconds, as with electromechanical switches, packet switching would be much faster.

The packet-switching half of Fig. 25.1 would have looked better if it had not been necessary to request permission to send before transmitting the data. In some situations, this is not necessary. In some cases, there is a *permanent* virtual circuit between the communicating parties and sufficient buffer storage is always kept available. Packet switching also compares more favorably if the message sent is short. A datagram network may transmit single packets only with no preliminary reservations.

On a packet-switching network, some of the data protocols apply to each separate physical link of the journey through the network. Physical link control with error-checking and acknowledgments is applied to each individual link. Buffering and queue management, and possibly routing and flow control decisions occur at each node. With circuit switching a single physical path exists, end-to-end. Buffering, queue management, error-checking, acknowledgments, and flow control, are not done repetitively for each step of the journey; they are done on an *end-to-end* basis. All of the Layer 2 functions we listed in Box 11.1 are done once only. This improves the response time and lessens the total amount of buffer storage and processing that is needed to relay the traffic.

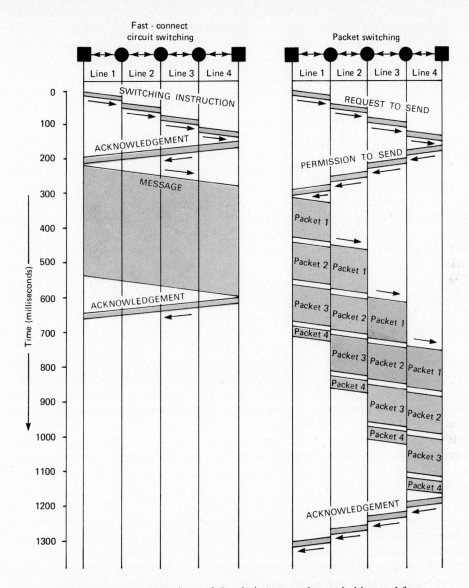

Figure 25.1 A comparison of the timing on packet switching and fast-connect circuit switching. In this illustration a 400-byte (3200-bit) message is sent on 9600 bps lines. The packet size is 1008 bits. No queuing delays are shown. If the lines were moderately highly utilized queuing delays would lengthen the end-to-end delay with packet switching more than with circuit switching.

Most data networks implemented today use packet-switching or store-and-forward concentrators rather than fast-connect circuit switching. The reason is often that off-the-shelf small computers can be used as the switches. The software and protocols needed for packet switching are well documented. However, several of the world's telephone administrations do now operate a fast-connect circuit-switched data network.

RELATIVE MERITS   There have been several detailed studies comparing the relative merits of packet switching and circuit switching [3, 4, 5]. Among their conclusions are the following. For datagrams or short messages *permanent* virtual circuits employing packet switching give the fastest delivery time. For long messages circuit switching is better. The crossover point is typically around 400 bits in message length but varies with network parameters [3]. With virtual calls (non-permanent virtual circuits) the operation of setting up the call swings the balance somewhat in favor of circuit switching.

The total cost of the lines required for a mesh-structured network tends to be less with packet switching [4]. Although the delivery time on the right-hand side of Fig. 25.1 is longer, the lines are occupied less because the individual physical links are used in short bursts.

The cost of the switching nodes tends to be less with circuit switching [4]. This is because packet-switching nodes store the messages and need buffer storage for packets and queuing software; circuit switches do not.

Figure 25.1 does not show the effects of congestion on the links. Congestion could delay the switching of the path before transmission on the left-hand side and cause queues to build up, delaying the sending of each packet on the right-hand side. With circuit switching, the queuing would be end-to-end. The required waiting time in a circuit-switched network for all the required tandem circuits to become simultaneously free tends to be shorter than the total queuing time for the links in a packet-switching network [5].

For very long-distance calls, e.g., international calls, packet switching may give a substantially longer delay than circuit switching because the virtual circuit passes through many switching nodes. In such a case circuit switching may be preferable.

The best of both worlds could be obtained by using packet switching for short messages and circuit switching for long messages or long-distance international calls. Some future data calls may use both, especially for international calls spanning multiple carriers. Today packet-switching networks can be easier to implement because off-the-shelf hardware and software can be used. A telephone administration deciding to offer a switched data network service for the first time can have a packet-switching network operational quickly.

To summarize, there are four main categories of switching in use, and several variations on each of these. They are:

1. Slow circuit switching such as conventional telephone switching.

2. Fast circuit switching capable of connecting and disconnecting paths in a small fraction of a second.

3. Conventional message switching in which messages are *filed* and routed.

4. Packet switching in which messages are chopped into slices (packets) and then routed at high speed.

   Box 25.1 summarizes the differences between these types of switching.

Both circuit-switched networks and leased line networks can use the CCITT Recommendation X.21. This Recommendation defines the physical characteristics and control procedures for a general purpose interface using synchronous digital transmission between user machines and DCEs. A real (i.e., not virtual) digital circuit links one DCE to another, possibly through circuit-switching equipment.

The X.21 interface provides for end-to-end digital transmission in a relatively simple fashion. It facilitates fully automatic call establishment and clearance with a repertoire of call progress and malfunction signals. Any bit sequence can be transmitted over the interface during the data transfer phase.

Simplicity was a prime objective. The connection between the user machine and the DCE uses substantially fewer circuits than the connection between a user machine and a modem (for analog transmission—the CCITT V.24 or EIA 232-C interface). These X.21 circuits are shown in Fig. 25.2. The three basic circuits are TRANSMIT (T), RECEIVE (R), and SIGNAL ELEMENT TIMING (S). The TRANSMIT and RECEIVE circuit carry the data in both directions simultaneously. The SIGNAL ELEMENT TIMING circuit gives the timing of the bits flowing from the network to the user machine.

The CONTROL circuit (C) is used by the user machine to indicate whether it is ON or OFF hook to the network (among other things). The INDICATION circuit (I) is used by the network to signal (among other things) the start of the data transfer phase during which any pattern of bits can be sent. This phase and other phases are indicated without the use of special characters or bit stuffing in the bit stream.

In addition to these five circuits there may be SIGNAL GROUND (G). A BYTE TIMING circuit (B) is also used on some systems to indicate the start of control bytes.

The interface is either in the *data transfer* phase or in one of many *control* phases. Control information is sent during the control phases by transmitting characters from the CCITT Alphabet No. 5. This use of streams of control characters gives an

BOX 25.1 Comparison of the main characteristics of circuit switching, message switching, and packet switching

Conventional Circuit Switching (e.g., telephone switching)	Fat-Connect Circuit-Switching Systems	Conventional Message Switching	Packet Switching
The equivalent of a wire circuit connects the communicating parties.	The equivalent of a wire circuit is connected between the end buffers for brief periods.	No direct electrical connection.	No direct electrical connection.
Real-time or conversational interaction between the parties is possible.	Real-time or conversational interaction between the parties is possible.	Too slow for real-time or conversational interaction.	Fast enough for real-time or conversational interaction between data machines.
Messages are not stored.	Messages are not stored.	Messages are filed for later retrieval.	Messages are stored until delivered, but not filed.
Designed to handle long continuous transmissions.	Designed to handle short sporadic transmissions.	Designed to relay messages.	Designed to handle bursts of data.
The switched path is established for the entire conversation.	The switched path is repeatedly connected and disconnected during a lengthy interaction.	The route is established for each individual message.	The route is established dynamically for each packet.
There is time delay in setting up a call and then negligible transmission delay.	A delay which ought to be less than one second, associated with setting up the call and delivering the message.	Substantial delay in message delivery.	Negligible delay in setting up the call. Delay of usually less than one second in packet delivery.
Busy signal if called party is occupied.	Delay, or busy signal, if called party is occupied.	No busy signal if called party is occupied.	Packet returned to sender if undeliverable.
Effect of overload: Increased probability of blocking, causing a network busy signal. No effect on transmission once the connection is made.	*Effect of overload:* Increased delay and/or increased probability of a busy signal.	*Effect of overload:* Increased delivery delay.	*Effect of overload:* Increased delivery delay (but delivery time is still short). Blocking when saturation is reached.

BOX 25.1 *Continued*

Electromechanic or computerized switching offices are used.	Computerized switching offices are used.	Fairly complex message-switching center is needed, with facilities.	Small switching computers are used with no filing facilities.
Protection against loss of messages is the responsibility of the end users.	The network may be designed to protect the users against loss of messages.	Elaborate procedures are employed to prevent loss of messages. The responsibility of the network for the message is emphasized.	Some protection against loss of packets. End user protocols can be employed in message protection because of the conversational interaction.
Relatively expensive to a user whose transmissions are very short.	Charges for short transmissions can be lower than over the telephone network.	Charges for message delivery lower than over the telephone network.	Charges for short transmissions can be lower than over the telephone network.
Any length of transmission is permitted.	Any length of transmission *may* be permitted.	Lengthy messages can be transmitted directly.	Lengthy transmissions are chopped into short packets. Very long messages must be divided by the users.
Economical with low traffic volumes if the public telephone network is employed.	High traffic volumes needed for justification.	Economical with moderate traffic volumes	High traffic volumes needed for economic justification.
The network cannot perform speed or code conversion.	*May* provide speed or code conversion.	The network can perform speed or code conversion.	The network can perform speed or code conversion.
Does not permit delayed delivery.	*May* permit delayed delivery if the delay is short.	Delayed delivery if the recipient is not available.	Does not permit delayed delivery (without a special network facility).
Point-to-point transmission.	Point-to-point transmission.	Permits broadcast and multiaddress messages.	Does not permit broadcast and multiaddress messages (without a special network facility).
Fixed bandwith transmission.	Users effectively employ small or large bandwidth according to need.		Users effectively employ small or large bandwidth according to need.

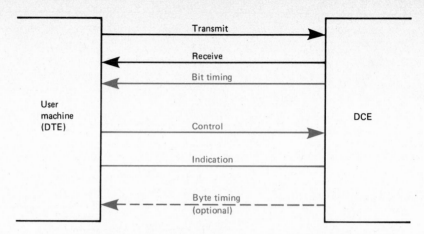

Figure 25.2   CCITT X.21 interchange circuits. This simple digital syn-chronous interface is much more flexible than the earlier analog inter-faces such as CCITT V.24 and EIA RS-232-C, because an endless di-versity of control signals could be sent as coded bytes on the data transfer circuit.

unlimited set of options for future control mechanisms. It is much more flexible than the use of multiple control circuits as on analog interfaces. It is necessary to establish the correct alignment of characters during the control phases. To do this any sequence of call control characters to or from the user machine may be preceded by two or more contiguous SYN characters. Optionally the BYTE TIMING circuit may be used for this purpose.

In an X.21 circuit-switched network the calling user machine sends to the network the address of the machine it wants to be connected to. It receives in response various control signals such as *number busy, out of order,* or *call connected.* The network "rings" the called machine by sending BEL characters to it. Normally the called ma-chine gives an affirmative response.

All of these control characters are sent on the TRANSMIT and RECEIVE cir-cuits.

CCITT Recommendation X.96 defines a variety by *call progress signals* for use on public data networks. These are shown in Box 25.2.

In addition to these a variety of optional new features are appearing on X.21 networks. These include the following:

• *Automatic answering.*

• *Automatic dialing.*

• *Direct call.* The call-request signal causes a call to be set up to a previously designated address. This, in effect, can appear like a nonswitched circuit.

BOX 25.2   Call progress signals for circuit-switched networks (from CCITT Recommendation X.96)

Call Progress Signal	Brief Description of Circumstances
Selection signal procedure error	The selection signals received did not conform to the specified procedure.
Selection signal transmission error	A transmission error was detected in the selection signals by the first DSE.
Invalid call	Facility request invalid.
Access barred	The calling DTE is not permitted to obtain a connection to the called DTE. Incompatible closed user group or incoming calls barred are examples.
Not obtainable	The called number is not assigned, or is no longer assigned or there is an incompatible user class of service.
Number busy	The called number is engaged in another call.
Out of order	The called number is out of order (DTE "uncontrolled" not ready). Possible reasons include: 1) DTE not functioning: 2) mains power off to DTE/DCE; 3) line fault between DSE and DCE.
Changed number	The called number has recently been assigned a new number.
Call the information service	The called number is temporarily unobtainable, call the information service for details.
Network congestion	The establishment of the connection has been prevented due to: 1) temporary congestion conditions; 2) temporary fault conditions, e.g. expiry of a time-out.
Terminal called	The incoming call was signalled to the DTE and call acceptance is awaited.
Controlled not ready	The called DTE is in the *Controlled not ready* state.

- *Closed user group*. Communication is permitted from a user machine only to other machines in the closed user group. A machine may belong to more than one group.

- *Outgoing calls barred*.

- *Incoming calls barred*.

- *Abbreviated address calling*. A brief address from a user machine is expanded into a full network address.

- *Calling line identification*. A user machine is notified of the address of the machine which is calling it.

- *Called line identification.* A user machine is notified of the address of the machine to which it has been connected.

- *Multiple lines* at the same address.

- *Charge transfer* (reverse charges call).

- *Connect when free.* Also known as comp-on, the called machine requests that a connection to a busy machine be established as soon as that machine becomes free.

- *Redirection of call.* Incoming calls are automatically transferred to a nominated address.

CCITT X.21 *BIS*

The use of X.21 requires a change in user machines and software. As an interim measure connection to some public networks may be made via a *conversion* interface facility defined in CCITT Recommendation X.21 *BIS*. This is designed for conventional analog connections using the CCITT V.24 or EIA RS.232C modem connections.

This requires no change to existing machines, but it cannot use the new features of X.21 networks.

HYBRIDS BETWEEN PACKET SWITCHING AND CIRCUIT SWITCHING

There are various forms of hybrid between packet switching and circuit switching. It is likely that some large networks of the future will contain elements of both.

Figure 19.4 illustrates that the delivery time of a packet-switching network is less if the packet size is less. The occupancy of a node (the vertical lines in Fig. 19.4) is also less if the packet size is less. The packet size should not be made too short, however, because each packet carries a header and trailer of fixed size (totaling 15 characters on some networks). If the packet was too small the ratio of data to overhead would be too small.

Suppose, however, that the network mechanisms were changed so that only the first packet of a message needs a full header. Subsequent packets of that message all take the same route as the first. Error checking is done on an end-to-end basis only, not on a node-to-node basis. In effect the first packet of a message would have established a switched path between the users, which would remain in effect until the last packet of the message is sent. When the first packet is sent, buffering and transmission capacity for a fast flow of subsequent packets is reserved and remains available until the end of the transmission. The first packet may contain no data—only a header. The last packet may also contain no data—only a trailer.

Packets could not arrive out of sequence because they follow each other along the same route, so message reassembly problems would be avoided. Acknowledgments and flow control are done on an end-to-end basis, thereby avoiding the duplication of function of conventional packet-switching networks which require multiple HDLC-level checks and acknowledgments and then the virtual-circuit checks and acknowledgments.

Such a mechanism would be a hybrid between packet switching and circuit switching, attempting to achieve a faster delivery time than conventional packet switching.

TIME-DIVISION SWITCHING

A digital trunk can handle either packets or continuous streams of bits. Similarly a digital switch could switch either packets or continuous streams of bits like a circuit switch. Both the trunks and the switches operate much faster than any of the users require; therefore they must be shared by many users.

Figure 25.3 illustrates the principle of time-division switching and transmission. Here tomatoes are shown rolling down a chute and being sorted by gates that open and close at exactly the right times. There are four types of tomatoes, A, B, C, and D and they must be switched to four outgoing paths.

The tomatoes may be thought of as being samples of four signals travelling together in a time-division-multiplexed fashion. Signal C is to be switched to path 1, signal A to path 2, and so on. The gate to path 1 opens at exactly the right moments to make the C samples travel down path 1. At other times it may be desirable to make signal C travel down path 4. This is accomplished by changing the timings with which the gates open.

The tomatoes of Fig. 25.3 could represent *bits* arriving at a switch; they could represent *8-bit bytes* or they could represent larger *blocks* of data. The same principle applies: the separation of the time-multiplexed elements is a switching process. They may be arriving at the rate of several million bits per second. There may be hundreds or thousands of paths, and the gates open and close at electronic speed like the logic circuits in a computer.

VARYING-SPEED STREAMS

In Fig. 25.3 the signals being switched are of equal speed. One of the attractive features of time-division switching for future networks is that it can handle streams at different speeds. The capacity of a high-speed channel and switch can be dynamically allocated between users needing high, medium, and low transmission rates.

Figure 25.4 illustrates the principle of a transmission line and switch handling channels of different speeds. A high-data-rate channel is switched to path 2. Low-data-rate channels are switched to paths 1 and 3.

When a user requires a channel in a time-division network employing different channel speeds, he will indicate the destination of the call, the channel speed he wants, and possibly the duration of the call. A network controller will then attempt to make a reservation for these requirements through the transmission channels and switches. If the operation is under computer control the reservation could be for a very short block of time. One user device might request a 200-bit-per-second channel for one second. Both of these may be derived from a digital carrier operating at say 2.048 million bits per second. With time division of the capacity under computer control,

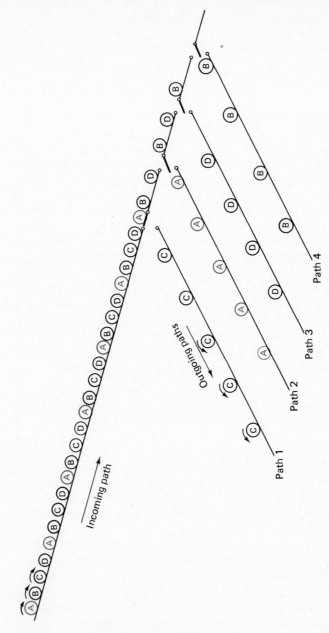

Figure 25.3 Synchronous time-division switching of a time-multiplexed stream.

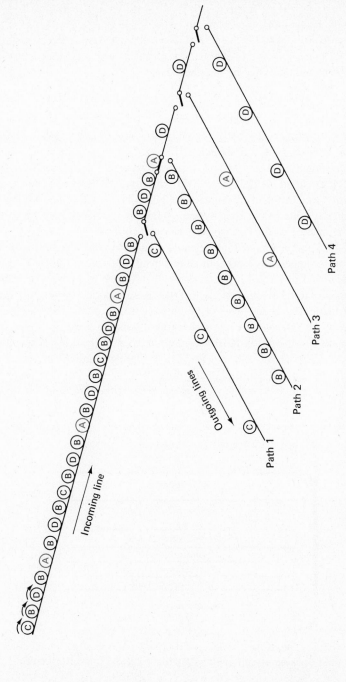

Figure 25.4 Synchronous time-division switching with different channels.

subchannels of large or small capacity may be allocated to users for very brief periods of time.

While some users specify the duration of their call when the reservation is made, others may request a channel for the foreseeable future, and at a later time request the disconnection of that channel. Telephone speech is being handled digitally on many systems, so speech and data may be interleaved.

PACUITS   A switch which uses these types of techniques and which has enough storage to store packets can act as both a circuit switch and a packet switch at the same time.

One such switch is manufactured by the Computer Transmission Corporation (TRAN) [(6)]. It is called a PACUIT switch (from the words PACket + circUIT). A PACUIT network was installed by TRAN in California for the Pacific Telephone and Telegraph Company, one of the Bell System operating companies, for interconnecting terminals and computers of the state universities and colleges.

The PACUIT equipment multiplexes onto a single digital line asynchronous traffic (from start–stop terminals), synchronous traffic (from buffered terminals), and *pacuits* (Fig. 25.5). A *pacuit* is a small block of data which travels in the network. A train of these blocks travels from a source node to a destination node carrying the data of all users who are using that route. They may be switched through multiple intermediate nodes but there is no *intermediate* error checking or acknowledgments. All error control is done on an end-to-end basis with cyclic redundancy checking at the source and destination nodes. This greatly reduces the node buffering requirements.

The pacuit system might be thought of as a passenger bus service with buses (pacuits) leaving at regular intervals for a given destination. Different buses leave for

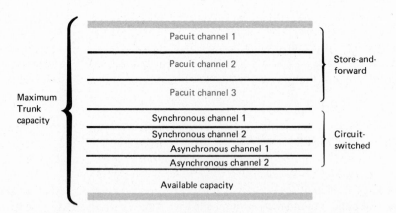

Figure 25.5   Use of the trunks on TRAN's *paciut* network which combines time-division circuit switching with store-and-forward operation.

other destinations. Each bus can carry bits *from* more than one user at the source node, and *for* more than one user at the destination node.

All logical links between network nodes are full-duplex. While one stream of buses goes from node A to node B, another different stream goes from node B to node A. This second stream can take a different route, but the pacuits follow each other so they cannot get out of sequence. Each pacuit contains an acknowledgment, positive or negative, of the accuracy of pacuits travelling in the opposite direction on that logical link. Only 5 bits are needed for acknowledging up to four pacuits. If a pacuit is received in error the source node will retransmit that and subsequent pacuits.

All intermediate nodes operate in a purely time-division circuit-switched mode for through traffic. The effect of this is to minimize the end-to-end delays.

While the circuit-switched nature lowers the buffer storage in intermediate nodes, the smallness of the pacuits lowers the buffer storage in the source and destination nodes. ARPANET allocates 1008-bit buffers to packets. The pacuit system uses very small buffers because the pacuits leave at frequent intervals.

If a terminal user does not enter any data between one pacuit department and the next to that terminal's destination, almost no space will be wasted for that terminal in the pacuit. The pacuit is serving multiple users and it is probable that at least one of them will have something to send. The pacuit is of variable length and an efficient compaction technique ensures minimal overhead. When a user machine disconnects from the node, it is completely deallocated from the pacuit channel.

How often should the buses depart for a given destination? That depends on how much traffic there is between the source and destination node. The software monitors the traffic and dynamically adjusts the departure rate of the pacuits. On almost all computer networks there is heavy traffic between certain destination pairs and little between others. If there is *any* traffic between a node pair, there may be a minimum bus departure rate in order to set a minimum on the virtual bandwidth between that node pair.

Not all terminals connected to the TRAN network *need* to employ packets or any other form of *burst* multiplexing. Some types of terminals transmit *continuous* data streams and have powerful error detection and retransmission schemes using polynomial error-detecting codes. These terminals are connected via the time-division circuit-switching facility of the network. File transmission does not need packet-switching.

HYBRIDS WITH SEPARATE MACHINES   While TRAN combines store-and-forward switching and circuit switching in the same machine, other systems use separate circuit-switching and store-and-forward-switching machines in the same network.

A large packet-switching carrier might find that it improves overall network performance to build circuit-switched links between certain packet-handling nodes. Again telephone companies of the future might have large packet-switching and circuit-switching networks installed using the same digital trunks. A customer may use the circuit-switched network for his file transfers and the packet-switched network for his interactive traffic. There is much to be said for a large organization having a datagram network and a circuit-switched network operating together, with each of them more efficient for its own type of traffic than virtual-call packet switching.

Both telephone company systems and corporate and government tie-line networks carry more telephone traffic than data. Common carriers are installing digital (PCM) trunks for telephone traffic at a rapid rate. Equipment using the trunks may be designed to meet the needs of four types of users, as shown in Fig. 25.6. Both circuit switching and datagram switching are used. Telephone and batch data users employ the circuit switching. Interactive users employ the datagram switching, some with virtual call facilities which perform message reassembly and sequence checking.

AT&T's TNS   AT&T's Transaction Network System uses a mixture of message switching and fast circuit switching. It is designed to serve large numbers of cheap interactive terminals which send fairly short messages to multiple computer centers and expect short replies. The most common applications are financial ones with transactions originating in stores, restaurants, offices, and banks, and being used for verifying credit, authorizing checks, dispensing cash, electronic fund transfer, and so on. Other applications with simple inquiries and responses can be handled.

AT&T wanted to serve this potentially vast number of terminals with its existing telephone cables and central offices. The terminals can be AT&T Transaction telephones, illustrated in Fig. 25.7, or other manufacturers' terminals with a compatible interface. In some cases a voice response to the terminal is used, in other cases a short data response.

Each terminal is attached to a local loop like a telephone. It might have a four-

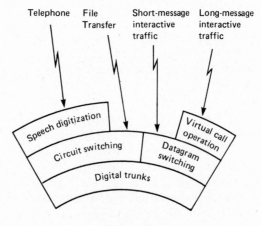

Figure 25.6

pin plug, to plug into a conventional telephone jack. The telephone wires connect it, like a telephone, to its local central office. There the wires are connected to a small solid-state circuit switch which can scan up to 60 such terminals. This is called a data station selector. When selected to transmit, a terminal either sends a message from its buffer or indicates that it has nothing to send. It scans the 60 terminals in about a second on average. It can also select a terminal and transmit a message *to* the terminal buffer.

The data station selector is connected by one two-wire telephone line to a *message switch* in a distant central office. The message switch is based on a processor used in electronic switching systems (ESS) for telephone switching. The message switch is connected to trunks going to the many data processing centers which serve the terminals.

The message switch controls the data station selectors. Normally it commands them to scan the terminals, i.e. switch to each terminal in turn and send a tone which instructs that terminal to send its buffer contents if it has anything to send. When the message switch has a response to send *to* a terminal, it interrupts the scanning cycle to send it.

The message switch may be several hundred miles from a data station selector and may control many such selectors. It can be any distance from the data processing centers it serves.

Both the message switch and the data station selectors are duplexed for reliability. Two identical halves of a data station selector normally scan up to 30 terminals each. If one half fails, the other half is commanded to scan up to 60 terminals. Parity is used for error detection. If a message from a terminal has an error when it reaches the message switch, that switch sends a negative acknowledgment which instructs the terminal to hold the message for retransmission on the next scan. Conventional error control is used between the message switch and the data processing centers.

Sometimes the data station selector is not a central office; for economic reasons, it may be in a shopping center or office building. Two data station selectors may be wired in tandem like those shown on the left of Fig. 25.7.

When voice response is used, the voice response unit is located at the message switch. The data processing center usually sends a sequence of three-character codes to the message switch. Each code corresponds to an English word, phrase, or number stored in digital form in the message switch. This response is read out and passed through a ditigal-to-analog converter to form telephone speech which is sent to the station's handset.

**FUTURE POTENTIAL
OF TNS TECHNOLOGY**   Perhaps the most attractive feature of this scheme is that it takes advantage of the vast quantity of local telephone loops in existence. The local loops of the USA represent a capital asset of $15–20 billion. They are wire pairs which radiate out from local central offices. It therefore makes sense to put scanning devices at the central offices. In this

AT & T's Transaction telephones
accept input from a keyboard
and magnetic stripe cards

AT & T's Transaction III telephone
responds on an 8 - character LED
display. It can be polled by the data
station selector.

AT & T's Transaction II telephone
responds on an 8 - character LED
display.

AT & T's Transaction I telephone
responds by voice answerback or
with green and yellow lamps.

SHOPPING CENTER

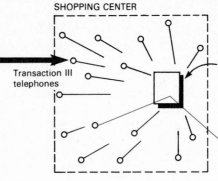

Transaction III
telephones

Local data station
selectors on user
premises, in tandem
with one at a central
office.

Asynchronous
transmission
on local loops.

OFFICE BLOCK

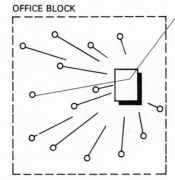

Transaction II
data-response
telephone

Transaction I
voice-response/keyed
answer-tone response
telephone

404

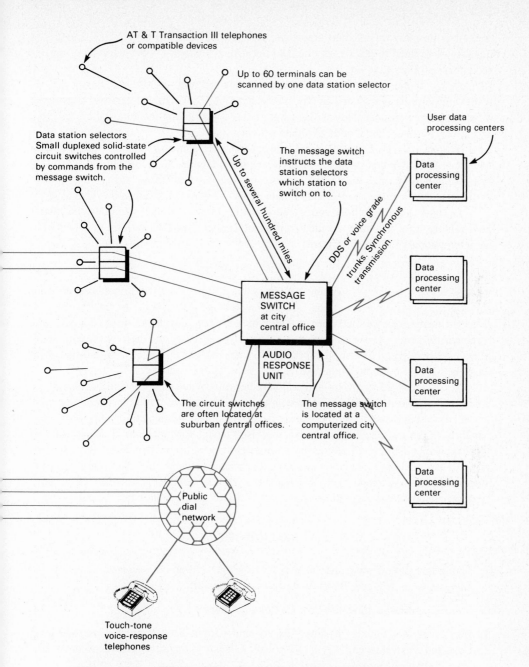

AT & T Transaction III telephones
or compatible devices

Up to 60 terminals can be
scanned by one data station selector

Data station selectors
Small duplexed solid-state
circuit switches controlled
by commands from the
message switch.

Up to several hundred miles

The message switch
instructs the data
station selectors
which station to
switch on to.

User data
processing centers

Data
processing
center

DDS or voice grade
trunks. Synchronous
transmission.

MESSAGE
SWITCH
at city
central office

AUDIO
RESPONSE
UNIT

Data
processing
center

Data
processing
center

The circuit switches
are often located at
suburban central offices.

The message switch
is located at a
computerized city
central office.

Data
processing
center

Public
dial
network

Touch-tone
voice-response
telephones

Figure 25.7 AT&T's TNS (Transaction Network System) used to connect large numbers of cheap terminals for applications such as credit checking, authorizing checks, etc., to multiple computer centers. It uses a combination of circuit switching and message switching. (Photos courtesy of AT&T.)

way, it is possible to link into a network with a relatively low investment cost a vast quantity of isolated terminals which could not take advantage of concentrators or cluster controllers at their location.

Many of the trunks from the central offices are now digital, carrying 1.5, 3.2, or 6.3 million bits per second in North America (T1, T1A, and T2 carriers) [7]. These digital circuits were installed for voice but are ideal for linking the data station selectors of Fig. 25.7 to the nearest node of a data network.

The local loops can carry a bit rate much faster than the 9600 bps of an analog telephone trunk. When used for DDS (Dataphone Digital Service) they carry 56,000 bps, without modems. Much faster, more sophisticated machines than those in Fig. 25.7 could therefore be connected to a data network by an extension of the TNS system.

Because local telephone loops and a central office serve all locations, no matter how remote, this provides an ideal means of connecting *all* locations to nationwide (or international) computer networks.

VARIETY   There can be various types of hybrids between conventional packet switching and circuit switching. Indeed, there are many possible mechanisms with which to build a switched data network. The mechanisms being used today are not necessarily the best, and new developments in transmission subsystems can be expected. It is desirable that the network interface standards being devised today should work with new types of networks.

If CCITT X.25 hardware and software becomes widespread, it will become desirable that machines using it should be able to establish calls on circuit-switched networks as well as on packet-switched networks. Some telephone administrations operating fast-connect, circuit-switched networks have devised means for machines to set up calls on these networks using X.25 protocols. Conversely it is desirable that X.21 usage spreads rapidly, and machines using the simple X.21 interface should have data sent by circuit-switched, packet-switched, or hybrid networks, without being able to tell the difference. Appropriate conversion would be done by the PTT or network operator.

REFERENCES

1. Traditional circuit switching is explained in the author's *Telecommunications and the Computer,* 2nd ed., Prentice-Hall, Englewood Cliffs, NJ, 1976.

2. See *Telecommunications and the Computer,* Chapter 25.

3. Kimmerle, K., and H. Rudin, "Packet and Circuit Switching: A Comparison of Cost and Performance," *Proc. National Telecommunications Conference,* Dallas, Nov. 1976.

4. Esterling, R., and P. Hahn, "A Comparison of Digital Data Network Switching," *Proc. National Telecommunications Conference,* New Orleans, Dec. 1975.

5. Closs, F., "Message Delays and Trunk Utilization in Line-Switched and Message-Switched Data Networks," *Proc. First USA–Japan Computer Conference*, Tokyo, 1972.

6. Sanders, R., and J. deSmet, *A Network Combining Packet Switching and Time Division Circuit Switching in a Common Network*, IFIP Conference, Nice, France, 1975. More information is available from the Computer Transmission Corporation, California.

7. Explained in the author's *Future Developments in Telecommunications*, 2nd ed., Prentice-Hall, Englewood Cliffs, NJ, 1977.

26 LOCAL WIDEBAND NETWORKS— ETHERNET

Most of this book is concerned with long-distance communication. This chapter, however, discusses short-distance communication as, for example, within a factory complex, an office building, a shopping precinct, a university campus, or possibly an area of a town connected with cable television links.

With the dropping cost of minicomputers and the rapid spread of distributed processing, there are many machines within an office building or local area. It is desirable that they should be able to communicate. In factories there will increasingly be large numbers of process control minicomputers; in an office there will increasingly be large numbers of word processing machines, electronic mail machines, and intelligent copiers. Organizations will have large numbers of intelligent terminals and desk-top computers. So local computer networks are needed. Furthermore the local area will often contain a node of a long-distance network, possibly an X.25 node, possibly a concentrator, or, increasingly in some countries, a small satellite earth station. It is desirable to connect the various machines which should communicate to this long-distance node.

Usually telephone lines have been used for the local interconnection, often going via the local PABX (private telephone exchange on the premises, which with modern technology is itself a small computer). There are disadvantages in this approach:

1. A separate pair of wires is needed for each device (or "extension") that is connected. With hundreds of extensions, this is a lot of wiring.

2. If all paths through the exchange happen to be busy a device cannot be connected. It encounters a busy signal.

3. *Most* installed telephone exchanges are electromechanical and switch slowly. Intercommunicating computers should be able to send messages to one another very quickly whenever they need (in a small fraction of a second).

4. Bandwidth is usually limited to that of the telephone line. For some uses of distributed processing, very high-speed bursts of short duration are desirable. Many "office-of-the-future"

uses, for example, need a facsimile document displayed on a screen with a fast response time. A typical page of a document needs 250,000 bits to encode it in facsimile form. Over a telephone-speed line it takes half a minute to transmit.

Techniques are now in use for employing, inexpensively, a transmission medium that transmits millions of bits per second within a local area. Usually coaxial cable is used; sometimes wire pair cable or radio. Many different devices are connected to this transmission path without going through a switch. In this way local networks have been built for a variety of purposes:

- Connecting factory terminals to a computer.
- Connecting distributed processing configurations.
- Interconnecting multiple local computers for resource sharing.
- Forming loosely coupled multiprocessor systems.
- Interconnecting word-processing machines.
- Connecting diverse communicating devices to a local satellite earth station.

THE DIGITAL WALL SOCKET

A future objective might be to have sockets in the walls of buildings into which digital devices can plug. The office of the future may have an electricity socket, a telephone socket, and a digital network socket. The digital socket can handle machines with low or high data rates, for example simple terminals, visual display terminals, digital facsimile machines, facsimile displays, word processing machines, copying machines, digital storage units, personal computers, minicomputers, and large computers.

EXPERIENCE WITH LOCAL NETWORKS

A variety of local network systems have been implemented. These include Bell Telephone Laboratories' Spider, IBM's loop architectures such as the 3790 system [1], University of California at Irvine Distributed Computing System [2, 3], Mitre's Mitrix [4], and Xerox's Ethernet [5].

From experience with such networks a number of characteristics have emerged as desirable for a local networking facility:

1. It needs to be highly flexible and easily changeable because new devices and offices are constantly added or removed.

2. A cable to which branches can be added is better than a loop (ring) cable because it makes it easy to add new locations.

3. The transmission medium and control system should be easily extendible, with minimum service disruption.

4. The system needs to be highly reliable. Single shared components should be minimized. The

transmission medium should be *passive* so the failure of an active element will not disable it, but will disable any one station only.

5. Distributed control rather than centralized control is preferable for reliability, and probably also for cost reasons because some systems will have few stations and will be unable to afford expensive centralized control.

6. Failure or malfunction of one connection to the transmission medium should not disable or jam transmission for other attachments.

7. The traffic will be *highly* bursty in nature, so simple multiplexing or time division multiple access would be much too inefficient. Asynchronous burst multiple access is needed.

8. The transmission medium and control mechanisms need to be cheap if they are to serve cheap microcomputers.

ETHERNET   A system which meets these criteria cheaply and elegantly is the Xerox Ethernet [5]. Local networking facilities like Ethernet have great future potential.

"Ether" was a hypothetical substance that was once thought to occupy all space so that radiation could be propagated. The Ethernet designers use the term to refer to their transmission medium, which could be coaxial cable, wire pairs, optical fibers, or radio. Like the ether once postulated by physicists it is *passive*. It has no amplifiers or active elements and continues to exist if active elements connected to it fail.

The first implementation used a coaxial cable as its "ether." This ran down the corridors of buildings, above the ceiling or below the floor. It could have branches like a tree structure. There is no central or master control point. Devices can be tapped into the cable using off-the-shelf CATV (cable television) taps. New taps or branches can be added anywhere, if the system capacity is not exceeded. This topology, shown in Fig. 26.1, is more flexible than a loop system. In most offices, stations and branches to the cable are likely to be added frequently.

Initially a cable transmitting 3 million bits per second was used, one kilometer in length. There is no reason why these figures could not be exceeded. Cheap CATV cable can trasmit far more than 3 million bits per second. Three million bps was a convenient data transfer rate for the minicomputers that were interconnected. A higher rate would have needed expensive special-purpose packet buffering. Up to 256 stations could be connected to the cable.

Different cables can be mixed on an Ethernet system. The first implementation used small-diameter coax for connection within station clusters and larger-diameter low-loss cable for runs between clusters.

The taps to the cable are connected to *transceivers,* at each using station. The transceiver can receive signals on the cable, and transmit signals sufficiently strong to reach the far points of the cable. Every signal sent on the cable will reach every other transceiver.

The transceivers are simple and cheap. A main consideration in their design is

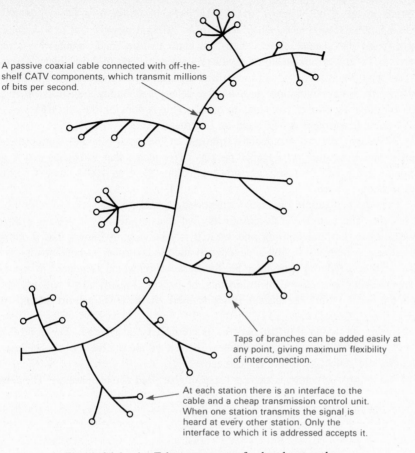

A passive coaxial cable connected with off-the-shelf CATV components, which transmit millions of bits per second.

Taps of branches can be added easily at any point, giving maximum flexibility of interconnection.

At each station there is an interface to the cable and a cheap transmission control unit. When one station transmits the signal is heard at every other station. Only the interface to which it is addressed accepts it.

Figure 26.1   An Ethernet system for local networks.

that if they develop a fault they cannot jam or pollute the ether. When unpowered, a transceiver disconnects itself from the ether. A watchdog timer circuit in each transceiver shuts down its transmitter if it behaves incorrectly.

PACKET BROADCASTING   When an Ethernet transceiver transmits a packet, it is received by every transceiver on the Ether. This is a form of *packet broadcasting*. The packet carries a destination address as its first 8-bit byte. Only the station to which it is addressed accepts the packet.

Packet broadcasting was previously used on radio networks, notably on the ALOHA system discussed in the following chapter. It is being used with *portable* radio terminals in an ARPA system in California. Each station in a packet radio system makes its own decision as to when it transmits. The problem is that two stations might transmit at the same time; their packets collide and cannot be received correctly. Techniques exist which could prevent collisions (polling, reservations, time division multiple access). These have disadvantages of different types, and in a packet broadcasting system with low propagation delays and bursty transmission it can be better to allow occasional collisions to occur. This is done on the ALOHA system, the ARPA portable terminal system, and on Ethernet.

When two stations accidentally transmit at the same time, they must detect the collision and retransmit the damaged packets. This means that 100% channel utilization cannot be achieved. Ethernet can, however, come close to 100%, which polling and other techniques cannot.

An Ethernet station transmits variable-length packets at a speed of millions of bits per second. The transceiver listens to its own transmission. If it notices a difference between what it is transmitting and what it is receiving, it knows that a collision is taking place. The transmission is abandoned and the controller reschedules it. The controller selects a random time interval, the duration of which is related to the load on the ether. After this interval it retransmits the packet. Usually there will not be a collision the second time the packet is transmitted. If there is, a third attempt will be made.

In this way *control* of the network is completely distributed. The control is simple and the control units are inexpensive. There is no alternative routing because of the simplicity and reliability of the coaxial cable.

The control structure is the converse of that used for telephones. The telephone

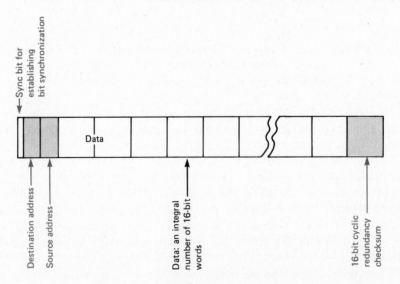

Figure 26.2   The Ethernet packet format.

system in a building has a cable to *each* station and *one* central switching system. Ethernet has *one* cable and a control unit at *each* station. Ethernet is appropriate for brief *bursts* of transmission at very high data rates between any of the stations. The telephone system is appropriate for lengthy *continuous* connections of low data notes between any stations. There could be enormous numbers of applications for a system with the characteristics of Ethernet.

PACKET FORMAT   The format of the packet is simple, like the control mechanism. It consists of an integral number of 16-bit words (Fig. 26.2). The first word contains the source and destination address, both 8 bits. The last word contains a 16-bit cyclic redundancy checksum for end-to-end detection of transmission errors.

The transmitting device encodes the bits it sends with phase encoding (as on magnetic tape) so that there is at least one transition during each bit time. The receiving machine can detect this signal; this is referred to as "detecting the presence of *carrier*." A SYNC bit precedes each packet transmitted. The receiving machine knows when a packet begins by detecting the carrier, and uses the SYNC bit to acquire bit phase. The receiving machine knows when a packet ends because the carrier ceases. It checks that an integral number of 16-bit words have been received. It assumes that the last 16-bit word is the cyclic redundancy checksum. This checksum is both created and checked by hardware, and the checksum does not go into the packet buffer.

When the hardware detects the start of a packet it checks its destination address. If that does not match its own address it ignores the packet.

CONTROLLERS   The hardware interface to the cable serializes and deserializes the data transmitted. It detects packets, checks to see if they are addressed to that station, creates and checks the cyclic redundancy checksum, and detects collisions.

The controller is a firmware or software device which must initiate the retransmission of packets (Fig. 26.3). It uses a random number generator to determine how long to wait before attempting retransmission. The mean wait is initially equivalent to an end-to-end round-trip delay on the cable. However if another attempt at retransmission is needed for a packet the controller doubles the mean delay time. It keeps doubling it every time an attempt at retransmission of that packet fails. In this way it adjusts its behavior to the load conditions on the cable at a given moment, attempting to minimize the probability of collisions.

When the load on the network is low, collisions are rare, and the mean delay time rarely exceeds its minimum value of one round-trip delay. As the traffic load becomes high the retransmission intervals increase in an attempt to sustain channel efficiency.

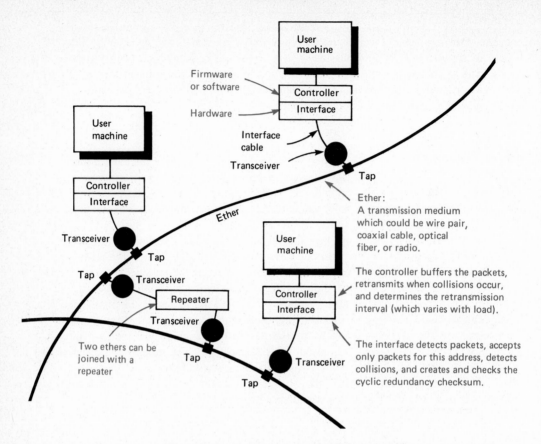

Figure 26.3 Connections to the Ethernet cables.

CARRIER DETECTION   When a packet is going by, a station interface can hear its carrier and so does not initiate a transmission of its own.

An electrical signal takes about 4 microseconds to pass from one end of a one kilometer coaxial cable to the other end. Within that 4 microseconds a station may begin to transmit, not knowing that a packet is already on its way. This is a very brief interval but two or more stations may be waiting to begin transmission at the same moment when a current transmission ends. They start at the same time, collide, and because of the collision pause for a random time and then retransmit (Fig. 26.4).

If the utilization rate of the cable is low, collisions will be rare; when the utilization is heavy collisions will be more common. Because of this the controllers dynamically adjust their behavior as the load on the cable increases; they increase their retransmission interval following collisions.

When collisions occur, transmission is aborted quickly so that damaged packets

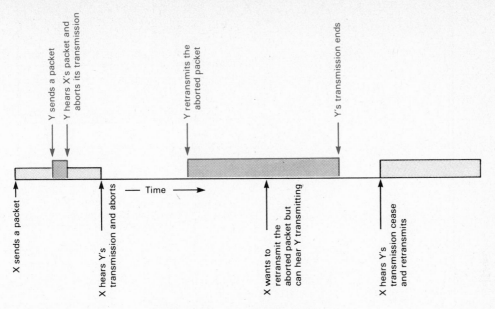

Figure 26.4   An Ethernet collision.

do not occupy much of the transmission time. Collisions are detected and the transmission aborted within an end-to-end round-trip time (e.g., within 16 microseconds on a 1-kilometer cable, this being the time of a 2-way trip and turnaround). The aborted packets are filtered out in hardware and do not reach the listening station's software.

If a station has been sending a packet for twice the round-trip delay without damage then it is safe. Every other station has heard it by then and will avoid colliding with it. If the round trip is 16 microseconds and the transmission rate is 3 million bps, 48 bits are sent during twice the round-trip delay time. In other words, if the packet is not damaged during its first 48 bits it will not be damaged at all. If the station is in the middle of the cable rather than at the end, the figure will be 24 bits.

Short packets, less than 48 bits, may be transmitted completely, damaged, and retransmitted. Long packets cannot suffer quite such a fate. They may be aborted after 48 bits and retransmitted. Only a fraction of them is transmitted twice, so the overall transmission efficiency is higher with longer packets. Figure 26.5 shows the overall transmission efficiency for different packet sizes and different numbers of stations queuing for transmission [5]. With packets of a few hundred bytes, transmission efficiency can be high even with hundreds of stations queuing for transmission. With very short packets the channel utilization drops to an asymptote of 0.368, $1/e$, the same asymptote as a slotted ALOHA channel. However it would not normally be the case that large numbers of terminals on a cable would be queuing for transmission. This would be a severe overload condition. On a reasonably heavily loaded cable, with a Poisson input distribution, the mean number of packets waiting for the channel to become free

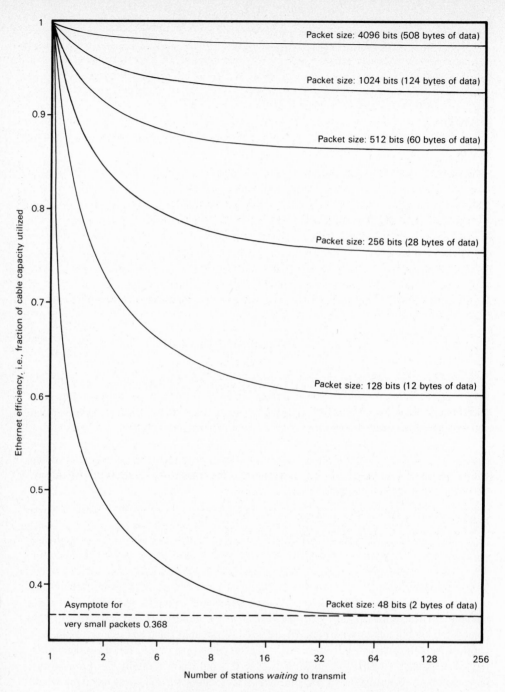

Figure 26.5 The Ethernet transmission efficiency is high when the packet size is large. When the packet size is small, there will be few stations *waiting* to transmit—usually less than one on average.

would be one or two. If the packets were short (say less than 500 bits), then a 3-million bps cable would have *very* little queuing—a mean number of items waiting much less than 1—and so there would be few collisions and a high transmission efficiency.

SUMMARY To summarize then, an Ethernet system can achieve good transmission efficiency, when not excessively overloaded. It uses a simple, inexpensive, distributed control mechanism. It is used for short-distance networks; its efficiency would drop severely if the distances became large. It can transmit at much higher rates than is common on long-distance networks, and so can be used for a high level of distributed processing or multiprocessing within a local area. It is ideal for use on CATV cables. It does not suffer from the inflexibility of some loop systems; stations can be added, moved, or removed easily. New branches can be easily added to the cable. The system can be extended by joining separate cables together with a repeat, and possibly with an extension of the 8-bit addresses. In practice a 3-million bps system designed for 256 stations has proven very reliable.

For local networking, factory control, word processing, and general office use, Ethernet or some similar system can find innumerable applications.

REFERENCES

1. *General Information Manual on 3790,* IBM Corp., Poughkeepsie, NY.

2. Faber, D. J., et al., "The Distributed Computing System," *Proc. 7th Annual IEEE Computer Soc. International Conference,* Feb. 1973.

3. Faber, D. J., *"A Ring Network," Datamation,* 21, 2 (Feb. 1975).

4. Willard, D. G., "Mitrix: A Sophisticated Digital Cable Communications System," *Proc. National Telecommunications Conference,* Nov. 1973.

5. Metcalfe, R. M., and D. J. Boggs, *"Ethernet: Distributed Packet Switching for Local Computer Networks," Communications of the ACM,* Vol. 19, No. 7, July 1976.

27 RADIO AND SATELLITE NETWORKS

Radio has a property which is particularly appealing for data networks; a signal transmitted at one location can be received at *any* location within a given area without any need for wires, switches, or routing strategies. Machines within that area could intercommunicate freely with each other like delegates around a table. But, like delegates around a table, some protocol would be nesessary so that they do not all talk at once.

There are various data radio networks now operating, many of them in an experimental environment. In the simpler ones transmission is one-way, e.g., transmission of information to be printed in specified police cars or delivery trucks; broadcasting a high-speed stream of data on public television channels from which the viewer can request items for display [1]. For computer applications, two-way transmission is usually needed. It was first widely used at the University of Hawaii by Abramson [2]. A radio unit, about the same cost as a modem, provides a two-way link with computers miles away, or with a radio repeater station or a node of a different type of network. Of particular interest, the terminals could be portable. The first system with portable two-way terminals was an ARPA system in California [3]. The potential now exists of three mass markets merging: pocket calculators, CB radios, and hobby computing, to provide data radio terminals of very widespread applicability.

Communications satellites extend the concept of wireless networks to a large geographical area. As satellites become larger their earth stations are becoming smaller. Satellite Business Systems (a subsidiary of IBM, COMSAT, and Aetna) is locating earth stations with 5- and 7-meter antennas at corporate premises throughout America [4]. A satellite designed for data networking and for launch by the space shuttle could have very low-cost earth stations, and could drastically change the techniques of networking [5].

PACKET RADIO

Packet radio is a technique in which data are formed into packets like those on a packet-switching or datagram network, and these are sent by radio. Packet radio is one alternative to the local telephone loops for interactive computer terminals. Because of this, it could be very valuable in countries with underdeveloped telephone systems. In highly developed countries, it could provide mobile or portable terminals. Its enthusiasts imagine a large market of pocket-calculator-sized machines containing microcomputers and a radio link to a nearby packet-switching node.

Packet radio needs a form of multiple-access control which permits many scattered devices to transmit on the same radio channel without harming each other's transmission. There is no control problem in broadcasting from the control station *to the devices*. The problem lies in transmitting *from the devices* to the central station—a central computer, concentrator, or packet-switching node.

Unlike a satellite channel, the transmitting devices need to be cheap and simple, and channel bandwidth is not great. The messages sent *from* the radio terminals are mostly very short. An elaborate form of multiple-access control with messages going back and forth to a control center presents too much overhead. Yet demand-assignment of channel capacity is definitely needed.

A simple form of control known as ALOHA control is used on such systems. It was first employed by Abramson at the University of Hawaii, where he applied it to satellite channels as well as to terrestrial radio links [2].

RANDOM PACKETS   ALOHA control is a very simple, but effective, contention scheme. Each terminal is attached to a transmission control unit with a radio transmitter and receiver. The data to be transmitted are collected in the transmission control unit which forms them into a "packet." The packet contains the addresses of the receiving location and the originating terminal, and some control bits, in a header. The Hawaii packet contains up to 640 bits of data following a 32-bit header, and is protected by a powerful error-detecting code which uses 32 redundant bits in each packet. The transmission control units cost $3000 to build in 1973. Abramson estimates that they could cost less than $500 to produce in quantity [6]. They could be cheaper than modems.

When the packet is complete, the transmission control unit transmits it at the maximum speed of the link. These packet transmissions take place *at random*. All devices receiving on that frequency receive the packet. They all ignore it with the exception of the device (or devices) to which the packet is addressed. A device which receives a packet addressed to it transmits an acknowledgment if the packet appears to be free from error.

The sending device waits for the acknowledgment confirming correct receipt. It waits for a given period and then if it has not received an acknowledgment, it transmits the packet again.

If one central station is transmitting to many outlying stations—for example, a computer transmitting to its terminals—the central station has control over the times at which the packets are sent. When the outlying stations transmit to the central station, the packets are transmitted at random times. Consequently, they occasionally collide. If two packets are transmitted at overlapping times, both will be damaged, and their error-detecting codes will indicate the damage. The transmission control units which sent the packets will therefore receive no acknowledgment. After a given time, each transmission control unit retransmits its packet. It is important that they should not retransmit simultaneously or the packets will again collide. Each transmission control unit should wait a different time before retransmitting.

The different waiting times could be achieved by giving each transmission control unit a different builtin delay. However, there are many such control units and the one with the longest delay would be at a disadvantage. Therefore, the ALOHA scheme gives each control unit a randomizing circuit so that the time it waits before retransmission is a random variable. The retransmitted packets are unlikely to collide a second time but there is a very low probability that this will happen. If so, a third retransmission will be made. A second, or even third collision does little harm if the delays before reattempting transmission are low compared to the desired terminal response time. If a packet is damaged by other causes, such as radio noise, it will similarly be retransmitted. The ALOHA protocol is illustrated in Fig. 27.1.

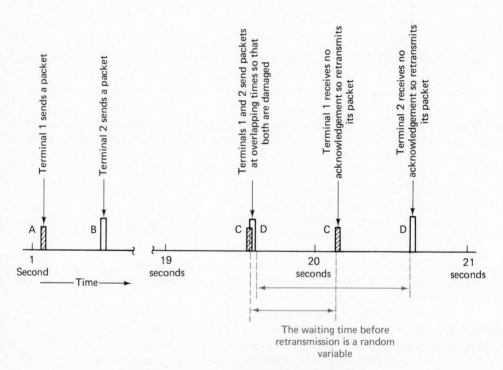

Figure 27.1   The "classical" ALOHA protocol.

Packet radio is a little like an unruly auction in which participants all shout their bids and the auctioneer acknowledges them. If a bid is not acknowledged, the person shouts it again. Occasionally, two persons shout a bid at once and then both have to repeat their bid.

FREQUENCIES   A packet radio system can use one frequency or two. The Hawaii system uses two 100-KHz channels in the UHF band at 407.350 MHz and 413.475 MHz, one for transmitting *to* the terminals and one for transmitting *from* them. If a separate channel is used for transmitting from the computer to the terminals, there is no problem with interference on this channel. (The bidders can hear everything the auctioneer says.) Fortunately in most computer dialogues, the terminal says much less than the computer, so the channel from the terminals, on which packets can collide, will be utilized much less than the channel *to* the terminals.

On the original Hawaii system, the 100-KHz bandwidth channels transmitted occupied the channel for approximately 29 milliseconds. Figure 27.1 is drawn approximately to scale using these figures.

Many different types of data-processing devices may be interconnected using ALOHA broadcasting (Fig. 27.2). The transmission control unit may be attached to a terminal, or concentrator or controller handling many terminals, a computer in a central data processing location, a node of a packet-switching network, a satellite earth station controller, and so on.

CHANNEL UTILIZATION   It is clear that the ALOHA protocol will work well if the number of transmissions is small compared with the total available channel time. A more interesting question is: what happens when the channel becomes busy? Abramson's analysis of the ALOHA channel proceeds as follows.

Suppose that all of the users of an ALOHA channel originate λ packets per second on average.

Suppose that the packets are of fixed length of duration T seconds.

The utilization of the channel as perceived by the users, which in conventional queuing theory is referred to as ρ, is then $\rho = \lambda T$,

$$\frac{\text{The total time the channel is in use for sending original packets}}{\text{The total time}} \text{ is } \rho$$

In reality, there will be more than λ packets using the channels because some packets have to be transmitted more than once due to collisions. Let the total number of packets per second, including retransmitted packets, be λ'.

Because of the retransmitted packets, the actual channel utilization will be greater

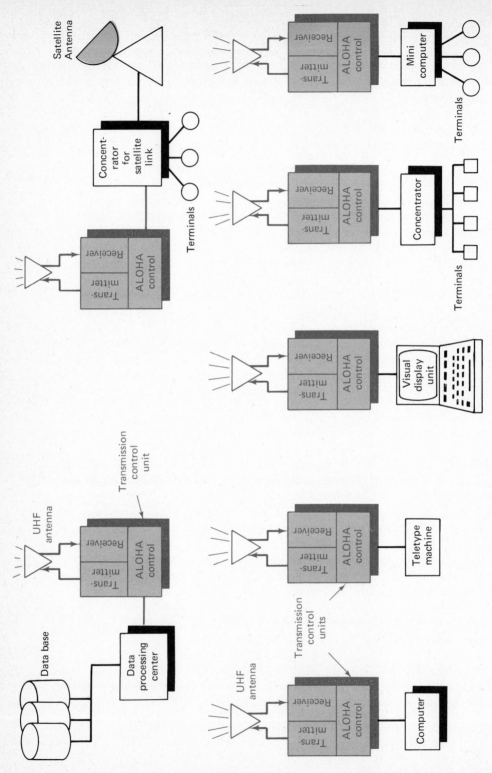

Figure 27.2 Many different data processing machines can be interconnected on a packet broadcasting network.

422

than that perceived by the users—greater than ρ. To understand how the channel behaves when it comes busy, we wish to know the relationship between ρ and λ'.

The assumption normally made in the analysis of interactive systems is that the users orginate messages *independently* and *at random*. In other words, the probability of a message starting in a small time Δt is proportional to Δt. If this assumption is valid, then there is a Poisson distribution of the number of messages originating per second. In this calculation, we assume a Poisson distribution of the number of packets per second.

The probability of n packets originating in a second is:

$$\text{Prob}(n) = \frac{\lambda'^n e^{-\lambda'}}{n!}$$

The probability of no packets originating in a time of duration t is:

$$[\text{Prob}(n = 0)]' = e^{-\lambda' t}$$

Suppose that one particular packet originates at a time, t_o. There will be a collision if any other packet originates between the times $t_o - T$ and $t_o + T$. In other words, there is a time period of duration $2T$ in which no other packet must originate if a collision is to be avoided.

The probability of no packet originating in the time $2T$ is $e^{-\lambda' \cdot 2T}$. This is the probability a packet will have no collision.

Let R be the fraction of packets that have to be retransmitted. Then:

$$R = 1 - e^{-\lambda' \cdot 2T} \tag{27.1}$$

The relation between the number of user-originated packets and the actual number of packets on the channel is therefore:

$$\lambda = \lambda'[1 - R] = \lambda' e^{-\lambda' \cdot 2T}$$

Substituting into $\rho = \lambda T$:

$$\rho = \lambda' T e^{-\lambda \cdot 2T}$$

Sometimes a retransmitted packet will collide a second time and have to be retransmitted again. The mean number of times a given data packet is retransmitted is:

$$N = 1 + R + R^2 + R^3 \ldots$$
$$= \frac{1}{1 - R} \tag{27.2}$$
$$= e^{\lambda' \cdot 2T}$$

Substituting $\lambda'T$ in Equation (27.1) we have

$$\rho = \frac{\log_e N}{2N} \tag{27.3}$$

In Fig. 27.3, ρ is plotted against N. It will be seen that as the channel utilization (as perceived by the user) increases, the traffic which attempts to use the channel builds up at an increasing rate. A chain reaction develops, with the retransmitted packets themselves causing retransmissions so that above a certain throughput the channel becomes unstable.

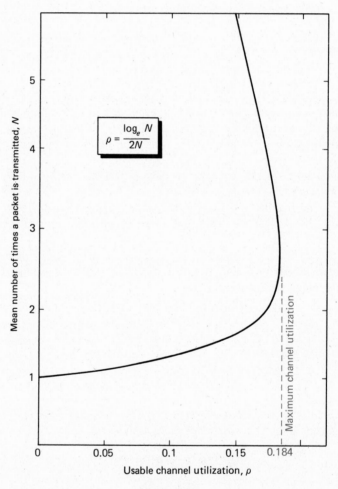

Figure 27.3

Differentiating Equation (27.2) shows that the maximum value of ρ is $1/2e = 0.184$.

The maximum utilization of a classical ALOHA channel is 18.4%.

It is clearly desirable to stop the users of an ALOHA channel from transmitting when they reach the unstable part of the curve in Fig. 27.3. Batch transmission devices might be made to pause for a while when any packet is retransmitted *twice*. Interactive users might be slowed down either by giving them an artificially long response time, or by giving them a visible warning. (Reference 7 discusses the stability of heavily loaded packet radio systems.)

PERFORMANCE   The teleprocessing expert who is used to optimizing land-
IMPROVEMENTS   line systems to give high line utilization will be horrified
                         by the figure of 18.4% maximum channel utilization. In
reality an ALOHA system is unlikely to run at more than about 16% channel utilization because of need to avoid the unstable part of the curve in Fig. 27.3.

There are, however, several ways to improve the channel utilization. We will discuss three techniques which have been used:

1. Slotted ALOHA.

2. Carrier sense.

3. FM discrimination.

With a combination of these three techniques, channel utilization becomes as high as that on typical land-line systems.

SLOTTED ALOHA   In the so-called "classical" ALOHA system packet, trans-
                         missions begin at completely random times. A varia-
tion called a "slotted" ALOHA system causes packets to begin transmission at the start of a clock interval [8]. The time for transmission approximately fills one fixed-length slot and the timing of the slots is determined by a system-wide clock. Each transmission control unit must be synchronized to this clock. Such a scheme has the disadvantage that packets must be of fixed length, but the advantage that collisions occur about half as frequently.

Figure 27.4 shows a slotted ALOHA channel. Packets C and D on this diagram are in collision.

Suppose again that the packet transmission time is T. The slot width is also T. If a given packet is transmitted beginning at time t_o, then another packet will collide with it if it originates between times $t_o - T$ and t_o. In other words, there is a time period of duration T in which no other packet must originate if a collision is to be avoided.

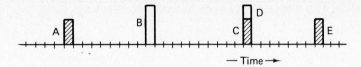

Figure 27.4 **A** slotted ALOHA channel. Each packet must begin on one of the time divisions.

The probability of no packet originating in this time, T, i.e., the probability of no collision is $e^{-\lambda' T}$. Consequently, Equation (27.1) is modified to:

$$\rho = \lambda' T e^{-\lambda' T} \tag{27.4}$$

Equation (27.2) is modified to:

$$N = e^{\lambda' T} \tag{27.5}$$

Substituting, we then have

$$\rho = \frac{\log_e N}{N} \tag{27.6}$$

This is plotted in Fig. 27.5. The channel utilizations for a given retransmission rate are double those for classical ALOHA channel.

The maximum utilization of a slotted ALOHA channel is 36.8%.

The transmission control unit is slightly more complicated because it must maintain the slot timing. A transmitter will send out periodic timing pulses for the entire system and each control unit must synchronize its activity to these pulses.

EARLY WARNING   Any technique which prevents the separate transmission control units from transmitting at the same instant will improve the utilization of a packet radio channel. One possibility is to use a reservation protocol which permits the control units to reserve certain time slots. Another technique is to use an early-warning system.

An early-warning system may divide up the terminals by priority. If there are two priority classes, the high-priority terminals send out a signal at a fixed interval before they transmit. All transmission control units hear this warning signal. The low-priority ones avoid the time slot in question, leaving it free for the high-priority use. If two high-priority terminals warn that they want the same slot, both must decide whether or not to reallocate the time of their transmission. This action lowers the probability of

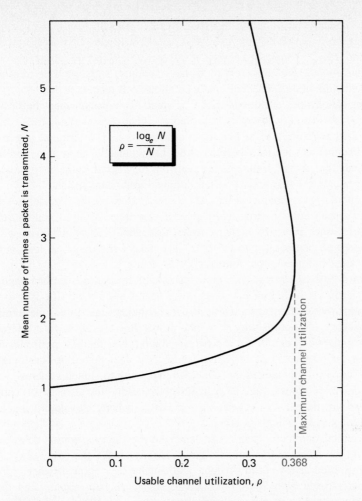

$$\rho = \frac{\log_e N}{N}$$

Figure 27.5 Traffic on a slotted ALOHA channel. The channel utilization is twice that of the classical ALOHA channel but only fixed-
length packets are sent.

collision, but could still result in either a collision or a slot being left empty. A multi-
ple-priority early-warning system could be used.

CARRIER SENSE   Somewhat simpler than an early-warning system is a *car-
                               rier sense* mechanism. Carrier sense implies that each ter-
minal can detect when another terminal is transmitting—it can detect its carrier. If
another terminal is transmitting, it will avoid starting its transmission at that instant
because it would cause a collision.

Unfortunately, while all terminals can receive the powerful transmission from the center, they may not all be able to receive the weaker transmission from other terminals. In this case, to make a carrier sense mechanism operate, the center must send out a *busy signal* saying when it is receiving. The busy signal will be transmitted on a narrow bandwidth control channel, and all stations will receive it.

What action does a terminal take if it wants to transmit when the busy signal is being sent? It could wait until the busy signal ceases and then immediately transmit. This is referred to as *persistent* carrier sense. The terminal is persistent and grabs the channel as soon as it becomes free. Unfortunately, there may be other persistent terminals that do the same. Then a collision may occur immediately after the busy signal ceases as more than one persistent terminal grabs the channel.

An alternative is *nonpersistent* carrier sense. Here, if the channel is sensed busy the terminal reschedules its transmission for a later time, using a random delay again, and then tries once more. A higher channel throughput can be achieved with nonpersistent, than with persistent, carrier sense. The delays are longer, at least at low channel utilizations, but usually not long enough to matter.

A third type of carrier sense gives maximum channel utilizations almost as high as nonpersistent carrier sense, but gives lower delays when the traffic is heavy. This is called *p-persistent* carrier sense. Here, if the channel is sensed idle, the terminal transmits the packet with a probability p. With a probability $1 - p$, it waits briefly and then repeats the process. p can be set at whatever figure gives the best performance.

These three types of carrier sense can be used with slotted or nonslotted ALOHA systems. They are summarized in Table 27.1, applying to slotted systems.

Figure 27.6 shows Fig. 27.5 redrawn to show the effects of carrier sense [9]. Using nonpersistent carrier sense or p-persistent where the value of p is low, channel utilization can be as high as 80%.

The effectiveness of carrier sense depends upon the propagation delay being short compared to the message transmission time. This is usually the case because the packets are transmitted at the speed of light, and usually over short distances. If a 24,000 bps channel is used with 704-bit packets as in the Hawaii system, and the average distance transmitted is 10 miles, the packet transmission time is 29 milliseconds and the radio propagation time is 0.054 milliseconds. The curves in Fig. 27.6 are drawn for a propagation time 1% of the packet transmission time. If for some reason the propagation time is long compared to the packet transit time, carrier sense can still be made effective by sending a warning "busy" signal before the packet is transmitted.

FM DISCRIMINATION   When the FM modulation is used, a radio receiver circuit can be built to discriminate between weak and strong signals, and reject the weak ones. Such a technique can greatly increase the efficiency of a packet radio system.

The transmission control units can be organized so that they vary substantially in power. There is then a high probability that two colliding packets will differ in power

Table 27.1   Three types of carrier sense mechanisms

	Nonpersistent Carrier Sense	Persistent Carrier Sense	$p-$Persistent Carrier Sense
IF THE CHANNEL IS SENSED IDLE:	The terminal transmits the packet.	The terminal transmits the packet.	With probability p, the terminal transmits the packet. With probability $1-p$, the terminal delays for one time slot and starts again.
IF THE CHANNEL IS SENSED BUSY:	The terminal reschedules the transmission to a later time slot according to a retransmission delay distribution. At this new time it repeats the algorithm.	The terminal waits until the channel goes idle and then immediately transmits the packet.	The terminal waits until the channel goes idle and then repeats the above algorithm.
		NOTE: This is a special case of $p-$persistent carrier sense	

sufficiently that one will be received correctly. The time slot is then not wasted, although the weaker packet would have to be retransmitted. It is interesting to note if one of the packets could survive in all collisions, then 100% channel utilization could be achieved on a slotted channel. In practice, the discrimination could never be this good, but it might be a reasonable objective that one packet should survive in half of the collisions. The maximum channel utilization could then be high, especially if carrier sense is also used.

Unless a transmission control unit had the ability to change its transmitting power, discrimination would have the effect that some terminals always had low priority. This may or may not be a disadvantage. It would be advantageous, for example, to give batch terminals a lower priority than interactive ones. Interactive terminals with a dialogue structure needing a fast response should be given priority over those for which a longer response time is acceptable.

REPEATERS   In a packet radio system the terminals are likely to transmit to some controlling location. This might be a computer center. It might be an ARPANET IMP or a Telenet Central Office. It might be a satellite earth station.

Some of the terminals may be too far away from the controlling location for an

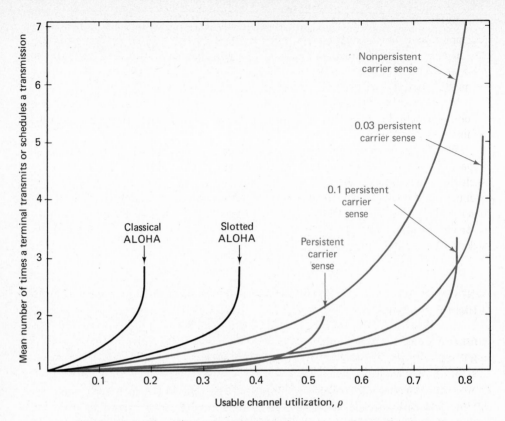

Figure 27.6   The effect of carrier techniques on packet radio channel utilization [4].

inexpensive transmitter to reach it. In such a case, radio repeaters are used. The transmitters used in the Hawaii system have a range of many miles, but repeaters are used for inter-island transmission and to reach terminals in the shadow of mountains.

Conventional radio repeaters cannot receive and transmit on the same frequency at the same time because the strong transmitted signal blots out the weak incoming signal. They receive on one frequency band, translate the signal to a different frequency band, and then transmit it. A packet repeater can, however, operate on a single frequency. It switches off its receiver momentarily while it transmits a packet. Some packets will be lost when this happens, and, as with a collision, they will have to be retransmitted. Operating at a single frequency saves the expense of the frequency translation equipment.

The Hawaii repeaters use a single frequency for relaying packets to the control location, and a different frequency for relaying packets back to the terminals. If two frequencies are used in this way, the repeater antennas pointing towards the central station can be highly directional.

When the terminals, perhaps hand-held terminals, are distributed over a wide geographic area, many repeater stations may be used (Fig. 27.7). Such may be the case in areas of low population density and large distances, where the alternatives to radio would be expensive. In areas of high population density, such as a city, repeaters may be used to avoid problems with high-rise buildings.

When large numbers of terminals are used, it is desirable to select the design options such that the central location is complex, the repeaters less expensive, and the terminals as inexpensive as possible.

When multiple repeaters are used, a problem that must be solved is the cascading of packets. A packet from certain terminals may reach more than one repeater, or reach the central station as well as a repeater. Unless the repeaters have directional antennas, packets from one repeater may reach other repeaters. Some packets might travel endlessly in loops. The unnecessary cascading of packets could substantially lower the effective channel capacity. It is necessary to devise a protocol that prevents packets from multiplying themselves.

HAND-HELD TERMINALS AGAIN

Let us return to the pocket terminal. Such devices might be used on a 50,000 bps UHF channel. In a terminal dialogue using the 256-character screen, the *average* transmission rate to the terminal from a distant computer over a long period of dialogue might typically be 10 characters per second. If these are transmitted as 7-bit characters, the channel might accommodate 500 active terminals. Many messages *to the computer* would be one-character responses and some would be longer data entries. The transmission rate to the computer might typically average one character per second. The channel requirement to the computer would not exceed that *from the computer* even with the low channel utilization of a classical ALOHA system. A single system might therefore have thousands of users of whom not more than 500 would be likely to be active at once.

A typical input packet would be a few milliseconds in duration. A full-screen output message would be about 50 milliseconds. The response time of the device could therefore be very fast. Its potential applications are as diverse as the computer industry itself.

SATELLITE CHANNELS

There are two ways of using communications satellites in a data network. They can be used as *point-to-point channels* or as *broadcast channels*. They have been mainly used as point-to-point channels so far. This means that the satellite channel simply replaces a terrestrial channel, and data switching nodes must determine what data they send over it. The main advantage of a satellite channel is that it is cheaper for long distances and a high bandwidth can be used. The main disadvantage is its 270 milliseconds propagation delay. This delay is not necessarily harmful by itself because an overall response time of less than a

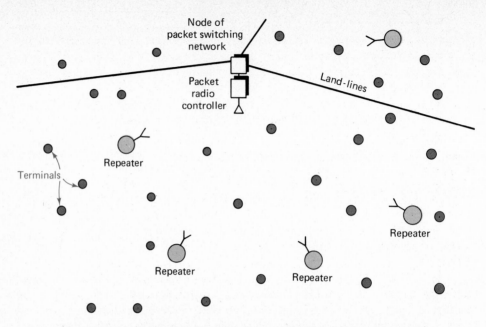

Figure 27.7 Terminals scattered over a wide geographic area may be served by multiple packet radio repeaters relaying transmissions to a central control station.

second is rarely needed. It is harmful if multiple satellite circuits are used in tandem, as with terrestrial circuits, because then a long delay builds up. It is harmful with an inappropriate physical link protocol because this can severely degrade the effective throughput (details in Reference [10]). It is also harmful if an inappropriate flow control or pacing mechanism is used which functions inefficiently when propagation is delayed.

To use a satellite merely for point-to-point channels wastes one of the most attractive features of satellites—their ability to directly interconnect all users within the satellite's range. A computer network could be built with a cheap earth station at every computer site and complete interconnectability between the sites. The system would be using *broadcast channels* like a packet radio net. As with a packet radio net, some means of controlling the transmission is necessary, either preventing two stations transmitting at once or dealing with the collision when they do.

The original ALOHA network used a satellite as indicated in Fig. 27.8. It employs classical ALOHA multiple-access control on the satellite channel. This restricts the channel utilization to 18.4% as shown in Fig. 27.3.

A satellite channel is expensive and it is desirable that it should be used with a higher maximum utilization than basic ALOHA systems permit. Unfortunately carrier sense does not work well on satellite channels because of the propagation delay.

Where a transmitting machine can detect another machine's packet almost as soon as it is sent, carrier sense can give a high channel utilization. The efficiency of carrier sense operation is affected by the ratio:

$$\frac{\text{Propagation time}}{\text{Packet transmission time}}$$

This ratio is typically 0.01 for a radio system with machines 20 miles or so distant, or an Ethernet system with a mile of coaxial cable. For a satellite voice grade circuit the ratio is about 2. For a satellite circuit transmitting at 1.544 mbps (T1 carrier speed) the ratio is over 400.

ROUND ROBIN PROTOCOL

There are several alternatives to an ALOHA protocol for transmitting sporadic bursts of data from small satellite earth stations. Perhaps the simplest is a protocol in which each earth station is allowed to transmit in turn in a round robin fashion. Each station transmits a burst, the length of which was predetermined. All stations listen to the bursts, listening for messages addressed to themselves.

The disadvantage of a round robin system is that the traffic load at a station may vary second-by-second. The station therefore wants a way to vary the amount of channel space it uses. It cannot vary its usage of channel space without informing the other earth stations that it is going to do so, or confusion will result. A variety of schemes are possible in which a station could *make a reservation* for time slots before it uses them.

RESERVATIONS

One difference between an ALOHA system and a conventional demand assignment system is that in the conventional system a *reservation* is made for a portion of the transmission capacity; in an ALOHA system it is not.

A system which takes channel space at random without reservations may be appropriate for brief sporadic transactions which need quick service—like individuals catching taxis at random in New York. Transactions from computer terminal users conform to this random pattern. A system *with* reservations can normally achieve higher channel utilization. However, the users have to wait longer on average before (successful) transmission. The taxis of New York could be fuller on average if all passengers had to make a reservation (there would be fewer taxis); however, the passengers would usually *have to wait longer* to obtain a taxi. Nonreservation systems tend to degrade more seriously when the load swings up to high levels, like trying to find a taxi in New York in a thunderstorm.

PACKET RESERVATIONS

It is possible to design a packet reservation system for interactive data transmission that will have the advantage of an ALOHA system in handling sporadic burst traffic, but which will give better utilization of the satellite channel capacity. It will not give as fast a mean response time as an ALOHA system but even so, it will complete a one-way trip in well under one second, and hence is fast enough for interactive computing.

L. G. Roberts [11] proposed a reservation system which could be used as an extension of terrestrial packet-switching networks such as ARPANET, using satellite channels of 50,000 bits per second or more. In this system all *protocol* messages are handled in an ALOHA fashion. The system is always in either a *reservation state* or an *ALOHA state*. In the reservation state, reserved blocks of data are sent; in the ALOHA state, protocol or short data messages are sent.

Fig. 27.8 illustrates the operation of the system. This illustration could relate to a 50,000 bit-per-second channel. The time allocated for reserved bursts is 25 milliseconds. Each such burst begins with a bit pattern which establishes synchronization, has a header giving the addresses of its destination and source, and ends with a comprehensive error-detection pattern. The burst would contain more than 1000 data bits.

At the left of the diagram, earth station A makes a request to transmit three blocks of data. The request travels on the ALOHA subchannel; 270 milliseconds later it listens to its own request and hears that it has not been relayed correctly. Another earth station had made a request at the same instant, causing an ALOHA collision. Station A makes its bid again, selecting a new ALOHA slot at random. This time it succeeds. All earth stations hear the request, know that station A is going to transmit 3 blocks, and calculate, knowing the present number of items in the queue, in which time slots these blocks will occur. No other earth station will then attempt to use those positions in the queue. Station A does not wait for reply to its request. It assumes that every station has acted upon it, and transmits the data to stations C to Z.

Every station receives the transmitted blocks and examines their destination addresses. Stations C and Z will recognize their addresses and accept the data. All other stations will ignore the data. Stations C and Z check the error-detection bits in the blocks, conclude that the data was received correctly, and transmit acknowledgment messages. The acknowledgment messages are sent, like the reservation request, in the period the channel is in ALOHA mode. Earth station A retains the data until correct acknowledgments have been received. If no such acknowledgments arrive, station A will transmit the data again.

At the right-hand side of the diagram, station A transmits a short message. This message is short enough to fit into one of the ALOHA slots and so no reservation is made for it. Again station A retains it until a correct acknowledgment is received.

VARYING THE MIX

It is not known how much of the traffic will be short and how much will consist of long messages. The scheme is therefore designed to vary the mix it can handle automatically. If the long messages

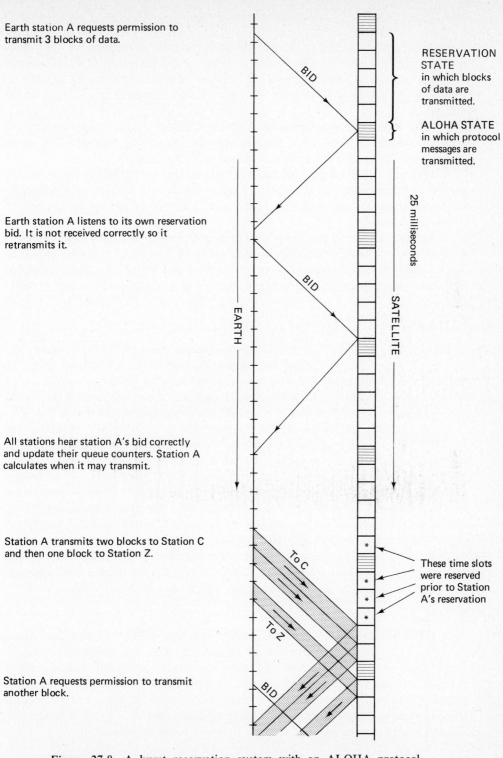

Earth station A requests permission to transmit 3 blocks of data.

RESERVATION STATE in which blocks of data are transmitted.

ALOHA STATE in which protocol messages are transmitted.

BID

25 milliseconds

EARTH

SATELLITE

Earth station A listens to its own reservation bid. It is not received correctly so it retransmits it.

BID

All stations hear station A's bid correctly and update their queue counters. Station A calculates when it may transmit.

Station A transmits two blocks to Station C and then one block to Station Z.

To C

These time slots were reserved prior to Station A's reservation

To Z

Station A requests permission to transmit another block.

BID

Figure 27.8 A burst reservation system with an ALOHA protocol mechanism [9].

435

predominate, the channel is in the ALOHA state one sixth of the time (as on the left-hand side of the diagram). This is enough to handle the necessary protocol messages without excessive ALOHA collisions. If there are no long messages, the channel reverts to a continuous ALOHA state. This can be seen happening in the center of the diagram.

If the channel is in a continuous ALOHA state, the first reservation request will cause it to allocate a time slot in reservation mode. As soon as the reservation queue goes to zero, the system reverts to a continuous ALOHA mode.

In Roberts' proposal [11] the reserved time slots were 1350 bits in length and the nonreserved slots were 224 bits. Both of these include the overhead of synchronization, error detection, and addressing. Other slot sizes may be appropriate to channels of different speeds.

To make a burst reservation system work, the protocol messages must be relayed accurately. There is scope for chaos if there are errors in some of the reservation messages. This is especially so when there is a large number of ground stations competing for access. The protocol messages should therefore have exceptionally safe error detection facilities.

COMPARISON

It is difficult to compare one protocol with another because the comparison must make assumptions about the traffic mix that is handled. For different situations, different techniques appear preferable. There is a great diversity of potential uses of satellite channels. Roberts [11] makes an interesting comparison of a packet reservation system like that in Fig. 27.8 with other systems, on the assumption that the traffic would be broadly similar to that on ARPANET, a multipurpose network of computers used mainly in universities. He assumes, for purposes of comparison, that all earth stations send and receive an equal volume of messages; half of these are single packets of 1270 bits (including the header) and half are multipacket blocks of 8 packets. Both the numbers of single packets and multipacket blocks arrive with a Poisson distribution. This assumption biases the results slightly in favor of a reservation system in that it does not have very short messages which would favor an ALOHA protocol, or large batches of data which would favor a *round robin* approach somewhat more. Figure 27.9 gives curves for such a traffic pattern. The round robin curves relate to a sytem in which each earth station in strict rotation has a time slot allocated to it in which one packet can be transmitted.

THE SBS SATELLITES

SBS (the satellite subsidiary of IBM, Comsat, and Aetna) employs an architecture with demand-assigned reservations. However, each station does not reserve *packets;* it reserves the *channel capacity* it needs, and can vary its demand for capacity from second to second. It is thus more akin to circuit switching than packet switching. The reason for this is that the majority of its revenue is likely to come from voice transmission (and other forms of continuous-channel transmission in general), and less from interactive data transmission.

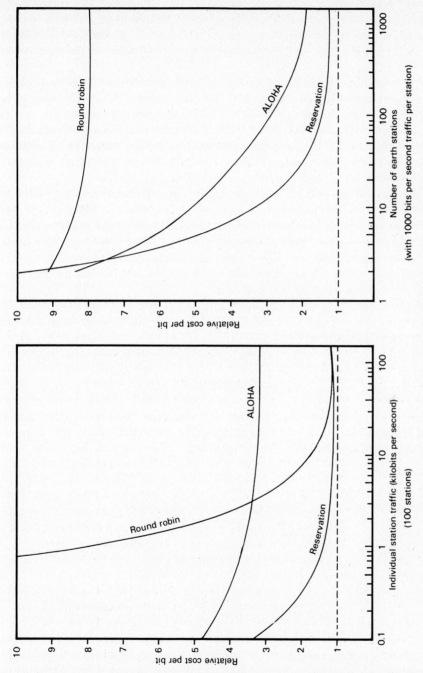

Figure 27.9 Comparison of a round robin, ALOHA, and burst reservation protocol.

437

The channels which are derived between any two stations can vary enormously in capacity from second to second. They are derived by transmitting brief bursts of bits at a speed of 48 mbps on each of 10 transponders (per satellite). These bursts are buffered at the earth stations which send and receive them so that continuous channels are created [12].

The continuous channels may be further subdivided to handle the *bursts* of data that are transmitted on computer networks. This may be done by concentrators, packet switches, circuit switches, or any of the mechanisms we have discussed. The result is an extremely flexible architecture with which integrated corporate networks can be built, carrying voice, video, and facsimile traffic as well as data. This is important because data transmission is a small fraction of the telecommunication expenditure in most corporations.

The users of the SBS satellites can employ channels of up to 6.312 mbps (T2 carrier speed). They can request such a channel at any time and transmit over it for only a second or so if desired. With such a channel a file or portion of a data base that would have taken a whole shift to transmit over a switched telephone circuit can be sent in 20 seconds. At the same time it should be economical to send small amounts of data, or handle interactive terminals, with earth stations cost-justified by their transmission of corporate telephone and mail traffic.

Such facilities will greatly change the design of corporate and government networks such as those in Figs. 4.14 and 4.17. Satellites could also lower the transmission costs on public data networks.

REFERENCES

1. Now a European standard—*Teletext*. The BBC has been broadcasting data for reception by television viewers since 1976. See the author's *Future Developments in Telecommunications*, 2nd ed., Chapter 11.

2. The ALOHA System is a research system at the University of Hawaii, supported by ARPA under NASA Contract No. NAS2-6700 and by the National Science Foundation under NSF Grant No. AJ-33220. N. Abramson, "The ALOHA System—Another Alternative for Computer Communication," Fall Joint Conference, *AFIPS Conf. Proc.*, Vol. 36, 1970.

3. Roberts, L., "Extension of Packet Switching to a Hand Held Personal Terminal," *AFIPS Conference Proceedings*, SJCC72, pp. 295–298.

4. *Satellite Business Systems, FCC Application for a Domestic Satellite System*, 1975. Vol. II contains a good technical description of the plans. Available from the FCC, Washington, DC.

5. Studies by NASA and associated companies have indicated that a large satellite, assembled in space with several space shuttle trips, would permit hand-held devices to communicate (i.e., hand-held earth stations). See Bekey, I., and H.

Meyer, "1980–2000 Raising Our Sights for Advanced Space Systems," *Astronautics and Aeronautics,* July/Aug. 1976.

6. Abramson, N., "Packet Switching with Satellites," *National Computer Conference AFIPS Conf. Proc.,* Vol. 82, 1973.

7. Kleinrock, L., and F. Tobagi, "Random Access Techniques for Data Transmission over Packet Switched Radio Channels," *AFIPS Conference Proceedings,* Vol. 44, 1975, AFIPS Press, Montvale, NJ.

8. Kleinrock, L., and S. Lam, "Packet Switching in a Slotted Satellite Channel," National Computer Conference, *AFIPS Conf. Proc.,* Vol. 42, 1973.

9. Kleinrock, L., and F. A. Tobagi, "Carrier Sense Multiple Access for Packet Switched Radio Channels," *Proc. International Conference on Communications,* IEEE, Minneapolis, 1974.

10. Martin, J., *Satellite Communications Systems,* Prentice-Hall, Englewood Cliffs, NJ, 1978.

11. Roberts, L. A., "Dynamic Allocation of Satellite Capacity through Packet Reservation," National Computer Conference, *AFIPS Conf. Proc.,* Vol. 42, 1973.

12. Barnla, J. D., and F. R. Zitzmann, *The SBS Digital Communication Satellite System,* EASCON-77, Washington, 1977.

Other Reading

Fralick, S., and J. Garrett, "A Technology for Packet Radio," *AFIPS Conference Proceedings,* Vol. 44, 1975, AFIPS Press, Montvale, NJ.

Fralick, S., D. Brandin, F. Kuo, and C. Harrison, "Digital Terminals for Packet Broadcasting," *AFIPS Conference Proceedings,* Vol. 44, 1975, AFIPS Press, Montvale, NJ.

Frank, H., I. Gitman, and R. VanSlyke, "Packet Radio Network Design—System Considerations," *AFIPS Conference Proceedings,* Vol. 44, 1975, AFIPS Press, Montvale, NJ.

Burchfiel, J., R. Tomlinson, and M. Beeler, "Functions and Structure of a Packet Radio Station," *AFIPS Conference Proceedings,* Vol. 44, 1975, AFIPS Press, Montvale, NJ.

Binder, R., et al., "Aloha Packet Broadcasting—A Retrospect,"*AFIPS Conference Proceedings,* Vol. 44, 1975, AFIPS Press, Montvale, NJ.

Cerf, V., and R. Kahn, "A Protocol for Packet Network Intercommunication," *IEEE Transactions on Communications,* May 1974, pp. 637–648.

Kahn, R. E., "The Organization of Computer Resources into a Packet Radio Network," *NCC 1975 Proceedings.*

28 MESSAGE COMPRESSION

The cost of processing and storage is dropping much faster than the cost of transmission. Processing and storage can be used to lower the number of bits transmitted, and the more the cost drops the more worthwhile this trade-off becomes. In some cases data compression techniques can achieve dramatic savings.

Data compression techniques fall into three categories:

1. Techniques which are application dependent. These cannot be built into general-purpose software. They can take advantage of intelligent terminals and distributed intelligence in general.

2. Editing and substitution techniques which can be built into general-purpose software.

3. Encoding techniques which can be built into hardware, microcode, or software.

The latter two could be regarded as Layer 4 control functions.

DIALOGUE COMPRESSION   Before the use of intelligent terminals every character of a dialogue with a remote machine had to be transmitted.

Now a good part of some dialogues can take place at the terminal, and transmission occurs when remote data must be read or written, or when more processing power is needed than that available locally.

With a theater booking or order entry dialogue using intelligent terminals the operator could collect the facts about the customer one at a time and then transmit them in a compressed block to a distant system. With a data base interrogation language a local machine can guide the user in the formulation of his query and then transmit it in a compact fashion to the data-base machine.

The dialogue can be expanded to be psychologically effective for the user, and at the same time the data transmitted can be compressed into a small number of bits. The data transmitted constitute an interface between the dialogue processing in the peripheral machine and the application processing in a host computer.

SUBSTITUTION   Much of what is printed or displayed at a terminal consists of English phrases to guide or help the terminal user. These need not necessarily be transmitted. They may be stored at the terminal location and selected when required. Instead of transmitting a lengthy phrase, an identifier of that phrase may be sent which occupies no more than one or two bytes.

Where English constitutes a substantial portion of the transmission, words or phrases may be substituted with code characters. Each 8-bit byte may contain combinations of bits that represent the 200 or so most commonly used words. Suppose, also, that 32 of the 256 possible combinations indicate that this character alone does not give the word in question but that the next character is also needed. This gives $32 \times 256 = 8192$ additional words that may be encoded. Another combination of bits in the first character indicates that the word is spelled out in ASCII code. The machine receiving this string of data converts it into verbal English with a table lookup operation.

The vocabulary required for many specific applications is small, and it may be necessary to store no more than, say, 256 words. Alternatively, such a scheme may generate not words but messages or phrases.

In general where only a limited set of attribute values exist, there is no need to spell out an attribute value in full. Instead a code can be used. With some data items, such as "type of license," a code would normally be used. Others, such as "name," are often spelled out in full.

Most of the names that are used in name data items belong to a relatively small set. The first names of persons, for example, could be encoded in one 8-bit byte. The 256 names which this makes possible could include almost all the first names that are used. The first bit may have the additional function of encoding sex, giving 128 female names and 128 male names. However, there would always be the occasional person seeking baptismal distinction whose first name would defy the encoding scheme. Therefore one 8-bit combination could serve as an exception byte which indicates that the following bytes spell out the name in full.

Surnames do not yield so well to code substitution, especially in the United States, where the names of so many national origins are mixed together. Nevertheless, even in the United States 128 entries could include about 80% of all surnames and 256 entries more than 90%. We will represent more than 90% of the names by 1 byte and spell the remainder out in full. Two bytes (65,536 combinations) would encompass almost all surnames, but the substitution table might be excessively large.

Substitution could be a function of the Layer 4 software.

When fields are stored in the form in which humans prefer to read them they often contain more characters than are necessary. Dates, for example, we may write as 12 NOV 1976, or, in our most compact written form 11.12.76, and so dates are often stored as 6 bytes in computer files. In the machine, however, the month needs no more than 4 bits, the day can be encoded in 5 bits, and the year usually needs no more than 7 bits—a total of 16 bits, or two 8-bit bytes. Conversion from the 2-byte form to human-readable form needs only a few lines of code.

Another common way of representing dates is in the Julian form proposed by Joseph Scalizer in 1582 for astronomical uses. Scalizer represented dates as the number of elapsed days since Jan. 1, 4713 B.C. Using this scheme, Jan. 1, 1976 is 2,445,701. Often, only the four low-order digits are used. May 23, 1968 and Oct. 9, 1995 are then each 0000, and dates are counted from those days, requiring 14 bits. Many other items such as part numbers and street addresses can often be compressed similarly. This is likely to be done by application code rather than network software.

AVOIDANCE OF EMPTY SPACE IN MESSAGES   When formatted records are transmitted they may contain a varying set of fields rather than a fixed set—in other words some of the fields may be missing. A data compression scheme may ensure that fields which are not present occupy no space. A bit map may precede the fields to indicate whether they are present or not.

Invoices or documents to be printed or displayed often contain much blank space. The blank areas need not be transmitted. Instead a code can instruct the cursor to move horizontally by a given amount or to skip lines.

Numeric fields in some files contain a high proportion of leading or trailing zeros. More than two zeros can be encoded into two (packed decimal) characters—one character to indicate repetition and the next to say how much repetition. Some messages contain repetitive blanks or other characters, and these can be dealt with in a similar manner.

EDITING   These are all examples of editing. The software can contain a variety of editing facilities which improve the attractiveness of printouts and displays while at the same time minimizing the number of bits transmitted.

Two types of editing can be used—one which is transparent to the application programmer and one which is not. The programmer need not know that leading zeros are removed or that blank fields are compressed. On the other hand he can make good use of an editing language which helps him to lay out displays attractively, and enables him to use pre-existing formats and panels. These formats and panels may be stored in the host computer or in a remote terminal node. The interface should be the same. The programming should be independent of where the display, printing, or dialogue function takes place.

The editing facility may be designed to select an existing screen display (panel) or document layout, and enable the programmer to add variable data to it. Only the variable data are transmitted. Similarly a terminal user may have a screen display into which he inserts variables, and only the variable data are transmitted to a distant host. The software which selects the display, edits the transmitted data, and puts the data in the correct place in the display, is part of the Layer 4 function.

The right type of editing and dialogue compression can give major savings in transmission costs—much more than intricate attempts to optimize the transport network topology.

CHARACTER ENCODING

One generally applicable way to compress transmitted data is to use the most efficient form of character encoding. The conventional U.S. ASCII code or CCITT Alphabet Number 5 which most transmission employs does not give tight encoding.

Numeric data is more economically transmitted in binary form, and alphabetic data could be encoded into 5 bits rather than 8. In fact, there is much to be said for using the code which telex machines use for compact data transmission.† It uses "letter shift" and "figures shift" characters to switch the meaning of the bit combinations between letters and figures (plus special characters), somewhat like the shift key on a typewriter. It is interesting to reflect that a 5-bit code with three shifts could carry all the data that most users would be likely to want to transmit. A minor modification of the telex code could achieve this, as shown in Fig. 28.1. The character 00010 has been given the meaning "transparency shift." When this character is transmitted, the characters following it have the meanings shown in the right-most column, until a "letters shift" or "figures shift" character is sent. Some of these are control characters. A variety of control characters is used on modern terminals. The remainder are 4-bit binary characters, bits 1, 2, 3, and 5 being used, with the fourth (always a 0) being ignored. Any 8-bit binary character can thus be sent in two of the 2-bit characters, and so programs could be transmitted in this code.

A somewhat tidier 5-bit, three-shift code could be devised if the telex code were ignored. The character 00010 is "carriage return" in the telex code and "transparency shift" in Fig. 28.1. To communicate with a telex code machine, a machine using the code in Fig. 28.1 need inhibit only its "transparency shift" feature and substitute "carriage return."

The translation circuitry could be on one LSI chip and would not be expensive. The throughput with alphanumeric data on a given data channel would be almost 40% higher than with the 8-bit codes in use.

VARIABLE-LENGTH CHARACTER ENCODING

Character-encoding schemes in normal use have a fixed number of bits per character. Tighter packing of data can be achieved with a code which employs a variable number of bits per character. With such a code the most commonly occurring characters would be short, and the infrequently occurring characters

---

†CCITT Alphabet Number 2. See the author's *Telecommunications and the Computer,* Chapter 3, 2nd ed., Prentice-Hall, 1976.

Code	Letters shift CCITT standard international telegraph alphabet No. 2	Figures shift	Transparency shift Control characters or four-bit binary combinations (T)
11000	A	—	T
10011	B	?	Control
01110	C	:	Control
10010	D	Who are you?	Control
10000	E	3	T
10110	F	Note 1	Control
01011	G	Note 1	Control
00101	H	Note 1	T
01100	I	8	T
11010	J	Bell	Control
11110	K	(	Control
01001	L	)	T
00111	M	.	Control
00110	N	,	Control
00011	O	9	Control
01101	P	0	T
11100	Q	1	T
01010	R	4	Control
10100	S	,	T
00001	T	5	T
11100	U	7	T
01111	V	=	Control
11001	W	2	T
10111	X	/	Control
10101	Y	6	T
10001	Z	+	T
00000	Blank		T
00100	Space		T
01000	Line feed		T
11111	Letters shift		
11011	Figures shift		
00010	Transparency shift		

Note 1: Not allocated internationally by CCITT available to each country for internal use

Figure 28.1 The Baudot code, used by telex machines, encodes alphanumeric formation with five bits per character. A third shift added to the Baudot code would permit it to encode characters not in its basic character set in binary form.

would be long. The shortest character—the most frequently occurring one—would be only one bit.

To provide a simple illustration, suppose that it were necessary to encode only four characters *A, B, C,* and *D.* To encode these in a conventional fixed-length manner would require two bits per character. Suppose the *A* is a frequently occurring character and that *C* and *D* are infrequently occurring. The relative popularity of the characters is as follows:

> *A:*   60%
>
> *B:*   25%
>
> *C:*   10%
>
> *D:*   5%

Because *A* occurs most frequently it will be coded with one bit, a 0 bit. To recognize the start of a character, every other character must begin with a 1 bit. *B* is the second most frequently occurring character, so *B* will be encoded with two bits: 10. To avoid confusion with *B*, no other character may now begin with 10. *C* and *D* must therefore be encoded with three bits, 110 and 111, respectively.

We thus have:

Character	Code	Length (bits)	Probability of Occurrence	Probability × Length
A	0	1	0.60	0.6
B	10	2	0.25	0.5
C	110	3	0.10	0.3
D	111	3	0.05	0.15
			Weighted mean length	= 1.55

The mean length of all characters is now 1.55 bits, which is better than the two bits of fixed-length encoding.

This type of coding was originally proposed by D. A. Huffman [1] and is called a Huffman code.

Note that such a scheme pays off only with the skewed character distribution. If all characters were used equally often, the mean number of bits per character would be $1 \times 0.25 + 2 \times 0.25 + 3 \times 0.25 = 2.25$—worse than with fixed-length characters.

The more skewed the character distribution, the more effective is Huffman and other variable-length encoding. In English text the letters of the alphabet occur with varying frequency, and Huffman encoding gives a mean of about 4.12 bits per character [2]. Most commercial data transmission has a distribution of characters which is more skewed than this. Often the proportion of numeric characters is high and the proportion of *zeros* is very high. On one commercial file the relative frequency of occurrence of characters was measured and found to be that shown in Fig. 28.2. Such a distribution is typical and can be encoded with a mean of about 3 bits per character.

Character	Frequency of occurrence (%)
0	55.5
1	6.7
2	4.5
8	3.5
3	3.3
A	3.2
5	3.0
6	2.7
4	2.7
9	2.2
7	1.9
F	1.5
B	1.2
Blank	1.1
D	1.0
E	0.9
Z	0.7
P	0.6
N	0.5
U	0.4
C	0.4
H	0.4
R	0.3
M	0.3
L	0.3
S	0.25
I	0.20
T	0.15
K	0.15
Y	0.13
X	0.12
G	0.10
J	0.10
O	0.06
Q	0.03
V	0.03
W	0.03
.	0.01
—	
,	
&	
/	
+	
<	below
)	0.001
(	
%	
=	
#	
?	
'	
@	

Figure 28.2 Where the distribution of characters is highly skewed, as here, variable-length character coding can be used to good effect.

A variety of variable-length codes can be used. Figure 28.3 shows one of them. The rule for determining the number of bits per character in Fig. 28.3 is as follows:

If the first bit is 0, the character has one bit.
If the first 2 bits are 10, the character has three bits.
Otherwise character length is the number of leading 1's + 3.

The result indicated in Fig. 28.3 is a mean of 3.01 bits per character.

Figure 28.4 shows a Huffman code which is slightly more efficient and gives a mean of 2.91 bits per character, but is somewhat more complex to decode.

Figures 28.3 and 28.4 give a low mean number of bits per character because one single character is far more common than any other. In some transmission two or more characters may share this distinction. If two characters are far more popular than any others, they may both be coded with 2 bits. The encoding in order of decreasing popularity may begin as follows:

$$00$$
$$01$$
$$100$$
$$101$$
$$1100$$
$$1101$$
$$111000$$

There are many possible variations on this idea. If variable-length encoding is used, it is desirable that the method best suited to the data in question be employed.

HUFFMAN CODE IMPLEMENTATION

Character conversion can be carried out in software, microcode, or hardware. It is usually done today by software in a communications processor or intelligent terminal. Special-purpose hardware is more efficient. The Codex Corporation has implemented hardware data compression in its 6000 Series of intelligent network processors [3]. Inexpensive microprocessors today can do Huffman encoding, decoding, and suppression of repeated characters, fast enough to keep pace with most terminals. The conversion function can be conveniently combined with the function of statistical multiplexing [4].

A simple method of doing Huffman encoding is to use the original character as a memory address with which to look up the compressed character. Because the memory positions are of fixed length and the characters variable, the memory position must contain an indication of which bits to use. For ease of implementation the longest Huffman code may be shorter than those in the ideal code. Figure 28.3 has 17-bit

Character	Frequency of occurrence (%)	Code	Number of bits
0	55.5	0	1
1	6.7	100	3
2	4.5	101	3
8	3.5	11000	5
3	3.3	11001	5
A	3.2	11010	5
5	3.0	11011	5
6	2.7	111000	6
4	2.7	111001	6
9	2.2	111010	6
7	1.9	111011	6
F	1.5	1111000	7
B	1.2	1111001	7
Blank	1.1	1111010	7
D	1.0	1111011	7
E	0.9	11111000	8
Z	0.7	11111001	8
P	0.6	11111010	8
N	0.5	11111011	8
u	0.4	111111000	9
C	0.4	111111001	9
H	0.4	111111010	9
R	0.3	111111011	9
M	0.3	1111111000	10
L	0.3	1111111001	10
S	0.25	1111111010	10
I	0.20	1111111000	10
T	0.15	11111111000	11
K	0.15	11111111001	11
Y	0.13	11111111010	11
X	0.12	11111111011	11
G	0.10	111111111000	12
J	0.10	111111111001	12
O	0.06	111111111010	12
Q	0.03	111111111011	12
V	0.03	1111111111000	13
W	0.03	1111111111001	13
.	0.01	1111111111010	13
—	↑	1111111111011	13
,		11111111111000	14
&		11111111111001	14
/		11111111111010	14
+		11111111111011	14
<		111111111111000	15
)	below	111111111111001	15
(	0.001	111111111111010	15
%		111111111111011	15
=		1111111111111000	16
#		1111111111111001	16
?		1111111111111010	16
'		1111111111111011	16
@	↓	11111111111111000	17
		11111111111111001	17

Average character length =
$0.555 \times 1 + 0.112 \times 3$
$+ 0.130 \times 5 + 0.095 \times 6$
$+ 0.048 \times 7 + 0.027 \times 8$
$+ 0.015 \times 9 + 0.0105 \times 10$
$+ 0.0055 \times 11 + 0.0029 \times 12$
$+ 0.0007 \times 13$
$= 3.01$ bits per character

Figure 28.3

Character	Frequency of occurrence (%)	Code	Number of bits
O	55.5	0	1
1	6.7	1000	4
2	4.5	1100	4
8	3.5	10010	5
3	3.3	10100	5
A	3.2	10101	5
5	3.0	10110	5
6	2.7	11100	5
4	2.7	11101	5
9	2.2	11110	5
7	1.9	100110	6
F	1.5	101110	6
B	1.2	111110	6
Blank	1.1	110110	6
D	1.0	110100	6
E	0.9	110101	6
Z	0.7	1011110	7
P	0.6	1111110	7
N	0.5	1101110	7
u	0.4	10011110	8
C	0.4	10011100	8
H	0.4	10011101	8
R	0.3	10111110	8
M	0.3	11111110	8
L	0.3	11111111	8
S	0.25	11011110	8
I	0.20	100111110	9
T	0.15	110111110	9
K	0.15	110111111	9
Y	0.13	1001111110	10
X	0.12	1001111111	10
G	0.10	1011111100	10
J	0.10	1011111101	10
O	0.06	10111111100	11
Q	0.03	10111111101	11
V	0.03	10111111110	11
W	0.03	101111111110	12
.	0.01	1011111111110000	16
—		1011111111110001	16
?		1011111111110010	16
&		1011111111110011	16
/		1011111111110100	16
+		1011111111110101	16
<	below	1011111111110110	16
)	0.001	1011111111110111	16
(		1011111111111000	16
%		1011111111111001	16
=		1011111111111010	16
#		1011111111111011	16
?		1011111111111100	16
'		1011111111111101	16
@		1011111111111110	16
		1011111111111111	16

Average character length =
0.555 x 1 + 0.112 x 4
+ 0.206 x 5 + 0.76 x 6
+ 0.018 x 7 + 0.24 x 8
+ 0.005 x 9 + 0.0045 x 10
+ 0.0017 x 11 + 0.0003 x 12
+ 0.0001 x 16
= 2.91 bits per character

Figure 28.4

characters, for example. A code in which the maximum length is 14 bits could be used without much gain in average character length.

Decompression could also use a table lookup, but a single simple lookup would require too large a table (e.g., 2^{14} positions) with many blank entries. Instead a tree-structured table search is used so that the table occupies less space. The tree structure will vary from one code set to another, so if multiple code sets are used it should probably be in software rather than hardware.

HOW EFFECTIVE IS HUFFMAN COMPRESSION?   Huffman coding of telegraph text without upper and lower case typically requires a mean character length of 4.2 bits. Coding of prose text with capitals, lower-case characters, digits, all punctuation, and machine control characters typically requires a mean character length of 4.9 bits. Data to and from a terminal in which most text transmission is avoided by peripheral storage of text phrases, formats and panels, is typically less than 4 bits per character on average. Assembly language source listings of programs have a typical mean character length of 4.8 bits.

The minimum possible mean character length based on the frequencies of characters is referred to by the term *entropy* in information theory. The mean character lengths in practice (the figures above) are typically 2 or 3% greater than the entropy figure.

Three typical files for a manufacturing application gave the following figures for possible size reductions:

Original File Size (bytes)	Reduction Using Suppression of Repeated Characters (%)	Reduction Using Huffman Code (%)
300,000	54	82
3 million	34	46
19 million	64	83

The reduction would have been greater if repeated characters had been suppressed first and then the Huffman code used. A few files give more dramatic savings.

A study of the use of the Huffman code for compacting programs gave savings in the range of 35 to 45% for object code and 55 to 75% for source code.

A combination of the techniques in this chapter, and especially dialogue compression, text substitution, and peripheral panel storage and editing can give dramatic reductions.

REFERENCES

1. Huffman, D. A., "A Method for the Construction of Minimum-Redundancy Codes," *Proc. I.R.E. 40,* Sept. 1952, 1098.

2. Gilbert, E. N., and E. R. Moore, "Variable-Length Binary Encodings," *Bell System Tech. J.,* July 1959, 933.

3. Forney, G. D., Jr., and W. T. Tao, "Data Compression Increases Throughput," *Data Communications,* May/June 1976.

4. Forney, G. D., Jr., and R. W. Stearns, "Statistical Multiplexing Improves Link Utilization," *Data Communications,* July/Aug., 1976.

29 UTILIZATION PATTERNS OF COMPUTER NETWORKS

How is a general-purpose computer network likely to be used? Can we make any statements about usage that should affect the design? The answer to these questions is likely to vary from one set of users to another. ARPANET kept exceptionally detailed statistics about its usage. From these we can draw conclusions, some of which would be valid on other networks. It is important, however, to understand that many networks, especially corporate and government networks, have utilization patterns entirely different from ARPANET, leading to the desirablilty of entirely different designs.

ARPANET TRAFFIC The ARPANET statistics we will quote are about the use of the network after it had been in operation for four years [1]. It had approximately 40 switching computers and 50 host computers. All but two of the 42 circuits operated at 50 kilobits per second. The traffic had grown spectacularly from the start and had now leveled out at about 4 million packets per day.

For a period of one week all packets were *traced* and the IMP's sent details of message lengths, sources, destinations, and timing, to a network measurement center where statistics were compiled.

PEAKS During the week the network accepted on average 47 messages per second from the hosts. The traffic varied as shown in Fig. 29.1. The average during the prime working hours of weekdays was about 80 messages per second. Traffic peaks went up to about 110 messages per second—2.34 times the average traffic. As on all networks there is much spare capacity for moving nontime-critical traffic at night.

It is common on corporate and government networks also that the peak traffic is

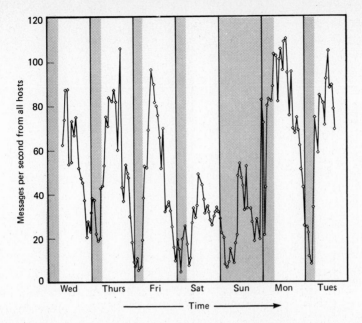

Figure 29.1 The arrival rate of messages on ARPANET. Nights and Sunday are shaded red [1].

about $2^1/_2$ times the average traffic. Sometimes on networks for specific applications there are peak loads of exceptional magnitude such as peak stock-market trading, lunch-time peaks in banks, and so on.

MESSAGE LENGTHS The lengths of the ARPANET messages were surprisingly short. 96% were single-packet messages. Furthermore most of the 4% which were multipacket messages were sent at night or on Sundays, as shown in Fig. 29.2. The points on the lower chart in Fig. 29.2 represent averages over one-hour spans. The peaks are for those hours in which file transfers dominated the interactive traffic. The users were able to do file transfers at any time. Some chose to do them at night when they obtained somewhat faster network throughput. The peaks of Fig. 29.2 represent a relative absence of interactive traffic, and this occurred during the night hours and Sunday afternoon.

The number of user bits in an average packet was small. A histogram of this is shown in Fig. 29.3. The mean packet length is 218 bits, which includes the 64-bit packet header, i.e., 154 bits ($19^1/_4$ characters) of user data. This surprisingly low figure reflects the fact that most messages sent in interactive dialogues with terminals are short.

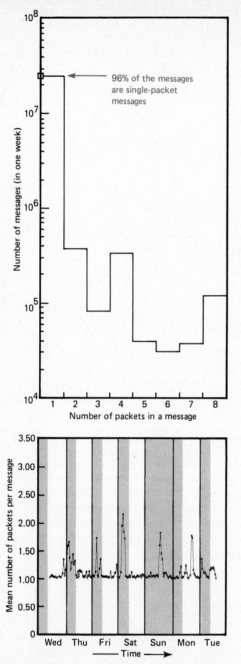

96% of the messages are single-packet messages

Number of messages (in one week)

Number of packets in a message

Mean number of packets per message

Wed   Thu   Fri   Sat   Sun   Mon   Tue

⟶ Time ⟶

Most of the multipacket messages occur at night or on Sunday (shaded red) when users tend to send files of data.

Figure 29.2 Message-length statistics from the usage of ARPANET [1].

454

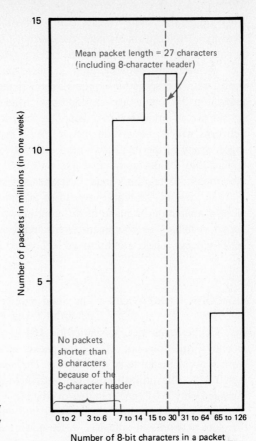

Figure 29.3 The packets sent by ARPANET users were mostly very small [1].

Most terminals used on ARPANET were teletype or typewriter-like terminals. With visual-display-unit dialogues some of the messages going *to* the terminals would be longer. On the other hand, many visual-display-unit dialogues use very brief messages *from* the operators. ARPANET used message buffers of 1008 bits—the maximum packet length. In view of the above evidence this was clearly too long.

OVERHEAD RATIO   Because the average message is short and the protocols are complex, the ratio of overhead bits to data bits is high—some would say "horrifying." The number of overhead bits transmitted is 8.22 times greater than the number of user bits transmitted [1]. The overhead includes the packet header of 64 bits (Layer 3), the frame header and trailer of 56 bits (Layer 2), and all the control messages such as RFNM's, requests for buffer allocation, allocation confirmations, etc.

Almost all of the network architectures that represent the current state of the art have a high level of overhead. Some transmit more overhead bits than ARPA. If the messages are long, on average, the overhead is not too significant. If the messages are as short as on ARPA the overhead ratio is serious.

A datagram network with 255-byte packets would handle 97% of ARPANET traffic with a respectable overhead ratio if the datagram header were kept short. The remaining 3% could use an additional header and separate protocols. With a wide-spread use of minicomputers handling the local batch processing, the traffic on many networks will be largely interactive. With distributed intelligence for editing the messages, many of the interactive messages will be short. There could therefore be a wide applicability of datagram networks with less overhead than X.25 networks. However the proposed datagram standard uses headers similar in length to those of X.25 packets.

In view of the high overhead of packet-switching networks it is important that a close examination be made of different network protocols and structures. Fast-connect circuit switching or combinations of circuit switching and packet switching may be a better scheme. These are discussed in Chapter 25.

NETWORK UTILIZATION   The total number of user bits being transmitted over ARPANET was much lower than the total network capacity: 47 messages per second with 154 user bits per message = 7238 bits per second. (This does not include the packet headers.) The overall utilization of the network was calculated to be 0.0077 [2]. The *maximum* hourly utilization during the week was 0.029. The utilization of the *most heavily loaded* line is plotted in Fig. 29.4; it averaged only 0.01 (not counting overhead).

These are very low figures compared with the utilization of conventional leased-line data networks in industry. A leased-line network for an airline reservation system or a sales office administrative system would be regarded as badly designed if its overall utilization were less than 10%. Such networks have the advantage that they can be optimized for a particular application.

The conclusion that might be drawn from this is that a packet-switching network of the ARPA type is economically justifiable only if it carries a *much higher traffic volume* than ARPANET. ARPANET could have been built with 9600-bps lines, but then it would not have achieved its response time objectives. Occasionally ARPA-like techniques have been proposed for private corporate networks with a substantially lower traffic volume per link than ARPANET. This is a mistake.

NETWORK DELAY   An objective of ARPANET was that a message's round trip should be sufficiently fast that the network delay is almost invisible to the user. He should perceive little difference between using a computer in the same building and using a computer a thousand miles away. To achieve this an average round-trip delay of less than 200 milliseconds was specified. Figure

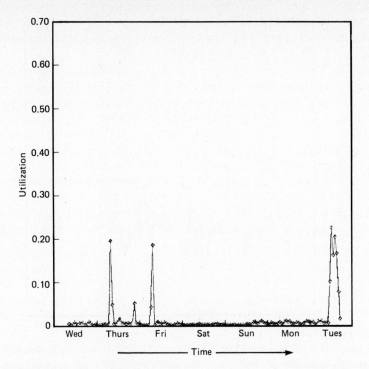

Figure 29.4 The utilization of the *most heavily loaded* line on the ARPA network. Its average utilization is 0.01 (not counting overhead bits) [1].

29.5 shows that this objective was more than met. The average delay measured was around 100 milliseconds. The average would have been higher if the messages had been longer, but even long messages have a handsomely fast delivery.

To achieve the fast delivery, wideband lines were needed (50,000 kbps). This accounts for the low utilization of the network. For a cost-effective network the objective of 200 milliseconds round-trip delay for all messages is questionable. A much longer delay is acceptable for many types of messages. This suggests the need for a priority scheme which allows the designer to request fast delivery of only the top-priority messages, and perhaps only of single-packet messages. A priority scheme can make the resulting network lower in cost.

TRAFFIC PATTERNS   An ARPANET packet traveled over 3.31 physical links between nodes, on average, to reach its destination. The mean number of physical links between nodes on the entire network was 5.32. These

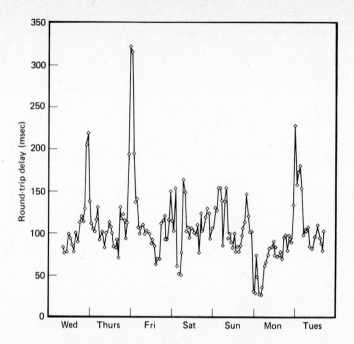

Figure 29.5 The round-trip delay on ARPANET messages was low enough to be almost invisible to the users [1].

figures tended to grow as the network acquired more nodes, and today they are much higher.

The network was designed with the assumption that traffic patterns would be random, i.e., a host would transmit to any other host with equal probability. In reality each user tended to have a favorite machine which was transmitted to, or a small group of favorites. Figure 29.6 illustrates favoritism. For each host the *favorite destination* was determined, i.e., that destination host to which it transmitted the most frequently. Figure 29.6 plots the percentage of messages which go to this single favorite destination. It is plotted for all sources on an hourly basis. The average is 61%.

In corporations the favoritism effect is much stronger. All sales offices tend to use the single computer with the sales and customer data base; the manufacturing computers tend to communicate with production planning; a head office computer draws its information from certain machines; and so on. There are well-established lines of control and paths of information flow. Many of them are hierarchical. To design a network with the assumption of *random* patterns of flow would give an unnecessarily complex and expensive result. Some much-touted design tools make this assumption.

The high proportion of favoritism suggests that on packet-switching networks using protocols like X.25, there will be a major use of *permanent virtual circuits,* as opposed to virtual calls. On corporate networks good reasons will remain for the use of *leased* lines. The latter view is strengthened by the fact that the utilization percent-

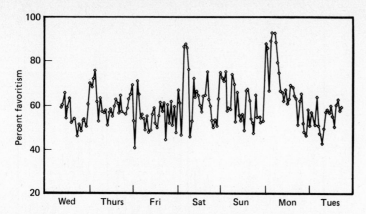

Figure 29.6 61% of the ARPANET messages are sent by users to their *favorite* destination [1].

ages of typical corporation leased lines are *much* higher than those on existing packet-switched networks.

On a network with N hosts, there are $N(N-1)/2$ host pairs. ARPANET at the time of these measurements had 1225 host pairs, i.e., 1225 different logical links between hosts. *Half* of the traffic used only 20 of them. Most of them were not used at all. Figure 29.7 shows the distribution of host pair traffic. In corporations this distribution is likely to be much more skewed.

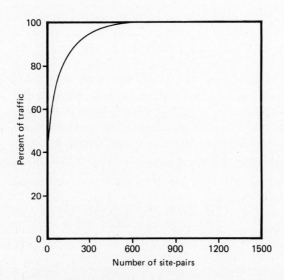

Figure 29.7 Most of the ARPANET traffic goes between a relatively small proportion of the site-pairs [1].

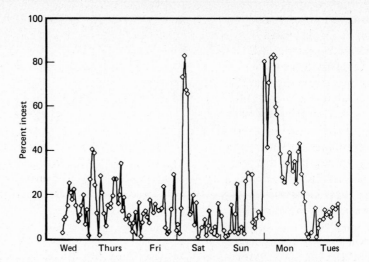

Figure 29.8   22% of the ARPANET traffic (and 80% at times) is incestuous, i.e., it is between hosts attached to the same node [1].

INCEST   Another interesting effect on ARPANET is referred to as *incest*. Incest was defined as a host machine using another host at the same location. Figure 29.8 shows the percentage of incest, and it is surprisingly high. On average 22% of the exchanges were incestuous. At times there was 80% incest. Incest tended to be at its height at night or in the wee hours of the morning.

The intent of ARPANET was that users should be able to use any machine anywhere on the network. The high level of incest and favoritism shows that machine *familiarity* plays a large part in computer usage, even among the fertile, exploring minds of university staff. If systems had been easier to use, more self-explanatory, with better use of catalogs and directories, and better designed dialogue structures, there might have been less favoritism and somewhat more even traffic distribution.

Incest will probably always be high because users of nearby machines visit each other's offices and talk to one another more. The nocturnal incest peaks were often caused by file transfers. Software designers should assume that incest will be common, for example between computers which share a common communications controller.

TOPOLOGY   The layout of the ARPA network changed repeatedly as more hosts were added and as traffic patterns changed. It remained a mesh-structured network on which any host could communicate with any other host.

Most corporate networks are hierarchical networks. There are several forms of hierarchical networks—star-structured, tree-structured, multidrop, concentrator, etc.

Some have their main computer centers at lower levels, shown in the illustrations in Chapter 6. In the mid-1970's many corporations began to build mesh-structured links between computer centers. Much of the traffic flow was still predominantly hierarchical, however. Sales traffic used the sales network; accounting information went to the head-office computer; and so on. In many cases there were hierarchical networks for separate divisions or applications, with lines running roughly parallel, so it paid to combine the networks. The traffic patterns in corporations tend to be orderly, predictable, often hierarchical, and often with nonhierarchical links between separate systems but with these links carrying a small proportion of the traffic. There is certainly not the any-to-any traffic pattern that might be assumed in a general-purpose resource-sharing network like ARPANET. Because of this, most computer manufacturers' network architectures stress hierarchical networks of high-line utilization, as well as peer-coupled links between data processing centers.

ADVANTAGES
OF SHARING

Most corporate networks do not have as good a response time as ARPANET. Some have a response time so long that it seriously inhibits interactive use. Some designers use the term "pain threshold." Pain-threshold design is not a good way to induce end users to employ the networks, especially if they are accustomed to fast responses from their standalone minicomputers.

ARPA can achieve fast responses because it employs 50,000 bps lines. Cost-conscious corporate designers can employ wideband lines only if they have high enough traffic volumes. Given the figures for typical dialogues of Table 9.1, it takes a large amount of traffic to achieve high utilization of 50,000 (or 48,000 or 56,000)-bps lines. There is thus a strong argument for lines being shared by multiple applications and divisions in a corporation, and also by multiple corporations.

REFERENCES

1. Kleinrock, L., and W. E. Naylor, *"On Measured Behaviour of the ARPA Network,"* *AFIPS Conference Proceedings,* Vol. 43, AFIPS Press, Montvale, NJ, 1974.

2. Ibid., page 775.

PART **IV** ERRORS, FAILURES,
AND
SECURITY

30 ERRORS AND RECOVERY

The recovery from errors, which is fairly straightforward on basic data communication links, becomes highly complex in a distributed processing environment. The reason for this is that many different types of malfunctions are possible, some of them subtle. In a simple teleprocessing system, all that is needed is recovery from transmission errors. A distributed system needs to recover from node failures, invalid protocol usage, traffic jams, missing packets, disrupted sessions, and other such conditions.

The following steps may be necessary in the recovery process:

1. Detect the error condition.

2. Report the error to the node and control layer responsible for recovery.

3. Initiate repair procedures if the fault condition is not self-correcting.

4. Select the appropriate restart point.

5. Reexecute the operation which failed.

6. Resynchronize if necessary, for example data file resynchronization.

LAYERED RECOVERY   As in other aspects of network design, recovery procedures should be built into the control layers (Fig. 30.1):

Layer 1:	Recovery from electrical circuit failure.
Layer 2:	Recovery from transmission errors.
Layer 3:	Recovery from virtual circuit problem.
Layer 4:	An end-to-end check on the delivery of messages.
Session Service Layers:	Recovery from protocol or session service problems.
User process:	Application program recovery.

464

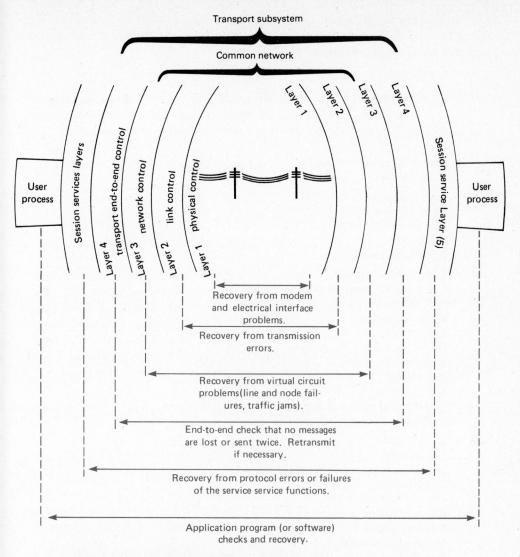

Figure 30.1   Problems should be dealt with at the lowest level without
affecting higher levels, unless unavoidable.

Where possible each layer should take care of its own problems without affecting
other layers. Bit transmission errors should be taken care of by the link control layer
(e.g., HDLC). Transport subsystem problems should be taken care of by the transport
subsystem without interfacing with protocols external to the transport subsystem, unless
unavoidable. Session problems should be resolved by the network software without
interfering with the application programs. Each set of concentric rings in Fig. 30.1 has
a job to do. It should do that job in spite of problems wherever possible.

It is a principle of layered architectures that problems should be dealt with at the lowest level possible without interfering with higher levels. Sometimes the failures are such that higher levels will inevitably be affected.

TYPES OF RECOVERY Procedures are needed for recovery from circumstances which include the following. They have been grouped into the 7 layers but some may be moved to a different layer than that indicated.

- Layer 1: *Electrical interface.*
  Modem problems.

- Layer 2: *Physical link.*
  Bit transmission errors.
  Brief circuit failures (dropouts) [1].
  Lost frames.
  Faulty frame headers.

- Layer 3: *Virtual circuit.*
  Link failure (bypassed by alternate routing).
  Node failure (bypassed by alternate routing).
  Traffic congestion.
  Traffic lockup.
  Insufficient buffer space in nodes.
  Error in packet protocols.
  Station busy.   ⎱ (Return packet to sender.)
  Station unavailable. ⎰
  Invalid virtual call set-up procedure.
  Invalid call dis-connect procedure.

- Layer 4: *End-to-end transmission.*
  Lost message.
  Incomplete message (not all packets delivered).
  Garbled message.
  Message delivered twice.
  Failure in mid-message.
  Security violation.
  Flow control violation.
  Failure of access to network. (An alternate transmission means may be available, e.g., dial telephone circuit.)
  Network deadlock.

- Layer 5: *Session control.*
  Invalid session request.
  Failure in session binding procedure.
  Station busy.
  Station not available.
  Security violation.
  Failure to disconnect the session.

- Layer 6: *Presentation control.*
  Failure to interpret Layer 6 header.
  Failure to establish appropriate session service resources.
  Receiver resources needed for session operation become temporarily unavailable.
  Contention for resources temporarily prevents the transaction being processed.
  Violation of message and response pattern.
  Pacing error.
  Recoverable program error in receiving machine.
  Security violation.
  Request for unavailable data.
  Session protocol violation.
  Chaining error.
  Error in transaction bracketing (grouping).
  Distributed file recovery.
  Invalid record found on remote file.
  File lockout due to contending users.
  Failure of file access mechanism.
  Request refused for security reasons.
  Recovery from previous failure requires resynchronization of file.
  Data unavailable.
  Data-base procedure violation.
  Search or access time exceeds limits.
  Deadlock.

- Layer 7: *Application programs.*
  Application program errors.
  Invalid data-base reference.
  Security violation.
  And so on.

A full-function computer network or distributed processing system will usually require recovery procedures at all layers.

At the physical link layer, procedures for bit error detection and data retransmission are needed. These are provided for in the standard data link control procedures such as HDLC, with error-detecting codes. On certain less common transmission links with a very high noise level, error-*correcting* codes are used.

Packets can have faults other than erroneous bits. The packet may be undeliverable for some reason; it may be of an invalid length; it may be addressed to a station which is not operating.

At the virtual-call layer, multipacket transmissions can run into problems which do not occur with single packets. It may not be possible to reassemble a multipacket message. A virtual call may have an invalid call setup procedure. Traffic congestion may prevent the completion of a call. A station may violate security by attempting to call a station in a closed user group.

At the session layer there can be faults which are external to the transport subsystem software or resources needed for the session may be unavailable.

Records requested in the session may be inaccessible. There may be security violations. A request may fail to receive a response. There may be procedural violations in a dialogue.

At the application layer, checks are often applied which are external to any of the network software, for example batch totaling, validity checks, application security checks. The number of errors made by operators of terminal devices far exceeds the errors caused by noise or failures. Accuracy controls need to be devised for human input, and tight controls used to prevent abuse or embezzlement.

END-TO-END CONTROL   The application designer must decide what end-to-end checks he feels are necessary. The transport subsystem may be designed never to lose a message or deliver it twice. Messages may be undeliverable because of failures or other reasons. In this case a fail-safe system returns the message to its sender, or at least notifies the sender of nondelivery.

Some transport subsystems are designed to have a higher degree of safety than others. Some software gives the system designer a choice of whether he requires guaranteed delivery or return of messages, or correct sequencing of messages. Some packet-switching systems have been safer than others. Some have occasionally lost messages.

For *most* applications the delivery capability of a public data network or private transport subsystem are perfectly adequate. For applications in which loss of messages would be a disaster, the application designer should probably build his own end-to-end safeguards, unless the Layer 4 software provides safe end-to-end controls. The message is retained at one end of the virtual circuit until the other end acknowledges receipt. The user programs keep totals of transaction amounts, for example cash, or of transaction identifiers such as order numbers, check numbers, account numbers, and so on, and periodically ensure that the running totals agree.

User program end-to-end checks may duplicate some of the checks built into the network layers of control. The user may have to devise his own sequence numbering scheme, for example. Nevertheless, end-to-end control is a prudent safeguard for a system handling cash transactions or messages vital to the functioning of a corportaion. The Postal Service does not normally lose letters, but systems using the mail for placing vital orders or sending money require confirmation of receipt of such letters.

The following chapter discusses recovery in Layer 2—the physical link. Chapter 32 discusses recovery in the transport subsystem. Chapter 31 discusses recovery at the session layer—Layer 4.

REFERENCES

1. Dropouts and other circuits failures are described in James Martin, *Telecommunications and the Computer,* 2nd ed, Part IV.

31 RECOVERY AT THE PHYSICAL LINK LAYER

The main form of recovery needed at the physical link layer is recovery from transmission errors which can occur in data or in any of the supervisory control bits. In addition to the physical link, protocol must deal with invalid transmissions, faulty headers, and lost data or supervisory packets. This recovery capability is built into physical link protocols such as HDLC and SDLC.

ARQ

The usual means of recovering from transmission errors is to employ an *error detecting* code on each block (or packet) that is transmitted. When an error is detected the block is retransmitted automatically. This is referred to as ARQ (Automatic Repeat reQuest).

ARQ procedures are built into physical link control protocols such as HDLC or binary synchronous. They typically employ 16 redundant bits at the end of a frame which are used to detect errors in that frame. They employ a powerful error detecting code—normally a polynomial code [1, 2].

The transmitting machine stores each block it sends until it receives acknowledgment that the block has been received correctly. If it does not receive this positive acknowledgment it retransmits the block. Data transmission codes such as the ASCII code or CCITT Alphabet No. 7 contain special characters for positive acknowledgment (referred to as an ACK character) and negative acknowledgment (a NAK character) which indicates that an error was detected in a block. Line control procedures such as *binary synchronous* line control have specially formatted positive and negative acknowledgment messages. More recent line control procedures do not necessarily employ negative acknowledgments. Instead the transmitting machine waits for a positive acknowledgment that the message has been received correctly. If it does not obtain it within a given time it automatically retransmits the message. It will attempt retransmission a given number of times and if repeatedly unsuccessful it will try to invoke a higher layer of recovery protocol.

CCITT
RECOMMENDATION
V.41

A recommended method of error control is given in CCITT Recommendation V.41 [2]. This can be implemented as part of the data terminal equipment or independently of it in the modem or circuit termination equipment. If it is part of the circuit termination equipment, the interface between it and the data terminal is the conventional CCITT V.24 interface that would be used with a normal modem (Fig. 31.1).

The system employs transmission of information in fixed length blocks containing 240, 480, 960, or 3840 bits of information. In addition, each block contains 4 *service bits* and 16 *error-detection bits*. The total lengths of the blocks are thus 260, 500, 980, or 3860 bits. If an error is detected the block is retransmitted. The error-correcting device may have a buffer in which errors are corrected by retransmission before the information is passed to the data terminal.

The four service bits are used to indicate the start of message, end of message, end of transmission, and the sequence of blocks sent. A count up to 3 is used to ensure that retransmitted blocks are not accidentally lost or received twice. The 16 error-detection bits employ a powerful polynomial code which we describe in the next chapter.

The modems used must provide simultaneous forward and backward channels. The backward channel, which may be of low speed, carries a binary 0 to indicate the acceptance of transmitted blocks and a binary 1 to indicate the need for repetition.

Physical link protocols such as HDLC, etc., have the error recovery procedures specified in the protocol, and hence built into terminals which use the protocol. Devices such as that shown in Fig. 31.1 can be used to protect simpler terminals.

CONTINUOUS ARQ

There are three types of ARQ:

1. Stop-and-wait ARQ.
2. Continuous ARQ with pull-back.
3. Selective repeat ARQ.

Stop-and-wait ARQ has been the most widely used.

After sending a block the transmitting terminal *waits* for a positive or negative acknowledgment from the receiving terminal. If the acknowledgment is positive it sends the next block. If it is negative it resends the previous block.

With *continuous* ARQ the transmitting terminal does not wait for an acknowledgment after sending a block. It immediately sends the next block. While the blocks are being transmitted the stream of acknowledgments is examined by the transmitting terminal. When there is a negative acknowledgment or the absence of a positive acknowledgment the terminal must determine which block was incorrect. The blocks must

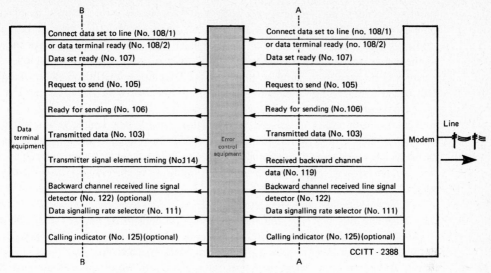

Error control equipment at the transmitting terminal

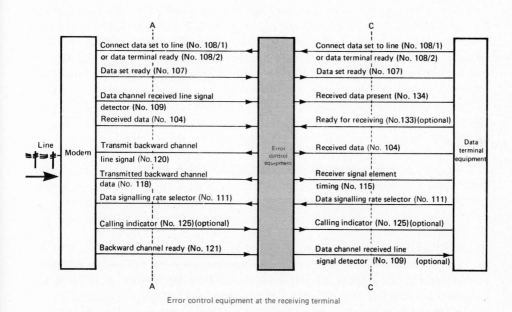

Error control equipment at the receiving terminal

Figure 31.1 Transmission error control equipment using CCITT Rec-omendation V.41 can be part of the data terminal, the modem, or the separate unit in between.

therefore be numbered, for example with a 3-bit binary number (modulo 8). The acknowledgment will contain the number of the transmitted block it refers to so that the transmitting terminal can identify it. If the transmission delay is such that the acknowledgment may be received more than 8 blocks after it was transmitted, then more than 3 bits will be needed to number the blocks. A satellite link may use 8 bits (modulo 256) because of its long propagation time.

On failing to receive a positive acknowledgment the transmitting terminal may back up to the block in error, and recommence transmission with that block. This is sometimes referred to as a *pull-back* scheme. A more efficient technique is to retransmit only the block with the error and not those blocks which follow it. This single-block retransmission requires more logic and buffering in the receiving terminals. It is referred to as *selective repeat* ARQ.

Figure 31.2 illustrates stop-and-wait ARQ and the two types of continuous ARQ.

Selective repeat ARQ, with retransmission of individual blocks, is the most efficient and also the most expensive. Whether it is worth the extra cost depends upon the number of blocks in error and the ratio of block transmission time to the time that elapses before an acknowledgment can be received. In most cases continuous ARQ with pull-back is preferable because it costs less and achieves almost as high an effective throughput.

For teletype transmission the time taken to transmit a block is long compared to the time taken to receive an acknowledgment; so stop-and-wait ARQ is normally used. On satellite circuits the transmission rate is high, and the time taken to receive an acknowledgment is as high as 750 milliseconds (satellite round trip plus two line turnaround times). Stop-and-wait ARQ would be highly inefficient so selective repeat ARQ should be used. In general, continuous ARQ is needed when the transmission rate is high and the propagation delay or line turnaround time is long. Many of the line control procedures of the 1960's were designed for stop-and-wait ARQ. Modern line control procedures such as HDLC are usually designed to allow *either* stop-and-wait *or* continuous ARQ.

Continuous ARQ operates best on a full-duplex line but is often used over a half-duplex line. On some full-duplex circuits with continuous ARQ, data is sent in both directions at once, the acknowledgment signals being interspersed with the data.

FRAME COUNTS   It sometimes happens that the control characters themselves or end-of-transmission characters are invalidated by a noise error. If this happens, then there is a danger that complete frames might be lost or two or more frames inadvertently joined together. It is possible that during the automatic transmission process a frame could be erroneously sent twice. To prevent these frame errors, sequence numbers are used. On some systems an odd/even (i.e., modulo 2) count has been used. At the start of a block, a control character is sent to indicate whether this is an odd-numbered or even-numbered block. If an odd-numbered

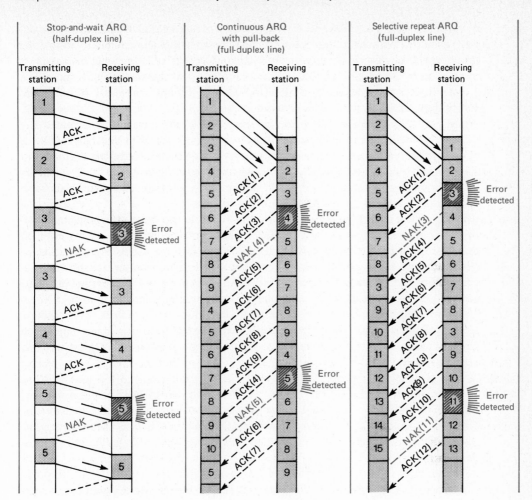

Figure 31.2 Three types of ARQ (Automatic Repeat ReQuest). The continuous and selective repeat examples here use modulo 8 (3-bit) sequence numbers.

block does not follow an even-numbered block, then the block following the last correct block is retransmitted. On some systems, two alternative start-of-transmission characters are used. With other schemes, the ACK characters contain this odd-even check. Two different ACK-type signals may be sent: ACK 0 and ACK 1. In the ASCII code there is only one ACK character; so if this code is used, a two-character acknowledgment sequence is sometimes employed.

HDLC etc. use a modulo 8 (3-bit) count for frame sequencing and continuous ARQ scheme. With fast transmission rates it is possible that more than one consecutive frame could be lost in a transmission dropout lasting a hundred milliseconds or more. The modulo 8 count would detect up to seven consecutive missing frames.

When a line interconnects several terminals in different locations, an addressing (or polling) technique is needed to make each device recognize when a frame is addressed to it, or to enable a computer to know which device originated a frame. It is difficult on multipoint lines to recover from *addressing* errors with certainty by means of answerback schemes with negative acknowledgments. The simplest method is a scheme with positive acknowledgments *only* and sequence-numbered frames. The receiver simply ignores incorrect frames. The transmitter sends a frame with a sequence number and waits for acknowledgment of its correct receipt. If no acknowledgment is received after a specified time, then it resends the frame with the same sequence number. One of two things might have gone wrong. First the frame might have been received with an error. In this case, it is retransmitted. Second, the positive acknowledgment might have been destroyed. In this case, when the receiver receives a second copy, it rejects it because it does not have the expected sequence number and sends another acknowledgment saying what number frame it expects next.

Providing that all errors are detected by the error-detecting code, this scheme is almost infallible on point-to-point or multipoint lines. It fails only in the improbable circumstance of a contiguous group of n frames being lost when a modulo n sequence number is used.

HDLC EXAMPLES   HDLC and similar protocols permit either continuous or stop-and-wait ARQ. Often the transmitting station sends several frames, then stops and waits for an acknowledgment. This is illustrated in Fig. 31.3.

Figure 31.4 shows continuous ARQ on a full-duplex line when the receiving station becomes unable to receive because of overload or some other condition. It sends a RECEIVE NOT READY S-frame. The transmitting station stops until it receives a RECEIVE READY indicating that the receiving station is ready to accept again. The N_R receipt sequence number in the RECEIVE NOT READY told the transmitting machine to hold frame $N_s = 4$ for retransmission. This implies that the frames prior to that had been received correctly.

In Fig. 31.5 continuous ARQ is used with data flowing in both directions on a full-duplex line (such as a line between nodes of a packet-switching network). Most acknowledgments are carried by the data frames themselves (the *I*-frames). An error occurs which destroys the flags which separate two frames. The two frames appear to be one erroneous frame. Station *B* ignores the erroneous frame and tells Station *A* that it expects to receive frame number 5 next ($N_R = 5$). Before Station *A* receives this signal it has already transmitted frame number 7. Station *B*, in this illustration, is

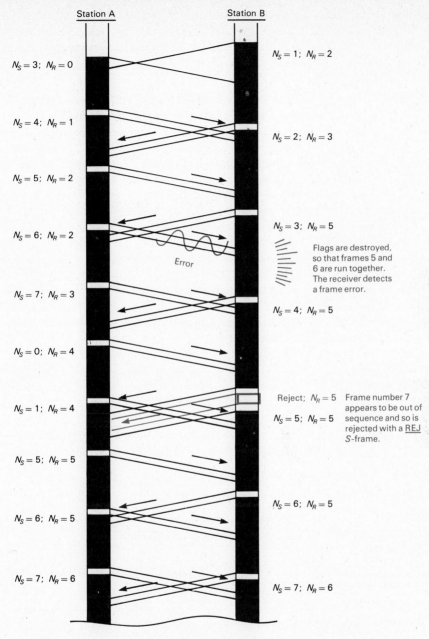

Figure 31.5 Envelope damage causes two packets to be merged during full-duplex transmission with HDLC.

designed to reject frames which are out of sequence. It therefore responds with a RE-JECT *S*-frame saying that frame 7 is out of sequence and that frame 5 is still the one that is expected next. Station *A* sends frame 5 and the ones that follow it in sequence.

TIME-OUTS   The *primary* station in HDLC etc. (*control* station or *master* station in other protocols) is responsible for orderly continuous operation of a physical link (except in balanced mode operations in which the responsibility is shared equally). The primary station must check that responses are received to its commands. To do this it uses *time-outs,* i.e., it uses a clock and takes action if a response is not received within a specified time. Usually the action is to retransmit the message in question. The primary station may retransmit a given number of times and if no response is received to any of these transmissions, within their time-out period, the primary station refers the problem to a higher layer of control (Chapters 32 and 33).

On many systems two time-outs are used, referred to as *idle detect* and a *nonproductive receive.*

An *idle detect* occurs when a primary station sends a command (in HDLC etc., a frame with the *poll* bit set) and receives *nothing* in response. A *nonproductive receive* is when the primary station receives a response that is unintelligible and so instructs the secondary station to retransmit it.

For an *idle detect* a time-out of 1 to 2 seconds is typical between the end of sending a message and the start of receiving a response. This time must be greater than the signal propagation time to and from the secondary station, the line turnaround time necessary to reverse the direction of transmission, and the processing time at the remote station.

For a *nonproductive receive* a time-out of 3 to 20 seconds is typical. This includes the time to transmit its frame and the time the secondary station waits before retransmitting.

THE NEED FOR HIGHER-LAYER INTERVENTION   The physical link layer of control attempts recovery actions which include the following:

1. Damaged frames are retransmitted.
2. Commands with no responses are resent.
3. Attempts to bring a secondary station on-line are retried.
4. Invalid frames are rejected and details returned to the sender.
5. Out-of-sequence frames are rejected and retransmitted.
6. When a station becomes busy it is polled until it is ready to accept again.

Recovery should be completed by the physical link layer if at all possible. The following are circumstances in which recovery cannot be completed by the physical link layer and the problem is passed to a higher-layer protocol:

1. Persistent noise is encountered on the line. To overcome it the transmission rate can be lowered by adjusting the modulation.

2. More than a specified number of attempts at retransmission fail. The number of attempts varies from one implementation to another. The transmission subsystem may attempt to send the data to its destination by using an alternate end-to-end route, or by establishing a dialed telephone connection.

3. The secondary station rejects a command with which it is not compatible. A higher layer of control examines the details of the rejected command.

4. A station has an internal malfunction. This is reported. It may be possible to switch to an alternate station.

Where possible these problems should be solved within the transport subsystem. In some cases operator intervention is necessary, and in others management may have to intervene.

REFERENCES

1. Polynomial codes are explained in the author's *Security, Accuracy and Privacy in Computer Systems*, Chapter 8, Prentice-Hall, Englewood Cliffs, NJ, 1973.

2. CCITT Recommendation V.41 describes a polynomial error detection code for analog circuits, CCITT, International Telecommunications Union, Geneva.

32 TRANSPORT SUBSYSTEM RECOVERY

In the previous chapter we were concerned with transmission errors on a circuit connecting two points. In this chapter we assume that the physical circuits have reasonably good ARQ, and raise our level of concern to the logical circuits and the transport subsystem as a whole, with its multiple nodes and multiframe messages.

Many new types of problems occur when we consider the transport subsystem, including node failures, protocol errors, equipment malfunctions, traffic jams, deadlocks, and inability to deliver the traffic in the required sequence. The transport subsystem should be designed to detect and as far as possible recover from these problems. There are also major concerns external to the transport subsystem but we save these for the following chapter.

Recovery in a *datagram* network with no virtual calls is much simpler than with full transmission capability. We will discuss datagram recovery first.

DATAGRAM RECOVERY   Datagram recovery is slightly more complex than basic physical-link recovery because a packet may be undeliverable or unacceptable for a variety of reasons. These must be indicated to the sender.

The most basic form of packet recovery is that when each packet is independent and in no way related to any other packet—in the words of the CCITT Study Group definition of a datagram: *A message which can be contained in the data field of only one packet is delivered to the destination in its address field. No referral is noted by the network to any other datagram previously sent or likely to follow.*

Box 24.2 describes the types of datagrams that a user device passes to the network and receives from it. Almost all datagrams transmitted are of the DATA type. The other types (with the exception of PADDED) are for various error, failure, congestion, and diagnostic situations.

A user device may *test* whether the network is functioning correctly by sending an IDENTIFY or an ECHO datagram. An IDENTIFY datagram returns the user's own address and in this way tests the user's interface to the network. An ECHO datagram travels to the destination port and is then returned to the sender. This permits a user machine to test the path through the network and, if it wishes, measure the transit and queuing delay.

A user machine may be receiving a stream of faulty datagrams from some other user machine, probably because of a hardware, software, of application program fault in that machine. The receiving machine can prevent this annoyance by sending a BLOCK datagram containing the address of the faulty sender.

A user machine may receive from the network a variety of datagram types designed to indicate that something has gone wrong. They include the following:

Type Code	Type	Purpose
3	BLOCKED	This instructs the receiving machine to stop sending datagrams to a given address. It is sent by the machine at that address (in the form of a BLOCK-type datagram) because, as mentioned above, it is being plagued by the receipt of faulty datagrams from the location in question.
7	NOT-ACCEPTED	This is a datagram which has been returned because the addressee is not accepting datagrams, probably because of failures or because the power is turned off.
8	NOT-DELIVERABLE	This is a datagram which has been returned because network failures prevent its being delivered.
10	CONGESTING	A datagram which is generated inside the network when congestion occurs to indicate that a certain link has excessive queues.
4	BAD-ADDRESS	This is a datagram returned because it has an invalid address. It may contain a nonexistent address or an address to which it is barred for security reasons, e.g., the address of a closed user group.
5	BAD-LENGTH	This is a datagram returned by the network because it is too long, or else too short to have a valid header.
6	BAD-TYPE	This is a datagram returned because its original type code was invalid.

Other types of systems have similar packet or block recovery problems and need equivalent means of reporting the problems and recovering from them.

VIRTUAL CALLS   When multipacket messages or virtual calls are sent, it is necessary to deal with incompleted calls, sequence errors, and errors in the call establishment or clearing process. Traffic deadlocks can occur, as described in Chapter 34, when multipacket messages are sent. Unlike a simple datagram network the expediency of deleting and later retransmitting a packet cannot be used. To recover from deadlocks (and other conditions) it is sometimes necessary to *reset* a logical channel or *restart* a network node or user machine.

SEQUENCING ERRORS   Sequencing problems can be avoided by not having alternate routing within a virtual call, and avoiding recovery techniques which cause the packets to arrive out of sequence. The packets for the call are then delivered in the same sequence as that in which they were sent. This simplifies the network control mechanisms without necessarily causing serious throughput or response time degradation. When a circuit or network node fails, the call may be restarted using an alternate route. The recovery procedure will ensure that all packets after a given number will be retransmitted by the alternate route.

On many networks, packets can arrive out of sequence. Probably the best way of controlling out-of-sequence packets is with the window concept illustrated in Fig. 20.5. The packets are allowed to get out of sequence up to the limits of the window. Beyond that the recovery procedure must come into operation. Packets beyond the right-hand edge of the window cannot be accepted, and are deleted; they must be retransmitted. A packet at the left-hand edge of the window might be missing, in which case the window cannot rotate. The receiving machine requests that this be retransmitted.

RESETTING   The mechanisms for a virtual call or virtual circuit attempt
A VIRTUAL CIRCUIT   to recover at the packet level. If the error, failure, or
                         congestion condition is such that this proves impossible,
then the call must be *reset*.

Resetting means that all packets in the network relating to that virtual circuit, traveling in either direction, are discarded, and the virtual circuit, is reinitialized. This does not mean that the virtual circuit is disconnected or that a virtual call must be reestablished; it means that the flow control windows for both directions of transmission are reset to zero. The sequence numbering of the packets transmitted after a reset starts from zero. The user machines involved are notified that a reset has taken place, so that they will retransmit what packets they can starting with the new sequence numbers.

A reset can be triggered either by a user machine or by transmission subsytem equipment. It could occur for a variety of reasons. The user machine might be having a problem. The network might have congestion conditions that normal flow procedures cannot cope with. Some form of deadlock might have occurred. A reset may be necessary because of a failure of a transmission node, and subsequent rerouting. It might be necessary because procedure orders were violated by the user machine—either the transmitting or receiving machine

RESTART

A reset can happen without fatally harming the call that is in process. A more disruptive level of recovery is a *restart*.

A *reset* affects only one virtual circuit. A *restart* affects all the virtual circuits employed by a user machine. A *restart* occurs when a using machine or segment of network which serves it cannot continue to function without briefly shutting down and restarting. All switched virtual calls are disconnected and *must be reestablished*. Permanent virtual circuits which cannot be disconnected are all reset. A request for restart says "Clear out everything and begin again."

If possible a *session* should not be terminated when a reset or restart occurs. There may be a pause in the session but it should not have to be rebound or begun again. There is, of course, the possibility of messages being lost. Reset and restart procedures have been designed on some systems so that messages are not lost. In other systems messages have been lost. To avoid the possibility of loss, sufficient buffering is needed. With a large flow control window or modulo 128 (rather than module 8) sequence numbers, this could be substantial.

On many systems the infrequent loss of a message does not matter. A terminal operator may simply reenter the message if he does not receive a response. A batch system may back up to its previous *checkpoint*. The application designer needs to have a clear understanding of whether the transmission subsystem occasionally loses messages, so that he knows what degree of end-to-end protection to build.

CCITT RESET AND RESTART

Resets and restarts are specified in the CCITT X.25 protocol. They can be initiated either by a user machine or by the network. In the former case the user machine sends a RESET REQUEST or RESTART REQUEST packet to the network (to its DCE). In the latter case the network sends a RESET INDICATION or RESTART INDICATION packet to the user machine. The response to these packets is a RESET CONFIRMATION or RESTART CONFIRMATION.

The packets initiating or giving information about a *reset* (shown in Fig. 22.13) contain the number of the logical channel in question, the cause of resetting and a diagnostic code. Four possible reasons are specified:

- Out of order.
- Remote procedure error.
- Local procedure error.
- Network congestion.

An 8-bit diagnostic code gives further information about any reset caused by a procedure error in a user machine.

The packets initiating or giving information about a *restart* (shown in Fig. 22.14) contain the cause of the restart. Two causes are specified:

- Local procedure error.
- Network congestion.

It is likely that more details about the cause of resets and restarts will be specified in the future.

The X.25 *logical channel* can be in one of the three states when it is transmitting data (as opposed to setting up or clearing a call):

1. *Reset-request state:* a user machine has requested a reset.
2. *Reset-indication state:* a transmission node has indicated that a reset is taking place.
3. *Flow-control-ready-state:* the logical channel can transmit data normally.

When the logical channel is in the *reset-request state* the network will confirm the reset by transmitting to the user machine a RESET CONFIRMATION packet. This places the logical channel in the *flow-control-ready* state ready to transmit data again.

When the logical channel is in the *reset-indication* state, the user machine will confirm the reset by transmitting a RESET CONFIRMATION packet, and this, again, places the logical channel in the *flow-control-ready* state so that data transmission can begin again.

Just as there are two *reset* states, so there are two *restart* states:

1. *Restart-request state:* a user machine has requested a restart.
2. *Restart-indication state:* a transmission node has indicated that a restart is taking place.

In both cases a response is needed to indicate that the restart is operative. Figure 32.1 shows state transition diagrams for CCITT X.25 reset and restart. If by any chance the user machine and network simultaneously exchange a RESTART REQUEST and RESTART INDICATION, then no RESTART CONFIRMATION is needed. Similarly if they exchange a *RESET* REQUEST and *RESET* INDICATION, then no RESET CONFIRMATION is needed.

CALL CONNECTION PROBLEMS   The telephone network is sometimes unable to connect a call which a subscriber has dialed. The subscriber hears signals which indicate why his call is not completed such as a slow busy signal indicating that the called party is busy, a fast busy signal indicating that the circuits or switches are busy, or a variety of recorded spoken messages saying that a nonworking number has been dialed or that there is a temporary problem.

A data network or transport subsystem may similarly have difficulties and inform

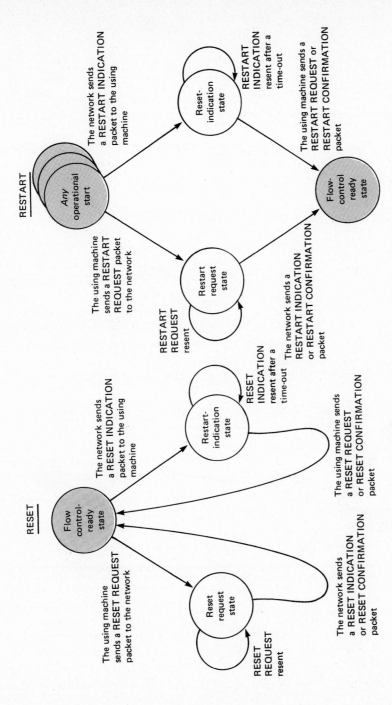

Figure 32.1 State transfer diagrams for reset and restart, from CCITT Recomendation X.25.

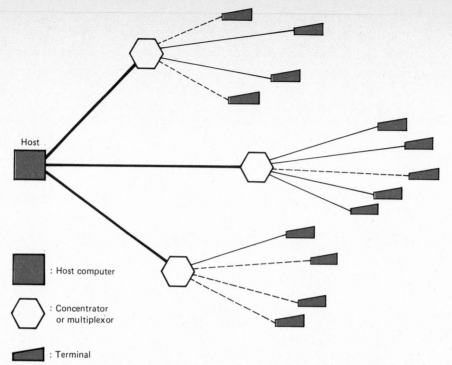

: Host computer

: Concentrator
  or multiplexor

: Terminal

1. Tree structured network. Vulnerable to line and concentrator failures.

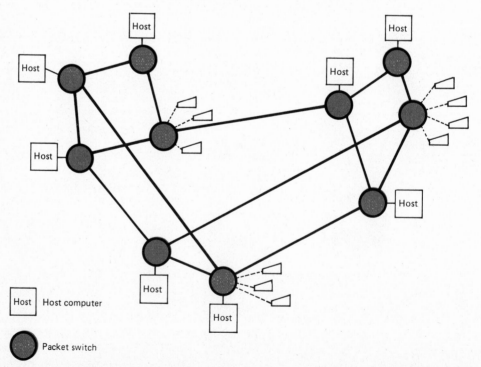

Host | Host computer

Packet switch

2. Early packet-switching systems, e.g., ARPANET and CYCLADES.

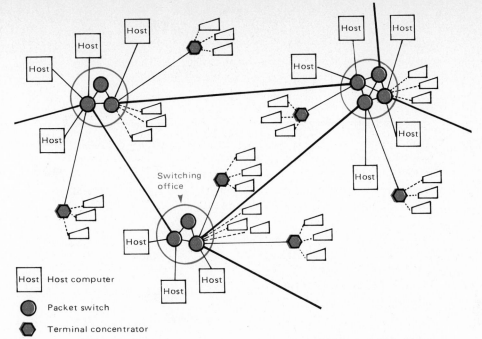

Host Host computer

⬤ Packet switch

⬢ Terminal concentrator

3. Early public service packet networks, e.g., TELENET, DATAPAC, EPSS, and TRANSPAC.

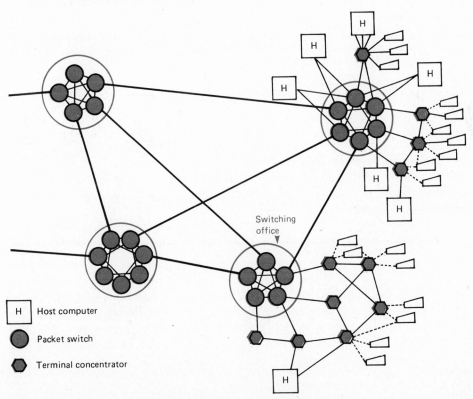

H Host computer

⬤ Packet switch

⬢ Terminal concentrator

4. Third generation of packet networks.

Figure 32.2 Network growth leading to higher availability.

the user machine why a virtual call cannot be completed. The reasons are somewhat similar to those with telephone calls. They include the following:

- *Number busy.*
  The called number has no free channels and cannot accept another call.

- *Network busy.*
  Congestion conditions within the network temporarily prevent the requested virtual circuit from being established.

- *Not obtainable.*
  The called number is not assigned or is no longer assigned.

- *Out of order.*
  The called number is not working. Possible reasons include:
  Subscriber link not functioning.
  User machine not functioning.
  Physical link control not working.

- *Invalid call.*
  An invalid facility was requested.

- *Reverse charging refused.*
  The call establishment request specified reverse charging and the called machine will not accept that.

- *Access barred.*
  The calling machine is not permitted to obtain the number that it has requested. A possible reason is that a *closed user group* is specified so that only users within that set can gain access to the number in question.

- *Local procedure error.*
  The machine making the call has made an error in procedure.

- *Remote procedure error.*
  The machine called has made an error in procedure.

All of these reasons relate to the transport subsytem. In the session services subsystem there are *many* more reasons why a session cannot be established. The transport subsystem layers are unconcerned with these. Session-level controls are discussed in the following chapter.

NETWORK RELIABILITY　　It is desirable that the paths through a transport network should be as failure-free as possible. Leased lines and switching machines will both fail [1]. To achieve a high level of reliability the network needs to be able to bypass the failures with alternate routing. A large network can afford more alternate paths than a small network. It is therefore economical to build a higher level of reliability into a large network than a small one. Public data networks should become highly reliable, the weakest link being the local subscriber loop which accesses the network.

There have been three generations of packet-switching networks, as illustrated in Fig. 32.2.

The first diagram of Fig. 32.2 shows a typical private network structure. It is vulnerable to failures of both its leased lines and concentrators. Its reliability could be increased with alternate routing and dial telephone backup.

The second diagram illustrates the early packet-switching networks such as ARPANET and CYCLADES. These are vulnerable to failures of the the packet switch (IMP) to which a host is connected. This is a single minicomputer which is typically inoperative 1% of the time.

The third diagram illustrates the first public packet-switching systems. A switching office of Telenet and other value-added carriers contains multiple minicomputer switches fully interconnected by wideband channels within the office. If one or more fails, the others in that office perform the switching task. The offices and multiple routes between them give a high reliability to the trunking network. However, links from customer machines are vulnerable to failures of the concentrators and lines which connect them to the switching offices.

As data networks grow, multiple access lines and alternate routes between the concentrators are added as in the fourth diagram of Fig. 32.2. In the third generation of packet-switching networks the switches are themselves built of multiple microprocessors on a common bus. This both lowers the cost and further enhances reliability.

There is one weak link left in such networks: the local loop to the subscriber's premises. If multiple lines are used to a subscriber's office they often go through the same telephone company cable. A dialed backup line also goes through the same cable. A failure of the cable breaks all these lines. When the local loop cable fails it often takes a long time to repair [1].

REFERENCE

1. Details of line failures and time to repair are given in the author's *Telecommunications and the Computer*, 2nd ed., Prentice-Hall, Englewood Cliffs, NJ, 1976.

33   SESSION
        RECOVERY

The transport subsystem recovery procedures do not solve all of the end-user failure problems. In this chapter we are concerned with recovery procedures external to the transport subsystem.

A well-designed transport subsystem is a great help. It would be ideal if we could assume that everything we feed into one end of a logical channel is delivered at the other end in sequence. In reality, however, the transport subsystem will cause an occasional *reset, restart,* or complete disruption of a session, and leave the external mechanisms to sort out whatever problems these may cause.

SESSION SURVIVAL   In general, failures are of two types: those which are sufficiently severe that the session must be *unbound,* and those for which repair or correction can take place. It is desirable that the latter category is made to apply to as many failures as possible but this objective considerably complicates the software. There is substantial difference in the *resilience* of different networking systems.

Recovery within a session may take place without a terminal operator being affected other than by a slight delay. Other forms of recovery do affect the operator. He may have to take certain types of action or may be sent a message telling him to wait until some recovery action is completed.

Problems which could necessitate the unbinding of a session include:

- A permanent hardware failure which cannot be bypassed.
- A permanent telecommunication failure which cannot be bypassed.
- A program bug which cannot be circumvented.

- Machines cannot communicate as required because of an error in systems generation.

- A mismatch exists in Layer 6 or 7 services so that one machine cannot do what another requests. This really implies a fault in the setting up of the session.

Problems which might be resolved without breaking a session include:

- A transport subsystem *reset* or *restart* as described in the previous chapter.

- Lost messages.

- Duplicate messages.

- Garbled messages.

- Sequence number errors.

- Contention problems.

- Insufficient resources available, temporarily.

- A transient hardware failure.

- A hardware problem which an operator can fix such as a printer running out of paper.

- A hardware or circuit failure which can be bypassed.

- An operator error.

- A nonsevere security violation.

- A loss of synchronization in the Layer 6 or 7 protocols.

- A nonrepeating program error.

- A higher-layer function cannot perform as requested. For example, a specified Presentation Control *format* does not exist in the distant node which is requested to use it (but it could be sent there without breaking the session).

INITIATION OF RECOVERY

If a network management module is involved in setting up and closing down sessions, then this module will become responsible for certain types of recovery actions. The simpler recovery actions should not involve network management but should be resolved directly between the communicating parties.

When a problem is detected, the node which detects it needs to send a control message to the node responsible for recovery. This may be the primary user station of a primary-secondary pair, the user station which originated the session, or a network management node. The control message contains a code which indicates the cause of the problem. These codes are defined in the network architecture. There are many of them in advanced architectures because there are many potential causes of problems. On interpreting the code, the node responsible for recovery initiates appropriate action.

SPECIFIC AND
GENERAL FAILURES
Some errors and failures affect only one message and its response. Others affect an entire session but are restricted to that session. Others are more general in the range of their damage, affecting all the sessions to a given node, unit, or portion of a network. The distinction between Reset and Restart in X.25 networks, discussed in the previous chapter, reflects this difference between failures which affect single sessions and failures more general in their effect. The distinction applies to higher layers also. Broad-ranging failure Session Services Subsystem could be caused by a computer failure or failure of a control program.

CHECKPOINT RESTART
In order to restart in an orderly fashion after a failure, *checkpoints* are taken. A checkpoint is a recording of data and the status of applications programs or system controls at a given time so that processing may restart in an orderly fashion by reconstructing the status when the checkpoint was made.

Checkpointing applies at two levels—the network software and the application environment. The checkpointing for the software stores the status of each station, recording information such as the terminal table entries, the destination queues, and the control blocks in use. This is usually recorded on a special disk data set. When the system restarts, this is used to restore the environment to its status prior to closedown.

There may be checkpointing in the software external to the network, for example data base software. This must ensure that no data is accidentally lost or made inaccessible by breaking a chain or losing an index entry, and that no records fail to be updated when they should be, or are accidentally updated a second time when the restart occurs.

The checkpointing for the application programs varies with the type of application. If the application is interrupted it should return to a preplanned point and restart at that point. In anticipation of trouble, the programmer needs to place these checkpoints in his program and test that when a return is made to a checkpoint no data is falsely processed or files falsely updated.

RECOVERY SETS
The data being transmitted over the network should be divided into *recovery sets*. A recovery set is the group of data which is transmitted from the time of one application checkpoint to the next. It is the group of data to which recovery is applied. One communicating party should acknowledge the receipt or completion of a recovery set to the other party.

The recovery set will differ in size and nature from one type of application to another. In an interactive session it may consist of one message from a terminal user and the response to that message. For the processing of documents such as invoices it may consist of the group of transactions that constitute one invoice. For a dialogue such as airline reservations it will consist of the group of messages that results in a booking or dealing with a customer. For remote file usage it might relate to one segment or track of a file. For batch processing it will be groups of transactions between check-points, perhaps several hundred transactions, which are controlled as a group and re-transmitted if an error or failure damages the group.

In some cases the recovery set is the concern solely of the application designer. It is desirable, however, that it be incorporated into the network software. Users of Uni-vac's Distributed Communications Architecture (DCA) define an ACKSET (Acknowl-edge Set) which represents the smallest set of recoverable data. The Session Services software controls and acknowledges the delivery of ACKSET's. In IBM's SNA (Sys-tems Network Architecture) the recovery set is called a *chain* (and sometimes a bracket). Code bits indicate whether a message is the first message of a chain, the last message, or one in the middle. If an error occurs the receiver aborts the entire chain and sends back a negative response indicating that the chain has been aborted. It dis-cards all other incoming messages which are part of that chain. The sender can decide whether or not to recover the chain. If yes, then the entire chain must be resent.

The application designer decides what messages are grouped into a chain and how this grouping relates to the application recovery philosophy, the structure of the termi-nal user dialogue, the allocation of batch check points, and the avoidance of losing a file update or updating a record twice when recovering from failures.

SEQUENTIAL NUMBERS In order to detect lost or duplicate messages, sequence numbers are used by the higher layer control mecha-nisms. A response to a message may be given the same sequence number as the message, and any exception or error messages may carry the sequence number of the items they relate to.

Sequence numbers are used for Layer 2 and Layer 3 control as described earlier. These are often 3-bit numbers giving a modulo 8 count. The Layer 4 sequence numbers may be longer because Layer 4 failures or out-of-sequence conditions may cover a larger range. IBM's SNA uses 16-bit sequence numbers (giving a modulo 65,536 count). These are used for linking together messages chopped up in packets as well as for recovery control at the higher layers.

IN-SESSION RECOVERY If recovery can take place within the session the necessary actions are as follows:

1. Detection of the error.
2. Reporting the error to the sender with an indication of what caused it.

3. Correction of the error if possible.

4. Selection of a restart point within the session and restarting in an orderly fashion.

The error is usually detected by the receiving node. It may be detected before it reaches the destination in which case the message may continue its journey to the receiving node but with an error indication. The receiving node notifies the sender of the error and the type of cause. Occasionally the sender does not receive any such indication. The message may have been lost, possibly because of a failure in the receiving node. The sender will detect the loss either by a time-out, i.e., it does not receive a reply within a specified time, or else because the next response it receives does not have the expected sequence number.

The responsibility for correcting the error and restarting the session may lie with the station which initiated the exchange of messages. On the other hand, it may lie with the primary station where a primary-secondary relationship exists between communicating parties. Exactly who is responsible must be specified when the session is *bound*.

The party responsible for recovery may:

1. Resynchronize the communicating protocols and resend the message or recovery set in question.

2. Correct the situation and then resynchronize and resend.

3. Request that an operator correct the situation, e.g., put more paper in the printer, and then resynchronize and restart.

4. Decide that the situation cannot be recovered automatically and terminate the session.

Simply resynchronizing and resending the data without corrective action may be done when a time-out indicates that a message is lost, when a duplicate message is received, when a message is rejected because of insufficient resources or contention, or when a sequence number error is detected. If one message is lost or not delivered because of contention, that message is resent. If the problem appears more complex, the recovery set is resent. Some systems always retransmit the recovery set rather than individual messages.

In some applications the recovery sets can be processed in any sequence. Each one might be an invoice, an order, a reservation, or an administrative message. They may be queued or stored before processing and if one is lost it can be retransmitted out of sequence. In other applications the recovery sets must be processed in sequence. They might be part of an ongoing terminal dialogue, part of a program, or part of a logical sequence of steps. The recovery process must then retransmit the data in sequence. Which procedure is followed must be defined in the recovery protocols. A general-purpose protocol might always use *sequential* recovery. If either is possible then the procedure to be followed must be specified when the session is *bound*.

When a session has to be terminated the disruption spreads to the application programs. A session can be terminated with differing degrees of abruptness. We will refer to *orderly, quick,* and *instant* closedowns.

An application program should be written in such a way that the programmer anticipates the possibility of a closedown. An exit routine should be written which is to be executed, if possible, when a closedown occurs. In some software this is called TPEND exit routine. This routine should store any important data so that the application program can be started again later without loss. It may notify the terminal users as graciously as possible that a closedown is occurring. It disassociates the program from further use of communications.

In an *orderly closedown* the application programs will be able to execute their TPEND exit routines. The software schedules each program's TPEND. It waits until all other programs in a node have terminated and then deactivates the node from further communications. When this closedown occurs a computer may be prevented from initiating new connections with terminals or accepting new messages, though it can send the pending messages in its output queue or currently in process. It can send closedown messages to its terminals, if desirable. The node should take a checkpoint of internal system control blocks in order to facilitate an orderly restart.

In a *quick closedown,* further transmission between terminals and application programs is not permitted. The software schedules each program's TPEND but does not allow any queues to be worked off or dialogue to be terminated gracefully. Only the messages currently being transmitted can be completed.

In an instant closedown the node is abruptly cut off from all communications. It may be cut off in mid-message.

HANGING SESSIONS
Usually when troubles occur the session will be terminated by the software. A particular annoying problem is when the software fails to terminate a session which has failed to function. The session is left hanging with nothing happening. Here intervention of a terminal operator or network operator is needed to close the session.

BYPASSING LAYER 4
FAILURES
Some failures in transport subsystems are bypassed by alternative routing, as we have discussed. To deal with Layer 4 failures it is sometimes necessary to use a different host computer, terminal or cluster controller. In some networks a *logical* machine can be moved from one physical machine to another and retain the same network address.

Figure 33.1 shows a network in which host computers perform Layer 4 functions and are responsible for setting up sessions for the user machines in the outlined

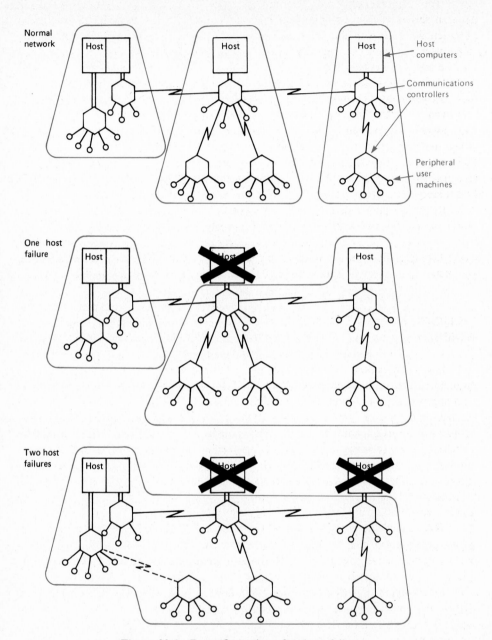

Figure 33.1 Reconfiguration after host failures.

areas. This diagram could represent an IBM SNA or Univac DCA System. The center diagram shows one of the host computers having failed. The network is reconfigured to lessen the impact of this loss. The bottom diagram shows two host failures. Some of the user machines now report to a different host which sets up sessions for them and may be able to run their jobs.

Unfortunately most jobs in a commerical environment cannot be switched from one host to another because they need files which are accessible only via the host. It improves the availability of files if storage units can be made accessible directly from the network, rather than necessarily via a host. Figure 33.2 shows a configuration in which the storage control units are accessible from the communications controllers. In other words, storage management is removed from the host. This amounts to a further step in distributing function. The bottom of Fig. 33.2 shows a host failure and that host's storage being incorporated into the area controlled by a different host.

Reconfigurations of the type shown in Figs. 33.1 and 33.2 can be done in a *nondisruptive* fashion or an *immediate* fashion. If the switchover is nondisruptive, existing sessions are allowed to continue. This might be the case when a working host is being taken off-line. In an immediate reconfiguration, sessions have to be terminated and restarted after the switchover. This should be an *orderly* termination if possible.

APPLICATION   When a session is disrupted it is desirable to protect the
INTEGRITY   application environment. This is done in different ways
                          depending on the type of application.

In an application with no file updating there is little risk of damage. The main problem is that of inconvenience to the end users. In some cases this can be minimized with appropriate use of checkpoints so that the whole of a job is not lost. If a computer becomes inaccessible it may be possible to run the job on a different computer, and sufficient information may be stored somewhere accessible in order to facilitate such a switch. In many session terminations a transaction will be lost, such as an inventory inquiry, a document being entered, an information retrieval attempt, a mathematical expression to be evaluated, and so on. The transaction may be reentered when a new session is established. An intelligent terminal or controller may store the half-processed transaction to lessen the terminal operator's work or inconvenience.

The situation is more of a problem when files are being updated. Control mechanisms must ensure that the record does not fail to be updated and is not accidentally double-updated during recovery. It is as bad to deduct money from a bank account by mistake as not to deduct it all.

Batch processing, where data are being taken from a magnetic tape, updated, and written on another magnetic tape, is relatively easy to control because the original tape still exists after a failure. The processing returns to the previous checkpoint and redoes the updating.

When data is updated on disk the original copy is overwritten. Therefore in order to start again from a checkpoint, a log must be written containing details of the data

Normal network

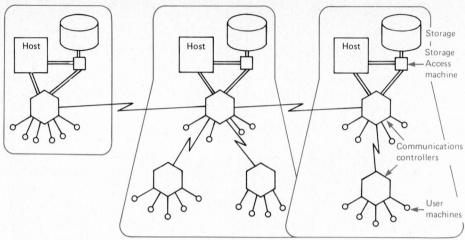

One host failure

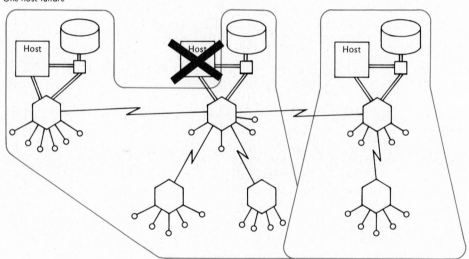

Figure 33.2   Reconfiguration with network-accessible storage units.

before updating and the transactions which updated it. This log may be stored only from one checkpoint to the next. Once a checkpoint is safely passed, the log of data prior to that checkpoint may be discarded. This is done automatically in some systems and reconstruction is done automatically after a session failure. The checkpoints may be fairly close together so that not too much data has to be stored.

In some systems, file update logs are stored for a long period in case of file destruction by fire, vandalism, or operator error. These logs (also called journals) are often different from the checkpoint-restart logs which are part of data base and network software [1].

If a file is being updated by only one session, the checkpoint-restart mechanism could relate to that session. Often, however, a file is being updated by *multiple* sessions simultaneously. For example, a file of bookings may be updatable from many terminals in different locations. In this case it is necessary to prevent the independent sessions from interfering with one another and to protect the data from both multiple-session and single-session failures. For the brief period when one transaction is in the process of updating a record, other updating transactions must be locked out of it as described in the next chapter.

USE OF SEQUENCE NUMBERS

A failure may occur when a terminal operator or application process is updating a distant file, and it may not be clear whether a particular transaction has in fact updated the file or not. The failure may have occurred just after writing on the file, or just before it. The terminal operator or application process must be told precisely whether or not it should resend the transaction.

To ensure safe recovery the messages and their responses are given sequential numbers as discussed above. This is part of the Layer 4 control in networking software. The use of the sequential numbers may be extended into Layers 6 and 7 and into the application environment to help correlate responses with the messages which require them and to help ensure correct file updating during recovery periods.

Figure 33.3 shows the normal use of sequential numbers networking software. Figure 33.4 shows the same numbers being used beyond Layer 4 to control storage updating. The sequential number assigned to a message is printed at the user terminal and is written on the record which that message updates. If a failure occurs when the message is being processed, the terminal user can check whether or not the record was in fact updated. Using the sequential numbers a precise set of rules can be given to an operator to ensure that the right recovery action is taken. Similarly, rigorous protocols can be given to application, file, and data base software which employ networks.

In general it is desirable that protocols for file updating be linked to network protocols in order to ensure safe recovery.

TERMINAL DIALOGUE INTERRUPTIONS

When the terminal user's dialogue is interrupted, it is sometimes advantageous that he should be able to start it again where he left off. If it is a lengthy dialogue, for example the reordering of complex machinery, it is certainly desirable that he should not have to go back to the beginning. For this reason, checkpoints may be built into the dialogue structure. At intervals the decisions made up to that point in the dialogue will be reviewed

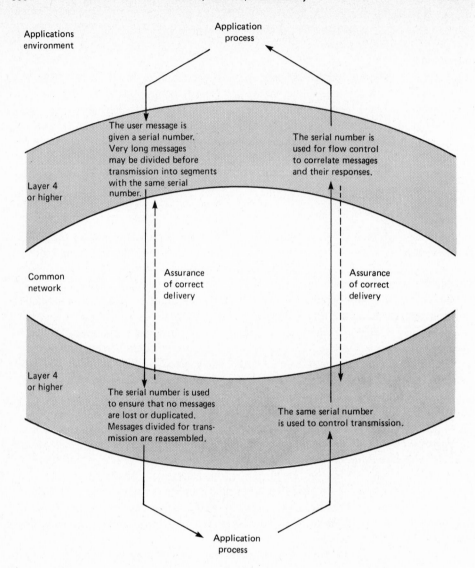

Applications
environment

Application
process

The user message is
given a serial number.
Very long messages
may be divided before
transmission into segments
with the same serial
number.

The serial number is
used for flow control
to correlate messages
and their responses.

Layer 4
or higher

Common
network

Assurance
of correct
delivery

Assurance
of correct
delivery

Layer 4
or higher

The serial number is used
to ensure that no messages
are lost or duplicated.
Messages divided for transmission are reassembled.

The same serial number
is used to control transmission.

Application
process

Figure 33.3   The use of serial numbers to control communications integrity.

(and can be changed if necessary). When the operator agrees that they are correct, they
will be recorded. If anything goes wrong from that point onward, the operator will be
able to restart the dialogue at the previous checkpoint.

In most terminal dialogues there are certain stages at which the set of decisions
recorded up to that point can be agreed upon as correct. Sometimes this can be re-

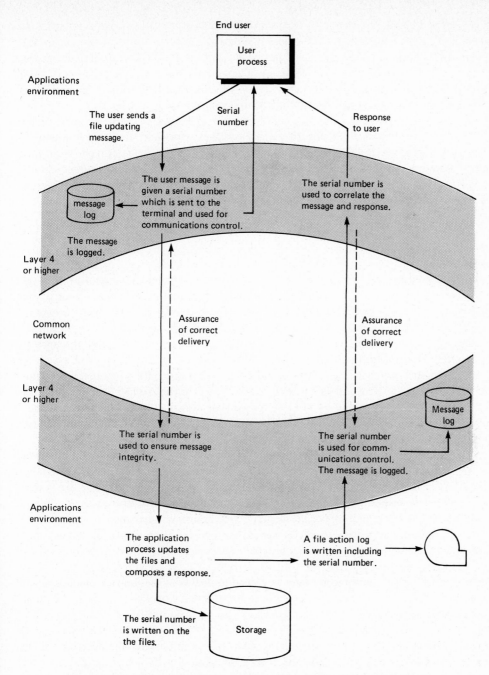

End user

User
process

Applications
environment

The user sends a
file updating
message.

Serial
number

Response
to user

The user message is
given a serial number
which is sent to the
terminal and used for
communications control.

message
log

The serial number is
used to correlate the
message and response.

The message
is logged.

Layer 4
or higher

Common
network

Assurance
of correct
delivery

Assurance
of correct
delivery

Layer 4
or higher

Message
log

The serial number is
used to ensure message
integrity.

The serial number
is used for comm-
unications control.
The message is logged.

Applications
environment

The application
process updates
the files and
composes a response.

A file action log
is written including
the serial number.

The serial number
is written on the
the files.

Storage

Figure 33.4 Extending the use of the serial number to control file updating.

501

garded as a mental *closure* in the decision-making process. Sometimes it is merely an arbitrary stage in data entry. Periodically, either at a natural closure or not, the operator should be given a recap of what has been established up to that point and asked to check it. If the operator is carrying out a complex data-entry sequence, the record being built up might be checked once every 10 screens or every few minutes. When the operator has agreed that this is correct, the computer will store it.

This checkpoint is often of more value for operator failures than for machine failures. The operator will sometimes make mistakes or become confused in a lengthy dialogue, and the checkpoint will give him a point from which to recover. We do, in fact, have *two entirely different types of checkpoints: one intended for accuracy control and recovery from hardware failure, the other primarily intended for bewilderment control and recovery from human dialogue failure*. With some dialogue structures the two checkpoints can be the same.

GRACEFUL DEGRADATION   The failure of a computer system may be total, although often it is only partial. A terminal or its line may go dead, in which case the failure can appear total to the terminal operator. An on-line data file may become unavailable. The main computer may go out, but peripheral line-control computers are still capable of giving a limited response to the terminal. In other situations, functions for which a fast response to terminals is not mandatory may be temporarily shelved.

The term *fallback* is used to mean that the system modifies its mode of operation to circumvent the error. In doing so it may give a degraded form of service, but still carry out the urgent part of its task. A real-time system may have a hierarchy of fallback procedures to deal with different eventualities, each circumventing an interruption of the more important functions of the system.

The term *fail softly* is used to mean that, when a component goes out, the system uses an alternative means of processing rather than collapsing completely. The euphemism "graceful degradation" is also employed for this, and implies that the system should be planned so that fallback procedures cause as little disturbance as possible to the more vital work, and especially the more vital real-time functions.

It is desirable that the fallback techniques used cause no change in the structure of the man–machine dialogue. Certain types of messages will no longer be permissible when the failure occurs, but the formats of those that are permissible should be unchanged. Ideally a full-time operator is trained to deal with the fallback condition, and detailed written instructions should be given in the terminal operator's manual. A "non-dedicated" operator will have to be guided by the terminal itself.

BYPASS PROCEDURES   When a system does fail and terminals become inoperative, the terminal users must still have some means of dealing with the situations that confront them. The bank teller must still be able to deal with customers who come in and ask to withdraw money. The insurance clerk, the shop foreman, and the telephone salesgirl must have some standby procedure that enables them to carry on their work without real-time assistance from the computer.

The computer may make periodic printouts of the key information in its files in anticipation of failure. These may be transmitted to the terminal operators at night or when the terminal is not in use. In a bank, for example, the balances of all branch accounts containing more than $500 may be printed at that branch, so that no amount greater than this will be paid out when the terminal is inoperative without checking the listing.

Alternatively, the terminal operator may make a telephone call to a central location to obtain key information. The terminal may be used off-line to obtain replies from staff at a central location. In most cases the terminal operator carries on as well as possible, and the computer sorts out what has happened when it comes back on the air. When the computer is used to control in an optimum fashion the events that are happening, the events will still go on when the machine has failed, but will no longer be optimized. The nonoptimum bypass procedure in such cases represents a loss in revenue, which may be roughly calculable.

CONTROLS DURING
FAILURE PERIODS

It is important that the system controls do not allow errors to be entered into the files, or information to be lost, during the brief periods of difficulty when failures are being encountered.

Some of the application checks can be designed so that they are continuous throughout the failure period. This is especially important with systems handling cash or accountable items.

When a bank teller's terminal ceases to obtain on-line responses, he can, on most systems, use the same terminal *off-line* to print transactions that are dealt with while the system is out. He saves these until the system is back on the air and then enters them. The check totals or running totals that are kept should be used to control this off-line procedure, ensuring that nothing is lost or double-entered. The terminal in a system well designed for control has its own accumulators. When the computer failure occurs, the teller makes the terminal print out control totals, kept in its own accumulators, showing net cash. These will also have been recorded in the computer up to the time when the failure occurred. The off-line operation continues, and, when the computer becomes usable again, the operator prints the totals. He then enters all the transactions into the computer, which updates its files accordingly. The computer totals are then printed and must agree with the terminal's off-line ones.

Continuity of the use of control totals or other checks throughout the period of bypass operation is important to ensure that nothing is misprocessed during this difficult period.

In general, the use of function distribution and processing distribution enables end-user machines to give continuity of control procedures and enables systems analysts to design safe fallback procedures. The intelligent terminals so employed need to be linked into the network protocols for integrity control.

REFERENCE

Martin, J., *Security, Accuracy and Privacy in Computer Systems,* Prentice Hall, Englewood Cliffs, NJ, 1973.

34 DEADLOCKS

Network deadlock is one of the worst things that can happen to a network. It has plagued various networks including some quite simple ones. The network suddenly jams with immovable traffic. It often takes the operators some time to realize that it has happened. When they do realize they may be unsure what to do about it. They usually have to recover manually by purging messages from the network nodes and restarting. It is usually necessary to deactivate the user applications. User messages are lost. Restarting does not remove the original cause of the deadlock and it may happen again. In some cases it has happened soon after restarting because the same traffic conditions are present.

Deadlocks are caused by a basic flaw in the control mechanisms. The causes of deadlocks are often subtle and very difficult to find. When they are found they usually cannot be corrected quickly. New control mechanisms are needed. So the network remains in a deadlock-prone condition for some time. The causes of deadlocks have usually been latent in manufacturers' or contractors' software. Sometimes an architectural concept has been inherently deadlock-prone.

It is very desirable that manufacturers and software producers understand the causes of deadlocks and test their protocols well enough to avoid them before such networks are implemented. Deadlocking networks are extremely objectionable to customers.

It is necessary to have protocols which avoid deadlocks, and also a means of *automatically* backing out of a deadlock if it does occur, as gracefully as possible.

THREE LAYERS OF DEADLOCKS

Deadlocks can be caused at three layers.

First, the *transport subsystem* can have traffic jams, some of which lock it solidly. Second, Session Service protocols can deadlock. While a transport deadlock may paralyze *all* traffic, a Layer

4 deadlock may affect only one node and its sessions. Third, the *application* subsystem may cause deadlocks, such as data base deadlocks. It may be difficult to tell which layer is causing the deadlock, who is to blame, or who should fix it.

TYPES   Some types of deadlocks are subtle and the implementor
OF DEADLOCKS   may be caught by surprise. Some are seemingly simple
                             and easily avoidable. All the following deadlocks have
happened in practice.

Pacing Deadlock

A concentrator is designed to stop polling the terminal controllers downstream of it when its buffers are full. It fills up with messages going to the terminal controllers but cannot deliver any of them until it receives a *pacing* message from a terminal controller. However, it cannot receive the pacing message because it has stopped polling.

The reason for this deadlock, and many like it, is that the control signals, in this case pacing, are sent like ordinary data messages. If the data messages cannot move then the control messages cannot move either, but the control messages are vital for unlocking the jam.

Control messages ought to travel on a separate subchannel. This may be achieved by giving the control messages a higher *priority* than the data messages, and always making them short so that buffers are permanently reserved for them. The control message may carry only one byte of information.

Deadwood Deadlock

A concentrator, cluster controller, or other network node fills up with undeliverable messages because the destination to which they are to be delivered has failed, or some line or device along the path has failed. This undeliverable traffic may back up to other nodes.

If this was caused by the failure of *one* terminal there is clearly a basic flow control fault. The source should not keep sending messages with no acknowledgements. However, the failure may be a computer or cluster controller which serves *many* users each of which by itself has adequate flow control. In total the traffic in flight to the inaccessible users is enough to jam a concentrator.

This jam is more likely to happen when *continuous* flow control is used, i.e., a source sends several messages to a user before receiving an acknowledgment to compensate for the in-flight delay. It is perhaps more prone to happen with communications satellite protocols, because here many messages may be in-flight before any acknowledgment is required.

In some packet-switching networks, undeliverable packets have roamed about from node to node. Each node routes them to somewhere else but none can reach its destination. Such roaming undeliverable packets need to be detected and deleted or retuned to their senders.

Every network must have some means of dealing with undeliverable messages. The best way may be to destroy them and notify their sender of the reason. The sender retains the messages until the destination user acknowledges correct receipt, so that the sender can retransmit them if necessary.

It is very important that the failure of any one component not paralyze or flood the network.

Reassembly Lockup

A serious form of jam called *reassembly lockup* plagued the original ARPA network when long messages from different sources converged on one destination. We will describe two kinds of reassembly lockup.

The destination IMP receives and acknowledges the first packets of several multipacket messages. It has only a certain amount of memory available for the assembly of messages, and when it starts to receive a message it does not know how many packets will arrive for that message. It may attempt the reception of more messages than it can handle. It is then in serious trouble. It runs out of memory for reception of more packets, but cannot deliver to the destination host the incomplete messages which are clogging its memory. The neighboring nodes continue to transmit packets to it but it cannot accept them. After several attempts the neighboring nodes try to send the packets to it by a different route. But the destination IMP is locked solid. The traffic piles up in neighboring areas like city streets after an accident.

The RFNM mechanism of Fig. 20.2 prevented a destination from being flooded by *one* source. It does not prevent excessive traffic reaching a destination node from *multiple* sources—one message from each. To prevent that a reservation mechanism was added to the ARPANET protocols. The buffer required for reassembly of a multipacket message must be reserved before that message is sent.

Reassembly Lockup with Reservation

Figure 20.3 shows the ARPANET mechanism for making a reservation for buffer space to reassemble multipacket messages. The IMP which serves the computer originating a multipacket message sends a REQUEST FOR ALLOCATION control packet to the destination IMP. If the destination IMP has space available it sends back an ALLOCATION control packet telling the source IMP that space has been reserved for its message. The source IMP then sends the data packets.

When the data packets have been delivered, a RFNM is sent to the source which contains an ALLOCATION message, i.e., buffers for another message are automatically reserved.

The reservation protocol lengthens the response time of the network somewhat, which is undesirable for interactive traffic. Most interactive traffic consists of short messages, often single-packet messages. No reservations were made for single-packet messages because these *do not have to be reassembled;* they are delivered to the destination host as soon as they arrive.

It was previously thought that if a buffer reservation is made for every message that has to be reassembled, there could be no reassembly lockout. That sounds logical. However, a more subtle form of lockout occurred.

Occasionally the destination IMP has no buffers remaining for single-packet messages. Single-packet messages are on their way to it; consequently the neighboring IMP's become full of single-packet messages waiting to be sent to it (Fig. 34.1). The packets are relayed in a first-in first-out (FIFO) manner, and because the adjacent nodes are clogged with single-packet messages the packets for longer messages for which space has been reserved cannot reach their destination. The destination IMP holds the reserved space which can never be filled and which keeps other packets out.

Delivery-sequence Lockup

The previous lockup can be avoided if the destination node accepts single-packet messages and discards them if it has no space. These packets will then have to be retransmitted by their source node. They will not clog the neighboring nodes, *A, B,* and *C* in Fig. 34.1. ARPA adopted this procedure along with reservations for multi-packet messages.

The destination node was constrained, however, to deliver the messages between two user processes *in sequence,* as specified by a sequence number. Figure 34.2 illustrates a situation in which this requirement caused a lockup.

Multipacket message *N* is received and is immediately followed by single-packet message *N* + 1. The latter is discarded because there is no space for it. Message *N* is delivered to the destination host, and this frees up some buffers. A RFNM can then be

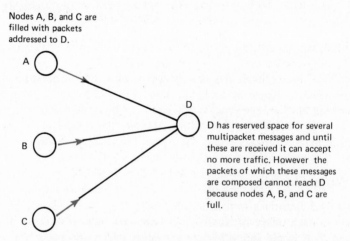

Nodes A, B, and C are
filled with packets
addressed to D.

D has reserved space for several
multipacket messages and until
these are received it can accept
no more traffic. However the
packets of which these messages
are composed cannot reach D
because nodes A, B, and C are
full.

Figure 34.1   Example of a reassembly lockup.

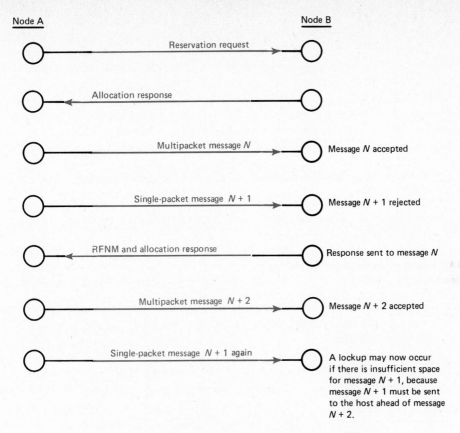

Node A

Node B

Reservation request

Allocation response

Multipacket message N — Message N accepted

Single-packet message $N + 1$ — Message $N + 1$ rejected

RFNM and allocation response — Response sent to message N

Multipacket message $N + 2$ — Message $N + 2$ accepted

Single-packet message $N + 1$ again — A lockup may now occur if there is insufficient space for message $N + 1$, because message $N + 1$ must be sent to the host ahead of message $N + 2$.

Figure 34.2 Example of a delivery-sequence lockup.

sent to the originating host, along with an automatic indication that space is reserved for its next multipacket message. Multipacket message $N + 2$ arrives and this again leaves no further space. Single-packet message $N + 1$ arrives again, but again has to be discarded again for space reasons. However, message $N + 2$ cannot be delivered to the host ahead of $N + 1$, so a lockup exists.

If $N + 1$ had been rejected or delayed because of transmission errors, a similar situation could have occurred.

Store-and-forward Lockup

Figure 34.3 illustrates a store-and-forward lockup. Two adjacent nodes want to send packets to each other, but each is full and cannot accept them. If A could send one packet to B, A would then have space to receive a packet from B and the deadlock would be broken.

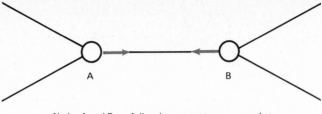

Nodes A and B are full and can accept no more packets.
A wishes to send packets to B, or via B.
B wishes to send packets to A, or via A.

Figure 34.3 Example of a direct store-and-forward lockup.

The previous lockup occurred with multipacket messages. Store-and-forward lockups can occur with single packets.

Indirect Store-and-forward Lockup

An indirect version of store-and-forward lockup can occur involving several nodes all trying to send traffic to one another in a pattern something like that in Fig. 34.4. Each is full and cannot become free because the node it is trying to send to is also full. Hence deadlock.

This may occur only very infrequently under heavy traffic conditions. However, there must be some means of avoiding or dealing with the situation.

SESSION SERVICE AND APPLICATION DEADLOCKS   The deadlocks discussed above relate to the transport subsystem. Deadlocks also occur in the software external to the transport subsystem, and also occasionally in the users' code.

Pacing mechanisms are used external to the transport subsystem. They have a variety of functions of which one important one is the regulation of traffic to synchronous devices such as remote line printer so it can print at maximum speed. All such pacing mechanisms need to be designed with caution because of the danger of deadlocks.

A subnetwork is sometimes used external to a common carrier network, for example in a system which uses both a manufacturer's network architecture and a valued-added carrier. To avoid deadlocks in the subnetwork, control messages have occasionally to be passed quickly through the carrier network. Nondelivery of a control message could deadlock the subnetwork.

DEADLY EMBRACE   A particularly important category of deadlock is that associated with distributed data, in which different users simultaneously updating records could cause deadlock.

It is necessary for a data user to *lock* a record between reading it and writing back

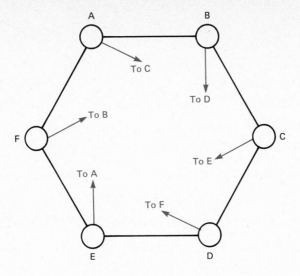

Buffers in all nodes are full
with packets flowing clockwise.

Figure 34.4 Example of an indirect store-and-forward lockup. There are many possible variations of this lockup, which may occur very infrequently.

an updated copy. This is to prevent another user from updating it between the first user's READ and WRITE. The users in question might be geographically separate.

A situation which is more difficult to control occurs when the updating process requires two records. Record Y is read, but cannot be updated until record Z is read. Record Y must be locked during the updating process. We therefore have the following sequence of events:

> Transaction A: 1. Locks record Y.
>   2. Reads record Y.
>   3. Reads record Z.
>   4. Updates record Y.
>   5. Unlocks record Y.

A situation referred to as a *deadly embrace* can occur if another transaction locks record Z and cannot release it until it has read record Y. The program for transaction B is as follows:

> Transaction B: 1. Locks record Z.
>   2. Reads record Z.
>   3. Reads record Y.
>   4. Updates record Z.
>   5. Unlocks record Y.

The two transactions form a deadly embrace as follows:

> Transaction A locks record Y.
>
> Transaction A reads record Y.
>
> Transaction B locks record Z.
>
> Transaction A tries to read record A but it is locked.
>
> Transaction B tries to read record Y but it is locked.

Both wait for the records they want to become unlocked but neither is programmed to release the record it has locked.

Deadlock!

In the above example, records Z and A may be in different geographical locations. More complex still, the deadly embrace may relate more than two transactions, for example:

> Transaction A locks record X until it has read Y.
>
> Transaction B locks record Y until it has read Z.
>
> Transaction C locks record Z until it has read X.

Figure 34.5 illustrates these deadly embrace situations.

There are two ways to deal with the deadly embrace problem. First, prevent it from happening, and second, back out of it when it does happen. Some software for a centralized data system prevents it from happening by establishing controls at message scheduling time. This would be difficult to accomplish efficiently in a distributed data system; therefore it is desirable to be able automatically to back out of deadly embrace situations.

To deal with a deadly embrace the software must detect that a transaction is hung up, and have a means of temporarily terminating one of the programs that is causing the deadlock. It must back out of the activities of the terminated program without affecting the integrity of the stored data. This back-out and subsequent restart of the program should be done automatically and be transparent to the program itself. To accomplish this the application programs require *synchronization points*. The system saves the transactions following a synchronization point until the program makes a *commitment*, i.e., the data is correctly updated. The system will back out of the dead-locked program to its synchronization point, pause long enough for the other dead-locked transactions to finish, and then restart the program.

If the programs in question are in different locations, rapid communication through the network with control messages is necessary. These may be INTERRUPT messages sent by Session Service software or by user programs or software.

Deadly embrace situations can sometimes occur when network resources other than data are used.

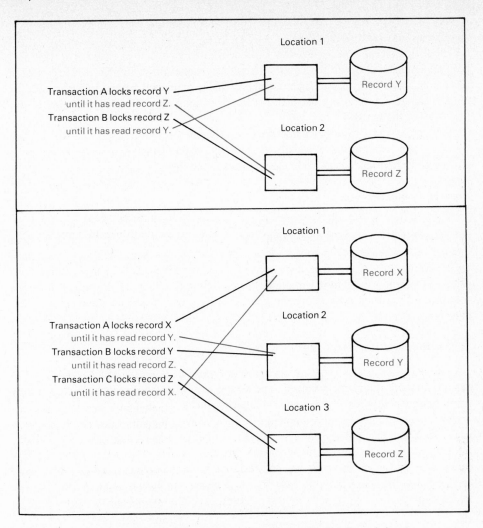

Figure 34.5　Deadly embrace situations with distributed data.

DEADLOCK
SOLUTIONS
We can make several general comments about techniques
which help avoid deadlocks.

Separate Control Channels

The control signals needed to unlock a jam must be able to flow during the dead-lock. There must, in effect, be a separate subchannel for control signals. This can be accomplished by giving the control messages priority so that they always jump the queues of data messages, and ensuring that buffer space for brief control messages is permanently reserved in the nodes.

It is important to recognize that deadlocks often have causes external to the transport subsystem and hence the control signal subchannel must be able to carry session service and user control messages as well as those employed by the transport subsystem. A public data network needs a facility for passing *user* INTERRUPT signals rapidly through the network.

Some systems have been implemented without a priority subchannel for control signals. Such systems have usually had deadlock problems, and have to resort to clumsy and often inadequate techniques for resolving them.

Reserve Capacity

Nodes which run out of buffer space are often the cause of deadlocks. To back out of such situations each node might have a little reserve capacity which is brought into use only when a lockup occurs. In a packet-switching system the nodes could have two overflow buffers [1]. The nodes would move certain packets to their destinations using the overflow buffers in an attempt to break the deadlock. The jammed traffic is shifted a packet at a time using the special buffers which can be used for no other purpose.

Destruction and Retransmission

Usually the easiest way of dealing with jammed or undeliverable packets is to delete them and notify their sender. The sender may store copies of them so that they are not permanently lost if the network deletes them.

A source node may store packets with Layer 3 until the destination node acknowledges their correct delivery. A user, Layer 4, or higher layer software will be likely to do the same. The user or higher layer software in some cases duplicates the safety precautions of Layer 3 if these are not designed in an integrated fashion. The user of an X.25 network, for example, may feel it necessary to have end-to-end precautions which duplicate to some extent the end-DCE-to-end-DCE controls of the carrier.

Automatic Back-out

When a lockup occurs it can paralyze a network. Most packet-switching network technicians have their war stories about the night of the great traffic lockup.

It is possible to restore a network to normal working by *manual* intervention. Often it has proved necessary to clear manually and restart the entire network. Manual restart has many problems associated with it, including the fact that it is sometimes very slow. It is highly desirable for a network to have its own automatic recovery, possibly sending RESET or RESTART packets to the users as described in Chapter 32. It should be able to detect a condition of severe congestion before it finally causes a lockup, and if a lockup does occur, to back out of it as quickly as possible.

Solutions to Reassembly Lockup

Reassembly lockup, which was the most serious form of lockup on the ARPA network, can be avoided in several ways.

First, reassembly lockup does not occur if *only single-packet messages* are sent. The hosts could be made to slice up and reassemble their own messages so that this is possible. Second, the lockout could be avoided if the destination IMPS's could pass incomplete messages to the receiving host. Third, unreassemblable messages could be deleted and their source hosts asked to retransmit them. None of these solutions was regarded as satisfactory because they complicate the protocols needed in the hosts. The intent of the design was that the network should appear transparent to the hosts, and that they should not have to be concerned with reassembling or resequencing packets or retransmitting the messages.

A third solution is to give the nodes a *backing store* so that they can temporarily move incomplete messages out of their main memory when lockouts occur. This would increase the cost of the nodes substantially, and lessen their reliability.

The solution which was adopted on the ARPA and similar networks was to prevent the originating nodes from sending a multipacket message until they were sure that enough space had been reserved in the destination node for its reception. To accomplish this, more control messages were needed. Many uses of networks consist of a rapid interchange of single-packet messages, and the overhead of sending reservation messages, and waiting for responses to them would increase the network response time and lower its traffic capacity. Single-packet messages were therefore sent without reservations, but had to be discarded if there was not enough space. Jams still occurred with this procedure (Fig. 34.2) but much less frequently. The jam in Fig. 34.2 could be avoided with appropriate use of the *window* mechanism for flow control of both single- and multipacket messages, as described in Chapter 20.

Decouple the Transport Network

ARPA repeatedly had to redesign the protocols of the transport network. However, the ARPA transmission protocols could be changed without affecting the end users because of the decision to make the transport subsystem independent of the higher-level protocols. This is an application of the principle of *layered* architecture. The transport network should be decoupled from the layers which use it.

Keep It Simple

Many deadlock problems can be avoided by using certain simplifications in the network.

Some deadlocks arise only in mesh-structured networks or networks with alternate routing strategies. Deadlocks are more easily avoided in tree-structured networks.

Moreover, many of the problems that develop are related to multipacket messages or to the requirement to deliver the messages to the using machine in a specified sequence. If the transport subsystem handles only single packets and is not required to deliver them in a fixed sequence, the problems of reassembly and resequencing, which cause most of the trouble, are avoided.

Because of this, many versions of networks are found which avoid the complexities associated with packet resequencing, alternate routing within a session, and selective repeat error control. Datagram networks are simple and relatively easy to control. The early implementations of IBM's SNA systems used only tree or loop structures with no alternate routing. This simplified the protocols in what was already a highly complex architecture. Early implementations of other manufacturers' network architectures contained similar simplifications.

Thorough Simulation

There are many subtleties and rarely occurring problems in multiple-route networks. These must be dealt with by the software and control mechanisms. The experience to date is that it is very difficult to debug network software completely because it must handle *all possible* traffic conditions.

It is important that network software should be tested by simulation as thoroughly as possible before networks become live. An *operational* network is an unfortunate place to discover an unexpected form of deadlock.

35 SECURITY AND PRIVACY

Security and privacy are important because many people in many places have access to a computer network. The information stored in some of the network machines may be of great value to a corporation. It must not be lost, stolen, or damaged. It is important to protect the data and programs from hardware and software failures, from catastrophies, and from criminals, vandals, incompetents, and people who would misuse it.

A network is often shared by users for whom security is of little or no importance, and users for whom it is vital. It may be shared by users who are highly responsible with urgent business and others who are irresponsible and likely to try anything.

Security refers to the protection of resources from damage and the protection of data against accidental or intentional disclosure to unauthorized persons or unauthorized modifications or destruction.

Privacy refers to the rights of individuals and organizations to determine for themselves when, how, and to what extent information about them is to be transmitted to others.

Although the technology of privacy is closely related to that of security, privacy is an issue which goes far beyond computer centers and networks. To a large extent it is a problem of society. To preserve the privacy of data about individuals, solutions are needed beyond technical solutions. Future society, dependent on a massive use of networks and data banks, will need new legal and social controls if the degree of privacy of personal information that is cherished today is to be maintained.

Data can be locked up in computers as securely as they can be locked up in a bank vault. Nevertheless, the data on many systems cannot be regarded as being highly secure because insufficient attention has been paid to the design or implementation of the security procedures.

Security is a highly complex subject because there are so many different aspects to it. A systems designer responsible for security needs to be familiar with all features of the system because the system can be attacked or security breached in highly diverse ways. Sometimes a great amount of effort is put into one aspect of security and other aspects are neglected. If a moat is seen as the way to make a castle secure, a great amount of security engineering could be applied to the moat. It could be very wide, and full of hungry piranha fish, and could have a fiercely guarded drawbridge. However, this alone would not make the castle secure. A determined intruder could tunnel under the moat. A security designer sometimes becomes so involved with one aspect of security design that he fails to see other ways of breaking into the system. It takes considerable knowledge and ingenuity to see all the possible ways.

EIGHT ESSENTIALS

Box 35.1 lists eight essentials of network security:

1. The users of a network must be positively *identifiable* before they use it.

2. The systems and possibly also the network management must be able to check that their actions are *authorized*.

3. Their actions should be *monitored* so that if they do something wrong they are likely to be found out.

4. Data, hardware, and software should be *protected* from fire, theft, or other forms of destruction.

5. They should be *locked* to prevent unauthorized use.

6. The data should be *reconstructible* because, however good the precautions, accidents sometimes happen.

7. The data should be *auditable*. Failure to audit computer systems adequately has permitted some of the world's biggest crimes.

8. The network and systems should be *tamperproof*. Ingenious programmers should not be able to bypass the controls.

9. Transmission should be *failsafe* so that when errors or failures occur messages are not lost, double-processed, or irrecoverably garbled.

10. Transmissions should be *private* with some being protected from eavesdropping and tampering by cryptography.

LAYERS
OF PROTECTION

The nucleus of security control lies in the technical design of the network and computer systems. Without tight controls in the hardware and software, no other precautions can make the system secure.

Design of tightly controlled systems, however, is not enough by itself. Several types of protection are needed. Security can be represented by another layer diagram as shown in Fig. 35.1. The layer of technical controls is surrounded by that of physical

BOX 35.1   The essence of network security

Network users should be:

• IDENTIFIABLE

Their actions should be:

• AUTHORIZED
• MONITORED

Data, hardware, and software should be:

• PROTECTED
• LOCKED

Data should be:

• RECONSTRUCTIBLE
• AUDITABLE
• TAMPERPROOF

Transmission should be:

• FAILSAFE
• PRIVATE

security. This refers to locks on the doors, guards, alarms, and other means of preventing unauthorized access, and includes fire precautions, protection of stored data files, and so forth. It is not enough to have good hardware and software if disks can be stolen or the tape library destroyed by fire.

The next layer is that of administrative controls to ensure that the system is used correctly. The programmers and data processing staff must be controlled so that they do not misuse the system. Controlled computer room and program testing procedures must be enforced. The administrative controls extend beyond the data processing section to the user departments, scattered far across the network, the auditors, and general management.

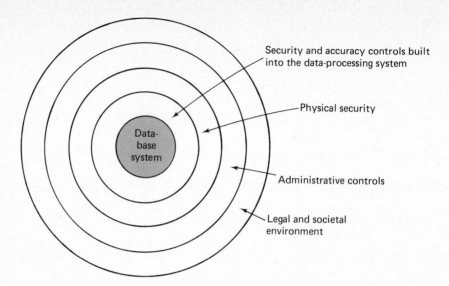

Figure 35.1   Four layers of control needed for data-base security and privacy.

The layers in Fig. 35.1 are not entirely separate. Physical security is not irrelevant when designing system techniques. The question of physical security affects what transmission and systems safeguards are used. The administrative procedures are very much related to the system design, especially with a real-time or terminal-based system. The auditors need to be involved in the system design, and the views of general management concerning security very much affect the system design.

The outermost layer of Fig. 35.1 is by far the most problematical. When the network revolution has run its course society will be very different. Many controls will no doubt have evolved, seeking to maximize the benefits and minimize the dangers of a technology of which George Orwell never dreamed. A legal framework is beginning to emerge in some countries which will relate to computers and networks.

TYPES OF SECURITY   There is a wide diversity of different types of security ex-
EXPOSURE   posure, most of them relating to the computer center, in-
                               dependent of networks [1]. Catastrophes such as major
embezzlements have resulted in dramatic headlines, but by far the most common cause of computer calamities is human carelessness and accidents. One company reported ''a $3.8 million deficiency'' caused by an error in cutover. Usually failures are less spectacular and more frequent.

Distributed systems, if they are poorly designed or loosely managed, could increase the probability of accidents through carelessness. Data, instead of residing in one highly secure center, may be distributed among locations with less protection. The greater complexity of a distributed system has sometimes increased the frequency of problems. Control, instead of residing in one location with one management, may be scattered.

A major exposure introduced by networks is the ease with which persons and machines can gain access to a computer center. It is necessary to prevent unauthorized access and unauthorized communication between machines.

Another exposure is that data transmitted may be seen by unauthorized persons, recorded, diverted, or even modified by tampering with lines or switching nodes.

THREE-LEVEL ATTACK　　Each security exposure must be attacked in three ways:

1. Minimize the Probability of It Happening at All

A major part of fire precautions should be preventive, and this is just as important with all other security breaches. Would-be embezzlers should be discouraged from ever beginning.

2. Minimize the Damage if It Does Happen

An intruder who succeeds in bypassing the physical or programmed controls that were intended to keep him out should still be very restricted in what he can accomplish. A fire once started, should be prevented from spreading. If the security procedures are compromised, it must be possible to limit the harm that could result. Some security designers have made the grave error of supposing that their preventive measures will always work.

3. Design a Method of Recovering from the Damage

It *must* be possible to reconstruct vital records or whole files if they become accidentally or willfully damaged or lost. It *must* be possible to recover from a fire sufficiently quickly to keep the business running. If an authorized person obtains a security code or a file of network passwords, it must be possible to change these quickly so that they are of no use to him. It is important to attack the security problem *in depth,* and recovery procedures are vital to the overall plan. The designers of the preventive mechanisms must not be allowed to become so infatuated with their security schemes that they neglect recovery techniques.

The various forms of failsafe recovery and deadlock avoidance discussed in the previous chapters are important. Along with these it is necessary to lock out unauthorized network users and prevent wiretapping or recording of the data transmitted.

PRIVACY LOCKS　　　　The question of *who* is authorized to do *what* on a network is very important. Before each operation a computer should check to verify that it is an authorized operation.

Authorization schemes vary from being very simple to highly complex. One of the simplest schemes requires that the user key in a *password* which only he should know. If it is an acceptable password for the program or file in question, he is allowed to proceed. The CODASYL Data Description Language uses *privacy locks* appended to the data. The privacy lock is a single value which is specified in the schema description. Data locked in this way cannot be used by a program unless the program provides a value which matches the privacy lock. It is rather like the user of a bank safe needing to know the combination which will open the safe. Unlike a bank safe, however, different combinations can be used for all different data types. The locking mechanism can be much more intricate than with a bank safe.

Figure 35.2 shows a possible sequence of events when a terminal is used, showing the variety of locks that could be applied. No one link through a network is likely to have all of these locks, but should have several.

AUTHORIZATION SCHEMES

The locks which are built into systems and networks are related to authorization schemes and tables saying who is authorized to do what, or what interconnections are permitted.

The authorization tables can relate to:

1. Individual users.
2. Groups or categories of users.
3. Security levels (top secret, corporate confidential, etc.).
4. Application programs.
5. Time of day (like a time lock on a bank vault).
6. Terminal or terminal location.
7. Network node (e.g., host computer, cluster controller, concentrator).
8. Transaction types.
9. Combinations of these.

Restrictions can be placed on the relationships between six different entities on a network—the users, the terminal or input/output devices that are used, the network nodes such as host computers or terminal cluster controllers, the application programs, the data sets or elements of data, and the volumes such as tapes or disks on which the data are recorded. Locks may be implemented on any of these relationships, and alarms may be used to bring attention to any suspected violation.

Figure 35.3 summarizes the relationships that may be locked:

1. The user himself may be identified and locked out of the terminal, or out of the node, program, data, or volume he requests.

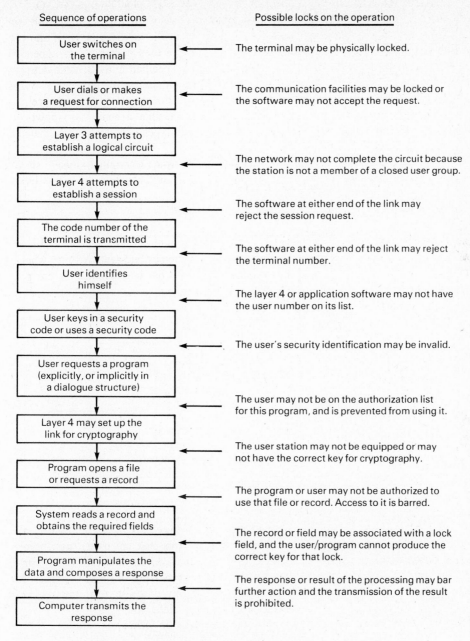

Sequence of operations	Possible locks on the operation
User switches on the terminal	The terminal may be physically locked.
User dials or makes a request for connection	The communication facilities may be locked or the software may not accept the request.
Layer 3 attempts to establish a logical circuit	The network may not complete the circuit because the station is not a member of a closed user group.
Layer 4 attempts to establish a session	The software at either end of the link may reject the session request.
The code number of the terminal is transmitted	The software at either end of the link may reject the terminal number.
User identifies himself	The layer 4 or application software may not have the user number on its list.
User keys in a security code or uses a security code	The user's security identification may be invalid.
User requests a program (explicitly, or implicitly in a dialogue structure)	The user may not be on the authorization list for this program, and is prevented from using it.
Layer 4 may set up the link for cryptography	The user station may not be equipped or may not have the correct key for cryptography.
Program opens a file or requests a record	The program or user may not be authorized to use that file or record. Access to it is barred.
System reads a record and obtains the required fields	The record or field may be associated with a lock field, and the user/program cannot produce the correct key for that lock.
Program manipulates the data and composes a response	The response or result of the processing may bar further action and the transmission of the result is prohibited.
Computer transmits the response	

Figure 35.2 A possible sequence of events when a terminal is used, and locks which could be applied at each stage.

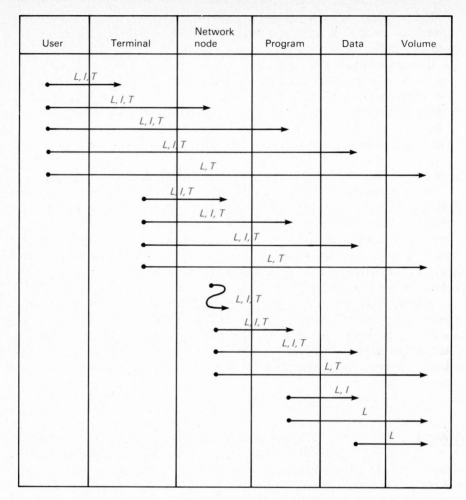

L = based on security *levels* (top secret, secret, corporate confidential).
I = based on *individual* items or persons, or groupings of these.
T = based on *time* of day (like a time lock on a bank vault).

Figure 35.3 Relationships covered by locks, alarms, and authorization tables.

2. A specific terminal may be in an insecure area and therefore be locked out of certain nodes, programs, data, or volumes.

3. A node such as a computer or terminal cluster controller may be locked out of other nodes, programs, data, or volumes.

4. A program may be prevented from accessing certain data or volumes.

5. Certain data may have a high security classification and so be prevented from being stored on any volume that has a lower classification.

The locks may be based on security classification levels, on the individual entities or groups of entities, or on time. These are indicated by the letters L, I, and T, repectively, in Fig. 35.3.

If security classification levels are used, the types of entities may each be assigned a classification, such as CONFIDENTIAL, SECRET, and so on. If a user is not security cleared for SECRET information, he will not be permitted to use a terminal classified for SECRET work, or permitted to use any program data, or volume classified SECRET. SECRET data may not be transmitted to an unclassified terminal. If a volume is not labeled SECRET, then SECRET data may not be written on it. And so on. As indicated in Fig. 35.3, any of the relationships may be based on such classification levels. There may be any number of levels.

Much greater precision is obtained by basing the relationships on individual users or entities. User A is only permitted to use program B, data C, and volumes D and E. Program X is only permitted to access data Y and Z. Or a certain file, volume, or program is labeled so that it can only be used by the person who created it. Some such schemes result in the need for large authorization tables. To lessen the size of the tables, the individual persons, items, or data entities can be arranged into groups, and the locks based on groupings.

Finally, the system may have time locks. Like a bank vault door, access may be permitted only at certain times of day. A *nocturnal* intruder will not be able to access data even if he knows the necessary passwords or security codes. A terminal in a secure area on the prime shift may be classified as insecure on other shifts. If a person is detected trying to use a magnetic-stripe card key on a terminal out of hours, he will immediately trigger an alarm.

ALARMS

To keep burglars out of a building or vault the locks on the windows and doors will be backed up by burglar alarms. The locks on networks, and surveillance methods designed to detect unauthorized entry, can sound alarms. Some systems send an immediate alarm message to a security officer's terminal, and possibly ring a bell there. Some systems inform a suitable authority at the user's location. Some do both. The potential intruder may be locked out of the system, or may be kept talking harmlessly while the local security officer investigates.

The existence of alarms, but not the details of how they work or what triggers them, should be well publicized to act as a psychological deterrent.

IDENTIFYING
THE TERMINAL USER

With some users of networks it is necessary to identify positively the person at the terminal. Until he is identified he should not be permitted to have access to any sensitive data or to make any modifications to the files. On other systems, it is not necessary to identify the terminal user, providing the computer knows which terminal it is, because only security-cleared personnel can use that particular terminal. There are three ways in which a person can be identified:

1. By Personal Physical Characteristics

For example, a device can be used for reading and transmitting a person's fingerprints or thumbprint, and the computer can have a program for identifying this. Less expensive, his telephone voice, speaking certain prearranged digits or words, can be transmitted to the computer; the computer will have a program for recognizing his voice by comparing his speech against a stored *voice print*. Some systems have a device which measures the lengths of a person's fingers on one hand, this being a set of variables which differs from one person to another like fingerprints, and not too expensive to measure and encode. Physical identification schemes are likely to be the most expensive of the three ways to recognize a person.

2. By Something Carried

A terminal user can carry a badge, card, or key. He inserts the badge into a terminal badge reader or the key into the terminal itself. Magnetically encoded cards like credit cards are used for this purpose.

3. By Something Known or Memorized

He can memorize a password or answer a prearranged set of questions. Techniques of this type require no special hardware. They are the least expensive of the three, and under most circumstances they can be made reasonably secure if applied intelligently. The user's identification number, however, must not be a number that might be guessed, such as his birth date or car license number.

Keys, locks, machine-readable badges, and credit cards all have one disadvantage: They can be lost. The user may fail to remove them from the terminal after the transaction is complete. If a sign-on action is used along with a badge or card, the user may forget to sign off. It may be possible to duplicate the key or badge. For these reasons, the use of the key, card, or badge is not necessarily more secure than identification of a terminal operator by a memorized security code or a sequence of questions. Keys on banking system terminals and badges in certain airline systems have been in operation for years, although nobody pretends that they would keep out an ingenious and persistent imposter, any more than an apartment lock would keep out an ingenious and determined burglar; but they are better than no lock at all.

On some military systems the terminal has a small fence around it, and the operator cannot leave the area without opening a gate with the same badge or key that he uses on the terminal.

A password has been used on a number of systems to identify the user. In its simplest form, all the terminal users, or users of a given category or at a given location, know the same password; until this is typed in, the system will take no action. For any reasonable measure of security, however, it is desirable to provide each of the individual terminal users with a different security code. He must type this code into the terminal. The computer will then check what the individual using that code is permitted to do. On some systems, the user keys in his own personal identification number, followed by a security code which has been issued to him. The computer checks that he has entered the correct security code and that the transactions he enters are authorized for that individual. A table such as that in Fig. 35.4 may be used. As a result of this check, categories of authorization may be established indicating what types of action the individual is permitted to take.

The security code must be changed periodically. On some systems, it is changed once per month. Each terminal user must take care not to let anyone else know his code. For example, the code for a user may be mailed in such a way that the code is

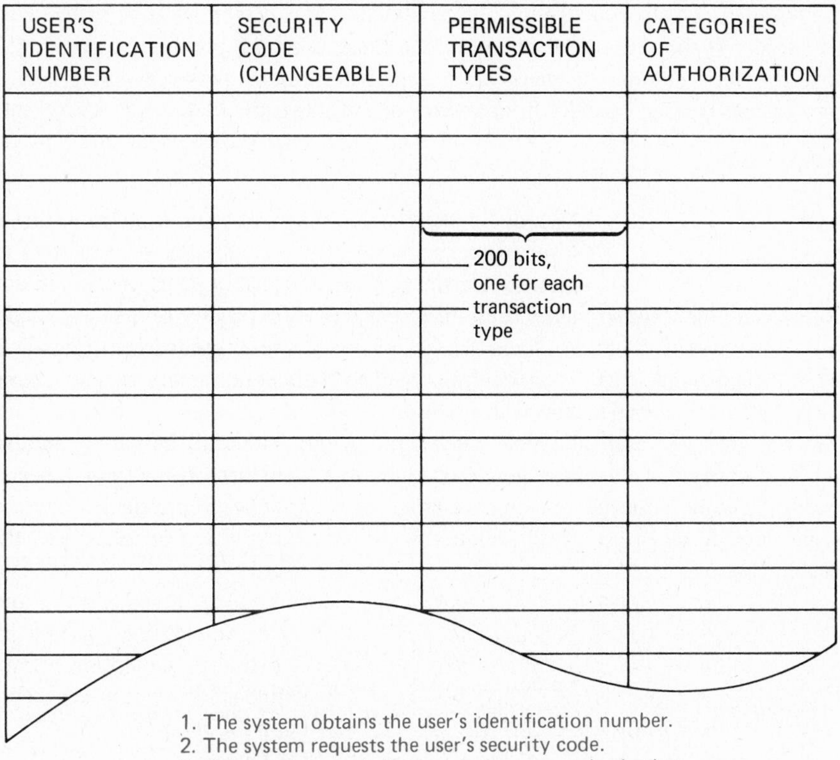

USER'S IDENTIFICATION NUMBER	SECURITY CODE (CHANGEABLE)	PERMISSIBLE TRANSACTION TYPES	CATEGORIES OF AUTHORIZATION
		200 bits, one for each transaction type	

1. The system obtains the user's identification number.
2. The system requests the user's security code.
3. If the security code is correct, the system checks that the user was permitted to enter the transaction type he did enter.
4. The listed categories of authorization are then used to control access to the data base.

Figure 35.4   Use of a simple authorization table.

on a detachable piece of card with nothing else written on it. The receiver is instructed to detach this piece of card immediately. If the card with the security code on it is lost, anybody finding it is unlikely to associate it with the correct personnel number. It must be possible to issue a user with a new security code whenever he wants it. If he feels that security has been compromised in any way—for example, by someone looking over his shoulder and seeing his security code as he types it in the terminal—then he should be able to ask immediately for a new security code. On some terminals, the security code is automatically prevented from being printed or displayed as it is keyed in.

The disadvantage of the password or security code technique is that the code can be given to another person without any physical loss by the giver and without anything having to be duplicated. There is no physical evidence of the other person's possession of it. This technique must, therefore, be accompanied by rigorous controls and a serious attempt to catch, quickly and automatically, any person who is using another person's code. If the terminal users think that there is a high probability that they will be caught if they attempt to enter the system with another person's code, then they may be deterred psychologically from making an invalid entry.

MESSAGE AUTHENTICATION

Message authentication refers to steps taken to ensure that a message came from a legitimate source or goes to a legitimate destination. It is possible in a network that data might be accidentally misrouted. There have been cases of highly sensitive data being printed at the wrong location. Even the telephone network occasionally gets wrong numbers. It is possible that the misrouting could be deliberate, or that an active wiretap is being used by an intruder who wants to gain access to files.

In one message authentication scheme the sender and receiver put unique pseudorandom numbers on the messages. Both have the same set of numbers. They may both have these numbers stored or may generate them. The receiving software compares the number on the received message with what it expects, and takes action if it is not identical.

CLOSED USER GROUPS

Some transport networks, including those using the CCITT X.25 standard, employ the concept of *closed user groups*. A closed user group is a defined set of user machines or processes; they can communicate with one another but can have no communication with machines or processes outside the group. A person at a terminal outside the group cannot use the network to contact a machine or process in the group. On one network there may be many closed user groups, and many users who are freely interconnectable because they are not members of such a group.

CRYPTOGRAPHY The safest way to have reasonable assurance that transmitted data have not been read, copied, or tampered with is to use cryptography. This means that the data are enciphered before they are transmitted and deciphered after transmission. The enciphering process scrambles the bits so thoroughly that a person wanting the information is unlikely to be able to unscramble them.

Cryptography has been used since the ancient Chinese by spies, lovers, and political schemers. Much has been written about it since the advent of radio and data transmission, and there has been massive expenditure on it in military and intelligence circles. There are spectacular stories from World War II about enemy codes being broken. Japanese messages planning the bombing of Pearl Harbor were deciphered and then not acted upon.

Cryptography is a fight between the person who enciphers and the person who tries to crack the code. The subject has drastically changed its nature with the advent of computers. The enemy will use a computer to work on cracking the code, searching at high speed through very large numbers of possible transformations. However, the enciphering will also be done by a computer and an inexpensive algorithm can scramble the data in a truly formidable way. On balance, if both sides act prudently, the sender is better off than the code cracker.

Microelectronics has further changed the applicability of cryptography. Now it can be done with a microprocessor or a special cryptography chip. With this the transmission from a terminal can be enciphered without great expense.

On networks, cryptography should be an *end-to-end* process, independent of the transport subsystem. It can thus be considered a Layer 4 function.

It is generally desirable for networks to interconnect many different machines, from different manufacturers. To use cryptography two communications machines must employ the same algorithm. One machine may need to contact many different machines on the network. It would help if all cryptography on the network used the same algorithm. If the same algorithm were used by large numbers of machines it could be implemented in the form of a cheap mass-produced LSI chip.

Would this be safe? If a mass-produced crypto chip were employed the enemy also could use it in attempts to break the code. To make such a scheme safe the enciphering must employ not only a suitably complex algorithm but also a *crypto key*. The key is a random collection of bits or characters which the transmitting and receiving stations use in conjunction with the algorithm for enciphering and deciphering (Fig. 35.5). If the enemy knows the crypto algorithm but not the key, it would take a large amount of work for him to break the code.

Some crypto devices use a key of 64 bits. If a code breaker attempted to decipher a message by using a computer to try out keys in a trial-and-error fashion, there would be 2^{64} possible keys to try. If an ultra-fast special-purpose computer were used for code breaking which could try out one key every microsecond, the average time taken to find the right key would be

$$\frac{2^{64}}{2} \text{ microseconds} = \frac{2^{64}}{2 \times 1,000,000 \times 3600 \times 24 \times 365.25} \text{ years}$$

That is, 292,271 years.

A key of 80 bits would require a time longer than the age of the universe.

With such keys, complete trial and error will not succeed in breaking cryptography codes. The cryptanalyst is therefore forced to find shortcuts which avoid full trial and error. Consequently the encoding technique must do everything possible to prevent shortcuts working; the data must be scrambled in a sufficiently complex fashion.

Most of the ciphers used prior to the development of computers can be broken by using computers. Today, however, a cheap LSI chip can execute an exceedingly complex cipher.

There are two ways to make codes uncrackable. One is sufficiently complex key usage; the other is sufficiently complex algorithms. Before computers, the safest systems used a key that was used once only. Sometimes the key was very long. Some Army Signal Corps systems used a key which occupied an entire paper tape roll 8 inches in diameter. Every tenth character was numbered so that the tape could be set up at any designated starting position.

With computer-to-computer transmission, such a technique could employ disks containing keys of many millions of random bits. The sending and receiving installations must both have the same key disk. The enciphering can be simple, quick, and virtually uncrackable if the contents of the key disk are changed frequently. However, this change may be time-consuming.

Data to be transmitted is enciphered with a crypto key and encipher algorithm:

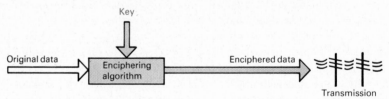

The data received is deciphered with the same crypto key and a decipher algorithm:

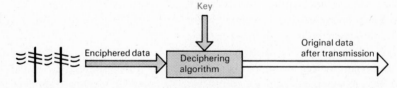

Figure 35.5   Cryptography. Both enciphering/deciphering algorithm and the key must be sufficiently complex.

KEY LEVERAGE   If a cryptographic system is to be secure it is necessary to *manage* the use of keys securely and on some networks it is desirable to transmit the keys. This is easier to accomplish if the keys are relatively small. A given quantity of keys can be made to encode a larger quantity of data by utilizing it with a more complex algorithm. This is referred to as *key leverage*.

Modern cryptographic hardware uses a relatively small key and scrambles it in association with the data in formidable ways. Figure 35.6 shows an enciphering technique employed by an IBM device called Lucifer which was used in conjuction with terminals and computers requiring highly secure transmission [2]. A very broadly similiar algorithm from IBM formed the basis of an American federal standard for cryptography.

DATA ENCRYPTION   A national as well as international standard for cryptogra-
STANDARD   phy is needed in order to permit the machines of many different manufacturers to be interconnected. Such a standard is likely to be secure and practical if:

1. It scrambles the data sufficiently thoroughly.
2. It uses a long enough key to prohibit trial-and-error methods of code breaking.
3. It does not add significantly to transmission overhead.
4. It can be implemented on a single mass-produced LSI chip.

The U.S. National Bureau of Standards created a Data Encryption Standard (DES) in 1977 [3]. It is now implemented on VLSI chips costing less than $50, though the extra equipment needed to employ them is much more expensive.

The Data Encryption Standard has two modes of operation called KAK (Key Auto Key) and CTAK (Cipher Text Auto Key). They are illustrated in Figs. 35.7 and 35.8.

In KAK mode the input data is read into a buffer 64 bits at a time. The 64 bits are then scrambled with a 64-bit key (somewhat similarly to Fig. 35.6) to produce 64 bits of output. The encoding operation starts with a START ENCIPHER command and then proceeds without further synchronization until the end of the data. The receiving machine knows when the data starts. If a bit is lost in transmission, synchronization is lost and the data will have to be retransmitted.

CTAK mode is more complex and proceeds 8 bits at a time. It is thus convenient for transmitting a stream of 8-bit characters. The input stream enters a 64-bit register in groups of 8 bits until the register is full. Enciphering then occurs using a 64-bit key to produce 64 bits of output. Only the left-hand eight bits of this are used. They are both transmitted and fed back to be combined with 8 bits of input as shown in Fig. 35.8. This technique is referred to as cipher-text feedback. It increases the difficulty of

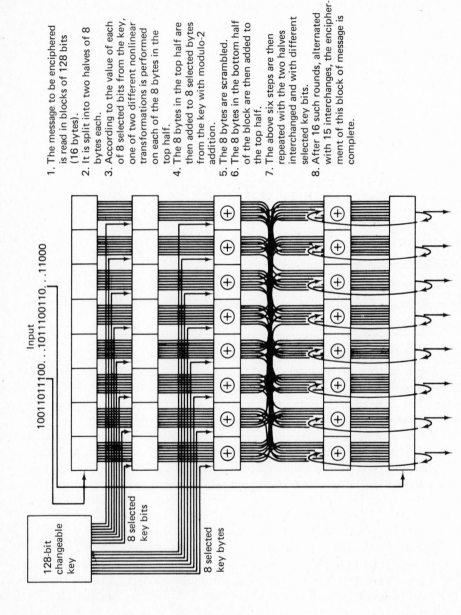

1. The message to be enciphered is read in blocks of 128 bits (16 bytes).
2. It is split into two halves of 8 bytes each.
3. According to the value of each of 8 selected bits from the key, one of two different nonlinear transformations is performed on each of the 8 bytes in the top half.
4. The 8 bytes in the top half are then added to 8 selected bytes from the key with modulo-2 addition.
5. The 8 bytes are scrambled.
6. The 8 bytes in the bottom half of the block are then added to the top half.
7. The above six steps are then repeated with the two halves interchanged and with different selected key bits.
8. After 16 such rounds, alternated with 15 interchanges, the encipherment of this block of message is complete.

Input

1001101110...1011100110...11000

128-bit changeable key

8 selected key bits

8 selected key bytes

Figure 35.6 The operation of the cryptography module.

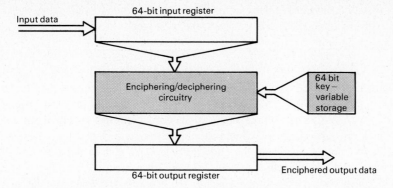

Figure 35.7 The U.S. Data Encryption Standard (DES) operating in Key-Auto-Key (KAK) mode. Figure 35.8 shows its other mode of operation.

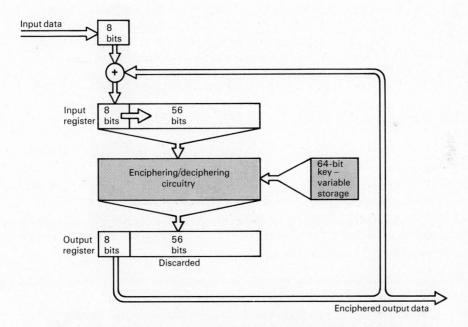

Figure 35.8 The U.S. Data Encryption Standard (DES) operating in Cipher Text Auto Key (CTAK) mode. 64 dummy bits are needed at start up and this degrades throughout especially when the message is short.

attempted code breaking, but it needs a dummy 64 bits entering into the circuit to start up the operation before live data are used. It adds this much overhead to the messages sent. The KAK mode adds no extra bits to the messages.

TIME AVAILABLE FOR BREAKING THE CODE   If a cryptanalyst has a very long time available for breaking a code, he is more likely to succeed. Again, he is more likely to succeed if he has a very large amount of text to work on. The computer system should be designed so that whenever possible it minimizes the time available to the code breaker. This can be done by designing the key so that it can be changed at suitably frequent intervals.

On some systems the time available for cracking the code can be made very short. The intruder may be trying to break into a computer system. However, the key is changed sufficiently frequently that if he takes a day to break the code the result will still not enable him to gain access to the system.

On the other hand, some commercial data are kept on disk or tape and retain their value for a very long time. Data concerning oil drillings or mineral prospecting, for example, could be of great value to a thief, and in some cases may retain their value for years. The thief has plenty of time to break the code. In such cases an especially complex algorithm and a long key may be used. If a standard algorithm must be employed, many keys may be used for different portions of the data, or the data may be enciphered more than once. An algorithm that uses a long once-only key might be used.

There are three ways in which the keys used for transmission can be changed sufficiently frequently.

1. They may be changed manually. Some enciphering devices have a small keyboard for the entry of keys.

2. The key may be changed at intervals by a computer which controls a session. The new keys are transmitted to the session participants and automatically loaded.

3. The key may be automatically selected and transmitted to the participants when a session is set up. It would be loaded and the crypto operation checked as part of the function of setting up the session.

In all three methods the new key is transmitted to one or both communicating parties. *That transmission must itself be enciphered.*

Which method is used may depend upon the application and the properties of the network software. In an electric fund transfer application with the machines permanently in session the keys may be changed automatically. In some banking systems a new key is inserted manually when the system is started up each day. For the once-only transmission of a sensitive file, manual key insertion might be used.

The most satisfactory and trouble-free scheme for many networks is the automatic allocation of keys when a session is established—this being part of the binding process. When a session is set up, a decision is made whether cryptography is necessary or not and if it is the keys are allocated. The session management software must be designed to control this process with a suitably high level of security. The fact that cryptography is used in the session can be made completely transparent to the session user.

TIGHT DISCIPLINE   A chip which executes the DES algorithm can be bought at a low cost. Unfortunately much more is needed than the chip in order to achieve disciplined, secure transmission. The algorithm must be interfaced to the current network equipment and procedures. The message headers *and* trailers must still work correctly. The keys must be generated and managed in a secure fashion. The transmission must recover from failures without giving information to a would-be code breaker.

A wiretapper attempting to break a cipher may deliberately cause failures on the communication line and observe the recovery action that takes place. To stop this technique from being of any value, when an erroneous block is retransmitted it should be enciphered in the same way as the previous block, *using the same key*. This may happen automatically if it is merely a Layer 2 error. If the intruder causes a Layer 3 failure, however, he might be able to cause retransmission of the same message with a different key. Comparing the two could assist him in cryptanalysis, especially if he could do it many times. The protocols should be designed to prevent this.

Synchronization between the transmitting and receiving machines is important with cryptography. Recovery from a loss of synchronization needs carefully thought out protocols. Everything that can possibly go wrong needs to be carefully tested with the enciphering and deciphering mechanisms: Cryptography + loose discipline = chaos.

KEY MANAGEMENT   When a new key is selected at one end of the link, the same key must also be used at the other end. It could be sent by courier. Both systems could have a file of keys and select the next one in the file. More often the key is *transmitted* to the other end.

When a key is transmitted, it must be done securely, so the key is itself enciphered for transmission. What key is used to encipher the key? It could be the previous key used by that machine. This would work if machine *A* always communicates with machine *B*. If, however, machine *A* communicates with machine *B* and then with machine *C*, how would machine *C* know what key to use? In some networks a terminal always communicates with the same host. In others there can be diverse interconnections between multiple machines. In the latter case the machines may have to communicate with a management node to set up a session. They have a permanent session

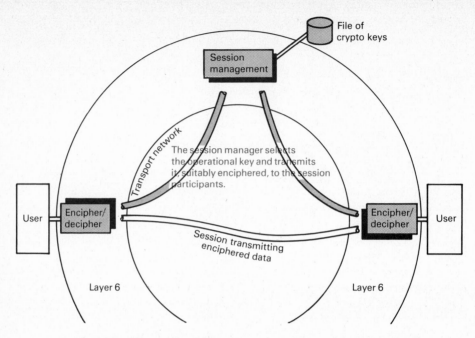

Figure 35.9 The cyptography key to be used in a session is selected at the start of the session by the session manager. The enciphering is completely transparent to the users.

with this node, as discussed earlier, and transmission on this session may be enciphered.

Figure 35.9 shows this situation. Machine *A* contacts its manager and requests a session of Machine *B*. The manager sets up the session, binding the user processes, and transmits the key to be used to both *A* and *B*. This transmission is enciphered with a key stored in both *A* and the manager, and another key stored in *B* and the manager.

The key which enciphers the data is sometimes called an *operational key*. The key which enciphers the transmission of the operational keys to machines which use them is sometimes called a *second-level key*.

The management node may store many keys—both operational keys and second-level keys. This file of keys must be kept *very* securely, so it is also enciphered, using a *third-level key*.

In IBM systems, software is available for the management of cryptographic keys—the Programmed Cryptographic Facility [4]. This generates keys using a pseudorandom number generator. It generates and stores operational keys, second-level keys, and third-level keys. The operational keys are employed for enciphering transmitted data or enciphering data stored on disks or tape. The second-level keys (called secondary keys) encipher the operational keys. The third-level keys (called primary

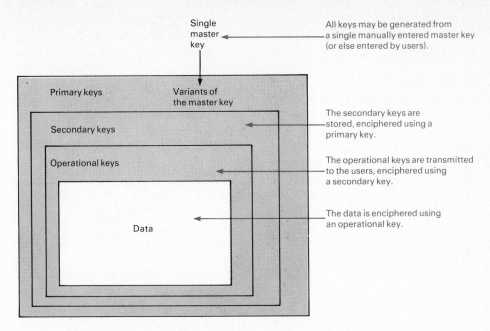

Figure 35.10 The operational cryptography keys must themselves be protected by further cryptography.

keys) encipher the file of keys in which all levels of key are stored. Figure 35.10 illustrates these layers of protection.

All the keys may be generated automatically from a single *master key* which is entered into the system manually. The set of keys may be changed as often as required by entering a new master key. When this is done some of the old keys must be kept because there are data on the files which are enciphered with them. Alternatively some or all of the keys may be entered manually. There are three types of second-level keys: those for communication between a host and terminal, those for communication between two hosts, and those used for enciphering data stored on disks or tape.

Along with these cryptographic safeguards it is necessary to have good *physical* security with physical locks to prevent the stealing of key files, and good administrative security to control who has knowledge of the master key or other keys.

VALIDATION   When keys have been established at each end of a link the machines may exchange a brief test message to ensure that the cryptography is synchronized and working correctly. With some systems validation can be done with a live message rather than a test message. It may be sufficient to check that valid characters are being received rather than a jumble of bits.

WHEN SHOULD CRYPTOGRAPHY BE USED

Given the right software and hardware, cryptography can be troublefree and automatic. All of the keys can be generated from a single master key at a major computer center. No overhead *need* be added to the messages except that involved in setting up the session.

Only a small fraction of network transmission needs enciphering and most terminals and controllers will not have crypto hardware. Wiretapping or tampering with network switching nodes is rare, although it is remarkably easy to accomplish. Most telephone junction boxes in office buildings are unlocked and unprotected. It is easy to connect a tap, via a small isolation transformer out of sight behind the terminal panel, which connects to another line at the end of which the wiretapper can operate in comfort. He may even be able to dial a connection to his tap from his own premises.

Examples of types of transmission which need protecting are:

1. Electronic fund transfer. Money transfers of millions of dollars are transmitted between banks in electronic form.

2. Cash dispensing machines. In some banks these are remote terminals and a customer can withdraw a large sum if it is in his account.

3. Military and intelligence information.

4. Work relating to military contractors.

5. Diplomatic communication.

6. Valuable commercial data such as oil or mineral prospecting results.

7. Data of value to competition such as lists of customers, invoices, development plans, details of unannounced products, classified research.

8. Sensitive police or personnel information; payrolls; payroll checks transmitted to a bank.

9. Communication with a system security officer.

A distributed system may be divided into portions which are secure and portions which are not (Fig. 35.11). Certain areas, such as where valuable data are stored, where the crypto keys are stored, and the security officer's area, need to be ultra secure. Physical and administrative security will be maintained in these areas. The transmission links between them should be regarded as nonsecure unless cryptography is used. Certain data should be entered and certain types of interactive usage should occur only at the secure terminals.

Cryptography may be used to make sure that an intruder cannot gain access to the system via the network with a terminal of his own and a false use of passwords.

INDIRECT ADDRESSING

Some networks are designed so that if an eavesdropper records part of a (nonenciphered) session he cannot tell what machines are participating in the session because the addresses carried by the messages are indirect addresses rather than machine addresses. This is so in Univac DCA

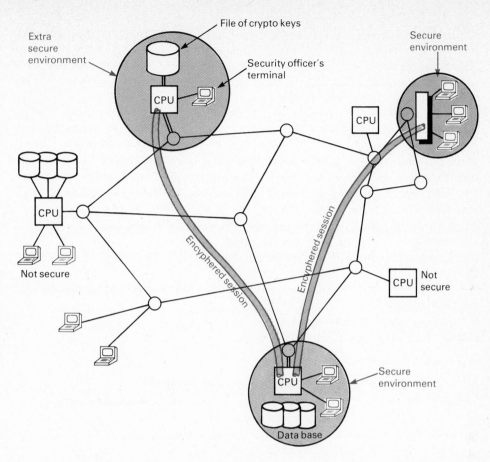

Figure 35.11   Some network facilities are secure and some are not.

networks. Two sessions between the same two machines carry different session identifiers which are allocated when the session is set up. Only the nodes which set up the session can convert these identifiers into machine identifications.

THE SYSTEM'S   To maintain high security in any building or organization,
POLICEMEN   policemen are needed. A secure computer system needs a
                          staff responsible for the security of the data files and the
control of the authorization to use these files. A security officer should be appointed
who will be the sole person able to change the authorization tables or file lockword
tables in the system. He will have details of what each individual is authorized to read
or change on the files. He is responsible for issuing passwords or security codes and
for ensuring that they are used correctly.

In a network environment there may be several security officers, possibly one associated with each host computer, or one associated with each corporate division or function. In a system with terminals in scattered locations, there should be a person responsible for security in each of these locations where sensitive data is handled. A suitable person with another job, such as an office manager, can be a local security officer. He takes instructions from the main security officer. The system sends him listings of all detected violations of correct procedure that occur in his location.

When the system detects a violation of correct security procedures it should immediately take some action. Most terminal users can be expected to make occasional mistakes. When a user's first violation is detected, the computer should ask him to reenter the data and log the fact that the violation occurred. However, if an operator who made one mistake immediately makes a second, again attempting to enter an invalid code or access an unauthorized file, this may be an indication that he is attempting to do something illegal on the terminal. The system then immediately informs the local security officer in the hope that the culprit will be caught red-handed. This miscreant may be "kept talking" by the system, but locked out of any sensitive files, until he is caught.

Another approach that has been used is to lock the terminal completely the moment the second violation occurs. The application programs are written in such a way that no more information is accepted from that terminal until the condition has been cleared. The only man who can clear it is the security officer for that location.

AUDIT AND CONTROL
PROCEDURES

Any persons contemplating an invasion of the files either through curiosity or malicious intent should be deterred by the thought that there is a high probability that the system will detect them and alert the appropriate security officer.

A log should be kept of all violations of correct procedure, for example, when a terminal user types in a security code that is not the one allocated to him or attempts to access a file for which he has no authorization. Details of these violations are printed and sent to the security officers. A branch security officer will receive a listing of all the violations that have occurred within his branch. A file owner will be sent details of all unauthorized attempts to read or change records in his file. This log of violations should be analyzed to detect any unusual activity. Most violations are accidental and caused by a genuine mistake on the part of the terminal operator. The sudden departure from the norm in this activity, however, may indicate that someone is tampering with the system, and possibly exploring to find a method of gaining unauthorized access. The list of violations may be printed out once a week; on the other hand, it may pay to do it more frequently on a system containing highly restricted and sensitive information. The location security officers may be sent a list of any violations that occur each night. Then a would-be intruder will have little time to practice.

It is particularly important to maintain extremely tight security over the authorization records, passwords, and file lockwords, etc. If an imposter can change them, then most of his problems are solved. No one should be given the authority to read or change these records except the file owners or the security officers. If any change is made, then the appropriate file owner or security officer will be sent details of that change the following day. Such changes may be detected on a nightly run by comparing last night's authorization records and file lock tables with those of tonight. If an unauthorized person has managed to make changes in them, it will be detected quickly.

It is advisable that a journal be kept in which all changes that are made to these security records are logged, indicating who made the change and where it was made.

A SOLVABLE
PROBLEM
There is much more to security than we have described in this chapter, and the reader who would like to read further on the subject should obtain Reference 1.

In general, network security should be regarded as a solvable problem. It needs to be solved at an appropriate cost for the systems in question. The systems analyst responsible for security needs the broadest possible view. Overemphasis on narrow security measures should be avoided.

REFERENCES

1. Computer security techniques in general are described in the author's *Security, Accuracy, and Privacy in Computer Systems,* Prentice-Hall, Englewood, NJ, 1973.

2. IBM's Lucifer system is described in IBM Research Reports, Vol. 7, No. 4. Published by IBM Research, Yorktown Heights, NY.

3. Data Encryption Standard (DES). Federal Information Processing Standard #46. National Bureau of Standards, 1977. Available from National Technical Service, U.S. Dept. of Commerce, 5285 Port Royal Road, Springfield, VA 22161.

4. Programmed Cryptographic Facility, OS/VS1 and OS/VS2 MVS, General Information Manual, IBM manual No. GC28–0942, Program No. 5740-XY5, IBM, Poughkeepsie, NY.

A bibliography on cryptography:

• Tuckerman, B., "A Study of the Vigenere-Vernam Single and Multiple Loop Enciphering Systems," IBM Report No. RC 2879, Thomas J. Watson Research Center, Yorktown Heights, NY, 1970. (A study of the use of APL for code breaking.)

Page 242 of *Security, Accuracy & Privacy* reproduces the whole bibliography.

• Morgan, B. D., and W. E. Smith, "Data Encryption: The High Cost of Installing a $50 Chip," *Data Communications,* Feb. 1977.

• IBM Cryptographic Subsystem: Concepts and Facilities, IBM manual No. GC 22-9063, Poughkeepsie, NY.

PART V FUTURE

36 THE FUTURE OF NETWORK ARCHITECTURES

The dominant factor affecting the long-range future of networks is that which will affect all other areas of the electronics industry: the growth of microelectronics.

Figure 36.1 shows the increase in numbers of electronic components in an integrated circuit. Since the production of the planar transistor in 1959 the number has been doubling every year. The curve in Fig. 36.1 was predicted in 1964 by the director of research at Fairchild Semiconductors, Gordon Moore, and became known as Moore's law. There are no signs in the research laboratories that this growth will slow down yet, although eventually it must. The technology is nowhere near the fundamental limits imposed by physics. New production techniques will be able to put far more components onto the same surface area, and the surface area of one chip will increase.

The dashed curve of Fig. 36.1 extrapolates Moore's law into the future. Whether the microelectronics industry grows as rapidly as indicated here depends more upon economics than on the basic physics. It appears technically possible to climb Moore's curve for another fifteen years at least. Individual components will become much smaller as the industry moves from optical etching of chips to electron beam etching (like an electron microscope) and then to X-ray etching. The yield (i.e., proportion of chips without defects) will increase as the industry swings from liquid etching to dry plasma etching and to automated manufacturing under computer control in a controlled atmosphere. As the yield increases it will be economical to have chips of larger area. Today a silicon wafer about 10 centimeters in diameter is etched and diced into individual chips a few millimeters in diameter. With a lower proportion of defects the wafer may not have to be diced; circuitry could be devised to use most of the wafer, automatically circumventing defective portions (like circumventing defective nodes in a network). Integrated wafers with a hundred times today's packing density will eventually be made and this could take us to the top of the dotted curve in Fig. 36.1. It is likely that before the mid-1980's we will have microcomputers on a chip with a million bits of memory.

544

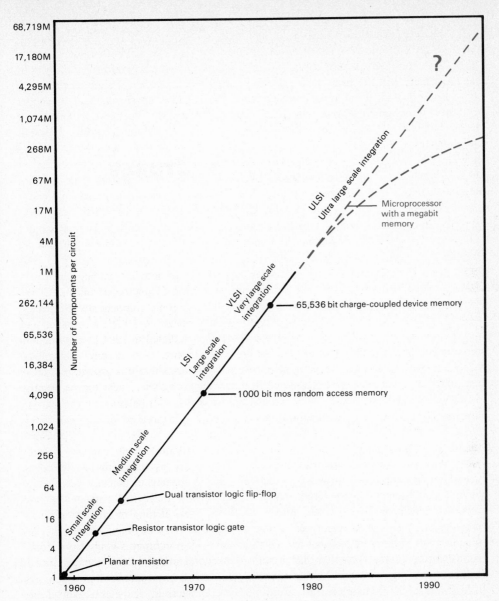

Figure 36.1 The growth of microelectronics.

In addition to conventional semiconductors, magnetic bubble and—later—bubble lattice memories will give relatively cheap solid state storage which does not lose its contents when the electricity is switched off. Microprocessors brought a revolution in the potential application of electronics. We are on the threshold of another revolution: *microfiles*. Today's magnetic bubble products store about 150,000 bits per square centimeter. A pocket calculator could have a megabit store. Before the end of the 1980's pocket devices may store ten million bytes.

Microelectronic devices will handle the protocols we have discussed in this book. The common carrier DCE's and DSE's are beginning to employ microcomputers, and there will be cheap mass-produced virtual call controllers for the users.

The potential user population will grow gigantically. Large numbers of people will have programmable machines with substantial memory. Pocket calculators will have alphanumeric displays so that users can carry out dialogue with programs. This will enormously extend the range and variety of programs that people find useful. Hobby and amateur use of computers will take on innumerable forms. The home television set in some countries will become a major interactive information medium with schemes like Viewdata [1]. Every store and restaurant will need financial terminals for credit checking, check validation, and possibly electronic fund transfer. Electronic mail will spread. Children of all ages will use electronic teaching facilities. Business people, sales people, scientists, maintenance staff—all will need their terminals and pocket machines.

CHEAP ACCESS TO NETWORKS

It will be desirable that these machines be able to access the data networks of the world *cheaply*. The main form of access will be via local telephone lines. It is desirable that the user machines be able to plug into the home or office telephone outlet, dial a local telephone number and be connected to a data network which gives a cost per packet in keeping with the cost of the technology. Both the Viewdata and X.25 schemes promise to make this possible, and promise a suitably low cost for the small user with a very low traffic volume. For the electronic eighties this is a social service of vital importance, but one cannot help wonder how many common carrier and telephone administrations will step on it.

We can now see the beginning of a new form of publishing of high social potential which depends for its growth on telecommunications access. The Viewdata scheme permits entrepreneurs, both large and in some cases very small, to make data and programs available for easy access from the home and office. The data or program provider is paid a small royalty each time his program or data are accessed. If such schemes can harness entrepreneurial spirits ranging from computer hobbyists to giant publishing conglomerates, then the growth of networks will be immense and society will need data highways comparable with today's telephone networks.

National X.25 networks, acquiring more and more nodes and links, will be connected by international circuits so that the industrial world becomes laced with X.25 networks.

If a packet travels over more links then its delivery time is lengthened. Networks need to be structured so that there are not too many links in tandem.

Let us suppose that a mean end-to-end delivery time of 100 milliseconds is required for packets of length 128 bytes. This objective could not be achieved with voice-grade circuits (transmitting at 9600 bps). With circuits transmitting at 56,000 bps the maximum number of hops permissible is three or four, depending on how long a packet waits in each node. AT&T states that three hops will be the maximum on its ACS trunk network. Such a restriction would be excessively restrictive on international networks. International packet switching using circuits of that speed is likely to encounter longer (but not unacceptable) delivery times.

To lessen the number of hops multilevel networks can be used with long distance hops spanning major centers. This higher level part of the network may operate at higher speeds if there is enough traffic to make that economical. Combinations of circuit switching and packet switching could also lower the delay on international networks.

As the traffic volume grows on packet networks higher bit-rate circuits will become justified. It is likely in North America that T1 carrier circuits will be used, transmitting 1.544 million bps. With such circuits a 128-byte packet could have an end-to-end delivery time of 100 milliseconds even if it travels over 60 or more hops. However, many millions of packets per circuit per day are needed to justify such circuits. Extensive sending of mail by networks will result in high speed circuits being used.

STANDARDS

Given this potential, the immense importance of *standards* is clear. There need to be universally accepted standards for the transport network, and for many functions external to the transport network such as file access protocols, cryptography, virtual terminals, access via the home television set, access via pocket machines, dialogue functions and programming language extensions.

X.25 is an appropriate standard for many uses of the transport network. It has been criticized by datagram enthusiasts for being too complex. However, given the rate of development of microelectronics X.25 interfaces on mass-produced chips will become cheap.

EXTENSIONS TO X.25

Many extensions to X.25 are being proposed, formally and informally. It has space for additional features in its headers and control packets. There is little doubt that it will be extended. Perhaps the most important extension would be to make it function with all types of networks.

There are many data networks other than packet-switching networks. Circuit-switching data networks have been implemented by major common carriers, and have advantages over packet switching in some circumstances. Many networks with intelligent multiplexers and concentrators are here to stay. Satellite systems like SBS show great promise. Cable TV is spreading rapidly and local wideband networks like Ethernet have enormous potential.

The ordinary user does not care to know how the transport network operates. He wants a standard interface which can couple his machine to all types of networks. X.25 interfaces are provided to circuit-switched networks such as the Scandinavian network.

PROPERTIES
OF VIRTUAL CIRCUITS

Users are concerned about properties of virtual circuits which affect how they would couple machines. Box 36.1 summarizes these properties. The packets which set up the circuit will request certain types of circuits and may eventually be able to request most of the properties shown in Box 36.1. For example, it may be possible to request different logical bandwidths, for some machines occasionally need very high bandwidths for a brief period.

Propagation delay can vary over a wide range. A few real-time applications for machine control need a very brief response time. Interactive terminals need a response time which sometimes has to be brief (say 2 seconds for the overall response time) and sometimes can be longer (say 7 seconds). Batch transmissions can tolerate a delay of many seconds. For electronic mail or message switching, delays of hours may be acceptable. A virtual circuit may be substantially cheaper if there is no guaranteed short delivery time.

Sometimes the extra delay caused by introducing a satellite circuit plays havoc with pacing mechanisms. By using a propagation delay parameter the user may cause the transport network to avoid satellite circuits.

The expression of a priority may be equivalent in effect to setting a required propagation delay, and the latter is more precise.

The transport network may enforce a maximum message size. Alternatively it may permit a stream of packets, and a message could be any number of packets.

The user may request that no tight restriction is placed on message length so that the transport network can establish a route which avoids any such restrictive mechanisms. In some cases the user needs *continuous* transmission rather than burst transmission. If he expresses this need he may be given a circuit-switched or time-division multiplexed circuit, rather than a packet-switched circuit.

One type of service should be datagram operation which is simpler and less expensive than packet switching and which guarantees first-in/first-out delivery. Datagram service and virtual-call service can be merged as discussed in Chapter 24.

The network may offer a choice between half-duplex transmission (one direction at a time) and full-duplex (both directions at once). The CALL REQUEST packet may specify one or the other.

The CALL REQUEST packet may ask for guaranteed delivery, in which case the transport network may execute end-to-end recovery. Alternatively the user machines may do end-to-end buffering and recovery.

The CALL REQUEST packet may ask for a circuit with guaranteed privacy, in which case the transport network enciphers the messages. On the other hand, the user machines may practice end-to-end cryptography if they need it.

BOX 36.1 Properties of a virtual circuit

- *Dedicated or switched circuit.*
  A dedicated circuit always connects the same machines and is always available. A switched circuit interconnects multiple machines.

- *Address range.*
  A switched circuit may be connectable to few machines or many. Eventually the address range will encompass as many machines as international telephone dialing.

- *Logical bandwidth.*
  The maximum overall transmission rate in bits per second.

- *Propagation delay.*
  The time between the first bit of a message leaving the sending machine and appearing at the receiving machine.

- *Priority.*
  Different messages may be given different priorities which affect the expected propagation delay and cost.

- *Maximum message length.*
  Some transport networks impose a maximum size on message lengths.

- *Half- or full-duplex.*
  Some logical links can transmit data in both directions at the same time (full-duplex). Some can transmit in only one direction at once (half-duplex).

- *FIFO.*
  Most transport networks deliver packets in the same sequence as that in which they were sent: first-in/first-out. Datagram networks do not and may be less expensive.

- *Guaranteed delivery.*
  Some networks guarantee to deliver messages or return them. Others give less assurance and end-to-end message control is necessary.

- *Privacy.*
  The virtual circuit might be made secure by the use of cryptography.

- *Continuous transmission.*
  The user may want to transmit continuously rather than in packets. This is desirable for speech, television, most facsimile machines, and some computer uses.

- *Cost function.*
  The cost of the virtual circuit may vary greatly depending upon the different features, grades of service, and distances.

In general a future thrust of architectures should be that transport networks are logically separate from their users, that many different types of transport mechanisms may be interlinked, and that a user should be able to request the logical properties of the circuit he asks for.

BALANCED PROTCOLS   *Unbalanced* protocols are those in which one machine of a communication pair is a primary or master station, and the other is a secondary or slave station. The main reason for this mode of operating is that the secondary machine is small and inexpensive and cannot economically perform all of the functions that a primary machine does, especially functions associated with recovery. With the increasing power of microelectronics it becomes economical to use balanced protocols in which each machine performs the same protocol functions and each machine is responsible for recovery of the messages it initiates.

The advantage of balanced protocols is that any machine can communicate with any other. In an unbalanced protocol, a secondary station cannot communicate directly with another secondary.

As microelectronic power grows, any-to-any communication will be perceived as a major advantage, and balanced protocols will be used increasingly. This applies at Layer 2; HDLC can operate in *balanced* mode. It also applies at Layers 3 and 4. X.25 nodes have identical interfaces to the transport network. Nodes of some computer and minicomputer networks can communicate in a balanced (horizontal) fashion using Layer 4 facilities. They can set up a session with each other directly without requiring this to be done by a separate manager node. It should be noted that there are some network services for which manager nodes may still be desirable, for example the management and allocation of cryptography keys.

HIGHER-LAYER   X.25 today relates only to the transport subnet-
EXTENSIONS   work. Important activities in the various subcommittees
                          of standards organizations are concerned with extensions of X.25 into Layer 4 and higher. The first to be implemented is the PAD (packet assembly/disassembly) interface to character mode terminals discussed in Chapter 21. Other devices which could become standardized or widely accepted (perhaps View-data sets), may also have interfaces in the future which connect them to X.25 net-works. They may be variations of the PAD interface. Eventually, perhaps, pocket calculators will be connectable to X.25, or at least datagram, networks.

A particularly important proposed standard is that for virtual network terminals. To write programs independently of the terminals they send to and receive from would greatly increase the portability of programs. Commands, PICTURE state-ments, or input/output routines relating to virtual terminals could be written into pro-gramming languages and software.

The main objection to this from manufacturers is that they are likely to produce terminals with much more capability than the standard virtual terminals. Probably both standard virtual terminals and terminals with more functions will exist. There may eventually be large numbers of standard virtual terminals and this mode of operation may be a selectable subset of more complex devices.

ACS-LIKE NETWORKS   It is possible to put a variety of programmed functions into the nodes of public as well as private networks. The structure of AT&T's ACS network is particularly appealing because it could allow customers, software houses, or the telephone company, to create new functions which would reside in the network nodes. Given the enormous inventiveness of the computer world this could result in a wide diversity of new network functions.

Viewdata-like networks go a step further and provide storage for potentially vast quantities of information. These data are distributed to the nodes of the network. The distinction between public data networks and computer service organizations could become blurred if Viewdata-like networks and ACS-like networks converge.

FOUR CATEGORIES   We can distinguish five types of public data networks:
OF NETWORK

1. *Dumb networks* without computerized networks, e.g., telephone and telex networks.
2. *Virtual circuit networks.* Basic X.25 networks like DATAPAC, TRANSPAC, etc.
3. *Distributed function networks,* like ACS, with a variety of functions in the nodes for data entry, editing, message storage and delivery, etc.
4. *Data providing networks,* like Viewdata, making a wide diversity of data available to subscribers.
5. *Computer service networks,* like time-sharing networks, which enable users to access computing power, programs, and data.

The latter two types of networks may employ the former three types for transmission.

DIALOGUE STANDARDS   Chris Evans [2], a psychologist who is a major authority on terminal dialogue for naïve users, goes further than terminal standardization and says that it is easier than most engineers realize to standardize various types of end-user dialogues. To do so would greatly extend the applicability of dialogue software and make it possible to build dialogue into hardware.

However, the most important reason for dialogues standards is that they would increase *familiarity* of usage for vast numbers of potential users. Most people are hesitant to approach computer terminals because they do not know what to do with them. To achieve the mass usage of terminals that is technically and economically desirable, the machines and their dialogues must be made familiar.

Standard dialogues might include menu-selection dialogues, dialogues used on future pocket calculator-like machines with alphabetic display and memory, standard keyboards for such dialogues (the pushbutton and rotary dials on U.S. telephones are a simple and familiar example of standardization), data base interrogation or information retrieval dialogues, and dialogues for high-volume applications such as banking terminals, credit checking, and electronic mail.

An important form of standard dialogue is that emerging for interactive use of home and business television sets with the British Prestel (Viewdata) network and its equivalent in other countries. Viewdata uses a menu-selection dialogue that is being used for a vast range of different types of applications. It makes effective use of color on the screen, and if Viewdata sets become widespread, they will become familiar to a large public who had never dreamed of using computers. The way we use the telephone has become standardized and familiar. The same must happen with some forms of terminal usage.

The standards committees talk little about dialogue standards. They are potentially very important.

DATA-BASE PROTOCOLS

A particularly desirable extension to network architectures is protocols for using remote files and data bases. An on-line file or data base serving a distributed environment might reside in a node which itself has no application programs. It is in a storage subsystem with file or data base management software. It may be in a vault or an area with exceptionally high physical security. An application program which employs it may be in a local or remote computer.

The file access protocols may specify the packets which make requests for data, the means of pacing, and the means of recovering from the various types of errors and failures without losing or falsifying information.

PROGRAMMING LANGUAGE EXTENSIONS

Programming languages need macroinstructions which permit the use of networks, virtual terminals, and remote files. These should be high-level instructions as close as possible to the natural structure of the language, e.g., GET, PUT, PICTURE statements, etc. In general, *language extensions* are needed for the use of remote data bases, files, and distributed processing.

The application programmer using advanced networking software may not know the location of the machine he is addressing or of the data he is using. Symbolic addresses are used. Data may be addressed by the name of a file and the networking software will have to use a directory to find the geographical location of that file, and obtain data from it. A program may be referred to by name, and the networking software will have to find the geographical locations of the program.

DIRECTORY OPERATIONS

Similarly a person at a terminal may refer to a needed program or logical file by name, without stating *where* it resides. A directory will establish the location of program or file.

An application program may refer to a predefined data subschema in a data base environment. A data base management system attempts to assemble the data the programmer wants; however, to do so it may have to execute network operations because the data is in a distant machine. Distributed data base software may employ a directory for finding the location of requested data.

OPERATING SYSTEM EXTENSIONS

Directory operations is one example of an extension to conventional operating systems. Today's networking software forms an adjunct to existing operating systems. It is built using the primitives that operating systems provide. This is because operating systems existed long before networking software.

It has been suggested that future operating system development might take a different approach. Operating systems for a distributed environment might be built out of networking primitives rather than the other way round [3, 4]. Primitives for communication via a channel may be the same as primitives for communication via a line or virtual circuit. Some operating systems are likely to become distributed, either among machines in the same room, machines on a wideband cable like Ethernet, or machines which are geographically separate. Different machines may do file management, input/output management, program library control, scheduling, directory operations, and so on. An evolution of operating systems into an environment of multiple machines will lead to systems of higher availability and ruggedness, capable of continuing to serve users when failures occur.

In general, extensions to higher layers of networks may eventually encompass all or most of the facilities listed in Box 15.1 and many more that are related to office-of-the-future requirements. Probably no one machine, or one architecture, will include quite all of them. Different features from that list are useful on different types of systems.

INCOMPATIBILITY

It is possible to see how the transport network could be made (theoretically) completely standard. If standards for the transport network exist, machines can be built which bridge the gap between other types of systems and the standard network. X.25 may form the basis of this standard bridge, but needs many additional features.

A few standards at Layer 5 to 7 are emerging. However, it is not likely that these will make computers generally interconnectable in the 1980's because different machines are so different in their software and operating systems. The *binding* process is highly complex. It has proven remarkably difficult to have general interconnection of *computers from the same manufacturer,* even of minicomputers as with DECNET.

The messages for setting up the session have very complex structures. To devise a set of such messages which could bind computers from different manufacturers is inconceivable for the near future.

There will be incompatibility problems in distributed processing networks between machines of different manufacturers for a long time to come. The machines may be interconnectable at Layer 3 but not capable of being generally *bound* at Layers 5 to 7. Process-to-process communication will then have to take place by sending transactions from one incompatible machine to another, as on ARPANET, rather than the tighter coupling of DECNET or SNA.

There is hope, however, that standard protocols for terminal access and file access will emerge.

HIGHER BANDWIDTH   Some computer architects consider that a major flaw in today's telecommunications is the difficulty of obtaining high bandwidth channels. It takes seven hours to transmit a magnetic tape over a voice-grade circuit. The problem was expressed by IBM vice president for engineering, programming and technology, B. O. Evans:

> We've always had to design hardware and software with costly interface devices, just to plug them into phone lines where they were locked into a guaranteed slow rate of transmission. For a time that was tolerable. We could live with it before computers became truly highspeed machines and before data communications became a widespread way of life. But today it's ridiculous [5].

Telecommunications does not *have* to operate at slow speeds. AT&T and others have been building high-speed digital trunks for a decade. AT&T's digital trunks operate at speeds of 1.544, 6.312, 44.7 and 274, million bits per second [6]. These are referred to as T1, T2, T3, and T4 carrier trunks. There is very widespread use of trunks at the lower of these speeds. However, they are designed mainly for voice transmission, so they are time-division multiplexed into the low-speed channels needed for the human voice. With a very few expensive exceptions, customers cannot use the high speeds. The same has been true with satellites. Each transponder on most of today's communications satellites is capable of relaying 60 million bits per second. However, the users are throttled down to voice-grade speeds.

Data networks could be built with the high-speed digital trunks, using transmission and switching of millions of bits per second — many millions on the high-capacity routes. This would not need fundamentally new technology, but a reconfiguring and reprogramming of today's facilities. High-speed transmission is also used on in-plant and short-distance systems like Ethernet and on cable television links. It is used on the new generation of satellites from Satellite Business Systems. Users of these satellites can have channels of a wide variety of speeds dynamically allocated to them, including channels of millions of bits per second [7].

Even if they were available, most users would not be able to afford *leased private* lines of many megabits per second. What they could afford is *virtual calls* of high bandwidth using these facilities. They may use the high-bandwidth circuit only for a fraction of the time in a day, but when they use it they do so at high speed. This gives them low response times, the ability to move a program quickly to a node where it will be executed, the ability to move a file from one machine to another, the ability to use graphics at high speed via networks, and so on. Another set of applications of high-speed transmission is those using facsimile images. These tend to be too long for conventional packet switching—hundreds of thousands of bits per record. Facsimile documents and images will be used increasingly in future office equipment. They will be filed, transmitted, printed, and displayed on terminals. A display user will want the image to appear on his display within a reasonable response time. When transmitted over a public telephone line in digital facsimile form, a typical document takes about a minute. It does not consume more transmission resources if it is sent fast—it is still the same number of bits, and the high-speed links exist, *if only they were usable.*

In general, high-bandwidth communications are needed for progress in computing and office automation. However, because few users can afford private high-bandwidth links there is a stronger argument for the *sharing* of public networks than with low bandwidths. Common-carrier networks will eventually be expanded by putting control equipment on the digital (PCM) telephone trunks to give high-bandwidth virtual circuits or virtual calls. It would be better if this happens soon because it will have a major effect on computer architectures and office automation.

PACKETIZED VOICE   An extremely thorough study by the Network Analysis Corporation [8] shows that the cheapest way to transmit telephone conversations in the future will be in the form of packetized voice. Packet switching for voice will have to have somewhat different network mechanisms from packet switching for data. It will have to use high capacity circuits such as T1 circuits (1.544 million bps), because substantial delays in packet delivery could not be tolerated. Burst switching and burst multiplexing is economical for voice because speech is not continuous in telephone conversations. It has a peak-to-average ratio of about three.

One of the attractive aspects of building packet networks for voice is that data, mail, and telephone conversations could be economically interleaved using the same facilities. This is desirable for the office-of-the-future.

COMMUNICATIONS   Satellites of the 1980's, starting with SBS's initial satel-
SATELLITES   lites and progressing to larger satellites *designed* for launch with the space shuttle, have the potential of lowering the costs of networking. It is desirable that they be used with demand-assigned, multiple-access forms of control. These offer the prospect of high-bandwidth bursts between machines when needed, but will substantially change the nature of the trans-

port subsystem. It is desirable that interfaces to the transport network become adopted which can employ satellite and other high-bandwidth burst communications. Some changes in protocols are needed because of the long propagation delay. Cheap earth stations will be made possible by large satellites. It is desirable that the earth station design and satellite design be done in an integrated fashion to provide the most cost effective network structure.

RADIO TERMINALS

Radio terminals offer the prospect of portable devices having network access, and of network access which is inexpensive because it bypasses the local telephone cables. As in the University of Hawaii system, radio may connect terminals directly to satellite earth stations. Radio protocols represent a fundamental change in the transport subsystem, but the interface to this transport network could be similar to X.25, or, more simply, a datagram interface.

LOCAL WIDEBAND NETWORKS

Local wideband links using coaxial cable, CATV systems, or radio, have great potential. Effective control mechanisms for such networks have been devised, including Ethernet (Chapter 6). These offer the possibility of a plug in the wall of an office to which all types of communicating data machines could be connected—terminals; typewriters; instrumentation; facsimile machines and document displays; word processing machines; filing systems; information retrieval systems; fire, smoke, and burglar detectors; Viewdata sets; copying machines and computers.

The plug and interface would need to be standardized, and be capable of accepting transmissions at a wide range of speeds. They should link to nationwide networks which give wideband transmission. The XTEN network of Xerox offers the promise of such an end-to-end facility for the office-of-the-future.

INTEGRATION OF SYSTEMS

There are economic reasons for wanting to combine different types of office machines. The copying machine can double as a facsimile transmitter. Word processing machines can accomplish multiple functions, and can double as computer terminals. The office of the future will contain a wide variety of such machines, interconnectable by telecommunications links which will need to be better than voice-grade links.

Computer systems until the late 1970's have consisted of a central processor with peripherals or terminals attached to it. Like the view of the universe before Copernicus, everything was subordinate to the central processor. Now a Copernican revolution is taking place in which a large processor is not necessarily the center of the universe. If anything is regarded as central in the new view it is the switch or network to which multiple machines are connected, including multiple processors.

There are many forms which the switch or network can take. It may be a computerized PABX (CBX) switching telephone and data traffic. It may be a supercontroller to which a CBX is attached, or which incorporates a CBX. This supercontroller will be critical to many manufacturers' product lines. The network may be a corporate telephone network adapted to also handle data; it may be a local wideband network like Ethernet; it may be a satellite system, concentrator network, or packet-switching system.

It is clear that network architectures have a long period of evolution ahead to encompass these diverse requirements. For the foreseeable future there will be multiple network architectures meeting different needs. They will utilize diverse protocols and there will be need for conversion modules to bridge the gap between the different protocols. Separate architectural layers with clean interfaces between them will make interconnection and evolution easier. The more these interfaces can be standardized and agreed upon the better for all involved. Competition between carriers and computer manufacturers is building up in countries where the law permits it, but both will benefit from lessening their customer problems and making interconnection of machines as easy as possible. That means standards upon which all agree.

THREE WORLDS   In most countries of the world telecommunications and public data networks are the province of government. Private corporations are not allowed to provide public networks; neither as common carriers nor value-added carriers.

Because of this telecommunications are evolving differently in North America compared to most of the rest of the world. The innovations of Xerox (XTEN), IBM (SBS), other new satellite carriers, television distribution companies (QUBE; Home Box Office), radio carriers, and others are not occurring in most of the world. (Incidently, note that none of the above are telephone companies.)

Without question Europe and other parts of the world need *competition* to spur innovation in telecommunications. However that is probably not going to occur so I expect that different facilities will evolve in North America.

There will probably be three world zones of telecommunications in the late 1980's:

1. North America with a rich diversity of competing networks including wideband networks which transmit at speeds above 64,000 bps. Japan may also have wideband networks.

2. Europe and countries which build X.25 networks: Europe will be laced with X.25-compatible networks of low virtual bandwidth. The price per packet may be low enough to discourage the building of based-line networks. The X.25 capability may be upgraded to provide the types of facilities which Bell is planning with ACS, but it seems doubtful. Viewdata-like resources may spread using the X.25 networks.

    There is talk about wideband digital public networks based on switching schemes like the British Post Office's System X designed for voice and data switching. However facilities like those of XTEN, SBS, etc. are not coming into existence at the time of writing. The emphasis is almost entirely on low-speed packet switching (and in Scandinavia, circuit switching).

3. Much of the rest of the world will have merely "plain old telephone service" (known affectionately as POTS), and telex networks.

This discrepancy will mean that many American machines will not be usable in Europe and elsewhere from 1985 to 1990. Many of these machines will be concerned with increasing the productivity of office workers, professionals, and executives. Today's studies show that there is great potential for this, and quote figures as high as 100 billion dollars per year in productivity improvements in the USA. Not all such productivity improvements need wideband transmission, but many do—including intelligent copying machines, fast electronic mail, office screens for multiple uses, video presentations, teleconferencing, access to facsimile filing systems, and so on.

Only part of the network infrastructure needed for a high-productivity electronic society will be available in Europe and elsewhere. While in the U.S. the FCC stresses as much deregulation as is practical, thus encouraging competition, Europe and elsewhere will pay heavily for having their networks in the slow-moving hands of government.

REFERENCES

1. Viewdata information is available from U.K. Post Office, Telecommunications Headquarters, Room 600 Lutyens House, 1–6 Finsbury Circus, London EC2M 7LY.

2. Evans, Christopher, "Human Factors and Standards in Data Communications," Fourth Data Communications Symposium, IEEE Catalog Number 75 CH1001–7 DATA, IEEE, New York, 1976.

3. Wecker, S., "A Design for a Multiple Processor Operating Environment," *Proc. of IEEE Compcom,* Feb. 1973.

4. Wecker, S., "A Building Block Approach to Multi-Functions Multiple Processor Operating Environment," *Proc. of AIAA Computer Network Conference,* Alabama, April, 1973.

5. B. O. Evans is quoted in IBM's magazine *THINK* in an article on satellite business systems entitled *Stitch in Time* by Harrison Kinney. Armonk, NY, Nov/Dec 1977.

6. Explained in the author's *Telecommunications and the Computer,* 2nd ed., Prentice-Hall, Englewood Cliffs, NJ, 1976.

7. Explained in the author's *Satellite Communication Systems,* Prentice-Hall, Englewood Cliffs, NJ, 1978.

8. Howard Frank's definitive study of packetized voice transmission is available from the Network Analysis Corporation, Long Island, NY.

INDEX

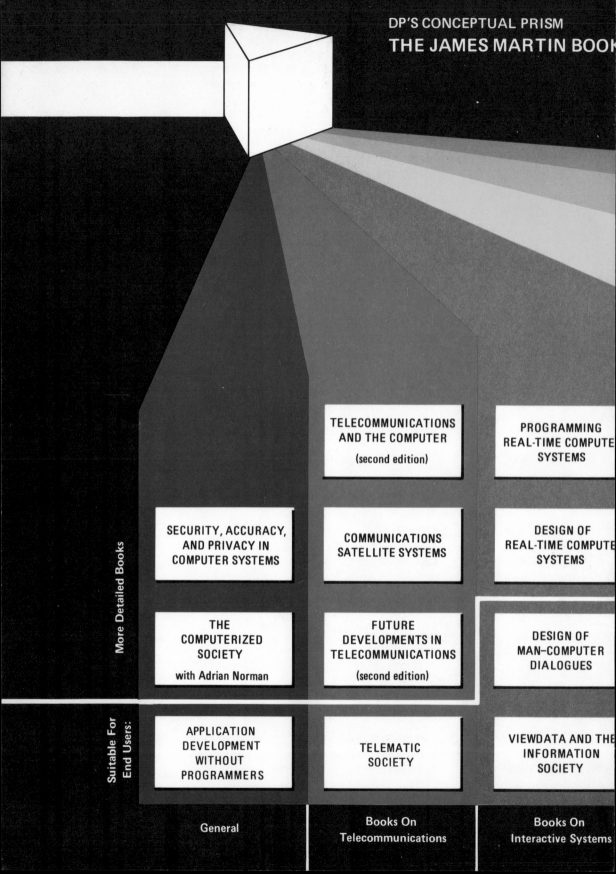

DP'S CONCEPTUAL PRISM
THE JAMES MARTIN BOOK

Suitable For End Users:

More Detailed Books

General	Books On Telecommunications	Books On Interactive Systems
	TELECOMMUNICATIONS AND THE COMPUTER (second edition)	PROGRAMMING REAL-TIME COMPUTE SYSTEMS
SECURITY, ACCURACY, AND PRIVACY IN COMPUTER SYSTEMS	COMMUNICATIONS SATELLITE SYSTEMS	DESIGN OF REAL-TIME COMPUTE SYSTEMS
THE COMPUTERIZED SOCIETY with Adrian Norman	FUTURE DEVELOPMENTS IN TELECOMMUNICATIONS (second edition)	DESIGN OF MAN–COMPUTER DIALOGUES
APPLICATION DEVELOPMENT WITHOUT PROGRAMMERS	TELEMATIC SOCIETY	VIEWDATA AND THE INFORMATION SOCIETY